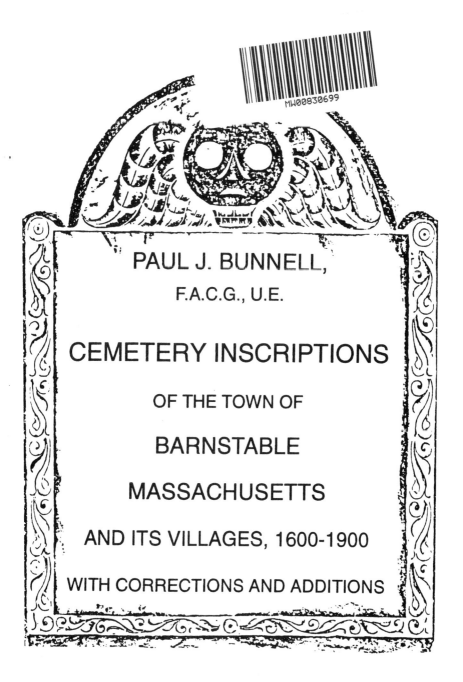

PAUL J. BUNNELL,
F.A.C.G., U.E.

CEMETERY INSCRIPTIONS

OF THE TOWN OF

BARNSTABLE

MASSACHUSETTS

AND ITS VILLAGES, 1600-1900

WITH CORRECTIONS AND ADDITIONS

HERITAGE BOOKS, INC.

Other Hertitage Books by Paul J. Bunnell:

Research Guide to Loyalist Ancestors

The New Loyalist Index

Published 1995 by

HERITAGE BOOKS, INC.
1540-E Pointer Ridge Place,
Bowie, Maryland 20716
(301) 390-7709

ISBN 0-7884-0176-9

SPECIAL THANKS TO THE FOLLOWING:

Leslie Diane Bunnell
and
Patricia Doreen White
For all the many hours they put into this project,
helping me collect the material while fighting off the
elements of nature and recording the inscriptions in some of
the cemeteries. Thanks for the support and encouragement
that helped make this book possible.

Thomas R. Lynch
(Mr. Wizard)
For all the computer support and guidance. His help was
greatly appreciated. Thank you Tom.

The Historical Commission
of the
Town of Barnstable
For recognition and support on this project. Thanks to
Pat Anderson and others on the Board.

The Barnstable Cemetery Department
To Steven Sundelin, Supervisor and Manager, and his
staff for their interest and support. They are doing a
wonderful job on their current stone restoration project.
Thanks for your encouragement to carry on with my project and
for being the first customer of this book.

The Sturgis Library
Located at Route 6A, Barnstable, Massachusetts. Thanks to Susan
Kline, Librarian and Manager for her help and support on
this project, Randy Mason for finding more material in the
cellar vaults, old desks and files and Jean Condito for some
last minute discoveries during this revision process. Randy's
dedication and concern to get as many records together for
this book as possible is greatly appreciated. My thanks to all
the other employees who helped me and who contributed to the
preservation of all the records that were found during the
revision work. And let us not forget all the contributing
researchers of this material found at this fine library.

Thomas R. Lynch
For taking the photographs for this book.

Leslie Diane Bunnell
For making the gravestone rubbing that was used for the
cover of this book.

SPECIAL THANKS, CONTINUED

Mr. and Mrs. Frank Maki, Sr.
Of Barnstable, who led me to other source materials like the
Blevin/Blivin maps, photographs, slides and rubbing projects, and
their work on Phinney's Lane Cemetery in Centerville and Hillside
Cemetery which was found during the revision work. In 1981, they
did the inventory of the Lothrop Cemetery which is included in
this book.

To all the various works and projects of Gustavus Hinkley, many
compiled by Allice Sperl. These records were located thoughout
the Sturgis Library which caused some to be overlooked, later
found during the revision work, some on microfilm, compiled
booklets and a Davis Family cemetery collection, many in the
cellar vaults. This valuable collection adds greatly to the
manual inventory project because it helps with stones that are
missing today. Some records were added in pencil, which I had noted
to help eliminate any inaccuracies from Hinckley's work.

The Cape Cod Synagogue of Hyannis and Marjorie Gibson of Cotuit
Who solved the problem of the mysterious cemetery that was reputed
to be located under one of the runways at the Barnstable Airport in
Hyannis. During my revision work Marjorie Gibson, a fellow member
of the Falmouth Genealogical Society, found a 1962 Public and Semi
Public Facilities map of the airport done by Atwood and Blockwell,
consulting planners of Boston, Mass. After lengthy research with
an attorney, Barnstable Airport officials and Blackburns Auto
Salvage, a lead from Blackburns brought me to the Cape Cod
Synagogue who quickly explained that there was no cemetery out
there and that a deal was struck with the town to allow the runway
to be built on the land of the proposed cemetery, in exchange for
a Jewish section opened at the Mosswood Cemetery in Cotuit.

Thanks: Marjorie Gibson of Cotuit
        Attorney David Cole, Administrator for Cobb Trust
        Mr. Blackburn of Blackburns Auto Salvage
        Philip Rilley, Barnstable Airport Manager, and his
          own interesting story of runway 1331 at another airport.
        Trish Jochnowitz of the Cape Cod Synagogue, Hyannis
        for solving the problem.

Hazal Oakley
For her contribution of the Native American Burial Grounds and
lots that she knew existed in Barnstable villages. All of these
graves are unmarked, and in one case a Native American cemetery in
West Barnstable is a designated burial ground for any ancient
remains found during construction digs, some over a thousand
years old.

SPECIAL THANKS, CONTINUED

Mr. and Mrs. Robert H. Dowes (Marjorie S. Dows, translation)
For their contribution of many typed pages of Barnstable and
other Cape communities transcibed around 1989. They now live in
Rochester, New York. The transcriptions were donated to the Sturgis
Library, in Barnstable, and found during the revision work unidexed
and filed in a desk.

Dr. Jim Gould of Cotuit
Who discovered the missing names in the first edition, which were
lost in the tranfer of information between myself and the publisher.
These names were mostly the Bassett's, Baxter's and unnamed people.
Thank you Jim!

Thank you Dr. Laird Towle, Karen Ackermann, Elaine Fiehrer and
Christopher Mohr, and all of Heritage Books, Inc. for your
support and quick action during the revision process.

This book is dedicated to
My Good Friends

Thomas, Carol, Sara and Holly Lynch
and
Bill and Rhonda Fitzgareld
and
Thomas, Colleen and Benjamin Higham

Cobb's Hill Cemetery (East) #9, one of the oldest, in downtown Barnstable.

TABLE OF CONTENTS

Cobb's Hill Cemetery (West) #9, stones white from restoration project.

Oak Grove Cemetery #18, a unique stone, victim of vandalism.

FOREWORD

I started this project over two years ago, realizing the need to record the early cemetery inscriptions of the Town of Barnstable, Massachusetts and its villages. Barnstable is one of the earliest settlements in America. Tens of millions of people living in the United States, England and Canada and probably other countries are descendants of these early pioneers. As time passes, many of the ancient stones and monuments marking these settlers are falling into decay and ruin. Many of them are being vandalized or stolen. As a professional genealogist, I felt compelled to take on this project for the town I live in, to preserve the memory of those ancestors who created the foundations of our society in America, some of whom became the early planters of Nova Scotia, the American Loyalists, and others searching out new lands in Connecticut, New York and New Jersey and others who went back to England or other places in the world.

While treading my way through the wintry snow, fighting off mosquitoes and black flies in the spring, thrusting through the hot and humid summer months enjoying the fall the best, I look back now and reflect back to every moment with enjoyment. It was an experience! Some days I was rewarded by visits from small animals that occupy the natural park settings we call cemeteries.

Other days, I felt great sadness as I tried to piece together vandalized stones, desperately trying to recover the information that was fragmented and scattered about. The pointless attack and destruction of monuments in these cemeteries is a disgrace and waste of recorded history. I make a desperate plea to all families living near cemeteries to question any suspicious activity and call your local police if you witness vandalism.

Several things were accomplished by the revised edition. Finding an error from electrically transferring materials and losing over 200 names was one major adjustment. I also eliminated the birth date estimations (b.c.) so no errors were transferred into the record incorrectly. Finding misplaced and unknown records was another discovery along the way, and adding the Native American cemeteries was something that came along after a discussion with Hazel Oakley of Mashpee. Plus this revision also benefits from the discovery of several other Hinckley records that were not included before because they were overlooked in the vault at the Sturgis Library. Thanks to the intense search and help of the staff, many more records were brought together. This revision will help make this work more accurate and complete. I thank all who helped during this period.

STRANGE ENDING TO A SPECIAL PROJECT

While working on this book, Steve Sundelin, Supervisor of the Barnstable Cemetery Department asked a favor. He had some stolen stones that had been recovered but didn't know their location in the cemeteries. They were:

KEZIAH C. HALLET, widow of William L. Hallet, born 1807 and died 1 Sept. 1822. With these records, her location was found on 21 Oct. 1991 at Oak Grove Cemetery on Oak Neck Road, Hyannis, MA.

ASA C. AMES, died 10 April, 1848, age 28 years. While conducting my inventory of the Old Mosswood Cemetery in Cotuit, I found an empty spot next to Caroline W. Ames (d. 1 January 1856, age 34), the widow of Asa C. Ames. The odd part of this happy ending was that I found the location of the missing stone on 10 April 1991, exactly 143 years from the day Asa C. Ames died. A fitting anniversary present!

OTHER REQUESTS FOR HELP

Mr. George G. Swain, Jr. of Bourne, Massachusetts requested my help in locating his ancestors who died out of the Barnstable area, but he noted one record saying that they were burried in the Barnstable district. Those relatives found are listed below:

EDWIN M. JONES, b. 1833, d. 1903. Found at the Old Mosswood Cemetery in Cotuit in October, 1991.
CAPT. EDWIN F. JONES, b. 1868, d. 1934, same cemetery.
ISAAC JONES, d. 12 Oct. 1809, age 90, Marstons Mills Cemetery, Marstons Mills.
ISAAC JONES, b. 1801, d. 1866, same cemetery.

OF INTEREST TO READERS

You may want to check the Lovell listings and be surprised to find "the friends of man" burried there along with their masters. I did not find any other accurences of pets buried in any of the cemeteries. The writings with each pet are heartwarming.

THE BEST QUOTE FOUND

Bradley Hall Wheeler was taken away at the age of twenty-six. Besides his favorite sport of golf inscribed on his stone is this quote left for all to read:

"Life flies by so fast.
You hardly get a chance to realize it.
So get a hold of what you can,
And make the best of it."

Bradley Hall Wheeler, born 1963 Aug. 4, died 1989 July 2.

USING THIS BOOK

Caution should be taken when looking for your ancestors in this book. Realize that the information placed on these stones was supplied by friends, relatives or others. Therefore, the vital statistics are only as accurate as the person supplying them. But this information, even if not absolutely accurate, will lay the ground work to lead you to the correct records that will verify the dates and places that were given to the stone cutter.

The information collected by the author was done with great care. Many stones were hard to read due to the poor condition of the stones. Every attempt was made to accurately transcribe the information. A question mark (?) was placed where there is doubt or condition of the stone makes it unreadable. By doing this, I have furnished at least what little information could be gathered.

Although the title of this book states that the records are from 1600 to 1900, there are several births in the 1500's. I used the year 1900 to give me a cut-off date for births. However, in a few cases I have recorded many stones with births into the 1900's. In some of the small cemeteries, I have recorded one hundred percent of the lot. There are some persons still living who are noted here because they were born before 1900. I hope this work will help you locate your ancestors and establish a record of these early settlers that lived and died in Barnstable.

Following is a list of codes and descriptions of all the cemeteries listed in this book. It includes records of other sources used along the way. Written records were consulted only to find lost or destroyed stones absent during the inventory process. Every attempt was made to insure accuracy, but some errors may have occured in the process. Where possible, I have cross referenced the sources to insure accuracy. When it is stated that 100% of the cemetery was inventoried, every stone and time period was recorded up to the time the information was gathered. In some of the cemeteries the size is noted. The following cemetery codes are included with each record to assist the researcher in finding the correct graveyard.

#1 - SOUTH STREET CEMETERY

Located at South Street, Hyannis, it is 0.83 acre. This cemetery was inventoried 100%, but many stones are missing. At one time, this was considered the "paupers" cemetery.

#2 - CONGREGATIONAL CHURCH CEMETERY

Located at Main Street, Centerville.

#3 - ANCIENT CEMETERY
Located at Phinney's Lane, Centerville. It is 0.73 acre. This cemetery was inventoried 100%. Many stones are missing.

#3R - PHINNEY'S LANE CEMETERY RECORDS (ANCIENT CEMETERY)
This collection was done by B.B. Bliven in 1978 and a copy is located at the Sturgis Library, Route 6A, Barnstable, Mass. Record is on microfilm.

#4 - BAPTIST CEMETERY
Located at North East School Street, Hyannis. This cemetery was inventoried 100%.

#5 - WEST BARNSTABLE CEMETERY
Located at Route 6A, West Barnstable. 5.03 acres.

#5R - WEST BARNSTABLE CEMETERY RECORDS
These are the Gustavas Hinckley Cemetery Records, by Allice Sperl of the West Barnstable Cemetery on Route 6A, West Barnstable. These records can be found at the Sturgis Library on Route 6A, Barnstable.

#5R2 - GUSTAVUS HINCKLEY CEMETERY RECORDS
Collected by Allice Sperl, this is a complete listing found downstairs in the vault during the revision, #R929.5 dated from 21 Nov. 1719 to 1894 for West Barnstable Cemetery. Located at the Sturgis Library, Route 6A, Barnstable, Mass.

#6 - SANDY STREET CEMETERY
Located at Route 6A, West Barnstable. 0.58 acres.

#7 - MARSTONS MILLS CEMETERY
Located at Route 149, Marstons Mills. 5.75 acres.

#8 - BEECHWOOD CEMETERY
Located at Route 28, Old Stage Road and Old Post Road, Centerville. 10.30 acres.

#9 - COBB HILL EAST CEMETERY
Located at Route 6A and Millway Road, Barnstable. This cemetery was renamed from the "Meeting House Cemetery".

#9R - GUSTAVUS HINCKLEY CEMETERY RECORDS
Collected by Allice Sperl. A partial listing found at the Sturgis Library, Route 6A, Barnstable, Mass.

#10 - COBB HILL WEST CEMETERY
Located at Route 6A and Millway Road, Barnstable. 0.41 acres. This cemetery also renamed from the "Meeting House Cemetery".

#11 - LOTHROP HILL CEMETERY
Located at Route 6A, Barnstable. 4.50 acres. This cemetery was inventoried 100%, but many old stones are missing.

#11R - LOTHROP HILL CEMETERY RECORDS

The is a collection done by Mr. and Mrs. Bliven and includes photography, rubbings, art work, mapping and historical writings. It is dated 1981. Very few of the Bliven records can be found. These records and the Lothrop Hill Cemetery inventory can be found at the Sturgis Library in the town of Barnstable.

#12 - HILLSIDE CEMETERY (EAST)

Located at Old Mill Road, Osterville. 9.87 acres.

#12R - HILLSIDE CEMETERY (EAST) (ANCIENT PART) RECORDS

This collection was done by B.B. Bliven in 1977. A copy exists at the Sturgis Library in the town of Barnstable on Route 6A. This record is found on microfilm.

#13 - HILLSIDE CEMETERY (WEST)

Located at Old Mill Road, Osterville. 2.0 acres.

#14 - MOSSWOOD CEMETERY (OLD)

Located at Putnam Avenue and Old Post Road, Cotuit. 11.0 acres.

#14R - MOSSWOOD CEMETERY (OLD) RECORDS

These are deed records found in the main cemetery office located at Putnam Avenue and Old Post Road, Cotuit.

#15 - MOSSWOOD CEMETERY (NEW)

Located at Putnam Avenue, Cotuit. 72.02 acres.

#15R - MOSSWOOD CEMETERY (NEW) RECORDS

Deed records found in the main cemetery office at Putnam Avenue in Cotuit.

#16 - SAINT XAVIER CATHOLIC CHURCH CEMETERY

Located in Hyannis.

#17 - OAK NECK CEMETERY

Located at Oak Neck Road, Hyannis. 5.40 acres.

#18 - OAK GROVE CEMETERY

Located in Hyannis. 15.00 acres.

#19 - CUMMAQUID CEMETERY (E. BARNSTABLE CEMETERY)

Mary Dunn Road, Cummaquid. 6.24 acres.

#20 - CROCKER PARK CEMETERY

Located at Church and Sandy Street, West Barnstable. 5.22 acres. This cemetery was inventoried 100%.

#21 - UNIVERSALIST CEMETERY

Located at Elm Street, Hyannis. 1.0 acre. This cemetery was inventoried 100%.

#22 - THE CAPE COD SYNAGOGUE CEMETERY (AS NAMED HERE)
This entry is to warn the researcher that the cemetery recorded as being located at the end of the Barnstable Airport in Hyannis on a 1962 Public & Semi Public Facilities, Barnstable, Massachusetts map done by Atwood & Blockwell, Consulting Planners of Boston, Mass., was only a proposed cemetery. It was agreed upon during the airport expansion that a Jewish section be placed at the new Mosswood cemetery in Cotuit in lieu of the proposed cemetery at the airport. The Public & Semi Public Facilities map was originally discovered by Marjorie Gibson of Cotuit.

#23 - WEST BARNSTABLE, CEDAR & CROCKER ROAD BURIAL GROUND
It is said that there are two Native American's buried here. Names are not available. Exact location unknown. Source from Hazel Oakley, Native American resident of Mashpee, Mass.

#24 - WEST BARNSTABLE NATIVE AMERICAN BURIAL GROUND
This area was given to the Wampanoag Tribe for remains of Native American's found elsewhere during various digs and finds. Exact location is unknown at this time. Source is from Hazel Oakley, Native American resident of Mashpee.

#25 - STONE MARKER COMMEMORATING CHIEF IANOUGH
A brass plate is placed on a large stone located on Route 6A in Barnstable near Cummaquid Cemetery (#19). The exact location of this Native American's burial place is unknown, but some sources say it could be located at the Cummaquid Cemetery.

#26R - HINCKLEY RECORDS ADDITION
Two volumes found in the basement in 1994 at the Sturgis Library, Route 6A, Barnstable, Massachusetts, R929.5, vault records under Loring. Memorial Inscriptions of West & East Parish Cemeteries. West - 21 Nov. 1719 to 1894 and East - Jan. 1683 to 1894, including Dimmocks Lane, Meeting House or Cobb Hill, Lothrop's Hill (The Ancient Burying Ground) and Parish Line. This also includes some misc. sheets found during the revision dated 11 Feb. 1880 at Roxbury, possibly by Hinckley. He states the work was done in 1878.

#27R - JOSIAH HINCKLEY DIARY
Barnstable, Massachusetts, from 1870 to 1881, Page 7. Found at Sturgis Library, Route 6A, Barnstable, Mass. in 1994.

#28R - GENEALOGICAL NOTES OF BARNSTABLE FAMILIES
By Amos Otis. Published 1979 by Genealogical Publishing Co., Baltimore, Maryland. Page 34. A copy of this book can be found at the Sturgis Library, Route 6A, Barnstable, Mass.

#29R - COBB HILL CEMETERY TRANSCRIPTIONS
Work done by Mr. & Mrs. Robert H. Dowes, Rochester, New York. Marjorie S. Dowes transcribed in 1989 (typed pages). Found in a desk (not cataloged yet) at the Sturgis Library, Route 6A, Barnstable, Mass.

#30R - BEECHWOOD CEMETERY TRANSCRIPTIONS
Work done by Mr. & Mrs. Robert H. Dowes, Rochester, New York. Marjorie
S. Dowes transcribed in 1989 (typed pages). Found in desk (not catalogued
yet) at the Sturgis Library, Route 6A, Barnstable, Mass.

#31 - SAINT PATRICK'S CEMETERY (CATHOLIC)
Located on Barnstable Road, Hyannis, appoximately 3/4 acre, mostly Irish
and Hispanic (Port./Mex.) are buried here. Care and upkeep done by Saint
Xavier Catholic Church, Hyannis. This cemetery was inventoried 100%.

#32 - SAINT PETER'S MEMORIAL GARDEN (CREMATION LOT)
Saint Peter's Episcopal Church, Osterville. For church members only,
there are approximately 24 people buried here. This lot was started
c.1984. A diagram of remains locations is in the church office, including
the names of each person. This source is listed only to establish location,
members not listed in this book due to early interment.

#33 - SAINT MARY'S MEMORIAL GARDEN (CREMATION LOT)
Saint Mary's Church, Route 6A, Barnstable. For church members only,
approximately 25 years old, no markers, but records in church office. This
source is listed only to establish location, members not listed in this book
due to early interment.

South Street Cemetery, #1, a hollow metal marker tried in the mid-1800's.

QUICK REFERENCE CHART

#1   South Street Cemetery
#2   Congregational Church Cemetery
#3   Ancient Cemetery
#3R Phinney's Lane Cemetery (called The Ancient Cemetery)
#4   Baptist Cemetery
#5   West Barnstable Cemetery
#5R West Barnstable Cemetery Records
#5R2 Gustavas Hinckley Cemetery Records
#6   Sandy Street Cemetery
#7   Marstons Mills Cemetery
#8   Beechwood Cemetery
#9   Cobb Hill East Cemetery
#9R Gustavas Hinckley Cemetery Records
#10 Cobb Hill West Cemetery
#11 Lothrop Hill Cemetery
#11R Lothrop Hill Cemetery Records
#12 Hillside Cemetery (East)
#12R Hillside Cemetery (East) (Ancient Part) Records
#13 Hillside Cemetery (West)
#14 Mosswood Cemetery (Old)
#14R Mosswood Cemetery (Old) Records
#15 Mosswood Cemetery (New)
#15R Mosswood Cemetery (New) Records
#16 Saint Xavier Catholic Church Cemetery
#17 Oak Neck Cemetery
#18 Oak Grove Cemetery
#19 Cummaquid Cemetery (East Barnstable Cemetery)
#20 Crocker Park Cemetery
#21 Universalist Cemetery
#22 The Cape Cod Synagogue Cemetery (as named here)
#23 West Barnstable, Cedar & Crocker Road Burial Ground
#24 West Barnstable Native American Burial Ground
#25 Stone Marker Commemorating Chief Ianough
#26R Hinckley Records Addition
#27R Josiah Hinckley Diary
#28R Genealogical Notes of Barnstable Families
#29R Cobb Hill Cemetery Transcriptions
#30R Beechwood Cemetery Transcriptions
#31 Saint Patrick's Cemetery (Catholic)
#32 Saint Peter's Memorial Garden (Cremation Lot)
#33 Saint Mary's Memorial Garden (Cremation Lot)

Cummaquid Cemetery #19 (East Barnstable Cemetery), Mary Dunn Rd., in Cummaquid, Mass. Signs of Hurricane Bob in the background.

? - Died 1885 (crypt located on road with metal door, no name) S:19

? - Died 1900 Aug 31 Age 63 yrs 10 mos Stone says "Mother good night" (between Capt David Anderson & Joseph H Hallet, no name listed on stone) S:19

? - (no name)(a large above ground stone crypt with no markings) S:31

? - (no name)(a metal cross with no markings, near Frank and Mary Souza) S:31

? - (no name)(this is an above ground crypt dated 1877 located right on the banks of the pond in the back of the cemetery) S:18

?, (Dad) - Died 1948 March 27 Born 1873 March 3 (next to Thatcher B Crocker & Thomas Percival Lewis) S:11

?, (Mother) - Died 1932 Born 1870 (near Clifford Jones & Myron Howland) S:13

?, Abigail - Daughter of ? (stone not clear) She is between Gage's, possibly a Gage? S:4

?, Abraham - Died 1777 July 7 Age 20 Son of Christefer & Bethia (buried next to Solomon Goodspeed who died the same day, possibly a battle?) S:7

?, Almon B - Died 1855 Jan 1 Born 1848 Dec 13 (last name not listed, but between Anjenette Young & Jenlima Hinkley) S:12

?, Bernard M - Died Son of Martin & Marie Stone says "Gone to be an angel" S:31

?, Brazillan - Died 1700's July (stone not clear) S:5

?, Elexander (Alexander) - Died 1785 June 29 Age 2 Son of Eban & Mary (stone not clear, but buried between Ebenezer Crocer (Crocker) & Pricilla Crocker) S:7

?, Elizabeth - Died 183? (stone worn) Wife of William (between George & Fannie Childs & Elizabeth Slade, wife of Willard Slade) S:14

?, Elisabeth A - Died 1851 Sept 13 Age 36 yrs 10 mos 4 days Father or husband was James K Next to Ben Handy S:4

?, Francis - Died 1907 Born 1903 (no last name listed, located between Stephen Bates & Tallman plot) S:12

?, George Capt - Died 1833 April 12 Age 40 (stone between the Stewart's & Snow's) S:4

?, Hannah - Died 1876 Born 1804 (stone not clear, located between Alice L Blossom & Watson Crocker, she probably is mother of Alice L Blossom because Alice's parents are listed as Henry & Hannah Blossom?) S:5

?, Hannah C - (stone not clear) Wife of John S:4

?, Harriet - Died 1843 Dec 6 Born 1811 Jan 25 (buried between Smith's & Crocker's) S:5

?, Idella - (no dates listed, little stone) Age 2 mos (located between Adresta G Hamblin & Elizabeth McDonald) S:14

?, Irene S - Died 1832 Oct 13 Age 32 yrs 2 mos Wife of ? (grave next to Ben Handy) S:4

?, Joseph - Died 1700's (stone not clear, buried between Jobe Howland & Dr John Russel) S:5

?, Louisa F - Died 1855 Dec 30 Age 15 yrs 4 mos 18 days Daughter of James K & Elizabeth A Next to William Handy S:4

?, Mabel - Died 1839 ? (stone badly worn, located next to Horton L Reynolds) S:14

?, Mary Ann - Died 1854 April 11 Born 1815 May 31 Buried between Smith's & Crocker's S:5

?, Mary L - Died 1872 Oct 5 Age 20 yrs 1 mo Wife of Charles A (stone not clear, located between Capt George Bracc & Lydia Crocker) S:5

?, Phinehas Capt - Died 1825 March 17 Age 33 Was drowned at sea (last name could be Stewart because his stone is

? (Cont.)
  located between the Stewart's)
  S:4
?, Sarah - Died 1809 Dec 25
  (buried between Allen Good-
  speed & Capt Owen L Adams)
  Daughter of Ansel & Relief (stone
  not clear) S:7
?, Susie M - Died 1883 Born 1880
  (stone says grandchild, possibly
  parents or grandparents were
  Joshua & Mary Backus) S:5
?, Temperance - Died 1775 Sept 7
  Age ? yrs 10 mos (stone not
  clear) Daughter of Capt ? &
  Abigail S:5
?, Theo - (stone not clear, but
  between the Baxter's & Mer-
  chant's) S:4
?, Thomas - (stone badly damaged)
  Son of Lemuel & Abigail S:4
A-pley or **Ap-ley**, Ziphia - Died
  1885 Apl 26 Age 69 years, 9
  months Wife of Oliver A-pley S:4
A-pley, Oliver G - Died 1870 Apl 6
  Age 56 Wife was Zilphia A-pley
  S:4
Abaran, Blanche M - Died 1987
  Born 1894 (with James R
  Abaran) S:17
Abaran, James R - Died 1969 Born
  1888 (with Blanche M Abaran)
  S:17
Abbott, Edna A - Died 1972 Born
  1884 Wife of Joseph Abbott (with
  him & J Clyde Abbott & others)
  S:18
Abbott, Ellen - Died 1912 Born
  1836 Wife of Job Abbott (with
  him & Thomas Abbott & others)
  S:18
Abbott, J Clyde - Died 1925 Born
  1924 (with Joseph & Edna
  Abbott & others) S:18
Abbott, Job - Died 1878 Born 1830
  (with wife, Ellen Abbott)
  S:18
Abbott, Joseph - Died 1954 Born
  1874 (with wife, Edna A Abbott
  & others) S:18
Abbott, Thomas - Died 1876 Born
  1856 (with Joseph Abbott &

Abbott (Cont.)
  others) S:18
Adams, Abagail - Died ? Feb 22 Age
  89 (stone not clear) (with Alphous Adams Sr & Jr) S:14
Adams, Aimee L -Died 1970 Born
  1891 Wife of William F Adams
  (with him) S:12
Adams, Albert S - Died 1984 Born
  1899 (with Sarah A Adams)
  S:15
Adams, Alexander Clinton - Died
  1910 Nov 24 Born 1847 April 9
  (with Anne Adams & others)
  S:14
Adams, Alphous - Died 1869? Nov
  16 in his 95th year (with Abagail
  Adams & others) S:14
Adams, Amelia E - Died 1945 Born
  1860 Wife of Herbert W Adams
  (with him) S:12
Adams, Anne - Died 1882 Oct 19
  Born 1809 Feb 26 Wife of Urial
  Adams (with him & others) S:14
Adams, Ansel - Died 1862 Feb
  Born 1842 April 7 Lost at sea
  (with Urial Adams) S:14
Adams, Beatrice - Died 1942 Born
  1887 Stone says only Beatrice,
  no last name but appears relat-
  ed to William F & Betsey F
  Adams (next to them) S:12
Adams, Benjamin - Died 1824 at
  New Orleans S:5R
Adams, Bertha Louise - Died 1874
  Born 1873 (with Abbie Dottridge
  Danforth) S:14
Adams, Bethuel - Died 1900 Mar 1
  Born 1813 Nov 9 (stone is a
  fancy metal hollow marker) (with
  Sarah Adams) S:12
Adams, Betsey F - Died 1953 Born
  1866 (with William F Adams)
  S:12
Adams, Charles Owens - Died 1919
  Born 1834 (with Sarah Frances
  Adams) S:14
Adams, David W - Died 1823 Dec
  10 Age 5 Son of Alphous &
  Abagail Adams (with them) S:14
Adams, Elizabeth Annie - Died
  1852 May 2 Born 1832 Jan 12

2

Adams (Cont.)
(with Malvina Cook & others)
S:14

Adams, Ethal A - Died 1911 Nov 22 Born 1909 Oct 26 (next to Margaretta F & Thornton R Adams) (stone says, "Tell papa baby's all right") S:13

Adams, Florence A - Died 1961 Born 1879 Wife of Charles Coleman (next to him) S:13

Adams, Freeman C - Died 1955 Born 1873 (with Mathide L Mutsch) S:12

Adams, Harry Alden - Died 1987 Born 1897 Was a Y2 in US Navy (next to Laurence Mouat Adams) S:15

Adams, Helen - Died 1980 Born 1893 Wife of William Tenney (with him) S:14

Adams, Heman - Died 1893 Oct 18 Age 66 years, 10 months S:14

Adams, Herbert W - Died 1892 Born 1865 (with wife, Amelia E Adams) S:12

Adams, Herbert W - Died 1893 Born 1867 (Has a large metal hollow marker with an anchor at the top) (with Walter Dodge) S:12

Adams, Isiah - Died 1920 Born 1839 (with Lizzie B Adams) S:12

Adams, John - Died 1800 Aug 1 in his 21st year (died at Havanah, Cuba) S:5

Adams, John F - Died 1932 Born 1844 (next to Julia Agnes Adams) S:13

Adams, Joseph F - Died 1913 Born 1833 (with Mary L Adams) S:12

Adams, Julia Agnes - Died 1915 Born 1852 (next to John F Adams) S:13

Adams, Laurence Mouat - Died 1990 Born 1898 (next to Harry Alden Adams) S:15

Adams, Lizzie B - Died 1905 Born 1842 (with Isiah Adams) S:12

Adams, Malcolm H - Died (still living 1991?) Born 1912 March 13 (a rock stone) (with wife, Mary M Derwin) S:12

Adams, Margaretta F - Died 1963 Feb 20 Born 1882 Feb 15 (between Ethal A & Thornton R Adams) S:13

Adams, Mary L - Died 1900 Born 1841 (with Joseph F Adams) S:12

Adams, Mary V - Died 1930 Born 1865 (with Mary L & Joseph F Adams) S:12

Adams, Ora - Died 1943 Feb 20 Born 1857 June 4 Wife of S Alexander Hinckley (with him & Isabel Hinckley & others) S:18

Adams, Owen L (Capt) - Died 1817 June 14 in his 28th year S:7

Adams, Relief - Died 1887 Jan 5 Age 81 years, 1 month, 28 days Wife of Ansell Adams S:7

Adams, S Edna - Died 1988 Born 1888 Daughter of Edson Fisher & Eleanor Lumbert (with them) S:14

Adams, Sarah - Died 1900 April 7 Born 1819 Sept 18 (stone is a fancy metal hollow marker) (with Bethuel Adams) S:12

Adams, Sarah A - Died 1988 Born 1904 (with Albert S Adams) S:15

Adams, Sarah Frances - Died 1918 Born 1840 (with Bertha Louise Adams) S:14

Adams, Susan E - Died 1901 Born 1848 (large metal hollow stone with anchor at top) (with husband, Watson F Adams & others) S:12

Adams, Theophilus (Capt) - Died 1863 Apr 16 in his 77th year S:7

Adams, Thornton Rosco - Died 1964 May 5 Born 1888 June 18 Was In Massachusetts CMM USN RF during World War 1 (next to Margaretta F Adams) S:13

Adams, Urial - Died 1893 July 13 Born 1803 Sept 12 (with Anne Adams & others) S:14

Adams, Watson F - Died 1903 Born 1842 (large metal hollow marker with anchor at top) (with wife, Susan E Adams) S:12

3

Adams, William F - Died 1920 Born 1864 (with Betsey F Adams) S:12

Adams, William F - Died 1975 Born 1886 (with Aimee L Adams, wife) S:12

Aguiar, John N - Died 1944 Born 1879 S:16

Ahearn, Maurice J - Died 1974 Born 1898 (with wife, Winifred A Ahearn) S:15

Ahearn, Winifred A - Died 1978 Born 1891 (with husband, Maurice J Ahearn) S:15

Ahonen, Axel - Died 1961 Born 1885 (with Johanna Sippola, wife) S:12

Ahonen, Toivo A - Died 1975 Dec 21 Born 1912 Sept 7 Was a PFC in US Army Air Force during World War I S:20

Aiello, John E - Died 1953 Born 1889 (flat stone covered with grass) S:16

Aikins, Florence McD - Died 1916 April 8 Born 1878 March 3 (next to Laurence P Aikins) (last name not clear, possibly Aikins?) S:31

Aikins, Laurence P - Died 1909 May 14 Born 1908 Dec 7 (with Margaret A Aikins) S:31

Aikins, Margaret A - Died 1910 Dec 22 Born 1910 Dec 17 (with Laurence P Aikins) S:20

Ainsworth, Eliza D - Died 1893 April 17 in her 90th year S:9R

Ainsworth, Elizabeth - Died 1838 July 29 Age 6 years, 10 months Daughter of Sidney & Mary Ainsworth (next to family) S:10

Ainsworth, Elizabeth C - Died 1850 April 29 in her 69th year Wife of Richard Ainsworth S:9R

Ainsworth, George Henry - Died 1852 July 22 in his 9th year Son of Sidney & Mary Ainsworth (next to family) S:10

Ainsworth, Helen D - Died 1853 June 25 in her 39th year S:9R

Ainsworth, James (Capt) - Died 1865 Dec 24 in his 54th year S:9R

Ainsworth, John - Died 1845 Dec 8 in his 26th year S:9R

Ainsworth, Richard - Died 1858 July 20 Age 74 Born in Anderton, County of Lancashire, England S:9R+26R

Ainsworth, Richard Jr - Died 1850 June 15 in his 27th year at San Diego S:9R

Ainsworth, Sidney - Died 1854 May 28 in his 17th year Son of Sidney & Mary Ainsworth (next to family) S:10

Ainsworth, Sophia W - Died 1863 Feb 22 in her 76th year S:9R

Ainsworth, William - Died 1876 Oct 25 Age 42 years, 10 months S:10

Aittaniemi, Frederick E - Died 1979 Born 1922 Was a Sargeant in US Army during World War II S:20

Aittaniemi, Irene E - Died 1990 June 11 Born 1913 March 1 Wife of John H Aittaniemi (with him) S:20

Aittaniemi, John H - Died (still living 1991?) Born 1912 June 2 Married 14 Nov 1934 (also has plaque & flag that says, "West Barnstable Fire Dept") (with Irene E Aittaniemi, wife) S:20

Albert, Charlotte M - Died 1962 Born 1887 Wife of Samuel H D Drew (with him & Theodore F Drew & others) S:18

Alcock, John - Died 1975 Born 1877 (with Mary S Alcock) S:13

Alcock, Mary S - Died 1970 Born 1888 (with John Alcock) S:13

Alden, Albert - Died 1883 Born 1811 S:10

Alden, Lizzie - Died (death date underground) Born April 24 Daughter of Albert & Susan M Alden S:10

Alden, Mary - Died 1865 May 24 Born 1841 Sept 18 S:10+26R

Alden, Mary E - Died 1937 Born 1885 (Crocker stone with Eleanor Crocker) S:11

Alden, Nancy F - Died 1867 June

Alden (Cont.)

24 Age 58 years, 10 months (next to Peter O Alden, husband) S:19

Alden, Peter O - Died 1873 Aug 23 Age 75 years, 2 months, 20 days (with wife, Nancy F Alden) S:19

Alden, Susan Monroe - Died 1895 Sept 13 Born 1813 Aug 5 S:10

Alden, Susie - Died 1855 May Stone says - "Our Darling" S:10

Aldrich (no first name) - Died (no dates, just a flat stone marker) S:21

Alexander, Elizabeth H - Died 1900 Born 1813 (with John G Crocker & others) S:18

Alexander, Harriet - Died 1869 Born 1790 (with Elizabeth H Alexander & others) S:18

Alexander, Sylvanus - Died 1819 Born 1784 (with Harriet Alexander & others) S:18

Alheit, Katheryn - Buried 1982 June 2 Age 90 S:15R

Allain, Abraham - Died 1951 Born 1869 (with Josephine Allain) S:16

Allain, Josephine - Died 1967 Born 1872 (with Abraham Allain) S:16

Allbee, Helen J - Died 1976 Born 1892 S:16

Alleman, Harriett M - Died 1966 Born 1884 S:15

Allen, Abigail T - Died 1826 Dec 22 or 29 in her 28th year (22nd date from Hinckley Ceme records) Wife of Capt Henry H Allen S:10

Allen, Abigail T Mrs - Died 1826 Dec 22 in her 26th year Wife of Capt Henry H Allen (next to him) S:10

Allen, Andrew - Died 1815 Aug 27 in his 78th year S:12

Allen, Asenath C - Died 1887 April 21 Born 1807 Feb 11 Wife of George Allen S:5R

Allen, Caroline Hastings - Died 1892 Born 1813 (In Allen plot with Abby Hallen Strawbridge & others) S:12

Allen, Daisy E - Died 1974 Born 1886 S:12

Allen, David - Died 1852 Son of David & Lydia M Allen S:12

Allen, David H - Died 1838 June Age 65 years, 3 months Son of Andrew & Dorcas Allen S:12

Allen, David L - Died 1807 Aug 18 Age 1 year 6 months Son of Homes 6 Lucy Allen (next to father) S:10

Allen, Deborah - Died 1763 Dec 8 in her 24th year Wife of Nathaniel Allen S:12

Allen, Dorcas - Died 1816 Dec 26 in her 77th year Widow of Andrew Allen (next to him) S:12

Allen, Elizabeth Dana - Died 1927 Born 1838 (in Allen plot with Alice Howitt Steele & others) S:12

Allen, Frank D - Died 1981 Born 1890 (next to Mary E Allen) S:12

Allen, Gardner B Sr - Died 1976 Born 1891 (undertaker plaque only) S:17

Allen, George - Died 1892 March 19 Born 1804 Aug 24 S:5R

Allen, Henry H (Capt) - Died 1827 Dec 3 in Amsterdam in his 26th year Removed and buried in June 16, 1828 S:10

Allen, Holmes Esq - Died 1809 Nov 17 in his 35th yr S:10R+26R

Allen, Homes Esq - Died 1809 Nov 17 in his 35th yr S:10

Allen, Leo - Died 1950 Born 1881 (there are 2 stones next to him that only say, RAB & ASB) S:12

Allen, Lillian Leah - Died 1983 Born 1892 (Jewish section) Stone says, "Mother" S:15

Allen, Lydia - Died 1788 July 1 in her 27th yr Husband or father of Jabez Allen Stone has "Relict" noted S:3+3R

Allen, Lydia - Died 1882 located in row 12 S:11R

Allen, Marguerite K - Died 1976 Born 1894 (with Gertrude M Crosby) S:17

Allen, Marth - Died 1736 June 21

Allen (Cont.)
Age 3 years, 2 months Daughter of James & Martha Allen S:11R

Allen, Mary E - Died 1923 Born 1923 (next to Daisy E Allen) S:12

Allen, Mary Elizabeth - Died 1849 Sept 7 Age 6 months Born 1849 Mar 9 Daughter of John & Eveline Allen S:10

Allen, Mary Swain - Died 1866? July (stone not clear) Age 18 months, 3 days Daughter of David A & Lydia M Allen S:12

Allen, Maurice B - Died 1980 Born 1896 (with Vernnette L Allen) S:15

Allen, Minnie G - Died 1952 Born 1866 (next to Bessie W Leonard) S:12

Allen Nathan Hastings - Died 1909 Born 1843 (in Allen plot with Caroline Hastings Allen & others) S:12

Allen, Rebeckah - Died 1761 Dec 3 in her 81st yr Relict of Ebenezer Allen Esq of Chilmark,Marthas Vinyard Island, Massachusetts S:11

Allen, Relience - Died (dates underground, stone leaning) Wife of Nathaniel Allen S:12

Allen, Sally - Died 1813 April 6 in her 31st yr Wife of Jabel Allen S:10

Allen, Susanna - Died 1753 Oct 4 in her 60th yr Wife of James Allen S:11R

Allen, Vernnette L - Died 1965 Born 1898 (with Maurice B Allen) S:14

Allen, William E - Died 1806 Aug 12 Age 10 months Son of Homes & Lucy Allen (next to father & David) S:10

Allen, Zacbeus - Died 1787 Aug 4 in his 7th yr Son of Jabez & Lydia Allen S:3

Alley, Churchill B - Died 1854 Aug 23 in his 17th yr Drowned in the Hudson River (next to Sarah Alley & Olive J Lawrence) S:13

Alley, Ernest S - Died 1906 Born

Alley (Cont.)
1869 (next to Joseph H Alley) S:13

Alley, Everett C - Died 1934 Born 1867 (next to Lena M Alley) S:13

Alley, Joseph H - Died 1881 Nov 2 Age 48 yrs 10 mos 23 days (next to wife, Sarah J Alley) S:13

Alley, Lena M - Died 1954 Born 1872 (next to Everett C Alley) S:13

Alley, Sarah - Died Age 40 Stone says, "Wife" (stone broken & worn) (between Churchill B Alley & Olive J Lawrence) S:13

Alley, Sarah J - Died 1877 June 22 Age 43 years 8 months Wife of Capt Joseph H Alley (next to him) S:13

Allin (Allyn), Susannah - Died 1753 Oct 4 in her 60th yr S:11

Allyn, (a son) - Died (stone worn badly) (next to sister, Elizabeth Allyn, d 1698) Son of Samuel & Hannah Allyn S:11

Allyn, (Child) - Died 1776 Oct 24 Age 4 years Child of James & Lydia Allyn (next to father) S:11

Allyn, (daughter) - Died 1753 April 16 Daughter of Thomas & Elizabeth Allyn S:11

Allyn, (girl) - Died 1808 Oct 1 Age 14 months, 6 days (next to Hannah Allyn) Daughter of Benjamin & Abby Allyn S:11

Allyn, ? - Died 1753 April 16 (stone worn) Daughter of Thomas & Elizabeth Allyn S:11

Allyn, ? - Died 1764 Oct 4 (stone worn) Son of Thomas & Elizabeth Allyn S:11

Allyn, ? - Died (stone badly worn off) (It does mention Thomas) (Next to Elizabeth Allyn, dau of Thomas & Elizabeth Allyn) S:11

Allyn, Ann Gorham - Died 1889 located in row 1 S:11R

Allyn, Benjamin - Died 1835 Mar 7 in his 78th (a stone is between him & another Benjamin which is worn and cannot be read)

6

Allyn (Cont.)
S:11

Allyn, Benjamin - Died 1811 Mar 19 (stone underground) (next to Benjamin Allyn d 1835) S:11

Allyn, Benjamin - Died 1814 Aug 14 in his 33rd yr in North Carolina Son of Lucy & Benjamin Allyn S:11R

Allyn, Benjamin - Died 1833 located in row 1 S:11R

Allyn, Benjamin - Died 1833 March 7 in his 78th yr S:11

Allyn, C Howard (Capt) - Died 1932 Born 1848 (with Sylvia D B Allyn & others) S:18

Allyn, Elizabeth - Died 1698 Dec 23 Age 17 Daughter of Samuel Hannah Allyn S:11

Allyn, Elizabeth - Died 1756 Jan 15 Daughter of Thomas & Elizabeth Allyn S:11

Allyn, Elizabeth - Died 1757 March 19, Age 31 years, 6 months, 24 days Wife of Thomas Allyn (buried next to her) S:11

Allyn, Elizabeth - Died 1776 located in row 2 S:11R

Allyn, Elizabeth - Died 1786? Jan 15 Daughter of Thomas & Elizabeth Allyn S:11

Allyn, Esther - Died 1862 Born 1814 (with Nathan Allyn & others) S:11

Allyn, Frederick - Died 1883 Dec 12 Age 74 years, 3 months? (next to large cedar tree by dirt road) S:11+26R

Allyn, Frederick - Died 1903 Born 1849 (with Nathan & Esther Allyn) S:11

Allyn, Hannah - Died (stone very small & badly worn) 1776 Oct 13 Age 8 lacking 7 days (date from Hinckley Ceme records, #11R) Daughter of Thomas & Hannah Allyn S:11

Allyn, James - Died 172? Dec 28 (worn) (next to Susannah Allyn, wife of James) S:11

Allyn, James - Died 1741 Oct 8 in his 51st yr S:11R

Allyn, James - Died 1774 located in row 2 S:11R

Allyn, James - Died 1796 Sept 22 in his 68th yr (next to wife, Lydia Allyn) S:11

Allyn, James - Died 17?6 June (stone badly worn) S:11

Allyn, James - Died 17?? June 21 Age 58 ? (next to Susannah Allyn, wife of a James Allyn) S:11

Allyn, James - Died ?? Oct 28 or 18 (stone badly worn) (next to Susannah & Elizabeth Allyn) S:11

Allyn, Joseph - Died 1871 Born 1792 (with Ann D Gorham, his wife) S:11

Allyn, Kezia or Keziah Mrs - Died 1809 May 12 or 15 Wife of Samuel Allyn S:11+26R

Allyn, Lucy - Died (stone badly worn) 1811 March 19 in her 55th yr Wife of Benjamin Allyn (a stone next to her is unreadable) (above date from Hinckley Ceme records 11R) S:11

Allyn, Lucy - Died 1785 Aug 31 Age 19 months, 15 days Daughter of Benjamin & Mrs Lucy Allyn S:11R

Allyn, Lydia - Died 1776 located in row 2 S:11R

Allyn, Lydia - Died 1776 Oct 24 Age 4 years, 10 months, 12 days Daughter of James & Mrs Lydia Allyn S:11R

Allyn, Lydia - Died 1808 Oct 1 Age 14 months, 6 days Daughter of Benjamin & Lydia Allyn S:11R

Allyn, Lydia - Died 1809 Feb 8 in her 71st yr or 1802 (1802 from Hinckley ceme records #11R) Widow of James Allyn (buried next to him) S:11

Allyn, Lydia M - Died 1882 May 30 Age 82 & 1 mo. S:11+26R

Allyn, Marston - Died 1757 Aug 20 Age 9 months 27 days Son of James & Lydia Allyn (next to brother, Marston Allyn) S:11

Allyn, Marston - Died 1766 July 22

Allyn (Cont.)

or 28 Age 6 years, 9 months, 11 days (next to Marston Allyn) Son of James & Lydia Allyn S:11

Allyn, Martha - Died (no date) located in row 2 S:11R

Allyn, Mary - Died 1762 July 25th (stone worn) in her 27th yr Wife of Thomas Allyn (next to him) S:11

Allyn, Nabby - Died 1861 May 10 Age 63 or 83? (stone not clear) Widow of late Benjamin Allyn S:11

Allyn, Nathan - Died 1862 Born 1814 (With Esther Allyn) S:11

Allyn, Nymphas - Died 1766 Sept 23 Age 2 Son of James & Lydia Allyn S:11

Allyn, Rebecca - Died 1761 located in row 7 S:11R

Allyn, Samuel - Died 1700 Dec 26 in his 40th yr Son of Samuel & Hannah Allyn S:11R

Allyn, Samuel - Died 1764 Oct Son of Thomas & Hannah Allyn S:11

Allyn, Samuel - Died 1810 July 29 in his 59th yr S:11

Allyn, Sarah E - Died 1900 Born 1852 (with Esther & Nathan Allyn) S:11

Allyn, Susannah - Died 1756 Aug 18 Age 2 (next to Elizabeth Allyn) Daughter of Thomas & Elizabeth Allyn (dates from Hinckley Ceme records 11R) S:11+26R

Allyn, Susannah - Died 1753 Oct 4 in her 60th yr Wife of James Allyn (between 2 James Allyn) S:11

Allyn, Susannah - Died 1756 ? (worn) Daughter of Thomas & Elizabeth Allyn S:11

Allyn, Sylvia D B - Died 1923 Born 1850 (with Fred B Livesley & others) S:18

Allyn, Thomas - Died 1776 Feb 24 in his 47th yr (stone worn) S:11

Allyn,(child) - Died 1794 Oct Age 4 Child of James & Lydia Allyn S:11

Almeida, Dorothy - Died 1986 Born 1900 (undertaker plaque) S:18

Almeida, Eugenia - Buried 1985 Dec 27 Age 84 S:15R

Almeida, Evelyn R - Died (still living 1991?) Born 1891 (listed with John M Almeida) S:14

Almeida, John M - Died 1974 Born 1889 (listed with Evelyn R Almeida) S:14

Almieda, Joaquin F - Died 1944 Born 1886 World War I Veteran S:16

Almiller, Cyrus - Died 1905? Born 1845 (buried with Loretta Almiller) S:8

Almy, Ruth Morel - Died 1977 May 15 Born 1896 July 7 (next to Samuel Cabot Almy) S:14

Almy, Samuel Cabot - Died 1959 Dec 6 Born 1895 May 7 From Massachusetts, was 1st Lieutenant in Field Artillery during World War I (next to Ruth Morel Almy) S:14

Alpheus, (Capt) - Buried 18 Feb 1869 S:14R

Alsop, Nathalie Hooper - Died 1937 Born 1880 S:14

Altmiller, Charles A - Died 1967 Born 1875 (with Mabel A Altmiller) S:13

Altmiller, Mabel A - Died 1966 Born 1883/4 (with Charles A Altmiller) S:13

Alves, Jacob - Died 1963 Born 1884 (undertaker plaque only) S:16

Alvezi, James N - Died 1981 Born 1915 (next to Ruth J Alvezi) S:19

Alvezi, Ruth J - Died (still living 1991?) Born 1916 (listed next to James N Alvezi) S:19

Alvin, Lillian M - Died 1920 Born 1879 (with Elba D Lucas & others) S:18

Amaral, Helen M - Died 1968 Born 1895 S:15

Amaral, Manuel - Died 1937 Born 1878 (with Mary Amaral) S:31

Amaral, Mary - Died 1950 Born 1879 (with Manuel Amaral) S:31

Ambrose, Joseph - Died 1949 Born 1880 S:16

Ames (Crosby), Sarah C - Died 1851 Born 1837 (large Ames stone) daughter of C F & H C Crosby S:12

Ames, (baby) - Died 1843 May 21 Child of Cephas & Rhoda Ames (next to them) S:14

Ames, (Mother) - Died 1921 Born 1858 (Ames stone) Wife of Samuel Ames (with him & others) S:12

Ames, Abigail H - Died 1845 Born 1806 (large Ames stone) S:12

Ames, Almira P - Died 1833 Born 1831 (large Ames stone) S:12

Ames, Angie L - Died 1984 Born 1890 April 8 (with husband, Bernard S Ames) S:15

Ames, Ann H - Died 1894 July 5 Age 78 years, 7 months Widow of Stephen Ames S:7

Ames, Asa C - Died 1848 April 10 in his 28th yr (next to wife, Caroline W Ames) (this stone was taken from cemetery, found & given to Barnstable Ceme Dept Manager, Steve Sundelin While on this project, this Author was asked to located its position which occured 10 Apr 91 exactly 143 years after his death) S:14

Ames, Asenath - Died 1892 Born 1832 Wife of Josiah a Ames (next to him) S:12

Ames, Benjamin F - Died 1845 Jan 31 in his 24th yr (between Miss Lydia L & Enos Ames Jr) S:13

Ames, Bernard S - Died 1964 July 29 Born 1887 April 15 (with wife, Angie L Ames) S:15

Ames, Beulah Mrs - Died 1831 June 25 in her 58th yr Wife of Thomas Ames (next to him) S:12

Ames, Bradford L - Died 1872 Born 1835 (stone says,"Lost at sea") (with James Parker & others) S:13

Ames, Bradford L - Died 1944 Born 1867 (with Granville Ames &

Ames (Cont.)
Thankful Hamblin) S:13

Ames, Bulah - Died 1865 June 26 Age 77 years, 3 months Stone says "Mother" (next to husband, Isaac I Ames) S:14

Ames, Caroline W - Died 1856 Jan 1 Age in her 34th yr (next to husband, Asa Ames) S:14

Ames, Cephas I - Died 1888 Nov 18 Age 78 (next to Rhoda H Ames) S:14

Ames, Chloe - Died 1828 Oct 18 in her 45th yr (with Josiah & Judson Ames) Widow of Josiah Ames S:12

Ames, Clara E - Died 1845 Sept 3 Age 7 mos 19 days Daughter of Asa & Caroline Ames (next to them)(omitted from the book) S:14

Ames, Doris - Died 1895 Born 1889 (Ames stone) (with Samuel & Mother Ames & others) S:12

Ames, Dorothy - Died 1927 Born 1895 (Ames stone) (with Samuel & Mother Ames & others) S:12

Ames, Edward W - Died 1859 May 31 Age 24 (between Sidney & Samuel Ames) S:13

Ames, Edwin - Died 1857 Oct 1 Age 12 years, 8 months S:3

Ames, Electa A - Died 1859, 2nd Age 54 (stone not clear & broken) (between Otis W Blount & Sidney Lovell) S:13

Ames, Enos - Died 1845 Dec 19 in his 54th yr (next to Mrs Mary Ames, wife) S:13

Ames, Enos Jr - Died 1844 Sept 26 in his 29th yr (next to possible mother, Mrs Mary Ames) S:13

Ames, Eunice - Died 1873 March 15 Age 28 years, 5 months Wife of Eugene B Coleman (next to Sophia & James Coleman) S:14

Ames, Eveline W - Died 1840 Born 1817 (Crowell stone) (with Sarah P Ames & others) S:14

Ames, Frederick - Died 1895 Born 1817 (Crowell stone) (with Eveline W Ames & others) S:14

Ames, Granville - Died 1886 Born 1834 (with wife, Thankful Hamblin) S:13

Ames, Harriet G - Died 1898 Born 1817 (large Ames stone) S:12

Ames, Isaac I - Died 1864 Oct 21 Age 80 years, 7 months (next to wife, Bulah Ames) S:14

Ames, Isadore A - Died 1915 Born 1843 Wife of Bradford Ames (with him & James Parker & others) S:13

Ames, John - Died 1 Oct 1857 Age 12 yrs 8 mos (next to Lucy P. Sturgess) S:3R

Ames, Josephine M (Cross) - Died 1973 May 4 Born 1901 May 3 Stone says "Mother" (next to Walcott Ames, his stone says "Father") S:13

Ames, Josiah - Died 1824 at New Orleans (with Chloe & Judson Ames) S:12

Ames, Josiah - Died 1885 Born 1804 (large Ames stone) S:12

Ames, Josiah A - Died 1900 Born 1827 (next to wife, Olive Ames) S:12

Ames, Judson - Died 1825 Nov in his 17th yr Son of Josiah & Chloe Ames (with them) S:12

Ames, Julius P - Died 1843 June 11 Age 1 year, 11 months Son of Cephas & Rhoda Ames (next to them) S:14

Ames, Lillie May - Died 1853 April Daughter of Josiah A & Asenath Ames S:12

Ames, Lucy F - Died 1893 March 9 Age 69 years, 9 months (with Rebecca S Ames & others) S:14

Ames, Lydis L Miss - Died 1845 April 9 in her 27th yr (next to Benjamin F Ames) S:13

Ames, Mary - Died 1830 Sept 5 Age 20 years, 1 month (stone worn) Wife of Nathan Ames S:14

Ames, Mary A - Died 1922 Born 1846 (with Osmond F Ames) S:12

Ames, Mary C - Died 1931 Born 1846 Wife of Nelson Bearse

Ames (Cont.)
(with him & others) S:12

Ames, Mary E - Died 1866 June 10 Age 79 years, 10 months Wife of Thomas Ames (next to him) S:12

Ames, Mary Mrs - Died 1865 April 15 in her 74th yr Widow of Enos Ames (between him & possible son, Enos Ames Jr) S:13

Ames, Maud - Died 1890 Born 1882 (with Alice M Jones) S:12

Ames, Olive Mrs - Died 1810 Aug 11 in her 26th yr (right side of stone broken) Wife of John Ames & daughter to Lothrop & Marcey Tu???? (Tucker?) S:12+12R

Ames, Oren P - Died 1845 Born 1842 (large Ames stone) S:12

Ames, Orlando - Died 1856 Born 1836 (large Ames stone) S:12

Ames, Orlando J - Died 1836 Born 1834 (large Ames stone) S:12

Ames, Osmond F - Died 1915 Born 1838 (with Mary A Ames) S:13

Ames, Prince L - Died 1832 Feb 15 in his 23rd yr (next to Chloe Ames, d 1828) S:12

Ames, Rebecca S - Died 1908 Born 1833 (with Carrie C Stratton & others) S:14

Ames, Rhoda H - Died 1903 March 18 Age 90 years 10 months (next to Cephas I Ames) S:14

Ames, Roland C - Died 1930 Born 1856 With wife, Alice M Jones S:12

Ames, Samuel L - Died 1846 June 25 Age 45 (next to Edward W Ames) S:13

Ames, Samuel M - Died 1929 Born 1858 (Ames stone) (with mother Ames & others) S:12

Ames, Sarah C - Died 1834 June 16 Age 5 years 10 months Daughter of Isaac & Bulah Ames (next to mother) S:14

Ames, Sarah E - Died 1847 Sept 3 Age 19 days Daughter of Asa & Caroline Ames (next to them) S:14

Ames, Sarah P - Died 1887 Born 1824 (Crowell stone) (with Wil-

Ames (Cont.)
liam L G Robbins & others) S:14

Ames, Sidney E - Died 1861 March 11 (stone broken) Age 1 year, 2 months (between Electa & Edward Ames) S:13

Ames, Simeon L - Died 1903 March 23 Age 80 years, 3 months, 17 days (with Lucy F Ames) S:14

Ames, Stephen C - Died 1840 Mar 1 Age 27 Born 1810 (buried next to wife, Ann H Ames) S:7

Ames, Thomas - Died 1814 Jan 14 Age 67 S:12

Ames, Thomas - Died 1860 June 15 Age 79 years, 11 months S:12

Amirault, Bertha M - Died 1987 Born 1898 (with Catherine S Leary) S:16

Anagnostou, Nicholas - Died 1966 Born 1886 S:15

Anderson, Annie H - Died 1854 Oct 31 Age 13? Daughter of David & Mary Anderson (next to father) S:19

Anderson, Annie H - Died 1896 Jan 27 Born 1863 Jan 4 (stone is down) (next to son, Arthur E Anderson) S:21

Anderson, Arthur E - Died 1887 Aug 3 Age 10 months Stone says,"Baby" Son of Joseph & Annie H Anderson (next to mother) S:21

Anderson, Clarence L - Died 1962 Born 1902 (with wife, Frances A Enos) S:19

Anderson, David (Capt) - Died 1863 Feb 8 Age 86 years, 4 months (next to daughter, Annie H Anderson) S:19

Anderson, Ellen - Died 1938 Dec 24 Born 1876 Aug 9 (next to Franklin C Lewis) Beloved with of Franklin Crocker Lewis, mother Beatrice, Madeleine, Thomas, Franklin She kept flying the flag of her unconquerable courage (new copper stone) S:8

Anderson, Frances A - Died (still

Anderson (Cont.)
living 1991?) Born 1896 (listed with Mabel A Nickerson & others) S:31

Anderson, George L - Died 1963 Born 1893 (with Pearl A Anderson) S:17

Anderson, Grace Cynthia - Died 1985 July 16 in Unity, Maine Age 83 yr 10 mo 20 days B 1901 Aug 26 at Woonsockett, Rhode Island (this is a rock stone with plaque) Wife of Charles Nelson Libby Jr (next to him) Married 26 Oct 1929 (also a scalptured stone w/gold leaf) S:19

Anderson, Ida F - Died 1974 Born 1891 (with Joel A Anderson) S:15

Anderson, Joel A - Died 1980 Born 1900 (with Ida F Anderson) S:15

Anderson, John - Died 1926 Born 1864 (buried with Eunice & Nelson Phinney & others) S:8

Anderson, John E - Died 1977 Born 1897 S:18

Anderson, Joyce K - Died 1989 June 16 Born 1932 April 23 S:19

Anderson, Lizzie E - Died 1950 Born 1869 S:8

Anderson, Marion C - Died 1978 Born 1902 (with Benjamin F Crosby & Mary S Eldridge) S:14

Anderson, Millidge T (Rev) - Died 1930 Born 1866 (buried next to Lizzie E Anderson) S:8

Anderson, Muriel H - Died 1980 Aug 8 Born 1900 Aug 1 (next to Stanley E Anderson) S:18

Anderson, Pearl A - Died 1964 Born 1896 (with George L Anderson) S:17

Anderson, Rishe Levine - Died 1988 Born 1932 (on reverse side of Margaret E Pinson stone) S:20

Anderson, Sarah Zilpha - Died 1981 Jan 2 Born 1891 Jan 28 Stone says,"Love Lillie" S:18

Anderson, Stanley E - Died 1954 Dec 14 Born 1894 Aug 24 From Massachusetts, was CM1 in

Anderson (Cont.)
USNRF during World War I (next to Muriel H Anderson) S:18

Anderson, Susan Jane - Died 1935 Born 1850 (buried with Eunice & Nelson Phinney) (she could have been a Clark?) S:8

Anderson, William - Died 1964 Born 1884 (with wife, Abbie B Dondale) S:15

Andrade, Antonio M - Died 1896 Born 1896 S:15

Andre, Manuel - Died 1977 Born 1892 Was a Pvt in US Army during World War I S:15

Andrews, Anthony J - Died 1954 Born 1884 (with Martha F Andrews) S:18

Andrews, Edward C - Died 1933 Born 1855 (this side of stone is marked "A" for Andrews on top) (with Mary J Andrews & others) S:21

Andrews, Elaine M - Died 1973 Born 1911 (in Tallman plot) (with Myrtle I Tallman & others) S:12

Andrews, Helen Whittemore - Died 1972 Born 1898 (next to William Andrews & Nellie & Hiram Whittemore) S:19

Andrews, Jessie - Died 1970 Born 1899 (undertaker plaque only) S:15

Andrews, Martha F - Died 1957 Born 1882 (with Anthony Andrews) S:18

Andrews, Mary J - Died 1926 Born 1851 (with Isaac P Laha & others) S:21

Andrews, Philip D - Died 1978 Born 1904 (he was a Mason) (in Tallman plot with Harry L Tallman & others) S:12

Andrews, William P - Died 1966 May 17 Born 1890 Dec 3 From Massachusetts, was FIFC in Med Det 302 Infantry during World War I (next to Helen Whittemore Andrews) S:19

Annabel ?, Patience - Died 178? ? 27th (stone laying on ground,

Annabel ? (Cont.)
not clear) S:11

Annabel, Lucretia - Died 1805 located in row 17 S:11R

Annabel, Patience - Died 1760 located in row 6 S:11R

Annabel, Prudence - Died 90th year (stone not clear) Widow of Samuel Annabel (stone next to hers could be his, but cannot read it) S:11

Annable, Abigail - Died 1784 March 17 in her 70th yr Wife of Thomas Annable S:11R

Annable, Annah Bacon - Died 1728 May 9 in her 31st yr Wife of Nathaniel Bacon S:11R

Annable, Ansel - Died 1851 Aug 2 Age 65 (next to dau, Polly, d 1834) S:11

Annable, David - Died 1806 April 14 Age 2 Son of Samuel & Desire (buried next to mothers stone) S:10

Annable, Davis - Died 1898 Dec 12/17 ? Born 1846 Sept 2 S:10

Annable, Desire - Died 1714 Feb 14 in her 18th yr Daughter of Samuel & Patience Doggett Annable S:11R

Annable, Desire - Died 1819 June 30 in her 39th yr Relict of Samuel Annable (on same stone with him) S:10

Annable, Edward - Died 1917 Jan 19 Born 1840 Dec 16 (possible son of Freeman & Hitty Annable buried with family) S:10

Annable, Elizabeth - Died 1906 Jan 20 1849 July 8 S:10

Annable, Elizabeth L - Died 1855 Sept 29 or 1835 Born 1831 June 25 Daughter of Freeman & Hitty Annable (above 1835 death date Hinckley Cem records #10R) S:10

Annable, Emma - Died 1908 Born 1844 Wife of Daniel W Percival (on same stone with him) S:10

Annable, Experience - Died 1815 Oct 13 in her 62nd yr Relict of Joseph Annable (next to him)

Annable (Cont.)
S:11
Annable, Hittie - Died 1896 Feb 9
Born 1807 Feb 7 Wife of Freeman Annable S:10
Annable, James Freeman - Died
1856 Feb 29 Born 1838 May 1
Son of Freeman & Hitty Annable
(buried next to mother) S:10
Annable, Joseph - Died 1811 Mar
24, Age 57 (worn)(erected to the
memory of...)(next to wife, Expe-
rience Annable) S:11+26R
Annable (Amable?), Lucretia - Died
1861 Sept 13 Age 70 years, 5
months Widow of Ansel D Annable
(there is an Ansel Annable who
died 1851?)(Hinkley shows
Amable spelling) (located at
Lothrop's Hill) S:11R+26R
Annable, Lucretia C - Died 1855
April 10 Age 24 Daughter of
Ansel D & Lucretia Annable
(Hinkey shows Amable - possible
error) S:11R+26R
Annable, Lydia Miss - Died 1837
Sept 10 in her 55th yr (next to
Thomas, Samuel & Polly Anna-
ble whos parents were Joseph &
Experience Annable) S:11
Annable, Mehitable - Died 1747
June 11 Daughter of Samuel &
Bethiah Russel S:11+26R
Annable, Parenee(?) Mrs - Died
(date worn off) Widow of Samuel
Annable S:11
Annable, Patience - Died 1760 Oct
in her 90th yr Wife of Samuel
Annable S:11R
Annable, Paulie - Died 1813 Dec 8
in her 26th yr Daughter of
Joseph & Experience Annable
S:11
Annable, Polly - Died 1834 Aug 1
Age 14 Daughter of Ansel &
Lucretia Annable (next to father)
(next to large cript above ground
with metal door, no names list-
ed, but dated 1876, also stone
down in front, buried) S:11
Annable, Polly Miss - Died 1813
Dec 8 in her 26th yr Daughter of

Annable (Cont.)
Joseph & Experience Annable
(on same stone with Samuel
Annable) S:11
Annable, Samuel - Died 1744 June
21 in his 75th yr S:11+26R
Annable, Samuel - Died 1811 Aug
2 in his 40th yr at Wilmington,
North Carollina (listed on same
stone with wife, Desire)(is this
the same Samuel who is listed in
source 11 with Miss Polly
Annable?) S:10
Annable, Samuel - Died 1814 Aug
23 in his 40th yr at Wilmington,
North Carolina (on same stone
with, Miss Polly Annable)(is this
the same Samuel who is listed in
source 10 with, wife Desire
Annable?) S:11
Annable, Samuel - Died 1814 Aug
23 in his 40th yr in Wilmington,
North Carolina Son of Joseph &
Mrs Experience Annable (on
same slate with Polly) S:11R
+26R
Annable, Thomas - Died 1798 Dec
6 in his 91st yr S:11R
Annable, Thomas - Died 1814 ?
17th Age 18 ? Son of Joseph &
Experience Annable S:11
Annable, Thomas - Died 1814 17th
Oct Age 18 (month & age from
Hinckley Ceme records 11R) Son
of Thomas & Experience Anna-
ble S:11+26R
Annand, Geneive - Died 1882 Born
1859 Daughter of James &
Isabella Annand S:12
Annand, Isabella B - Died 1895
(with James Annand) S:12
Annand, James - Died 1889 (with
Isabella B Annand) S:12
Annible, Martha - Died 26 April
1741 Age 7 Daughter of Samuel
& Remember Annible S:5R
Antone, Lurana - Died 1836 Dec 8
in her 18th yr (age is from
Hinckley Ceme records) Wife of
Joseph Antone S:5
Appleton, (infant) - Died 1807 Mar
25 in Boston Daughter of Capt

Appleton (Cont.)
Oliver & Hannah Appleton S:10

Appleton, Thomas H - Died 1814 Jan 13 Age 12 years,10 months Son of Capt Oliver & Hannah Appleton (with Infant Appleton) S:10

Araugo, Frank D - Died 1965 Born 1881 S:15

Archer, Charles A - Died 1966 Born 1895 (with wife, Vera S Archer) S:18

Archer, Rosalinda D - Died 1907 Feb 2 Born 1829 June 5 S:5

Archer, Vera S - Died 1984 Born 1909 Wife of Charles A Archer) S:18

Archondis, Constandinos - Died 1984 Born 1896 Was a Private in US Army during World War I S:15

Arenovski, Julia - Died 1925 Born 1853 S:31

Arenovski, Louis - Died 1937 Jan 29 Born 1861 Nov 4 (large stone) (buried with Louis V Arenovski) S:8

Arenovski, Louis V - Died 1959 Oct 20 Born 1892 May 20 (large stone) (buried with Louis Arenovski) S:8

Arico, Cora M Stevens - Died 1954 Born 1906 Has a Veteran star which says, "1944-46" (next to Richard A Stevens) S:13

Arington, Frances - Died (still living 1991?) Born 1912 Wife of Joseph Novak (next to him) S:11

Arkwell, Helen F - Buried 1985 Nov 8 Age 84 Located in section 11, lot 77, grave 2 S:15R

Arms, Elda B - Died 1971 Born 1904 (with Francis E Arms) S:11

Arms, Francis E - Died 1987 Born 1904 (with Elda B Arms) S:11

Arms, Frank L - Died 1935 Born 1861 (with Henrietta F Arms) S:11

Arms, Henrietta F - Died 1956 Born 1864 (with Frank L Arms) S:11

Arms, Richard Woodworth - Died

Arms (Cont.)
1988 Mar 27 Born 1900 Feb 21 Was Private in US Army during World War I (with Ruth Adams Arms) S:11

Arms, Ruth Adams - Died 1980 Born 1903 (with Richard W Arms) S:11

Arnold, Edward T - Died 1951 Born 1881 (next to Lillian C Arnold) S:17

Arnold, Lillian C - Died 1975 Born 1890 (next to Edward T Arnold) S:17

Arvanitis, George - Died 1988 Oct 2 Born 1894 May 21 (with Mary Arvanitis) S:15

Arvanitis, Mary - Died (still living 1991?) Born 1911 Sept 8 (listed with George Arvanitis) S:15

Ashe, Francis B - Died 1934 Born 1877 S:17

Ashe, Minnie - Died 1953 Born 1884 Stone says,"Mother" S:16

Ashley, Cora H - Died 1874 Feb 23 Born 1841 July 1 Wife of Rev William Ashley (with him & others) S:14

Ashley, William (Rev) - Died 1878 Oct 1 Born 1823 Nov 11 (with Addie L Childs) S:14

Ashley, William Meredith - Died 1973 Born 1893 S:11

Ashworth, Belle Fenner - Died 1956 Born 1894 (next to Joseph L Ashworth) S:11

Ashworth, Joseph L - Died 1977 Born 1895 Was PVT in US Army in World War I (flag at stone) S:11

Askew, Bertha A - Died 1960 Born 1888 (with Edwin Askew) S:17

Askew, Edwin - Died 1974 Born 1885 (with Bertha A Askew) S:17

Atkins, Helen - Died 1883 Born 1882 Daughter of James & Helen Atkins S:2

Atkins, Helen D - Died 1898 Born 1831 (buried next to James R Atkins) S:2

Atkins, James R - Died 1864 Born 1831 S:2

Atkins, Sheldon - Died 1892 Born 1891 Son of James & Helen Atkins S:2

Atkins, Temperance - Died 1896 July 29 Age 77 years, 6 months S:10

Atsalis, Katina K - Died 1988 Born 1900 (with Konstantinos D Atsalis) S:15

Atsalis, Konstantinos D - Died 1980 Born 1894 (with Katina K Atsalis) S:15

Atwater, Jean Howe - Died 1975 Jan 20 Born 1876 Sept 7 Wife of James H Morse (with him) S:14

Atwater, Miley Benner - Buried 1986 March 26 Age 87 section, 11 lot 55 S:15R

Atwood, Doris S - Died (still living in 1991?) Born 1907 (listed with Ralph F Atwood) S:13

Atwood, James R - Died (no dates) He was a Landsman in US Navy (next to other military stones like William Ward & Philip Hughes) S:18

Atwood, Ralph F - Died (still living in 1991?) Born 1906 (listed with Doris S Atwood) S:13

Auglair, Kenneth T - Died 1985 Born 1951 S:19

Austin, Margaret A - Died 1932 Born 1852 (with Mary E O'Donnell) S:16

Austin, Mary Louise - Died 1990 July 14 Born 1921 Feb 17 (with Paul Howe Austin) S:20

Austin, Paul Howe - Died (still living 1991?) Born 1920 Dec 28 (he has 2 stones, one says,"Howe", the other, "Austin"?) (with Mary Louise Austin) S:20

Avery, Earle Rexford - Died 1954 Born 1881 (with wife, Florence Hanson) S:18

Ayling, Alice S - Died 1988 Born 1893 S:8

Ayling, Charles L - Died 1970 Born 1875 (with Alice S Ayling) S:8

Ayling, Edith Cornish - Died 1965 Jan 31 Born 1871 Mar 28 (in

Ayling (Cont.)
Ayling & Cornish plot) S:8

Ayling, Robertson - Died 1930 Feb 9 Born 1907 Mar 24 He was an Aviator S:8

Aylmer, George - Died 1914 March 8 Born 1913 Sept Son of George Aylmer & Catherine Tuohy (with them & George F Aylmer Jr & others) S:31

Aylmer, George F - Died 1945 Oct 23 Born in County Limerick, Ireland Son of Michael Aylmer & Ellen Bray (with them & Catherine V Tuohy & others) S:31

Aylmer, George F Jr - Died 1975 Jan 11 Born 1916 July 16 Son of George Aylmer & Catherine Tuohy (with them & Martin J Aylmer & others) S:31

Aylmer, Henry J - Died (no date) Born 1912 June 23 Son of George F Aylmer & Catherine Tuohy (with them & George Aylmer & others) S:31

Aylmer, John P - Died 1941 Born 1878 S:16

Aylmer, Martin J - Died 1919 May 10 Born 1917 Aug 4 Son of George Aylmer & Catherine Tuohy (with them & George Aylmer d1914 & others) S:31

Aylmer, Mary Josephine - Died 1954 Born 1883 S:16

Aylmer, Michael - Died 1933 Oct 27 Born in Ireland (with wife, Ellen Bray & son, George Aylmer & others) S:31

Azadian, Harry P - Died 1967 Born 1887 (with wife, Mary N Ryder & M Jean Brushaber & others) S:19

B A S, - Died (this only says,"ASB", another stone there too which says, "RAB", they are between Leo Allen & Russell L Cousins) S:12

B F, - Died 1836 (this is on a foot stone which is also out of the ground, no main head stone) S:21

B R A - Died (a small stone that

B R A (Cont.)

only says "RAB", next to this one is another that says,"ASB", these stones are between Leo Allen & Russell L Cousins) S:12

B, ? Silva - Died Died in 1700's (stone badly worn) S:1

Babbidge, Mary - Died 1861 Aug 25 Age 77 years, 8 months S:4

Babbitt, Alice C - Died 1986 Born 1900 S:17

Babies In Purgatory Plot - Died (this listing is for all the (undertakers plaques) children who were not baptised and laid to rest down a hill away from the others in the cemetery, these markers will soon be gone never to know which child is in the right plot, most are dated 1950-70's) S:16

Backer, Anna Mrs - Died 1739 Mar 21 or 1732/3 in her 57th yr (per Hinckley ceme records) Wife of Deac John Backer S:5

Backus, (infant son) - Died 1852 Son of Joshua & Mary Backus S:5

Backus, Abagail - Died 1814 Jan 9 in her 67th yr Wife of Thomas Backus S:7

Backus, Abby B - Died 1845 Dec 5 Age 4 yrs 7 mos Daughter of Calvin Backus Jr and Betsy S:5R2

Backus, Alfred - Died 1900 Born 1844 (buried next to Elizabeth Backus) S:8

Backus, Alonzo - Died 1909 Born 1838 Son of Urial & Sarah Backus S:7

Backus, Alton G - Died 1851 Born 1849 Child of Joshua & Nary Backus S:5

Backus, Bessie C - Died 1938 Born 1867 (buried next to Alfred & Elizabeth Backus) S:8

Backus, Betsey W - Died 1888 Born 1806 S:5

Backus, Calvin - Died 1816 or 1846 in his 70th yr Born 1776 (1846 date from Hinckley Cem

Backus (Cont.)

records #5R) S:5

Backus, Calvin Jr - Died 1879 Born 1807 S:5

Backus, Christina - Died 1859 Aug 23 Born 1807 May 28 Wife of John J Backus (buried next to him) S:7

Backus, Delia E - Died 1905 Nov 8 Born 1831 Dec 25 Stone says, "At rest" (next to Otway B Backus) S:14

Backus, Elizabeth - Died 1922 Born 1848 S:8

Backus, Elizabeth C - Died 1897 Born 1836 Daughter of Urial M & Sarah Backus S:7

Backus, George O - Died 1895 Born 1846 Son of Urial & Sarah Backus S:7

Backus, Gilbert Irving - Died 1867? June 1 Born 1859 Aug 25 Son of Simeon & Tryplosa Backus (listed with Simeon & Minnie Backus) S:12

Backus, Helen M - Died 1878 Mar 2 Died at Malden, Massachusetts) Born 1838 July 4 Daughter of John C & Christina Backus S:7

Backus, J Francis - Died 1882 Age 37 years, 8 months Born 1844 Son of Urial & Sarah Backus S:7

Backus, John J - Died 1894 Feb 8 Born 1804 Apr 27 S:7

Backus, Joseph - Died 1852 Dec 23 Age 52 years, 9 months, 11 days (between wife, Tryphosa Backus & Sarah D Backus) S:21

Backus, Joseph H - Died 1901 Born 1829 Stone says, "GAR" (there is also a plaque that says, "Iyanough Tribe #14 Hyannis") with wife Seraphina De Backus) S:21

Backus, Joshua - Died 1896 May 21 Born 1822 Apr 8 S:5

Backus, Lemuel F - Died 1918 Born 1866 (buried next to Alfred, Elizabeth, Bessie Backus) S:8

Backus, Lucy H - Died 1871 Sept 7

Backus (Cont.)
Age 40 years, 10 months Widow
of Simeon Backus & daughter of
Solomon & Sally Hinckley (next
to parents) S:19

Backus, Lydia - Died 1850 in her
78th yr Born 1772 Widow of
Calvin Backus S:5

Backus, Mary - Died 1856 June 3
Born 1822 May 19 Wife of
Joshua Backus S:5

Backus, Mary C - Died 1876 Feb 25
in her 72nd yr S:6

Backus, Mary M - Died 1935 Born
1846 Daughter of Urial & Sarah
Backus S:7

Backus, Minnie Augusta - Died
1867 May 26 Born 1861 April 27
(listed with Simeon & Gilbert
Backus) S:12

Backus, Otway B - Died 1897 Feb
25 Born 1817 Mar 14 Stone
says, "Father" (next to Delia E
Backus) S:14

Backus, Patience - Died 1853 July
29 in her 77th yr Wife of Reuben
D Backus (buried next to him)
S:7

Backus, Reuben D - Died 1844 Aug
3 in his 73rd yr (buried next to
wife, Patience Backus) S:7

Backus, Sarah - Died 1892 Born
1809 (entire family buried near
each other) S:7

Backus, Sarah D - Died 1870?
March 2 Age 56 (stone down &
broken) (next to Joseph Backus)
S:21

Backus, Seraohina De - Died 1931
Born 1836 Wife of Joseph
Backus (with him) S:21

Backus, Simeon - Died 1865 Oct
Born 1829 Nov 1 (with Minnie
Augusta Backus) Sailed from NY
20 Oct 1865 Master of Stir DH
Mount for Jacksonville, Florida,
supposed lost in gale immediately after S:12

Backus, Susie M - Died 1883 Born
1880 (stone says grandchild)
Grandchild of Joshua & Mary
Backus S:5R

Backus, Tryphosa - Died 1863
June 17 Age 32 Wife of Simeon
Backus (next to Minnie,Gilbert &
Simeon Backus) S:12

Backus, Tryphosa Mrs - Died 1846
Oct 12 in her 45th yr Wife of
Joseph Backus (next to him)
S:21

Backus, Urial M - Died 1891 Born
1811 S:7

Bacon, (Infant) - Died 1827 July 2
(small stone) Daughter of
Freeman & Rebecca Bacon S:10

Bacon, (Infant) - Died 4 months old
Daughter of John & Eliza Bacon
(next to John Bacon Esq) S:9

Bacon, Abagail - Died 1859 Jan 18
Born 1862 Nov 6 Relict of
Honorable, Ebenezer Bacon S:9

Bacon, Abagail C - Died 1801 Dec
30 in her 18th yr Daughter of
Ebenezer & Rebecca Bacon S:9

Bacon, Abba G - Died 1879 Mar 10
Age 82 years,6 months (next to
George G Bacon) S:10

Bacon, Abigail - Died 1781 Aug 15
or 16 Age 7 weeks,14 or 4 days
Daughter of Ebenzer & Abigail
Bacon S:5

Bacon, Abigail - Died 1781 July 1
(Sunday) Consort of Ebenezer
Bacon (Hinckley records #5R say
she died Sunday, July 1 age 22)
S:5

Bacon, Abigail - Died 1859 Jan 18
Born 1769 Nov 6 Relict to
Honorable Ebenezer Bacon S:9R

Bacon, Abigail Miss - Died 1801
Dec 30 Age 18 Daughter of
Ebenezer & Rebecca Bacon Esq
S:9R

Bacon, Albert J - Died 1927 Born
1857 (with wife, Alice E Stickney) S:18

Bacon, Alexander - Died 1842 Sept
17 Age 6 months Son of Alex &
Mary M Bacon S:12

Bacon, Alioe T(or P) - Died 1885
July 12 Born 1796 Sept 27
(stone is on the ground, broken)
S:10

Bacon, Ann - Died 1768 Aug 27

Bacon (Cont.)
Wife of Nathaniel (buried next to Nathaniel Baker?) S:9

Bacon, Anna - Died 1804 Oct 29 Age 39 Wife of Isaac Bacon Jr S:10

Bacon, Anna - Died 1806 Aug 7 (stone small & worn) Daughter of Otis & Abigail Bacon (Hinckley Ceme records #10R say date of death the 17th, Age 2 years, 5 months) S:10

Bacon, Anna - Died 1832 Oct 31 Age 82 (buried next to Capt Samuel Bacon) S:9

Bacon, Annah/Annable - Died 1728 May 9 in her 31st yr Wife of Nathaniel Bacon (located on Lothrop's Hill) S:26R

Bacon, Betsey L - Died 1809 Sept 30 Age 3 Daughter of Isaac & Anna Bacon (Hinckley Ceme records #10R say 1802 for death age of four years, 7 days) S:10

Bacon, Betsey Mrs - Died Sept (underground) Widow of Oris Bacon (buried next to him) (Hinckley Ceme records #10R say Sept 14, 1824 in her 85th yr for death record) S:10+26R

Bacon, Carolin P - Died 1916 Sept 15 Born 1834 Apl 11 S:4

Bacon, Carrie M - Died 1941 Born 1870 Wife of Alfred T Small (with him) S:18

Bacon, Corrina A - Died 1849 Sept 20 Age 3 Daughter of Alex & Mary Bacon S:12

Bacon, Corrina L - Died 1856 April 20 Age 13 or 19 months Daughter of Alex & Mary Bacon S:12

Bacon, David - Died 1869 May 8 Born 1802 May 20 S:9R

Bacon, David G - Died 1869 May 8 Born 1802 May 29 S:9

Bacon, Deborah - Died 1721 April 2 in her 29th yr Wife of Samuel Bacon S:9+26R

Bacon, Desire Miss - Died 1811 Mar 2 in her 73rd yr S:10

Bacon, Desire Mrs - Died 1747 April 25 in her 23rd yr (Age from

Bacon (Cont.)
Hinckley Ceme records #11R) S:11+26R

Bacon, Ebenezer - Died 1793 Nov 3 in his 18th yr (age from Hinckley Ceme records #11R) Son of James & Joanna Bacon S:11 +26R

Bacon, Ebenezer - Died 1864 or 1868 June 24 Born 1794 Aug 28 Son of Ebenezer & Abagail Bacon (buried next to wife, Phoebe Bacon)(1868 death date from Hinckley Ceme records #9R) S:9

Bacon, Ebenezer (Honorable) - Died 1811 Nov 28 Born 1756 Aug 30 S:9

Bacon, Edward - Died 1825 Nov 1 Age 4 (age 4 from Hinckley Ceme records #9R) Son of Ebenezer & Phoebe Bacon S:9+26R

Bacon, Edward (Capt) - Died 1811 Aug 20 in his 69th yr S:10

Bacon, Edward (Capt) - Died 1853 June 18 Born 1796 Apr 10 S:9

Bacon, Edward (Esq) - Died 1783 Mar 6 Age 68 (next to Patience Bacon who died 1764) S:9+26R

Bacon, Eleanor - Died 1853 Aug 21 Age 9 years, 3 months Daughter of Owen & Eleanor Bacon S:4

Bacon, Elisha - Died 1891 Born 1825 Son of Ebenezer & Phoebe Bacon (buried next to sister, Emily Bacon) S:9

Bacon, Elisha (Rev) - Died 1863 Jan 11 Age 63 years, 6 months (buried with wife, Emeline V Bacon & family) S:8

Bacon, Elisha W - Died 1859 Sept 7 Age 21 years, 8 months, 19 days Fell from a loft on board ship, Skylark into ocean 300 miles off Hong Kong (stone is with George B Bacon too) (also listed with Rev Elisha Bacon & family) S:8

Bacon, Eliza B - Died 1871 or 1874 Feb 13 Born 1809 Oct 21 Wife of Francis Bacon (buried next to him) (1874 death date from

Bacon (Cont.)

Hinckley Ceme records #9R) S:9

Bacon, Elizabeth Vaughan - Died 1891 March 8 Born 1855 March 14 Daughter of George & Olivia Buckminster Bacon S:9R

Bacon, Eloisa Miss - Died 1835 Oct 27 Age 29 S:10

Bacon, Emeline V - Died 1887 Mar 20 Born 1802 Oct 7 (buried with husband, Rev Elisha Bacon & family) S:8

Bacon, Emily - Died 1883 Jan 15 Born 1818 Jan 3 Daughter of Ebenezer & Phoebe Bacon (buried next to brother, Edward Bacon) S.9

Bacon, Emily A - Died 1845 Nov 18 in her 20th yr Wife of James M Bacon S:4

Bacon, Emily A - Died 1929 Born 1861 (with Henry Bacon & Winthrop & Millicent Bassett) S:18

Bacon, Everett L - Died 1960 Born 1880 (with Nellie E Bacon) S:18

Bacon, Ferdenand - Died 1836 March 30 Age 3 months, 24 days Son of Nathaniel & Mary F Bacon (next to father) S:21

Bacon, Francis - Died 1877 May 9 Born 1804 Dec 21 (buried next to wife, Eliza B Bacon) S:9

Bacon, Francis E - Died 1854 or 1834 Oct 2 Age 2 years, 9 months, 27 days Son of Freeman & Rebecca C Bacon (1834 death date from Hinckley Ceme records #10R) S:10

Bacon, Francis William - Died 1849 Oct 31 Age 26 Died in Macao, China Son of Ebenezer & Phoebe Bacon (stone in family plot) S:9

Bacon, George - Died 1873 June 28 Born 1819 Aug 9 Son of Ebenezer & Phoebe Bacon S:9

Bacon, George B - Died 1856 Apr 9 Age 23 years,3 or 7 months, 21 days Died in New Orleans (stone is with Elisha W Bacon) (also listed with Sarah L Bacon) S:8

Bacon, George F - Died 1887 Oct

Bacon (Cont.)

10 Born 1825 Feb 10 (with Margaret F Bacon) S:18

Bacon, George G - Died 1877 Mar 14 Age 32 S:10

Bacon, Georgianna - Died 1959 Born 1874 Wife of James Kenney (with him) S:17

Bacon, Gertrude - Died 1958 Born 1900 Wife of William E Lewis (with him & next to Ens E Wesley Lewis & others) S:18

Bacon, Gracie Gloria? - Died 1892 Jan 13 Born 1888 Oct 6 Daughter of Oliver & Mary Bacon (two stones away from them & with, Jonnie Maynard Bacon) S:18

Bacon, Hannah - Died 1708 May (worn stone) Wife of ? S:11

Bacon, Hannah - Died 1753 May 8 in her 59th yr (age from Hinckley Ceme records #9R) Wife of Samuel Bacon S:9+26R

Bacon, Hannah - Died 1804 Oct 29 Wife of Isaac Bacon S:10

Bacon, Hannah G - Died 1822 Mar 30 Age 46 Wife of Capt Josiah Bacon (next to him) S:10

Bacon, Henry - Died on the 19th (stone small & worn) Son of (possibly Isaac & Anna Bacon) (buried next to Betsey Bacon, possible sister)(Hinckley Ceme records #10R say death date was 12 July 1773 age 14 years, 22 days) S:10

Bacon, Henry C - Died 1939 Born 1859 (with Emily A Bacon & others) S:18

Bacon, Ira B - Died 1895 Dec 24 Born 1828 July 11 S:4

Bacon, Ira W - Died 1929 Born 1866 (with wife, Sabina F Lavell & others) S:18

Bacon, Isaac (Capt) - Died 1819 June 24 in his 87th yr S:10+26R

Bacon, Isaac Jr (Capt) - Died 1810 Aug 21 Age 46 (buried next to wife, Anna Bacon) S:10

Bacon, Jeremiah - Died 1722 Oct 17 Age 4 months Son of Isaac & Mary Bacon S:9R

19

Bacon, Jeremiah - Died 1724 May 30 in his 29th yr S:9R+26R

Bacon, John (Esq) - Died 1731 Aug 20 in his 67th yr (buried next to Mary Bacon-Her stone is broken) S:9+26R

Bacon, John Mrs - Died 1745 May 24 in her 50th yr S:9+26R

Bacon, Jonnie Maynard - Died 1891 Dec 29 Born 1886 Oct 23 Son of Oliver & Mary Bacon (two stones away from them & with sister, Gracie Gloria Bacon) S:18

Bacon, Josephine L - Died 1928 Born 1841 (listed with husband, Nelson & Willis P Bacon & others) S:18

Bacon, Josiah (Capt) - Died 1825 Aug 3 Born 1776 Feb 24 S:10

Bacon, Judah - Died 1865 Mar 12 in his 63rd yr S:4

Bacon, Leveret Taylor - Died 1782 Feb 29 Age 6 Son of Capt Nathan Bacon S:10

Bacon, Lillian L - Died 1933 Born 1905 (with Sabina Lavell & William Elliott Lewis & others) S:18

Bacon, Lois H - Died 1882 Sept 21 Age 76 years, 10 months, 16 days Widow of Almoran Bacon S:18

Bacon, Louisa Davis - Died 1891 Born 1816 Daughter of Ebenezer & Phoebe Bacon S:9R

Bacon, Lovy - Died 1843 June 13 Age 61 years, 1 month Wife of Capt Nath Bacon S:4

Bacon, Lydia - Died (dates not clear) Age 2 months, 23 days Daughter of Edward & Patience Bacon (Hinckley Ceme records #9R say death date was 1745 April 28) S:9+26R

Bacon, Lydia - Died 1802 Jan 19 Age 16 Daughter of Ebenezer & Rebecca Bacon (Hinckley Ceme records #9R say death year was 1802) S:9+26R

Bacon, Lydia Gorham - Died (before 1811) Oct Daughter of Henry & Nabby Bacon S:10

Bacon, Mahala - Died 1885 Aug 19 in her 81st yr Wife of Judah Bacon S:4

Bacon, Marcy - Died 1722/3 Feb 23 of her 13th yr Daughter of Samuel & Sarah Bacon (next to them) S:11+26R

Bacon, Marcy - Died 1722 located in row 16 S:11R

Bacon, Margaret F - Died 1924 Oct 25 Born 1837 March 28 (with George F Bacon) S:18

Bacon, Marietter Frances - Died 1840 Oct 5 Age 5 months, 15 days Daughter of Alex & Mary M Bacon S:12

Bacon, Mary - Died (stone is broken and not clear) (next to John Bacon Esq & Mercy Bacon) (Hinckley Ceme records #9R say death date was 1726 March 5 in her 62th yr) S:9+26R

Bacon, Mary - Died 1783 July 24 in her 84th yr Widow of Capt Samuel Bacon S:7

Bacon, Mary A - Died 1923 Born 1864 (with Oliver F Bacon) S:18

Bacon, Mary A - Died 1941 Born 1850 (stone says, "Wife") (with William Scudder) S:12

Bacon, Mary M - Died 1871 Dec 8 Age 53 Wife of Alex Bacon S:12

Bacon, Mercy - Died 1765 Mar 19 Age 31 yrs 2 mos Daughter of John & Elizabeth Bacon S:9+26R

Bacon, Nabby - Died 1824 Oct 16 Age 41 or 40 Widow of Capt Henry Bacon (age 40 from Hinckley Ceme records #10R) S:10

Bacon, Nath (Capt) - Died 1843 Sept 27 Age 67 years, 3 months June S:4

Bacon, Nathaniel - Died 1875 Oct 30 Age 73 years, 3 months, 10 days (listed next to Capt Nathaniel Bacon) S:21

Bacon, Nathaniel - Died 1878 Aug 25 Age 40 years, 6 months (with wife, Cornelia Williams) S:18

Bacon, Nathaniel (Capt) - Died

Bacon (Cont.)
1853 May 23 Age 44 years, 5
months, 7 days Erected by wife,
Mary F Bacon Died in Kingston,
Jamaica with Yellow Fever (next
to Nathaniel Bacon) S:21

Bacon, Nathaniel (Deacon) - Died
1737/8 Jan 8 in his 64th yr
(stone worn) (next to wife, Ruth
Bacon, d1756) S:11+26R

Bacon, Nellie E - Died 1952 Born
1885 (with Everett L Bacon) S:18

Bacon, Nelson - Died 1893 Born
1841 Lost at sea (listed with
wife, Josephine L Bacon &
others) S:18

Bacon, Nelson W - Died 1946 Born
1870 (with Harrison D Doty &
others) S:18

Bacon, Oliver F - Died 1930 Born
1861 (with Mary A Bacon) S:18

Bacon, Oris - Died 1813 or 15 in
his 69th yr (stone worn) S:10+
26R

Bacon, Orris Mr - Died 1773 July
11 in his 58th yr (footstone is
broken in many pieces) S:10+
26R

Bacon, Patience - Died (no date)
located in row 6 S:11R

Bacon, Patience - Died 1718 Jan
13 Age 27 Wife of Nathaniel
Bacon S:11R

Bacon, Patience - Died 1728? June
in her 27th yr (stone turned
over) Wife of Nanael(?) Bacon
S:11+26R

Bacon, Patience - Died 1764 Oct ?
(day not clear) in her 44th yr
Wife of Edward Bacon S:9+26R

Bacon, Patience (Annable) - Died
1746/7 Mar 1 in her 42nd yr
Wife of Joseph Bacon (Annable
from Hinckley Ceme records
#11R) S:11+26R

Bacon, Patience ? - Died 1728 May
19 (stone not clear) (next to
Patience Bacon) S:11

Bacon, Phoebe - Died 1865 June
10 Age 32 Daughter of Ebenezer
& Phoebe Bacon (buried in
Bacon plot) S:9

Bacon, Phoebe - Died 1882 Mar 27
Born 1797 Feb 10 Wife of
Ebenezer Bacon (buried in
family plot with children and
next to husband) S:9

Bacon, Polly - Died 1849 Sept 18 in
her 81st yr Widow of Capt Jabez
Bacon S:4

Bacon, Rebecca - Died 1790 or
1791 June 1 in her 28th yr Born
1763 Nov 5 Wife of Ebenezer
Bacon & daughter of Nathan
Jenkins (1791 date from Hinckley Ceme records #9R) S:9+26R

Bacon, Ruth - Died 1756 July 9 in
her 80th yr Wife of Deacon,
Nathaniel Bacon, d1757/8 (next
to him) S:11+26R

Bacon, Samuel (Capt) - Died 1781
(died in a New Jersey prison ship
Obviously captured by the British during the American Revolution) (next to Anna Bacon) S:9

Bacon, Samuel (Deacon) - Died
1728 April 29 in his 46th yr
Deacon of East Church of Christ
in Barnstable, Mass S:11+26R

Bacon, Sarah - Died 1753 Sept 24
Age 74 Widow of Deacon, Samuel
Bacon (next to him, d1728)
S:11+26R

Bacon, Sarah - Died 1776 Apr 11
in her 24th yr Daughter of
Edward & Patience Bacon S:9

Bacon, Sarah - Died 1812 Jan 27
in her 74th yr Widow S:10R

Bacon, Sarah - Died 1823 June 23
Age 14 Daughter of Hon Ebenezer & Abagail Bacon S:9

Bacon, Sarah - Died 1916 Oct 2
Born 1827 Nov 26 Daughter of
Ebenezer & Phoebe Bacon
(buried next to brother, Elisha
Bacon) S:9

Bacon, Sarah L - Died 1834 Nov 23
Age 6 months, 20 days Daughter
of WW Bacon (stone says-At
Rest) (buried with George B
Bacon) S:8

Bacon, Simeon - Died 1739 Mar 19
in his 4th yr Son of John &
Elizabeth Bacon S:9+26R

Bacon, Susannah - Died (date underground) Daughter of Isaac & Aphia (or Anna) Bacon (Hinckley Ceme records #10R say death was 1802 Oct 14 Age 14 years, 3 months, 8 days & Anna for mothers name) S:10

Bacon, Temerance - Died 1843 Nov 13 Age 55 Daughter of Ebenezer Bacon Esq S:9

Bacon, Thomas - Died 1828 Oct 23 S:10R

Bacon, Willis P - Died 1903 Born 1866 (with Nelson W Bacon & others) S:18

Bagg, Lucy Mather - Died 1990 Born 1900 (undertaker plaque only) S:20

Bailey, Frank L - Died 1963 April 24 Born 1882 Sept 29 S:17

Bailey, Gideon - Died 1834 Mar 27 Age 49 S:10

Bailey, Harry Louis - Died 1962 May 26 Born 1877 Nov 13 at Manchester, New Hampshire Son of Charles Wesley Bailey & Lucretia Eastman Converse (with Helena Margherita Chesia Ravi) S:14

Bailey, Sarah G - Died 1822 Dec 22 Age 9 months, 9 days Daughter of Rev Stephen & Sarah Bailey S:5R

Bain, George HA - Died 1953 Born 1881 (with Emillie Larsen) S:12

Baken, Annah G - Died (date not clear) Wife of David Baken S:9

Baker, (baby) - Died 1874 Died for love (with Luther & Celia Baker) S:14

Baker, (baby) - Died 1876 Child of Luther & Celia Baker (with them) S:14

Baker, (infant) - Died 1820 Oct 13 Age 13 days Son of Silvester & Hannah Baker S:4

Baker, Abigail - Died 1847 Jan 11 Born 1761 May 11 Wife of Timothy Baker (last name not clear, but buried next to Timothy Baker) S:4

Baker, Abigail L - Died 1876 Dec

Baker (Cont.)
26 Born 1789 Sept 26 Wife of Timothy Baker S:4

Baker, Abijah - Died 1872 March 4 Age 52 years, 9 months Was in 40th Regimant Massachusetts Volunteers S:14

Baker, Abijah - Died 1879 Aug 9 Born 1795 Jan 20 Age 84 years, 6 months, 20 days (next to Alexander Baker) S:14

Baker, Abner - Died 1854 Apl 13 Age 18 Supposed lost at sea while on passage from Glasgow for Baltimore on ship, Bark Gov Briggs Son of Obed & Phebe Baker S:4

Baker, Adaline - Died 1892 Mar Born 1822 Dec S:7

Baker, Adelia, Frances - Died 1855 Oct 19 Age 1 year, 2 months, 14 days Daughter of Gorham F & CH? Baker S:4

Baker, Adolphus A - Died 1873 Feb 18 Born 1872 June 22 (with Isaac R Baker & others) S:18

Baker, Albert - Died 1918 Born 1918 Son of Albert Baker Wing & Lena Lewis (with them) (his last name should be Wing?) S:18

Baker, Albert P - Died 1888 Feb 18 Age 62 years, 2 months Stone says, "Father" (next to Esther A Baker & Willie Abner Baker) S:18

Baker, Alexander - Died 1867 June 8 Age 25 years, 2(?) months (next to Abijah Baker) S:14

Baker, Alice W - Died 1947 Born 1888 (this is an undertakers plaque which is just laying on grass, have no idea where plot is) S:21

Baker, Allen - Died 1900 Jan 20 Age 73 Stone says, "Father" & he was a "Mason" S:18

Baker, Alvah D - Died 1931 Born 1852 (with Susan I Baker) S:18

Baker, Alvin - Died 1899 Born 1814 (with Delana Baker) S:12

Baker, Ann - Died 1768 Aug 27 in her 68th yr Wife of Nathaniel

22

Baker (Cont.)
Baker S:9R+26R

Baker, Ann H - Died 1901 Feb 7 bc
1829 Sept 12 (on stone with
Harace S Baker) S:4

Baker, Ann M - Died 1822 Apl 22
Born 1882 May 1 S:4

Baker, Anna G - Died 1859 Feb 17
in her 58th yr Wife of David
Baker S:9R

Baker, Anna M - Died 1964 Born
1896 Wife of William H Baker
(with him) S:16

Baker, Anna Marie - Died 1979
Born 1912 (listed with John D
Baker) S:13

Baker, Anna Mrs - Died 1848 Dec
21 in her 83rd yr Wife of Benjamin Baker (next to him, d1851)
S:11

Baker, Asenath - Died 1870 Born
1805 (with Charles Baker) S:8

Baker, Avis E - Died 1948 Born
1887 S:14

Baker, Benjamin - Died 1846 Nov
18 Age 30 (next to possible
parents, Anna (1848) & Benjamin (1851) Baker) S:11

Baker, Benjamin - Died 1851? May
6 Age 83 (next to wife, Anna,
d1848) S:11

Baker, Bernard H - Died 1950 Born
1890 (on large Baker stone) S:11

Baker, Bessie - Died (no
dates)(there is a small white
stone behind her,like a childs
stone, no markings?)(not sure of
her last name?) S:18

Baker, Branda F - Died 1956 Born
1954 (on large Baker stone) S:11

Baker, Carroll E - Died 1964 Born
1924 Son of Charles & Henrietta
Baker (with them) S:18

Baker, Catherine M - Died 1932
Born 1881 (with Thomas Baker)
S:14

Baker, Celia K - Died 1924 Born
1842 (with Baby Baker & Luther
Baker) S:14

Baker, Charles - Died 1864 Feb 18
in his 28th yr Lost at sea in Sch
Breadnaught on same stone

Baker (Cont.)
with George Baker d: 1882 S:4

Baker, Charles - Died 1891 Born
1807 (with Asenath Baker) S:8

Baker, Charles G (Capt) - Died
1881 Mar 27 Age 53 years, 7
months S:4

Baker, Charles H - Died 1906 Born
1836 (with Susan P Baker) S:8

Baker, Charles L - Died 1962 Born
1883 (with wife, Henrietta B
Baker) S:18

Baker, Chester A - Died 1897 Born
1896 (next to Chester L & Mary
A Baker) S:31

Baker, Chester A - Died 1961 Born
1870 (with Marietta Baker) S:14

Baker, Chester L - Died 1941 Born
1863 (next to wife, Mary A
Baker) S:31

Baker, Clarence Eleazer - Died
1904 Born 1880 (with Fostina
Henrietta Baker & others) S:18

Baker, Clarence L - Died 1931 Born
1843 (with Maria J Baker) S:12

Baker, Clyde T - Died 1892 Oct 4
Age 2 months (with Martha
Baker & others) S:18

Baker, Cordelia - Died (no dates)
Age 14 years, 3 months, 12 days
Stone says, "Our Darling"
Daughter of Jeptha & Philena
Baker (next to them) S:18

Baker, Corinnie M - Died 1958
Born 1887 S:13

Baker, Cyrus A - Died 1836 July 21
Age 6 months Son of Cyrus &
Leonora Baker (next to mother)
S:18

Baker, David - Died 1872 May 7 in
his 80th yr S:9R

Baker, Delana - Died 1905 Born
1821 (with John Baker & Alvin
Baker) S:12

Baker, Dorinda - Died 1865 Dec 30
Age 51 Wife of Nehemia Baker
S:4

Baker, Dorothy A - Died (still living
1991?) Born 1901 (listed with J
Lincoln Baker) S:16

Baker, Edith S - Died 1925 Born
1893 (with Henry Harrison

Baker (Cont.)
Baker & others) S:18

Baker, Edward A - Died 1894 Born 1862 (with Mabel L Baker & others) S:18

Baker, Edwin - Died 1895 Born 1813 (with Persis Sears Baker) S:18

Baker, Eldred - Died 1849 Apr 30 Age 76 years, 9 months (buried next to wife, Ruth Baker) S:7

Baker, Eleazer - Died 1876 Dec 1 Born 1823 Jan 5 S:4

Baker, Eleazer - Died 1913 Born 1851 (with Fostina Bassett Baker & others) S:18

Baker, Eliza - Died 1859 Dec 14 Age 18 years, 6 months, 10 days Wife of Reuben Baker S:4

Baker, Eliza E - Died 1942 Born 1865 (with Cynthia R Jenckes & others) S:21

Baker, Elizabeth - Died 1855 Aug 24 Age 5 days Daughter of Reuben Baker S:4

Baker, Elizabeth B - Died 1855 Aug 19 Age 19 years, 2 months Wife of Reuben Barker & daughter of Capt Frederick Lovell (she obviously died giving birth to her daughter Elizabeth who is buried next to her & who was born 1855 Aug 19) S:4

Baker, Ella M - Died (no date) Born 1852 (stone over from vandals) Wife of William H Baker (with him & next to Toilston Phinney) S:18

Baker, Emma C - Died 1925 March 5 Born 1840 Nov 29 (with Ralph L Baker) S:18

Baker, Emma Jane - Died 1837 Apl 15 Age 22 years, 4 months, 7 days Wife of Capt Charles G Baker S:4

Baker, Emmeline - Died 1812 June 28 Age 3 years, 7 months, 20 days Daughter of Silvester & Hannah Baker S:10

Baker, Emy A - Died 1953 Born 1869 S:17

Baker, Esther A - Died 1907 June

Baker (Cont.)
25 Age 73 years, 8 months stone says,"Mother" (next to Albert P Baker) S:18

Baker, Etta - Died 1864 Born 1861 (with Susan P Baker) S:8

Baker, Eugene F - Died 1963 Born 1875 (with wife, Lola M Baker) S:14

Baker, Eugene S - Died 1976 Born 1897 (with Eugene & Lola Baker) S:14

Baker, Evelyn C - Died 1899 Nov 11 Born 1880 Aug 4 (next to Isaac B Baker & others) S:18

Baker, Everett D - Died 1959 Aug 23 Born 1894 June 27 From Massachusetts, was a Cook in Quartermaster Corp, during World War I S:18

Baker, Everett Hale - Died 1897 Born 1875 (with George Francis Baker & others) S:18

Baker, Ezra - Died (no date) located in row 17 S:11R

Baker, Ferdinand - Died 1932 Born 1852 (large Baker stone) S:11

Baker, Fostina Bassett - Died 1943 Born 1857 (with Christina Charlotta Bassett & others) S:18

Baker, Fostina Henrietta - Died 1897 Born 1885 (with Fostina Bassett Baker & others) S:18

Baker, Frances N - Died (still living in 1990?) Born 1928 (on large Baker stone) S:11

Baker, Frastus - Died 1899 Mar 3 Born 1842 Jan 12 Was a Soldier for 3 years in Company A, 24th Massachusetts Regiment (with Robert Evans) S:12

Baker, George F - Died 1882 Dec 24 Age 49 years, 6 months On the same stone with Charles Baker d: 1864 S:4

Baker, George Francis - Died 1906 Born 1842 (with James H Emery Baker & others) S:18

Baker, George W - Died 1868 Dec Born 1799 Mar S:7

Baker, Georgiana Howes - Died 1904 Born 1851 (with Everett

Baker (Cont.)
Hale Baker & others) S:18

Baker, Hannah - Died 1837 July
17 in her 54th yr Wife of Silvester Baker S:4

Baker, Hannah S - Died 1889 Born
1823 (with Charles H Baker) S:8

Baker, Harriet - Died 1884 Aug 6
Age 71 years, 8 months, 20 days
(with Winfield Scott Baker &
others) S:18

Baker, Henrietta B - Died 1950
Born 1884 Wife of Charles L
Baker (with him & son, Carroll E
Baker) S:18

Baker, Henry Adams - Died 1850
Born 1850 Son of Persis &
Martha Baker) S:18

Baker, Henry B - Died 1970 Born
1886 (with Thomas & Catherine
Baker) S:14

Baker, Henry C - Died 1897 Aug 6
Born 1857 Feb 26 S:4

Baker, Henry - Died 1900 April 18
Born 1835 March 23 (with Lucy
AR Baker & others) S:18

Baker, Henry Harrison - Died 1913
July 16 Born 1871 May 24 (with
Louise Stewart Baker & next to
Henry H Baker & family plot)
S:18

Baker, Horace S - Died 1925 Born
1852 On stone with Ann H
Baker S:4

Baker, Horatio - Died 1863 Apl 4
Age 33 years, 8 months Lost at
sea S:4

Baker, Howard - Died 1844 Born
1843 Son of Persis & Martha
Baker (with them) S:18

Baker, Irving - Died 1905 May 17
Born 1863 Aug 31 (next to
Edward J Carroll) S:18

Baker, Isaac B - Died (no dates)
(with Isabel F Baker, his wife)
S:18

Baker, Isaac R - died: 1874 March
12 Born 1873 Sept 29 (with
Henry Baker & others) S:18

Baker, Isabel F - Died 1931 Born
1874 Wife of Isaac B Baker (with
her) S:18

Baker, Izra C - Died (no markings)
Belonged to the Corp Co, 28
Massachusetts Infantry (American flag placed at grave) S:11

Baker, J Lincoln - Died 1956 Born
1889 (with wife. Dorothy A
Baker) S:16

Baker, James H - Died 1952 Born
1862 (with Everett Hale Baker &
others) S:18

Baker, Jany - Died 1811 Jan 15
Age 6 weeks Dec Daughter of
Hiram & Patty Baker S:4

Baker, Jeptha - Died 1886 Jan 9
Age 65 Stone says, "Father"
(with Philena Baker) S:18

Baker, John - Died 1853 Born
1845 (with Alvin & Delana
Baker) S:12

Baker, John D - Died (still living in
1991?) Born 1900 (listed with
anna Marie Baker) S:13

Baker, John F - Died 1916 Born
1836 (buried with Louise H
Baker) S:8

Baker, John W - Died 1872 March
31 Age 58 years, 10 months, 10
days (with Mary H Baker) S:18

Baker, Joseph - Died 1884 March 8
Age 73 years, 4 months, 28 days
(with Harriet Baker & others)
S:18

Baker, Joshua - Died 1900 Born
1840 (with Leslie Baker & others) S:18

Baker, Katharine C - Died 1914
Born 1868 Stone says,"Clover"
on top (next to Mary Carroll
Baker) S:18

Baker, Leonora - Died 1870? March
29 Born 1810 July 19 Stone
says, "Mother" Wife of Cyrus
Baker (next to son, Cyrus A
Baker) S:18

Baker, Leslie - Died 1905 Born
1890 (with Leslie Baxter Baker &
others) S:18

Baker, Leslie Baxter - Died 1878
Nov 21 Born 1874 Dec 22 (with
Rodney Baxter Sr & Jr & others)
S:18

Baker, Lillian R - Died 1868 April 7

Baker (Cont.)
Born 1866 Jan 26 (with Adolphus A Baker & others) S:18

Baker, Lizzie A - Died 1933 Born
1874 Wife of James Freeman
Crowell (with him & James L
Crowell & others) S:21

Baker, Lola M - Died 1961 Born
1876 Wife of Eugene F Baker
(with him & others) S:14

Baker, Loren H - Died 1900 Born
1828 Stone says, "Father"
(next to Lucy Baker) S:21

Baker, Louise H - Died 1895 Born
1838 (buried with John F Baker)
S:8

Baker, Louise Stewart - Died 1908
March 2 Born 1867 April 16
(with Walter Durell Baker &
others) S:18

Baker, Lucy AR - Died 1926 March
27 Born 1840 March 23
(with Edward A Baker & others)
(next to Loren H Baker) S:18

Baker, Ludencia - Died 1883 Feb 5
Age 33 years, 3 months Wife of
Benjamin Baker (next to Evelyn
C Baker & others) S:18

Baker, Luther - Died 1821 Nov 17
Son of Samuel & Temperance
Baker S:11+26R

Baker, Luther C - Died 1913 Born
1832 (with Celia K Baker) S:14

Baker, Lydia - Died 1820 Oct 3 in
her 26th yr S:1

Baker, Lydia - Died 1867 May 25
Age 64 years, 4 months Stone
says, "Thou wast a kind mother"
Wife of Abigah Baker (next to
him) S:14

Baker, Lydia G - Died 1877 Feb 21
Age 50 years, 5 months, 18(?)
days Wife of Bwer(?) Baker
(Middle initial found in Hinckley
ceme records) S:14

Baker, Lydia L - Died 1878 Jan 11
in her 78th yr S:4

Baker, Mabel - Died (still living ?)
Born 1917 wife of Walter Baker
(listed with him) S:12

Baker, Mabel Kimball - Died 1965
April 29 Born 1871 Sept 20

Baker (Cont.)
(with Edith S Baker & others)
S:18

Baker, Mabel L - Died 1904 July 6
Born 1868 Oct 9 (has 2 stones)
(with Mary R Baker & others)
S:18

Baker, Mabel N - Died 1985 Born
1888 (on large Baker stone) S:11

Baker, Maria J - Died 1915 Born
1844 Stone says, "God keep her
from harm" (with Clarence L
Baker) S:12

Baker, Marianna - Died 1913 Born
1842 (with Joshua Baker &
others) S:18

Baker, Marietta - Died 1928 Born
1849 (with Chester A Baker)
S:14

Baker, Marion - Died 1967 Born
1890 Wife of Jose Godoy (with
him) S:18

Baker, Martha G - Died 1944 Born
1886 (with Lola & Eugene Baker)
S:14

Baker, Martha J - Died 1916 Born
1858 (with Clyde T Baker &
others) S:18

Baker, Martha Sears - Died 1856
Born 1822 (with Persis Sears
Baker & others) S:18

Baker, Marther Mrs - Died 1776
April 3 Age 37 Wife of Samuel
Baker S:10R

Baker, Mary A - Died 1924 April 22
Born 1841 Mar 31 (with Robert
Evans & Molly Church & others)
S:12

Baker, Mary A - Died 1941 Born
1860 wife of Chester L Baker
(next to him & Chester A Baker)
S:31

Baker, Mary Carroll - Died 1913
Born 1842 Stone says, "Mother"
Wife of Reuben Baker (next to
him) S:18

Baker, Mary D - Died 188? March
Age 65 (stone down due to
vandals) Wife of William Baker
(next to him) (also down from
vandals) S:18

Baker, Mary E - Died 1932 Born

26

Baker (Cont.)
1853 (on large Baker stone) S:11

Baker, Mary H - Died 1872 Jan 7
Age 52 years, 4 months, 5 days
(with John W Baker) S:18

Baker, Mary P - Died 1900 Born
1844 Wife of L A Baker S:18

Baker, Mary R - Died 1865 March
30 Born 1863 Aug 31 (with Lillian R Baker & others) S:18

Baker, Maude H - Died 1956 Born
1886 (on large Baker stone) S:11

Baker, Melinda - Died Widow of
John W Baker Stone not clear
S:4

Baker, Mercy B - Died 1909 March
11 Born 1826 Oct 26 (with
Sidney Baker) S:19

Baker, Merrill - Died 1934 Born
1888 (with Mary H Nickerson &
Benjamin Small) S:14

Baker, Nathan (Capt) - Died 1837
Dec 28 in his 53rd yr (next to
wife, Patty Baker) S:21

Baker, Nathaniel - Died 1750 May
7 in his 71st yr S:9R

Baker, Nathaniel - Died 1791 Mar
20 in his 81st yr (next to Ann
Bacon who was the wife of a
Nathaniel?) S:9

Baker, Olive - Died 1879 Born
1811 (with Hannah Baker) S:8

Baker, Ozial P - Died 1921 Born
1837 (with Marietta Baker) S:14

Baker, Patty Mrs - Died 1864 April
11 in her 79th yr Widow of
Nathan Baker (next to him) S:21

Baker, Persis Sears - Died 185?
Born 1818 (with Martha Sears
Baker) S:18

Baker, Phebe - Died 1851 Nov 23 in
her 60th yr Wife of Eleazer
Baker S:4

Baker, Phebe - Died 1876 July 26
in her 71st yr Wife of Abed
Baker S:4

Baker, Philena - Died 1886 March
22 Age 61 Stone says, "Mother"
(with Jeptha Baker) S:18

Baker, Preston N - Died 1966 Born
1916 (on large Baker stone) S:11

Baker, Priscilla - Died 1835 Aug 29

Baker (Cont.)
in her 82nd yr Wife of Capt Seth
Baker S:1

Baker, Ralph L - Died 1892 Nov 1
Born 1862 Jan 31 stone says,
"Son" (with Emma C Baker) S:18

Baker, Rebecca W - Died 1851 Sept
28 in her 18th yr (with William
G Baker) S:21

Baker, Reuben - Died 1928 Born
1831 Stone says, "Father" (next
to wife, Mary Carroll Baker &
Irving Baker) S:18

Baker, Reuben (Capt) - Died 1856
May 30 Age 55 years, 1 month,
17 days S:4

Baker, Ruth - Died 1842 Dec 14 in
her 69th yr Wife of Eldred Baker
(buried next to him) S:7

Baker, Samuel Ely - Died 1897
Born 1830 (with Clarence Eleazer Baker & others) S:18

Baker, Sarah Hale - Died 1846
Born 1845 Daughter of Persis &
Martha Baker (with them) S:18

Baker, Seth - Died 1783 Son of
Seth & Priscilla Baker S:1

Baker, Seth (Capt) - Died 1847 Dec
24 in his 49th yr (next to wife,
Sophia L Baker) S:21

Baker, Sidney - Died 1885 Sept 6
Born 1831 March 15 (with Mercy
B Baker) S:19

Baker, Silvester Esq - Died 1838
Dec 27 in his 63rd yr S:4

Baker, Sofie C - Died 1958 Born
1897 (with Lola & Eugene Baker)
S:14

Baker, Sophia L - Died 1875 Dec
14 in her 76th yr Widow of Seth
Baker (next to him) S:21

Baker, Susan I - Died 1934 Born
1854 (with Alvah D Baker) S:18

Baker, Susan P - Died 1916 Born
1829 (with Etta Baker) S:8

Baker, Thomas F - Died 1938 Born
1881 Stone says, "In god we
trust" (with Catherine M Baker)
S:14

Baker, Timothy - Died 1871 Apl 10
Age 82 years, 6 months, 2 days
S:4

Baker, Timothy (Capt) - Died 1816 Dec 19 in his 57th yr S:4

Baker, Timothy J - Died 1925 Born 1849 S:4

Baker, Walter Durell - Died 1941 Feb 9 Born 1874 Oct 1 (with Mabel Kimball Baker & others) S:18

Baker, Walter E - Died 1964 Born 1900 (with Mabel Baker) S:12

Baker, William - Died 1846 Aug 15 Age 87 (stone down from vandals) (next to wife, Mary D Baker) (stone also down from vandals) S:18

Baker, William C - Died 1946 Born 1885 (with Thomas & Catherine Baker) S:14

Baker, William G - Died 1852 March 7 at Rio Janeiro, (Brazil) Age 20 (listed with Rebecca W Baker) S:21

Baker, William H - Died 1924 Born 1847 (stone over from vandals) (with wife, Ella M Baker) S:18

Baker, William H - Died 1952 Born 1897 (with Anna M Baker, wife) S:16

Baker, Willie Abner - Died 18?? Oct Born 1867 or 57 July 28 (next to Albert Abner Baker & Albert Baker Wing) S:18

Baker, Winfield Scott - Died 1898 Born 1848 (with Georgiana Howes Baker & others) S:18

Baker, Zemira - Died 1921 Sept 18 in her 72nd yr (stone loose) S:8

Balboni, Argia - Died 1956 Born 1878 (with Robert Balboni) S:16

Balboni, Robert - Died 1931 Born 1878 (with Argia Balboni) S:16

Baldwin, Abbott L - Died 1978 Born 1897 (with Blandine Baldwin) S:15

Baldwin, Blandine - Died (still living in 1991?) Born 1897 (listed with Abbott L Baldwin) S:15

Baldwin, Margaret May - Died 1986 Born 1895 (listed with Vera Baldwin Diaz) S:18

Ball, Alice H - Died 1937 Born

Ball (Cont.)
1887 Wife of William G Ball, next to her) S:15

Ball, William G - Died 1976 Born 1883 (next to wife, Alice H Ball) S:15

Ballou, Addie L - Died 1953 Born 1872 S:18

Balstok, Desire - Died (stone down, worn & broken) Wife of Emil Balstok (next to him) S:11

Balstok, Emil - Died 18?? May 11 (stone broken down, near dirt road) S:11

Banas, Felicia A (MD) - Died 1972 Born 1902 (with Edmund Z Dymza) S:16

Bang, (?) Sigrid Marie - Died 1970? Born 1878 (undertaker plaque only) S:15

Banks, Alexandria - Died 1985 Born 1890 (next to John Banks) S:15

Banks, John - Died 1980 Born 1891 (next to Alexandria Banks) S:15

Banks, Josephine M - Died 1966 Born 1893 Stone says,"Mother" (next to son or in-law John & Bertha Medeiros, possible daughter) S:15

Bansmere, Harry - Died 1973 Nov 29 Born 1887 Dec 8 From Massachusetts, was a Cpl in US Army during World War I S:17

Baptista, John F Sr - Died 1952 Born 1885 (next to Lena Rose Baptista) S:16

Baptista, Lena Rose - Died 1936 Born 1900 (next to John F Baptista Sr) S:16

Barboza, Alfred - Died 1977 Born 1883 (with Emily C Barboza) S:16

Barboza, Emily C - Died 1953 Born 1878 (with Alfred Barboza) S:16

Barboza, Mary Gomes - Died 1931 Born 1901 (with Mary O'Connor Gomes & others) S:31

Barker, Eliza - Died 1872 Sept 2 Born 1798 Mar 29 S:12

Barlow, Gertrude Hartley - Died

Barlow (Cont.)
1954 Born 1876 (next to John W
Barlow) S:14

Barlow, John W - Died 1962 Born
1871 (next to Gertrude Hartley
Barlow) S:14

Barlow, Sarah L - Died 1925 Born
1845 (next to Grace Barlow
Brooks) S:14

Barnaby, Madeline E - Died 1974
Born 1895 (with Roland E
Barnaby Sr) S:15

Barnaby, Roland E Sr - Died 1974
Born 1892 (with Madeline E
Barnaby) S:15

Barnard, Freddie Sears - Died 1888
Aug 28 Born 1875 Nov 21 (with
Lydia Carsley Barnard & others)
S:18

Barnard, George Worth - Died 1907
May 8 Born 1845 April 12 (with
wife, Mary Adelaide Barnard &
others) S:18

Barnard, Joseph A - Died 1905
Born 1833 (with Ruth A Barnard) S:18

Barnard, Lydia Carsley - Died 1900
May 6 Born 1814 Nov 9 (with
George Worth Barnard & others)
S:18

Barnard, Mary Adelaide - Died
1898 Nov 26 Born 1840 Jan 20
Wife of George Worth Barnard
(with him & Freddie Sears &
Lydia Carsley Barnard) S:18

Barnard, Ruth A - Died 1911 Born
1831 (with Joseph A Barnard)
S:18

Barraclough, Herbert H - Died
1970 March 5 Born 1896 July
12 From Massachusetts, was
Capt in Sig Corps during World
War I & II S:15

Barrett, Arthur R A - Died 1959
Oct 4 Born 1882 May 28 Stone
says, "Father" (2 stones) (with
Rosalinda M Barrett) S:16

Barrett, Rosalinda M - Died 1980
Dec 25 Born 1896 April 10 (with
Arthur RA Barrett) S:16

Barrett, Verile L - Died (still living
1991?) Born 1896 Feb 18 (listed

Barrett (Cont.)
next to Wilson H Barrett) S:14

Barrett, Wilson H - Died 1964 Born
1874 (next to Verile L Barrett)
S:14

Barrington, Nellie - Died 1979
Born 1885 S:17

Barros, Anna F - Died 1987 Born
1896 (with Antonio Barros) S:16

Barros, Antonio - Died 1958 Born
1876 (with Anna F Barros) S:16

Barros, Michael A - Died 1987 May
6 Born 1964 Mar 18 Stone says,
"You touched our hearts" (in
Watt plot) S:13

Barrow, Lillian Sparrow - Died
1978 Sept 30 Born 1887 Sept 21
(on same stone with Gordon
Medbury Spooner & others) S:11

Barrow, Ralph Sheldon - Died 1978
May 20 Born 1886 Nov 6 (on
same stone with Lillian Sparrow
Barrow & others) S:11

Barrows, Desire H - Died 1882
June 5 in her 60th yr Wife of
Samuel Barrows S:7

Barrows, Francies - Died 1738 Mar
17 Born 1738 Feb 5 Son of
Silvanus & Ruth Barrows S:5

Barrows, Sarah Paul - Died 1987
Born 1897 S:15

Barrus, Hester J - Died (still living
1991?) Born 1894 (with Howard
E Barrus) S:19

Barrus, Howard E - Died 1974
Born 1888 (with Hester J Barrus) S:19

Barry, Elizabeth M - Died 1957
Born 1888 (with Joseph J Barry)
S:16

Barry, Joseph J - Died 1972 July 3
Born 1889 Feb 28 From Massachusetts, was Wagoneer, Co C,
301 Eng during World War I
(with Elizabeth M Barry) S:16

Barse, John - Died 1716 May 2 Age
73 (possible husband of Elenour
Bears) S:1

Barstow, Desire - Died 1874 April 6
Age 78 yrs 10 mos Wife of Ichiel
Barstow (located at Lothrop's
Hill) S:26R

Barstow, Ichiel - Died 1855 March 14 Age 57 (located at Lothrop's Hill) S:26R

Bartlett, Bessie - Died 1987 Born 1897 S:15

Bartlett, Charles Lothrop - Died 1978 July 8 Born 1898 June 23 (flag at grave, with Lydia Ruth Bartlett) S:11

Bartlett, Diman - Died 1756 March 25 Age 15 days (stone is down on ground) Son of Ebenezer & Abigail Bartlett S:11

Bartlett, Lydia Ruth - Died 1982 Dec 6 Born 1900 Aug 27 (with Charles Lothrop Bartlett) S:11

Bartlett, Maion (Marion?) Swan - Died 1945 Sept 6 Born 1870 March 18 Wife of Stephen Smith Bartlett (buried next to him) S:11

Bartlett, Nelson - Died 1941 (or 1914?) Born 1853 S:10

Bartlett, Stephen Smith - Died 1942 June 3 at Boston Born 1861 Feb 14 (next to wife, Maion Swan Bartlett) S:11

Barton, Ellen Randolph - Died 1921 Feb 5 Born 1900 Aug 21 (with Mary Lowell Barton) S:14

Barton, Mary Lowell - Died 1957 Nov 3 Born 1868 Aug 14 (with Ellen Randolph Barton) S:14

Bateman, James TD - Died 1970 Born 1886 (with Katherine T Bateman) S:14

Bateman, Katherine T - Died 1965 Born 1885 (with James TD Bateman) S:14

Basett, Elisha - Died 1807 Oct 20 Age 95 S:5

Basett, Mary - Died 1783 June 18 Age 28 Wife of Samuel Basett S:5

Bassat, Daniel - Died 1836 Oct 10 Age 65 S:4

Bassat, Prudence - Died 1821 June 12 Age 49 Wife of Daniel Basset S:4

Basset, (infant) - Died 1849 Aug 23 Age 3 mos 4 days Son of Theodore & Lucy HI Basset (near

Basset (Cont.)
father) S:18

Basset, (infant son) - Died 1844? Born 1844 Nov 22 Son of ? (stone not clear)(with Francis P Basset & others) S:18

Basset, Alice A - Died 1850 Nov 2 Born 1850 June 4 (with Annie B Basset & others)

Basset, Annie B - Died 1862 Jan 20 Born 1860 April 6 (with Hersilia B Basset & others) S:18

Basset, Betsy C Miss - Died 1817 May 15 Age 18 Daughter of Daniel & Prudence Basset S:4

Basset, Edwin Albert - Died 1848 Aug 6 Age 1 month (last name listed on his foot stone, next to Prince L Basset) S:21

Basset, Eliaha B - Died 1889 Jan 27 Age 25 yrs 8 mos 13 days Stone says "Our Son" (next to Eudora E Coffin & Theodore F Bassett) S:18

Basset, Francis P - Died 1897 April 25 Born 1853 Sept 18 (with Frank P Hallett & others) S:18

Basset, Hazel C - Died 1981 Born 1895 (with Zenas D Basset) S:18

Basset, Herselia - Died 1886 April 11 Born 1825 April 27 (with Alice A Basset & others) S:18

Basset, Hersilia B - Died 1937 Dec 3 Born 1856 April 4 (with Alice A Basset & others) S:18

Basset, Horace S - Died 1850 Born 1833 (with Zenas DB Hallett & others) S:18

Basset, Lillian - Died 1934 Born 1862 Wife of Theodore F Basset (with him) S:18

Basset, Lucy H - Died 1894 March 16 Born 1823 Stone says "Mother" (with Theodore E Basset) S:18

Basset, Minnie N - Died 1885 June 11 Age 27 yrs 10 mos Wife of GL Basset S:18

Basset, Prince L Mr - Died 1852 Aug 13 Age 32 at New Orleans (listed next to Edwin Albert Basset) S:21

Basset, Sarah - Died 1746 Nov 1 Age 55 Wife of William Basset S:3

Basset, Sarah L - Died 1874 Born 1802 (with Maria L Bearse & others) S:18

Basset, Theodore E - Died 1893 May 12 Born 1821 May 13 (with Lucy H Basset) S:18

Basset, Theodore F - Died 1903 Born 1859 Stone says "Erected by his business associates in loving rememberance" (with wife, Lillian Basset) S:18

Basset, Zenas D - Died 1864 Born 1786 (with Sarah L Basset & others) S:18

Basset, Zenas D - Died 1881 Sept 16 Born 1818 Oct 24 (with Herselia Basset & others) S:18

Basset, Zenas D - Died 1964 Born 1892 (with Hazel C Basset) S:18

Bassett, ? - Died 1775 Nov 18 (stone not clear) Son of Nathan & Thankful Bassett (located between Elkanah Hamblen & Lydia Marston) S:5

Bassett, (infant) - Died 1873 (with Capt Jacob Bassett & others) S:18

Bassett, A - Died 1844 Feb 2 Age 56 Widow of John Bassett S:6

Bassett, Abigail - Died 1881 Born 1811 Wife of Nelson Scudder (listed on large stone with others in the family plot) S:11

Bassett, Abner T Capt - Died 1887 Feb 12 Born 1819 July 14 (with Melintha L Bassett & others) S:18

Bassett, Anna - Died 1844 Feb 2 in her 56th yr Widow of John Bassett S:26R

Bassett, Bethiah G - Died 1893 Sept 27 Born 1819 Dec 19 (with Gerry & Ferdinand Bassett & others) S:18

Bassett, Betsy - Died 1801 Nov 16 Age 19 S:7

Bassett, Caroline E - Died 1915 Jan 13 Born 1846 May 24 (with Elisha & Gerry Bassett & others)

Bassett (Cont.) S:18

Bassett, Charles - Died 1872 Dec 6 Age 57 (buried next to both wives, Fanny & Eriza) S:6

Bassett, Charles - Died 1873 Feb 24 Age 77 yrs 7 mos S:7

Bassett, Chester L - Died 1968 Born 1882 (with Laura E Bassett & others) S:11

Bassett, Christina Charlotte - Died 1816 Born 1830 (with Samuel Ely Baker & others) S:18

Bassett, Cleone C - Died 1882 July 17 Born 1880 Jan 11 (with Mildred Bassett & others) S:18

Bassett, Edwin A - Died 1898 Born 1823 S:2

Bassett, Elisha - Died 1807 Oct 20 in his 25th yr S:5R2

Bassett, Elisha B - Died 1936 Born 1877 (with Gerry & Lillie Bassett & others) S:18

Bassett, Eliza L - Died 1883 March 26 Age 75 yrs 4 mos S:6

Bassett, Elizabeth - Died 1790 May 24 in her 41st yr 2nd wife to Samuel Bassett S:5R2

Bassett, Elizabeth Sherwood - Died 1960 Born 1879 (with baby Bassett) S:19

Bassett, Eriza - Died 1855 Sept 6 Age 27 yrs 6 mos Wife of Charles Bassett S:6

Bassett, F Clifton - Died 1964 Born 1876 (with Stella F Bassett) S:18

Bassett, Fanny - Died 1849 Aug 24 Age 27 yrs 5 mos Wife of Charles Bassett S:6

Bassett, Ferdinand H - Died 1902 Dec 12 Born 1842 Mar 28 (with Gerry & Caroline Bassett & others) S:18

Bassett, George - Died 1886 Aug 31 Age 25 yrs 9 mos S:6

Bassett, Gerry - Died 1895 March 28 Born 1870 July 12 (with Bethiah & others) S:18

Bassett, Gershom - Died 1775 Nov 1 in his 18th yr Son of Deacon Nathan and Thankful Bassett S:5R2

Bassett, Ira Baxter - Died 1919 Born 1848 (with Phebe S Bassett & others) S:18

Bassett, Ira S - Died 1959 Feb 22 Born 1876 Oct 16 From Massachusetts, was Sergeant in Company B, 10th Regiment (but then says?) Ohio Infantry during Spanish American War (next to Ira S Bassett & others) S:18

Bassett, Jacob P H Capt - Died 1924 July 19 Born 1844 Dec 25 (with Sallie Crowell Bassett & others) S:18

Bassett, Janet - Died 1918 Born 1915 (next to Ira S Bassett & others with Alfed Johnston too) S:18

Bassett, John - Died 1839 Feb 2 Age 55 S:6

Bassett, John - Died 1902 Born 1819 S:6

Bassett, Laura E - Died 1964 Born 1880 (with Chester L Bassett & others) S:11

Bassett, Lillie W - Died 1909 Born 1881 (with Gerry & Elisha Bassett & others) S:18

Bassett, Luther - Died 1801 Oct 15 Age 24 S:7

Bassett, Martha P - Died 1899 Born 1840 S:6

Bassett, Mary - Died 1783 June 18 in her 28th yr Wife of Samuel Bassett S:5R2

Bassett, Melintha L - Died 1871 Sept 3 Born 1817 Sept 27 (with Capt Jacob P H Bassett & others) S:18

Bassett, Mildred - Died 1961 Born 1895 (with Millicent Bassett Trefry & Bertram Johnson) S:18

Bassett, Mildred - Died 1895 May 18 Born 1894 June 15 (with Cleone C & Capt Jacob Bassett & others) S:18

Bassett, Millicent L - Died 1974 Born 1883 (with Winthrop D Bassett & others) S:18

Bassett, Nathan Deacon - Died 1791 Dec 27 Age 77 S:5

Bassett, Norman L - Died 1971

Bassett (Cont.) Born 1898 (large rock stone plus another one that says "Bassett") S:19

Bassett, Olive - Died 1873 May 1 Age 61 yrs 1 mon Wife of Charles Bassett S:7

Bassett, Phebe S - Died 1937 Born 1848 (with Fred HR Bassett & others) S:18

Bassett, Rachel - Died 1823 April 3 in her 62nd yr Wife of Samuel Bassett S:5

Bassett, Sallie - Died 1945 May 5 Born 1851 July 31 (with Capt Abner T Bassett & others) S:18

Bassett, Samuel - Died 1824 Jan 4 Age 77th yr Next to wife Rachel S:5

Bassett, Sarah - Died 1746 Nov 1 in her 57th yr Wife of William Bassett S:3R

Bassett, Sherrold E - Died 1966 Born 1904 (with Laura Bassett & others) S:11

Bassett, Stella F - Died 1961 Born 1878 (with F Clifton Bassett) S:18

Bassett, Susan - Died 1878 April 7 Age 82 yrs 8 mos (stone is down) S:21

Bassett, Winthrop D - Died 1947 Born 1880 (with Millicent Bassett & Henry & Emily Bacon) S:18

Bassette (Bassett), Charlotte L - (no markings) Wife of Sherrold E Bassett (with him & others) S:11

Bates, Juliet F - Died 1935 Born 1840 Mother of Mabel F Lewis (on Lewis stone with others) S:11

Bates, Merion H - Died 1961 Sept 8 Born 1897 Dec 7 Listed as private (PFC) in Massachusetts Company 151, Depot R CAD S:12

Bates, Norine J - Died 1980 Born 1899 (undertaker plaque only) S:17

Bates, Stephen H - Died 1947 March 12 Born 1863 Aug 31 Was private in Commpany G, 13th Regiment, Infantry during

Bates (Cont.)

Civil War? (this must be an error and probably should say World War I) S:12

Bates, Susan S - Died 1864 Feb 23 Age 75 yrs, 5 mos S:7

Batterbury, William J - Died 1974 Born 1899 S:15

Bauch, Charles A - Died 1949 Born 1865 (with Charles Hallett & others) S:19

Bauch, Nellie M - Died 1942 Born 1875 (with Charles A Bauch & others) S:19

Baxter, (infant) - Died 1829 Sept 19 Age 8 days Son of Silvester & Sally H Baxter S:4

Baxter, Abigail - Died 1836 May 17 Age 41 at North Providence Wife of Nicholas? Baxter (next to him & Leander Baxter) S:21

Baxter, Abner Ely - Died 1807 June 13 Age 3 Son of Obed & Bridget Baxter S:4

Baxter, Alexander Capt - Died 1816 Sept 2 Age 45 S:4

Baxter, Alexander 2nd - Died 1869 May 2 Age 46 yrs 6 mos 13 days Stone says "Father" (next to wife, Persis L Baxter) S:21

Baxter, Alexina F - Died 1867 Jan 17 Age 10 yrs 3 mos 21 days (possibly daughter of Alexander & Persis Baxter, next to them) S:21

Baxter, Amy W - Died 1947 Born 1873 (with Gorgie Baxter & others) S:18

Baxter, Annie - Died 1883 Born 1873 (with Benjamin D Baxter & Elizabeth W Baxter) S:18

Baxter, Argo L - (stone not clear) Son Silvester & Sally Baxter S:4

Baxter, Babb - (no dates)(with Edwin A Baxter & others) S:18

Baxter, Barnabas - Died 1865 Born 1833 (with Mary T Baxter) S:21

Baxter, Bemon B - Died 1865 Dec 15 Age 20 yrs 8 mos (stone has an anchor on top of it) S:18

Baxter, Benjamin - Died 1897 Born 1839 (with Elizabeth A Baxter)

Baxter (Cont.)

S:18

Baxter, Benjamin - Died 1886 Born 1810 (with Emeline B Baxter) S:21

Baxter, Benjamin D - Died 1945 Born 1870 (with Annie & Eliz Baxter) S:18

Baxter, Bessie W - Died 1875 Jan 21 Age 12 yrs 5 mos 8 days Daughter of Capt Benjamin D Baxter (next to Hellen M Baxter) S:21

Baxter, Blanche H - Died 1975 May 30 Born 1884 June 25 (next to Horace P Baxter) S:18

Baxter, Bridget - Died 1807 April 7 Age 27 Wife of Obed Baxter S:4

Baxter, Bridget E - Died 1807 March 7 Age 13 days Daughter of Obed & Bridget Baxter S:4

Baxter, Caroline B - Died 1807 Feb 24 Age 2 Daughter of Obed & Bridget Baxter S:4

Baxter, Charles L - Died 1917 Born 1833 (with Josephine W Baxter) S:14

Baxter, Clara B - Died 1927 Born 1885 (with Fred S Baxter) S:18

Baxter, Clarence - Died 1888? Aug 9 Born 1875 Feb 1 (with Jennie? Baxter & others) S:18

Baxter, Ebed - Died 1903 Sept 16 Born 1882 July 24 (with Mary J Baxter & others) S:18

Baxter, Ebed L - Died 1923 Born 1860 (with John Baxter & others) S:18

Baxter, Eben S - Died 1907 Born 1845 (with Elnora Baxter) S:21

Baxter, Edgar A - Died 1924 Born 1863 (with wife Sarah E Baxter) S:18

Baxter, Edmund H - Died 1893 March 25 S:4

Baxter, Edward - Died 1793 May 1 in his 20th yr S:5R2

Baxter, Edward - Died 1816 April 4 Age 9 mos Son of Henry & Apphia Baxter S:10

Baxter, Edwin A - Died 1953 Born 1869 (with Amy W Baxter &

Baxter (Cont.)
  others) S:18
Baxter, Eleanor - Died 1875 Dec 21
  Born 1818 March 17 (with
  Rodney Baxter Jr & Sr & others)
  S:18
Baxter, Elen - Died 1879 Nov 7
  Born 1879 Nov 2 (with Ebed
  Baxter & others) S:18
Baxter, Eliza S - Died 1852 Born
  1790 (with Shubael Baxter &
  others) S:13
Baxter, Elizabeth - Died 1867 April
  28 Age 88 yrs 10 mos S:7
Baxter, Elizabeth A - Died 1921
  Born 1844 (with Benjamin
  Baxter & Bessie W Raymond)
  S:18
Baxter, Elizabeth C - Died 1898
  Born 1836 Wife of Charles
  Hinkley (with Maurice Careleton
  Bond & Cecil H Bond & hus-
  band) S:18
Baxter, Elizabeth W - Died 1952
  Born 1878 (with Ben & Annie
  Baxter) S:18
Baxter, Ella Butterfield - Died 1958
  Born 1871 S:17
Baxter, Elnora - Died 1919 Born
  1848 (with Eben and next to
  Lola Baxter) S:21
Baxter, Emeline B - Died 1896
  Born 1813 (with Ben & next to
  Bessie Baxter) S:21
Baxter, Emily D - Died 1876 Born
  1849 (with Howard Baxter) S:21
Baxter, Esther - Died 1877 Feb 22
  Age 76 yrs 5 mos 14 days S:4
Baxter, Eunice - Died 1889 July 4
  Born 1810 Jan 7 Wife of John B
  Baxter (with him) S:14
Baxter, Eva W - Died 1899 Born
  1852 (with Babb Baxter & oth-
  ers) S:18
Baxter, Frances H - Died 1942
  Born 1858 (with Shubael Baxter
  & others) S:13
Baxter, Frank A - Died 1863 Born
  1862 Son of Zenas & Mahala
  Baxter (next to brother, Zenas B
  Baxter) S:21
Baxter, Fred S - Died 1933 Born

Baxter (Cont.)
  1865 (with Clara B Baxter) S:18
Baxter, Georgie - Died 1880 Nov 17
  Born 1856 Sept 16 (a small
  stone) Daughter of Sturgis & Eva
  Baxter (with them & others) S:18
Baxter, Hannah Taylor - Died 1936
  Born 1876 Wife of Arthur M
  Coville (with him) S:19
Baxter, Harriet D - Died 1944 Born
  1872 (with James E Baxter) S:31
Baxter, Harriet W - Died 1874 Dec
  20 Born 1836 March 23 (stone
  down from vandals) Wife of
  Samuel W Baxter (she is located
  between Charles Goodspeed, d
  1888 & Dorcas Lovell) S:18
Baxter, Hellen M - Died 1865 Oct
  24 Age 24 yrs 6 mos 17 days
  (top of stone is gone, but next to
  him is Bessie W Baxter) S:21
Baxter, Henry Capt - Died 1846
  Feb 18 Age 60 S:10
Baxter, Henry Delano - (stone not
  clear, worn) Son of Ira & Sally
  Baxter (next to brother, Ira
  Baxter) S:21
Baxter, Horace P - Died 1954 Oct 9
  Born 1881 Dec 12 (next to
  Blanche H Baxter) S:18
Baxter, Howard - Died 1904 Born
  1847 (with Emily D Baxter) S:21
Baxter, Ida May - Died 1917 Born
  1866 Wife of Judah Crowell
  (next to him, stone down) S:21
Baxter, Ira Capt - Died 1853 Born
  1798 (there is a stone missing
  next to him which is very old
  with Sally Baxter) S:21
Baxter, Ira - Died 1847 Jan 16
  Born 1829 May 12 Lost at sea,
  latitude 4624, longitude 3120
  (listed next to Ira & Sally Baxter)
  S:21
Baxter, James - Died 1856 Sept 11
  Age 8 mos 6 days Son of Richard
  & Lydia Baxter (next to them)
  S:12
Baxter, James D (or B) - Died 1904
  Feb 3 Born 1817 June 5 S:10
Baxter, James E - Died 1943 Born
  1872 (with Harriet D Baxter)

34

Baxter (Cont.)
S:31

Baxter, James H - Died 1852 Sept 23 Age 4 yrs 4 mos Son of James D & Phebe B Baxter S:10

Baxter, James T - Died 1844 Born 1824 (with Shubael Baxter & others) S:13

Baxter, Jennie? - Died 1890 Jan 31 Born 1871 July 31 (with Ebed L Baxter & others) S:18

Baxter, John - Died 1914 Aug 18 Born 1869 April 14 (with Elen Baxter & others) S:18

Baxter, John - Died 1806 Feb 11 Age 27 S:4

Baxter, John B - Died 1887 July 25 Born 1809 July 15 (with wife Eunice Baxter) S:14

Baxter, Joseph F - Died 1900 July 15 Born 1873 March 14 (with Lucretia & Lymane Baxter) S:18

Baxter, Josephine W - Died 1909 Born 1831 (with Charles Baxter) S:14

Baxter, Leander - Died 1872 Dec 28 Age 52 (next to Nicholas? & Abigail Baxter) S:21

Baxter, Leone - Died 1891 Oct 7 Age 1 yr 20 days Son of CM Baxter (mother) S:4

Baxter, Lola - Died 1878 Sept 8 Age 2 yrs 10 mos 17 days Daughter of Eben & Elnora Baxter (next to them & Ben Baxter) S:21

Baxter, Lucretia A - Died 1939 Born 1854 Wife of Lymane Baxter (with him & Joseph F Baxter) S:18

Baxter, Lucy E - Died 1875 Feb 19 Age 28 yrs 2 mos 1 day Wife of Eldridge Baxter S:21

Baxter, Lucy R - Died 1866 March 8 Age 13 yrs 1 mon 11 days Daughter of Richard E & Lydia F Baxter (next to them) S:12

Baxter, Lydia H - Died 1913 Born 1825 (with Richard E Baxter) S:12

Baxter, Lymane - Died 1898 June 25 Born 1852 Nov 19 (with wife

Baxter (Cont.)
Lucretia A & Joseph F Baxter)
S:18

Baxter, Mary A - Died 1904 Born 1834 S:31

Baxter, Mary J - Died 1880 Sept 10 Born 1834 Dec 25 (with Clarence Baxter & others) S:18

Baxter, Mary M - Died 1911 Born 1834 (with Shubael Baxter & others) S:13

Baxter, Mary T - Died 1862 Born 1836 (with Barnabas Baxter) S:21

Baxter, Mercy B - Died 1822 Aug 11 Age 20 yrs 4 mos 11 days Wife of Capt Silvester Baxter S:5

Baxter, Minerva E - Died 1945 Born 1862 (with Shubael Baxter & others) S:13

Baxter, Nella P - Died 1854 April 17 Age 15 mos Daughter of Alexander & Persis Baxter (next to Alexina F Baxter) S:21

Baxter, Nicholas? (Mxm?mas?) - Died 1850 Jan 6 Age 62 (first name not clear, between Abigail & Leander Baxter) S:21

Baxter, Orin B - Died 1848 Aug 18 Born 1847 June 8 Son of John B & Eunice Baxter (with them) S:14

Baxter, Persis L - Died 1864 Dec 20 Age 40 yrs 10 mos 2 days Wife of Alexander Baxter 2nd (next to him & daughter, Nella P Baxter) S:21

Baxter, Phebe B - Died 1883 Sept 2 Born 1804 July 1 Wife of James D Baxter (next to him) S:10

Baxter, Pricilla - Died 1802 Nov 14 Age 9 weeks Daughter of Alexander Baxter & Sarah Leverett S:21

Baxter, Ralph L - Died 1941 Born 1882 S:4

Baxter, Richard E - Died 1859 Born 1826 (with Lydia H Baxter) S:12

Baxter, Rodney - Died 1880 Feb 5 Born 1875 Nov 3 (with Elen Baxter & others) S:18

Baxter, Rodney - Died 1888 July 17 Born 1815 March 8 (with Eleanor Baxter & others) S:18

Baxter, Rodney Jr - Died 1847 Sept 23 Born 1845 Aug 24 (with Marianna Baker & others) S:18

Baxter, Sally - Died 1839 Oct 21 Age 31 Wife of Silvester Baxter S:4

Baxter, Sally - Died 1843 Born 1800 (with Capt Ira & Sylvia Baxter) S:21

Baxter, Sara E - Died 1947 Born 1869 Wife of Edgar Baxter (with him & Belle Baxter Carlton) S:18

Baxter, Sarah L - Died 1843 May 3 Age 65 Widow of Capt Alexander Baxter S:4

Baxter, Samuel S - Died 1907 Born 1828 (with Shubael Baxter & others) S:13

Baxter, Shubael - Died 1857 Born 1785 (with Eliza S Baxter & others) S:13

Baxter, Simeon Capt - Died 1835 Age 31 Lost at sea in 1835 S:4

Baxter, Stugis G - Died 1931 Born 1850 (with Eva W Baxter & others) S:18

Baxter, Sylvia A - Died 1850 Born 1830 (with Sally & Ira Baxter) S:21

Baxter, Thomas Capt - Died 1806 May 10 Age 32 (a tall pointed stone) S:12

Baxter, Thomas PD - Died 1862 Aug 19 Age 40 yrs 5 mos (next to James B Baxter) S:10

Baxter, Walter - Died 1838 May 14 Age 58 S:4

Baxter, Zenas B - Died 1863 Born 1856 Son of Zenas & Mahala Baxter (next to brother Frank A Baxter) S:21

Bayardi, Adeline P - Died 1980 Nov 27 Born 1893 July 20 S:15

Beale, Arthur M - Died 1962 Born 1874 (round slate plaque for stone, but another marker a few feet away too) (with wife, LM Beale) S:11

Beale, Edith - Died 1954 Aug 16 in

Beale (Cont.)
Barnstable Born 1878 May 28 in Boston Wife of Laurence Mortimer S:11

Beale, L M - Died 1972 Born 1880 Wife of Arthur M Beale (with him) S:11

Beales, Alonzo R - Died 1949 Born 1890 (spray paint all over stone by vandals) (with Luella & William Beales) S:17

Beales, Luella - Died 1937 Born 1866 (silver spray paint all over stone by vandals) (with Alonzo & William Beales) S:17

Beales, William T - Died 1948 Born 1862 (silver spray paint all over stone by vandals) (with Luella Beales) S:17

Bears, Benjamin - Died 1748 May 15 Age 66 S:1

Bears, Elenour - Died 1766 Feb 11 in her 84th yr Wife of John Bears S:1

Bears, Lemuel Jr - Died 1816 Sept 9 in his 44th yr S:3

Bears, Prince - Died 1815 June 9 in his 84th yr Husband of Desire Bearse S:1

Bears, Sarah - Died 1808 Aug 18 in her 32nd yr Wife of Asa Bears S:4

Bears, Sarah S - Died 1808 Aug 8 Age 14 days July 25 Daughter of Asa Bears S:4

Bears, Thankful - Died 1762 Feb 26 Age 7 weeks 1 day Daughter of Lemuel & Patience Bears S:3

Bearse, (infant) - Died (death not listed) Born 1857 Aug 12 (stone is broken leaning against other family stones) (next to sister, Emily Bearse & other family members including parents, Phebe & Sylvester Bearse) S:18

Bearse, (infant) - Died (no date) Daughter of Chester & Harriet Bearse (buried with them) S:8

Bearse, (infant) - Died 1826 Apl 7 Son of Capt Isaac & Sally Bearse S:4

Bearse, (infant) - Died 1859 Oct 11

Bearse (Cont.)

Age 11 weeks Son of Allen & Sophia Bearse (with mother) S:21

Bearse, Abigail - Died 1830 Dec 16 in her 27th yr Daughter of Isaac & Mercy Bearse S:3

Bearse, Abigail S - Died 1869 April 10 Age 76 years, 10 months Widow of Freeman Bearse (next to him) S:21

Bearse, Ada May - Died 1908 Born 1854 (with John Sturgis Bearse) S:18

Bearse, Adelaide Lovell - Died 1932 Born 1845 (with William Henry Bearse) S:12

Bearse, Adeline F - Died 1928 Born 1847 (next to Mary A Bearse) S:14

Bearse, Albree N - Died 1910 Aug 13 Born 1848 June 30 (next to Eliza Jane Bearse) S:18

Bearse, Alfred - Died 1884 Sept 21 Age 77 years, 9 months Stone says,"Father" (next to wife, Mary A Bearse) (death date from Hinckley ceme records) S:14

Bearse, Alice L - Died (still living 1991?) Born 1894 (listed with Martha L Crowther & Edgar L Knapp) S:17

Bearse, Allen H - Died 1886 Sept 24 Age 73 years, 2 months (stone cracked) S:21

Bearse, Almira - Died 1882 Born 1810 (listed on same stone with Arthur Bearse) S:8

Bearse, Alton C - Died 1898 Feb 19 Born 1851 Aug 24 (with Flora J Hallett & others) S:18

Bearse, Alvin - Died 1893 Feb 22 Born 1849 June 22 (stone down from vandals) (next to Mercy S Bearse) S:18

Bearse, Amanda - Died 1832 Dec 14 Age 1 year Daughter of Hiram & Caroline Bearse (next to them) S:21

Bearse, Amanda A - Died 1895 Aug 26 Born 1814 Aug 7 (next to Lincoln B & Owen Bearse) S:18

Bearse, Amanda J - Died 1871 Dec 3 Age 32 years, 3 months, 6 days in Brooklyn, New York Born 1839 Aug 28 Wife of Cranville G Hallett & daughter of Owen & Amanda Bearse (next to parents) S:18

Bearse, Amelia - Died 1865 Apl 6 Age 44 years, 6 months Wife of Daniel Bearse S:4

Bearse, Andrus - Died 1901 Born 1807 S:2

Bearse, Angenora - Died 1842 Aug 29 Age 6 months, 19 days Daughter of Capt Amaziah & Martha Bearse (next to brother, Franklin Bearse) S:21

Bearse, Ann - Died 1876 Feb 4 Age 63 years, 6 months (buried next to husband, Frederic Bearse) S:8

Bearse, Ann Harwood - Died 1956 Sept 4 Born 1881 Sept 18 (with William Amasa Bearse) S:18

Bearse, Anne Howland - Died (no dates) (listed with Alton Irwin Carr Clark) S:18

Bearse, Annie R - Died 1933 Born 1857 (this is a small plaque, 4X10" that says, "Christ My Refuge") S:8

Bearse, Annie W - Died 1979 Aug 13 Born 1882 Oct 5 (with Harry C Bearse) S:18

Bearse, Arrandnh ? - Died 1877 Jan 16 (stone very hard to read) (buried next to Oliver Bearse) S:8

Bearse, Arthur - Died 1870 Born 1812 Listed on same stone with Almira Bearse) S:8

Bearse, Asa - Died 1879 Born 1812 (with wife, Bridget Bearse & others) S:18

Bearse, Asa (Capt) - Died 1852 June 5 in his 75th yr (in downtown Hyannis, Mass there is a restaurant called the Asa Bearse House, this was his home) S:4

Bearse, Asa F - Died 1910 Born 1832 (with wife, Sara L Bearse) S:14

Bearse, Augusta C - Died 1912 Aug

Bearse (Cont.)

14 Born 1831 June 2 (with Joseph Crowell & Abigail Crowell) S:18

Bearse, Austin (Capt) - Died 1881 Dec 21 Born 1808 Apr 3 Stone says, Loving & kind S:8

Bearse, Azuba S - Died 1885 Born 1832 (buried with Nathan H Bearse) S:8

Bearse, Belinda J - Died 1923 Born 1852 (with Osborne W Bearse) S:14

Bearse Benjamin F - Died 1828 July 22 in his 22nd yr S:4

Bearse, Benjamin F - Died 1854 Jan 5 Age 16 years, 5 months Aug Son of William & Bethiah L Bearse S:4

Bearse, Bernice O - Died (still living 1991?) Born 1909 (with Vernon B Bearse) S:18

Bearse, Bessie - Died 1844 June 12 Infant daughter of Richard Bearse & Bethiah Baxter (with them) S:21

Bearse, Bethiah L - Died 1849 Apl 29 Age 36 years, 8 months Wife of Capt WM Bearse (William) S:4

Bearse, Betsey - Died 1869 July 6 b: 1785 May 4 Widow of Capt Richard Bearse S:4

Bearse, Betsey P - Died 1863 June 6 Age 42 years, 7 months Wife of Robert L Bearse (next to son, Robert Sears Bearse) S:18

Bearse, Betsy - Died 1881 Born 1807 S:2

Bearse, Bridget - Died 1865 Born 1812 Wife of Asa Bearse (with him & Joseph T Beckett & others) S:18

Bearse, Caroline - Died 1830 Sept 13 in her 43rd yr Wife of Capt Asa Bearse S:4

Bearse, Caroline B - Died 1865 Feb 3 Age 57 years, 4 months, 20 days (next to husband, Hiram Bearse) S:21

Bearse, Carrie H - Died 1866 Nov 15 Age 6 years, 2 months, 15 days (small stone and off its

Bearse (Cont.)

base) Daughter of Henry & Mary Bearse (next to them) S:19

Bearse, Catherine - Died 1855 Sept 28 Age 61 years Wife of William Bearse (next to Wallace F Bearse) S:18

Bearse, Catherine R - Died 1914 Dec 17 Born 1843 or 45 May 3 (next to James & Jimmie Bearse) S:18

Bearse, Charles C - Died 1889 Feb 24 Age 77 (next to Penelope P Bearse) (middle initial of G found in Hinkley records, Jim Gould of Cotuit has found that the middle initial is C) (correction is from page 31) S:14

Bearse, Charles E - Died 1916 Born 1842 (was in Company D, 45th Regiment, Mass Vol Militia) (with Frances P Bearse) S:8

Bearse, Charles Edward - Died 1921 Born 1848 (stone is a raw stone with engraving in front) S:8

Bearse, Charles G - Died 1889 Feb 24 Age 77 (next to Penelope P Bearse)(middle initial found in Hinckley ceme records) S:14

Bearse, Charles H - Died 1938 Born 1886 Stone says,"Father" (with Lauretta S Bearse) S:18

Bearse, Charles O - Died 1950 Born 1879 (with Henrietta Bearse) S:18

Bearse, Charles W - Died 1909 Born 1845 (with Lora A Bearse) S:8

Bearse, Chester - Died 1935 Aug 7 Born 1859 Sept 27 (buried with Harriet F Bearse & others) S:8

Bearse, Clara A - Died 1862 Oct 26 Age 10 years, 4 months, 18 days Daughter of Lemuel & Hannah Bearse (next to them) S:18

Bearse, Clara F - Died 1899 Born 1840 (with Maynard Bearse & others) S:18

Bearse, Clarance Freeman - Died 1841 Jan Infant son of RL & Eliza Bearse (next to Robert

Bearse (Cont.)
Sears Bearse, brother) S:18

Bearse, Clarence L - Died 1948 Born 1892 (with Florence B Cook) S:18

Bearse, Clarissa J - Died 1849 Born 1826 S:21

Bearse, Daniel (Capt) - Died 1870 Born 1816 (with wife, Lydia F Crowell) S:18

Bearse, David - Died 1881 Dec 19 Born 1812 Nov 20 (with wife, Lucy Bearse) S:18

Bearse, Davis B - Died 1897 Nov 22 Born 1831 Nov 23 On the same stone with Sophronia B Bearse, wife S:4

Dearse, Delia M - Died 1934 Aug 12 Born 1848 Dec 10 (with Joseph & William H Bearse) S:18

Bearse, Desire - Died 1799 June 24 in her 71st yr Wife of Prince Bearse S:1

Bearse, Dora P - Died 1959 Born 1875 (with Helen M Field) S:18

Bearse, E Lewis - Died 1853 (no other markings) (buried next to Kate Bearse, possible wife) S:8

Bearse, Edson W - Died 1945 Born 1868 (large Bearse stone) (buried with Lucinia K Bearse) S:8

Bearse, Edward T - Died 1901 Born 1881 (with Belinda J Bearse) S:14

Bearse, Edwin W - Died 1909 July 13 Born 1839 March 12 (next to wife, Maria A Bearse) S:18

Bearse, Eleanor C - Died 1984 Born 1895 (with William P Bearse & others) S:18

Bearse, Eleazer H - Died 1843 Mar 26 Age 56 years, 1 month, 25 days Stone says, Father (buried next to wife, Rebecca Bearse) S:8

Bearse, Eliot F - Died 1889 May 27 Age 39 years, 13 days (next to Robert L Bearse) S:18

Bearse, Elisha B - Died 1934 Born 1853 (buried with Sophia C Bearse) S:8

Bearse, Eliza Jane - Died 1889 March 3 Born 1826 Dec 17 (next

Bearse (Cont.)
to George P Bearse) S:18

Bearse, Eliza S - Died 1850 June 1 Age 35 years, 4 months S:4

Bearse, Elizabeth B - Died 1876 Sept 27 Age 85? years, 3 months (stone broken & not clear) Widow of Joseph Bearse (next to him) S:18

Bearse, Ella - Died (no dates) Daughter of Edwin W & Maria A Bearse (next to them) S:18

Bearse, Elza N (Capt) - Died 1861 Sept 16 in his 34th yr S:4

Bearse, Elza N Jr - Died 1882 Oct 25 Age 22 years, 8 months (died at Ellsworth, Maine) Son of Capt Elza & Rebecca Bearse is on the same stone as his mother) S:4

Bearse, Emeline - Died 1900 Oct 28 Born 1836 Dec 25 (with Eleanor C Bearse & others) S:18

Bearse, Emily H - Died 1860 Dec 3 Age 23 years, 1 month, 18 days Daughter of Sylvester & Phebe Bearse (next to brother, Theodore Bearse and he is next to parents) S:18

Bearse, Emmaetha? - Died 1821? Nov 14 Age 6 months (stone worn & down from vandals) (next to Levi W Bearse) S:18

Bearse, Ethel - Died 18?? May (small stone, behind Bearse stone, not very clear) (next to Frank Scudder Bearse & Henrietta Rosella Fletcher) S:8

Bearse, Frances P - Died 1918 Born 1839 (with Charles E Bearse) S:8

Bearse, Francis B - Died 1921 Born 1838 (next to wife, Martha Bearse, her stone is down from vandals) S:18

Bearse, Frank H - Died 1904 July 27 Born 1840 July 13 (with Lucy S Bearse & others) S:18

Bearse, Frank P - Died 1890 Born 1874 Son of Nelson & Mary Bearse (with them) S:12

Bearse, Frank Scudder - Died 1928 Mar 3 Born 1846 Aug 20 (buried

Bearse (Cont.)
with Henrietta Rosella Fletcher)
S:8

Bearse, Franklin - Died 1843 Oct
11 Age 4 years, 11 months, 7
days Son of Amaziah & Martha
Bearse (next to sister, Angenora
Bearse) S:21

Bearse, Franklin - Died 1895
March 12 (with wife, Nancy
Bearse & others) S:18

Bearse, Franklin C - Died 1932
Born 1898 (with Osbourne
Bearse & Genieve Crosby) S:14

Bearse, Frederic - Died 1871 Feb 1
Age 56 years, 10 months Stone
says, Company E, 13 th Regiment of New Hampshire Vols S:8

Bearse, Frederick - Died 1909 June
5 Born 1834 Jan 29 (buried next
to Temperance Bearse) S:8

Bearse, Frederick L - Died 1941
Born 1873 (with wife, Winnifred
M Bearse) S:18

Bearse, Freeman - Died 1854 Jan 6
Age 66 years, 9 months (next to
wife, Abigail S Bearse) S:21

Bearse, Gertrude M - Died 1911
Born 1877 (buried next to Azuba
S Bearse) S:14

Bearse, George A - Died 1877?
March 31 Age 25? (stone worn)
S:18

Bearse, George H - Died 1863 Jan
5 Son of William & Susan Bearse
S:8

Bearse, George H - Died 18?? Dec
29 Born 1812? June 25 (stone
badly worn & broken off at base,
but still standing) (there is a
stone next to him that is missing, but next to Mary D Bearse
d1844) S:21

Bearse, George P - Died (no dates
from vandals) (next to Eliza Jane
Bearse) S:18

Bearse, George W - Died 1815 Mar
16 (listed on Isaac Bearse stone)
Age 22 years, 1 month Stone
says: "Who was lost at sea"
(obviously, stone is only in
memory of him) S:3+3R

Bearse, Gertrude M - Died 1985
Dec 12 Born 1898 May 20 (next
to Osborne Warren Bearse) S:14

Bearse, Genevra Frances - Died
1845 May 1 Age 2 years, 1month
bc 1843 April Daughter of
Lemuel & Betsey Bearse S:3+3R

Bearse, Granville H - Died 1871
Jan 27 Age 22 years, 1 month,
28 days Son of Capt Warren &
Lucinda Bearse (with them) (tall
stone down from vandals) S:18

Bearse, Hannah - Died 1867 Feb
21 in her 65th yr Widow of Asa
Bearse S:4

Bearse, Hannah Mrs - Died 1832
June 7 in her 52nd yr Wife of
Solomon Bearse (stone missing
next to her Is it Solomon?) S:14

Bearse, Hannah S - Died 1884
June 7 Age 64 years, 16 days
(with Lemuel F Bearse, husband)
S:18

Bearse, Harriet F - Died 1891 Mar
2 Born 1862 Oct 9 (buried with
Chester Bearse & others) S:8

Bearse, Harrison G - Died 1863
April Born 1837 Oct 29 Lost at
sea on passage from New York to
Port Royal (next to Lucy & Capt
David Bearse) S:18

Bearse, Harry C - Died 1968 Oct 21
Born 1875 Aug 30 (with Annie W
Bearse) S:18

Bearse, Hattie P - Died 1865 Oct 24
Age 22 years, 10 months Daughter of William & Mary (next to
her are 3 small stones, Freddie,
Baby & Freddie (buried next to
husband) S:8

Bearse, Henrietta - Died 1953 Born
1882 (with Charles O Bearse)
S:18

Bearse, Henrietta H - Died 1848
Born 1835 (with Sarah L Crowell
& others) S:18

Bearse, Henry A - Died 1878 Dec 2
in his 43rd yr Drowned going
from Schi(?) Hattie, N Cove to
New London Harbour (Connecticut?) (stone next to wife, Sarah L
Bearse) S:8

Bearse, Henry A - Died 1894 Sept 20 Born 1831 Nov 23 (next to wife, Mary S Bearse) S:19

Bearse, Henry E - Died 1971 Born 1888 (buried with Grace M Chandler, wife) S:8

Bearse, Hiram - Died 1852 Oct 26 Age 45 years, 11 months, 4 days (next to wife, Caroline B Bearse) S:21

Bearse, Horace - Died 1902 April 14 Born 1844 March 10 (with wife, Lucy S Bearse & Mary & Frank Bearse) S:18

Bearse, Horace M - Died 1928 Born 1873 (buried with Azubah F White) S:8

Bearse, Idella F - Died 1861 Dec 17 Age 3 years, 1 month (died in Harwich, Mass) S:4

Bearse, Imogene(?) - Died 1878? Sept 13 Age 21 years (stone not very clear) (buried next to Nelson Bearse) S:8

Bearse, Inis - Died 1865 June 20? Born 1861, 21st of month (not clear) (stone is small with a small lamb on top of it)(buried next to Imogene Bearse) S:8

Bearse, Isaac - Died 1835 May 16 Age 90 years, 2 months, 21 days (George W. Bearse mentioned with him) S:3+3R

Bearse, Isaac H - Died 1841? Sept 20 Born 1809 Nov 23 (next to Capt Isaac Bearse Jr) S:21

Bearse, Isaac Jr (Capt) - Died 1834 Sept 28 in his 54th yr (next to wife, Mrs Sally Bearse) S:21

Bearse, Isaiah L - Died 1844 Feb 9 in his 66th yr (next to wife, Rachel Bearse) S:21

Bearse, James - Died 1758 Oct 11 in his 65th yr (next to Thankful Bearse) S:3R

Bearse, James - Died 1812 Sept 30 in his 42nd yr S:3

Bearse, James - Died 1857 April 23 in his 44th yr Son of Isaac & Mercy Bearse (stone does not have last name on it due to ware, but parents name verifies

Bearse (Cont.)
they are the Bearse family) S:3

Bearse, James - Died 1857 Mar 12 Age 75 years, 3 months S:4

Bearse, James (Jimmie) - Died 1898 May 12 (next to James A & Catherine R Bearse) S:18

Bearse, James A - Died 1874 May 14 Age 48 years, 9 months Was in Company A, 64th Regiment, Kansas Calvery (between Catherine & Jimmie Bearse) S:18

Bearse, James Ira - Died 1844 Aug 6 Age 19 years, 5 months, 20 days Son of James & Polly Bearse S:4

Bearse, James Jr - Died 1812 Sept 14 in his 17th yr Son of James Bearse S:3

Bearse, Jemima - Died 1845 Feb 16 in her 72nd yr Widow of James Bearse? Jemima's stone does not show her last name clearly, but James Bearse is near her? S:3

Bearse, Jemima H - Died 1918 Born 1839 Wife of Simeon F Jones (buried in same grave) S:9

Bearse, Joan F - Died 1848 July Born 1833 May 24 (with William P Bearse & others) S:18

Bearse, John C - Died 1936 Born 1887 (with Laura R Bearse) S:18

Bearse, John S - Died 1892 Jan 14 Age 51 years, 9 months Son of Sylvester & Phebe Bearse (next to them) S:18

Bearse, John Sturgis - Died 1916 Born 1843 (with Ada May Bearse) S:18

Bearse, Joseph - Died 1863 July 28 Born 1785 April 19 Age 78 years, 3 months, 3 days (stone worn) (next to wife, Elizabeth B Bearse) S:18

Bearse, Joseph Howard - Died 1904 Jan 29 Born 1847 Jan 31 (with Delia M Bearse & others) S:18

Bearse, Joseph P - Died 1891 Born 1825 S:4

Bearse, Julia Ann - Died 1831 Mar

Bearse (Cont)
21 in her 15th yr Daughter of
Isaac & Mercy Bearse S:3

Bearse, Kate - Died 1857 (possible
wife of E Lewis) (buried next to
him) S:8

Bearse, Laura - Died 1850 Born
1838 S:2

Bearse, Laura M - Died 1926 Dec
13 Born 1856 Dec 14 Daughter
of Nelson & Gloria A Bearse,
buried next to Nelson S:8

Bearse, Laura R - Died 1927 Born
1878 (with John C Bearse &
others) S:18

Bearse, Laura W - Died 1850 Oct 9
Age 17 years, 2 months, 20 days
Daughter of Andrus & Belseu L
Bearse S:2

Bearse, Lauretta S - Died 1974
Born 1893 Stone says,"Mother"
(next to Charles H Bearse) S:18

Bearse, Lemuael - Died 1863 Aug 6
Age 41 years, 4 months S:3+ 3R

Bearse, Lemuel - Died 1799 April
25 in his 68th yr (next to wife
Patience) S:3R

Bearse, Lemuel - Died 1816 Sept 9
in his 44th yr (next to Genevra
Frances Bearse) S:3R

Bearse, Lemuel F - Died 1895 May
14 Age 78 years, 7 months (with
wife, Hannah S Bearse) S:18

Bearse, Levi - Died 1888 March 20
Born 1800 Oct 15 (stone down
from vandals) (next to Mercy S
Bearse) S:18

Bearse, Levi W - Died 1860 Aug 14
Born 1857 Sept (small stone,
down from vandal) (next to Alvin
Bearse) S:18

Bearse, Lillah - Died 1873 June
Age 11 months, 6 days Daughter
of Owen & Amanda A Bearse
(next to sister, Sarah Adeline
Bearse) S:18

Bearse, Lincoln B - Died 1877 June
3 Age 39 years, 8 months (next
to Amanda Bearse) S:18

Bearse, Lora A - Died 1923 Born
1855 (with Charles W
Bearse)(others listed on same

Bearse (Cont.)
stone but with later dates
Probably children) S:8

Bearse, Louisa B - Died 1873 Born
1814 (with Marietta Bearse) S:18

Bearse, Lucinda - Died 1873 Jan 2
Age 44 years, 11 months, 22
days (tall stone down from van-
dals) Wife of Capt Warren H
Bearse & daughter of Nathan &
Climena Basset (with husband &
Willis & Granville Bearse) S:18

Bearse, Lucinia K - Died 1947 Born
1867 (large Bearse stone) (buried
with Edson W Bearse) S:8

Bearse, Lucy - Died 1884 Aug 5
Age 72 years, 5 months, 17 days
(next to Isaiah L Bearse) S:21

Bearse, Lucy - Died 1895 Aug 19
Born 1814 Aug 29 Wife of Capt
David Bearse (with him) S:18

Bearse, Lucy S - Died 1927 Sept 12
Born 1846 May 3 or 8? Wife of
Horace Bearse (with him &
others) S:18

Bearse, Luther H - Died 1850 May
15 Age 38 S:4

Bearse, M Harriet - Died 1976 Born
1890 (with Zenas DB Bearse &
others) S:8

Bearse, M Juliette - Died 1954
Born 1894 (with Maurice S
Bearse) S:16

Bearse, M P - Died (stone is missing, info taken from foot stone)
(next to Stacy B Bearse &
Benjamin Davis) S:19

Bearse, Mabel - Died 1910 Born
1866 Wife of Gilbert L Coleman
(next to him) S:14

Bearse, Maria A - Died 1916 May 5
Born 1852 June 29 (next to
husband, edwin W Bearse) S:18

Bearse, Maria L - Died 1913 Born
1829 (with Henrietta H Bearse &
others) S:18

Bearse, Marietta - Died 1871 Born
1846 (with Louisa B Bearse)
S:18

Bearse, Mark L - Died 1884 July 2
Age 6 years, 5 months Son of
Owen & Amanda Brease (with

Bearse (Cont.)
    them & others) S:18
Bearse, Martha - Died 1882 Nov 29
    Age 45 years, 4 months Stone
    says,"She still lives" Wife of FB
    Dearse (Francis D Dearse, next
    to her) Stone is down from
    vandals S:18
Bearse, Martha (or Mary) A - Died
    18?? Jan 12 Age 3 years, 7
    months, 17 days (stone worn)
    Daughter of ? (next to Mary
    Bearse) (not sure if last name is
    Bearse?) S:21
Bearse, Mary - Died 1817 Oct 11
    Age 22 (next to Martha or Mary
    A Bearse?) S:21
Bearse, Mary - Died 1955 Born
    1864 (with Zenas DB Bearse &
    others) S:8
Bearse, Mary A - Died 1882 March
    15 Age 71 years, 5 months Stone
    says,"Mother" Wife of Alfred
    Bearse (next to him) S:14
Bearse, Mary D - Died 1844 Dec 29
    Age 25 years, 10 months, 12
    days Wife of Allen H Bearse
    (near him) S:21
Bearse, Mary E - Died 1874 Feb 13
    Age 32 years, 9 months, 13 days
    Wife of Frank Bearse (with him)
    S:18
Bearse, Mary F - Died 1830 Oct 10
    Age 2 years, 10 months Daugh-
    ter of Capt Asa & Caroline
    Bearse S:4
Bearse, Mary G - Died 1905 July
    12 Born 1837 Oct 5 (buried with
    husband, Capt Prince Bearse)
    (this is a very large stone with
    engraved flowers on it) S:8
Bearse, Mary H - Died 1934 Born
    1876 (with Nelson & Mary
    Bearse) S:12
Bearse, Mary Helen - Died 1884
    Born 1840 (with Clara F Bearse
    & others) S:18
Bearse, Mary S - Died 1864 Oct 26
    Age 63 years, 10 months (buried
    next to husband, William W
    Bearse) S:8
Bearse, Mary S - Died 1903 Dec 11

Bearse (Cont.)
    Born 1846 Dec 10 Wife of Henry
    Bearse (next to him & daughter,
    Carrie H Bearse) S:19
Bearse, Mary W - Died 1912 Mar 2
    Born 1825 May 25 (perpetual
    care for stone) Wife of Capt
    Dennis Sturgis (buried with him)
    S:8
Bearse, Maurice S - Died 1968
    Born 1896 (with M Juliette
    Bearse) S:16
Bearse, Maynard - Died 1898 Born
    1833 (with Mary Helen Bearse &
    others) S:18
Bearse, Melintha - Died 1874 Sept
    16 in her 79th yr Widow of Ira
    Bearse S:2
Bearse, Mercy - Died 1856 Oct 15
    in her 75th yr Widow of Isaac
    Bearse S:3
Bearse, Mercy S - Died 1862 Feb
    22 Born 1815 May 21 (stone
    down from vandals) (next to Levi
    Bearse) S:18
Bearse, Mildred - Died 1891 Sept
    25 Born 1890 Nov 29 (small
    stone) Daughter of EW & MA
    Bearse (next to sister, Ella & she
    is next to parents) S:18
Bearse, Miriam H - Died 1935 May
    2 Born 1870 Mar 29 Wife of
    Chester Bearse (buried with him
    & others) S:8
Bearse, Moses H - Died 1843 Dec
    15 in his 63rd yr S:4
Bearse, Nancy - Died 1873 March
    19 (with Joan F Bearse & others)
    S:18
Bearse, Nathan H - Died 1875 Born
    1823 (buried with Azuba S
    Bearse) S:8
Bearse, Nathan H - Died 1930 Born
    1859 (buried with Carrie L
    Chase, wife) S:8
Bearse, Nathaniel - Died 1805 Oct
    3 Age 1 year, 2 months Son of
    John & Susanna Bearse S:1
Bearse, Nathaniel F - Died 1820
    Oct 20 (Infant) Son of Isaac &
    Sally Bearse S:4
Bearse, Nelson - Died 1883 Born

Bearse (Cont.)
1861 S:8

Bearse, Nelson - Died 1889 Aug 16
Born 1812 Feb 15 (buried next
to Laura M Bearse) S:8

Bearse, Nelson - Died 1988 Born
1898 Was Ensign in US Navy
during World War I (with flag)
(another flag says, "In Memory of
Fireman") S:11

Bearse, Nelson 2nd - Died 1890
Born 1875 Son of Nelson & Mary
Bearse (with them) S:12

Bearse, Nelson H - Died 1933 Born
1844 (with Mary C Ames &
others) S:12

Bearse, Olive H - Died 1877 Mar 4
Born 1812 Oct 31 S:8

Bearse, Oliver - Died 1877 July 2
in his 34th yr Son of Nelson &
Clorida A Bearse (buried next to
them) S:8

Bearse, Oliver - Died 1885 Oct 14
Born 1816 July 19 S:4

Bearse, Osborne W - Died 1922
Born 1848 (with Stephen &
Linda Richards) S:14

Bearse, Osborne Warren - Died
1948 Born 1877 (with wife,
Genieve S Crosby) S:14

Bearse, Osmond W - Died 1905
Born 1845 (with Harriet A
Hamblin, wife) S:18

Bearse, Owen - Died 1807 Nov 27
(infant) Son of Isaac & Sally
Bearse S:4

Bearse, Owen - Died 1887 Sept 24
Born 1812 Aug 27 (next to
Amanda A Bearse) S:18

Bearse, Patience - Died 1777
March 9 in her 40th yr Wife of
Lemuel Bearse (next to him)
S:3R

Bearse, Penelope P - Died 1905
March 14 Age 64 (next to
Charles C Bearse) S:14

Bearse, Phebe Hallett - Died 1902
Born 1814 (with Sylvester
Bearse) S:18

Bearse, Phyllis Jerauld - Died 1966
Born 1898 Wife of Nelson Bearse
(with him) S:11

Bearse, Polly - Died 1858 Feb 8 Age
71 years, 6 months Wife of
James Bearse S:4

Bearse, Polly - Buried 1834 Nov 21
Age 15 S:14R

Bearse, Prince (Capt) - Died 1901
Oct 11 Born 1832 Mar 12
(buried with wife, Mary G
Bearse) S:8

Bearse, Prince H - Died 1822 Oct
24 (Infant) Son of Capt Isaac &
Sally Bearse S:4

Bearse, Prudance - Died 1816 Sept
27 Age 65 Wife of Gershom
Bearse S:1

Bearse, Prudence H - Died 1838
Feb 16 in her 29th yr Daughter
of Moses H & Rebecca Bearse
S:4

Bearse, Rachel - Died 1797 Mar 11
in her 38th yr Consort to James
Bearse S:11+26R

Bearse, Rachel - Died 1842 March
30 in her 62nd yr Wife of Isaiah
L Bearse (next to him) S:21

Bearse, Ray Huntington - Died
1983 Born 1901 S:20

Bearse, Rebecca - Died 1857 May
12 in her 70th yr Widow of
Moses H Bearse S:4

Bearse, Rebecca - Died 1873 June
5 Age 87 years, 1 month, 13
days Wife of Eleazer H Bearse
Stone says, Mother S:8

Bearse, Rebecca - Died 1876 Aug 5
Age 41 years, 2 months, 19 days
(listed on same stone as Elza N
Bearse Jr She was the wife of
Capt Elza N Bearse S:4

Bearse, Rebecca B - Died 1903
Born 1825 S:4

Bearse, Rebecca J - Died 1906
Born 1830 Wife of Warren H
Bearse S:8

Bearse, Rebecca W - Died 1882 Oct
8 Born 1813 July 27 Wife of WM
Bearse and the Widow of the late
JB Crowell S:4

Bearse, Richard - Died 1881 July 6
Born 1814 April 15 (with Bethiah Baxter & Bessie Bearse) S:21

Bearse, Richard (Capt) - Died 1852

Bearse (Cont.)
Dec 7 Age 73 years, 3 months S:4

Bearse, Robert L - Died 1899 May 19 Born 1814 June 7 (next to Eliot F Bearse) S:18

Bearse, Robert N - Died 1876 Oct 21 Born 1820 Nov 14 S:21

Bearse, Robert Sears - Died 1854 July 31 Age 2 years, 6 months Son of Robert L & Betsey Bearse (next to mother) S:18

Bearse, Russell B - Died 1979 Born 1889 (with M Harriet Bearse & others) S:8

Bearse, Sally - Died 1844 June 14 Age 31 Wife of Isaac Bearse S:3

Bearse, Sally L - Died 1901 Dec 7 S:4

Bearse, Sally Mrs - Died 1864 March 25 Age 83 years, 5 months Stone says,"Our Mother" Widow of Isaac Bearse Jr (next to him) S:21

Bearse, Samuel H - Died 1854 April 13 Stone says,"Supposed lost at sea while on his passage from Glasgow from Baltimore in Brig Gov Briggs" (listed with Sarah A Bearse) S:18

Bearse, Sara L - Died 1893 Born 1840 Wife of Asa F Bearse (with him) S:14

Bearse, Sarah A - Died (dates under ground) (listed with Samuel H Bearse who was lost at sea 1854) S:18

Bearse, Sarah Adeline - Died 1846 Aug 31 Age 1 year, 10 months, 24 days Daughter of Owen & Amanda Bearse (next to sister, Amanda J Bearse) S:18

Bearse, Sarah F - Died 1971 Born 1880 (grandchild of Augustine & Sarah Childs) (other names on stone are dated later) S:8

Bearse, Sarah L - Died 1876 July 2 Born 1835 Nov 8 Wife of Henry Bearse (his stone next to hers) S:8

Bearse, Sophia C - Died 1934 Born 1859 (buried with Elisha B

Bearse (Cont.)
Bearse) S:8

Bearse, Sophia H - Died 1859 Aug 17 Age 32 years, 9months, 7 days Wife of Allen H Bearse (near him & with to infant son, d1859) S:21

Bearse, Sophronia B - Died 1892 June 27 Age 72 years, 10 months Wife of Davis B Bearse and the former wife of John H Hallett She is listed on same stone with David B Bearse S:4

Bearse, Stacy B - Died 1852 Nov 2 Age 14 years, 11 months (stone off the base) (next to MP Bearse, but stone is missing) S:19

Bearse, Sturges - Died 1860 Jan 2 Age 49 years, 11 months, 21 days Son of Isaac & Mercy Bearse S:3

Bearse, Susan - Died 1859 Oct 10 in her 77th yr 1782 Widow of Ebenezer Bearse S:4

Bearse, Susan E - Died 1915 Born 1842 Wife of William E) (listed on same stone) S:8

Bearse, Susan F - Died 1967 Born 1872 (with Eleanor C Bearse & others) S:18

Bearse, Susanna - Died 1804 Aug 15 in her 27th yr Wife of John Bearse S:1

Bearse, Sylvester - Died 1882 Born 1814 (with Phebe Hallett Bearse) S:18

Bearse, Sylvester - Died 1903 Born 1845 (next to John S Bearse, brother? & possible parents, Phebe & Sylvester Bearse) S:18

Bearse, Temperance - Died 1912 Nov 21 Born 1828 Sept 6 (buried next to Frederick Bearse) S:8

Bearse, Thankful - Died 1759 June 7 in her 63rd yr Wife of James Bearse (next to him) S:3R

Bearse, Theodore H - Died 1863 Dec 6 Age 21 years, 6 months Son of Sylvester & Phebe Bearse (next to them) S:18

Bearse, Thomas - Died 1853 Sept 11 in his 74th yr S:4

Bearse, Vernon B - Died 1969 Born 1900 (with Bernice O Bearse & others) S:18

Bearse, W M (Capt) - Died 1889 Jan 9 Age 78 years, 4 months This is probably William Bearse S:4

Bearse, Wallace F - Died 18?? Oct 4 Age 2 years, 1 month (stone worn and down from vandals) (next to Emmaetha? Bearse & Catherine Bearse) S:18

Bearse, Warren H (Capt) - Died 1874 Jan 2 Age 53 years, 3 months, 5 days (tall stone down from vandals) (with Lucinda Bearse & others) S:18

Bearse, Watson H - Died 1922 May 19 Born 1844 Jan 3 (next to Clara A Bearse) S:18

Bearse, William Amasa - Died 1920 Sept 24 Born 1883 May 27 S:18

Bearse, William E - Died 1918 Born 1838 (listed on same stone with wife, Susan E Bearse) S:8

Bearse, William H - Died 1829 Born 1805 S:2

Bearse, William H - Died 1952 Oct 17 Born 1873 Sept 3 (with Virginia Kennedy & Joseph Howard Bearse) S:18

Bearse, William Henry - Died 1923 Born 1843 (with Adelaide Lovell Bearse) S:12

Bearse, William P - Died 1872 June 8 Born 1837 July 22 (with Emeline Bearse & others) S:18

Bearse, William P - Died 1962 Born 1872 (with Susan F Bearse & others) S:18

Bearse, William W - Died 1850 May 15 at Chelsea, Boston,Ma hospital Age 45 years S:8

Bearse, William W - Died 1865 Sept 25 Age 21 years, 3 months (buried next to wife, Hattie who also died that same year) (next to them are 3 small stones that say, Freddie, Baby & Freddie) S:8

Bearse, Willis B - Died 1886 Dec 8 Born 1886 Dec 14 (tall stone

Bearse (Cont.) down from vandals) (with Granville Bearse & others) S:18

Bearse, Winnifred M - Died 1961 Born 1879 Wife of Frederick L Bearse (with him) S:18

Bearse, Zenas DB - Died 1917 Born 1846 (on same stone with Mary Bearse & others) S:8

Bearse, Zipporah - Died 1846 Oct 13 Age 70 Wife of Solomon (stone missing between her and Solomon's other wife, Mrs Hannah Bearse Is it Solomon?) S:14

Beaudry, George J - Died 1973 Born 1900 S:15

Beaumont, Alphonse J - Died 1990 Born 1893 (undertaker plaque only) (next to Margaret M Beaumont) S:15

Beaumont, Leo Edmond - Died 1925 Aug 23 Born 1896 Aug 27 Was a Corporal in 101 Engineers, 26th Division (next to William Beaumont) S:31

Beaumont, Margaret M - Died 1989 Born 1900 (undertaker plaque only) (next to Alphonse J Beaumont) S:15

Beaumont, William - Died 1924 Born 1855 (next to Leo Edmond Beaumont) S:31

Beaupre, George H - Died (still living 1991?) Born 1926 Jan 21 (listed with Barbara F Hallett & others) S:19

Beckett, Caroline S - Died 1915 Born 1844 Widow of Joseph Beckett (with him & Asa Bearse & others) S:18

Beckett, Eleanor B - Died 1860 Born 1840 Wife of Joseph T Beckett (with him & Caroline S Beckett & others) S:18

Beckett, Joseph T - Died 187? Born 183? (stone worn) (with wife, Eleanor B Beckett & others) S:18

Beckloff, Peg - Died 1974 Born 1919 S:11

Bedard, Alexander - Died 1965

Bedard (Cont.)
Born 1881 (with Annie Bedard)
S:17

Bedard, Annie - Died 1975 Born
1882 (with Alexander Bedard)
S:17

Begg, Howard Bolton - Died 1967
Born 1896 (with wife, Katherine
Clasby) S:15

Behlman, Annie Myron - Died 1919
Born 1881 (with Arthur Henry
Behlman) S:14

Behlman, Arthur H - Died 1990
Born 1910 (with Capt George N
Fuller & others) S:14

Behlman, Arthur Henry - Died
1973 Born 1880 (with Annie
Myron Behlman) S:14

Behlman, Helen M - Died 1979
Born 1914 (with Capt George N
Fuller & others) S:14

Belden, Henritta - Died 1817 Sept
22 Age 5 years, 3 months S:5

Bell, Bessie B - Died (1 week old)
Born 30th 1894 (stone not clear)
Parents were, F & Annie S:13

Bell, Helen Wilson - Died 1953 May
31 Born 1895 June 2 (with
Kenneth Corwin Bell) S:14

Bell, Isabel P - Died 1959 Born
1887 (next to Robert O Bell) S:14

Bell, Jessie - Died 1963 Born 1894
wife of Hanson Washington (with
him & Sallie Crudup) S:18

Bell, John F - Died 1933 Born
1846 (with Annabelle Gass) S:13

Bell, Josephine - Died 1961 Born
1875 (with Henry Russo) S:16

Bell, Kenneth Corwin - Died 1971
April 16 Born 1892 June 11
(with Helen Wilson Bell) S:14

Bell, Minnie E - Died 1968 Nov 14
Born 1885 Oct 7 (with Lester
Prince Lovell) S:12

Bell, Robert O - Died 1964 Born
1887 (next to Isabel P Bell) S:14

Bender, Edward J - Died 1975
Born 1907 Stone says,"Beloved
husband & father" S:13

Benjamin, Emanuel W (MD) - Died
1971 Born 1899 (Jewish section)
S:15

Bennan, Mary - Died 1988 Born
1897 S:18

Bennett, ? - Died (this is an above
ground cript very lary (about 1
story high, next to pond in back
of cemetery) S:18

Bennett, Anna M - Died 1973 Born
1910 (with Holland Bennett)
S:13

Bennett, EA Leslie - Died 1973
Born 1892 (with Inez Kirk) S:15

Bennett, Edward L - Died 1982
Born 1897 (with Eva N Bennett)
S:16

Bennett, Eva N - Died 1957 Born
1898 (with Edward L Bennett)
S:16

Bennett, Holland - Died 1976 Born
1909 (with Anna M Bennett)
Also has military stone that
says, "Sgt in US Army during
World War II S:13

Bennett, Irene M - Died 1985 Born
1908 (with Robert G Bennett)
S:15

Bennett, Robert G - Died 1975
Born 1900 He was a Mason
(with Irene M Bennett) S:15

Bennett, William D - Died 1965
Sept 16 Born 1898 July 19 From
Massachusetts, was AS in
USNRF during World War I S:15

Bennett, William H - Died (no date
listed) Listed in Company C,
26th Massachusetts Infantry
S:12

Benson, Ada M - Died 1983 Born
1893 Age 90 (age from Hinckley
ceme records) S:15

Benson, Emaline - Died 1880 Born
1840 S:5

Benson, Margaret R - Died 1969
Born 1899 (with Robert G
Benson) S:16

Benson, Robert G - Died 1981 Born
1902 (with Margaret R Benson)
S:16

Benson, Sarah A - Died 1881 Jan
22 Age 28 years, 6 months Wife
of Calvin Benson S:5

Bentinck-Smith, William Frederick
- Died 1924 Aug 30 Born 1872

Bentinck-Smith (Cont.)
July 22 (with wife, Marion Jordan) S:14

Benttinen, Edytha Bearse - Died 1988 Born 1924 (with Ronald E Benttinen & others) S:20

Benttinen, Helmi Syryala S - Died 1984 Dec 29 Born 1901 Jan 20 (with Edytha Bearse Benttinen & others) S:20

Benttinen, Ronald E - Died 1988 Born 1928 (has 2 stones, one has fishing and hunting figures engraved on it) (with William Benttinen & others) Was a Private in US Army during Korea S:20

Benttinen, William - Died 1965 Dec 4 Born 1902 May 13 (has 2 stones, one with boating on it) (with Helmi Syryala S Benttinen & others) S:20

Benttinnen, Wilhelmina - Died 1938 Born 1864 (buried with H Marie Gonzales) S:8

Bergeron, Helen L - Died 1983 Born 1906 Wife of William Bergeron (with him) S:13

Bergeron, William - Died 22 Nov 1965 Born 26 July 1902 With with Helen L Bergeron Was from Massachusetts as a Private in BTRG D, 8 FA TNG Regiment during World War I & II (has a veteran star at grave too) S:13

Berry, Albree W - Died 1844 Dec 30 Age 6 years, 18 days (stone out of ground and broken) (next to parents, Benajah & Lucy Berry) S:21

Berry, Allen A - Died 1955 Born 1878 (with Joseph & Nancy Berry) S:18

Berry, Anna - Died 1810 June 10 in her 40th yr S:10+26R

Berry, Arthur CF - Died 1949 Born 1866 (with Ella F Berry & others) S:18

Berry, Benajah - Died 1868 Born 1789 (flat stone) (with Lucy Berry) S:21

Berry, Charles G - Died 1900 Dec

Berry (Cont.)
17 Born 1830 Aug 23 (with Thankful H Berry & others) S:18

Berry, Charles L - Died 1927 Born 1858 (with Lillian M Berry & others) S:18

Berry, Charlotte Louise - Died 1954 Born 1872 Wife of Richard T Greene (buried with him) (others listed on stone with later dates, possible children?) S:8

Berry, Clara D - Died 1854 Oct 2 Age 5 months, 17 days Daughter of Zerih? D & Eliza J Berry) S:21

Berry, Ella F - Died 1904 Oct 30 Born 1867 April 16 (with John R Dodge & others) S:18

Berry, Ephraim - Died (dates not clear) (Hinckley Ceme records #10R says death date 1804 June 25 in his 74th yr) (next to Mercy Berry) S:10+26R

Berry, Frank H - Died 1920 Born 1860 or 80 (stone not clear) (with Laura A Berry & others) S:18

Berry, Jane - Died 1837 Sept 11 Age 74 years, 7 months S:4

Berry, Joseph - Died 1797 May 7 Age 7 days Son of Joseph & Mercy Berry S:11R

Berry, Joseph - Died 1848 Mar or April 20 in his 82nd yr S:11

Berry, Joseph A - Died 1923 Feb 26 Born 1835 July 13 Stone says,"Father" (with Nancy & Allen Berry) S:18

Berry, Laura A - Died 1905 Born 1863 (with Charles L Berry & others) S:18

Berry, Lillian M - Died 1941 Born 1862 (with Frank H Berry & others) S:18

Berry, Lucy - Died 1874 Born 1791 (with Benajah Berry & next to son, Albree W Berry) S:21

Berry, Mercy - Died 1817 Nov 23 in her 80th yr Relict of Ephraim Berry S:10+26R

Berry, Mercy Mrs - Died 1798 April 13 in her 28th yr Wife of Joseph Berry (next to him) S:11 +26R

Berry, Nancy C - Died 1899 March 18 Born 1846 Feb 10 Stone says,"Mother" (with Joseph & Allen Berry) S:18

Berry, Phineas S - Died 1862 Born 1820 (with Rebecca P Crowell, his wife) S:18

Berry, Susanna - Died 1796 July 20 Age 2 years, 1 month Daughter of Joseph & Mercy Berry S:11R

Berry, Thankful H - Died 1898 March 22 Born 1832 March 29 (with Frank H Berry & others) S:18

Berth (or Baker), Richard? - Died 1848 Aug 2 Age 6 months, 8 days (stone worn, not clear) Son of Capt Seth & Sophia Berth or Baker (next to Rebecca & William Baker) S:21

Berth, Cora L - Died 1881 July 20 Age 7 weeks (next to Everett L Berth) S:21

Berth, Everett L - Died 1867 Feb 28 Age 2 months Son of William & Sophia L Berth (next to Cora L Berth) S:21

Besse, Agnes Merrill - Died 1980 Born 1895 (rock stone) (next to Edward Linden Besse) S:14

Besse, Edward Linden - Died 1951 Born 1862 (rock stone) (next to Agnes Merrill Besse) S:14

Bestford, Anna C - Died 1971 Born 1888 S:16

Bexter, Alexina F - Died 1857 Jan 17 Age 10 years, 3 months, 21 days (possible daughter to Alexander & Persis Baxter, next to them) S:21

Bickel, Edward R - Died 1988 Born 1904 (undertaker plaque only) (next to Edward P Deveney) S:19

Bigelow, John Rev - Died 1884 June 20 Born 1818 April 25 (stone says, "DD") S:12

Bigelow, Sophronia L - Died 1900 Oct 27 Born 1819 March 9 Wife of Rev John Bigelow (next to him) S:12

Bill, Frederic L - Died 1927 Born

Bill (Cont.)
1873 (with Georgina Daniel, his wife) S:12

Bingham, Clyde H - Died 1966 June 20 Born 1900 Mar 4 From New York & was Major in Army Air Force during World War II (next to Francis J Bingham) S:13

Bingham, Francis J - Died 1961 Jan 31 Born 1894 May 16 From Massachusetts & was a 2nd Lieutenant in the infantry Res during World War I (next to Clyde H Bingham) S:13

Birch, Alfred H - Died 1969 Born 1891 (with Anna K Birch) S:15

Birch, Anna K - Died 1966 Born 1888 (with Alfred H Birch) S:15

Birtwistle, Anna M - Died 1962 May 25 Born 1892 Oct 21 From Massachusetts, was Nurse in US Army Nurse Corps during World War I (with Matthew S Birtwistle) S:14

Birtwistle, Matthew S - Died 1960 April 20 Born 1888 March 30 From Massachusetts, was Commander (HC) in US Navy during World War I & II (with Anna M Birtwistle) S:14

Bishop, (infant) Chase - Died (no dates) (small stone) Child of Anthony & Clarissa Bishop (next to them) S:18

Bishop, Alexander - Died 1884 May 23 Age 60 years, 9(?) months, 14 days Stone says,"Father" (next to Betsey B Bishop) S:18

Bishop, Bessie - Died 1880 June 28 Age 14 years, 9 months, 5 days Stone says, "We miss our darling" Daughter of Lafayette F & Hannah S Bishop (next to Walter Bishop) S:18

Bishop, Betsey B - Died 1884 June 6 Age 61 years, 1(?) month, 24 days Stone says,"Mother" (next to Alexander Bishop) S:18

Bishop, Hamilton - Died 1846 June 26 Age 52 (next to wife, Susan H Bishop) S:21

Bishop, Lafayette F - Died 1891

Bishop (Cont.)
Nov 11 Age 45 years, 11 months (next to Clarence H Coffin) S:18

Bishop, Mary - Died 1969 Born 1881 S:15

Bishop, Susan H - Died 1846 Dec 16 in her 49th yr Widow of Hamilton Bishop (next to him) S:21

Bishop, Walter - Died 1880 or 2 Dec 4 Age 14 years, 10 months, 11 days Son of Lafayette F & Hannah S Bishop (next to Clarence H Coffin) S:18

Bixby, Alice Parker - Died 1905 Born 1889 (with Lillie Bixby & others) S:18

Bixby, Lillie - Died 1934 Born 1859 (with Alice Parker Bixby & others) S:18

Bjerke, Sverre - Died 1974 Born 1902 S:12

Bjornholm, Rachel H E - Died (still living 1991?) Born 1908 (with T Frederick Bjornholm) S:20

Bjornholm, T Frederick - Died 1973 Born 1906 (with Rachel H E Bjornholm) S:20

Black, Deborah - Died 1827 August 15 in her 75th yr Wife of Thomas Black S:5R

Black, Gabrielle C - Died (still living 1991?) Born 1937 (with Robert R Black Jr) S:20

Black, George M - Died 1967 Born 1895 S:11

Black, Margaret M - Died 1977 Born 1905 (with Robert Black Sr) S:20

Black, Olive - Died 1809 Oct 8 Age 25 S:5

Black, Robert R Jr - Died (still living 1991?) Born 1935 (with Gabrielle C Black) S:20

Black, Robert R Sr - Died 1982 Born 1900 (Also has a West Barnstable Fire Dept plaque) (With Margaret Black) S:20

Black, Thomas - Died 1880 in his 18th yr (lost at sea) S:5

Black, Thomas Jr - Died 1804 March 15 in his 18th yr Lost at

Black (Cont.)
sea Eldest son of Thomas & Deborah Erected by the only surviving son & brother S:5R

Blackburn, Catherine - Buried 1984 Oct 27 Age 83 S:15R

Blackinton, Florence W - Died 1868 Dec 14 Age 30 years, 5 months Wife of Allen A Blackinton S:21

Blagden, Clora M - Died 1967 Nov 14 Born 1886 Feb 2 (with William R Blagden) S:14

Blagden, Daniel S - Died 1923 Born 1850 (with Mary S Blagden, wife) S:21

Blagden, Deborah - Died 1858 Aug 6 Age 59 years Wife James Blagden (next to him) S:21

Blagden, Isabel - Died (this stone says only Isabel, but is only 6 inches away from James R Blagden) S:21

Blagden, JW - Died 1896 (next to James R Blagden) S:21

Blagden, James - Died 1882 April 10 Age 70 years, 5 days (next to wife, Deborah Blagden) S:21

Blagden, James R - Died 1864 June 15 at Alexandria, Virgina Age 40? (stone falling over) Was in Company A, 5th Regiment in Massachusetts Volunteers (next to JW Blagden) S:21

Blagden, Mary S - Died 1915 Born 1857 Wife of Daniel Blagden (with him) S:21

Blagden, William R - Died 1961 July 2 Born 1883 May 8 (with Clora M Blagden) S:14

Blais, Alice M - Died 1971 Born 1890 (next to Pierre O Blais) S:15

Blais, Pierre O - Died 1964 Born 1890 (next to Alice M Blais) S:15

Blake, Justina - Died 1833 Apl 6 Age 39 years, 6 months Wife of Dudley Blake S:4

Blake, Samuel - Died 1715 April 29 Age 24 (Latin inscription) Son of John & Hannah Blake of Dorchester (the letters "AM" are

Blake (Cont.)
listed after Samuel's name)
S:11R

Blanchard, Saidee I "Marshall" - Died 1962 Born 1876 (in Marshall plot) S:11

Blanche, Edith C - Buried 1986 Aug 12 Age 85 S:15R

Blish, Abraham - Died 1760 Jan 11 in his 48th yr S:5

Blish, Chloe - Died 1798 Sept 21 in her 36th yr S:5

Blish, Ebenezer - Died 1803 in his 58th yr or 2 Sept 1801 (1801 death date from Hinckley ceme records) S:5

Blish, Elisha - Died 1836 May in his 77th yr S:5R

Blish, Elisha - Died 1846 May 28 in his 86th yr S:3

Blish, George - Died 1869 May 16 in his 75th yr S:5

Blish, Hannah - Died 1732 Nov 11 in her 56th yr Wife of Joseph Blish S:5R

Blish, Hannah - Died 1807 Jan or June 2 in her 75th yr (stone not clear, but found record in Hinckley ceme records too) (stone fist appeared to read age 15?) S:5

Blish, Hannah - Died 1847 Nov 11 Age 19 years, 11 months (died in Boston) Daughter of George & Rebecca Blish S:5

Blish, Joseph - Died 1730 June 14 in his 83rd yr S:5

Blish, Joseph - Died 1754 March 14 in his 80th yr S:5R

Blish, Joseph (Dea) - Died 1780 June 21 in his 77th yr S:5

Blish, Joseph (Maj) - Died 1849 Oct 14 in his 82nd yr S:5

Blish, Joseph Lieut - Died 1815 May 19 in his 84th yr Listed as a Revolutionary War Veteran S:5

Blish, Mercy - Died 1756 Aug 17 in her 50th yr Wife of Joseph Blish (buried next to her) S:5

Blish, Rebecca A - Died 1868 Nov 17 in her 36th yr (died in Boston) Daughter of George & Rebecca Blish S:5

Blish, Rebecca P - Died 1886 Dec 16 Born 1800 Sept 25 Wife of George Blish S:5

Blish, Rebekah - Died 1830 Nov 16 in her 86th yr Wife of Elisha Blish S:3

Blish, Sarah - Died (date not clear)(death record, 25 Nov 1802 in her 69th yr was found in Hinckley records) Wife of Joseph Blish S:5

Blish, Sarah - Died 1790 May 6 in her 28th yr Wife of ? S:11+26R

Blish, Sarah - Died Stone not clear, but lived in 1700's Buried between Sarah Bliss & Deac Nathan Bassett S:5

Blish, Sarah Miss - Died 1816 May 1 in her 44th yr (Miss was found in Hinckley ceme records) S:5

Blish, Susie S - Died 1874 Apr 9 in her 39th yr (died in Baltimore, Maryland) (Daughter of George & Rebecca Blish) S:5

Blish, Sylvester - Died 1826 March Age 33 Lost at sea S:5R

Blish, Temperance - Died 1767 Aug 10 in her 52nd yr Wife of Abraham (buried next to her) (1767 death date found in Hinckley ceme records) S:5

Blish, Temperance S - Died 1854 Aug 20 in her 87th yr Wife of Maj Joseph Blish S:5

Blish, Timothy - Died 1778 June 6 in his 3rd yr Shot in ye head and died immediately Son of Joseph & Sarah Blish S:5R

Bliss, Caroline H - Died 1886 Born 1817 (with Owen Bliss) S:12

Bliss, Elizabeth P - Died 1884 Feb 24 in her 54th yr S:4

Bliss, Horace B - Died 1875 Feb 1 in his 15th yr S:4

Bliss, Owen - Died 1879 Born 1802 (with Caroline H Bliss) S:12

Blodgett, Dorothy - Died 1989 July 9 Born 1904 Nov 20 (with John William Herron) S:13

Blossm (Blossom), Alice L - Died 1872 Age 2 Born 1870 Daughter of Henry & Hannah Blossom S:5

Blossom, (infant) - Died 1814 July 10 (death date not clear on stone but found in Hinckley ceme records) Son of Josiah & Eunice Blossom S:5

Blossom, ? - Died 1858 Born 1854 (next to Henry Crocker Blossom) S:5

Blossom, Abby - Died 1895 Feb 23 in her 74th yr S:5

Blossom, Alice - Died 1829 Nov 11 in her 81st yr Wife of Joseph Blossom S:5

Blossom, Alice H - Died 1851 April 28 Age 14 Only child of John A & Eliza Blossom S:12

Blossom, Anna - Died 1809 Mar 30 in her 24th yr Wife of Samuel Blossom S:5

Blossom, Benjamin - Died 1864 Feb 14 in his 78th yr S:5

Blossom, Bennett W - Died 1865 Mar 13 in his 48th yr S:5

Blossom, Churchill - Died 1841 Nov 20 in his 93rd yr S:5

Blossom, Edith C - Died 1882 Age 1 year Born 1881 Daughter of Henry & Hannah Blossom S:5

Blossom, Eliza - Died 1874 Sept 24 Age 63 years, 11 months Wife of John A Blossom (next to John A Blossom) S:12

Blossom, Eliza T - Died 1938 Born 1857 Wife of Eugene F Blossom (with him) S:12

Blossom, Eugene F - Died 1927 Born 1847 With wife, Eliza T Blossom S:12

Blossom, Eunice - Died 1828 Aug 12 Born 1790 (on the same stone as Josiah Blossom) in her 38th yr Wife of Josiah Blossom & dau of Benjamin & Deliverance Crocker (most info listed here was found in Hinckley ceme records) S:5

Blossom, Hannah - Died 1814 Aug 1 in her 61st yr Wife of Churchill Blossom S:5

Blossom, Hannah - Died 1876 Born 1804 (Stone not clear Located between Alice L Blossom

Blossom (Cont.) and Watson Crocker She is probably mother of Alice L Blossom because Alice's parents were Henry & Hannah B) S:5

Blossom, Hannah - Died 1975 Born 1890 (undertaker plaque only) (three stones away from a Cecile M Bylund) S:21

Blossom, Henry Crocker - Died 1812 July 24 Age 2 years, 11 months, 2 days Son of Peter & Tryphosap Blossom S:5

Blossom, John A - Died 1878 July 2 Age 69 years, 10 months, 9 days S:12

Blossom, Joseph - Died 1749 Nov 3 or 13 in his 78th yr (Nov 3 date comes from Hinckley ceme records) S:5

Blossom, Joseph - Died 1833 Nov 13 in his 86th yr S:5

Blossom, Josiah - Died 1851 July 25 Born 1785 (on the same stone as Eunice Blossom) in his 66th yr (month, day and age from Hinckley ceme records) S:5

Blossom, Laura A - Died 1894 Jan 8 Born 1843 Nov 17 Stone says, "We miss thee everywhere" S:12

Blossom, Luther C - Died 1846 Mar 22 in his 23rd yr S:5

Blossom, Maria M - Died 1896 Sept 30 Born 1864 Oct 18 Stone says, "Our home is lonely without you" S:12

Blossom, Mehetable - Died 1752 Feb 27 in her 34th yr (1752 from Hinckley ceme records) S:5

Blossom, Mehitable - Died 1868 Jan 15 Age 77 Born 1791 Wife of Benjamin Blossom S:5

Blossom, Peter C - Died 1894 Oct 27 Age 82 years, 15 days S:5

Blossom, Ruth H - Died 1836 Aug 8 Age 19 Born 1816 Nov 20 Wife of Peter Blossom S:5

Blossom, Salley H - Died 1812 June 15 Age 13 months, 7 days Daughter of Edward & Mercy Blossom S:10

Blossom, Sally - Died 1806 March

Blossom (Cont.)
24 in her 25th yr Wife of Edward
Blossom S:10+26R

Blossom, Sally H - Died 1812 June
15 Age 13 months, 7 days
Daughter of Edward & Mercy
Blossom S:10

Blossom, Samuel - Died 1758 Feb
6 in his 46th yr S:5

Blossom, Samuel - Died 1856 Jan
25 Age 73 years, 9 months S:5

Blossom, Sarah - Died 1829 Dec
23 in her 52nd yr Daughter of
Joseph & Alice Blossom S:5

Blossom, Sarah - Died 1855 Oct 17
Age 62 years, 10 months Wife of
Samuel Blossom S:5

Blossom, Sarah A - Died 1884 Jan
22 Age 28 years, 6 months Wife
of Calvin Blossom S:5R

Blossom, Tryphosap - Died 1851
Nov 20 Age 34 years, 7 months
Wife of Peter Blossom S:5

Blount, ? - Died 1822 Dec 13 Age
10 months, 9 days (stone broken
near base Between Eliza Ann
Crocker & SH Blount) S:12

Blount, Ada F - Died 1871 Oct 1 in
her 39th yr Wife of Otis W
Blount (next to him) S:13

Blount, Eliza - Died 1870 Aug 13
Age 81 years, 9 months, 11 days
Wife of William Blount (next to
him) S:12

Blount, Emilly Wing - Died 1858
Sept 20 Age 34 years, 11
months, 22 days Daughter of
Williamn and Eliza Blount
(Buried next to parents) Stone
says, "Our sister pleasant in life
and thou art lovely in death"
S:12

Blount, Everette - Died 1865 March
28 in East Boston, Massachusetts Age 7 years, 4 months, 22
days Son & only child of Otis &
Ada Blount   (next to them) S:13

Blount, Otis W - Died 1866 Nov 11
Age 37 yrs 7 mos 28 days (next
to Ada F Blount) S:13

Blount, S H - Died 184?, 28th Age
21 (stone broken near base

Blount (Cont.)
Between Eliza Ann Crocker and
Emilly wing) S:12

Blount, William - Died 1871 April
16 Age 80 years, 10 months
S:12 +12R

Blush, Joseph - Died 1754 Mar 14
in his 80th yr (buried next to
Joseph Blish) S:5

Blute, Louis J - Buried 1985 Aug
10 Age 82 S:15R

Boden, Clara Nickerson - Died
1959 Born 1883 (next to Clarence H Boden) S:14

Boden, Clarence H - Died 1951
Born 1879 (next to Clara Nickerson Boden) S:14

Bodfish, (infant) - Died 3 months
(stone not clear) Son of Sylvanus
& Ann Bodfish S:5

Bodfish, ? - Died 1773 Sept 23 Age
22 (stone not clear for first
name, buried between Mrs Lydia
Bodfish & Rachel Bodfish) S:5

Bodfish, Abegail - Died 1735 Mar
31 in her 45th yr Wife of Nathan
Bodfish (or Nathaniel Bodfish)
(some info here from Hinckley
ceme records) S:5

Bodfish, Abigail G - Died 1847 Jan
30 Born 1809 March 1 Daughter
of Eben & Nancy Bodfish S:5R

Bodfish, Alfred - Died 1846 Nov 5
Age 1 year, 8 months, 20 days
S:5

Bodfish, Alvan - Died 1872 Apr 21
Age 81 years, 21 days S:5

Bodfish, Ann G - Died 1888 Sept 9
Age 70 years, 10 days Wife of
Sylvanus Bodfish S:5

Bodfish, Anna W - Died 1920 Born
1859 (with James Webb) S:14

Bodfish, Asa - Died 1850 Feb 16 in
his 32nd yr Son of Alvin &
Rhoda Bodfish S:5

Bodfish, Asenath C - Died 1893
Apr 5 Born 1809 June 22 S:5

Bodfish, Barnabas B - Died 1875
Born 1819 S:5

Bodfish, Benjamin - Died 1745 Apr
8 Age 2 Son of Solomon Bodfish
S:5

Bodfish, Benjamin - Died 1746 May 10 Age 3 months (with bro Solomon Bodfish) Son of Solomon Bodfish (stone not clear, but info found in Hinckley ceme records) S:5

Bodfish, Benjamin - Died 1760 Mar 25 in his 77th yr (Age from Hinckley ceme records, not sure if other Benjamin Bodfish d1760 is one in the same person?) S:5

Bodfish, Benjamin - Died 1760 Mar in his 93rd yr (not sure if other Ben Bodfish is same person?) S:5

Bodfish, Benjamin - Died 1827 Jan 14 in his 71st yr S:5

Bodfish, Benjamin - Died 1833 Feb 11 in his 32nd yr S:5

Bodfish, Betsey T - Died 1836 Oct 7 Age 14 Daughter of Josiah & Mehitable Bodfish S:5R

Bodfish, Catherine G - Died 1895 Dec 10 Born 1810 Nov 28 S:5

Bodfish, Clarissa - Died 1878 Mar 12 Age 75 years, 1 month, 10 days Wife of Prince Bodfish S:5

Bodfish, Deborah - Died 1887 Apr 18 Age 78 years, 1 month S:5

Bodfish, Desire - Died 1813 Apr 8 in her 81st yr Wife of Jonathan Bodfish S:5

Bodfish, Eben C - Died 1878 March 12 in Austrailia Born 1823 Sept 19 S:5R

Bodfish, Ebenezer - Died 1832 or 1839 Jan 16 in his 88th yr (the 1832 death date was found in Hinckley ceme records) S:5

Bodfish, Ebenezer - Died 1857 Feb 10 Born 1776 July 14 S:5R

Bodfish, Elisabeth - Died 1774 Oct 7 or 17 in her 74th yr (the 17th date from Hinckley ceme records) Wife of Robert Bodfish S:5

Bodfish, Elizabeth - Died 1818 Oct 16 in her 62nd yr Wife of Ebenezer Bodfish S:5

Bodfish, Elizabeth - Died 1848 Sept 5 Age 10 months Born 1847 Nov 8 S:5

Bodfish, Elizabeth - Died 1868 Nov

Bodfish (Cont.)
4 Age 90 years, 3 months Wife of Isaac Bodfish S:5

Bodfish, Ellen Desire - Died 1845 Sept 3 Age 16 years, 2 months Daughter of Josiah & Mehitable Bodfish S:5R

Bodfish, George H - Died 1868 May 9 in California Born 1820 Jan 2 S:5R

Bodfish, Hanah - Died 1777 Oct 5 in her 69th yr Wife of Solomon Bodfish S:7

Bodfish, Hannah - Died 178? Oct 2 Age 36 S:5R

Bodfish, Hannah - Died 1895 May 4 Age 79 years, 6 months S:5

Bodfish, Hannah Clay - Died 1879 June 11 Age 68 years, 2 months Born 23 June 1831 Son of Benjamin & Asenath Bodfish (most info here from Hinckley ceme records) S:5

Bodfish, Henry Clay - Died 1831 July 1 Age 8 days S:5

Bodfish, Herbert C - Died 1849 June 24 Age 11 days Son of Joseph & Adelia Bodfish S:5R

Bodfish, Isaac - Died 1837 Aug 30 in his 75th yr S:5

Bodfish, Isaac - Died 1865 Feb 28 Born 1814 Feb 20 S:5

Bodfish, Isaac W - Died 1848 Sept 22 Age 6 years, 4 months Born 1842 May 19 S:5

Bodfish, Jemima - Died 1730 July 16 in her 36th yr (Age & Joseph info from Hinckley ceme records) Wife of Robert Bodfish (or Joseph Bodfish) S:5

Bodfish, Jemima - Died 1785 June 23, 1 year, 2 months, 11 days Daughter of Ebenezer & Hannah Bodfish (Age from Hinckley ceme records) S:5

Bodfish, John - Died 1846 Sept 30 Born 1761 Mar 14 S:5

Bodfish, John DW - Died 1956 Born 1878 (with Louie E Bodfish, wife) S:18

Bodfish, Jonathan - Died 1810 Sept 2 in his 15th yr Son of

Bodfish (Cont.)

John & Mary Bodfish S:5

Bodfish, Jonathan - Died 1818 Jan 21 in his 91st yr S:5

Bodfish, Joseph - Died 1735 May 13 in his 38th yr S:5R

Bodfish, Joseph - Died 1744 Dec 2 in his 94th yr (day & month from Hinckley ceme records) S:5

Bodfish, Joseph - Died 1865 Sept 15 Age 84 years, 3 months, 19 days S:5R

Bodfish, Joseph - Died 1869 Feb 1 in his 76th yr S:5

Bodfish, Josie - Died (stone not clear) Age 5 months S:5

Bodfish, Lizzie - Died 1851 Oct 10 Age 6 months Daughter of ? (not listed) S:5R

Bodfish, Louie E - Died 1932 Born 1879 Wife of John DW Bodfish (with him & their children which have later dates and not listed here) S:18

Bodfish, Luella Wentworth - Died 1896 Dec 28 Infant Daughter of Julius & Minnie Bodfish S:5

Bodfish, Lydia - Died 1780 Mar 27 in her 94th yr (stone not clear) Widow of Benjamin Buried next to Brazillan ? (date found in Hinckley ceme records) S:5

Bodfish, Lydia Ann - Died 1830 Mar 31 Age 6 months, 26 days Daughter of Benjamin & Asanath Bodfish S:5

Bodfish, Lydia Mrs - Died 1774 Mar in her 24th yr S:5

Bodfish, Mary - Died 18?? June 11 Born 17?? July 19 (stone not clear) Widow of John Bodfish (Hinckley Ceme records #5R says death was 1854, birth 1772 June) S:5

Bodfish, Mary E - Died 1892 Mar 4 Age 40 years, 3 months Wife of Julius Bodfish S:5

Bodfish, Mehitable - Died 1864 Jan 3 Age 74 years, 10 months Wife of Josiah Bodfish S:5R

Bodfish, Mehitable - Died 1919 Born 1825 S:5

Bodfish, Nancy - Died 1847 July 19 Born 1786 June 7 Wife of Eben Bodfish S:5R

Bodfish, Nathan - Died 1773 Sept 23 in his 22nd yr S:5R

Bodfish, Prince - Died 1793 (or 1795) Oct 4 Age 3 Son of John & Mary Bodfish Stone says, "To see a first born slain" (stone message & 1795 date from Hinckley ceme records) S:5

Bodfish, Prince - Died 1840 Feb 1 Age 46 S:5

Bodfish, Rachel - Died 1772 Aug 15 Age 19 years (day of death from Hinckley ceme records) S:5

Bodfish, Rhoda - Died 1857 Jan 13 Wife of Alvin Dodfish S:5

Bodfish, Silvanus - Died 1740 Dec 13 in his 30th yr S:5

Bodfish, Silvanus - Died 1802 Apr 2 or 7 Age 48 S:5

Bodfish, Simeon - Died 1778 Jan 1 or 2 Age 7 (year not clear on stone) Son of Jonathan & Desire Bodfish (death dates from Hinckley ceme records) S:5

Bodfish, Solomon - Died 1747 Jan 2 Age 3 Son of Solomon Bodfish (with Benjamin Bodfish, his brother) S:5R

Bodfish, Solomon - Died 1798 July 20 in his 83rd yr S:7

Bodfish, Sophronia - Died 1816 May 21 Born 1815 Feb 2 Daughter of Eben & Nancy Bodfish S:5R

Bodfish, Sylvanis - Died 1892 June 1 in his 78th yr S:5

Bodfish, Tabitha - Died 1834 Dec 10 in his 40th yr Wife of Joseph Bodfish S:5

Bodfish, William B - Died 1847 Aug 11 Age 22 Son of Prince & Clarrissa Bodfish S:5

Bodfish, William P - Died 1822 Oct 21 Age 12 Son of Josiah & Mehitable Bodfish S:5R

Bohn, Harry - Died 1984 Nov 6 Born 1918 May 22 Stone says,"Loving husband" (With Hazel E (Kelley) Bohn) S:19

Bohn, Hazel E (Kelley) - Died 1971
July 16 Born 1914 March 7
Stone says,"In loving memory of
beloved wife and mother" (With
Harry Bohn) S:19

Bolekos, Catharine G - Died 1939
Born 1877 (with Christos G
Bolekos) Stone says, "Remem-
bered by her son" S:12

Bolekos, Christos G - Died 1976
Born 1901 in Greece (with
Catharine G Bolekos) Also a
marker that says, 1903 & was a
PVT in US Army during World
War II S:12

Bolekos, Mary G - Died 1972 Born
1900 in Greece wife of James K
Kalas (with him) S:12

Bolle, Reginald Fairfax - Died 1967
Born 1877 (next to Claudia
Elizabeth Bolles) S:14

Bollerer, Clara S - Died 1971 Born
1889 (with husband, George
Bollerer) S:15

Bollerer, George - Died 1973 Born
1885 (he was a Mason) (next to
wife, Clara S Bollerer) S:15

Bolles, Claudia Elizabeth - Died
1969 Born 1884 (next to Reginald Fairfax Bolles) S:14

Bond, Cecil H - Died 1931 Born
1878 (with Maurice Carleton
Bond & Elizabeth C Baxter &
Charles W Hinckley) S:18

Bond, Maurice Careleton - Died
1902 Born 1874 (with Cecil
Bond & Elizabeth Baxter) S:18

Bond, Nathan Oscar - Died 1914
Born 1836 (with Alice Simmons
& others) S:18

Bond, Nellie May - Died 1885 Born
1871 (with Haratio Simmons &
others) S:18

Bonous, Ada E - Died 1984 Sept 21
Born 1894 Dec 19 S:15

Boody, Louis Milton - Died 1936
Dec 2 Born 1866 Sept 6 (next to
Mabelle Boody) S:18

Boody, Mabelle MH - Died 1936
Feb 27 Born 1873 Feb 8 (next to
Louis Milton Boody) S:18

Booker, Mearl F - Died 1967 Dec

Booker (Cont.)
25 Born 1899 Aug 2 From
Massachusetts, was a PVT in Co
A, 5th Eng during World War I
S:15

Borges, Maria E - Died 1983 Born
1894 S:16

Botelho, Edward - Died (still living
1991?) Born 1933 (listed with
Evelyn Botelho) S:20

Botelho, Evelyn - Died 1976 Born
1946 (listed with Edward Botelho) S:20

Botello, Jesse - Died 1947 Born
1877 (with Mary C Botello) S:16

Botello, Mary C - Died 1971 Born
1884 (with Jesse Botello) S:16

Boudreau, Gustave - Died 1970
June 25 Born 1892 Sept 8 Stone
says,"Husband" (next to Margaret H Boudreau) S:15

Boudreau, Margaret H - Died 1975
July 7 Born 1891 Oct 27 Stone
says,"Wife" (next to Gustave
Boudreau) S:15

Boult, (daughter) - Died 1808 Feb
25 Daughter of Charles &
Rebecca Boult S:12

Boult, Charles - Died 1835 Nov 13,
Osterville, Massachusetts Born
1783 Oct 16 at Amsterdam,
Holland Stone erected by daughter, Eliza G Boult S:12

Boult, Charles W - Died 1904 Born
1821 (with Harlotte H Boult)
S:12

Boult, Frank M - Died 1941 Born
1860 S:12

Boult, Hallett - Died 1968 Oct 18
Born 1897 Jan 21 Was a Private
in Massachusetts 813 CML
Company, Air Operations, World
War 1 & 2 S:12

Boult, Harlotte H - Died 1904 Born
1830 (with Charles W Boult)
S:12

Boult, Isabella C - Died 1933 Born
1850 (next to Simeon L Boult)
S:14

Boult, Isabella D - Died 1850 Mar
17 Age 21 years, 10 months Wife
of Charles W Boult S:12

Boult, Jennie Hinckley - Died 1943 Born 1862 (next to Ella V Hinckley) S:12

Boult, Jesse - Died (still living 1991?) Born 1899 Wife of Burleigh Leonard (with him & James Leonard & Lucy Crosby on Leonard stone) S:12

Boult, Rebekah L - Died 1861 Sept 10, Osterville, Mass Born 1781 April 9 at Osterville, Mass (this stone was made by McGrath Brothers, Quincy, Mass) S:12

Boult, Rozilla - Died 1882 Nov 30 Age 63 Wife of Simeon L Boult (next to him)(Jim Gould reports that she was daughter to Nathan Coleman & located behind his grave) S:14

Boult, Simeon L - Died 1893 March 16 Age 75 (next to wife, Rosilla Boult) S:14

Bourget, Ida V Gauthier - Died 1989 April 23 Born 1895 Dec 4 (next to Thomas J Bourget) S:15

Bourget, Thomas J - Died 1972 Sept 18 Born 1896 May 17 Was from Massachusetts & was a PFC in CoH, 18th Infantry during World War I (next to Ida V Gauthier Bourget) S:15

Bournazo, Charles G - Died 1974 Sept 6 Born 1890 Oct 25 Stone says,"Father" (next to Georgia E Bournazo) S:14

Bournazo, Georgia E - Died (still living 1991?) Born 1897 Nov 17 Stone says, "Mother" (next to Charles G Bournazo) S:14

Bourne, Charles - Died (under ground) Son of Silvanus Bourne (stone small, next to William S Bourne another small stone) S:10

Bourne, Hannah - Died 1826 Mar 5 in her 85th yr (next to Dr Richard Bourne, died same year possible husband?) S:11

Bourne, Hannah Mrs - Died 1826 March 5 Age 85 Wife of Dr Richard Bourne S:11R

Bourne, Lydia - Died 1835 July 9

Bourne (Cont.)
in her 45th yr (?) or 49th Wife of Silvanus Bourne & Widow & Relict of Capt Jeremiah Farris (Farris is listed on her marker) (age 49 from Hinckley Ceme records #10R) S:10

Bourne, Mary - Died 1896 Jan 31 Born 1805 Oct 30 Wife of Alexander Scudder (next to him) S:14

Bourne, Olive - Died 1798 June 30 Age 41? S:11

Bourne, Olive Mrs - Died 1708 ? 30 (worn) (between Capt Benjamin Gorham & Mrs Mehitable Hall) S:11

Bourne, Richard Dr - Died 1826 April 25 Age 86 (see William Allen Bourne) S:11+26R

Bourne, Russell - Died 1898 Born 1824 S:10

Bourne, Sally - Died 1822 Jan 13 Age 32 Wife of Silvanus Bourne (next to another wife of his, Lydia Bourne) S:10

Bourne, Sally - Died 1855 Oct 21 Age 65 Widow of Silvanus Bourne (next to him) S:10

Bourne, Silvanus - Died 1846 Aug 16 Age 59 S:10

Bourne, William Allen - Died 1783 Oct 3 Age 2 years, 2 months Son of Dr Richard & Hannah Bourne Stone says "Such friends shall meet again" (possibly entered on Dr Richard Bourne's stone) (located at Lothrop's Hill) S:11R+26R

Bourne, William S - Died (under ground) Son of Silvanus Bourne (stone small and next to possible mother, Sally Bourne) S:10

Bowen, ? - (Block of wood for marker, no other markings) S:31

Bowen, Arnold D - Died 1925 Born 1910 (with William & Alethena Lovell) S:21

Bowen, John P - Died 1931 Born 1866 (with Lydia H Bowen & others) S:18

Bowen, Lydia H - Died 1946 Born

Bowen (Cont.)

1868 (with John P & Virginia Bowen & others) S:18

Bowen, Marjorie L - Died 1972 Mar 14 Born 1892 Feb 23 (also on maine family stone) Wife of Wallace Ryder Jr (with him) S:14

Bowen, Norman P - Died 1954 Sept 23 Born 1895 March 29 From Massachusetts, was Wagoner in Btry A, 321 Fa, during World War I S:18

Bowen, Virginia - Died (still living 1991?) Born 1907 (with Lydia & W Clifton Bowen & others) S:18

Bowen, W Clifton - Died 1943 Born 1898 (with Virginia & Walter Bowen & others) S:18

Bowen, Walter S - Died 1931 Born 1921 (with W Clifton Bowen & others) S:18

Bowers, Mary B D - Died 1901 July 31 S:11

Bowes, James N - Died 1933 Born 1875 (next to John D Bowes) S:20

Bowes, John D - Died 1934 Born 1873 (next to James N Bowes) S:20

Bowes, John J - Died 1887 Jan 24 Age 40 years, 6 months, 28 days (next to Mary N Bowes) S:31

Bowes, Mary N - Died 1893 April 6 Age 53 years, 5 months, 14 days (next to John J Bowes) S:31

Bowie, Jessie - Died 1980 Born 1893 (undertaker plaque only) S:17

Bowker, Leona Card - Died (still living 1991?) Born 1900 (next Oscar S Bowker) S:19

Bowker, Oscar S - Died 1989 Born 1900 (next to Leona Card Bowker) S:19

Bowles, Adelaide H S - Died 1949 Jan 22 Born 1861 Sept 6 Wife of Francis T Bowles & daughter of Samuel H & Catherine D Savage (in Bowles plot) S:10

Bowles, Francis Tiffany - Died 1927 Aug 3 at Barnstable, Mass Born 1858 Oct 7 at Springfield, Mass

Bowles (Cont.)

Son of Benjamin F & Mary E Bowles (in Bowles plot) S:10

Bowles, Lucia Gordon - Died 1952 Jan 24 at Baden, Germany Born 1864 July 20 at Springfield, Mass Wife of Otto Cursch (in Bowles plot) S:10

Bowles, Thomas Savage - Died 1910 Aug 14 at Nurenberg, Germany Born 1888 Nov 6 at Boston Son of Francis T & Adelaide S Bowles (in Bowles plot) S:10

Bowman, Eliza L - Died 1902 Jan 31 Born 1830 June 2 (has two markers) (with husband, Daniel H Sturgis) S:14

Bowman, Henry Weldin - Died 1973 March 8 Born 1887 Nov 3 From New Jersey, was Cpl in 302nd Bn Tank Corps during World War I (with Marian B Bowman) S:15

Bowman, Marian B - Died 1974 Oct 17 Born 1896 Oct 23 (with Henry Weldin Bowman) S:15

Boyd, Douglas - Died 1962 Born 1889 (with Marcelle Boyd) S:12

Boyd, James - Died 1937 Born 1855 (with Margaret S Boyd) S:12

Boyd, Lucille M - Died 1974 Born 1904 Wife of Wallace P Boyd (with him) S:17

Boyd, Marcelle - Died 1977 Born 1891 S:12

Boyd, Margaret S - Died 1952 Born 1886 S:12

Boyd, Wallace P - Died 1972 Born 1894 (with wife, Lucille M Boyd) S:17

Boyek, Charlotte B - Died 1922 Born 1845 Wife of EF Robbins (with him) S:14

Boyle, John Raymond - Died 1965 Born 1890 (with wife, Lydia May Boyle) S:19

Boyle, Lydia May - Died 1976 Born 1891 Wife of John Raymond Boyle (with him) S:19

Boylston, Kenneth - Died 1973

Boylston (Cont.)
May 5 Born 1897 Feb 8 From Massachusetts, was Cox in US Navy during World War I S:15

Boyne, Margaret K - Died 1942 Born 1862 S:8

Boyne, William - Died 1948 Born 1860 S:8

Boynton, James - Died 1875 Born 1850 (with George Bragg) S:12

Bracc (Brace?), William (Capt) - Died 1853 May 14 Age 74 years, 17 months (buried next to Relict, Elizabeth Bracc (Brace?) S:5

Bracc (Brace?), Elizabeth - Died 1864 July 28 Age 83 years, 3 months Relict of Capt William Bracc (Brace?) S:5

Bracc, George (Capt) - Died 1886 May 10 Born 1811 Sept 30 S:5

Brackett, Clarence E - Died 1962 Born 1879 (with Evelyn G Brackett) S:14

Brackett, Etta M - Died 1942 Born 1872 Wife of John A Holway (with him & daughter, Margarilla) S:11

Brackett, Evelyn G - Died 1981 Born 1887 (with Clarence E Brackett) S:14

Brackley, Alva A - Died 1973 Born 1891 (with Frank, Lola & Martha Crocker) S:18

Bradbury, Abbie W - Died 1958 Born 1898 S:14

Bradbury, Ethel E - Died 1951 Born 1883 (with James T Bradbury) S:18

Bradbury, James T - Died 1954 Born 1879 (with Ethel E Bradbury) S:18

Bradford, Clarabel - Died 1917 Born 1850 (with Daniel Bradford) S:18

Bradford, Coroline - Died 1836 July 6 in her 37th yr Widow of Nye Bradford (or Noah Bradford) (Noah info from Hinckley ceme) S:5

Bradford, Daniel P - Died 1928 Born 1850 (with Clarabel Bradford) S:18

Bradford, Elfleda J - Died 1940 Oct 13 Born 1871 Feb 12 (with Noah & Sarah Bradford) S:18

Bradford, Ellen L - Died 1959 April 25 Born 1872 Jan 1 (with Stuart E Bradford) S:18

Bradford, Emelie F - Died 1912 Born 1850 (with Harry Bradford & others) S:18

Bradford, Ernest S - Died 1956 Nov 9 Born 1867 Feb 20 (with Ellen L Bradford) S:18

Bradford, Eva C - Died 1942 Sept 8 Born 1856 April 10 (with William Wilson & others) S:18

Bradford, George A - Died 1917 Born 1888 (with Sarah Bradford & others) S:18

Bradford, Harry - Died 1878 (with Noah A Bradford & others) S:18

Bradford, Hitty - Died 1809 Feb 9 Age 29 Erected by Capt Lemuel Bradford in rememberance of Mrs Hitty Bradford, his amiable wife S:11

Bradford, James M - Died 1911 April 11 Born 1874 Feb 25 S:18

Bradford, Lila L - Died 1879 Born 1851 (with Emelie F Bradford & others) S:18

Bradford, Maria Mrs - Died 1816 June 18 Age 28 Consort to Jesse Bradford S:12

Bradford, Mary Mrs - Died 1809 Feb 9 in her 29th yr "This monument erected by Capt Lemuel Bradford in remembrance of Mrs Mary Bradford his aimiable wife" S:11R+26R

Bradford, Myron C - Died 1932 Oct 22 Born 1856 Feb 27 (with Eva C Bradford & others) S:18

Bradford, Noah - Died 1824 Sept 14 Age 2 years, 4 months, 16 days Son of Noah & Caroline Bradford (mothers name found in Hinckley ceme records) S:5

Bradford, Noah - Died 1872 (or 1832) Jan 22 Age 34 Came here from Kingston & lived here for 12 years (note & 1832 date found in Hinckley ceme records)

59

Bradford (Cont.)
S:5

Bradford, Noah - Died 1905 Jan 29 Age 76 years, 10 months, 14 days (next to wife, Sarah A Bradford) S:18

Bradford, Noah A - Died 1929 Born 1853 (with Lila L Bradford & others) S:18

Bradford, Sarah A - Died 1882 May 3 Age 55 years, 5 months Wife of Noah Bradford (with him & Elfleda J Bradford) S:18

Bradford, Sarah E - Died 1940 Born 1872 (with Millie Williams & others) S:18

Bradford, Stuart E - Died 1962 Dec 1 Born 1897 Oct 8 (with Ernest Bradford) S:18

Bradford, Sylvanus - Died 1851 Dec 31 in his 22nd yr Born 1830 July 4 S:5

Bradlee, Clara D - Died 1963 Born 1868 (with Eliot Robinson & Helen Bradlee) S:14

Bradlee, Helen W - Died 1975 Born 1877 Wife of Eliot Robinson (with him) S:14

Bradlee, Thelma Elaine - Buried 1985 Nov 6 Age 84 S:15R

Bradlee, W Loring - Died 1985 Born 1898 S:14

Bradley, E Fannie - Died 1926 Sept 21 Born 1850 Mar 6 S:8

Bradshaw, Bessie M - Died 1930 May 29 Born 1882 Nov 9 Wife of Carl A Bradshaw (with her & Lena Burke) S:18

Bradshaw, Carl A - Died 1947 Dec 21 Born 1878 Nov 26 (with wife, Bessie M Bradshaw) S:18

Bradshaw, Catherine E - Died 1977 March 22 Born 1908 Oct 22 Wife of Ireton C Bradshaw (with him & others) S:18

Bradshaw, Ireton C - Died 1981 Aug 31 Born 1905 Oct 6 Son of Carl & Bessie Bradshaw (with them & wife, Catherine E Bradshaw) S:18

Bragg, ?laur? - Died 1842 Jan 8 Age 22 (stone badly worn,

Bragg (Cont.)
cannot read first name) Wife of Allen Bragg (next to only child, John Allen Bragg) S:21

Bragg, Allen - Died 1899 Aug 20 Born 1815 Nov 22 Stone says, "Erected by his friends" (next to ?laur? Bragg) S:21

Bragg, Baxter - Died 1859 May 6 Age 76 Stone says,"Our Father" (stone down & broken) (next to wife, Polly Bragg) S:21

Bragg, Betsey - Died 1870 Oct 27 Age 76 years, 6 months Wife of Allen Bragg S:4

Bragg, Cyrena - Died 1904 Born 1817 (with Capt John Bragg) S:21

Bragg, Elizabeth - Died 1864 July 28 Age 83 years, 3 months Relict of Capt William Bragg S:5R

Bragg, George - Died 1854 Born 1832 (with James Boynton) S:12

Bragg, George (Capt) - Died 1886 May 10 Born 1811 Sept 30 S:5R

Bragg, Georgiana - Died 1884 Jan 14 Age 33 years, 8 months Wife of William W Bragg (next to him) S:21

Bragg, John (Capt) - Died 1884 Born 1817 (with Cyrena Bragg) S:21

Bragg, John Allen - Died 1842 Sept 21 Age 11 months Only child of Allen & Lauura? Bragg (next to mother, ??laur? Bragg) S:21

Bragg, Polly - Died 1858 April 8 Age 76 Stone says,"Our Mother" Wife of Baxter Bragg (next to him & Thomas Bragg) S:21

Bragg, Thomas - Died 1839 June 14 Age 23 (stone down & broken) (next to Polly & Baxter Bragg) S:21

Bragg, William (Capt) - Died 1853 May 14 Age 74 S:5R

Bragg, William W - Died 1887 March 18 Age 37 years, 8 months (next to wife, Georgiana Bragg) S:21

Brailey, Margaret L - Died 1855 Sept 30 (age 2 years, 7 months)

Brailey (Cont.)
(buried with twin, Mary L Brailey) Daughter of Charles & Margard P Brailey S:8

Braily, Mary L - Died 1855 Sept 21 Age 2 years, 7 months, 1 day Daughter of Charles & Margard P Brailey (buried with twin Margaret L Brailey) S:8

Braley, Charles A - Died 1896 Born 1827 (stone says, Thanks be to God who give us the victory) (buried next to Margaret P Braley) S:8

Braley, Endora F - Died 1932 Born 1861 (with S Frank Braley) S:12

Braley, Irene W - Died 1943 Born 1971 Wife of Charles N Collins (with him & others) S:14

Braley, Margaret P - Died 1901 Born 1831 (buried next to Charles A Braley) S:8

Braley, Rhoda J - Died 1865 May 20 Age 14 years, 6 months Daughter of Charles A & Margret P Braley S:8

Braley, Roy V - Died 1947 Born 1889 (with S Frank Braley) S:12

Braley, S Frank - Died 1936 Born 1855 (with Endora F Braley) S:12

Braman, Bethiah - Died 1792 April 25 in her 69th yr Wife of James Braman S:11+26R

Bramhall, Mary E - Died 1932 Born 1843 Wife of George N Bramhall S:12

Brand, Lizzie L - Died 1886 Mar 26 Age 25 years, 8 months, 9 days Wife of Frank Brand (stone cemented and restored) S:12

Brandt, Mabel C - Died 1985 Born 1893 S:15

Bratti, Concettina C - Died 1958 Born 1884 (with John P Bratti) S:16

Bratti, John P - Died 1958 Born 1869 (with Concettina C Bratti) S:16

Bratton, Elizabeth L - Died 1981 Born 1892 Wife of Stephen Novak (on same stone) S:11

Bray, Ellen - Died 1932 Jan 31 Born in Ireland Wife of Michael Aylmer (with him & son, George Aylmer & others) S:31

Breed, Charles S - Died 1921 Born 1850 (with wife, Aurilla C Nickerson) S:14

Breidenthal, Marion L - Died 1973 Born 1897 Stone says, "Mother" S:18

Brennan, Ella E - Died 1943 Born 1861 (buried next to Zenas Brennan) S:8

Brennan, Janice D Twombley - Died 1985 Born 1908 Was a Captain, in nurse corps World War II (next to Daisy, Winfield & Helen Twombley) S:11

Brennan, Mary Clark - Died 1974 Born 1898 S:15

Brennan, Zenas - Died 1940 Born 1855 (buried next to Ella E Brennan) S:8

Bresnihan, John - Died 1979 Born 1924 Was a Sargeant in US Army during World War II S:20

Brewster, George W - Died 1972 Oct 27 Born 1897 March 10 From Massachusetts, was an Engineer I in US Navy during World War I (with Mary M Grondin) S:14

Bridges, Benjamin Franklin - Died 1974 Born 1887 S:17

Bridges, Edward I - Died 1907 Feb 11 Born 1872 June 29 (he was a Mason) S:19

Briggs, Annie Cordelia - Died 1881 Oct 25 Born 1848 Jan 9 Wife of Casper W Briggs (next to Mary Phinney & Gordelia Gorham) S:19

Briggs, Irving Fleet - Died 1969 Dec 11 Born 1894 Jan 21 From Massachusetts & was a SFC Med ib Det, 47th Infantry, AEF during World War I (next to Leila Howard Briggs) S:15

Briggs, Leila Howard - Died 1977 Dec 1 Born 1894 Sept 29 (next to Irving Fleet Briggs) S:15

Briggs, Pauly D - Died 1902 Born

Briggs (Cont.)
1812 (with Mary & Daniel Snow) S:8

Brigham, Joseph W - Died (no date shown) Born 1882 (with wife, Vila R Nickerson) S:14

Bright, Charles W - Died 1968 Born 1900 (was a Mason) S:15

Brinton, Mabel G - Died 1971 Born 1892 Wife of Ralph M Knowland (with him) S:17

Brister, Orrin F - Died 1883 March 10 Age 59 Has a star of 1861-65 Veteran of the Civil War S:19

Brito, Eugenia L - Died 1980 Born 1895 From Cape Verde Island (with Joseph M Brito) S:16

Brito, Joseph M - Died 1989 Born 1900 From Cape Verde Island (with Eugenia L Brito) S:16

Britton, Priscilla, Jean, Gauley - Died 1971 April 13 Born 1927 May 21 S:11

Brockway, Mary L - Died 1965 Born 1891 (with Rowley Brockway) S:20

Brockway, Rowley J - Died 1965 Born 1890 (also has a West Barnstable Fire Dept flag & plaque) (with Mary L Brockway) S:20

Broderick, Edward Henry - Died 1958 Jan 13 Born 1884 May 21 S:16

Brodie, Ada L - Died 1985 Born 1900 S:15

Brogan, Frank D - Died 1979 Born 1887 (with wife, Mary Foley) S:16

Brogan, Rita - Died 1938 Born 1918 Daughter of Frank Brogan & Mary Foley (with them & Margaret Foley & others) S:16

Brook, John - Died 1972 Jan 10 Born 1897 Dec 7 Was PFC in US Army during World War I from New Jersey (next to Mary M Brook, wife) S:19

Brook, Mary M - Died (no dates) Wife of John Brook (next to him) S:19

Brooks, ? - Died (no dates, but stone says,"Wife" and next to Lester Brooks? who's stone is same style) (also next to John L Brooks?) S:21

Brooks, Grace Barlow - Died 1946 Born 1874 (next to Gertrude H Barlow) S:14

Brooks, John L - Died 1842 March 13 Was a Private in Massachusetts 1 CL US Marine Corp (next to two stones that say just Lester & wife, possible Brooks?) S:21

Brooks, Katherine G - Died 1987 Born 1906 (with Winfield S Brooks) S:11

Brooks, Lester - Died (no dates, small stone, next to wife & John L Brooks) S:21

Brooks, Winfield S - Died 1963 Born 1902 (rock stone) (with Katherine G Brooks) S:11

Brow, Mercy Elizabeth - Died 1906 Born 1850 S:5

Brown, Adeline - Died 1987 Born 1899 (with Frank E N Brown & Randall Brown) S:31

Brown, Adeline S - Died 1909 Born 1847 S:18

Brown, Charles H - Died 1936 Born 1857 (listed on Paine, Titcomb & Brown stone) S:11

Brown, Clara M - Died 1978 April 27 Born 1889 Aug 16 (next to Walter S Brown) S:11

Brown, Edmund G - Died 1959 Born 1890 (with Lidia N Brown) S:11

Brown, Eliza Miss - Died 1892 Sept 30 S:1

Brown, Elizabeth A - Died (still living 1991?) Born 1894 June 19 (listed next to Francis C Brown) S:15

Brown, Elizabeth M - Died 1929 March 17 Born 1908 Oct 29 S:31

Brown, Florence E - Died 1966 Sept 7 Born 1895 Oct 10 S:16

Brown, Francis - Died 1895 Born 1809 (next to wife, Joanna

Brown (Cont.)
Brown) S:21

Brown, Francis C - Died 1972 March 14 Born 1893 Aug 15 From Massachusetts, was LDSOM in USARF during World War I (next to Elizabeth A Brown) S:15

Brown, Frank EN - Died 1950 Born 1895 (with Randall N Brown) S:31

Brown, Frederick - Died 1981 Born 1894 Son of John Easton & Jessie Templeman S:15

Brown, Gordon - Died 1974 Born 1896 (with Jeanette B Brown) S:15

Brown, Hetty A (Lothrop) - Died 1884 Oct 7 Born 1843 Nov 2 Wife of Francis H Brown S:9R

Brown, Ira D Sankey - Died 1898 Nov 3 Born 1877 April 7 Stone says,"Our boy" (next to John EN Brown) S:18

Brown, Jeanette B - Died 1984 Born 1904 (with Gordon Brown) S:15

Brown, Joanna - Died 1876? June 27 (stone worn) Wife of Francis Brown (next to him) S:21

Brown, John E N - Died 1930 Born 1850 (next to Ira D Sankey Brown) S:18

Brown, Lidia N - Died 1971 Born 1896 (with Edmund G Brown) S:11

Brown, Margaret T - Died 1942 Born 1872 (perpetual care) stone references, Ralph Curtiss Brown S:11

Brown, Martha J - Died 1968 Born 1896 (also 1917-18 US Veteran plaque) (with Mary L Brown & next to Robert N Brown) S:19

Brown, Mary L - Died 1979 Born 1901 (with Mary L Brown) S:19

Brown, Mattie A - Died 1931 Nov 10 Born 1862 Nov 2 Wife of Everett W Lewis S:8

Brown, Ouida N - Died 1958 Born 1893 (with Joseph Burlingame & Inez Garder) S:14

Brown, Phebe B - Died 1945 Born 1858 (listed of Paine, Titcomb & Brown stone) S:11

Brown, Phebe Amelia - Died 1862 Jan 20 Age 32 yrs 6 mos Wife of Henry W Brown S:26R

Brown, Randall N - Died 1929 Born 1926 (with Frank EN Brown) S:20

Brown, Robert N - Died 1990 Born 1928 (next to Martha J Brown) S:19

Brown, Rosie T - Died 1886 July 5 Born 1851 Oct 27 Wife of Henry Brown S:4

Brown, Walter Francis - Died 1870 July 24 Age 8 months, 7 days Son of Francis H & Hettie A Brown S:9R

Brown, Walter S - Died 1953 June 5 Born 1878 Sept 3 Was PVT Co A 23rd Infantry during Spanish American War S:11

Bruce, Mertie Louise - Died 1918 Born 1895 (with Ella & Howard Goodspeed) S:14

Brueggeman, Olive L - Died 1966 Born 1903 Mother of Donald F Chrisholm S:13

Brueggeman, Robert John - Died 1949 Aug 1 Born 1944 Sept 2 Son of Olive L Brueggeman S:11

Brundage, George S - Died 1950 Born 1869 Has a World War I Veteran Star (with Gertrude B Brundage) S:14

Brundage, Gertrude B - Died 1969 Born 1879 (with George S Brundage) S:14

Brundrett, Marion W - Died 1960 Born 1881 S:14

Brury, Lorenzo G - Died 1880 June 15 Age 60 years, 5 months Was in CoE, 40th Massachusetts Regiment S:18

Brushaber, M Jean - Died 1988 Born 1829 (with Mary E Hallett & others) S:19

Bryant, Belina May - Died 1924 Born 1847 Wife of Ambrose Lewis (buried with him) S:8

Bryant, David L - Died 1907 Born

Bryant (Cont.)
1827 (with Mary M Murray & others) S:18

Bryant, Edwin G - Died 1962 Born 1884 (with wife, Florence R Bryant) S:17

Bryant, Florence R - Died (no date listed) Born 1887 Wife of Edwin G Bryant (listed with him) S:17

Bubniak, John - Died 1970 Born 1887 S:16

Bucci, Michael - Died 1957 Oct 24 Born 1894 Sept 29 Was from Massachusetts and was a Private in Co 171 Infantry during World War 1 (next to Ethel Bucci) S:13

Buck, Calvin - Died 1869 March 21 Age 52 Stone says, "Father" (next to Martha Buck) S:21

Buck, Cornelia - Died 1904 July 23 Born 1849 Nov 15 (with Ebenezer & Martha Eldridge) S:21

Buck, Ellen A - Died 1972 Born 1901 (with J Jerauld Buck) S:15

Buck, Herbert - Died 1905 Born 1850 (with Rosella Buck & others) S:21

Buck, J Jerauld - Died 1968 Born 1893 (with Ellen A Buck) S:15

Buck, Marianna - Died 1948 Born 1886 (with John W Baxter & others) S:21

Buck, Martha - Died 1901 April 20 Age 82 Stone says, "Mother" (next to Calvin Buck) S:21

Buck, Rosella - Died 1914 Born 1855 (with Marianna Buck) S:21

Buckley, Anthoney L - Died 1967 Born 1888 Stone says, "God bless Mom & Pop" (with Mary E Buckley) S:16

Buckley, Francis T - Died 1980 Born 1892 (with Mary J Buckley & others) S:31

Buckley, Jane - Died 1865 Born 1865 (with Francis T Buckley & others) S:31

Buckley, John - Died 1900 March 2 Born 1822 June 17 (with wife, Grace Jane Thornton & others) S:31

Buckley, Mary E - Died 1972 Born 1893 Stone says,"God bless Mom & Pop" (with Anthoney L Buckley) S:16

Buckley, Mary J - Died 1977 Born 1889 (with John Buckley & others) S:31

Buckley, Timothy - Died 1862 Born 1862 (with Jane Buckley & others) S:31

Buckminster, Olivia - Died 1900 Oct 2 Born 1823 Mar 2 Wife of George Bacon Esq S:9

Bullock, Elwood P - Died 1983 July 29 Born 1900 May 22 (with Harriett E Carr) S:19

Bumpus, Albert G - Died 1979 Born 1910 (small undertakers plaque only) (next to Mildred K Bumpus) S:13

Bumpus, Mildred K - Died 1986 Born 1913 (small undertakers plaque only)(next to Albert g Bumpus) S:13

Bunker, Laura - Died 1958 Born 1866 (with Frank & George Clifford) S:18

Bunting, Keith WT - Died 1990 Born 1930 (undertaker plaque only) S:20

Buratti, Felix - Died 1952 Oct 19 Born 1886 Feb 5 S:16

Burbank, Helen C - Died (still living 1991?) Born 1896 Aug 20 (next to James A Burbank) S:14

Burbank, James A - Died 1974 March 1 Born 1894 Jan 21 Was Lieutenant in US Navy (next to Helen C Burbank) S:14

Burbine, Annie - Died 1953 Born 1878 Wife of John Burke (with him) S:16

Burge, Clayton A - Died 1986 Oct 17 Born 1909 Aug 10 (with Laura M Lothrop Burge & others) S:18

Burge, Laura M Lothrop - Died (still living 1991?) Born 1908 July 13 (with Frank G Lothrop & others) S:18

Burges, Mercy - Died 1822 Feb 20 Age 78 Wife of Nathaniel Burges

Burges (Cont.)
S:4

Burgess, Arthur Ellery - Died 1985 Born 1899 (with Gertrude Adeline Hickey Burgess) S:15

Burgess, Earl Died (still living 1990) Born 1907 (with Catherine Chandler) S:11

Burgess, Elizabeth A - Died 1887 Dec 30 Age 79 Wife of Moses Burgess S:5R

Burgess, Gertrude Adeline Hickey - Died 1988 Born 1903 (with Arthur Ellery Burgess) S:15

Burgess, Hartley A - Died 1969 Born 1901 (with Olga T Burgess) S·13

Burgess, Mishey - Died 1983 Born 1890 (with Sara Myers) S:17

Burgess, Moses - Died 1885 March 28 Age 80 years, 5 months, 19 days S:5R

Burgess, Moses R - Died 1887 Born 1849 S:5

Burgess, Olga T - Died 1977 Born 1901 (with Hartley A Burgess) S:13

Burgess, Rebecca - Died 1899 Born 1835 (with Nelson Rhodehouse) S:14

Burgess, Sarah B - Died 1845 Oct 31 Age 29 years, 6 months S:4

Burke, Caroline PM - Died (still living 1991?) Born 1888 (with William H Burke) S:16

Burke, Elizabeth A - Died 1959 Born 1878 Stone says,"Mother" (next to Garrett M Burke) S:31

Burke, Garrett M - Died 1924 Born 1864 (next to Elizabeth A Burke) S:31

Burke, John - Died 1940 Born 1869 (with wife, Annie Burbine) S:16

Burke, Lena - Died 1970 Dec 14 Born 1907 April 2 (with Carl & Bessie Bradshaw, her parents) S:18

Burke, Michael P - Died 1984? Born 1917 S:20

Burke, William H - Died 1948 Born 1887 (with Caroline P Burke)

Burke (Cont.)
S:16

Burkholder, Christian H - Died 1922 Born 1841 (with Carman H Butler) S:12

Burleigh(?), Corrinna Ann Died 1854 Dec 20 Age 2 years, 4 months, 18 days Daughter to J Burleigh(?) & Olive Ann Hunt S:13

Burlingame, Abbie A - Died 1882 June 10 Age 2 years, 7 months, 29 days (small stone) (with Walcott Burlingame) S:14

Burlingame, Alvan C - Died 1906 Born 1851 (with Effie D Burlingame) S:14

Burlingame, Alvan L - Died 1951 Born 1892 S:14

Burlingame, Alvin C - Died 1851 Oct 13 Age 31 years, 5 months, 28 days Lost from Bargue Hexina, 30 miles east from Gibraltar (listed with William S Felker) S:14

Burlingame, Anna - Died 1885 March 29 Age 90 years, 3 days Widow of Pardon A Burlingame (with him) S:14

Burlingame, Aurilla - Died 1847 Born 1823 (with Zenas & Lydia Lovell & others) S:12

Burlingame, Charlotte M - Died 1911 Nov 30 Age 71 Wife of Capt PA Burlingame (next to him & other wife) S:14

Burlingame, Effie D - Died 1931 Born 1858 (with Alvan C Burlingame) S:14

Burlingame, Ella F - Died 1929 Born 1881 (with Joseph Burlingame & Inez Garder) S:14

Burlingame, Forrest - Died 1936 Born 1890 (with Joseph Burlingame & Inez Garder) S:14

Burlingame, George C - Died 1948 Born 1892 (with Joseph Burlingame & Inez Garder) S:14

Burlingame, James H - Died 1896 Born 1853 (with wife, Lillian R Handy) S:14

Burlingame, Joseph H - Died 1950

Burlingame (Cont.)
Born 1888 (with Inez I Garder)
S:14

Burlingame, Laura A - Died 1875
Feb 14 Age 44 Wife of Capt PA
Burlingame (next to him) S:14

Burlingame, PA (Capt) - Died 1881
Dec 21 Age 55 (next to wife,
Laura A Burlingame) S:14

Burlingame, Pardon A - Died 1854
July 25 Age 62 years, 2 months,
20 days His last words were, "I
am going home" (next to wife,
Anna Burlingame) S:14

Burlingame, Polly - Died 1837 Oct
17 Age 39 years, 4 months, 10
days Wife of Pardon A Burlingame (with William S Felker)
S:14

Burlingame, Walcott - Died 188?
March 9? (stone small & worn)
(with Abbie A Burlingame) S:14

Burlington, Louis Herbert - Died
1946 Born 1880 (with Grace
Semple) S:12

Burman, Hyman - Died 1975 Aug
23 Born 1893 Nov 29 (Jewish
section) S:15

Burns, Anna M - Died 1981 April 6
Born 1889 Aug 31 (In a large
Mausoleum) (with James E
Burns) S:16

Burns, Dorothy J - Died 1969 Born
1894 (next to husband, Herbert
N Burns) S:15

Burns, Herbert N - Died 1971 Born
1892 (next to wife, Dorothy J
Burns) S:15

Burns, James E - Died 1973 June
16 Born 1887 Dec 27 (in a large
mausoleum) (with Anna M
Burns) S:16

Burns, Sarah F - Died 1985 Born
1893 S:17

Burrage, Margaret - Died 1969
Born 1892 (with Russell Burrage) S:16

Burrage, Russell - Died 1959 Born
1889 (with Margaret Burrage)
S:16

Burrows, Elias W - Died 1917 Sept
30 Born 1831 May 5 (with wife,

Burrows (Cont.)
Temple P Harlow) S:14

Burrows, Sarah G - Died 1875 Dec
13 Born 1873 Sept 29 Daughter
of EW & TP S:14

Bursley, (daughter) - Died 1888
Sept 19 (stone is a tiny lamb)
Daughter of GA & HF Bursley
(next to David Bursley) S:18

Bursley, (infant child) - Died (dates
worn off) (located on large Bursley family plot stone) Child of
David & Mary L Bursley S:10

Bursley, ? - Died 1800 July 10 Age
94 (stone not clear) S:5

Bursley, ?, A - Died 1806 Dec 12 ?
(stone badly worn, but in Bursley plot on large stone with
others, like just over Ruth E
Chipman) S:10

Bursley, Abigail - Died 1835 Aug
18 in her 56th yr Widow of
Josiah Bursley S:5

Bursley, Abigail Mrs - Died 1790
Aug 29 in her 40th yr S:5

Bursley, Allen (Capt) - Died 1835
Feb 1 Age 31 (listed in Bursley
plot) Who was wrecked &
drowned at Port Patrick, Scotland by the loss of the ship,
Lyon of Boston S:10

Bursley, Ann E - Died 1905 Born
1839 (in large Bursley plot) S:10

Bursley, Ausmond - Died 1871
Sept 28 Age 75 years, 1 month,
18 days S:5

Bursley, Bethiah Mrs - Died 1794
Feb 2 in her 79th yr 1715 Relect
& wife of Joseph Bursley S:5

Bursley, Carrie - Died 1878 Oct 1
Age 20 years, 10 months Daugh-
ter of James & Mary A Bursley
S:9R

Bursley, Charles A - Died 1904 Feb
26 Born 1859 Sept 10 (with
Hattie F Bursley) S:18

Bursley, Cleone - Died 1884 Sept
18 Age 61 Wife of David Bursley
(in Bursley plot) S:10

Bursley, Daniel P - Died 1828 Oct
17 Age 21 Son of Josiah & Abi
gail Bursley S:5

Bursley, David - Died (dates under ground) (a very small stone) It says,"Our darling baby" (next to (Dau) Bursley d1888) S:18

Bursley, David - Died 1881 Feb 8 (Bursley plot) S:10

Bursley, David Jr (Capt) - Died 1879 Nov 10 Age 43 Son of David & Ruth Bursley (in Bursley plot) S:10

Bursley, Delia - Died 1867 Oct 11 Age 79 S:5

Bursley, Elizabeth - Died 1831 Jan 23 Age 20 (in Bursley plot) Youngest daughter of John & Susannah Bursley S:10

Bursley, Ellen M - Died 1895 July 15 Born 1830 Dec 18 (with Francis A Bursley) S:18

Bursley, Enoch - Died 1849 Aug 10 Age 1 year Born 1848 Jan 11 Son of Washington & Sophronia Bursley S:5

Bursley, Enoch P - Died 1847 Apr 22 Age 28 Born 1819 Aug 3 (middle initial was found in Hinckley ceme records) S:5

Bursley, Francis A - Died 1896 June 12 Born 1827 May 6 (with Ellen M Bursley) S:18

Bursley, Grace - Died 1834 Mar 20 Born 1778 Oct 5 (inscribed on door of Bursley tomb, found in Hinckley ceme records) S:5

Bursley, Hattie F - Died 1936 Dec 6 Born 1858 Feb 22 (next to Charles A Bursley) (2 stones missing next to her due to vandalism) S:18

Bursley, Hemam - Died 1850 Nov 3 Born 1770 Jan 1 S:5

Bursley, Henry Green - Died 1857 May 29 in New York Age 8 years, 10 months Son of Ira & Louisa M Bursley (in Bursley plot) S:10

Bursley, Huldah - Died 1860 Oct 16 Age 66 years, 4 months Wife of Ausmond Bursley S:5

Bursley, Ira - Died 1830 Age 51 (in large Bursley plot) Lost in the ship, ocued(?) on the coast of ? (stone badly worn) S:10

Bursley, Ira - Died 1890 Oct 18 at New York Born 1832 Feb 9 at Barnstable, Ma Son of Ira & Louisa M Bursley (in same Bursley plot) S:10

Bursley, Ira (Capt) - Died 5 August ? (stone worn, but on large Bursley plot stone with other family members like Cleone Bursley) S:10

Bursley, Jabez - Died 1732 Jan 15 in his 51st yr S:5

Bursley, James - Died (he is listed on stone with Temperance Bursley who died 1734 - stone not clear for his info) S:5

Bursley, Jemima - Died (stone not clear) (Hinckley Ceme records #5R says death date was 1846 Sept 7 age 78) Wife of Lemuel Bursley S:5

Bursley, Joanna - Died 1851 Jan 11 Born 1802 Mar 12 S:5

Bursley, John - Died 1810 Apr 14 Age 63 or 65 (age 65 found in Hinckley ceme records) S:5

Bursley, John - Died 1827 Feb 16 Age 85 years, 3 months, 16 days S:5

Bursley, John - Died 1836 Feb 17 Age 64 (in Bursley plot) S:10

Bursley, John - Died 1842 ? Age ?5 (in Bursley plot, badly worn) Son of Ira & Louisa Bursley S:10

Bursley, John Jr - Died 1726 Dec or 5 Aug Age 75 Born 1652 (5 Aug date in Hinckley ceme re cords) S:5

Bursley, John Jr - Died 1835 April 15 in his 31st yr Son of John & Susannah Bursley (in Bursley plot) S:10+26R

Bursley, John W - Died 1833 Sept 16 Born 1803 Sept 2 (on Bursley tomb per Hinckley ceme records) S:5

Bursley, Johne - Died 1830 or 39 Sept 11 Age ? (stone worn, but in Bursley plot) Son of David & Ruth Bursley S:10

Bursley, Joseph - Died 1716 Oct 26 in his 4th yr (this slate was

Bursley (Cont.)
removed from the Methodist Cemetery to David Bursley's lot in the Unitarian West Cemetery and erroneously inscribed as having been found in all cemetery at Calves Pasture) Son of Joseph Bursley S:11R+26R

Bursley, Joseph - Died 1750 Born 1686 Age 63 (found in Hinckley ceme records) (buried next to Lemuel Bursley, his son & wife Sarah) S:5

Bursley, Joseph - Died 1778 Born 1714 Age 65 (found in Hinckley ceme records) S:5

Bursley, Joseph - Died 1825 Feb 21 Age 2 years, 7 months Son of Josiah & Abigail Bursley S:5

Bursley, Josiah - Died 1830 May 14 Age 55 years, 1 months, 7 days S:5

Bursley, Lemuel - Died 1744 July 29 in his 26th yr Son of Joseph Bursley (buried next to him) S:5

Bursley, Lemuel - Died 1846 May 2 Age 78 S:5

Bursley, Louisa - Died (stone worn badly, in large Bursley plot) Daughter of David & Ruth Bursley S:10

Bursley, Louisa M - Died 1867 Sept 15 Age 50 or 60 Wife of Capt ira Bursley (located in same Bursley plot) S:10

Bursley, Mary - Died 1820 Jan 24 Age 77 years, 11 months, 26 days Jan 28 Wife of John Bursley S:5

Bursley, Mary L - Died 1897 Born 1854 Wife of Ansel Lothrop (on same stone with him and others) S:10

Bursley, Ruth E - Died 1923 Mar 3 Age 89 years, 2 months, 10 days (in Bursley plot) Widow of William Chipman (on same large Bursley stone) S:10

Bursley, Samuel C(Capt) - Died 1825 Sept 1 Age 28 (in Bursley plot) S:10

Bursley, Sarah - Died 1743 Oct 3

Bursley (Cont.)
Age 55 Wife of Joseph Bursley (buried next to him) S:5

Bursley, Sarah Anne - Died 1817 Dec 29 Age ? (stone worn, but in Bursley plot) Daughter of David & Ruth Bursley S:10

Bursley, Silas - Died 1800 July 10 Age 24 S:5R

Bursley, Sophronia - Died 1872 Jan 10 Age 60 years, 10 months Wife of Washington Bursley S:5

Bursley, Susannah - Died 1828 Aug 31 Age 56 (in Bursley plot) Wife of John Bursley & daughter of Capt Samuel Crocker S:10

Bursley, Temperance - Died 1734 Sept 30 in his 39th yr (notation says that James may be buried with her) S:5

Bursley, Washburn - Died 1886 Oct 29 Born 1812 Oct 5 Husband of Deborah l Turner S:5

Bursley, Washington - Died 1884 Apr 4 Age 74 years, 8 months (buried next to wife, Sophronia Bursley) S:5

Burt, Annie EE - Died 1873 May 8 Age 21 years, 9 months Daughter of Nathaniel & Diana Burt (with them) S:18

Burt, Diana P - Died 1890 Sept 29 Age 64 years, 5 months (with husband, Nathaniel & daughter Annie Burt) S:18

Burt, Nathaniel B - Died 1870 May 14 Age 52 years, 7 months (with Diana & Annie Burt) S:18

Burton, Charles W - Died 1967 Born 1892 S:15

Bushe, Ellen - Died 1982 Born 1900 S:15

Buster, Karen - Died 1969 March 26 Born 1956 March 22 S:13

Butler, Alice M - Died 1949 Born 1893 S:16

Butler, Carman H - Died 1946 Born 1908 (with Carman H Butler) S:12

Butler, E Ruth Brown - Died 1976 Dec 10 Born 1908 Jan 30 (next to Clara M Brown) S:11

68

Butler, Emma M (or B) - Died 1943 Born 1878 Wife of Stanley B Butler (with him) (middle initial B is from Hinckley ceme records) S:14

Butler, Francis P - Died 1977 Born 1887 Was a Cy in US Navy during World War I S:15

Butler, Frederick J - Died 1952 Born 1875 (with Merrill W Butler) S:12

Butler, Helen E - Died 1983 May 17 Born 1898 Jan 19 Wife of William F Sullivan (with him) S:16

Butler, Irene F - Died 1901 Born 1840 (with Zidon A Butler) S:14

Butler, Joseph - Died 1944 Born 1869 (undertaker plaque only) S:16

Butler, Margaret J - Died Still living in 1991? Born 1920 Wife of Merrill W Butler (listed with him) S:12

Butler, Merrill W - Died 1981 Born 1913 (Listed with Margaret J Butler, wife) He was a Mason S:12

Butler, Stanley B - Died 1960 Born 1872 (was a Mason) (with wife, Emma M Butler) S:14

Butler, Submit A - Died 1958 Born 1876 Wife of Frederick J Butler (with him) S:12

Butler, Zidon A - Died 1905 Born 1839 (with Irene F Butler) S:14

Butterfield, Ida Whittemore - Died 1951 Oct 10 Born 1894 Oct 12 Wife of Leo Butterfield (with him & others) S:19

Butterfield, Leo L - Died 1952 Sept 22 Born 1897 May 8 (With wife, Ida Whittemore Butterfield & Nellie & Hiram Whittemore) S:19

Butts, Bethana - Died 1906 Jan 11 Born 1832 July 6 S:8

Buxton, Ada C - Died 1963 Born 1873 (with Charles W Buxton) S:14

Buxton, Charles W - Died 1958 Born 1869 (with Ada C Buxton) S:14

Bylund, Cecile M - Died 1946 Born 1894 (with Frederick & Sarah Taylor) S:8

C, L E - Died (no dates or other info) (next to Azuba Baxter) S:21

Cabral, John P - Died 1925 Born 1873 (has a Fire Department flag placed at grave) (with wife, Mary G Cabral) S:31

Cabral, Joseph P - Died 1980 Born 1920 (with John P & Mary G Cabral) S:31

Cabral, Manuel B - Died 1940 Born 1871 (with Mary Luiz, wife) S:14

Cabral, Mary - Died (still living 1991?) Born 1900 Wife of David Leland (listed with him) S:14

Cabral, Mary G - Died 1957 Born 1879 Wife of John P Cabral (with him) S:31

Cadigan, Anna M - Died 1990 Born 1906 (with John F Cadigan) S:15

Cadigan, John F - Died 1976 Born 1898 (with Anna M Cadigan) S:15

Cadigan, Mary A - Died 1979 Born 1900 (next to John F Cadigan) S:15

Cadwick, Kelley - Died (no dates-quartz stone with plaque, nothing else listed but name) S:8

Cahoon, Anna - Died 1854 Mar 10 Age 87 Widow of John Cahoon S:3

Cahoon, Clarissa J - Died 1876 July 22 Age 44 years, 9 months, 28 days Wife of William G Cahoon (stone notation says that he is buried with her) Stone says, "We morn the loss" S:8

Cahoon, Clinton Herbert - Died 1959 Born 1888 (with Effie Butlers Cahoon) S:18

Cahoon, Didah (?) - Died 1853 Aug 9 Age 39 (?) years, 17 days (stone badly worn) (same stone with daughter, Sarah Cahoon) S:8

Cahoon, Delia L - Died 1931 Born 1881 Wife of Horace N Cahoon (with him) S:31

Cahoon, Edith - Died 1929 Born

Cahoon (Cont.)
1904 (with Rebbeca M & Lora M Cahoon) S:13

Cahoon, Effie Butlers - Died 1942 Born 1881 (with Clinton Herbert Cahoon) S:18

Cahoon, Hannah - Died (no markings on stone, next to Minerva W Cahoon) S:13

Cahoon, Horace N - Died 1919 Born 1875 S:31

Cahoon, Irving F - Died 1915 Born 1876 (with Lora M Cahoon) S:13

Cahoon, John - Died 1820 Aug 25 in his 56th yr (next to wife Anna) S:3R

Cahoon (Cohoon), John - Died 1820 July 21 in his 16th yr Son of John and Anna Cahoon S:3R

Cahoon, Lora M - Died 1925 Born 1882 (with Irving F & Edith F Cahoon) S:13

Cahoon, Lucy - Died (no markings, next to Obed A Cahoon) S:13

Cahoon, Marion E - Died 1974 Born 1885 Wife of William S P Lovejoy (in Lovejoy plot) S:11

Cahoon, Merhane (?) - Died 1825 Apr 1 (?) (stone not very clear) Died in Harwich, Massachusetts (buried with Didah? Cahoon) S:8

Cahoon, Minerva W - Died 1854 Mar 26 Age 36 Widow of Obed Cahoon (next to him) S:13

Cahoon, Obed - Died 1818 July 6 Age 34 (next to wife, Minerva W Cahoon) S:13

Cahoon, Obed A - Died 1863 Nov 21 Age 18 at Beaufort, South Carolina A member of Company F, 104 (?) Regiment, Massachusetts Vol (also star marker that says, Civil War Veteran 1861-1865 S:13

Cahoon, Rebbeca M - Died 1954 Born 1902 (with Lora & Edith Cahoon) S:13

Cahoon, Russell H - Died 1979 Born 1960 S:20

Cahoon, Sarah - Died 1918 Jan 10 Age 81 years, 9 months (in same grave with mother, Didah (?)

Cahoon (Cont.)
Cahoon) S:8

Cahoon, Stephen - Died (no markings, next to Obed A Cahoon) S:13

Cahoon, Timmy - Died 1969 Born 1952 (a small rock with info painted in red on it) (also has a West Barnstable Fire Dept plaque) S:20

Cahoon, William G - Died (no dates listed) (possibly buried with, Clarissa J Cahoon because her stone says he is buried with her?) S:8

Cain, Joseph Lambert - Died 1956 April 26 Born 1896 Sept 17 From Massachusetts, was 2nd Lieutenant in Air Res during World War I SS (with Lora Lillian) S:14

Calvin, Edwin E - Died 1983 Born 1912 S:11

Cameron, George Arthur - Died 1981 Jan 30 Born 1899 Oct 20 Was a SC2 in US Navy S:15

Cammett, Anna - Died 1847 Aug 5 Age 66 years, 11 Wife of Peter Cammett (with him) S:14

Cammett, Benjamin B - Died 1852 July 1 Age 31 years, 1 day at Independence, Jackson County, Missouri (with Joseph Cammett, possible father) S:14

Cammett, Betsey H - Died 1872 Jan 10 Age 60 Wife of Samuel S Lovell (next to William L Cammett) S:13

Cammett, Cynthia - Died 1878 Sept 29 Born 1796 Dec 2 S:7

Cammett, David - Died 1874 Mar 25 Age 65 years, 6 months (with John H Cammett) S:12

Cammett, Edward B - Died 1849 Sept 23 Age 13 years, 9 months, 4 days, drowned off Cape Horn (with Nabby Cammett, possible mother) S:14

Cammett, Eliza B - Died 1870 Aug 11 Age 79 years, 6 months, 11 days (next to David Cammett) S:12

Cammett, Eliza H - Died 1915 Born 1830 (with Franklin Cammett) S:14

Cammett, Emeline Robbins - Died 1902 Born 1841 (next to Henry D Robinson Cammett) S:12

Cammett, Franklin - Died 1826 March 18 Age 52 months, 4 days? Son of Peter & Anna Cammett (with them) S:14

Cammett, Franklin - Died 1901 Born 1827 (with Eliza H Cammett) S:14

Cammett, Henry D Robinson - Died 1945 Born 1868 (next to Emeline Robbins Cammett) S:12

Cammett, John H - Died (date is underground) Only son of David & Mercy Cammett (next to father) S:12

Cammett, John H (Capt) - Died 1864 Aug 4 Age 73 years, 11 months, 2 days S:12

Cammett, John Henry - Died 1907 Born 1833 (next to Emeline Robbins Cammett) S:12

Cammett, Joseph - Died 1875 May 18 Age 77 years, 10 months, 7 days (listed with Benjamin B Cammett) S:14

Cammett, Mercy - Died 1874 Dec 7 Age 66 years, 7 months (next to David Cammett) S:12

Cammett, Nabby - Died 1878 Aug 18 Age 84 years, 6 months, 10 days Wife of Joseph Cammett (next to him) S:14

Cammett, Peter - Died 1830 March 7 Age 41 years, 4 months (with wife, Anna Cammett) S:14

Cammett, Robert - Died 1884 Aug 19 Born 1798 Sept 27 S:7

Cammett, Ruth Wing - Died 1884 Jan 10 Born 1823 Aug 17 S:7

Cammett, Tryphena G - Died 1854 Dec 31 Age 20 years, 8 months Daughter of Peter & Anna Cammett (next to them) S:14

Cammett, Tryphosa - Died 1851 Aug 27 Age 11 years Daughter of Peter & Anna Cammett (next to them) S:14

Cammett, Warren - Died 1906 Jan 19 Born 1840 Sept 13 (next to wife, Persis C Scudder) S:13

Cammett, William L - Died 1870 April 11 Age 28 Son of John & Betsey H Cammett (next to Betsey) S:13

Campbell, Alexander R - Died 1973 Born 1900 (with Martha Campbell) S:20

Campbell, Lillah A - Died 1881 Nov 1 Born 1853 June 21 Wife of John R Campbell & daughter of Owen & Amanda Bearse (next to parents & family) S:18

Campbell, Margurete B - Died 1989 Born 1896 (next to husband, Wallace F Campbell) S:15

Campbell, Martha W - Died (Still living 1991?) Born 1905 (With Alexander Campbell) S:20

Campbell, Mary - Died 1935 Born 1876 S:16

Campbell, Mary E - Died 1975 Born 1880 Wife of Peter Campbell (next to him) S:14

Campbell, Peter - Died 1942 Born 1874 (next to wife, Mary E Campbell) S:14

Campbell, Wallace F - Died 1969 Born 1891 (next to wife, Margurete B Campbell) S:15

Canarias, Julio - Died 1986 Born 1898 Stone says,"Beloved godparents" (with Margaret M Canarias) S:15

Canarias, Margaret M - Died 1967 Mar 17 Born 1900 Dec 23 S:15

Canarias, Margaret M - Died 1967 Born 1900 Stone says, "Beloved godparents" (with Julio Canarias) S:15

Canary, Ann - Died (no dates) (with Mary E Canary) S:31

Canary, Bridget - Died (no dates) (with Mary E Canary) S:31

Canary, Hanah - Died 1892 Nov 6 Age 28 years, 4 months, 15 days Daughter of Patrick & Mary Canary (next to them & sister, Nellie H Canary) S:31

Canary, James - Died (no dates)

71

Canary (Cont.)
(with Mary E Canary) S:31

Canary, Mary - Died (no dates)
(with Mary E Canary) S:31

Canary, Mary - Died 1871 Born
1842 (next to Hanah Canary,
daughter & husband, Patrick
Canary) S:20

Canary, Mary E - Died 1885 June
26 Age 26 years, 8 months
(listed with her are, James, Ann,
Mary & Bridget Canary) S:31

Canary, Nellie H - Died 1897 June
17 Age 27 years, 8 months, 7
days Daughter of Patrick & Mary
Canary (next to them & sister,
Hanah Canary) S:31

Canary, Patrick - Died 1902 Born
1825 (next to Mary Canary) S:31

Canning, Grace C - Died 1984 Feb
14 Born 1900 Sept 18 (next to
Thomas F Canning Jr) S:15

Canning, Thomas F Jr - Died 1968
Sept 4 Born 1897 Mar 22 From
Massachusetts, was SFL Med
Dep during World War I (next to
Grace C Canning) S:15

Cannon, Alice G - Died 1945 Born
1872 (with Ralph J Cannon &
others) S:18

Cannon, James Newton - Died
1826 Oct 22 Age 6 weeks, 2 days
Son of Lothrop Cannon & Harriet Davis S:10

Cannon, Loton J - Died 1929 Born
1876 (with Alice G Cannon) S:18

Cannon, Lucinda T - Died 1931
Born 1853 (with Rufus Henry
Cannon) S:18

Cannon, Ralph J - Died 1919 Born
1918 (with Alfred C Ritchie &
others) S:18

Cannon, Rufus Henry - Died 1929
Born 1848 (with Lucinda T
Cannon) S:18

Cannon, Sarah - Died 1829 Nov 10
Age 2 months Daughter of
Lothrop Cannon & Harriet Davis
S:10

Capitell, Winifred J - Died 1986
Born 1888 (with Arthur A Capitell) S:16

Captitell, Arthur A - Died 1975
Born 1889 (with Winifred J
Capitell) S:16

Card, Charles C - Died 1938 Born
1882 (next to Leona Card
Bowker) S:19

Carley, S Elizabeth - Died 1942
Born 1859 S:8

Carley, Sarah A - Died 1867 Born
1835 (with Ben F & Temperance
H Crocker) S:13

Carlin, Margaret G - Died 1977
Born 1889 (with Ralph L Carlin)
S:15

Carlin, Ralph L - Died 1936 Born
1888 (with Margaret G Carlin)
S:15

Carlson, Adeline S - Died 1956
Born 1882 (with Carl & J Frederick Carlson) S:20

Carlson, Carl A - Died 1960 Born
1880 (With Adeline & J Frederick Carlson) S:20

Carlson, Celia M - Died 1971 Born
1899 S:15

Carlson, Eulah H Farnsworth -
Died 1986 Born 1913 (military
stone) S:12

Carlson, Frederick R - Died 1981
Born 1897 (has military stone
that says,"SN US Navy during
World War 1") S:12

Carlson, George A - Died 1982
Born 1896 (with wife, Violet B
Carlson) S:17

Carlson, George W - Died 1972
April 5 Born 1896 May 9 From
Massachusetts, was Cpl in CoL,
3rd Pioneer Inf during World
War I S:15

Carlson, J Frederick - Died 1987
Born 1912 Son of Carl & Adeline
Carlson (With them) S:20

Carlson, John A - Died 1971 Born
1901 S:12

Carlson, Roger E Jr - Died 1980
Born 1944 (also has a West
Barnstable Fire Dept plaque &
rock stone) Was a SN in US Navy
during Vietnaum S:20

Carlson, Violet, B - Died 1973 Born
1901 Wife of George A Carlson

Carlson (Cont.)
(with him) S:17

Carlton, Belle Baxter - Died 1948 Born 1897 (with Edgar & Sara Baxter) S:18

Carmo, Joseph - Died 1978 Born 1898 (undertaker plaque only) S:17

Carney, Ada R - Died 1926 Born 1865 (with Charles H Carney) S:18

Carney, Benjamin J - Died 1933 Born 1856 (with Hannah Carney & others) S:18

Carney, Charles H - Died 1925 Born 1863 (with Ada R Carney) S:18

Carney, Deborah - Died 1880 Oct 27 Age 84 years, 6 months, 2 days Wife of Patrick Carney Buried with Husband, Patrick (same stone) S:4

Carney, Eliza AS - Died 1887 Dec 1 Born 1832 Dec 4 (with John A Carney) S:18

Carney, Gertrude L - Died 1951 Born 1896 (with Alonzo Lothrop & others) S:18

Carney, Hannah B - Died 1953 Born 1859 (with Gertrude L Carney & others) S:18

Carney, John A - Died 1867 Feb 7 Born 1828 April 10 (with Eliza AS Carney) S:18

Carney, Patrick - Died 1854 Aug 3 Age 73 years, 10 months Buried with Deborah Carney (same stone) S:4

Carney, Priscilla M - Died 1964 Born 1899 (with William L Carney) S:15

Carney, William L - Died 1973 Born 1895 (with Priscilla M Carney) S:15

Caron, Joseph P - Died 1967 Jan 20 Born 18?? May 18 From Massachusetts, was Pvt in Co F, 101 Ammo Tran during World War I (next to Odile M Caron) S:15

Caron, Odile M - Died 1988 June 27 Born 1893 Jan 10 (next to

Caron (Cont.)
Joseph P Caron) S:15

Carpenter, Daniel - Died 1791 Nov 4 in his 57th yr S:5

Carpenter, Marian - Died 1940 Feb 17 Born 1857 Oct 24 (stone down from vandals) (next to Eliza P Hamblin) (stone also down) S:18

Carpenter, Temperance - Died 1817 Dec 13 in her 84th yr Relicte & Wife of Daniel Carpenter S:5

Carr, Bertrand Jr - Died (still living 1990) Born 1920 Jan 23 (in Turpin plot) S:11

Carr, Edwin S - Died 1883 Sept 8 Age 47 (with Esther H Carr & others) S:18

Carr, Esther H - Died 1907 Dec 23 Age 71 (with Edwin S Carr & others) S:18

Carr, Harriett E - Died (still living 1991?) Born 1908 Feb 1 (listed with Elwood P Bullock) S:19

Carrit, Temperance - Died 1739 Sept (stone not clear for day) Age 27 Wife of Andrew Carrit S:9

Carroll, Edward J - Died 1875 July 24 Born 1815 Sept 27 (next to Ralph L Baker) S:18

Carroll, Katherine - Died 1930 Born 1845 (next to Bessie Baker?) S:18

Carsley, Rachel - Died 1834 Oct 2 Age 77 years, 9 months, 1 day Stone says, "Grandmother" (with Rachel Carsley) S:14

Carsley, Rachel - Died 1884 July 27 Age 82 years, 10 months, 12 days (with Rachel Carsley, Grandmother) S:14

Carsley, Susanna A - Died 1851 Feb 25 Age 92 Widow of Seth Carsley S:7

Carter, Irving W - Died 1956 Born 1887 S:17

Carter, John E - Died 1985 Born 1894 (with Mary G Carter) S:19

Carter, Mary G - Died 1984 Born 1898 (with John E Carter) S:19

Cary, Grace H - Died 1983 Born

Cary (Cont.)
1905 (with Robert O & Robert F Cary) S:19

Cary, Louis Favrean? - Died 1987 Born 1915 (with Mary Bradley Cary) S:20

Cary, Mary Bradley - Died (still living 1991?) Born 1912 (listed with Louis Cary) S:20

Cary, Robert F - Died (still living 1991?) Born 1935 (listed with Robert O & Grace H Cary) S:19

Cary, Robert O - Died 1981 Born 1900 (with Grace & Robert Cary) S:19

Cary, Roberta M - Died 1933 Born 1933 (next to Robert O Cary & others) S:19

Case, Ebenezer - Died 1842 Aug 18 in his 86th yr S:3

Case, Eliza - Died 1842 Apr 8 Age 44 Wife of Lot Case (buried next to him) S:8

Case, Eliza Ann - Died 1835 Oct 17 Age 5 years, 11 months, 14 days Daughter of Lot & Eliza Case S:8

Case, Eliza Ann - Died 1841 Apr 20 Age 3 years, 6 months, 3 days Daughter of Lot & Eliza Case S:8

Case, Isaac - Died 1798 Aug 25 in his 15th yr Son of Ebenezer and Martha Case (located at Cobb Hill East Cemetery)(Goodspeed or Meeting House Hill East) S:26R

Case, John C (Capt) - Died 1869 Nov 1 in his 43rd yr Lost overboard from schooner Emma Bacon in Delaware River S:8

Case, Lillian Parker - Died 1912 Born 1885 (with I Fenno Elliot & others) S:18

Case, Lot - Died 1871 June 15 Age 77 years, 4 months (stone says "Father") S:8

Case, Lucy P - Died 1899 Born 1826 (with Willis Leslie Case & others) S:18

Case, Lydia S - Died 1858 Apr 23 Age 26 years, 10 months, 3 days Wife of Capt John Case (his stone next to her) S:8

Case, Martha - Died 1843 Feb 2 Age 82 Widow of Ebenezer Case S:3

Case, Mary Elizabeth - Died 1921 Born 1855 (with Lillian Parker Case & others) S:18

Case, Olive S - Died 1887 June 7 Age 46 years, 10 months S:8

Case, Philander - Died 1851 Born 1821 (with Lucy P Case & others) S:18

Case, Sarah - Died 1875 May 25 Age 67 years, 5 months Wife of Lot Case (buried next to him) S:8

Case, Sophronia - Died 1854 Dec 27 Age 10 years, 7 months, 19 days Daughter of Lot & Eliza Case (buried next to them) S:8

Case, Willis Leslie - Died 1919 Born 1850 (with Mary Elizabeth Case & others) S:18

Casey, John Louis - Died 1961 July 15 Born 1893 Aug 26 From Massachusetts, was Y1 in US NRF during World War I (next to Ruth Jones Casey) S:16

Casey, Ruth Jones - Died 1955 Dec 27 Born 1898 June 5 (next to John Louis Casey) S:16

Casey, Stephen Randolph - Died 1978 Born 1887 S:15

Casey, William T - Died (no information) (with George A Moors) Stone says, "Friends" S:13

Cash, Adulsa N - Died 1906 Born 1847 (with Gustavus Cash) S:14

Cash, Alexander G - Died 1922 Born 1840 (with wife, Phoebe A Cash) S:18

Cash, C Maurice - Died 1894 Born 1868 (with Gustavus & Adulsa Cash) S:14

Cash, Edward - Died 1941 Born 1878 (with Raymond L Cash) S:18

Cash, Edward H - Died 1906 Born 1900 (next to Mary H Cash) S:31

Cash, Elizabeth - Died 1963 Born 1882 S:14

Cash, Elizabeth B - Died 1929 Born 1855 S:4

Cash, George H - Died 1935 Born

Cash (Cont.)
1850 S:4

Cash, Gustavus M - Died 1889
Born 1841 (with Adulsa N Cash)
S:14

Cash, Hannah E - Died 1922 Born
1863 (with William & Leon Cash)
S:18

Cash, Horace (Capt) - Died 1878
March 6 Age 68 years, 4
months, 6 days (next to wife,
Polly Cash) S:14

Cash, Horace C - Died 1878 Born
1878 (with Gustavus & Adulsa
Cash) S:14

Cash, Irene B - Died 1922 Born
1848 (with Nellie Cash & others)
S:21

Cash, Leander B - Died 1882 Born
1844 (stone marked with large
"C" at top of stone for Cash) Was
in Iyanough Tribe #14 Hyannis
(plaque) (with Irene B Cash &
others) S:21

Cash, Leon B - Died 1974 Born
1890 (with Hannah & William
Cash) S:18

Cash, Lillie - Died 1888 Born 1872
On the same stone with 2
Theodosia Cash's S:4

Cash, Mary H - Died 1941 Born
1876 (next to Edward H Cash)
S:31

Cash, Nellie - Died 1879 Born 1870
(with Edward C Andrews &
others) S:21

Cash, Pauline - Died 1911 Born
1882 (with Gustavus & Adulsa
Cash) S:14

Cash, Phoebe A - Died 1900 Born
1838 Wife of Alexander Cash
(with him) S:18

Cash, Polly - Died 1885 Dec 13 Age
74 years, 5 months Wife of
Horace Cash (next to him) S:14

Cash, Raymond L - Died 1957 Feb
10 Born 1899 June 13 From
Massachusetts, was Sea, US Navy
during World War I (next to
Edward Cash) S:18

Cash, Raymond W - Died 1945
Born 1898 (next to Selina V

Cash (Cont.)
Cash) S:17

Cash, Selina V - Died 1934 Born
1895 (next to Raymond W Cash)
S:17

Cash, Thedosia BD - Died 1875
Born 1875 On same stone with
Lillie & Theodosia Cash S:4

Cash, Theodosia - Died 1902 Born
1877 On the same stone with
Theodosia & Lille Cash S:4

Cash, William S - Died 1952 Born
1861 (with Hannah & Leon
Cash) S:18

Casley, Hannah - Died 1801 (stone
not clear for rest) Age 57 (next to
Capt Samuel Bacon)(she was a
widow & died March 8 per
Hinckley Ceme records #9R) S:9

Castonquay, (no name) - Died (no
dates) (a large mound cript at
front gate of cemetary) S:18

Caswell, Gertrude S - Died 1947
Born 1906 Stone says, "Mother"
(with Harry Leon Caswell, son)
S:12

Caswell, Harry Leon - Died 1953
Born 1932 Son of Gertrude S
Caswell (with him) S:12

Catalini, Bruno - Died 1984 Born
1940 (rock stone) S:20

Cathcbt, Rachel - Died 1868 Mar 2
Age 97 S:4

Cessford, Edgar - Died 1960 Born
1903 (with Isabel M Cessford)
S:19

Cessford, Isabel M - Died 1957
Born 1906 (with Edgar Cessford)
S:19

Chadwick, Adrian - Died 1939
Born 1871 (next to wife, Florence Rich) S:12

Chadwick, Bernice - Died 1976
Born 1908 Daughter of Adrian &
Florence Chadwick (with them)
S:12

Chadwick, Bertha Y - Died 1960
Born 1882 S:12

Chadwick, Burton Lovell - Died
1975 Oct 10 Born 1897 Nov 27
Was a PVT in US Army during
World War I (next to Grace

Chadwick (Cont.)
Ashley Chadwick) S:12

Chadwick, Elsie R - Died (still living 1991?) Born 1903 Daughter of Adrian & Florence Chadwick (listed with them) S:12

Chadwick, Etta G - Died 1903 Born 1849 S:12

Chadwick, Grace Ashley - Died 1984 Dec 2 Born 1900 May 24 Wife of Karl Chadwick (next to him) S:12

Chadwick, Joseph H - Died 1903 Born 1833 S:12

Chadwick, Karl W - Died 1970 July 5 Born 1895 Nov 3 Was a Massachusetts Sea, US Navy World War I Veteran Also has Vet star at grave S:12

Chadwick, Lucia A - Died 1896 Born 1837 Daughter of David & Olive P Fuller (next to them) S:12

Chadwick, Maude F - Died 1895 Born 1893 Daughter of Adrian & Florence Chadwick (with them) S:12

Chadwick, Philip B - Died 1968 Oct 4 Born 1888 Nov 30 From Massachusetts and was a Private, 1 Co, 151 Depot Brigd, during World War 1 S:13

Chadwick, Walter L - Died 1899 Born 1899 Son of Adrian & Florence Chadwick (with them) S:12

Chamberlain, Joshua - Died 1880 June 30 Age 72 S:11R

Chamberlan, Agnes M - Died 1986 Born 1897 S:15

Chamberland, Allen Taylor - Died 1865 Age 23 yrs 6 months Born 1842 (Hinkley did not reference birth date) (on large family stone with Capt Joshua Chamberland & others) S:11+26R

Chamberland, Betsey Loring - Died 1890 Age 80 yrs 9 mos 25 days Born 1810 (Hinkley records middle name as T. and doesn't reference birth off stone) (on large family stone with Capt

Chamberland (Cont.)
Joshua Chamberland & others) S:11

Chamberland, Eliza Anne - Died 1870 June 20 Age 33 yrs 9 mos Born 1836 (Hinkley does not record birth off stone) (on large family stone with Capt Joshua Chamberland & others) S:11

Chamberland, Ellen - Died 1898 Born 1839 (on large family stone with Capt Joshua Chamberland & others) S:11

Chamberland, Joshua - Died 1879 Feb 20 Age 32 yrs 8 mos Born 1846 (Hinkley does not record birth off stone)(on large family stone with Capt Joshua Chamberland & others) S:11

Chamberland, Joshua (Capt) - Died 1880 June 30 Age 72 yrs Born 1808 (Hinkley does not record birth off of stone) (a large family stone, square with others) S:11+26R

Chamberland, Lucretta - Died 1948 Born 1854 (on large family stone with Capt Joshua Chamberland & others) S:11

Chamberland, Phebe Thatcher - Died 1926 Born 1844 (on large family stone with Capt Joshua Chamberland & others) S:11

Chamberlin, Cyrus - Died 1819 June 25 Age 8 months, 20 days Son of Dr Cyrus & Eliza Chamberlin S:10

Chamberlin, Cyrus (Doctor) - Died 1820 Dec 9 in his 39th yr S:10 +26R

Chamberlin, Emily Nickerson - Died 1819 Aug 25 Age 3 years, 6 months Daughter of Dr Cyrus & Eliza Chamberlin S:10

Chamberline, Eliza Mrs - Died 1820 Mar 20 in her 40th yr Wife of Dr Cyrus Chamberlin (buried next to him) S:10+26R

Champaigne, Florence - Died 1989 Born 1896 (undertaker plaque) S:18

Chandler, Catherine - Died 1987

Chandler (Cont.)
Born 1908 (with Earl Burgess)
S:11

Chandler, Grace M - Died (death date not listed which could mean she is not buried here) Born 1885 Wife of Henry E Bearse, listed on this stone S:8

Chapman, Earle M - Died 1990 May 13 Born 1903 July 29 (next to Virginia Giles) Stone says, "Sleep peacefully my darling" S:13

Chapman, Ella DC - Died 1907 Born 1844 (next to John W Chapman) S:14

Chapman, Harriet B - Died 1960 Born 1869 S:14

Chapman, Indianna M - Died 1971 Aug 31 Born 1881 March 21 S:17

Chapman, John W - Died 1897 Born 1828 (next to Ella DC Chapman) S:14

Chapman, Sarah W - Died 1981 Born 1898 S:17

Chappelle, Mabel D - Died 1975 Born 1899 S:18

Chas, Dorcas E - Died 1834 Sept 9 Age 8 months Jan Daughter of Daniel & Dorcas Chas S:3

Chase, (Baby) - Died 1959 May (located between Ellen C McClusky & Mary A Terry) S:31

Chase, ? - Died 1884 Jan 14 (stone broken in half) Widow of Heman Chase (next to him) S:21

Chase, ?nnie C - Died 1891 Dec 6 Age 6 years, 2 months, 4? days Born 1885 Sept 25 Son of Edgar & Emma C Chase (next to Leonard Chase) S:21

Chase, Ada Loring - Died 1923 Born 1870 On family stone with Frances Fressenben Chase & others S:11

Chase, Adelaide C - Died 1937 Born 1852 (with Thomas S Chase & others) S:18

Chase, Albert - Died 1896 May 10 Age 88 years, 6 months, 22 days (with wife, Elizabeth P Chase)

Chase (Cont.)
S:18

Chase, Albert F - Died 1905 Born 1853 (with Sarah Leavitt & others) S:18

Chase, Albert T - Died 1983 Born 1898 In US Army during World War I (next to Hattie A Chase) S:18

Chase, Alexander B - Died 1922 Born 1848 (with Lucy H Chase & others) S:18

Chase, Allan H - Died (still living 1990) Born 1927 (large Chase grinding wheel stone for marker) S:11

Chase, Allan J - Died 1933 Dec 9 Born 1844 Dec 3 at Conway, New Hampshire (on Chase stone with others) S:11

Chase, Anthony Jr - Died 1862 Nov 20 Age 39 years, 5 months Stone says, "Passed on" (with Clarissa Chase) S:18

Chase, Benjamin F - Died 1947 Born 1868 (with Hector E Chase) S:18

Chase, Bertha M - Died 1905 Feb 12 Born 1882 Feb 1 (with Sarah C Basset & others) S:18

Chase, Carrie L - Died 1940 Born 1860 Wife of Nathan Bearse, buried next to him) S:8

Chase, Charles Henry - Died 1819 Oct 7 Age 9 months Son of Leonard & Cynthia Chase S:10

Chase, Charles M Sr - Died (still living 1991?) Born 1912 (listed with Frances Chase) S:20

Chase, Clara - Died 1898 Jan 10 Age 49 years, 1 month (next to Luke & Susan Chase) S:21

Chase, Clarence - Died 1946 Born 1882 (with Margaret L Chase) S:19

Chase, Clarence F - Died 1891 Born 1890 (with Reuben & Elizabeth Chase) S:18

Chase, Clarence Milton - Died 1963 June 26 Born 1882 Oct 22 (with Edith A Chase) S:18

Chase, Clarissa - Died 1894 Feb 6

Chase (Cont.)
Age 66 years, 4 months (with Anthony Chase Jr) S:18

Chase, Cleone B - Died 1947 Born 1854 (with Edward Sr & Jr Chase & others) S:18

Chase, Cynthia - Died 1834 ? 29th (stone broken) Wife of Leonard Chase (Hinckley Ceme records #10R say death was in March age 52) S:10

Chase, David - Died 1828 Feb 24 Age 69 S:3

Chase, Davis - Died 1858 Feb 16 Age 23 years, 7 months Son of Heman & Nabby A Chase S:21

Chase, Davis A - Died 1807 Dec 22 Age 11 weeks Son of Capt Davis & Hannah Chase S:4

Chase, Dorcas - Died 1943 Born 1870 (with Thomas & Catherine Baker) S:14

Chase, Dorcas E - Died 1834 Sept 4 Age 8 mos 18 days Daughter of Daniel and Dorcas Chase (next to sister Harriot) S:3R

Chase, Dorcas H - Died 1852 Feb 16 wife of Daniel Chase (next to daughter Harriot Chase) S:3R

Chase, Edgar - Died 1902 Born 1842 (with wife, Emma C & with Leonard C Chase) S:18

Chase, Edith A - Died 1970 July 17 Born 1880 Dec 10 (with Clarence Milton Chase) S:18

Chase, Edward L - Died 1920 Born 1857 (with Cleone B Chase & others) S:18

Chase, Edward L Jr - Died 1920 Born 1885 (with Edward Sr & Cleone & Josephine Chase & others) S:18

Chase, Eliza L - Died 1904 Born 1857 Stone says, "Our loved one" (with Lysander A Chase) S:18

Chase, Elizabeth - Died 1981 Born 1898 (with Alice Simmons & others) S:18

Chase, Elizabeth F - Died 1890 Born 1872 (with Reuben & Clarence Chase) S:18

Chase, Elizabeth P - Died 1890 Oct 29 Age 79 Wife of Albert Chase (with him & next to daughter, Amanda E Henton) S:18

Chase, Ellen - Died 1904 Jan 6 Born 1838 Sept 10 (with Erastus B Chase) S:14

Chase, Emily F - Died 1850 Born 1820 (with Heman & Martha Chase) S:21

Chase, Emily H - Died 1857 May 8 Age 3 months Daughter of Heman & Martha Chase (next to them) S:21

Chase, Emma C - Died 1955 Born 1860 Wife of Edgar Chase (with him & Leonard Chase) S:18

Chase, Emma T - Died 1847 Age 13 months, 3 days Born 1846 Sept 18 Daughter of Heman & Martha Chase (next to them) S:21

Chase, Enoch E (2nd) - Died 1880 Born 1875 (with Nellie S Chase & others) S:18

Chase, Enoch E (Rev) - Died 1887 Aug 21 Born 1804 March 27 (with Rebekah Chase & others) S:18

Chase, Erastus B - Died 1877 March 26 Born 1837 July 10 (with Eunice & John Baxter) S:14

Chase, Eva - Died 1945 Born 1867 (with Irving & Frank Chase) S:18

Chase, Frances - Died 1818 May 20 Age 12 yrs 9 mos who drowned at Albany Son of Capt Daniel and Dorcas Chase (next to sister Dorcas E Chase) S:3R

Chase, Frances Fessenben - Died 1967 Born 1880 (on family stone with others) S:11

Chase, Frances M - Died (still living 1991?) Born 1920 (listed with Charles Chase Sr) S:20

Chase, Frank - Died 1958 Born 1874 (with Irving Chase) S:18

Chase, Frederic - Died 1830 Aug 15 Age 7 Son of Leonard & Cynthia Chase S:10

Chase, Freeman - Died 1862 Born 1805 S:14

Chase, Freida A - Died 1987 Born 1900 (with husband, Roy L Chase) S:15

Chase, Garfield - Died 1960 Born 1881 S:11

Chase, George - Died 1939 Born 1879 (with Hattie Chase) S:18

Chase, Grace H - Died 1955 April 13 Born 1877 Sept 18 (next to Walter B Chase) S:18

Chase, Harriot - Died 1839 Feb 17 Daughter of Daniel & Dorcas Chase (stone not clear for last name, but parents are Chase) S:3

Chase, Hattie A - Died 1932 Born 1875 (next to George Chase) S:18

Chase, Hector E - Died 1983 Born 1900 (with Benjamin F Chase) S:18

Chase, Heman (Capt) - Died 1848 March 31 Age 49 (next to widow, ? Chase d1884) S:21

Chase, Heman B - Died 1880 Born 1825 (with Emily & Martha Chase) S:21

Chase, Henry B - Died 1902 March 19 Born 1823 April 25 (with Rebecca B Chase & others) S:18

Chase, Horatic S - Died 1862 Nov 13 Age 5 years, 10 months, 25 days Son of Luke B & Susan S Chase (next to them) S:21

Chase, Irving - Died 1932 Born 1887 (with Frank & Eva Chase) S:18

Chase, Josephine S - Died 1918 Born 1884 (with Edward Jr & Sidney C Chase & others) S:18

Chase, Joshua A (Capt) - Died 1883 Born 1823 (with Mary T Chase & others) S:18

Chase, Julius B - Died 1926 Born 1851 (with Mary C Chase) S:21

Chase, Leon F - Died 1953 Born 1897 (with Margaret E Chase) S:16

Chase, Leonard - Died 1850 July 22 Age 71 (stone worn) S:10+26R

Chase, Leonard - Died 1880 Sept

Chase (Cont.)
12 Age 79 (with wife, Susan Chase) S:14

Chase, Leonard - Died 1892 March 11 Age 73 (next to ?nnie C Chase) S:21

Chase, Leonard C - Died 1891 Born 1885 (with Edgar & Emma Chase) S:18

Chase, Lucy H - Died 1929 Born 1852 (with Enoch E Chase 2nd & others) S:18

Chase, Luke B - Died 1892 Aug 16 Age 72 years, 3 months Stone says, "Father" (next to wife, Susan S Chase) S:21

Chase, Lysander (Capt) - Died 1881 Born 1819 (stone leaning off base) (next to wife, Ruth Crowell) S:21

Chase, Lysander A - Died 1915 Born 1854 (with Eliza L Chase) S:18

Chase, Margaret C - Died 1963 Born 1900 S:17

Chase, Margaret E - Died 1967 Born 1883 (with Leon F Chase) S:16

Chase, Margaret L (Maggie) - Died 1959 Born 1882 (with Clarence Chase) S:19

Chase, Martha - Died 1915 Born 1825 (with Heman & Emily Chase) S:21

Chase, Mary C - Died 1909 Born 1862 (with Julius B Chase) S:21

Chase, Mary HE - Died 1856 Born 1829 Daughter of Enoch E & Rebekah Chase (with them & Henry B Chase & others) S:18

Chase, Mary T - Died 1901 Born 1825 (with Albert M Homer & others) S:18

Chase, Mertis E - Died 1948 Born 1879 Wife of Thomas Chase (with him) S:18

Chase, Nellie S - Died 1896 Born 1886 (with Mary HE Chase & others) S:18

Chase, Olive - Died 1869 Aug 5 Wife of Luke Chase S:4

Chase, Oliver L (Capt) - Died 1871

Chase (Cont.)
June 9 Born 1807 July 21 (next to wife, Mercy C Lothrop) S:19

Chase, Patricia G L - Died 1966 Born 1931 (large Chase grinding wheel stone for marker) S:11

Chase, Rebecca B - Died 1908 Jan 31 Born 1835 April 10 (with Alexander B Chase & others) S:18

Chase, Rebekah - Died 1898 March 23 Born 1808 March 31 (with Alexander B Chase & others) S:18

Chase, Reuben E - Died 1940 Born 1859 (with Elizabeth F & Clarence F Chase) S:18

Chase, Roy L - Died 1973 Born 1902 (with wife, Freida A Chase) S:15

Chase, Sarah Anna - Died 1976 Sept 7 Born 1893 Oct 23 S:16

Chase, Sidney C - Died 1906 March 4 Born 1881 Oct 27 (with Bertha M Chase & others) S:18

Chase, Sidney C - Died 1985 Born 1911 (with Josephine S Chase & others) S:18

Chase, Susan - Died 1872 July 16 Age 70 (stone missing next to them) (with husband, Leonard Chase) S:14

Chase, Susan - Died 1892 May 25 Born 1830 Oct 18 Wife of Phillip Chase S:19

Chase, Susan S - Died 1897 Oct 11 Age 74 years, 5 months Stone says, "Mother" (next to husband, Luke B Chase & Clara Chase) S:21

Chase, Tbyphosa F - Died 1869 Sept 22 Wife of Leonard Chase S:4

Chase, Thomas B - Died 1940 Born 1886 (with wife, Mertis E Chase) S:18

Chase, Thomas S - Died 1929? Born 1847 (with Adelaide C Chase & others) S:18

Chase, Tranvis B - Died 1848 May 26 Age 12 years, 9 months Son of Capt Daniel & Dorcas Chase

Chase (Cont.)
S:3

Chase, Walter B - Died 1870 Aug 11 Age 2 years, 9 months, 3 days Son of Heman & Martha Chase (next to them) S:21

Chase, Walter B - Died 1970 June 8 Born 1879 March 12 (next to Grace H Chase) S:18

Chase, Walter F - Died 1965 Born 1900 S:17

Chatfield, Belle - Died 1912 Oct 15 Born 1870 Oct 2 (with Alton Churbuck) S:14

Chatfield, Florentine - Died 1918 Jan 28 Born 1833 Dec 13 (with Alton Churbuck) S:14

Chatfield, Florrie - Died 1961 July 3 Born 1876 Oct 17 Wife of Alton G Churbuck (with him) S:14

Chatfield, Thomas - Died 1922 July 17 Born 1831 May 30 (with Alton Churbuck) S:14

Chatterdon, Bonnie - Died 1973 Born 1884 S:18

Chausse, Albina M - Died 1985 Born 1894 (with Leon P Chausse) S:15

Chausse, Leon P - Died 1974 Born 1893 (with Albina M Chausse) S:15

Cheney, MacGregor, Alfred - Died 1941 Jul 23 Born 1906 Dec 21 S:12

Cheney, Sarah MacGregor - Died 1953 Oct 8 Born 1873 Sept 16 S:12

Chesbro, Addilo - Died 1962 Born 1873 (with Rev J Wallace Chesbro & Ronald A Chesbro) S:12

Chesbro, Albert L - Died 1990 Born 1905 (with Grace P & Marie S Chesbro) S:12

Chesbro, Grace P - Died (still living in 1991?) Born 1905 (with Ronald A & Albert L Chesbro) S:12

Chesbro, J Wallace Rev - Died 194? Born 1871 Stone says, "Thy word is a light unto my path" (with Addilo Chesbro) S:12

Chesbro, Marie S - Died 1973 Born 1905 (with Albert L Chesbro) S:12

Chesbro, Ronald A - Died 1960 Born 1903 (with Grace P & Addilo Chesbro) S:12

Chesley, Herbert William - Died 1989 Born 1897 (with Gladys Loveland) S:11

Chessman, Christina H - Died 1848 Dec 13 in her 58th yr Widow of Rev Daniel Chessman & daughter of Benjamin Hallett Esq S:4

Chessman, Daniel Rev - Died 1839 May 21 in his 52nd yr He died 21 years of his ministry & 6th year as Reverned of this Baptist Church S:4

Cheston, Alice - Died 1936 Born 1856 (buried with Eunice & Nelson Phinney) S:8

Cheuard, Ellen R - Died 1980 Born 1899 Wife of Louis H Cheuard (with him) S:18

Cheuard, Louis H - Died 1986 Born 1900 (with wife, Ellen R Cheuard) S:18

Chicoine, Aurore - Died 1987 Born 1893 (with Frederic Chicoine) S:16

Chicoine, Frederic - Died 1960 Born 1896 (with Aurore Chicoine) S:16

Child, Blanche Colby - Died 1967 Born 1876 Stone says, "Mother" S:15

Child, Temperance - Died 1771 June 23 in her 25th yr Wife of Josiah Child S:9

Childs, (Father) - Died 1952 Born 1859 (next to (Mother) Childs) S:8

Childs, (infant) - Died 1844 Oct 12 Age 13 days Daughter of Thomas & Ann Childs (with mother) S:14

Childs, (Mother) - Died 1939 Born 1864 (buried next to "Father" Childs) S:8

Childs, A Seabury - Died 1948 Born 1863 (with wife, Ella M Hunnewell) S:14

Childs, Abagail - Died 1820 Dec 3 Age 69 Wife of Josiah Childs (next to him) S:10

Childs, Addie L - Died 1928 Oct 14 Born 1851 March 12 (with Rev William W Ashley) S:14

Childs, Adulsa H - Died 1848 May 11 Age 21 years, 7 months Wife of Joseph G Childs S:14

Childs, Alden B Jr - Died 1960 April 7 Born 1897 Feb 17 From Massachusetts, was Private in 1st Co, 151 Depot Brigade during World War I (next to Fannie C Childs) S:14

Childs, Alexander C (Rev) - Died 1896 Born 1823 (next to Eunice H Childs) S:14

Childs, Alexander G (Capt) - Died 1872 Sept 5 Born 1799 Nov 20 (with wife, Lucy C Childs & others) S:14

Childs, Alonzo - Died 1865 Nov 17 Age 16 years, 3 months, 24 days Son of William & Sophia Childs (stone is next to sister, Susan A Childs) S:14

Childs, Ann - Died 1844 Oct 4 Age 21 years, 3 months, 4 days (with Infant Childs d1844) Wife of Thomas Childs S:14

Childs, Augustine F (Capt) - Died 1914 July 28 Born 1829 Aug 9 (with wife, Sarah F Childs) S:8

Childs, Augustus F - Died 1910 Born 1827 (on same stone with Mary G Childs) S:8

Childs, Benjamin - Died 1826 Mar 13 Age 3 years, 8 months Son of Samuel & Sarah S:11

Childs, Benjamin Franklin - Died 1919 Born 1824 (buried with Thirza Maria Childs) S:8

Childs, Betsey S - Died 1870 Nov 28 Born 1787 June 2 S:9

Childs, Caroline W - Died 1932 Born 1871 (with Mary E Childs) S:14

Childs, Charlotte W - Died Aug 10 or 16 ? (stone broken to ground) Widow to Deacon, Samuel Childs S:11

Childs, Clarence L - Died 1923 Born 1893 S:20

Childs, Clarisa J - Died 1876 Born 1802 Wife of Jacob Childs (stone says) S:8

Childs, Daniel - Died 1857 Jan 26 Age 23 (next to wife, Susannah Childs) S:14

Childs, David - Died 1882 Aug 19 Age 80 years, 1 month, 13 days S:3

Childs, David (Capt) - Died 1813 June 8 Age 75 (Hinckley Ceme records #10R say death date was 1815) S:10

Childs, David H (Capt) - Died 1919 Feb 24 Born 1827 Sept 20 (buried with wife, Janet A Childs) S:8

Childs, Drusilla D - Died 1911 Born 1820 (stone has perpetual care) (buried with Simeon C Childs) S:8

Childs, Ebenezer Deacon - Died 1756 Jan 17 Age 66 (wife, Hannah one stone away from his) S:5

Childs, Edward - Died 1869 Oct Age 41 yrs 9 mos Son of David and Sally Childs (next to Sally) S:3R

Childs, Edward (Eddie) W - Died 1855 Sept 8 Born 1836 Nov 19 Son of ER & NL Childs Stone says, "Our Darling" S:8

Childs, Edward W - Died 1931 Born 1842 (stone has perpetual care) (was in Company D, 45th Regiment, Mass Vol militia) (with F Albertine Childs) S:8

Childs, Edward W (Eddie) - Died 1889 Sept 8 Born 1888 Nov 13 Stone says "Our Darling" Son of EP & NL Childs S:8

Childs, Egbert H - Died 1876 Oct 11 Age 16 years, 9 months, 20 days Son of Jacob & Clarisa Childs (buried next to them) S:8

Childs, Elijah - Died 1828 Dec 20 Age 67 (next to his widow, Mary Childs, d1832) S:11

Childs, Elijah - Died 1884 Mar 11

Childs (Cont.) Born 1806 Sept 28 (listed with Lucy A Childs) S:11

Childs, Elizabeth - Died 1872 Jan 28 Age 75 Wife of James Childs (next to him) S:14

Childs, Elizabeth C - Died 1928 Born 1858 (next to Rev Alexander C Childs) S:14

Childs, Ella M - Buried 1951 S:14R

Childs, Elsie - Died 1875 March 11 Born 1873 March 31 (small stone) Daughter of George & Fannie Childs (next to father) S:14

Childs, Elsie - Died 1877 Born 1872 Daughter of George & Fannie Childs (with them) S:14

Childs, Emma J - Died 1937 July 8 Born 1866 May 7 Wife of Wilton (with him) S:16

Childs, Eunice H - Died 1901 Born 1832 (next to Rev Alexander C Childs) S:14

Childs, Eveline W - Died 1842 Oct 29 Age 1 year, 7 months, 2 days Daughter of William & Sophia Childs (next to brother, Alonzo Childs) S:14

Childs, Everett P - Died 1944 Born 1859 (buried next to Edward W Childs and with Nancy L Childs) S:8

Childs, F Albertine - Died 1936 Born 1846 (wife of Edward W Childs, with him) (place into side of hill) S:8

Childs, Fannie C - Died 1975 Aug 30 Born 1891 May 17 Stone says, "Mother" (next to Alden B Childs Jr) S:14

Childs, Fannie W - Died 1923 Born 1849 Wife of George Childs (with him) S:14

Childs, Felix S (Rev MSGR) - Died 1969 Sept 10 Born 1891 Oct 23 (with Emma & Wilton Childs) S:16

Childs, Frankie - Died 1868 June 22 Age 5 years, 9 months, 3 days Son of Augustus F & Mary Childs S:8

Childs, Frederick H - Died 1961 Born 1882 (with Mary A Childs) S:14

Childs, George W - Died 1849 Oct 31 Age 5 years, 9 months S:14

Childs, Gcorgc W   Died 1920 Born 1843 (with wife, Fannie W Childs) S:14

Childs, Gladys E - Died 1965 Born 1883 (with Harold J Childs) S:14

Childs, Guy Parkman - Died 1919 Nov 10 From Massachusetts, Private in 153 Depot Brigade (next to William & Minnie Childs) S:14

Childs, Hannah - Died 1755 Feb 23 Age 37 (age from Hinckley ceme records) Wife of Ebenezer Childs (buried next to husband) S:5

Childs, Hannah - Died 1811 Jan 17 Age 72 years, 8 months Consort to Capt David Childs (next to him) S:10

Childs, Hannah B - Buried 1855 Oct 31 S:14R

Childs, Hannah Mrs - Died 1777 Sept 20 in her 66th yr Widow of David Childs S:9R+26R

Childs, Harold J - Died 1967 Born 1888 (with Gladys E Childs) S:14

Childs, Herman F - Died 1918 Born 1891 (next to two stones that say only "Mother" and "Father" Childs) S:8

Childs, Irene - Died 1968 Born 1899 (buried next to Herman and "Father" and "Mother" Childs) S:8

Childs, Isabelle C - Died 1948 Nov 27 Born 1867 Feb 16 Stone says, Daughter of Augustine & Sarah Childs S:8

Childs, Jacob - Died 1864 July 2 Age 79 years Stone says, Father (buried next to family) S:8

Childs, James - Died 1772 April 3 in his 47th yr (large stone next to him worn off) S:11+26

Childs, James - Died 1867 May 30 Age 69 (next to wife, Elizabeth Childs) S:14

Childs, James (Capt) - Died 1834 or 1831 Jan 1 Age 66 (1831 came from Hinckley ceme records) (near the other two James Childs) S:14

Childs, James B - Died 1850 March 25 Age 21 (stone next to him, face down & buried) Son of James & Elizabeth Childs (next to him) S:14

Childs, Janet A - Died 1914 May 30 Born 1845 Feb 19 (buried with Capt David Childs) S:8

Childs, Jennie - Died (no date) Burial location is section 7, lot 10, grave 4 S:14R

Childs, Joseph F - Died 1970 Jan 3 Born 1895 Aug 10 (has 2 stones) From Massachusetts, was PFC in US Army during World War I (with Mary E Childs) S:16

Childs, Josiah - Died 1833 June 8 Age 88 S:10

Childs, Julia A - Died 1874 Dec 26 Age 20 Daughter of Simeon C & Drusilla D Childs Stone says, "At Rest" (buried next to brother, Simeon C Childs) S:8

Childs, Leo A - Died 1953 Born 1898 Stone says, "Father" (with Marion C Childs) S:16

Childs, Lewis W - Died 1960 Nov 25 Born 1877 June 20 (buried in back of Olive L Childs) S:8

Childs, Lucy A - Died 1897 Feb 20 Born 1807 Oct 31 (listed with Elijah Childs) S:11

Childs, Lucy C - Died 1891 Jan 12 Born 1811 June 20 Wife of Capt Alexander G Childs (With William Ashley & others) S:14

Childs, Marion C - Died 1949 Born 1898 Stone says, "Mother" (with Leo A Childs) S:16

Childs, Mary - Died 1762 Jan 15 in her 35th yr S:5

Childs, Mary - Died 1793 Mar 15 in her 64th yr Wife of Samuel Childs (next to him, stone down) S:11+26R

Childs, Mary - Died 1832 Sept 3 (a little stone next to her, broken

Childs (Cont.)
and cannot read) Widow of
Elijah Childs (next to her d1828)
S:11

Childs, Mary A - Died 1970 Born
1882 (with Frederick H Childs)
S:14

Childs, Mary E - Died 1895 Born
1857 (with Caroline W Childs)
S:14

Childs, Mary E - Died 1989 Born
1898 (with Joseph F Childs)
S:16

Childs, Mary G - Died 1915 Born
1838 (buried with Augustus F
Childs) S:8

Childs, Mary Miss - Died 1811 Nov
6 Age 50 Born 1762 Feb 3 S:11R

Childs, Mary Mrs - Died 1796 May
26 Age 63 Widow of Capt James
Childs S:11R

Childs, Minnie E - Died 1953 Born
1871 Wife of William Childs
(with him) S:14

Childs, Nabby - Died 1871 May 24
Born 1790 Mar 2 S:9

Childs, Nancy L - Died 1929 Born
1866 (buried with Everett P
Childs & next to Edward W
Childs) S:8

Childs, Olive - Died 1873 Dec 24
Age 3 (a small stone located in
back of Olive & Lewis Childs) S:8

Childs, Olive L - Died 1878 Dec 24
Born 1870 Dec 3 (buried in front
of Lewis W Childs) S:8

Childs, Phebe - Died 1823 Jan 22
in the 38th yr Wife of James
Childs S:10+26R

Childs, Richard - Died 1805 May
22 in his 63rd yr S:11R+26R

Childs, Rodolphus E - Died 1907
Mar 16 Born 1838 Feb 23 Listed
in Company E, 40th Regiment of
Massachusetts Vols (buried with
Hannah G Lewis, wife) S:8

Childs, Rosa J - Died 1936 Born
1860 Wife of Ezra Hobson (with
him) S:14

Childs, Sally - Died 1852 Oct 20
Age 50 yrs 10 mos Wife of David
Childs S:3R

Childs, Sally - Died 1869 Oct Age
44 years, 9 months S:3

Childs, Samuel - Died 1876 Dec 15
or Oct 16 Age 82 (next to wife,
Sarah Childs, d1834) S:11+26R

Childs, Samuel - Died Nov (underground & laying down) (Hinckley
Ceme records #11R say death
was on the 29th, 1784 in his
62nd yr) S:11+26R

Childs, Samuel H - Died 1919 Born
1852 (with Mary E Childs) S:14

Childs, Sarah - Died 1854 or 1834
Feb 21 Age 35 (Hinckley Ceme
records say death was 1854,
possible typo) Wife of Samuel
Childs (next to him d1876) S:11
+26R

Childs, Sarah B - Died 1836 June
9 Wife of Alexander Childs S:6

Childs, Sarah B - Died 1905 Born
1834 Home at last Wife of Alonzo
L Phinney (next to him) S:14

Childs, Sarah F - Died 1913 Feb 24
Born 1836 Jan 18 (buried with
husband, Capt Augustine
Childs) S:8

Childs, Simeon C - Died 1864 Oct
2 Age 18 Died at USA General
Hospital, Beverly, NJ Was in the
14th Massachusetts Light Army
during Civil War Son of Simeon
C & Drucilla D Childs (his stone
is next to sister, Julia A Childs)
S:8

Childs, Simeon C - Died 1914 Born
1819 Was in Company D, 45th
Massachusetts Vol Militia
(buried with Drusilla D Childs)
S:8

Childs, Sophia - Died 1876 Jan 25
Age 29 years, 3 months, 11 days
Daughter of William & Sophia
Childs (next to mother) S:14

Childs, Sophia I - Died 1903 March
8 Born 1821 Feb 5 (next to
husband, William Childs) S:14

Childs, Susan A - Died 1890 Feb 4
Age 36 years, 4 months, 21 days
Daughter of William & Sophia
Childs (next to Sophia Childs)
S:14

Childs, Susannah - Died 1855 Oct 28 Age 19 years, 4 months Wife of Daniel Childs (next to him) S:14

Childs, Temperance Mrs - Died 1771 June 23 in her 25th yr Wife of Josiah Childs S:9R+26R

Childs, Thirza Maria - Died 1927 Born 1830 Wife of Benjamin Childs (buried next to him) S:8

Childs, Tirzah - Buried 1825 May 2 Age 59 S:14R

Childs, Tyyne J - Died 1965 Born 1906 (next to Winslow Childs Sr) S:18

Childs, William - Died 1896 March 11 Born 1820 Oct 3 (next to wife, Sophia I Childs) S:14

Childs, William C - Died 1840 May 16 Age 9 months Son of William & Sophia I Childs (next to Eveline W Childs) S:14

Childs, William F - Died 1943 Born 1869 (he was a Mason) (with wife, Minnie E Childs) S:14

Childs, William F - Died 1973 Born 1916 S:31

Childs, William S - Died 1894 Aug 3 Born 1838 Dec 27 (with Rev William Ashley & others) S:14

Childs, Willie R - Buried 1901 Sept 28 S:14R

Childs, Wilton L - Died 1968 Aug 19 Born 1866 Dec 17 (with Emma J Childs, wife) S:16

Childs, Winslow F Sr - Died 1961 Sept 29 Born 1896 June 26 From Massachusetts, was Pvt in Co11, 156th Depot Brig during World War I (next to Tyyne J Childs) S:18

Childs, Zena C - Died 1808 Aug 8 Age 7 months Son of James & Trizah Childs S:7

Chipman, (?) Abiah - Died 1736 in his 40th yr Wife of ? (stone not clear Possibly Chipman) S:5

Chipman, (?) Joseph - Died (stone not clear located between Parker & Chipman) Son of Samuel & Mary S:5

Chipman, (infant) - Died 1832 Feb

Chipman (Cont.)
22 (with mother, Phebe Winslow Chipman) Son of Walter & Phebe Winslow Chipman S:10

Chipman, ? - Died 1780's 5th of month Age 76 (stone not clear) S:5

Chipman, Abagail - Died 1775 Sept 10 Age 7 years, 8 months, 11 days Daughter of Timothy & Elizabeth Chipman (Hinckley cemetery records state she died Aug 1757 age 6?) S:5

Chipman, Abiah - Died 1736 July 15 Age 40 Wife of Deacon Samuel Chipman S:5R

Chipman, Abigail - Died 1759 Sept 10 Age 1 year, 1 month, 11 days Daughter of Deacon Timothy & Elizabeth Chipman S:5R

Chipman, Alice - Died 1781 Jan 3 Age 76 Widow of Deacon Barnabas Chipman S:5R

Chipman, Barnabas - Died 1794 Jan 29 Age 5 Son of Joseph & Temperance Chipman S:7

Chipman, Betsey - Died 1786 June 11 Age 1 year, 8 months Daughter of William & Hannah Chipman S:5R

Chipman, Daniel Crocker - Died 1835 Feb 1 Age 18 years, 7 months, wrecked and drowned at Port Patrick, Scotland, the loss of the ship Lyon of Boston Son of Walter & Phebe W Chipman S:10

Chipman, Elizabeth - Died 1768 Sept 6 Age 1 year, 7 months Daughter of Deacon, Timothy & Elizabeth Chipman S:5

Chipman, Elizabeth - Died 1817 Oct 2 in her 19th yr Daughter of Joseph & Temperance Chipman (next to them) S:10+26R

Chipman, Elizabeth - Died 1818 Mar 12 Age 94 Relict of Dea Timothy Chipman S:5

Chipman, Elizabeth Mrs - Died 1753 Mar 6 Age 49 (stone marked "Barnstable") Wife of Barnabas Chipman who was

Chipman (Cont.)
from Barnstable (some of this record is from the Hinckley ceme records) S:5

Chipman, Fannie Foster - Died 1874 May 15 Born 1857 Nov 16 S:9

Chipman, Hannah - Died 1838 July 6 Age 72 Widow of John Chipman S:5R

Chipman, Hannah - Died 1851 April 19 Age 16 at Boston Daughter of David & Sarah Lewis S:10

Chipman, Hannah L - Died 1878 Oct 12 Age 67 Wife of William Chipman S:5R

Chipman, Hope - Died 1683 Jan 8 Age 54 Wife of Elder, John Chipman Stone says, "Who changed this life for a better" Daughter of John Howland of the Mayflower S:11+26R

Chipman, Huldah - Died 1807 Wife of Peter Chipman S:5R

Chipman, Joanna - Died 1838 July 6 Age 72 Widow of John Chipman S:5

Chipman, Joseph - Died 1741 May 28 Age 6 weeks, 3 days Son of Samuel & Mary Chipman S:5R

Chipman, Joseph - Died 1811 Aug 16 in his 10th yr Son of Joseph & Temperance Chipman (next to them) S:10+26R

Chipman, Joseph (Deacon) - Died 1827 Feb 17 Born 1758 May 14 S:10

Chipman, Mary - Died 1779 Jan 26 in her 51st yr Wife of Barnabas Chipman S:7

Chipman, Mary - Died 1792 Sept 10 in her 37th yr S:5

Chipman, Mary - Died 1883 June 4 Born 1794 Aug 22 (Aunt Polly is noted on stone) S:5

Chipman, Mary (?) - Died 1713 ? July (this is a small & worn down stone, next to Hope Chipman, d1683) S:11

Chipman, Mehitable - Died 1865 June 25 Age 39 years, 6 months

Chipman (Cont.)
Wife of Walter Chipman (buried next to him) S:9

Chipman, Nancy - Died 1817 June 11 Age 1 year, 3 months, 4 days Daughter of Samuel & Nancy Chipman S:4

Chipman, Phebe W - Died 1826 Aug 7 Age 1 year, 10 months Daughter of Walter & Phebe W Chipman S:10

Chipman, Phebe Winslow - Died 1832 Feb 19 Age 37 (with infant son) Wife of Walter Chipman S:10

Chipman, Ruth E - Died 1923 Mar 3 Age 89 (in large Bursley plot) S:10

Chipman, Samuel - Died 1776 Feb 28 in his 22nd yr (of small pox) Eldest Son of Deacon, Timothy & Elizabeth Chipman S:5

Chipman, Samuel (Deacon) - Died (stone not clear, but buried 5 stones from another Deacon Samuel Chipman?) S:5

Chipman, Samuel (Deacon) - Died 1753 Mar 17 Age 64 S:5

Chipman, Sarah - Died 1713 July 10 Age 14 years, 8 months Daughter of Deacon Samuel Chipman & grand daughter of Hope Chipman S:11R

Chipman, Sarah - Died 1818 Dec 4 in her 52nd yr Consort of Timothy Chipman S:5

Chipman, Sarah - Died Jan 8 1742/3 Age 81 (stone not clear) Widow of Deacon, Samuel Chipman (death year & age from Hinckley ceme records) S:5

Chipman, Temperance Mrs - Died 1844 Jan 28 Born 1764 Mar 25 Widow of Deacon, Joseph Chipman (next to him) S:10

Chipman, Timothy - Died 1842 Dec 10 Age 79 S:5R

Chipman, Timothy - Died 1842 Dec 10 in his 79th yr S:5

Chipman, Timothy Deacon - Died 1770 Aug 24 Age 48 S:5

Chipman, Walter - Died 1792 Nov

Chipman (Cont.)
7 Age 2 Son of Temperance Chipman S:7

Chipman, Walter - Died 1821 July 7 Age 1 year, 1 month, 12 days Son of Walter & Phebe W Chipman S:10

Chipman, Walter - Died 1837 Mar 13 Age 44 S:10

Chipman, Walter - Died 1882 Sept 10 Born 1822 Aug 8 S:9

Chipman, Walter - Died Nov 6 ?(year not clear) Son of Walter Chipman (buried one stone from him) S:9

Chipman, William - Died 1786 May 11 in his 27th yr S:5

Chipman, William - Died 1887 May 21 Age 81 years, 4 months S:5R

Chipman, William (Capt) - Died 1866 Oct 4 Age 39 Born in Barnstable (in Bursley plot) Perished by the foundering of the steamship, Evening Star S:10

Christian, Frederick B - Died 1972 Born 1892 (he was a Mason) (with Helene C Christian) S:15

Christian, Helene C - Died 1987 Born 1894 (with Frederick B Christian) S:15

Christianson, Mathida - Died 1923 Born 1887 Wife of Elisha Robbins (with him) S:14

Christie, Anna J - Died 1974 Born 1891 (stone is a rock) (with Frank T Auglair) S:19

Christie, Frank K - Died 1973 Born 1894 (marker is a rock) (with Anna J Christie) S:19

Churbuck, Alton G - Died 1918 Dec 23 Born 1877 May 30 (with wife, Florrie Chatfield) S:14

Church, Isabelle A - Died 1973 Born 1899 (with Vallette S Church) S:14

Church, Molly - Died (death not recorded) Born in Derry Cerre, County Derry, Ireland Wife of Robert Evans (buried with him & others) S:12

Church, Vallette S - Died 1975

Church (Cont.)
Born 1894 (with Isabelle A Church) S:14

Churchill, Martha - Died 1750 June 4 in her 23rd yr Wife of James Churchill S:11+26R

Churchill, Mercy - Died 1756 Sept 20 Age 26 years, 10 months, 26 days Second wife of James Churchill & daughter of Silvanus & Mercy Cobb S:9R

Chute, Eunice H - Died 1979 Jan 7 Born 1892 June 10 (next to James L Chute) S:14

Chute, James L - Died 1971 Oct 1 Born 1896 Aug 3 From Massachusetts, was Commander in US Navy during World War II (next to Eunice H Chute) S:14

Cicak, Anna Lukacz - Died 1989 Born 1898 S:15

Civill, Grace W - Died 1982 Born 1886 S:18

Clagg, Charles F - Died (someone scratched 1989, May on stone) Born 1904 Oct 31 S:11

Clagg, Clara E - Died 1983 June 4 Born 1902 April 16 Wife of John Harold Thomas (with him) S:11

Clagg, Elizabeth F - Died 1901 Born 1871 (on family stone with others) S:11

Clagg, Elizabeth R - Died 1925 Born 1849 (on family stone with others) S:11

Clagg, Harry B - Died (still living in 1990?) Born 1942 Sept 10 Son of Charles F Clagg & Marjorie B Ryder S:11

Clagg, Ira T - Died 1865 July 12 Age 22 years, 9 months, 17 days Son of John Mary Clagg S:19

Clagg, J Henry - Died 1941 Born 1870 (on large family stone with others) S:11

Clagg, James - Died 1925 Born 1841 (on family stone with others) S:11

Clagg, John - Died 1881 April 16 Age 80 years, 2 months (stone worn) (war star plaque there) (with wife, Mary Clagg) S:19

Clagg, Mary - Died 1889 Aug 30 Age 80 Wife of John Clagg (with him) S:19

Clagg, Nathalin R - Died 1958 Born 1872 (with others on family stone) S:11

Claghorn, (female) - Died 1810 Dec 3 Age 58 (next to Mrs Eunice Claghorn, d1787) S:12

Claghorn, ? - Died (stone badly worn) (next to Thankful Claghorn) S:11

Claghorn, Benjamin - Died 1754 Mar 12 Age 21 (stone worn) Son of Robert & Thankful Claghorn S:12

Claghorn, Bethia - Died 1733 Oct 30 in her 65th yr Wife of Robert Claghorn S:11R+26R

Claghorn, Ebenezer - Died 1754 Mar 18 Age 12 Son of Robert & Thankful Claghorn S:12

Claghorn, Eunice Mrs - Died 1787 Aug 18 Age 31 ? Wife of Jabez Claghorn S:12

Claghorn, Jabez - Died 1821 June 20 Age 86 S:12

Claghorn, Nathaniel - Died 1729 July 23 in his 22nd yr S:11R +26R

Claghorn, Nathaniel (?) - Died July 25 (stone worn bad) (between Patience Davis & Thankful Claghorn) S:11

Claghorn, Robert - Died 1750 July 11 Age 51 S:12

Claghorn, Temperance - Died 1763 Jan 4 Age 17 Daughter of Jabez & Unice (Eunice) Claghorn S:12

Claghorn, Thankful - Died (stone worn bad) (next to Nathaniel Claghorn) S:11

Claghorn, Thankful - Died 1725? July 25 Age 22 S:11

Claghorn, Thankful - Died 1754 Mar 8 (stone worn) Daughter of Robert & Thankful Claghorn S:12

Claghorn, Thankful - Died 1770 April 17 in her 71st yr Wife of Robert Claghorn (next to Robert d1750) S:12

Claire, Ruth - Died 1990 Born 1891 (undertaker plaque only) S:15

Clamens, Marie Louise Blane (Blanc) - Died 1953 Born 1888 S:14

Clancy, Benjamin - Died 1930 Born 1879 (with Ellen Wiley Scudder & others on Wiley/Scudder stone) S:12

Clancy, Benjamin Jr - Died 1915 Jan 22-24 (with Benjamin Clancy & others on Wiley/Scudder stone) S:12

Clap, Mary - Died 1776 June 8 Age 62 Relict of Capt Stephen Clap (located at Cobb Hill East Cemetery)(Goodspeed or Meeting House Hill East) S:26R

Clapp, Abby Elizabeth - Died 1865 July 8 Born 1840 Mar 27 Wife of David Clapp S:9

Clapp, Adaline H - Died 1941 Born 1854 (next to Charles H Clapp) S:21

Clapp, Benjamin A - Died 1960 Born 1883 (located in back of family stone) (with wife, Ethel Clapp) S:18

Clapp, Charles H - Died 1937 Born 1858 (next to Adaline H Clapp) S:21

Clapp, Elizabeth Zappey - Died 1964 Born 1906 (next to Maude E & Arthur F Zappey) S:11

Clapp, Ethel - Died 1951 Born 1881 (located in back of family stone) (with husband, Benjamin A Clapp) S:18

Clare, Edna LM - Died (still living 1991?) Born 1906 (listed with Herbert F Clare) S:13

Clare, Herbert F - Died 1981 Born 1901 (listed with Edna LM Clare) S:13

Clark, Alton Irwin Carr - Died (no dates) (listed with Anne Howland Bearse) S:18

Clark, Annie - Died 1929 Born 1850 (with Collins E Clark) S:11

Clark, Charles H - Died 1975 Born 1895 S:17

88

Clark, Collins E - Died 1937 Born 1852 (with Annie Clark) S:11

Clark, Desire C - Died 1844 June 29 Age 25 years, 7 months (buried next to husband, Reuben Clark) S:8

Clark, E A (Edward?) - Died Was in 5th Massachusetts Infantry (on GAR plaque next to wife, Margaret Clark) S:19

Clark, Earle Richardson - Died 1987 Jan 26 Born 1894 June 28 (has 2 stones) Was an ENS in US Navy during World War I (with Helen Browne Clark) S:16

Clark, Emily A - Died 1914 Jan 2 Born 1832 Feb 17 S:21

Clark, Frank A - Died 1985 Born 1905 (with Ida K Clark & others) S:18

Clark, Georgia Mary - Died (no info listed, is she buried here?) (on stone with Andrew Turnbull MacCoy) S:8

Clark, Gertrude M - Died (no dates) (with Sidney Clark & others) S:18

Clark, Helen Browne - Died 1988 Feb 27 Born 1896 Feb 5 (with Earle Richardson Clark) S:16

Clark, Ida K - Died 1975 Born 1906 (with Frank A Clark & others) S:18

Clark, Jeanne - Died 1945 Nov 25 Born 1888 Nov 25 S:11

Clark, Josiah - Died 1877 Sept 24 in his 75th yr (Hinckley Ceme records #10R say death date 1837) S:10+26R

Clark, Kenneth E - Died 1922 Born 1895 (buried with Rosa & Orren Kelley & family) S:8

Clark, Madaline Salome - Died 1841 Apl 31 Age 1 year, 8 months Daughter of Rev Presbery Clark S:4

Clark, Margaret - Died 1887 Jan 29 Age 61 years, 10 months Wife of Edward A Clark (next to him) S:19

Clark, Morton H - Died 1968 Born 1888 S:15

Clark, Nelson - Died 1849 Born 1848 (buried with Nelson & Eunice Phinney & others) S:8

Clark, Nelson - Died 1931 Born 1852 (buried with Eunice & Nelson Phinney & others) S:8

Clark, Percy L - Died 1975 Born 1890 (with Mary F Enos & others) S:18

Clark, Rachel - Died 1857 Nov 24 in her 86th yr Widow of the late Josiah Clark S:10+26R

Clark, Reuben - Died 1885 June 1 Born 1818 Feb 18 (buried between Desire C Clark & Tirzah Clark, both wifes) Stone says, "My heavenly home is bright and fair" S:8

Clark, Ruth - Died (still living 1991?) Born 1900 (listed with Sharn Clark) S:18

Clark, Sarah Maria - Died 1870 Aug 28 Born 1804 Sept 3 Late of Brookfield, Mass Widow of Hiram B Clark S:21

Clark, Sharn - Died 1983 Born 1900 Stone says,"Knights of Columbus" (with Ruth Clark) S:18

Clark, Sidney - Died (no dates) (with Gertrude M Clark, Marjorie Clark Mitchell & others) S:18

Clark, Temperance - Died 1864 Oct 6 Age 23 years, 6 months Wife of Isaac Clark S:4

Clark, Tirzah - Died 1897 Dec 20 Born 1819 Oct 3 Wife of Reuben Clark Stone says, "We loved her because she loved us" (buried next to husband) S:8

Clark, William N Gilbert - Died 1933 Born 1858 (with Adelaide M Nickerson) S:14

Clarke, Anna A - Died 1975 Born 1911 (with Earle L Clarke) S:13

Clarke, Earle L - Died 1966 Born 1907 (with Anna A Clarke) S:13

Clarke, Esther C - Died 1986 Born 1894 (with John Clarke & others) S:11

Clarke, James F - Died 1950 Born 1874 S:17

Clarke, James J - Died 1970 Born 1896 (with Jessie A Clarke) S:16

Clarke, Jessie A - Died 1975 Born 1898 (with James J Clarke) S:16

Clarke, John - Died 1925 Born 1920 (with Esther Clarke & James Coggeshall Jr) S:11

Clarke, Nellie B - Died 1973 Born 1879 S:18

Clarkin, Bertha M - Died 1981 Born 1884 (with William L Fitzgeral) S:16

Clarner, Louis K Jr - Died 1936 Born 1881 (with wife, Laura C Harlow) S:14

Clasby, Katherine - Died 1978 Born 1905 Wife of Howard Bolton Begg (with him) S:15

Claussen, Charles Edward - Died 1927 Born 1927 (still born) (from Hinckley ceme records) Son of Howard Claussen & Florence Gifford (with them) S:14

Claussen, Florence G - Buried 1975 Age 78 S:15R

Claussen, Florence G - Buried 1975 Dec 28 S:14R

Claussen, Howard P - Died 1973 Born 1894 (with Charles L Gifford & wife Florence S Gifford) (he was creamated) (from Hinckley ceme records) S:14

Clay, Levenia H - Died 1954 Born 1858 (with Helen C Hartford) S:18

Clayman, James - Died 1988 Dec 3 Born 1897 Feb 9 (Jewish section) S:15

Clayton, Charles D - Died 1864 August 17 Age 2 years, 10 months (stone is down) (next to mother, Mary H Clayton) Son of Charles D & Mary H Clayton S:14

Clayton, Charles D - Died 1898 Feb 6 Age 68 years, 4 months, 6 days Stone says, "Father" (stone is down) (next to wife, Mary H Clayton) S:14

Clayton, Laura B - Died 1937 Born 1864 Wife of Wallace Ryder (with him) S:14

Clayton, Mary H - Died 1886 June 8 Age 53 years, 7 months Stone says, "Mother" Wife of Charles D Clayton (next to him) S:14

Clement, Julietta M - Died 1902 June 21 Born 1833 Feb 10 Wife of Thomas R Clement MD (next to him) S:12

Clement, Thomas R MD - Died 1898 Sept 18 Born 1824 Nov 25 (next to Julietta M Clement, wife) S:12

Clifford, Frank L - Died 1950 Born 1866 (with Laura Bunker & George W Clifford) S:18

Clifford, George W - Died 1914 Born 1901 (with Frank Clifford & Laura Bunker) S:18

Clifton, Theodore E - Died 1972 Born 1900 S:18

Cliggott, Denis J - Died 1978 Born 1897 Was a Sea 2 in US Navy during World War I S:15

Clinghan, Jane M - Died (still living 1991?) Born 1915 (listed with William Clinghan) S:20

Clinghan, William J - Died 1988 Born 1912 (has 2 stones) Was a PFC in US Army during World War II (with Jane Clinghan) S:20

Cloghorn, Joseph - Died 1745 Feb 21 Age 2 years, 4 months, 12 days Son of Ebenezer & Sarah Cloghorn S:3

Cloud, Leonard - Died 1970 May 5 Born 1921 May 10 Was from Massachusetts and a PFC in Battery C, 211 AAA AW BN, CAC during World War II (with wife, A Hope Whiteley) S:13

Clough, Elvia - Died 1958 Born 1895 Wife of George Davis (listed with him) S:14

Clough, Ivia M - Died 1956 Born 1895 Wife of Arthur Coleman (with him) S:14

Clouter, Florence B - Died 1980 Born 1900 Wife of James Graham (with him) S:14

Clowery, Bryce Hugh - Died (still living 1990?) Born 1924 (listed with Angie Walker & John

Clowery (Cont.)
Francis Clowery) S:11

Clowery, John Francis - Died 1970 Born 1892 (with wife, Angie Walker) S:11

Coan, Mary - Died (no date) Born 1860 wife of Thomas Ormsby (listed with him) S:16

Coates, Sarah B - Died 1898 Sept 8 Born 1811 May 12 (stone over from vandals) S:18

Cob, Frederick - Died 1867 Nov 12 Age 67 years, 9 months S:10

Cob, Samuel - Died 1757 Sept 7 in his 75th yr (next to wife Elizabeth Cobe) S:9

Cobb, (male) - Died 1801 ? 30th Son of Samuel & Abigail Cobb S:10

Cobb, ? - Died (broken sandstone marker, worn & info nearly gone) (located between Rebecca Hinckley & Elizabeth Cobb d1843) S:10

Cobb, Abiah - Died 1846 June 10 Age 47 years 6 months 13 days (in Cobb plot) Wife of Enoch T Cobb S:10

Cobb, Abigail - Died 1778 Oct 20 in her 26th yr Consort to Ebenezer Cobb S:10+26R

Cobb, Abigail - Died 1811 Aug 8 in her 40th yr Wife of Samuel Cobb S:10+26R

Cobb, Alfred - Died 1829 Nov 28 Born 1829 July 21 (in Cobb plot) Son of Enoch T & Abiah Cobb S:10

Cobb, Alice F - Died 1963 Born 1872 Wife of John H Cobb (with him) S:18

Cobb, Anna Mrs - Died 1785 June 21 in her 59th yr Wife of Benjamin Cobb S:10R+26R

Cobb, Asa - Died 1884? May 22? Age 52 years, 10 months Born 1801 July 26 (stone worn) (next to wife, Mercy G Cobb) S:19

Cobb, Asa Crocker - Died 1837 Nov 20 Born 1837 Oct 1 (in Cobb plot) Son of Enoch T & Abiah Cobb S:10

Cobb, Bartlett W - Died 1885 March 24 Born 1801 July 4 S:18

Cobb, Bartlett W - Died 1908 Born 1842 (with Georgianna Cobb) S:18

Cobb, Benjamin - Died 1803 Jan 6 in his 78th yr S:10

Cobb, Benjamin - Died 1800 May 26 in his 48th yr (in Cobb plot) (1800 death year from Hinckley Ceme records #10R) S:10+26R

Cobb, Bethia - Died 1871 Dec 23 Age 76 years, 2 months, 5 days S:7

Cobb, Betsey (Miss) - Died 1894 March 9 Age 93 years, 7 months (next to Mercy T Cobb) S:19

Cobb, Charles Jackson - Died 1849 May 26 Born 1849 April 11 (in Cobb plot) Son of Enoch T & Mary J Cobb S:10

Cobb, Daniel - Died 1813 Sept 20 (Etatis - 20) Son of Daniel & Elizabeth Cobb S:10

Cobb, Daniel - Died 1813 Sept 20 Age 20 Son of Daniel & Elizabeth Cobb S:10R

Cobb, Daniel - Died 1823 May 19 Age 71 S:10

Cobb, Daniel Mr - Died 1823 (front of stone worn off) (next to Elizabeth Cobb) S:10

Cobb, David - Died 1757 May 23 in his 37th yr S:9R+26R

Cobb, David Mr - Died 1823 Jan 11 in his 72nd yr S:10+26R

Cobb, Davis Rev - Died 1848 Feb 12 Born 1818 May 12 Born in Barnstable & Died in Chatham, Mass S:4

Cobb, Ebenezer - Died 1757 Jan 5 in his 32nd yr S:9R+26R

Cobb, Ebenezer - Died 1826 Dec 1 Age 75 S:10

Cobb, Eleazer - Died 1731 Sept 21 in his 36th yr S:9R+26R

Cobb, Eleazer - Died 1826 Dec 1 in his 75th yr S:10R+26R

Cobb, Eleazer Jr - Died 1824 Dec 31 Age 48 S:10R

Cobb, Elizabeth - Died 1721 May 4 in her 66th yr Wife of Samuel

Cobb (Cont.)
Cobb S:9R+26R

Cobb, Elizabeth - Died 1800 Sept 13 in her 46th yr Wife of Ebenezer Cobb (next to him) (above 13th from Hinckley Ceme records #10R) S:10+26R

Cobb, Elizabeth - Died 1841 July 26 Age 77 Widow of Joseph Cobb S:10

Cobb, Elizabeth - Died 1843 Sept 28 Age 84 Widow of Daniel Cobb (next to him) S:10

Cobb, Elizabeth Miss - Died 1821 June 10 in her 68th yr S:10R+ 26R

Cobb, Elizabeth Mrs - Died 1843 (front of stone worn) (located between Cobb, ? & Daniel Cobb d1823) S:10

Cobb, Elizabeth Mrs - Died 26 July 1811 Age 76 Wife of Joseph Cobb, buried next to him S:8

Cobb, Ellen Maria - Died 1879 Dec 9 Born 1843 April 14 Daughter of Matthew & Phebe Cobb (buried next to them) S:9

Cobb, Enoch T - Died 1876 Feb 26 Age 78 years, 2 months (in Cobb plot) S:10

Cobb, Eva B - Died 1892 Oct 21 Born 1868 Nov 1 (next to Bartlett W Cobb) S:18

Cobb, Evelyn Bradford - Died 1901 Oct 23 Born 1861 July 15 (with Mayhew A Luce & others) S:18

Cobb, George - Died 1936 Born 1879 S:19

Cobb, Georgianna - Died 1936 Born 1847 (with Bartlett W Cobb) S:18

Cobb, Hannah - Died (no date) located in row 5 (could be the same as Hannah Cobb d 1747) S:11R

Cobb, Hannah - Died 1713 located in row 12 (flat) S:11R

Cobb, Hannah - Died 1788 Jan 11 in her 26th yr Wife of Ebenezer Cobb S:10R+26R

Cobb, Hannah - Died April 1700's (next to Johny Cobb) (Hinckley

Cobb (Cont.)
Ceme records #11R say Johny was her husband & she died 1747 April 3 in her 66th yr) S:11+26R

Cobb, Harold F - Died 1932 Born 1903 (with Alice F Cobb) S:18

Cobb, Henry - Died 1855 Jan 5 at Tazewell (?), Tennessee Born 1833 Feb 5 (in Cobb plot) Graduate of Harvard Unv class of 1851 Was a civil engineer, mortal remains rest here Errected in love by his deely afflieted father S:10

Cobb, Henry - Died 1892 Dec 31 Age 95 years, 6 months, 7 days S:7

Cobb, Henry (Elder) - Died 1679 (a tall monument with metal fence around it) Ancestor of the Cobb family in Barnstable Errected by Enoch T Cobb a descendant in 1871 S:11

Cobb, Horace - Died 1921 Oct 1 Born 1858 Feb 12 (with Evelyn Bradford Cobb & others) S:18

Cobb, Isaac (Capt) - Died 1826 Nov 13 Age 39 Drowned at sea S:10R

Cobb, Isaac H Died 1901 Jan 11 Age 80 (next to Mercy G Cobb) S:19

Cobb, James - Died 1790 Jan 16 Age 4 years 11 months 16 days Son of Joseph & Susannah Cobb (buried next to mother) S:10

Cobb, James - Died 1824 Dec 18 Age 64 S:10R

Cobb, James Died 1872 June 21 Age 74 years, 10 months S:10

Cobb, Job G - Died 1916 Born 1836 (with Martha V Cobb & others) S:18

Cobb, John - Died (no date) (no location or info) S:11R

Cobb, John - Died 1713 Mar 1 in his 2nd yr (stone made of sandstone, very worn) Son of John & Hannah Cobb) S:11+26R

Cobb, John - Died 1736 May 25 Age 17 Son of John & Hannah Cobb S:11R

Cobb, John - Died 1754 Aug 24 in his 77th yr S:11R

Cobb, John - Died 1857 Oct 26 Age 55 years, 9 months S:19

Cobb, John - Died Aug 1794 ? (stone not clear) (located next to Hannah & Johny Cobb) S:11

Cobb, John (Capt) - Died 1800 June 6 Age 45 (age from Hinckley Ceme records #10R) (buried next to wife, Martha Cobb) S:10

Cobb, John H - Died 1944 Born 1869 (with wife, Alice F Coob) S:18

Cobb, Johny - Died 1775 Age 17 Son of John J & Hannah Cobb S:11

Cobb, Jonathan - Died 1829 Dec 11 Age 18 or 48 (age 48 from Hinckley Ceme records #10R) S:10

Cobb, Joseph - Died 11 Aug 1856 Age 74 Buried next to wife, Elizabeth Cobb (not sure if this is the same person as Joseph Cobb who died 1836 and in #10 ceme?) S:8

Cobb, Joseph - Died 1836 Aug 11 in his 74th yr (with Elizabeth Cobb) (not sure if this person is the same as the Joseph Cobb who died 1856 and is buried in #8 ceme?) S:10+26R

Cobb, Joseph - Died Feb (stone underground) (located between Elizabeth Crocker & Mary Lewis) (Hinckley Ceme records #10R say death date was 20 Feb 1796 in his 63rd yr) S:10+26R

Cobb, Joseph Mr - Died 1824 Dec 18 in his 64th yr (another stone located next to him but broken & gone, person on other side of this broken stone is Susan Cobb) S:10+26R

Cobb, Josephine - Died (still living 1991?) Born 1918 Jan 23 Wife of Wayland L Cobb (with him) S:17

Cobb, Lucy - Died 1867 May 1 Age 77 Daughter of David & Lucy Cobb S:10

Cobb, Lucy Mrs - Died (dates

Cobb (Cont.)
underground) Relict of David Cobb (buried next to him) (Hinckley Ceme records #10R say death date was 2 Oct 1823 age 73) S:10

Cobb, M - Died (no dates, but located in large cript on hill over looking street with stoned in door) S:10

Cobb, Marietta Frances - Died 1841 Aug 7 Age 16 years, 26 days Daughter of Davis & Ellen M Cobb S:4

Cobb, Martha - Died 1831 Dec 6 Age 72 Widow of Capt John Cobb S:10

Cobb, Martha V - Died 1913 Born 1842 (with Job G Cobb & Elizabeth E Crocker & others) S:18

Cobb, Mary - Died 1823 May 14 in her 89th yr Widow of Matthew Cobb (buried next to him) S:9+26R

Cobb, Mary AB - Died 1917 Born 1842 (with Samuel & William Cobb) S:19

Cobb, Mary J Mrs - Died 1873 Aug 4 Age 64 years, 11 months (Cobb plot) 2nd wife of Enoch T Cobb S:10

Cobb, Mary L - Died 1877 Oct 18 Age 83 (stone worn) Wife of Wil liam Cobb (next to him) S:19

Cobb, Matthew - Died 1762 Jan 24 in his 43rd yr (buried next to Matthew Cobb who died 1863) S:9+26R

Cobb, Matthew - Died 1863 May 18 Born 1788 July 20 S:9

Cobb, Matthew - Died 1888 Oct 23 in New York Born 1835 July 1 S:9

Cobb, Mehitable - Died 1801 Jan 30 in her 5th year Daughter of Samuel & Abigail Cobb S:10R+ 26R

Cobb, Mercy G - Died 1886 March 2? Age 73 (this is probably an error if you look at husbands record) Wife of Asa Cobb (next to him) (stone worn and off its

Cobb (Cont.)
base) S:19

Cobb, Mercy T - Died 1914 Born 1830 (next to Miss Betsey Cobb) S:19

Cobb, Mr - Died (no date or first name) Located in row 5 S:11R

Cobb, Olive - Died 1866 Feb 15 Age 75 S:10

Cobb, Patience M - Died 1886 Jan 19 Age 82 years, 6 months, 1 day Wife of Henry Cobb S:7

Cobb, Peris Mrs - Died 1845 Jan 8 Age 86 Widow of Benjamin Cobb (in Cobb plot) S:10

Cobb, Phebe Bliss Farnham - Died 1875 Aug 30 Born 1801 July 8 Wife of Matthew Cobb S:9

Cobb, Pierce W - Died 1987 Born 1898 Stone says,"Beloved father" S:18

Cobb, Priscilla - Died 1987 Born 1926 S:13

Cobb, Rachal - Died 1746 Jan 25 Age 60 Wife of Thomas Cobb S:9 +26R

Cobb, Rebekah - Died 1756 Oct 2 Age 17 years, 5 months, 19 days Daughter of Silvanus & Mercy Cobb S:9R

Cobb, Richard - Died 1826 May 9 Age 30 S:10

Cobb, Richard Henry - Died 1821(?) Mar 16 Age 2 months 26 days Infant son of Matthew & Mary Cobb S:10

Cobb, Sally T - Died 1832 June 12 Age 46 years 7 months S:10

Cobb, Samuel - Died 1727 Sept 7 in his 73rd yr (church record says, Dec 7) S:9R+26R

Cobb, Samuel - Died 1905 Born 1818 (with Mary AB & William Cobb) S:19

Cobb, Sarah - Died 1835 Sept 23 Age 72 Wife of Ebenezer Cobb S:10

Cobb, Sephrenia - Died 1805 April 28 Daughter of Samuel & Abigail Cobb (Hinckley Ceme records #10R say death date was 1807 age 2) S:10

Cobb, Silvanus - Died 1756 Sept 30 Age 55 years, 9 months, 22 days S:9R

Cobb, Sophia - Died 1837 Oct 10 Age 36 years, 9 months (with Temperance Cobb) S:21

Cobb, Sophronia - Died 1807 April 28 in her 2nd yr Daughter of Samuel and Abigail Cobb (located at Cobb Hill East Cemetery) (Goodspeed or Meeting House Hill East) S:26R

Cobb, Susan - Died 1823 April 20 Age 33 Daughter of Joseph & Susan Cobb (stone broken & gone next to her) (Hinckley Ceme records #10R say death year was 1825) S:10

Cobb, Susannah - Died 1835 April 7 in her 75th yr Widow of Joseph Cobb (stone broken, laying on ground, covered in grass) S:10+26R

Cobb, Temperance - Died 1862 June 20 Age 63 years, 9 months Wife of Bartlett Cobb (with Sophia Cobb) S:21

Cobb, Temperance (Mrs) - Died 1865 July 19 Age 65 (stone down & broken) Wife of Charlie Cobb S:19

Cobb, Thankful Mrs - Died 1821 Oct 4 Age 28 S:10R

Cobb, Thomas - Died 1742 Oct 1 in his 60th yr S:9+26R

Cobb, Thomas F - Died 1869 Born 1831 S:18

Cobb, Wayland L - Died 1972 Sept 3 Born 1900 July 17 (with wife, Josephine Cobb) S:17

Cobb, Wellington - Died ? Feb 19 (stone worn) Infant son of Matthew & Mary Cobb S:10

Cobb, William - Died (stone under ground, cannot read) (next to wife, Mary L Cobb) S:19

Cobb, William - Died 1900 Born 1867 (with Samuel & Mary Cobb) S:19

Cobb, William L - Died 1842 Oct 6 Age 9 months, 9 days Son of Davis & Ellen M Cobb S:4

Cobe (Cobb), Elizabeth - Died 1721 May 4 in her 66th yr Wife of Samuel Cobe S:9

Coburn, Ida May - Died 1900 June 3 Born 1853 Dec 12 (with WB Hallett & others) S:18

Cocks, Rowland Eillis - Died 1952 Born 1887 S:14

Coffin, Adeline D - Died 1945 Born 1863 (with Oliver C Coffin) S:12

Coffin, Alice F - Died 1971 May 20 Born 1890 March 16 (next to Donald O Coffin) S:12

Coffin, Anna - Died 1901 Born 1871 S:5

Coffin, Augusta B - Died 1964 Born 1870 (with husband, Edwin H Coffin & Edwin H Coffin Jr) S:12

Coffin, Clarence H - Died 1921 Born 1849 (next to Lafayette F Bishop) S:18

Coffin, Donald O - Died 1970 May 8 Born 1895 March 7 (plus 2 military stones) Was PFC in US Army during World War I for Massachusetts S:12

Coffin, Edwin H - Died 1933 Born 1867 (with wife, Augusta B Coffin) S:12

Coffin, Edwin H Jr - Died 1940 Born 1900 Son of Edwin Sr & Augusta Coffin (with them) S:12

Coffin, Elizabeth - Died 1797 April 28 Age 34 Born 1763 S:10

Coffin, Elizabeth - Died 1859 Born 1827 (with Harriet C Coffin & others) S:18

Coffin, Esther H - Died 1907 Born 1854 (with Herbert S Coffin & others) S:18

Coffin, Eudora E - Died 1893 Nov 21 Age 43 years, 3 months, 6 days Stone says,"Wife" (next to Elisha B Basset) S:18

Coffin, Hannah Bishop - Died 1933 Born 1851 (next to Bessie Bishop) S:18

Coffin, Harriet C Coffin - Died 1891 Born 1836 (with Henry H Coffin & others) S:18

Coffin, Henry H - Died 1858 Born

Coffin (Cont.) 1856 (with Lilie A Coffin & others) S:18

Coffin, Herbert S - Died 1908 Born 1850 (with Henry H Coffin & others) S:18

Coffin, Joseph C - Died 1890 Born 1829 (with Thyphema Coffin) S:12

Coffin, Joseph H - Died 1897 Born 1818 (with Elizabeth Coffin & others) S:18

Coffin, Lecia - Died 1904 Born 1834 S:5

Coffin, Lilie A - Died 1866 Born 1864 (with Esther H Coffin & others) S:18

Coffin, Madelyn A - Died (still living 1991?) Born 1904 (listed with Robert P Small) S:12

Coffin, Oliver C - Died (no markings) (with Adeline D Coffin who died 1945) S:12

Coffin, Sophia - Died 1832 April 2 Age 14 A colored person S:10R

Coffin, Thyphema - Died 1897 Born 1832 (with Joseph C Coffin) S:12

Coffin, Zora - Died 1955 Born 1889 Wife of Walter White (with him) S:12

Coggeshall, George Knowles - Died 1978 June 5 on Cape Cod, Massachusetts Born 1902 Dec 27 "Beloved husband" S:11

Coggeshall, James Jr - Died 1976 Born 1896 (with Esther C Clarke) S:11

Cohoon, John - Died 1820 Aug 25 in his 50th yr S:3

Cohoon, John - Died 1820 July 21 in his 16th yr Son of John & Anna Cohoon S:3

Colby, Maria Otis - Died 1821 May 20 in her 24th yr or 34th (stone says, At rest) She was the Consort to Rev Phillip Colby of Middlebough (Hinckley ceme records say that she was 34 and died at home) S:5

Colella, Pasquale J - Died 1972 Sept 8 Born 1897 Dec 9 S:15

Coleman, Abigail - Died 1907 Born 1831 (with Leonard E Goodrich & others) S:18

Coleman, Abraham - Died 1881 Jan 22 Born 1811 April 25 (with Patience Coleman) S:13

Coleman, Adeline L - Died 1906 Oct 6 Born 1824 March 2 Wife of Isaac Coleman (with him) S:21

Coleman, Albert B (Capt) - Died 1907 Born 1845 (with Emma L & L Esther Coleman) S:18

Coleman, Albert P - Died 1961 Born 1884 (with Mae Schenck Coleman) S:13

Coleman, Alcott N - Died 1850 Oct 7 Age 6 mos Child of Nathan & Temperance Coleman (next to Temperance and with Alcott N d1847) S:14

Coleman, Alcott N - Died 1847 May 2 Age 7 months Child of Nathan and Temperance Coleman (next to Temperance and with Alcott N d1850) S:14

Coleman, Alice - Died 1873 Sept 22 Age 12 years, 10 months (small stone) Daughter of James H & CF Coleman (next to father) S:14

Coleman, Arthur A - Died (still living 1991?) Born 1895 (listed with wife, Ivia M Clough) S:14

Coleman, Asa Elery - Died 1940 Born 1879 (listed with Joseph & Jeannette Hamlin) S:14

Coleman, Bacon - Died 1894 Born 1821 (with Abigail Coleman & others) S:18

Coleman, Bernice Eliza - Died 1956 Born 1883 (with Asa Elery Coleman) S:14

Coleman, Bethiah - Died 1815 July 17 in her 75th yr Wife of Ebenezer Coleman S:3R

Coleman, Braddock - Died 1873 March 11 Age 68 years, 4 months (next to children & wife, Martha Coleman) S:14

Coleman, Braddock - Died 1952 Born 1866 (with wife, Lydia S Howes) S:14

Coleman, Carl Chester - Died 1954

Coleman (Cont.)
Nov 19 Born 1954 Aug 4 Stone says,"sweet baby god is near" Son of Vernon E & Thelma A Coleman (next to Lucy & Harry Coleman) S:21

Coleman, Caroline W - Died 1941 Born 1864 Wife of Marshall Robbins (with him) S:14

Coleman, Carrie M - Died 1944 Born 1862 Wife of James Hill (buried with him in Lowry plot) S:8

Coleman, Cecil Adams - Died 1983 Born 1910 Has military stone too which reads, "RD2 in US Navy during World War II" (listed with Helen E Coleman) S:13

Coleman, Charles - Died 1840 Jan Son of James & Mercy Coleman 8next to them) S:14

Coleman, Charles - Died 1863 April 15 Born 1858 Dec 2 (next to Ellen Coleman) S:13

Coleman, Charles H - Died 1941 Born 1876 (with wife, Florence A Adams) S:13

Coleman, Chloe A - Died 1923 Born 1838 (with Francis B Coleman) S:14

Coleman, Chloei - Died 1843 Nov 18 Age 31 years, 4 months S:12

Coleman, Clara E - Died 1936 Born 1865 (with Heman I Coleman Jr & others) S:18

Coleman, Corinna - Died 1848 Aug 26 Daughter of Braddock & Martha Coleman (next to them & Isadore A Coleman, sister?) S:14

Coleman, Cynthia L - Died 1933 Born 1876 (with Seth & Cynthia L Coleman) S:14

Coleman, David - Died 1896 Born 1840 S:7

Coleman, Dorcas - Died 1874? April 26 Born 1803 Oct 26 (stone located under tree & worn) Wife of John Coleman (next to him) S:14

Coleman, Dorothy - Died 1854 Oct 15 Age 86 wife of Hezekiah Coleman (next to him) S:14

Coleman, Effie L - Died 1974 Born 1895 (with William F Coleman) S:14

Coleman, Ellen - Died 1930 Aug 27 Born 1848, 6th (next to Charles Coleman) S:13

Coleman, Ellen L - Died 1931 Born 1862 (with William F Coleman) S:14

Coleman, Emily - Died 1843 Oct 17 Age 11 months(?) Daughter of James & Mercy Coleman (next to them) S:14

Coleman, Emma - Died 1864 Sept 3 Age 25 (base of stone cracked) Wife of Charles Loring (next to him) S:14

Coleman, Emma L - Died 1922 Born 1848 (with Capt Albert & L Esther Coleman) S:18

Coleman, Evelyn M - Died (still living 1991?) Born 1902 (listed with H Wesley Coleman) S:15

Coleman, Flora - Died 1866 Sept 8 Born 1864 Sept 13 Daughter of James & Sophia Coleman (one stone away from both of them) S:14

Coleman, Francis B - Died 1909 Born 1836 (with Chloe A Coleman) S:14

Coleman, Francis F - Died 1880 Born 1874 (with Francis & Chloe Coleman) S:14

Coleman, Francis M - Died 1873 Born 1872 (with Francis & Chloe Coleman) S:14

Coleman, Francis M - Died 1882 Born 1840 (with Phebe C Coleman) S:14

Coleman, Frederick W - Died 1911 June 9 Born 1823 May 24 S:8

Coleman, Gilbert L - Died 1939 Born 1863 (next to wife, Mabel Bearse) S:14

Coleman, H Arthur - Died 1922 Born 1901 (with Florence Adams & Charles Coleman) S:13

Coleman, H Wesley - Died 1986 Born 1899 (with Evelyn M Coleman) S:15

Coleman, Harry E - Died 1938

Coleman (Cont.) Born 1865 (with Lucy B Coleman) S:21

Coleman, Helen E - Died (still living 1991?) Born 1912 (listed with Cecil Adams Coleman) S:13

Coleman, Heman I - Died 1909 March 19 Born 1815 Aug 13 (he was a Mason) (with Mary J Coleman & Mary A Ready & others) S:18

Coleman, Heman I Jr - Died 1921 Born 1861 (with Clara E Coleman & others) S:18

Coleman, Hezekiah - Died 1861 Nov 15 Age 89? years, 7 months (stone down, was repaired once before) (next to wife, Dorothy Coleman) S:14

Coleman, Hezekiah - Died 1836 July 8 Age 8 months Child of Nathan & Lydia Coleman S:14

Coleman, Irma A - Died 1964 Born 1899 Wife of Carlton Taylor (with him) S:14

Coleman, Irving F - Died 1956 Born 1903 (with wife, Albertina Young) S:13

Coleman, Isaac - Died 1885 Jan 9 Born 1837 Nov 8 Was in 5th Massachusetts Volunteers (with Adeline L Coleman) S:21

Coleman, Isadore A - Died 1845 Sept 9 Age 4 years, 1 month, 11 days (next to possible parents, Braddock & Martha Coleman) S:14

Coleman, James - Died 1781 April 25 in his 78th yr S:3+3R

Coleman, James - Died 1873 Oct 8 Age 66 Stone says, "Father" (next to wife, Sophia Coleman) S:14

Coleman, James H - Died 1892 Oct 17 Born 1831 Nov 27 Stone says "Husband" (next to daughter, Alice Coleman) S:14

Coleman, James(?) - Died 16 July (date?) (Small worn stone) Son of Braddock & Martha Coleman (next to Corinna Coleman, sister) S:14

Coleman, John - Died 1888 June 7 Born 1801 Dec 12 (next to wife, Dorcas Coleman) S:14

Coleman, John F - Died 1896 Mar 14 Born 1852 Sept 28 (buried next to Frederick W Coleman) S:8

Coleman, John W - Died 1840 July 9 at Boston Age 13 years, 8 months, 21 days Son of Nathaniel & Mehitable Coleman S:12

Coleman, Kenneth B - Died 1896 Born 1895 (next to Mabel Bearse & Gilbert Coleman) S:14

Coleman, L Esther - Died 1953 Born 1888 (with Capt Albert & Emma Coleman) S:18

Coleman, Lizzie A - Died 1923 Born 1857 (with Chester H Wilbar & others) S:18

Coleman, Lizzie W - Died 1895 June 10 Age 13 years, 4 months Daughter of William A & Lucy A Coleman (with mother) S:13

Coleman, Lucy A - Died 1900 June 20 Born 1849 March 19 (with Lizzie W Coleman) S:13

Coleman, Lucy B - Died 1951 Born 1866 (with Harry E Coleman) S:21

Coleman, Lydia - Died 1836 Sept 26 Age 37 Wife of Nathan Coleman S:14

Coleman, Mae Schenck - Died 1983 Born 1891 (with Albert P Coleman) S:13

Coleman, Marin - Died 1889 Apr 30 Age 68 years, 6 months (buried next to Daniel Lumbert) S:8

Coleman, Martha - Died 1887? Born 180? (stone not clear) Wife of Braddock Coleman (next to him) S:14

Coleman, Martha J - Died 1888 March 30 Age 64 Wife of William Coleman (with him) S:14

Coleman, Mary J - Died 1884 Nov 22 Born 1826 Aug 7 (with Heman 1 Coleman & others) S:18

Coleman, Mary S - Died 1855 June 26 Age 33 years, 2 months, 21

Coleman (Cont.)
days Wife of Bacon? S:21

Coleman, Mehitable - Died 1800 May 18 Age 83 years, 3 months Widow of Nathaniel Coleman S:12+12R

Coleman, Mercy - Died 1858 Sept 18 Stone says,"Mother" (next to James Coleman Possible other wife?) S:14

Coleman, Minna H - Died 1965 Born 1889 (with Nathaniel P Coleman & others) S:18

Coleman, Miriam - Died 1843 Aug 30 Age 6 months Child of Nathan & Temperance Coleman S:14

Coleman, Nathan - Died 1875 May 26 Age 75 yrs (between "Mother, Temperance Coleman & Mother, Lydia Coleman")(alleged to be the richest man in Barnstable) (information furnished by Jim Gould of Cotuit) S:14

Coleman, Nathaniel - Died 1829 Feb 8 Age 67 years, 8 or 3 months S:12+12R

Coleman, Nathaniel P - Died 1961 Born 1886 (with Heman & Clara Coleman & Minna H Coleman & others) S:18

Coleman, Patience - Died 1784 Jan 28 Wife of James Coleman (next to him, stone is broken in half) S:3R

Coleman, Patience - Died 1888 Sept 15 Born 1813 May 7 (with Abraham Coleman) S:13

Coleman, Phebe C - Died 1912 Born 1834 (with Francis M Coleman) S:14

Coleman, Reliance Mrs - Died 1742 June 11 Age 38 Wife of John Coleman S:9R

Coleman, Sarah P - Died 1820 March 1 Age 11 months Child of Nathan & Lydia Coleman S:14

Coleman, Sophia - Died 1896 Feb 28 Age 56(?) (next to husband, James Coleman) S:14

Coleman, Sophronia - Died 1809 Dec 15 Age 56 years, 4 months,

Coleman (Cont.)

23 days S:12+12R

Coleman, Temperance - Died 1874 Sept 8 Age 58 wife of Nathan Coleman S:14

Coleman, Thomas Whitman - Died 1908 March 10 Born 1883 Aug 2 (with Nathaniel P, Heman & Clara Coleman & others) S:18

Coleman, William - Died 1873 Mar 4 Age 59 years, 5 months (with Martha J Coleman, wife) S:14

Coleman, William A - Died 1951 Born 1886 (with William F Coleman) S:14

Coleman, William F - Died 1938 Born 1857 (with Ellen L Coleman) S:14

Collier, John N (Rev) - Died 1871 Feb 11 at Auburndale, Age 39 S:13

Collins, (infant) - Died (possibly) 1840 May 25 (buried with mother, Maria O Collin) Father was Camaliel (?) Collins S:7

Collins, Alphonso E - Died 1958 July Born 1896 (modern flat stone on ground level already buried by dirt & grass) (he was in 212 Engineers during World War I, flag at grave, plaque says, 1917-18, he is listed on two stones) S:11

Collins, Anna B - Died 1950 Born 1888 (with parents, Virgil Collins & Martha Fuller) S:14

Collins, Benajah - Died 1878 March 6 Age 85 years, 4 months, 15 days Stone says, "Father" (next to wife, Rebecca Collins) S:14

Collins, Charles N - Died 1958 Born 1866 (with wife, Irene Braley & his parents, Virgil Collins & Martha Fuller) S:14

Collins, Clara N - Died 1970 Born 1872 (with parents, Virgil Collins & Martha Fuller) S:14

Collins, Elizabeth A - Died 1935 Born 1855 (with husband, Howard A Dottridge) S:14

Collins, G Elliot - Died 1936 Born

Collins (Cont.)

1914 (with Virgil Collins & Martha Fuller) S:14

Collins, John - Died 1939 Born 1884 S:18

Collins, Maria O - Died 1840 May 25 Age 23 (infant child buried with her) Wife of Camaliel (?) Collins S:7

Collins, Marion G - Died 1973 Sept 1 Born 1900 Jan 8 From Massachusetts, was a Y2 in US Navy during World War I (next to William F Collins) S:16

Collins, Marion H - Died 1978 Born 1896 (with Seth Collins) S:14

Collins, Marion W - Died 1926 Born 1904 (with Virgil Collins & Martha Fuller & Elliot Collins) S:14

Collins, Rebecca - Died 1876 Sept 5 Age 86 years, 8 days Stone says,"Mother" Wife of Benajah Collins (next to him) S:14

Collins, Seth - Died 1961 Born 1896 (with Marion H Collins) S:14

Collins, Virgil B - Died 1875 Born 1830 (with wife, Martha A Fuller) S:14

Collins, William F - Died 1958 Nov 30 Born 1892 May 4 From Massachusetts, was 1st Lt, Agd Res during World War I (next to Marion G Collins) S:16

Colliton, Hugh F Jr - Died 1983 Born 1899 S:15

Collo, John - Died 1765 March 15 in his 60th yr S:9R+26R

Colman, Bethiah - Died 1815 July 17 in her 72nd yr Wife of Ebenezer Colman S:3

Colman, Patience - Died 1784 Jan 28 in her 81st yr Wife of James Colman S:3

Colman, Reliance - Died 1749 June 11 Wife of John Colman S:9

Conant, Charles H - Died (stone not clear) Born 1842 Nov 11 S:5

Conant, Helen P - Died (still living in 1991?) Born 1907 (listed with Roger F Conant) S:13

Conant, Lydia - Died (stone not clear)(Hinckley Ceme records #5R say death was 1889 April 22, born 1810 March 10) Wife of John Conant S:5

Conant, Roger F - Died 1989 Born 1908 (with Helen P Conant) S:13

Conant, Sarah Mrs - Died 1754 Mar 16 Age 97 Wife of George Conant (Hinckley ceme records say that she was only 27 years old?) S:5

Conant, Susanna - Died 1736 Nov 7 in her 37th yr Wife of George Conant S:5

Condinho, Hortense - Died 1953 Born 1887 Wife of Joseph Condinho (with him) S:16

Condinho, Joseph - Died 1937 Born 1883 (with wife, Hortense Condinho) S:16

Congdon, Sarah G - Died 1928 Born 1850 (with Etta D Robinson & others) S:18

Conger, Edward B - Died 1991 Born 1903 (with Helen W Conger) S:20

Conger, Helen W - Died (still living 1991?) Born 1906 (listed with Edward B Conger) S:20

Conkling, Gunhild W - Died 1986 Born 1900 (with Warren & Milton Conkling) S:20

Conkling, Milton W - Died 1967 May 3 Born 1895 Nov 27? (has 2 stones) From Massachusetts, was a PFC in US Army during World War I (with Warren & Gunhild Conkling) S:20

Conkling, Warren B - Died 1961 Born 1869 (with Gunhild & Milton Conkling) S:20

Connell, Alice F - Died 1979 Born 1896 Stone says, "Mother" (with George T Connell) S:15

Connell, George T - Died 1965 Born 1893 Stone says, "Father" (with Alice F Connell) S:15

Connell, Muriel J - Buried 1984 Feb 29 Age 84 S:15R

Conners, Herbert A - Died 1971 Jan 19 Born 1883 Feb 25 From

Conners (Cont.)
Massachusetts, was 1st Lieutenant Air Service during World War I S:14

Conney, Thomas J - Died 1978 May 28 Born 1900 Dec 8 S:15

Connolly, Mary F - Died 1964 Born 1888 (with Peter F Connolly) S:16

Connolly, Peter F - Died 1958 Born 1883 (with Mary F Connolly) S:16

Connor (Conner), Briah K - Died 1987 Born 1904 Was 1st Lieutenant in US Army during World War II (flag at stone) S:11

Connor, Briah A - Died 1958 Born 1875 (in Connor plot with others) S:11

Conroy, Gertrude M - Died 1990 Born 1897 (with Joseph W Conroy) S:16

Conroy, Joseph W - Died 1976 Born 1898 (with Gertrude M Conroy) S:16

Conway, Helen F - Died 1982 Born 1933 (next to John C Conway) S:19

Conway, John C - Died 1981 Born 1928 (next to Helen F Conway) S:19

Coogins, Abbie F - Died 1890 July 28 Born 1855 Aug 21 Stone says,"Mother" S:18

Coogins, Clinton B - Died 1914 Born 1848 (a sailors anchor on stone) (with Rosella & Clinton Coogins) S:18

Coogins, Clinton H - Died 1916 Born 1872 (with Clinton B & Rosella Coogins) S:18

Coogins, Rosella P - Died 1923 Born 1850 (with Clinton B & Clinton H Coogins) S:18

Cook, Benjamin - Died 1938 Born 1880 (a rock marker) (with Valina B Cook) S:18

Cook, Edward B - Died 1954 Jan 2 Born 1884 July 30 S:31

Cook, Florence B - Died 1969 Born 1888 (with Clarence L Bearse) S:18

Cook, Herbert E - Died 1961 Born 1875 (with Lillian S Cook) S:17

Cook, John - Died 1824 in his 31st yr (stone says, "Father") (listed on stone with Sally Cook) He was lost in US Ship, Hornet in war of 1812 (veteran star at grave) S:8

Cook, Joseph W - Died 1922 Born 1854 (with Mary A Cook) S:18

Cook, Lillian S - Died 1962 Born 1881 (with Herbert E Cook) S:17

Cook, Malvina - Died 1853 May 10 Born 1836 June 11 (with Ansel Adams & others) S:14

Cook, Mary A - Died 1936 Born 1857 (with Joseph W Cook) S:18

Cook, Sally - Died 1869 Mar 29 in her 80th yr (stone says "Mother") (John Cook listed on her stone, he died at sea in 1812) S:8

Cook, Valina B - Died 1987 Born 1885 (a rock marker) (with Ben Cook) S:18

Cook, William E - Died 1886 April 4 Age 44 years, 15 days Served on board the USS Sacramento (next to Willie C Cook) S:21

Cook, Willie C - Died 1898 March 27 Born 1880 Aug 20 (stone off base) (next to William E Cook) S:21

Coolidge, Ada A - Died 1888 Mar 22 Born 1856 Mar 2 (with Ensign & Ruth Nickerson) S:14

Coolidge, Angeline M - Died 1893 Aug 22 Age 50 years, 11 months Wife of Charles S Coolidge S:14

Coombs, Caroline - Died 183? Jan 31 Born 1827 Sept 21 (with Franklin Coombs) S:8

Coombs, Emily - Died 1864 July 3 Born 1824 Dec 19 With of Edward Coombs Stone says, "At evening time shall be ?(not clear)" S:8

Coombs, Eunice Ames - Died 1902 Oct 23 in Natich, Mass Born 1825 Oct 12 in West Natick, Mass Wife of Edwin Coombs S:8

Coombs, Franklin - Died 1826 Aug 9 (stone not clear) Born July 31

Coombs (Cont.) (with Caroline Coombs) S:8

Coombs, Henry C - Died 1861 Aug 16 Born 1820 Mar 11 (Mason sign on stone) S:8

Coombs, Henry P - Died 1966 May 3 Born 1892 Sept 10 (flat metal plaque marker) From Massachusetts, was an F2 in USNRF during World War I S:21

Coombs, Herbert E - Died 1965 Aug 8 Born 1911 June 18 Was a Sargeant in Massachusetts 580 Field Artilery during World War II S:13

Coombs, Isabella - Died 1880 Oct 14 Born 1828 Sept 18 (name listed with her is Ranres?) (wife of Capt Henry Coombs) S:8

Coombs, Jessie - Died 1885 July 22 Born 1871 April 16 Daughter of Edwin & Eunice Coombs S:8

Coombs, Mary - Died 1828 Sept 30 Born 1821 May 11 (with Nelson Coombs) S:8

Coombs, Nathan? (Sr) - Died 1838 Oct 26 Born 1790 Oct 17 (with Mary Coombs & others) S:8

Coombs, Nellie G - Died (not clear) May Born Sept (buried next to Jessie Coombs) S:8

Coombs, Nelson - Died 182? Oct Born 1822 Aug (stone worn) (buried with Mary Coombs) S:8

Coombs, Sally Shuttleworth - Died 1978 Born 1917 (with Walter Shuttleworth Jr & Sr & Bridget Walls) S:31

Coombs, Sarah - Died 1861 Oct 1 Born 1832 Jan 19 Wife of Edward Coombs Stone says, "He leadth me besides the still water" S:8

Coombs, Simeon Rev - Died 1819 Nov 14 in his 60th yr Died 33 years of his ministry S:4

Coombs, Susie T - Died 1911 Born 1856 Stone says, "Mother" S:21

Coon, Etta L - Died 1834 Born 1861 I am going to sleep (with James Coon & Lorenzo E Coon) S:14

Coon, James - Died 1870 Born 1818 Drowned off Cape Henlopen, Delaware while attempting to reach shore from the wreck of the Schooner, JE Simmons A Loving father & brother (listed with Etta L Coon & Lorenzo E Coon Lorenzo died with him) S:14

Coon, James H - Died 1967 Born 1888 (with Myra B Coon) S:14

Coon, Lorenzo E - Died 1870 Born 1859 Perished on the wreck of the Schooner, JE Simmons His body was not recovered (listed with Etta L Coon) S:14

Coon, Mary B - Died 1904 Born 1822 (possible wife of James Coon, listed with him & Etta & Lorenzo Coon) Stone says, "A devoted wife & mother" S:14

Coon, Myra B - Died (sill living 1991?) Born 1898 (listed with James H Coon) S:14

Cooper, Benedict A - Died 1988 Born 1896 S:15

Cooper, Margaret J - Died 1987 Born 1893 Was a Nurse in US Army during World War I S:14

Coots, Ray (H?) - Died 1982 Born 1936 (next to Scott (C?) Coots) S:12

Coots, Scott (C?) - Died 1985 Born 1964 Stone says,"Here lies a loved man" (next to Ray (H?) Coots) S:12

Copelakis, Alex N - Died 1976 Born 1897 (with Constance Copelakis) S:15

Copelakis, Constance - Died (still living 1991?) Born 1910 (listed with Alex N Copelakis) S:15

Copeland, (infant) - Died (under ground) Son of Jason & Rebecca Copeland (next to father) S:21

Copeland, Georgie Gay - Died 1879 Feb 5 Age 14 Son of Jewett & Georgiana Copeland (next to brother, Winthrop Copeland) S:18

Copeland, Jason - Died 1831 or 18?4 Nov 12 Age 46 (stone badly

Copeland (Cont.) worn) (next to wife, Rebecca Copeland) S:21

Copeland, Jewett - Died 1874 Sept 2 Age 35 (stone down, nearly buried) (one stone away from children, Winthrop & Georgie Copeland & next to Alexander H Hallett who is in between them) S:18

Copeland, Rebecca - Died 1876 July 17 Age 74 years, 8 months Wife of Jason Copeland (next to him) S:21

Copeland, Richard B - Died 1875 July 10 Age 47 (with Rebecca N White) S:18

Copeland, Winthrop J - Died 1884 Sept 15 Age 15 years, 2 months Son of Jewett & Georgiana Copeland (next to brother, Georgie Copeland) S:18

Copithorn, Webster F - Died 1966 Born 1833 S:16

Corbell, John F - Died 1990 Feb 19 Born 1900 June 16 Was EM3 US Navy during World War I S:15

Corcoran, Robert - Died 1967 Born 1899 S:16

Cordeiro, Mary J - Died 1985 Born 1897 S:16

Cormier, Blanche L - Died 1963 Born 1896 (next to Frank Cormier) S:13

Cormier, Emily Marie - Died 1975 Dec 9 Born 1893 Sept 21 Wife of Thelex Cormier (with him) S:16

Cormier, Frank - Died 1972 March 19 Born 1893 May 26 From Massachusetts and was a Private in TRP 1, 14th Cavalry during World War 1 (next to Blanche L Cormier) S:13

Cormier, Thelex F - Died 1960 May 6 Born 1891 Aug 14 (with wife, Emily Marie Cormier) S:16

Cornell, Ethel L (Phd) - Died 1963 Born 1892 Stone says,"Educator, Author, Pioneer, Diplomate in Clinical Psychology Distinguished Teacher & Friend of Children (between Judith & Vera

Cornell (Cont.)
Norton) S:19

Cornevaux, Justin E - Died 1945 Born 1855 S:16

Cornish, Aaron S - Died 1902 Born 1848 (marker is a large rock) S:12

Cornish, Adeline - Died 1846 June 16 Age 29 years, 3 months, 19 days Wife of James Cornish (buried next to him & Eliza, another wife of his) S:8

Cornish, David H - Died 1983 Jan 22 Born 1896 Sept 10 S:17

Cornish, Eliza - Died 1883 May 29 Age 63 years, 5 months, 18 days Wife of James Cornish (Buried next to him) S:8

Cornish, Elizabeth Constance - Died 1907 Nov 22 Born 1893 Mar 5 Daughter of John B & Susan Cornish S:8

Cornish, Ellis G - Died 1955 Born 1868 (with wife, Mary A Sears & others) S:19

Cornish, James - Died 1891 Feb 1 Age 77 years, 10 months (stone says - At Rest) (buried next to wife, Eliza) S:8

Cornish, John Beals - Died 1919 Aug 29 Born 1846 July 11 (buried with Elizabeth Constance Cornish) S:8

Cornish, John Jervis - Died 1959 Born 1871 (large cross stone) Buried with wife, Maude Brayton Cornish S:8

Cornish, Julia A - Died 1913 Born 1832 Wife of Capt Joseph Hinckley (buried with him & Eliza S Hinckley) S:8

Cornish, Maude Brayton - Died 1962 Born 1874 (buried with other family members with later dates) S:8

Cornish, Ruth L - Died (no dates) Wife of William Poers (listed with him & Mary Sears & Ellis G Cornish) S:19

Cornish, Susan Jane - Died 1935 May 10 Born 1850 Oct 13 (buried with John Beals Cornish)

Cornish (Cont.)
S:8

Cornwell, Henry W - Died 1851 Sept 8 Age 1 year, 1 month, 4 days Son of William & Augusta Cornwell S:2

Correia, Dominga J - Died 1939 Born 1867 S:16

Costa, June - Died 1974 Born 1928 (listed with mother, Ethel Pina) S:16

Cotell, Bridget M - Died 1959 Born 1882 (with Clarence Y Cotell) S:16

Cotell, Clarence Y - Died 1956 Born 1885 (with Bridget M Cotell) S:16

Cotell, Nettie E - Died 1932 Born 1879 (has 2 stones) (with Harris Cotell) S:18

Cottele, Deborah Mrs - Died 1793 Oct 8 in her 34th yr Wife of Peter Cottele S:5

Cotell, Harris - Died 1948 Born 1872 (with Nettie E Cotell) S:18

Cotter, John J - Died 1960 Born 1886 (next to Mary C Cotter) S:14

Cotter, Mary C - Died 1962 Born 1896 (next to John J Cotter) S:14

Cottrell, Clarence A - Died 1948 Born 1874 S:14

Cottrell, Sarah E - Died (no dates) Burial location is section 7, lot 14, grave 1 S:14R

Coughlin, Mildred - Died 1982 Born 1900 S:16

Cousins, Minerva N - Died (still living in 1991?) Born 1899 Wife of Russell Cousins (listed with him) S:12

Cousins, Russell L - Died 1948 Born 1896 (next to Minerva N Cousins) S:12

Coute, Jilda F - Died 1988 Born 1910 (next to Manuel J Coute) S:11

Coute, John - Died 1932 Born 1928 (old worn stone with metal plaque on it) S:31

Coute, Manuel J - Died 1989 Born

Coute (Cont.)

1911 Was in US Navy in World War II (next to Jilda F Coute) S:11

Cova, Mary - Died 1974 Born 1898 S:17

Covell, Edward B - Died 1958 Born 1880 (with Dorothy C Story) S:16

Covell, Evelyn M - Died 1913 Born 1907 S:20

Coveney, Effie M - Died 1971 June 6 Born 1893 April 14 Stone says, "Best mom & nana" S:15

Coville, Arthur M - Died 1939 Born 1858 (with wifes, Katharine Hawes & Hannah Baxter) S:19

Coville, Elsie O - Died 1981 Born 1889 Wife of Lester Coville (next to him & with Manya A Coville) S:19

Coville, Lester - Died 1962 Born 1887 (with Richard Coville & next to wife, Elsie O Coville) S:19

Coville, Manya A - Died (still living 1991?) Born 1914 Wife of Richard Coville (next to him & with Elsie Coville) S:19

Coville, Richard P - Died 1986 Born 1911 (has two stones) Was Staff Sargeant in US Army during World War II (with Lester Coville) S:19

Cowell, Abbie L - Died 1901 Feb 28 Age 50 (with Henry A Cowell) S:12

Cowell, Henry A - Died 1888 Oct 13 Age 48 (with Abbie L Cowell) S:12

Cox, Irving Knapp - Died 1971 Nov 3 Born 1899 April 12 From Wisconsin & was a PVT in US Army during World War I S:15

Cox, Marjorie L - Died (no dates) Born 1900 (next to Thomas M Cox) S:18

Cox, Thomas M - Died 1937 Jan 15 Born 1886 Sept 5 From Massachusetts, was Corp in 401 Tel Bn(war not listed) (next to Marjorie L Cox) S:18

Coyle, Charles A - Died 1979 Born

Coyle (Cont.)

1897 Was in the US Navy S:15

Craddock, Kevin J - Died 1991 Born 1951 (undertaker plaque) S:20

Craig, William D - Died 1973 Dec 20 Born 1897 June 22 Was Ensign in USNRF during World War I S:15

Cram, Albina A - Died 1913 March 27 Born 1835 Oct 16 S:13

Crane, Catherine F - Died 1991 Feb 18 at Westwood, Massachusetts Born 1907 Dec 26 (With Cornelius Miller Trowbridge Jr) S:20

Cranmer, Evelyn A - Died 1986 Born 1913 (with James T Cranmer) S:11

Cranmer, James T - Died 1980 Born 1911 (with Evelyn A Cranmer) S:11

Craven, Isaac - Died 1941 Aug 8 Born 1866 April 17 (With Hattie A Jones) S:11

Crawford, Ann C - Died 1970 Born 1889 (next to husband, Frederick S McLane) S:15

Crawford, Audrey Bowles - Died 1971 Nov 22 Born 1908 June 29 (listed with Frederick Coolidge Crawford) S:15

Crawford, Calvin D - Died 1964 Born 1889 (with Nita M Crawford) S:14

Crawford, Etta M - Died 1964 Born 1888 S:14

Crawford, Frederick Coolidge - Died (still living 1991?) Born 1891 March 19 (listed with Audrey Bowles Crawford) S:15

Crawford, Mary A - Died 1902 Apr 20 Born 1830 Sept 13 Wife of Stephen H Crawford (buried with him) S:8

Crawford, Nita M - Died 1975 Born 1890 (with Calvin D Crawford) S:14

Crawford, Stephen H - Died 1902 June 7 Born 1829 Feb 15 (buried with Mary A Crawfordwife) S:8

Creighton, Lilian E - Died 1983

Creighton (Cont.)
Born 1903 (with William J
Creighton) S:16

Creighton, William J - Died 1988
Born 1900 (has 2 stones) Was in
US Navy during World War I
(with Lilian E Creighton) S:16

Croce, David N - Died 1884 Jan 6
Born 1822 July 16 (with Esther
Croce) S:11

Croce, Esther - Died 1901 Sept 3
Born 1838 July 5 (with David N
Croce) S:11

Crocer (Crocker), Ebenezer - Died
1779 May 9 in his 68th yr (buried
next to wife, Zeroias) S:7

Crocker, (Baby) Died 1871 Child
of Clarington & Rebecca E
Crocker (next to them) S:12

Crocker, (dau) - Died 1760 Dec 4
Age 3 months, 1 day Daughter of
Thomas & Mercy Crocker S:5R

Crocker, (infant) - Died 1836 Born
1835 Daughter of Walter &
Caroline Crocker S:6

Crocker, (infant) - Died 1888 Apr 4
Age 4 months Son of Oliver A &
Minnie S Crocker S:7

Crocker, ? Loring - Died 1813 Sept
22 Age 10 weeks Son of Loring &
Temperance Crocker S:10

Crocker, ary (Mary?) - Died 1777
April (stone not clear) Widow of
Lt John Crocker S:5

Crocker, ? - Died (stone is broken
& sunken into ground) (next to
David & Elizabeth Crocker) S:11

Crocker, A Howard - Died 1951
Born 1872 (with wife, Flora C
Crocker) S:18

Crocker, Abagail - Died 1844 June
2 Age 63 Born 1782 Mar 19 Wife
& relick of Deacon Shubael
Crocker (the word relick came
from the Hinckley ceme records)
S:7

Crocker, Abiah Mrs - Died 1825
June 7 in her 77th yr Relict of
Cornelius Crocker (Hinckley
Ceme records #10R say death
year was 1825) S:10+26R

Crocker, Abigail - Died 1756 Feb 7

Crocker (Cont.)
Age 25 S:5R

Crocker, Abigail - Died 1825 Aug
20 in her 81st yr Wife of Joseph
Crocker S:5

Crocker, Abigail - Died 1833 Sept
22 in her 69th yr Wife of Capt
John Crocker S:5

Crocker, Abigail - Died 1849 Mar 6
in her 76th yr Widow of Francis
Crocker S:5

Crocker, Ada S - Died 1855 Born
1855 S:5

Crocker, Addie L - Died 1880 Born
1861 S:5

Crocker, Adeline A - Died 1860
(with Benjamin & Olive Crocker)
S:14

Crocker, Alanson - Died 1855 (in
California) Born 1816 S:7

Crocker, Albert - Died 1837 June
19 Age 51 (stone covered in
heavy moss) (Hinckley Ceme
records #10R say age was 31)
S:10

Crocker, Albert - Died 1910 Born
1821 (with Rebecca Crowell
Crocker & others) S:18

Crocker, Alexander - Died 1890
Born 1842 He was a Mason
Stone says, "Husband" (next to
Lucie A Crocker Stone in back of
theirs is gone, possibly a child of
theirs?) S:18

Crocker, Alexander H - Died 1880
Mar 5 Age 25 years, 10 months,
1 day S:7

Crocker, Alfred - Died 1930 Oct 31
Born 1844 Nov 3 He lived in a
house by the side of the road
and was a friend to man S:10

Crocker, Alice - Died 1810 May 25
Age 5 years, 11 months Daugh-
ter of Loring & Temperance
Crocker S:10

Crocker, Alice - Died 1827 Dec 4 in
her 33rd yr Widow of George
Crocker S:5

Crocker, Alice - Died 1829 Feb 5
Age 54 Wife of Loring Crocker
(next to him) S:10

Crocker, Alice - Died 1836 Jan 18

Crocker (Cont.)
Age 18 years,7 months Daughter
of Loring & Alice Crocker (next
to them) S:10

Crocker, Alice - Died 1933 June 9
Born 1848 April 13 S:10

Crocker, Alice M - Died 1868 Feb
26 Born 1857 Dec 15 (with Ellen
M Crocker & Nellie A Crocker &
others) (Hinckley Ceme records
#18R say death date was 1867
age 10 years, 2 months, 11 days)
S:18

Crocker, Alicia D - Died 1913 Oct 7
Born 1817 Aug 14 Wife of Eben
B Crocker S:10

Crocker, Alicia D - Died 1931 Jan
18 Born 1844 Feb 27 Daughter
of Alicia D & Eben B Crocker
S:10

Crocker, Allen - Died 1799 Dec in
his 57th yr S:5

Crocker, Alvan - Died 1829 Feb 15
Age 82 S:7

Crocker, Alvan - Died 1862 Nov 22
in his 86th yr (buried next to
wife Lucy F Crocker) S:7

Crocker, Angeline B - Died 1918
Sep 13 Age 73 years, 7 months,
15 days (next to Asa & Rebecca
Crocker) S:18

Crocker, Anna - Died 1730 or 1750
Apr 19 in her 80th yr (d1750
from Hinckley Cemerec) Wife of
Joseph Esq (buried next to
Joseph Bodfish They were born
the same year?) S:5

Crocker, Anna - Died 1810 Oct 14
Age 75 Widow of Capt Samuel
Crocker S:10

Crocker, Arthur B - Died 1878 Jan
20 Born 1794 July 29 S:6

Crocker, Arthur Bixby - Died 1894
Born 1883 (with Elizabeth E
Crocker & others) S:18

Crocker, Arthur W - Died 1852 Feb
19 Age 45 (next to wife, Mary I
Crocker) S:14

Crocker, Asa - Died 1774 Nov 15
Age 33 in Boston (listed with
Thankful Crocker) S:10R

Crocker, Asa - Died 1824 July 21

Crocker (Cont.)
Age 15 months, 10 days Son of
Lot & Betsey Crocker S:4

Crocker, Asa Mrs - Died 1822 April
17 in her 47th yr S:10+26R

Crocker, Asa S - Died 1888 Oct 20
Age 82 years, 8 months, 10 days
(next to wife, Rebecca K Crocker)
S:18

Crocker, Augusta - Died 1888 Born
1838 (with Louisa Crocker &
others) S:18

Crocker, Augusta H - Died 1922
Born 1838 (with Eloise H Crocker & others) S:18

Crocker, Augustus - Died 1835
Aug 20 Age 23 months Born
1831 Sept 18 Son of William &
Sarah H Crocker (Written on
slate to the memory of Mehitable
H Crocker) S:5

Crocker, Augustus - Died 1867
April 13 Age 57 S:10

Crocker, Aurin B - Died 1926 Born
1832 (with Sarah C Crocker &
others) S:18

Crocker, Barnabas - Died 1847 Feb
4 in his 66th yr S:5

Crocker, Bathsheba - Died (Date
not clear) Widow of Benjamin
Crocker (buried next to him) S:7

Crocker, Bathsheba - Died 1808
located in row 10 S:11R

Crocker, Benjamin - Died 1827 Feb
(Day not clear on stone) Age 85
years, 6 months S:7

Crocker, Benjamin - Died 18?? Dec
9 (stone not clear buried next to
Benjamin & Bathsheba Crocker
His parents?) S:7

Crocker, Benjamin (Capt) - Died
1757 June 20 Age 62 S:5R

Crocker, Benjamin F - Died 1865
Born 1780 (with Temperance H
Crocker) S:13

Crocker, Benjamin Franklin - Died
1906 Feb 5 Born 1822 June 17
(with Caroline Pulsifer Crocker)
S:18

Crocker, Benjamin Sampson - Died
1929 Born 1855 (with Olive Rice
Jenks Crocker) S:14

Crocker, Bertha - Died 1947 Aug 15 Born 1867 March 13 (with Willard Crafts Crocker MD & others) S:18

Crocker, Bethiah - Died 1829 Dec 7 in her 49th yr Wife of Moses Crocker (buried next to him) S:5

Crocker, Bethsheba - Died 1803 Nov Age 69 Widow of Daniel Crocker (next to him) (Hinckley Ceme records #11R say death date was Nov 2 age 62) S:11

Crocker, Bethuel - Died 1853 Sept 13 Age 60 years, 11 months, 24 days (buried next to wife, Nancy E Crocker) S:7

Crocker, Betsey - Died (date not clear) Daughter of Heman & Elisa Crocker S:7

Crocker, Betsey - Died 1839 Mar 2 in her 47th yr Wife of Lot Crocker S:4

Crocker, Betsey - Died 1843 Sept 27 Age 34 years, 11 months, 24 days Widow of Timothy Crocker S:4

Crocker, Betsey C - Died 1895 Feb 22 Born 1810 May 22 Wife of Wilson Crocker (buried next to him) S:7

Crocker, Braddock - Died 1841 March 6 Age 58 (next to Holmes Crocker) S:14

Crocker, Braddock W (Capt) - Died Age 38 Lost at sea in 1861 (on same stone with Emily A Lovell & others) Born 1884 S:12

Crocker, Bridgham - Died 1853 May 8 in his 53rd yr (buried next to son, Henry & wife Sophia) S:5

Crocker, Bursley - Died 1838 Sept 20 in his 84th yr S:7

Crocker, Calvin, (Capt) - Died 1840 Nov 28 in his 78th yr (buried next to Eunice Crocker-wife) S:5

Crocker, Caroline - Died 1941 May 27 Born 1852 May 19 Daughter of Alicia D & Eben B Crocker S:10

Crocker, Caroline J - Died 1885 Oct 11 Age 83 years, 8 months

Crocker (Cont.)
Wife of Walter Crocker S:6

Crocker, Caroline M - Died 1878 Born 1825 S:6

Crocker, Caroline Pulsifer - Died 1922 June 4 Born 1829 Dec 14 (with Ella Pulsifer Crocker) S:18

Crocker, Carrie C - Died 1860 March 21 Age 24 years, 6 months Wife of Melatiah B Crocker (another one)(next to him) S:14

Crocker, Catherine L - Died 1915 Born 1851 (with Mary A Crocker & others) S:18

Crocker, Charles - Died 1812 Mar 5 in his 39th yr S:5

Crocker, Charles C - Died 1922 Born 1831 (with Priscilla H Crocker & others) S:18

Crocker, Charles E - Died 1867 Born 1860 (with Gilbert & Phebe & Louise C Crocker & others) S:14

Crocker, Charles F - Died 1897 Jan 13 Born 1832 April 28 (next to Arthur W Crocker) S:14

Crocker, Charles J - Died 1864 May 27 Age 1 year, 3 months, 12 days Son of Josiah & Pamelia A Crocker S:5R

Crocker, Charles W - Died 1907 Born 1847 (with Emily M Crocker) S:18

Crocker, Charlotte Howes - Died 1902 Born 1834 (on same stone with Daniel Chipman Crocker) S:10

Crocker, Chauncey B - Died 1967 May 22 Born 1907 April 13 S:13

Crocker, Chloe P - Died 1835 (month & day not clear) Age 3 days S:7

Crocker, Clara R - Died 1856 Born 1856 (with Lott Crocker & others) S:18

Crocker, Clarington - Died 1914 Born 1840 (either son or husband of Rebecca E Crocker) S:12

Crocker, Cloe - Died 1776 Age 3 months, 1 day Daughter of Thomas & Mercy Crocker S:5

Crocker, Cornelius - Died 1784 Dec 12 in his 81st yr S: 10R+26R

Crocker, Cornelius - Died 1789 Sept 13 in his 50th yr S: 10R+ 26R

Crocker, Cornelius - Died May 7 (stone worn) (buried between Josiah & Elizabeth Crocker) S: 10

Crocker, Cyruss - Died 1845 Nov 11 Age 21 years, 7 months Son of Ezekiel & Deborah Crocker S: 7

Crocker, Damaris - Died 1825 Jan 11 in her 32nd yr Wife of Watson Crocker S: 5

Crocker, Daniel - Died 1811 April 22 (on same stone with Josiah Crocker) (Hinckley Ceme records #10R say he died in his 50th yr) S: 10+26R

Crocker, Daniel - Died 1833 June 27 in New York in his 33rd yr Son of Daniel & Sally Crocker (on same stone with mother) S: 10+26R

Crocker, Daniel (Capt) - Died 1788 Nov 12 (Hinckley Ceme records #11R says died in his 64th yr) S: 11+26R

Crocker, Daniel Chipman - Died 1908 Born 1834 (on same stone with Charlotte Howes Crocker & others) S: 10

Crocker, David - Died (stone broken laying on ground) (next to Elizabeth Crocker) S: 11

Crocker, David - Died 1734 June 28 in his 9th yr Son of David Crocker Esq (located at Lothrop's Hill) S: 26R

Crocker, David - Died 1843 Jan 29 Age 65 (in Crocker plot) S: 10

Crocker, David - Died 1875 May 29 Born 1805 Jan 24 Stone says, "Father" (next to Elizabeth C Crocker) S: 14

Crocker, David - Died 1879 May 3 Age 68 years, 2 months, 7 days S: 5

Crocker, David (Capt) - Died 1833 Sept 22 in his 48th yr S: 5

Crocker, David L - Died 1983 Dec 9 Born 1909 Nov 22 (with wife, Louise A Crocker) (Barnstable Fire Dept plaque near stone) S: 19

Crocker, David or Daniel - Died 1774 ? (stone badly worn, one other next to him worn badly, can't read) Son of Daniel (Hinckley Ceme records #11R say death date was 1734 June 28 age 94 & that he was an Esquire) S: 11

Crocker, Davis - Died (no date) located in row 6 S: 11R

Crocker, Davis - Died 1846 July 5 Age 72 S: 10

Crocker, Deborah - Died 1744 March 28 Age 23 Daughter of Benjamin & Priscilla Crocker S: 5R

Crocker, Deborah - Died 1841 Dec 28 in her 75th yr Widow of Edmund Crocker S: 5

Crocker, Deborah - Died 1843 Oct 1 Age 61 Widow of Naler Crocker Esq (next to him) S: 10

Crocker, Deborah - Died 1875 July 31 Age 83 years, 6 months Wife of Ezekiel Crocker S: 7

Crocker, Deliverance - Died 1818 Mar 27 in her 67th yr Relict of Allen Crocker S: 5

Crocker, Desire - Died 1806 Apr 7 in her 29th yr Wife of Isaac Crocker S: 7

Crocker, Dewey - Died 1890 Born 1869 (with Gilbert & Phebe Crocker & Mary Fuller & others) S: 14

Crocker, Dorcas H - Died 1868 Dec 11 Age 51 years, 1 months, 4 days Wife of Reuben Crocker Jr (next to him) S: 14

Crocker, Eben Bacon - Died 1902 Sept 21 Born 1854 April 28 (with Ella Delap Crocker) S: 10

Crocker, Ebenezer - Died 1725 Jan 21 Age 7 years (stone worn) S: 11

Crocker, Ebenezer - Died 1785 located in row 10 S: 11R

Crocker, Ebenezer - Died 1818 Feb

Crocker (Cont.)
14 Age 19 Died at St Pierre, WI,
Martinico In memory of Mrs
Abigail Crocker (most of above
info from the Hinckley Ceme
records) S:5

Crocker, Ebenezer (Esq) - Died
1817 Feb 17 in his 65th yr S:7

Crocker, Ebenezer Mr - Died 1785
Jan 1 in his 71st yr S:11R

Crocker, Edmund - Died 1813 July
24 in his 24th yr S:5

Crocker, Edmund - Died 1821 Apl
24 in his 75th yr S:5

Crocker, Edward B - Died 1929
Born 1882 (with Elizabeth M
Crocker) S:21

Crocker, Edward J - Died 1859
Born 1847 S:5

Crocker, Edward S - Died 1948
Born 1872 (with wife, Hortense
M Heller) S:12

Crocker, Eleanor - Died 1945 Born
1885 (Crocker stone with others)
S:11

Crocker, Elijah - Died 1821 Sept
27 in his 19th yr Son of Daniel
& Sally Crocker S:10+26R

Crocker, Elijah (Capt) - Died (no
date) Age 67 years With Sarah F
Crocker (same stone) (this grave
site is at street level cut into a
hill in a square plot) Another
stone located here but looks like
it was broke S:8

Crocker, Elisabath - Died 17?? Nov
23 (stone not clear) Wife of
Francis Crocker S:7

Crocker, Elisha (Capt) - Died 1817
May 15 (Hinckley Ceme records
#10R say died in his 50th yr)
S:10+26R

Crocker, Eliza - Died 1816 Apr 19
Age 4 years Daughter of Alvan &
Phebe Crocker S:7

Crocker, Eliza - Died 1830 July 30
in her 27th yr Wife of Arthur
Crocker S:6

Crocker, Eliza - Died 1902 Apr 27
in her 85th yr S:7

Crocker, Eliza A - Died 1840 April
25 Age 7 months, 6 days

Crocker (Cont.)
Daughter of Ignatius & Mehitable Crocker (with John H Crocker, brother) S:14

Crocker, Eliza A - Died 1880 Oct
17 Age 38 years, 6 months
Widow of Melatiah B Crocker
(next to him) S:14

Crocker, Eliza Ann - Died 1845
April 8 Age 27 years, 8 months
Daughter of William & Eliza
Blount S:12

Crocker, Eliza B - Died 1893 Born
1815 (with Isaiah C Crocker)
S:12

Crocker, Eliza E - Died 1831 Aug 5
Age 25 years, 10 months, 1 day
Wife of Otis R Crocker S:5R

Crocker, Elizabeth - Died 1737
located in row 6 (could be same
as Elizabeth d 1757) S:11R

Crocker, Elizabeth - Died 1737
Sept 23 in her 27th yr S:5

Crocker, Elizabeth - Died 1757 in
her 28th yr (stone is stuck in
tree trunk, cut off) Wife of Daniel
Crocker S:11

Crocker, Elizabeth - Died 1757
June 13 Wife of Samuel Crocker
S:11

Crocker, Elizabeth - Died 1818 Feb
8 Relict of Capt Joseph Crocker
(on same stone) S:10

Crocker, Elizabeth - Died 1820
May 6 Age 6 years, 8 months (in
Crocker plot) Daughter of David
& Rachel Crocker (on same
stone with Jane Crocker) S:10

Crocker, Elizabeth - Died 1832 Nov
28 Age 69 S:10

Crocker, Elizabeth - Died 1842 Aug
3 Age 70 Wife of Morton Crocker
(next to James P Crocker) S:12

Crocker, Elizabeth - Died 1849
July 4 in her 76th yr Widow of
William Crocker S:6+26R

Crocker, Elizabeth - Died 1904
Born 1817 (perpetual care for
stone) (with William Jones,
possibly husband) S:8

Crocker, Elizabeth C - Died 1897
Sept 23 Born 1826 Oct 22 Stone

Crocker (Cont.)
says, "Mother" (next to David
Crocker) S:14

Crocker, Elizabeth E - Died 1955
Born 1881 (with Capt William
Crocker & others) S:18

Crocker, Elizabeth H - Died 1865
Dec 30 Born 1839 Mar 25
Daughter of Loring & Temper-
ance Crocker S:10

Crocker, Elizabeth Jane - Died
1826 Sept 21 Age 11 months
Daughter of David & Rachel
Crocker (there is another marker
next to her & Cyrus Chamberlin,
but front is worn off) S:10

Crocker, Elizabeth M - Died 1921
Born 1881 (with Edward B
Crocker) S:21

Crocker, Elizabeth Mrs - Died 1811
Feb 5 Age 74 Relict of Capt
Joseph Crocker S:10R

Crocker, Ella Delap - Died 1937
July 11 Born 1853 June 6 (with
Eben Bacon Crocker) S:10

Crocker, Ella Pulsifer - Died 1864
April 12 Born 1862 July 6 (with
Bertha Crocker) S:18

Crocker, Ellen - Died 1838/9 Age 2
Born 1837 (1839 from Hinckley
ceme records) Daughter of Capt
William Crocker & Martha
Crocker Starbuck S:5

Crocker, Ellen A - Died 1861
March 20 Age 3 years, 2
months, 22 days Daughter of
Marcus & Ellen M Crocker S:5R

Crocker, Ellen M - Died 1908 May
2 Born 1840 Nov 22 (with
Marcus M Crocker & others)
S:18

Crocker, Elmira - Died 1838 Jan 2
Age 27 Born 1811 Feb 8 Wife of
Wilson Crocker & daughter of
Zaccheus & Sarah Hinckley S:7

Crocker, Eloise H - Died 1965 Born
1876 (with Walter F Hinckley &
others) S:18

Crocker, Emily - Died 1822 Oct 11
Age 1 year, 9 months Daughter
of Ezekiel & Deborah Crocker
S:7

Crocker, Emily D - Died 1906 Sept
19 Born 1835 May 7 (with William H Crocker) S:21

Crocker, Emily M - Died 1912 Born
1855 (with Charles W Crocker)
S:18

Crocker, Emma B - Died 1847 Apl
30 in her 31st yr S:4

Crocker, Emma H - Died 1957
Born 1873 (with Gilbert & Phebe
& Isabelle Crocker & others)
S:14

Crocker, Enoch - Died 1854 Nov 28
Age 65 years, 10 months, 2 days
S:7

Crocker, Enoch - Died 1861 (died
in the battle of Bull Run) Born
1829 S:7

Crocker, Ephraim - Died (stone not
clear) (buried between Jonathan
Crocker & Huldah Howland)
(Hinckley ceme records say he
died 7 Oct 1725 Age 2 years, 5
days & was the son of Jonathan
& Elizabeth Crocker) S:5

Crocker, Ephraim - Died 1798 May
5 Age 37 S:5R

Crocker, Erastus - Died 1831 Sept
1 Age 18 years, 5 months (died
at sea) Son of Francis & Abigail
Crocker S:5

Crocker, Esther - Died 1960 Born
1887 (with Walter I Fuller) S:12

Crocker, Eunice - Died 1813 Dec 4
in her 79th yr Widow of Capt
Calvin Crocker (Hinckley Ceme
records #5R say death year was
1843) S:5

Crocker, Eunice - Died 1972 Born
1880 (perpetual care) (next to
Frank Crocker in Crocker plot)
(small stone in back of them that
says "Baby", nothing more) S:8

Crocker, Eunice Bourn - Died 1809
Apl 27 Age 16 Daughter of Zenas
& Hannah Crocker S:7

Crocker, Eunice G - Died 1868
Born 1787 (with Ben F &
Temperance H Crocker) S:13

Crocker, Eunice Mildred - Died
1915 Born 1878 (with Mary E
Wing) S:14

Crocker, Evelyn Bassett - Died
(still living 1991?) Born 1918
(next to Willis G Crocker Jr)
(stone has a happy face with X's
in both eyes, one hair coming
from top of head and the letters,
M on both sides of the head
Stone says, "Till we meet again")
S:13

Crocker, Evelyn M - Died (still
living 1991?) Born 1918 Dec 3
Wife of Willis G Crocker Jr
d1971 (with him) S:13

Crocker, Experience - Died 1740
Feb 15 in her 67th yr S:5R

Crocker, Ezekial - Died 1835 July
10 in his 65th yr S:10

Crocker, Ezekiel Died 1812 Jan
29 Age 10 months 19 days Son
of Ezekiel & Temperance Crocker
S:10

Crocker, Ezekiel - Died 1829 Nov 5
in his 48th yr S:7

Crocker, Ezra - Died 1843 Apr 9
Age 68 S:7

Crocker, F Chessman - Died 1953
Born 1877 (next to Sarah
Robbins Crocker) S:13

Crocker, Fear - Died 1833 Sept 8
in his 74th yr Wife of Joshua
Crocker & Daughter of Rowland
Thatcher S:7

Crocker, Flora C - Died 1948 Born
1877 (with A Howard Crocker &
others) S:18

Crocker, Francis - Died 1815 Apr
24 in his 62nd yr S:5

Crocker, Francis - Died 1932 Born
1845 (next to Mary E Crocker)
S:21

Crocker, Francis Bacon - Died
1921 July 9 Born 1861 July 4
Son of Henry H & Mary A Crocker S:9

Crocker, Francis W - Died 1839
Apr 29 Age 14 years, 6 months
Son of Arthur B & Almira Crock-
er S:6

Crocker, Frank E - Died 1951 Born
1872 (with wife, Martha W
Crocker & others) S:18

Crocker, Frank Elliott - Died 1934

Crocker (Cont.)
Born 1868 (Crocker plot, raw,
natural stone) (next to Eunice
Crocker, possible wife same kind
of stone) S:8

Crocker, Franklin - Died 1830 Jan
3 Age 23 Son of Loring & Alice
Crocker (next to them & on same
stone with Mathihas Crocker)
(Hinckley Ceme records #10R
say age was 22) S:10

Crocker, Franklin - Died 1908
Born 1834 (with Augusta H
Crocker & others) S:18

Crocker, George - Died 1823 Mar
10 in his 32nd yr (next to wife
Alice) S:5

Crocker, George - Died 1855 Oct 5
Age 36 S:6

Crocker, George B - Died 1862
Born 1839 S:6

Crocker, George B - Died 1912 Nov
28 Born 1822 July 25 S:5

Crocker, George F - Died 1946
Born 1864 (with wife, Nettie
Brown Crocker & others) S:18

Crocker, George H - Died 1865
June 21 Age 41 years, 10
months S:5

Crocker, George H - Died 1895
Born 1838 Son of JB & R Crocker S:5

Crocker, Georgianna AM - Died
1875 June 10 Age 24 years, 4
months Daughter of George &
Hannah Crocker S:6

Crocker, Georgianna F - Died 1857
May 30 Age 8 years, 4 months, 8
days Daughter of Josiah &
Pamelia Crocker S:5R

Crocker, Gershom - Died 1786 Nov
26 S:5

Crocker, Gideon H - Died 1866
Sept 5 Age 41 years, 6 months
(stone is down) (next to Rebecca
H Crocker, wife of Zenas) S:14

Crocker, Gilbert F - Died 1906
Born 1825 (with Phebe A Crocker) S:14

Crocker, Gorham D - Died 1933
Nov 26 Born 1868 Jan 21 (with
Seth & Nellie Crocker & others)

Crocker (Cont.)
S:18

Crocker, Greta O - Died (still living 1991?) Born 1902 (listed with Mansfield I Crocker) S:13

Crocker, Gustavus B - Died 1833 Feb 12 Age 23 Died and intered in Trinidad de Cuba (listed with Mrs Temperance L Crocker) S:14

Crocker, Hannah - Died 1723 Jan 23 in her 33rd yr Wife of Thomas Crocker S:5

Crocker, Hannah - Died 1743 May 14 Age 85 Widow of Deacon, Job Crocker S:11

Crocker, Hannah - Died 1785 (no located noted) S:11R

Crocker, Hannah - Died 1787 Mar (day not clear) Wife of William Crocker S:5

Crocker, Hannah - Died 1801 Nov 15 Daughter of Zenas & Hannah Crocker S:7

Crocker, Hannah - Died 1829 Oct 5 Age 29 Daughter of William & Elizabeth Crocker S:6

Crocker, Hannah - Died 1831 June 3 Age 73 Widow of Davis Crocker S:10

Crocker, Hannah - Died 1833 Dec 16 in her 49th yr Relict of Charles Crocker S:5

Crocker, Hannah - Died 1833 Sept 25 in her 67th yr Widow of Zenas Crocker (buried next to him) S:7

Crocker, Hannah - Died 1839 Mar 26 in her 21st yr Wife of Jacob P Crocker S:7

Crocker, Hannah - Died 1875 Born 1788 Wife of Watson Crocker S:5R

Crocker, Hannah C - Died 1899 Born 1828 (with Clara R Crocker & others) S:18

Crocker, Hannah E - Died 1937 Born 1849 (with Benjamin & Olive Crocker) S:14

Crocker, Hannah Kent - Died 1775 Jan 9 in her 84th yr Widow of Eben Crocker & William Kent & possible wife of or daughter of

Crocker (Cont.)
(Deacon) Joseph Hall S:7

Crocker, Hannah L - Died 1837 Born 1821 First wife of Joseph W Crocker (with him & other wife) S:13

Crocker, Hannah M - Died 1858 Aug 6 Age 31 Wife of George Crocker S:6

Crocker, Hannah M - Died 1951 Born 1871 Wife of James Odell (with him & Catherine R Gleason & others) S:31

Crocker, Harriet - Died 1843 Dec 6 Born 1811 June 28 "Our sister" Daughter of Moses & Bethia Crocker S:5R

Crocker, Harriet - Died 1896 Born 1818 (with Timothy Crocker & next to Alexander Crocker) S:18

Crocker, Harry - Died (no year listed) Age 8 Son of Capt Braddock & Emily Crocker (listed on their stone) y A 12 1888 Oct 13 age 48 S:12

Crocker, Harry C - Died 1946 Born 1857 (with Blanche Emerton) S:11

Crocker, Hattie Davis - Died 1896 Nov 26 Born 1878 April 3 Daughter of Alfred & Mary Annie Crocker S:10

Crocker, Hattie Estelle - Died 1845 or 1848 April 5 Born 1862 Aug 3 (with Daniel Harvey Handy & others) (death date of 1848 from Hinckley ceme records) S:14

Crocker, Hattie W - Died 1879 Born 1871 S:5

Crocker, Hazel Wilds - Died 1976 Born 1888 Wife of Neil L Crocker (with him) S:14

Crocker, Helen (Nellie) Sarah - Died 1895 Feb 6 Born 1871 Oct 6 (next to Henry Scudder Crocker) S:12

Crocker, Helen Howard - Died 1936 Born 1850 (with Henry Ellis Crocker) S:12

Crocker, Hemand - Died 1793 Feb 26 in his 30th yr S:7

Crocker, Henry - Died 1844 Nov 13

Crocker (Cont.)

Age 18 months Son of Bridgham & Sophia Crocker (Hinckley Ceme records #5R says death year was 1845) S:5

Crocker, Henry (Harry) Scudder - Died 1889 June 27 Born 1874 Mar 28 (next to Helen Sarah Crocker) S:12

Crocker, Henry B - Died 1883 May 18 Age 12 years, 7 months Son of Frank & Mary E Crocker (next to them) S:21

Crocker, Henry C - Died 1847 Oct 26 Age 5 months (with Sylvester H Crocker) S:14

Crocker, Henry Ellis - Died 1918 Born 1848 (with Helen Howard Crocker) S:12

Crocker, Henry H - Died 1893 Jan 6 in New York Born 1820 Feb 28 (wife also died in New York, stone next to him) S:9

Crocker, Henry Horace - Died 1904 Sept 24 Born 1853 Nov 17 Son of Henry H & Mary A Crocker S:9

Crocker, Henry P (Capt) - Died 1903 Jan 5 Born 1848 Jan 20 (stone is off the base) S:12

Crocker, Hiram - Died 1917 Born 1820 (with Benjamin & Hiram Crocker) S:14

Crocker, Hodiah - Died 1812 Aug 6 Consort to Samuel Crocker & daughter to Simon Jenkins S:7

Crocker, Holmes - Died 1844 Dec 30 Age 31 (next to Braddock Crocker) S:14

Crocker, Hope - Died 1760 Dec 13 in her 99th yr S:5

Crocker, Horace - Died 1913 Born 1849 (with Abbie W Crocker & others) S:18

Crocker, Howard F - Died 1869 May 15 Age 15 years, 3 months (stone vandalized) Son of Timothy & Harriet Crocker (near them and next to brother, Judson Crocker) S:18

Crocker, Ignatius - Died 1881 Oct 17 Born 1813 June 6 Stone says,"Father" & "Gone Before"

Crocker (Cont.)

(next to wife, Mary P Crocker) S:14

Crocker, Imogene F - Died 1900 Born 1846 (with Job G Cobb & others) S:18

Crocker, Ira (Capt) - Died 1812 at Edenton, North Carolina S:10R

Crocker, Irene - Died 1853 Feb 26 Age 1 year, 4 months Born 1851 Oct 25 Daughter of Nathan & Susan D Crocker S:9R

Crocker, Irvin H - Died 1903 Born 1819 S:5

Crocker, Irving F - Died 1930 Born 1843 (with wife, Julia Crocker) S:21

Crocker, Isaac - Died 1832 Jan 19 Age 85 years, 11 months S:7

Crocker, Isabelle - Died 1945 Born 1876 (with Gilbert & Phebe & Emma H Crocker & others) S:14

Crocker, Isadore M - Died 1901 Born 1863 S:5

Crocker, Isaiah C - Died 1892 Born 1813 (with Eliza B Crocker) S:12

Crocker, Israel - Died 1918 Born 1832 (with Martha W Crocker & others) S:12

Crocker, James - Died 1795 Dec 25 Son of Ephriam & Mercy Crocker S:5

Crocker, James B - Died (stone not clear) July Son of Joseph & Joanne Crocker (Hinckley Ceme records #11R say death was 1803 July 15 Age 4 months, 6 days) S:11

Crocker, James B - Died 1836 Oct 24 (3 weeks old) Son of James B & Thankful D Crocker S:6

Crocker, James D - Died 1876 Feb 16 Age 63 S:10

Crocker, James G - Died 1864 Sept 13 Age 28 Listed in the US Navy S:5

Crocker, James P - Died 1814 Nov 16 in his 23rd yr S:12+12R

Crocker, Jane - Died (stone not clear and broken in half, possibly dated 1700's) Wife of Thomas Crocker (next to Capt Thomas

Crocker (Cont.)

Crocker) (Hinckley Ceme records #10R say death was 1795 July 5 in her 47th yr) S:10+26R

Crocker, Jane - Died 1810 Dec 6 Age 7 weeks (in Crocker plot) Daughter of David & Rachel Crocker (with Elizabeth Crocker) S:10

Crocker, Jemima Miss - Died 1833 Feb 23 Age 63 Daughter of Isaac & Lydia Crocker S:7

Crocker, Jennie - Died 1875 Born 1844 S:5

Crocker, Joanna - Died 1831 Dec 15 in her 58th yr Wife of Joseph Crocker S:6+26R

Crocker, Joanna - Died 1861 Jan 20 in her 73rd yr Widow of Barnabas Crocker S:5

Crocker, Joanne - Died 1807 April 21 Age 8 months, 27 days Daughter of Joseph & Joanne Crocker S:11

Crocker, Job - Died 1731 May 21 in his 38th yr "Virtuous and much lamented" S:11R+26R

Crocker, Job (Deacon) - Died 1718 Mar 20 in his 75th yr (stone next to him is worn down, cannot read it) He was Deacon of Church of Christ in Barnstable, served 34 years (Hinckley Ceme records #11R say death year 1718) S:11+26R

Crocker, Johanna - Died 1728/9 Jan 23 Age 53 Wife of Thomas Crocker S:5R

Crocker, Johanna - Died 1732 Aug 4 Wife of Seth Crocker S:5

Crocker, John - Died 1736 Dec 23 in his 73rd yr S:5

Crocker, John - Died 1775 (no location noted) S:11R

Crocker, John - Died 1790 Feb 1 in his 81st yr S:5

Crocker, John - Died 1865 Born 1791 S:5

Crocker, John (Capt) - Died 1802 Aug 19 in his 55th yr S:5

Crocker, John (Capt) - Died 1807 Aug 4 Age 53 S:5R

Crocker, John (Deacon) - Died 1773 Feb 7 Age 89 yrs 11 mos S:11+26R

Crocker, John G - Died 1883 Born 1811 (with Mary A Crocker & others) S:18

Crocker, John H - Died 1841 June 17 Age 14 months, 8 days Son of Ignatius & Mehitable Crocker (with sister, Eliza A Crocker) S:14

Crocker, John Howland - Died (still living 1991?) Born 1914 (stone is a rock, he was a Mason) (with Mary Hinckley & C Stuart Hinckley) S:20

Crocker, John Lt - Died 1776 (stone not clear) (buried next to Mary Crocker - wife) (Hinckley Ceme records #5R says death was 14 June age 56) S:5

Crocker, Jonah - Died 172? Feb 23 (stone not clear) Age 28 S:5

Crocker, Jonathan - Died 1746 Aug 24 in his 84th yr S:5

Crocker, Jonathan - Died 1885 Jan 15 at Bridgewater, Mass Age 77 years, 11 months (stone is leaning) (next to wife, Lydia Crocker) S:19

Crocker, Jonathan (Deacon) - Died 1796 Dec 4 in his 65th yr (died same year as wife with small pox buried next to her) S:6+26R

Crocker, Joseph - Died 1728/9 Feb 23 Age 28 S:5R

Crocker, Joseph - Died 1741 Apr 7 in his 24th yr S:5

Crocker, Joseph - Died 1824 July 24 Age 11 months Son of David & Lydia Crocker S:5

Crocker, Joseph - Died 1826 Mar 12 in his 85th yr S:5

Crocker, Joseph - Died 1858 Feb 7 Age 88 Born 1770 S:6

Crocker, Joseph (Capt) - Died 1764 Aug 25 Age 29 at New Foundland (with Elizabeth Crocker) S:10

Crocker, Joseph (Deacon) - Died 1825 July 3 in his 78th yr (buried next to wife, Mary) S:7

Crocker, Joseph Esq - Died 1741 Jan 12 Age 74 S:5R

Crocker, Joseph W - Died 1885 Born 1812 (with John York & others in York plot on street) S:13

Crocker, Josiah - Died 1784 May 4 in his 36th yr Bachelor of Arts of Harvard College (located at Cobb Hill East Cemetery) (Goodspeed or Meeting House Hill East) S:26R

Crocker, Josiah - Died 1807 Aug 13 in New Orleans Age 26 (on same stone with Daniel Crocker) S:10

Crocker, Josiah - Died 1868 Born 1823 S:5

Crocker, Josiah Dr - Died 1834 Jan 1 Age 38 S:5

Crocker, Judson - Died 1873 Nov 20 Age 27 years, 10 months (stone vandalized) Son of Timothy & Harriet Crocker (near them) S:18

Crocker, Julia - Died 1842 Sept 16 Age 32 Wife of David Crocker (next to him) Stone says "An affectionate & devoted wife & mother" S:14

Crocker, Julia - Died 1903 Oct 6 Born 1870 Dec 31 (stone ready to fall over) Stone says "She brought life, light and joy to loving hearts" Daughter of William L & Ellen T Gage (near them) S:18

Crocker, Julia - Died 1924 Born 1847 Wife of Irving F Crocker (with him) S:21

Crocker, Julia Maria - Died 1862 Oct 22 in her 27th yr Wife of Edmund Crocker S:5

Crocker, Katharine - Died 1824 Aug 5 in her 85th yr Widow of Nathaniel Crocker S:5

Crocker, Lizzie (Hinckley) - Died 1951 Born 1872 Wife of Heman P Hinckley S:11

Crocker, Lois - Died 1808 Jan 19 Age 21 Wife of Lot Crocker S:5R

Crocker, Lois C - Died 1885 Sept

Crocker (Cont.)
22 Age 26 years, 8 months, 4 days Wife of Oliver Crocker S:7

Crocker, Lola W - Died 1988 Born 1895 Daughter of Frank & Martha Crocker (with them & Alva A Brackley) S:18

Crocker, Loring - Died 1841 Mar 21 Age 67 S:10

Crocker, Loring - Died 1887 Mar 6 Born 1809 Aug 16 S:10

Crocker, Loring - Died 1924 May 1 Born 1853 Jan 17 S:10

Crocker, Lot - Died 1934 Born 1861 He was a Mason (with Miriam S Crocker & wife, Marian MacLeod & others) S:18

Crocker, Lot Dea - Died 1856 Aug 15 Born 1782 Sept 13 S:4

Crocker, Lot Gage (Capt) - Died 1822 Sept Age 31 years, 5 months S:5

Crocker, Lot N - Died 1914 Born 1848 S:5

Crocker, Lott - Died 1860 Sept 30 Age 2 years, 10 months (stone is pulled up & located near church with another stone that says mother which may not be related to the above) Son of Aurin B & Sarah Crocker S:21

Crocker, Lott - Died 1860 Born 1857 (with Hannah C Crocker & others) S:18

Crocker, Louis - Died 1808 Jan 19 in her 21st yr Wife of Lot Crocker S:5

Crocker, Louisa - Died 1844 Jan 1 Age 18 months, 10 days Daughter of Lot & Betsey Crocker S:4

Crocker, Louisa - Died 1918 Born 1844 (with Sylvanus Alexander & others) S:18

Crocker, Louise A - Died (still living 1991?) Born 1915 July 21 Wife of David L Crocker (with him) S:19

Crocker, Louise C - Died 1867 Born 1863 (with Gilbert & Phebe & Dewey Crocker) S:14

Crocker, Lucie A - Died 1900 Born 1842 Stone says, "Wife" (next to

Crocker (Cont.)
Alexander Crocker, also stone in back of theirs is missing, possibly a child?) S:18

Crocker, Lucretia - Died 1799 Sept 15 Age 22 Wife of Naler Crocker S:10R

Crocker, Lucretia - Died 1807 Sept 12 Age 16 months Daughter of Naler & Deborah Crocker S:10

Crocker, Lucy - Died 1825 Nov 26 Age 16 months, 11 days Daughter of Timothy & Betsey Crocker S:4

Crocker, Lucy - Died 1885 Oct 3 Age 82 years, 4 months, 10 days S:5

Crocker, Lucy F - Died 1872 Oct 17 Age 79 years, 7 months Widow of Alvan Crocker S:7

Crocker, Lura A - Died 1968 Born 1881 Wife of Ottis C Crocker (with him) S:12

Crocker, Lurann - Died 1895 Jan 8 Age 72 years,6 months,25 days Wife of Oliver Crocker (next to Sarah B Crocker, daughter) S:13

Crocker, Luther - Died 1874 Born 1873 Son of Clarington & Rebecca E Crocker (next to them) S:12

Crocker, Lydia - Died 1788 Mar 1 in her 78th yr Wife of John Crocker S:5

Crocker, Lydia - Died 1809 Jan 14 in her 63rd yr (drowned) Wife of Isaac Crocker (buried next to him) S:7

Crocker, Lydia - Died 1824 in her 27th yr Wife of David Crocker S:5

Crocker, Lydia - Died 1843 Dec 10 in her 52nd yr Wife of Enoch Crocker S:7

Crocker, Lydia - Died 1855 Feb 15 Age 42 years, 7 months Wife of Jonathan Crocker (next to him) S:19

Crocker, Lydia - Died 1870 Feb 3 in her 93rd yr Wife of Ezra Crocker S:7

Crocker, Lydia - Died 1887 Mar 24

Crocker (Cont.)
Born 1805 Oct 19 S:5

Crocker, Lydia Mrs - Died 1773 Aug 5 in her 69th yr Wife of Cornelius Crocker S:10R+26R

Crocker, Lydia P - Died 1855 Born 1856 (with Benjamin & Olive Crocker) S:14

Crocker, Mansfield I - Died 1970 Born 1903 (listed with Greta O Crocker) S:13

Crocker, Marcus M - Died 1912 March 29 Born 1834 Aug 14 (with Ellen M Crocker & others) S:18

Crocker, Marcy - Died 1813 Dec 6 Age 56 Wife of Winslow Crocker S:5R

Crocker, Margaret G - Died 1928 Born 1850 (with William O Crocker) S:12

Crocker, Maria O - Died 1915 Jan 15 Born 1840 Oct 28 S:5

Crocker, Martha - Died 1858 Oct 18 Age 81 years, 4 months Wife of Prince Crocker S:6

Crocker, Martha - Died 1877 July 7 Born 1795 June 25 S:5

Crocker, Martha M - Died 1824 Sept Daughter of Samuel Crocker S:10R

Crocker, Martha Miss - Died 1859 Mar 10 Age 86 years, 6 months S:5

Crocker, Martha W - Died 1915 Born 1841 (with Maurice C Crocker & others) S:12

Crocker, Martha W - Died 1960 Born 1877 Wife of Frank Crocker (with him & daughter Lola Crocker & Alva Brackley) S:18

Crocker, Mary - Died (underground) Wife of William Crocker (next to him) S:11

Crocker, Mary - Died 1777 April 29 Age 54 Widow of Lt John Crocker S:5R

Crocker, Mary - Died 1784 Feb 7 in her 18th yr Daughter of William & Mary Crocker S:11R+ 26R

Crocker, Mary - Died 1838 July 9 in her 76th yr Relict of Ebenezer

Crocker (Cont.)

Crocker Esq (buried next to him) S:7

Crocker, Mary - Died 1841 June 24 in her 93rd yr Widow of Deacon, Joseph Crocker S:7

Crocker, Mary - Died 1849 Oct in her 95th yr Widow of Bursley Crocker S:5

Crocker, Mary - Died 1901 Born 1833 S:6

Crocker, Mary - Died 1911 Jan 11 Born 1841 June 21 Daughter of Alicia D & Eben B Crocker S:10

Crocker, Mary - Died Feb (stone in pieces between tree & Mehetable Russel) S:11

Crocker, Mary A - Died 1876 Dec 6 in New York Born 1823 Oct 8 Wife of Henry H Crocker S:9

Crocker, Mary A - Died 1902 Born 1810 (with Sylvanus Alexander & others) S:18

Crocker, Mary A - Died 1960 Born 1879 (with Timothy Crocker & others) S:18

Crocker, Mary Ann - Died 1854 April 14 Born 1817 May 31 Daughter of Moses & Bethia Crocker S:5R

Crocker, Mary Betsey - Died 1888 Born 1869 (a large stone with fence around it facing side street) (with Daniel & Charlotte Crocker) S:10

Crocker, Mary E - Died 1923 Born 1852 (possible wife to Francis Crocker, next to him & son, Henry B Crocker) S:21

Crocker, Mary I (or B) - Died 1836 March 17 Age 30 (stone worn) Wife of Arthur Crocker (next to him) S:14

Crocker, Mary Lydia - Died (date not clear) Daughter of Edmund & Julia Crocker (Hinckley ceme records #5R say death was 1859 Feb 4 age 2 years, 9 months, 4 days) S:5

Crocker, Mary Mrs - Died 1744 July 27 in her 57th yr Wife of Deacon John Crocker S:11R+

Crocker (Cont.)
26R

Crocker, Mary Mrs - Died 1817 March 20 in her 86th yr Wife of William Crocker S:11R+26R

Crocker, Mary N - Died 1881 Born 1821 S:5

Crocker, Mary P - Died 1890 Aug 1 Born 1817 Nov 28 Stone says, "Mother" (next to husband, Ignatius Crocker) S:14

Crocker, Mary S - Died 1881 Born 1847 (with Benjamin & Olive Crocker) S:14

Crocker, Mary Sampson - Died 1951 Born 1882 (with Benjamin & Olive Crocker) S:14

Crocker, Mathias (?) - Died 1812 Sept 9 Age 11 months Son of Loring & Temperance Crocker S:10

Crocker, Mathihas - Died 1828 Aug 19 Age 23 at Philadelphia, Pa S:10

Crocker, Maurice C - Died 1937 Born 1868 (with Israel Crocker & others) S:12

Crocker, Mehitable - Died 1827 Sept 10 Age 2 Born 1825 Aug 13 Daughter of William & Sarah Crocker S:5

Crocker, Mehitable - Died 1851 August 3 Age 35 years, 1 month, 18 days Wife of Ignatius Crocker (next to son, Sylvester H Crocker) S:14

Crocker, Mehitable - Died ?? March 11 (year not clear) Wife of Thomas Crocker (Hinckley Ceme records #9R say death was 1728/9 March 11 age 23) S:9

Crocker, Melatiah - Died 1737 Dec 31 in her 37th yr Wife of Ensign, Timothy Crocker (buried next to him) S:5

Crocker, Melatiah B - Died 1870 May 10 Age 35 years, 18 days (next to wife, Eliza A Crocker) S:14

Crocker, Mercy - Died 1813 Dec 6 in her 56th yr Wife of Winslow Crocker S:5

117

Crocker, Mercy - Died 1839 Dec 30 Age 63 Born 1776 Widow of Moody Crocker S:5

Crocker, Mercy - Died 1883 Oct 23 Born 1797 Jan 5 Daughter of Capt Joseph Esterbrook & Mercy Davis (says, wife for 68 years) S:10

Crocker, Milton H - Died 1986 Born 1894 (with Harry T Crowell) S:14

Crocker, Milton L - Died 1951 Born 1868 (with Israel Crocker & others) S:12

Crocker, Minnie S - Died 1891 Oct 2 Age 32 years, 11 months, 3 days Wife of Oliver Crocker S:7

Crocker, Miriam S - Died 1964 Born 1900 (with Flora C Crocker & others) S:18

Crocker, Moody - Died 1839 Oct 1 in his 70th yr (buried next to wife Mercy) S:5

Crocker, Moses - Died 1835 Mar 17 in his 55th yr S:5

Crocker, Naler Esq - Died 1829 Mar 28 Age 56 S:10

Crocker, Nancy - Died 1909 Feb 13 Born 1825 May 4 S:7

Crocker, Nancy E - Died 1864 Apr 17 Age 72 years, 7 days Widow of Bethuel Crocker S:7

Crocker, Nathan - Died 1880 Jan 28 Age 65 years, 4 months, 12 days S:9R

Crocker, Nathan N - Died 1866 July 13 Born 1810 Dec 30 S:6

Crocker, Nathaniel - Died 1740 Feb 8 in his 69th yr S:5

Crocker, Nathaniel - Died 1806 Nov 28 Age 3 Son of Willard & Mary Crocker (buried next to Willard) (Hinckley Ceme records #5R say death year was 1826) S:5

Crocker, Nathaniel - Died 1821 Nov 1 in his 86th yr S:5

Crocker, Nathaniel - Died 1930 Born 1851 (buried with Nancy H Lapham-same stone) S:8

Crocker, Nathaniel H - Died 1876 Sept 13 Age 70 years, 11 months

Crocker (Cont.)
S:7

Crocker, Neil Lowell - Died 1969 Born 1889 (with Hazel Wilds Crocker) S:14

Crocker, Nellie A - Died 1861 March 20 Born 1858 Dec 29 (with Alice M Crocker & others) S:18

Crocker, Nellie G - Buried 1977 Sept 25 S:14R

Crocker, Nettie Brown - Died 1958 Born 1866 Wife of George F Crocker (with him & Charles C Crocker & others) S:18

Crocker, Nymphas P - Died 1829 Oct 25 in his 31st yr S:6

Crocker, Olive J (Lollie) - Died 1889 April 17 Born 1858 May 17 Wife of Capt Henry P Crocker (next to him) S:12

Crocker, Olive Rice Jenks - Died 1928 Born 1859 (with Benjamin & Olive Crocker) S:14

Crocker, Olive Sawyer - Died 1978 Born 1897 S:15

Crocker, Oliver - Died 1898 Aug 18 Born 1822 Aug 24 S:7

Crocker, Oliver H - Died 1898 June 12 Age 77 years 5 months 27 days S:13

Crocker, Ottis C - Died 1951 Born 1869 (with Lura A Crocker) S:12

Crocker, Pamelia A - Died 1882 Born 1826 S:5

Crocker, Patience - Died 1727 Oct in her 87th yr Wife of Bacon William Crocker S:11+26R

Crocker, Paul - Died 1774 Sept (day not clear on stone) Son of Thomas & Marcy Crocker S:5

Crocker, Persis S - Died 1844 Born 1811 Wife of Joseph W Crocker (with him) S:13

Crocker, Phebe - Died 1765 Dec 22 in her 31st yr Wife of Daniel Crocker (next to him) S:11+26R

Crocker, Phebe - Died 1795 located in row 10 S:11R

Crocker, Phebe - Died 1825 Oct 18 in her 45th yr Wife of Alvan Crocker (buried next to him) S:7

Crocker, Phebe A - Died 1923 Born 1842 (with Gilbert F & Charles E Crocker & others) S:14

Crocker, Pricila - Died 1809 Sept 3 in her 21st yr Daughter of Kenelm & Martha Crocker S:5

Crocker, Pricilla - Died 1779 Dec 19 in her 87th yr Widow of Capt Benjamin Crocker S:7

Crocker, Prince - Died 1862 July 15 Born 1772 Sept 6 S:6

Crocker, Priscilla H - Died 1917 Born 1831 (with Willis H Crocker & others) S:18

Crocker, Rachel - Died 1836 Oct 13 in her 60th yr Widow of Thomas Crocker S:6

Crocker, Rachel - Died 1848 June 11 (in Crocker plot, metal fence all around) Wife of David Crocker S:10

Crocker, Rachel H - Died 1890 Born 1815 S:6

Crocker, Rebecca Crowell - Died 1905 Born 1823 (with Clarence Alton Eldridge & others) S:18

Crocker, Rebecca E - Died 1900 Aug 1 Born 1814 Dec 2 Wife of Clarington Crocker (next to a Clarington Not sure if son or husband?) S:12

Crocker, Rebecca H - Died 1887 Jan 25 Age 87 years, 2 months, 23 days Wife of Zenas Crocker (next to him) S:14

Crocker, Rebecca J - Died 1848 June 13 in her 63rd yr Widow of Rowland Crocker (buried next to him) S:7

Crocker, Rebecca K - Died 1883 June 22 Age 71 years, 6 months, 22 days Wife of Asa S Crocker (next to him & Angeline B Crocker) S:18

Crocker, Rebecca Miss - Died 1814 May 8 in her 30th yr S:5

Crocker, Rebecca Miss - Died 1832 Apr 23 in her 25th yr S:5

Crocker, Rebecca Sampson - Died 1901 Born 1821 (with Benjamin & Hiram Crocker) S:14

Crocker, Rebecca W - Died 1856

Crocker (Cont.)
June 25 Age 23 years, 6 months Daughter of Willard & Mary Crocker (buried next to brother & father) S:5

Crocker, Rebeckah - Died 1756 May 9 in her 47th yr Wife of Thomas Crocker (buried next to him) S:5

Crocker, Rebekah - Died 1756 July 11 Wife of Seth Crocker (buried next to him) S:5

Crocker, Reuben Jr - Died 1889 Oct 25 Age 79 years, 4 months, 15 days (next to wife, Dorcas H Crocker) S:14

Crocker, Robert F - Died 1873 Sept 17 Age 10 months, 5 days Son of PR & EC S:5R

Crocker, Rose DP - Died 1970 Nov 22 Born 1886 July 31 Wife of Willis G Crocker Sr(d1953) (next to him) S:13

Crocker, Rowland T - Died 1846 Oct 22 in his 77th yr S:7

Crocker, Ruth - Died 1854 Born 1785 (with Herbert F Gifford) S:14

Crocker, Ruth - Died 1874 Born 1800 Wife of ? (stone not clear) S:5

Crocker, Ruth S - Died 1925 Sept or Dec 13 Age 21 (year could be 1825?) Daughter of Davis & Hannah Crocker S:10

Crocker, Sally - Died 1837 Oct 3 Age 78 Widow of Daniel Crocker (on same stone with son, Daniel) S:10

Crocker, Samuel - Died 1866 Mar 19 Age 87 years, 7 months S:7

Crocker, Samuel (Capt) - Died (stone underground) (next to wife, Anna Crocker) (Hinckley Ceme records #10R say death was 1804 April 28 age 72) S:10

Crocker, Samuel S - Died 1851 Nov 28 Age 38 (next to Jonathan & Lydia Crocker) S:19

Crocker, Sarah - Died 1739 Jan 2 in her 36th yr S:5

Crocker, Sarah - Died 1784 July

Crocker (Cont.)
13 in her 21st yr Wife of William Crocker S:7

Crocker, Sarah - Died 1796 (died of small pox) Widow of Deacon, Jonathan Crocker S:6

Crocker, Sarah Abby - Died 1850 June 12 Daughter of Wilson & Betsey Crocker S:7

Crocker, Sarah B - Died 1841/51? Nov 9 Age 21 years, 7 months, 10 days Daughter of Oliver & Lurann Crocker (next to mother) S:13

Crocker, Sarah C - Died 1875 Born 1836 (with Clara R Crocker & others) S:18

Crocker, Sarah F - Died Age 64 (located on street with Capt Elijah Crocker) S:10

Crocker, Sarah Jones - Died 1839 May 2 Age 12 years, 2 months Daughter of Walter & Caroline J Crocker S:6

Crocker, Sarah Robbins - Died 1963 Born 1878 (next to F Chessman Crocker) S:13

Crocker, Seth - Died 1770 Mar 25 in his 69th yr S:5

Crocker, Seth B - Died 1908 March 9 Born 1861 March 14 (with Gorham D & Nellie A Crocker & others) S:18

Crocker, Sharon Lee - Buried 1950 S:15R

Crocker, Shubael H (Deacon) - Died 1847 Jan 19 Age 68 Born 1779 Oct 7 (family buried next to each other) S:7

Crocker, Sophia - Died 1835 Sept 18 in her 19th yr Daughter of George & Alice Crocker S:5

Crocker, Sophia - Died 1889 May 15 in her 77th yr (buried next to Bridgham Crocker-husband) S:5

Crocker, Sophia A - Died 1876 Born 1836 S:5

Crocker, Sophia Miss - Died (stone not clear) (located between Francis & Abigail Crocker) (Hinckley Ceme records #5R say death was 1819 Nov 12 age 26)

Crocker (Cont.)
S:5

Crocker, Sophronia - Died 1862 Born 1824 Daughter of JB & R Crocker S:5

Crocker, Stanton Whitney - Died Age 3 years, 10 months 22 days (located on street with Sarah F & Capt Elijah Crocker) S:10

Crocker, Staton, Whitney - Died Age 3 years 10 months 22 days (no date) (with Sarah & Elijah Crocker, located at street level cut into a hill) S:8

Crocker, Stephen - Died 1826 Age 24 (lost at sea) Born 1802 Sept 22 Son of Shubael Crocker S:7

Crocker, Stephen - Died 1882 Apr 30 Born 1830 Jan 10 S:5

Crocker, Stephen - Died 1889 Mar 5 in his 75th yr S:7

Crocker, Stephen R (Capt) - Died 1888 Nov 12 Born 1807 Oct 3 S:5

Crocker, Susan - Died 1888 Aug 29 at Salem Born 1837 Mar 24 in Barnstable,Mass Daughter of Ira & Louisa Bursley (in same Bursley plot) S:10

Crocker, Susan A - Died 1934 Born 1845 (next to Elizabeth C Crocker) S:14

Crocker, Susan Agusta - Died 1914 Sept 13 Born 1834 Aug 2 (with Hattie Estelle Crocker & others) S:14

Crocker, Susan D - Died 1873 Aug 7 Age 58 years, 3 months, 24 days Wife of Nathan Crocker S:9R

Crocker, Susan F - Died 1836 Feb 27 Age 3 months 17 days Daughter of Joseph W & Persis Crocker S:12

Crocker, Susan T - Died 1872 Oct 16 in her 83rd yr Widow of Joseph Crocker S:6

Crocker, Susanna - Died 1878 April 22 Age 91 years, 2 months, 22 days S:14

Crocker, Sylvester H - Died 1850 Nov Age 13 years, 1 month, 15

Crocker (Cont.)

days Son of Ignatius & Mehitable Crocker (with Henry C Crocker) S:14

Crocker, Sylvia - Died 1830 Jan 1 in her 82nd yr Relict of Alvan Crocker (buried next to him) & daughter of Rowland Thacher S:7

Crocker, Sylvia - Died 1843 Jan 5 Age 63 (next to Zerviah Crocker) S:14

Crocker, Sylvia R - Died 1926 Born 1845 (wife of Alfred Crocker) S:8

Crocker, Tabitha - Died 1845 May 14 Born 1807 July 7 Wife of Wilson Crocker S:7

Crocker, Taul - Died 1774 Sept 30 Age 18 months Son of Thomas & Marcy Crocker S:5R

Crocker, Temperance - Died 1736 July 11 Age 25 Wife of Seth Crocker S:5R

Crocker, Temperance - Died 1807 July 15 Age 5 Daughter of Isaac & Desire Crocker S:7

Crocker, Temperance - Died 1812 Jan 5 in her 36th yr Wife of Ezra Crocker (buried next to him) S:7

Crocker, Temperance - Died 1865 Mar 12 Age 76 Widow of Loring Crocker (next to him) S:10

Crocker, Temperance - Died 1872 April 15 Born 1809 Aug 12 Wife of Loring Crocker S:10

Crocker, Temperance - Died March (stone not clear) Relict of Joseph Crocker (Hinckley Ceme records #5R say death was 1741 March 29 age 85) S:5

Crocker, Temperance H - Died 1807 Born 1786 (with Ben F Crocker & others) S:13

Crocker, Temperance L Mrs - Died 1839 Feb 21 Age 56 (stone is down) Wife of Braddock Crocker (listed with Gustavus B Crocker) S:14

Crocker, Thankful - Died (year not clear) March Age 70 Wife of Samuel Crocker S:7

Crocker, Thankful - Died 18

Crocker (Cont.)

months (no year) Daughter of Thomas & Rachel Crocker S:6

Crocker, Thankful - Died 1815 April 28 in her 70th yr Relict of Asa Crocker S:10R+26R

Crocker, Thankful Mrs - Died 1735 Oct 1 Daughter of Deacon, Job Crocker (next to him) (Hinckley Ceme records #11R say age was 36) S:11

Crocker, Thatcher B - Died 1921 Born 1860 S:11

Crocker, Thomas - Died (dates underground, stone not clear) (next to his wife, Jane Crocker) S:10

Crocker, Thomas - Died 172? Apr (stone not clear) (Hinckley Ceme records #5R says death was 1720 April 8 age 58) S:5

Crocker, Thomas - Died 1756 (stone not clear) (Hinckley Ceme records #5R say death was on 9 Sept age 53) S:5

Crocker, Thomas - Died 1814 Jan 24 in his 50th yr S:6

Crocker, Thomas - Died 1826 March 2 Age 24 Son of Capt Ira Crocker S:10R

Crocker, Thomas - Died 1855 Dec 29 Age 59 years, 4 months, 15 days S:5R

Crocker, Thomas (Capt) - Died (dates under the ground) (buried next to Jane Crocker, wife) S:10

Crocker, Thomas (Capt) - Died 1800 Nov 9 Age 57 S:10R

Crocker, Thomas Mr - Died 1826 Mar 9 Age 24 Son of Capt Ira Crocker who died at Edmonton, North Dakota in 1812 S:10

Crocker, Timothy - Died 1737 Jan 31 Age 57 (buried next to wife, Melatiah) (Hinckley Ceme records #5R has death written in pencil as, 1837?) S:5

Crocker, Timothy - Died 1827 Nov 8 Age 10 years, 10 months, 18 days S:4

Crocker, Timothy - Died 1890 Born 1815 (with Harriet Crocker) S:18

Crocker, Timothy - Died 1925 Born 1857 (with Catherine L Crocker & others) S:18

Crocker, Turzy - Died Age 19 months (no year) Parents are Thomas & Rachel Crocker S:6

Crocker, W Abbie - Died 1889 Born 1857 (with Augusta Crocker & others) S:18

Crocker, Wallace F - Died 1884 Born 1856 (with Isaiah & Eliza Crocker) S:12

Crocker, Walley - Died 1772 Dec 9 Age 57 or 67? S:5R

Crocker, Wally - Died (no date) located in row 17 S:11R

Crocker, Walter - Died 1860 Sept 9 in his 74th yr (buried next to wife, Caroline J Crocker) S:6

Crocker, Walter Morrison - Died 1844 Dec 16 Age 16 Son of Walter & Caroline Crocker S:6

Crocker, Watson - Died 1876 Born 1788 (next to wife Damaris Crocker) (Hinckley Ceme records #5R say death year was 1875) S:5

Crocker, Watson E - Died 1921 Born 1839 S:5

Crocker, Willard - Died 1833 Aug 2 in his 35th yr S:5

Crocker, Willard C - Died 1914 Oct 9 Born 1870 Mar 26 S:5

Crocker, Willard Crafts (MD) - Died 1912 Sept 4 Born 1859 June 26 (with James Varnum Turner & others) S:18

Crocker, Willard R - Died 1885 (with Benjamin & Olive Crocker) S:14

Crocker, William - Died 1740 Mar 5 in his 63rd yr S:5

Crocker, William - Died 1787 Apr 15 in his 34th yr (buried next to wife, Sarah Crocker) S:7

Crocker, William - Died 1791 (?) Jan 22 Age 3 years, 5 months, 14 days Son of Ephriam & Mercy Crocker (date on stone not clear) (Hinckley Ceme records #5R say age was only 5 months, 14 days) S:5

Crocker, William - Died 1791 in his 81st yr S:5

Crocker, William - Died 1810 located in row 10 S:11R

Crocker, William - Died 1819 May in his 89th yr S:11+26R

Crocker, William - Died 1836 Jan 18 Age 40 Born 1796 Nov S:5

Crocker, William - Died 1844 June 24 in his 75th yr S:6

Crocker, William - Died 1879 Born 1809 S:6

Crocker, William (Capt) - Died 1837 Lost at sea Born 1814 (On same stone with Martha Crocker Starbuck & Ellen Crocker) S:5

Crocker, William (Capt) - Died 1893 Born 1840 (with Imogene F Crocker & others) S:18

Crocker, William H - Died 1900 Sept 13 Born 1856 Feb 8 (with Emily D Crocker) S:21

Crocker, William H - Died 1931 Born 1858 S:5

Crocker, William O - Died 1929 Born 1857 (with Margaret G Crocker) S:12

Crocker, William W - Died 1893 Born 1849 (with wife, Caroline A Nickerson) S:14

Crocker, Willis G Jr - Died 1971 Dec 25 Born 1914 May 19 (with Evelyn M Crocker, with her) (he is just two stones away from Willis Garfield Crocker Jr & Evelyn Bassett Crocker ?) S:13

Crocker, Willis G Sr - Died 1953 Aug 8 Born 1881 May 29 (next to wife, Rose D P Crocker) S:13

Crocker, Willis Garfield - Died 1971 Born 1914 Stone says,"Free at last" (next to Evelyn Bassett Crocker) S:13

Crocker, Willis H - Died 1871 Born 1859 (with George F Crocker & others) S:18

Crocker, Wilson - Died 1885 Dec 12 Born 1808 Apr 28 S:7

Crocker, Winslow - Died 1821 Dec 16 in his 66th yr S:5

Crocker, Zena - Died 1807 Feb 15 in his 46th yr (buried next to

Crocker (Cont.)
wife, Hannah S:7

Crocker, Zenas - Died 1877 May 6 Age 81 years, 2 months (next to wife, Rebecca H Crocker) S:14

Crocker, Zenas - Died 1898/9 Nov 22 Born 1831 June 7 (with Susan Agusta Crocker) S:14

Crocker, Zenas Jr - Died 1960 Born 1887 (with Merle MacDonald) S:14

Crocker, Zeroias - Died 1810 Nov 18 in her 88th yr Widow of Ebenezer Crocker S:7

Crocker, Zerviah - Died 1874 March 13 Age 32 years, 8 months, 15 days (next to Sylvia Crocker) (Hinckley ceme records has a Zerviah at age 92?) S:14

Croker, Walley - Died 1772 Sept 9 in his 67th yr S:5

Cronin, Marion Hart - Died 1926 Born 1892 (with Mildred Hart Pritchard) S:18

Crooks, Celena H - Died 1986 Nov 7 Born 1895 May 11 (next to William A Crooks) S:17

Crooks, Lillian L - Died 1990 Born 1894 (with John J Rogers & next to William & Celena H Crooks) S:17

Crooks, William A - Died 1975 March 5 Born 1893 Feb 25 Was a PFC in US Army during World War I (next to Celena H Crooks) S:17

Crosbay, Allen - Died 1801 Aug 15 in his 18th yr Son of Jesse & Ruthy Crosbay S:3

Crosbay, Jesse - Died 1804 Feb 24 in his 72nd yr S:3

Crosbay, Ruthy - Died 1797 May 28 in her 58th yr Wife of Jesse Crosbay S:3

Crosby, (baby) - Died (no dates listed) Child of Horace & Mary E Crosby (next to them) S:12

Crosby, (infant) - Died 1840 Sept 21 Son of Alvin & Ploomy Crosby S:2

Crosby, (infant) - Died 1856 Apr 3 Born 1856 Feb 11 Son of Hilman

Crosby (Cont.)
& Louisa Crosby S:2

Crosby, (infant) - Died 1857 Sept 18 Born 1857 July 23 Daughter of Hilman & Louisa Crosby S:2

Crosby, Abagail - Died 1857 Oct 1 Age 76 years, 9 months Wife of Lewis Crosby S:2

Crosby, Abigail - Died 1860 May 30 Age 54 years, 2 months, 16 days Widow of Daniel Crosby (next to him, d1854) S:12

Crosby, Abigail L - Died 1840 Born 1796 Wife of Jesse Gifford Crosby (buried next to him) S:5

Crosby, Abigail L - Died 1886 Jan 6 Age 67 (stone is in bad condition) (buried next to Maude Shaw (Crosby))(wife of Jehiel Crosby) S:8

Crosby, Abner - Died 1838 Dec 25 Age 51 years, 3 months S:5

Crosby, Abner F - Died 1892 June 18 Born 1866 or 1816? Sept 9 (stone not clear) Stone says, "Husband" (next to Charlotte Crosby, wife of Capt Abner Crosby) S:14

Crosby, Abner H - Died 1872 March 31 Age 57 years, 8 months, 24 days Stone says, "Father" (next to wife, Christina H Crosby) S:14

Crosby, Addie G - Died 1939 Born 1853 (next to Abner F & Charlotte Crosby) S:14

Crosby, Alexander - Died 1810 June 17 Age 6 years, 6 months, 4 days Son of Alvin & Ploomy Crosby S:2

Crosby, Alice Connor - Died 1947 Born 1884 Wife of Samuel C Crosby (with him) S:14

Crosby, Allen - Died 1801 August 15 Age 18 Son of Jesse and Ruth Crosby S:3R

Crosby, Almira E - Died 1843 Nov 11 Born 1843 Aug 7 (buried next to Uberto Crosby) S:8

Crosby, Alonzo P - Died 1935 Born 1846 (buried with Sarah H Crosby & many others, also with

Crosby (Cont.)
later dates) S:8

Crosby, Alonzo W - Died 1890 Born 1840 S:4

Crosby, Alvin - Died 1894 May 15 Age 10 years, 11 months S:2

Crosby, Amy L - Died 1961 Born 1888 Wife of Lawrence Crosby (with him) S:14

Crosby, Andrew W - Died 1931 Born 1883 S:12

Crosby, Angelina L - Died 1921 Born 1881 With Herbert B Crosby S:12

Crosby, Arebella (Ryder) - Died 1905 Born 1845 (buried with children with later dates into 1880's & with Gorham Freeman Crosby) (this plot area is very nicely done and well kept) S:8

Crosby, Asa - Died 1871 June 29 Age 55 years, 11 months, 12 days (next to wife, Cordelia Crosby) S:13

Crosby, Asa Gorham - Died 1905 Aug 22 Born 1845 Feb 2 He was a Mason, member of 4 bodies, Maryland, Maine, Portland, Maine He was a member of Scotish Rite bodies, 32 New York City Mecca Temple, NYC (next to Cordelia Crosby) S:13

Crosby, Beatrice Cowan, Dill - Died 1973 Born 1893 (with Frederick SS Dill) S:12

Crosby, Benjamin F - Died 1900 March 14 Born 1846 April 14 (with Lydia A Crosby) S:14

Crosby, Benjamin F - Died 1952 Born 1870 (with wife, Mary S Eldridge) S:14

Crosby, Bessie J - Died 1927 Born 1874 (buried with Alonzo P Crosby & many others, also with later dates) S:8

Crosby, Caroline Lewis - Died 1882 Born 1813 S:2

Crosby, Carroll P - Died 1952 Aug 26 Born 1896 Feb 20 Was a PFC in Massachusetts Company F, 101 Engineers during World War I (also has separate military

Crosby (Cont.)
stone) (with wife, Sarah E Crosby) S:12

Crosby, Charles H - Died 1936 Born 1854 (with Edith M Robbins) S:12

Crosby, Charlotte - Died 1855 or 1887 Sept 25 Born 1815 Oct 30 Wife of Capt Abner F Crosby (next to him) (1887 death date from Hinckley ceme records) S:14

Crosby, Chester A - Died 1988 Born 1905 (with Ida K Crosby) S:12

Crosby, Chloe H - Died 1905 Born 1834 S:8

Crosby, Christina H - Died 1887 Sept 2 Age 72 years, 6 months, 16 days Stone says, "Mother" Widow of Abner H Crosby (next to him) S:14

Crosby, Claribel C - Died 1970 Nov 24 Born 1884 Feb 12 (with Henry Crosby) S:14

Crosby, Cora L - Died 1949 Born 1874 Wife of Ernest O Dottridge (next to him) S:14

Crosby, Daniel - Died (Crosby plott with names listed only) S:12

Crosby, Daniel - Died 1828 Oct 31 Age 63 S:12

Crosby, Daniel - Died 1833 Mar 11 Age 1 year, 3 days Son of Daniel & Abigail Crosby (near them) S:12

Crosby, Daniel - Died 1854 Feb 4 Age 50 (next to Abigail Crosby, d1860) S:12

Crosby, Darius - Died 1883 Born 1808 S:2

Crosby, David H - Died 1982 April 23 Born 1963 Dec 16 Stone says, "Loved by all" (next to Roy G Crosby) S:31

Crosby, Dertus E - Died 1842? Sept 1 Age 17 Son of Asa & Cordelia Crosby (next to father) S:13

Crosby, Donald P - Died 1945 Born 1926 (with Carroll & Sarah Crosby) S:12

Crosby, Dorcas H - Died 1810 Feb 6 Age 8 years Daughter of Daniel & Dorcas Crosby S:12

Crosby, Dorcas H - Died 1841 Nov 23 Age 72 Wife of Daniel Crosby S:12

Crosby, Doris C - Died 1985 July 10 Born 1892 Sept 11 (next to Tom O Crosby) S:11

Crosby, Edith M - Died 1955 Born 1866 (with Joseph G Crosby) S:12

Crosby, Eleanor L - Died 1923 Born 1838 (buried with Isaac Crosby) S:8

Crosby, Eliza - Died 1879 Mar 3 Age 71 years, 8 months, 10 days Wife of Samuel Crosby S:2

Crosby, Eliza Bradford - Died 1850 Oct 13 Age 15 years, 1 month, 10 days Daughter of Alvin & Ploomy Crosby S:2

Crosby, Ellen - Died (Crosby plot with names listed only) S:12

Crosby, Ellen - Died 1875 Feb 17 Born 1875 Jan 26 (with Benjamin F Crosby) S:14

Crosby, Elliott - Died 1951 Born 1871 S:12

Crosby, Emily - Wife of Daniel (Crosby plot with names listed only) S:12

Crosby, Emily E - Died 1910? Mar 9 Born 1859? Sept 2 (stone worn) Daughter of Owen & Nancy Crosby, buried with them S:8

Crosby, Emma B - Died 18?? Dec 21 Age 32 years, 2 months, 23 days Daughter of Lewis & Olive J Crosby, buried next to them S:8

Crosby, Emma C - Died 1863 Dec 14 Born 1845 Feb 25 Daughter of MC & MC Crosby (probably is Uberto C & Mary C Crosby) S:8

Crosby, Enoch P - Died 1858 Born 1812 Son of Jesse & Susannah Crosby S:5

Crosby, Eunice - Died 1883 Feb 24 Born 1808 July 18 S:2

Crosby, Frederic W - Died 1864

Crosby (Cont.)
June 4 Born 1825/8 June 15 (With Hope D Crosby, wife) S:8

Crosby, Frederick W - Died 1864 June 4 Born 1828 June 15 (four small stones near him which say, MC, MAC, WC in Crosby plot) S:8

Crosby, Freelove - Died 1857 July 15 Age 52 years, 11 months Wife of Oliver Crosby (buried next to her) S:8

Crosby, Freeman M - Died 1907 July 14 Born 1858 Sept 17 (with Malvine M Crosby) S:8

Crosby, Genieve S - Died 1949 Born 1880 Wife of Osbourne Bearse (with him) S:14

Crosby, George H - Died 1846 Oct 29 age 4 months, 13 days Son of Hilman & Louise Crosby S:2

Crosby, Gertrude M - Died 1970 Born 1891 (with Marguerite K Allen) S:17

Crosby, Gorham - Died 1883 April Born 1809 Oct 12 (stone badly worn) (buried in Crosby plot - tall stone) S:8

Crosby, Gorham Freeman - Died 1914 Born 1838 (with Arabella Crosby (Ryder)) S:8

Crosby, Hannah A - Died 1896 Born 1835 (next to Oaks S Crosby) S:12

Crosby, Harriet - Died 1943 Born 1860 (with Elliott Crosby) S:12

Crosby, Harriet D - Died 1896 Mar 4 Age 71 years, 5 month Wife of Capt Hilman Crosby S:8

Crosby, Helen F - Died 1970 Born 1904 (with Merrill B Crosby) S:13

Crosby, Henry - Died 1960 July 12 Born 1883 May 23 (with Claribel C Crosby) S:14

Crosby, Henry Jr - Died 1967 Dec 26 Born 1907 Oct 17 (with Henry Sr & Claribel Crosby) S:14

Crosby, Herbert B - Died 1935 Born 1877 With Angelina L Crosby S:12

Crosby, Herbert F - Died 1936

Crosby (Cont.)
Born 1853 (with Sarah H Crosby) S:12

Crosby, Hilman (Capt) - Died 1880 Jan 20 Age 60 years, 7 months S:8

Crosby, Hope D - Died 1860 July 20 Born 1833 May 2 (buried with husband, Frederic Crosby) S:8

Crosby, Horace A - Died 1955 Born 1895 (with wife, Mary E Welsh) S:12

Crosby, Horace Manley - Died 1959 Born 1871 (with Velina Parker, his wife) S:12

Crosby, Horace Manley Jr - Died 1990 Jan 12 Born 1907 Nov 29 (with Viola J Crosby Nicknamed "Bumpa" On 2 stones) S:12

Crosby, Horace S - Died 1894 Born 1826 (with Horace Manley Crosby) S:12

Crosby, Ida K - Died 1990 Born 1907 (with Chester A Crosby) S:12

Crosby, Isaac D - Died 1889 Born 1833 (with Eleanor L Crosby) S:8

Crosby, Isaac H - Died 1840 Oct 19 Born 1845 May 9 (buried with Isaac h Crosby) S:12

Crosby, Isaac H - Died 1884 June 26 Born 1830 Dec 23? (with Isaac H Crosby b1840) S:8

Crosby, Isaiah - Died Age 1 year, 1 month Son of Capt Hilman & Harriet Crosby S:8

Crosby, James - Died 1857 Aug 1 Age 89 years, 4 months, 17 days S:3

Crosby, James - Died 1880 Dec 14 Born 1806 Jan 30 S:2

Crosby, James P - Died 1892 May 26 Age 65 years, 8 months, 3 days (next to Hannah A Crosby) S:12

Crosby, Janet Joy - Died 1964 Born 1874 (next to Harding F Joy) S:12

Crosby, Jehiel - Died 1885? Nov 24 (stone is in very bad condition & not clear) (buried next to Abigail

Crosby (Cont.)
L Crosby) S:8

Crosby, Jehiel Reed - Died 1931 Born 1852 (buried with Maude Shaw, wife) S:8

Crosby, Jesse - Died 1804 Feb 24 Age 72 (next to wife, Ruthy) S:3R

Crosby, Jesse - Died 1850 Born 1770 S:5

Crosby, Jesse Gifford - Died 1840 Born 1790 Wife was Abigail L Crosby & son of Jesse & Susannah Crosby) S:5

Crosby, Joseph F - Died 1860 Mar 25 Lost at sea Born 1832 Sept 9 (buried with Hope Crosby) S:8

Crosby, Joseph Franklin - Died 1916 Born 1866 S:12

Crosby, Joseph G - Died 1922 Born 1859 (with Edith M Crosby) (There is a hand made stone that says Crosby but nothing else just 5 feet away) S:12

Crosby, Julia - Died 1899 Born 1813 (listed in front of very large stone with Philander Crosby & many others, also with later dates) Stone says, "Thy Sleep Shall Be Sweet" S:8

Crosby, Laura J - Died 1894 Nov 10 Born 1821 July 3 S:12

Crosby, Lawrence G - Died 1981 Born 1888 (with wife, Amy L Crosby) S:14

Crosby, Leonor - Died 1857 May 5 in her 20th yr Daughter of Daniel & Caroline Crosby S:2

Crosby, Lewis - Died 1811 July 12 in his 68th yr S:2

Crosby, Lewis (Capt) - Died 1872 Sept 3 in his 56th yr S:8

Crosby, Louisa - Died 1846 Sept 2 Age 21 years, 6 months, 8 days Wife of Hilman Crosby S:2

Crosby, Louisa S - Died 1915 July 15 Born 1848 Oct 26 S:8

Crosby, Louisa W - Died 1852 June 21 Age 60 years, 8 months, 12 days (buried next to Jehiel Crosby d1885?) S:8

Crosby, Lucy - Died 1927 Born 1864 Wife of James Leonard

Crosby (Cont.)
(with him) Leonard stone with
fireman's flag) S:12

Crosby, Lucy A - Died 1911 Nov 12
Age 76 (with William C Crosby)
S:14

Crosby, Lucy A - Died 1921 Born
1835 (with Horace Manley &
Viola J Crosby Jr) S:12

Crosby, Lydia A - Died 1930 June
21 Born 1849 Oct 12 (with
Benjamin F Crosby) S:14

Crosby, MAC - Died (no dates) (In
back of Frederick Crosby) S:8

Crosby, MC - Died (no dates) (In
back of Frederick Crosby) S:8

Crosby, Malcolm - Died 1979 Born
1893 Was a PFC in US Army
during World War II With Alta E
Battle, his wife S:12

Crosby, Malvine M - Died 1945 Jan
12 Born 1863 Nov 13 S:8

Crosby, Marcia M - Died (still living
1991?) Born 1932 Wife of Clin-
ton Davies (with him & John
Davies & others) S:19

Crosby, Martha K - Died 1851 Born
1809 Daughter of Jesse &
Susannah Crosby S:5

Crosby, Martha K - Died 1859 Born
1809 Daughter of Jesse &
Susannah Crosby S:5R

Crosby, Mary A - Died 1847 Nov 21
Born 1804 Jan 2? (stone worn)
Wife of Wilson Crosby S:8

Crosby, Mary C - Died 1880? Sept
23 Born 1823 Mar 3 (buried next
to husband Uberto & family) S:8

Crosby, Mary Eldrige - Buried 1953
S:15R

Crosby, Mary Williams - Died 1904
Jan 5 Born 1841 Aug 15 (large
stone) (buried with husband,
Mazeppa Nickerson) S:8

Crosby, Mellisa - Died 1898 April 4
Born 1848 Feb 24 (with William
Crosby) S:14

Crosby, Melora - Died 1882 Oct 29
Born 1808 Dec 12 Wife of wilson
Crosby S:8

Crosby, Mercy - Died 1902 Apr 10
Born 1881? Dec 8 Wife of Owen

Crosby (Cont.)
Crosby Jr, buried with him &
others S:8

Crosby, Merrill B - Died 1977 Born
1901 (with Helen F Crosby) S:13

Crosby, Myrtle - Died (Crosby plot
with names listed only) S:12

Crosby, Nancy - Died 1810 Nov 20
Age 20 Daughter of Nathan &
Pasha Crosby S:12

Crosby, Nancy C - Died 1906 Jan
31 Born 1831 Nov 16 (stone
worn) (buried with husband,
Owen Crosby) S:8

Crosby, Nancy G - Died 1831 June
8 Age 27 Wife of Darius Crosby
S:5

Crosby, Nathan - Died 1838 Sept
28 Age 78 S:12

Crosby, Oaks S - Died 1887 Born
1829 (next to Hannah A Crosby)
S:12

Crosby, Olive J - Died 1887 Oct 28
in her 71st yr Wife of Capt Lewis
Crosby, buried next to him) S:8

Crosby, Olive Mrs - Died 1856 Sept
14 Age 59 years, late of Centerville, Massachusetts Widow to
Watson Crosby S:21

Crosby, Oliver - Died 1890 Dec 1
Age 89 years, 1 month (buried
next to Freelove Crosby) S:8

Crosby, Owen - Died 1833 July 10
Age 24 S:12

Crosby, Owen - Died 1913 Apr 19
Born 1832 Dec 29 (very big
stone with others) (buried with
Nancy C Crosby, wife) S:8

Crosby, Owen Jr - Died 1933 July
10 Born 1889? Aug 19 (stone
worn) (buried with wife, Mercy
Crosby & others) S:8

Crosby, Pasha Mrs - Died 1811
May 5 Age 43 Wife of Nathan
Crosby (next to him) S:12

Crosby, Percy Reed - Died 1886
June 18 Born 1829 Mar 10 son
of GF & B (buried next to Gorham
Crosby) S:8

Crosby, Philander - Died 1853
Born 1814 (buried with Julia
Crosby, listed in front of very

Crosby (Cont.)
large stone with many others)
Stone says, "Thy Sleep Shall be
Sweet" S:8

Crosby, Ralph - Died (Crosby plot
with names listed only) S:12

Crosby, Rolinza - Died 1848 March
17 Age 54 years, 5 months (next
to William Crosby) S:14

Crosby, Rosa - Died 1884 Jan 22
Born 1861 Oct 22 Wife of Joseph
C Crosby S:12

Crosby, Rose W - Died 1869 Dec 19
Age 22 years, 11 months, 6 days
(next to Abner H Crosby) S:14

Crosby, Roy G - Died 1971 Nov 6
Born 1953 Nov 12 Stone says, "I
am loved" (next to David H
Crosby) S:31

Crosby, Russell M - Died 1846
Born 1844 (buried with Melissa
J Hamblen & many others, also
with later dates) S:8

Crosby, Ruthy - Died 1707 May 28
Age 58 Wife of Jesse Crosby
(next to him) S:3R

Crosby, Sally - Died 1813 Nov 13 in
her 31st yr Wife of Samuel
Crosby S:12R

Crosby, Samuel - Died 1869 Nov
24 Age 81 yrs 2 mos 13 days
(next to wives, Martha Smith
and Sally Crosby) S:12R

Crosby, Samuel (Deacon) - Died
1888 Dec 3 Age 79 years, 1
month, 15 days S:2

Crosby, Samuel C - Died 1950
Born 1876 (with Alice Connor
Crosby) S:14

Crosby, Sarah - Died 1811 Jan 8 in
her 65th yr of her age Relict of
Nathaniel Crosby S:12R

Crosby, Sarah - Died 1830 Oct 15
in her 82nd yr Widow of Jesse
Crosby S:3

Crosby, Sarah - Died 1835 June 29
Born 1812 Nov 6 Wife of Gorham
crosby (buried next to him in
Crosby plot) S:8

Crosby, Sarah - Died 1893 Sept 16
Born 1824 Oct 20 (Marston plot)
(buried with husband, Russell

Crosby (Cont.)
Marston) S:8

Crosby, Sarah E - Died 1977 Born
1898 (with Carroll P Crosby)
S:12

Crosby, Sarah H - Died 1920 Born
1855 (with Herbert F Crosby &
Alcott N Hallett) S:12

Crosby, Sarah H - Died 1937 Born
1846 (buried with Alonzo P
Crosby & many others, also with
later dates) S:8

Crosby, Susannah - Died 1849
Born 1775 Wife of Jesse Crosby
S:5

Crosby, Temperance - Died 1858
Mar 30 Age 84 years, 2 months,
1 day Wife of James Crosby S:3

Crosby, Tempy F - Died 1858 Oct
14 Age 32 years, 7 months S:2

Crosby, Tom O - Died 1972 Dec 15
Born 1896 Dec 12 Was MM1 in
US Navy during World War I
(next to Doris C Crosby) S:11

Crosby, Uberto - Died 1872 June
11 Born 1819 Jan 6 (buried next
to wife, Mary C & family) S:8

Crosby, Uberto - Died 1925 Oct 4
Born 1845 July 29 S:8

Crosby, Viola J - Died (still living?)
Born 1913 (listed with Horace
Manley Crosby Jr) S:12

Crosby, WC - Died (no dates) (In
back of Frederick Crosby) S:8

Crosby, Watson - Died 1848 Dec
26 Age 18 years, 4 months, 13
days Son of James & Eunice
Crosby S:2

Crosby, William - Died 1848 May 5
Age 57 years, 4 months (next to
Rolinza Crosby) S:14

Crosby, William B - Died 1914 May
29 Born 1852 Sept 10 (with
Mellisa Crosby) S:14

Crosby, William C (or G) - Died
1895 or 1885 Feb 17 Age 84?
(with Lucy A Crosby) (1885 date
from Hinckley ceme records)
S:14

Crosby, Wilson - Died 1874 Dec 16
Born 1804 Mar 10 (with Mary A
Crosby, wife) S:8

Crosby, Wilton B - Died 1980 Born 1898 (with Lucy AE Sawyer, his wife) S:12

Crosby, Wilton B Jr - Died (still living 1991) Born 1923 (listed on parents stone, Wilton Sr & Lucy AE Sawyer) S:12

Crose, Mercy A - Died 1935 Sept 18 Born 1867 Oct 4 S:19

Cross, Annie F - Died 1968 Born 1878 (with Robert F Cross & Honora O'Sullivan) S:16

Cross, Elizabeth Breckinridge - Died 1952 Feb 22 Born 1890 Sept 29 (next to Virginia Castleman Breckinridge Cross) S:13

Cross, Ellen - Died 1938 Born 1879 (with Vincent Cross) S:16

Cross, John D - Died 1964 Born 1878 Stone says,"Father" (next to Lizzie C Cross) S:17

Cross, Lizzie C - Died 1952 Born 1883 Stone says,"Mother" (next to John D Cross) S:17

Cross, Mary Cabell Breckinridge - Died 1907 Aug 4 Born 1856 Dec 30 (with Richard K Cross) S:13

Cross, Richard K - Died 1909 Aug 28 Born 1842 July 21 Married 1883 June 6 (with Mary Cabell Breckinridge Cross) (Has Civil War star 1861-65) S:13

Cross, Robert F - Died 1958 Born 1875 (with Annie F Cross & Honora O'Sullivan) S:16

Cross, Vincent - Died 1936 Born 1879 (with Ellen Cross) S:16

Cross, Virginia Castleman B - Died 1963 Jan 21 Born 1888 April 13 (next to Richard K Cross) (middle name above was Breckinridge) S:13

Crowell, (infant) - Died 1861 Born 1861 Daughter of Susan & Elkanah Crowell (with them) S:18

Crowell, Abigail - Died 1832 April 14 Age 40 (with Joseph Crowell & Augusta C Bearse) S:18

Crowell, Abner (Capt) - Died 1868 Dec 28 Age 65 years, 1 month (stone leaning) (next to wife,

Crowell (Cont.)
Melinda Crowell) S:21

Crowell, Abner Jr - Died 1853 Sept 2 Age 22 years, 21 days Son of Abner & Melinda Crowell (next to mother) S:21

Crowell, Adebert Freeman - Died 1846 Aug 25 Age 16 months Son of Timothy & Rebecca w Crowell S:4

Crowell, Adelaide G - Died 1834 Sept 1 Age 1 year, 5 months Daughter of Capt Henry & Betsey Crowell S:21

Crowell, Agnes L - Died 1945 Born 1852 (between Willis E Crowell MD & son, Robert Dudley Crowell) S:18

Crowell, Alexander - Died 1891 Born 1816 (with wife, Ruth Nickerson) S:21

Crowell, Alice L - Died 1917 Born 1814 (with Ella F Crowell & others) S:21

Crowell, Allen - Died 1891 March 17 Age 71 years, 4 months (with wife, Phebe G Crowell) S:18

Crowell, Allen S - Died 1900 Aug 21 Born 1836 Oct 29 S:8

Crowell, Almond - Died 1864 March 30 Age 41 Lost at sea (listed with Eleanor A Crowell & others) S:21

Crowell, Alonzo - Died 1832 Oct 22 Age 1 year, 7 months Son of William & Betsy Crowell S:4

Crowell, Anna M - Died 1971 Born 1896 S:16

Crowell, Ansel H - Died 1884 Jan 25 Age 26 years, 10 months, 11 days Stone says, "My husband" (next to Jessie Crowell) S:14

Crowell, Arabella E - Died 1903 Jan 11 Born 1835 Oct 8 (with Gorham F Basset & others) S:18

Crowell, Betsey B - Died 1882 Dec 11 Age 77 years, 11 months, 14 days Wife of William Crowell (next to him & Willis T Crowell & others) S:18

Crowell, Braddock P - Died 1841 Sept 17 Age 10 days Son of

Crowell (Cont.)
  Joseph & Huldah Crowell
  (buried next to them) S:8
Crowell, Caroline P - Died 1918
  Nov 5 Born 1849 Aug 22 (a
  hollow metal marker with one
  panel missing) (with Oren H
  Crowell & Henry Hallett) S:18
Crowell, Carroll S - Died 1950
  Born 1886 (next to Mott C
  Crowell) S:18
Crowell, Charles C - Died 1931
  Born 1844 (with Eugenia D
  Gyder & others) S:19
Crowell, Charlotte - Died 1833 July
  21 Age 2 years, 2 months
  Daughter of Julius & Sarah
  Crowell (next to them) S:18
Crowell, Clara P - Died 1884 Sept 7
  in her 24th yr Daughter of
  George W & Mary E Crowell S:4
Crowell, Clarence - Died 1960 Jan
  22 Born 1899 Aug 27 From
  Massachusetts, was PFC in Co1,
  38th Inf (DSM) during World
  War I S:17
Crowell, Constant - Died 1913
  Born 1846 S:21
Crowell, Daniel - Died 1888 Feb 2
  Born 1816 June 10 (with Phebe
  Crowell & others) S:18
Crowell, Daniel 2nd - Died 1882
  March 17 Born 1853 Sept 29
  Son of Ebenezer & Helen Crowell
  (with them) S:21
Crowell, Deborah H - Died 1866
  Dec 9 Age 66 Daughter of Ezra &
  Deborah Crowell S:11
Crowell, Deborah H - Died 1942
  Born 1868 (with Claude Nicker-
  son & Myrtle Savery) S:14
Crowell, Deborah Mrs - Died 1858
  Feb 18 (stone is broken, says
  "our Mother was ready") Widow
  of Capt Ezra Crowell (next to
  him) (Hinckley Ceme records
  #11R say death was on 18 Feb
  age 84) S:11+22R
Crowell, Eben D - Died (no dates)
  Age 9 months (with Prentiss
  Crowell & others) S:18
Crowell, Ebenezer - Died 1904

Crowell (Cont.)
  April 10 Born 1828 April 19
  (with Helen & Daniel Crowell)
  S:21
Crowell, Edmond - Died 1875 Jan
  27 Age 76 (next to wife, Mrs
  Mary Crowell) (his name is also
  spelled Edmund on wifes stone)
  S:21
Crowell, Edmund - Died 1879 ?
  11th Age 68 years, 10 months,
  17 days (stone broken in three
  pieces) S:21
Crowell, Edward G - Died 1884
  March 26 Born 1833 May 31
  (next to William Crowell & oth-
  ers) S:18
Crowell, Eleanor A - Died 1890
  May 6 Age 63 Wife of Almond
  Crowell (listed with him & Gil-
  bert F Crowell and others) S:21
Crowell, Eleazer - Died 1880 Feb 6
  Age 56 years, 11 months, 5 days
  (next Sally Crowell) S:21
Crowell, Elisha - Died 1807 (no
  location noted) S:11R
Crowell, Elisha - Died 1857 (no
  location noted) S:11R
Crowell, Elisha H - Died 1837 June
  28 Age 29 Son of Ezra & Debo-
  rah Crowell S:11
Crowell, Eliza - Died 1875 Feb 9
  Age 34 years, 1 month, 15 days
  Wife of Judah C Crowell (next to
  him) S:21
Crowell, Eliza B Miss - Died 1850
  Nov 13 Age 28 Daughter of Ezra
  & Deborah Crowell S:11
Crowell, Eliza Miss - Died 1830
  Nov 13 Age 28 Daughter of Ezra
  and Deborah Crowell (located at
  Lothrop's Hill) S:26R
Crowell, Elizabeth - Died 1858 (no
  location noted) S:11R
Crowell, Elkanah - Died 1917 Born
  1829 (with Emily Hawes &
  Susan Crowell & others) S:18
Crowell, Elkanah Lincoln - Died
  1867 Born 1865 (with Elkanah
  & Susan Crowell & others) S:18
Crowell, Ella F - Died 1903 Born
  1893 (with James Freeman

Crowell (Cont.)
Crowell & others) S:21

Crowell, Ellen R - Died 1957 Born 1881 S:31

Crowell, Emily C - Died 1887 Jan 1 Age 89 Widow of Capt Washington Crowell (next to him & Emily Clark) S:21

Crowell, Emma - Died (stone not clear) Daughter of Augustus & Mary Ann Crowell S:4

Crowell, Eugene - Died 1937 Born 1852 (Crowell stone) (with Mary E Crowell & others) S:14

Crowell, Evelena - Died 1877 Aug 14 Age 26 years, 3 months Daughter of Abner & Betsey Crowell S:21

Crowell, Everett W - Died 1921 Born 1842 Was in Company D, 10th New York Calvary Vols (buried with Julia A Crowell) S:8

Crowell, Ezra (Capt) - Died 1839 April 26 Age 67 (stone is broken) S:11

Crowell, Fidelia L - Died 1934 Born 1862 (with Mott C Crowell) S:18

Crowell, Frank HD - Died 1930 Jan 29 Born 1854 Mar 3 (buried next to Joseph D Crowell) S:8

Crowell, Frank W - Died 1925 Born 1854 (with Georgia E Crowell & others) S:21

Crowell, George H - Died 1931 Born 1853 (with Josephine Crowell) S:14

Crowell, George W - Died 1823 Apl 1 in his 48th yr S:4

Crowell, Georgia E - Died 1926 Born 1855 (with Almond Crowell & others) S:21

Crowell, Gilbert F - Died 1862 Nov 5 Age 6 Son of Almond & Eleanor Crowell (with them & others) S:21

Crowell, Gorham - Died 1890 Dec 15 Age 67 (stone has been cemented back together again) (next to wife, Mary T Crowell) S:21

Crowell, Hannah C - Died 1895 Dec 22 Born 1836 Jan 13 (next

Crowell (Cont.)
to Edward G Crowell & others) S:18

Crowell, Harold B - Died 1918 Born 1888 S:19

Crowell, Harriet - Died 1874 April 14 Born 1813 Feb 21 (stone down, vandalized) Wife of Joseph Crowell (next to him) S:18

Crowell, Harry T - Died 1915 Born 1885 (with George & Josephine Crowell) S:14

Crowell, Helen - Died 1901 May 9 Born 1829 Nov 29 (with Ebenezer & Daniel Crowell) S:21

Crowell, Helen A - Died 1910 March 26 Born 1840 March 2 (with Osborne Crowell) S:18

Crowell, Herbert L - Died 1912 Born 1872 Stone says,"We will meet again" (next to Mary E Crowell) S:19

Crowell, Howard G - Died 1845? Sept 9 Age 13 months, 19 days Son of Oren & Hannah S Crowell (next to father) S:18

Crowell, Howes - Died 1860 Aug 8 Age 10 months, 21 days (next to Maria B Crowell) S:21

Crowell, Huldah S - Died 1900 Mar 26 Born 1817 Dec 23 Wife of Joseph Crowell (buried same grave) S:8

Crowell, Ida F - Died 1902 Mar 4 Born 1879 June 17 S:5

Crowell, Isabel F - Died 1858 March 22 Age 1 year?, 10 months, 4 days (stone worn) Daughter of Gorham & Mary Crowell (next to mother) S:21

Crowell, James Freeman - Died 1941 Born 1868 (with wife, Lizzie A Baker & others) S:21

Crowell, James H - Died 1871 Sept 16 Age 13 years, 2 months Son of Allen & Phebe Crowell (next to them & sister, Nellie Crowell) S:18

Crowell, James L - Died 1909 Born 1909 (with Alice L Crowell & others) S:21

Crowell, Jessie - Died 1915 Born

Crowell (Cont.)
1855 (next to Ansel H Crowell) S:14

Crowell, Joseph - Died 1836 Age 50 (with Abigail Crowell & Augusta C Bearse) S:18

Crowell, Joseph - Died 1889 Nov 10 Born 1816 Nov 11 (next to wife, Harriet Crowell) S:18

Crowell, Joseph D - Died 1846 Aug 9 Age 1 year, 1 day Son of Joseph & Huldah Crowell (buried next to them) S:8

Crowell, Joseph D - Died 1849 Oct 20 Son of Joseph & Huldah Crowell (buried next to them) S:8

Crowell, Joseph D - Died 1887 Sept 13 Born 1812 Feb 22 (on same stone with Huldah S Crowell, wife) S:8

Crowell, Joseph L - Died (no dates) Age 15 months, 27 days (with Luther Crowell & others) S:18

Crowell, Josephine - Died 1941 Born 1858 (with George H Crowell) S:14

Crowell, Judah - Died 1939 Born 1865 (next to wife, Ida May Baxter) S:21

Crowell, Judah C - Died 1866 Jan 6 Age 24 years, 4 months, 22 days (next to wife, Eliza Crowell) S:21

Crowell, Julia A - Died 1939 Born 1845 (buried with Everett W Crowell, husband) S:8

Crowell, Julius W - Died 1867 Nov 30 Age 28 years, 8 months, 23 days He was a Mason (with wife, Sarah L Crowell Next to children, Sarah, infant son & Charlotte Crowell) S:18

Crowell, Junius - Died 1860 Aug Son of Ebenezer & Helen Crowell (next to them) S:21

Crowell, Kelley H - Died 1855 Born 1818 (with Mary L & Leonard Crowell) S:18

Crowell, Leander - Died 1847 Aug 1 Age 35 years, 8 months (stone is down) S:21

Crowell, Leonard - Died 1848 Born

Crowell (Cont.)
1839 (with Kelley & Mary Crowell) S:18

Crowell, Levina L - Died (no dates) Age 9 months (with Eben D Crowell & others) S:18

Crowell, Luther - Died (no dates) Age 8 months, 26 days (with Levina L Crowell & others) S:18

Crowell, Lydia F - Died 1914 Born 1839 Wife of Capt Daniel Bearse (with him) S:18

Crowell, Lydia Mrs - Died 1842 Nov 6 Age 46 Widow of Capt Prentiss Crowell (listed on same stone) S:11

Crowell, Maria B - Died 1919 Born 1851 (next to Christopher Crowell Curtis) S:21

Crowell, Martha - Died 1867 March 22 Age 35 Wife of Christopher Crowell (next to child, Howes Crowell) S:21

Crowell, Mary Ann - Died 1851 Oct 7 Age 35 years, 5 days Wife of Augustus Crowell S:4

Crowell, Mary C - Died 1936 Born 1856 (Crowell stone) (with Mary E Crowell & others) S:14

Crowell, Mary E - Died 1890 Born 1853 (Crowell stone) (with Mary C Crowell & others) S:14

Crowell, Mary E - Died 1918 Born 1867 (next to Herbert L Crowell) S:19

Crowell, Mary L - Died 1905 Born 1820 (with Kelley & Leonard Crowell) S:18

Crowell, Mary Mrs - Died 1855 Jan 17 Age 46 years, 3 months, 10 days Wife of Edmund Crowell (next to him) S:21

Crowell, Mary T - Died 1880 April 30 Age 54 (stone is down) Wife of Gorham Crowell (next to him) S:21

Crowell, Melinda Mrs - Died 1831 or 1834 Oct 10 Age 25 Wife of Capt Abner Crowell (next to him) S:21

Crowell, Mott C - Died 1927 Born 1862 (with Fidelia L Crowell)

Crowell (Cont.)
S:18

Crowell, Nellie - Died 1854 Feb 2 Age 1 year, 4 months Daughter of Allen & Phebe Crowell (next to them) S:18

Crowell, Nellie C - Died 1977 Born 1895 Wife of Milton Crocker (with him) S:14

Crowell, Nellie R - Died 1879 Born 1878 (buried with Julia Crowell) S:8

Crowell, Olive - Died 1851 Oct 1 Age 78 yrs 11 mos Widow of Paul Crowell (next to him) S:3R

Crowell, Oren - Died 1858 July 13 Age 50 (next to Howard G Crowell, son) S:18

Crowell, Oren H - Died 1908 Dec 9 Born 1845 Oct 13 (a metal marker with one panel missing) (with Henry Hallett & Caroline P Crowell) S:18

Crowell, Osborne - Died 1905 Dec 15 Born 1848 Aug 1 (with Helen A Crowell) S:18

Crowell, Paul - Died 1831 Nov 2 Age 65 (next to Olive Crowell) S:3R

Crowell, Phebe - Died 1892 Aug 30 Born 1814 Oct 29 (with Joseph L Crowell & others) S:18

Crowell, Phebe G - Died 1887 Sept 17 Age 64 years, 10 months Wife of Allen Crowell (with him) S:18

Crowell, Prentiss - Died 1882 Born 1825 (with Luther Crowell & others) S:18

Crowell, Prentiss (Capt) - Died 1830 Aug 20 Age 38 Lost at sea (listed on same stone with wife, Mrs Lydia Crowell) (Hinckley Ceme records #11R say death year was 1830) S:11+22R

Crowell, Rebecca P - Died 1886 Born 1822 Wife of Phineas S Berry (with him) S:18

Crowell, Robert Dudley - Died 1880 Dec 26 Son of Dr Willis & Agnes Crowell (next to them) S:18

Crowell, Ruth - Died 1906 Born 1820 Wife of Lysander Chase

Crowell (Cont.)
(next to him) S:21

Crowell, Ruth Mrs - Died 1799 March 26 in her 28th yr Wife of James Crowell & daughter of Ebenezer Howes S:10R+22R

Crowell, Sally - Died 1893 Aug 15 Age 70 years, 10 months, 5 days (with Eleazer Crowell) S:21

Crowell, Sarah - Died 1829 Dec 29 Age 5 months Daughter of Julius & Sarah Crowell (next to Charlotte Crowell) S:18

Crowell, Sarah L - Died 1849 Born 1825 (with Horace S Basset & others) S:18

Crowell, Sarah L - Died 1876 Jan 6 Age 35 years, 7 months Widow of Julius W Crowell (with him) S:18

Crowell, Sidney - Died 1890 Aug 30 Born 1828 March 21 (with Arabella Crowell & others) S:18

Crowell, Susan - Died 1908 Born 1831 (with Emily Hawes & Elkanah Crowell & others) Wife of Elkanah S:18

Crowell, Sylvia - Died 1894 Nov 13 Age 89 years, 11 months (next to Edmond Crowell) S:21

Crowell, Teresa - Died 1901 Feb 5 Born 1821 July 3 (with W Wallace Frost) S:18

Crowell, Timothy B(Capt) - Died 1848 May 21 Age 33 years, 7 months Wife was Rebecca Crowell S:4

Crowell, Washington (Capt) - Died 1844 Feb 24 Age 45 (next to wife, Emily C Crowell) S:21

Crowell, William - Died 1865 Feb 26 Age 59 years, 4 months (next to wife, Betsey B Crowell) S:18

Crowell, William A - Died 1874 Nov 25 Age 25 years, 11 days Drowned in Mobile Bay, Alabama (next to James & Nellie Crowell) S:18

Crowell, Willis E (MD) - Died 1929 Born 1850 (next to down stone from vandals, cannot read it) (also next to Agnes L Crowell)

Crowell (Cont.)
S:18
Crowell, Willis T - Died 1879 June 11 Age 27 years, 8 months (stone off base) (next to Hannah C Crowell & others) S:18

Crowell, Zenas E - Died 1886 May 10 Born 1820 Dec 3 (with Teresa Crowell & others) S:18

Crowell?, (infant) - Died 1828 May 5 Age 8 days Son of Julius W & Sarah L Crowell? (next to Sarah Crowell) S:18

Crowther, Martha L - Died 1981 Born 1892 (with Edgar L Knapp & Alice L Bearse) S:17

Crudup, Sallie L - Died 1943 Born 1871 (with Hanson Washington) S:18

Cummings, William Gerald - Died 1976 Feb 26 Born 1894 Sept 18 He was a 1st Lieut in US Army in World War 1 (flag at his grave) S:11

Cunha, Helen P - Died 1967 Born 1894 S:15

Cunha, John S Sr - Died 1976 Born 1899 (one stone away from Helen P Cunha) S:15

Cunningham, Hannah - Died 1747 July 28 in her 41st yr Wife of Alexander Cunningham S:9R+ 22R

Curtis, Christopher Crowell - Died 1956 Born 1871 S:21

Curtis, Dorothy M - Died 1978 June 2 Born 1889 May 3 (with John A Curtis) S:13

Curtis, Elizabeth S - Died 1894 Jan 20 Age 70 years, 10 months, 4 days Wife of Capt John Curtis S:19

Curtis, Frederick N - Died 1969 May 28 Born 1948 June 18 Stone says, "Massachusetts SP4, TRP, C10 Calvary, 4th infantry Division, Vietnam BSM-PH" (he has a military star at his grave too) S:13

Curtis, James Everett - Died 1914 Born 1854 S:18

Curtis, John A - Died 1970 Oct 11

Curtis (Cont.)
Born 1886 March 16 (with Dorothy M Curtis) S:13

Curtis, Robert L - Died 1965 Born 1876 (with Vera E Curtis) S:15

Curtis, Vera E (or B) - Died 1985 Born 1893 (with Robert L Curtis) S:15

Cusick, (baby girl) - Died 1963 (undertaker plaque) (next to Nellie Sears & William Cusick) S:19

Cusick, William W - Died 1972 June 27 Born 1931 Dec 15 From Massachusetts, was a Cpl in 172 Infantry Reg during the Korean War (next to Nellie Sears & Baby Girl Cusick) S:19

Cypres, Hagar - Died 1809 Apr 27 Wife of George Cypres S:5

Cypres, Martha - Died Dec (stone not clear) Wife of George Cypres S:5

Dahill, Dora M - Died 1957 Born 1903 Daughter to Mary Dahill (with her & others) S:31

Dahill, James - Died 1902 Born 1865 (with Dora M Dahill & others) S:31

Dahill, Mary - Died 1949 Born 1876 Stone says,"Wife" (is she the wife of Richard McDonough who heads up the stone?) (also with son, Richard Dahill & others) S:20

Dahill, Richard - Died 1911 Born 1911 Son of Mary Dahill (with her & Dora Rooney & others) S:31

Daley, George T - Died 1956 Born 1879 (listed with Mary T Daley) S:16

Daley, Mary T - Died (still living 1991?) Born 1878 (note: this would make this person 113 years old or she is buried elsewhere?) S:16

Dalomba, Julio - Buried 1982 March 30 Age 85 S:15R

Dalur, Manuel A - Died 1964 Born 1900 S:15

Daly, John - Died 1948 Born 1889

Daly (Cont.)
(next to Marie Daly) S:16

Daly, Marie - Died 1956 Born 1896 (next to John Daly) S:16

Damaso, Barbosa - Died 1966 Born 1882 S:15

Danaher, Catherine M - Died (no dates) Wife of Robert Elliott (listed with him) S:16

Danforth, Abbie Dottridge - Died 1946 Born 1870 (with Kenneth Adams Danforth) S:14

Danforth, Kenneth Adams - Died 1897 Born 1895 (with Robert Lemuel Shedd) S:14

Daniel, (Baby) - Died 1895 (with Annie Daniel & others) S:31

Daniel, Annie - Died 1904 Born 1897 (with Bridget Morris & others) S:31

Daniel, Charles - Died 1913 Born 1832 or 1887 Stone says, "Father" (with wife, Kate M Daniel & all their children) S:31

Daniel, Charles J - Died 1959 Born 1875 (with brother, Edward G & sister, Margaret Daniel & others) S:31

Daniel, Edward G - Died 1961 Born 1889 (with brother, Charles & sister, Margaret & Baby Daniel & others) S:31

Daniel, Georgina - Died 1960 Born 1879 Wife of Frederic Bill (with him) S:12

Daniel, John - Died 1958 Born 1887 (next to Lillian (Mcardle) Daniel) S:16

Daniel, Joseph M - Died 1969 Born 1892 (next to Marion (Childs) A Daniel) S:16

Daniel, Kate M - Died 1939 Born 1854 Stone says,"Mother" (with husband, Charles Daniel & Margaret M Daniel & their other children) S:31

Daniel, Lillian (Mcardle) - Died 1978 Born 1882 (next to John Daniel) S:16

Daniel, Margaret M - Died 1942 Born 1882 (with brother, Charles J Daniel & others) S:31

Daniel, Marion A (Childs) - Died 1970 Born 1892 (next to Lillian (Mcardle) Daniel) S:16

Daniel, Robert M - Died 1935 Born 1875 (with wife, Blanche Lovell) S:16

Darling, Elizabeth A - Died 1954 Born 1862 Daughter of Daniel Sturgis & Eliza Bowman (with them) S:14

Darling, Roland Rice - Died 1986 Born 1896 (middle name from Hinckley ceme records) S:15

DaRosa, Sebastiao - Died 1951 Born 1878 S:18

Dauce, Ivy M - Died 1983 Born 1894 Wife of Henry Morris S:11

Daudelin, Doris Cutler - Buried 1984 March 10 Age 86 S:15R

David, Joseph A - Died 1953 Dec 6 Born 1868 Aug 27 (Veteran plaque that says, 1917-18) (next to Susie E David) S:19

David, Mary L - Died 1937 May 16 Born 1875 Oct 19 (next to Susie E David) S:19

David, Susie E - Died (still living 1991?) Born 1890 Sept 1 (101 years old?) (next to Joseph A David) S:19

Davidson, Dawn Marie - Died 1976 Born 1958 Stone says, "Unique" S:20

Davidson, Emil H - Died 1978 Born 1900 (with Ira A Davidson) S:20

Davidson, Herbert A - Died 1966 July 19 Born 1924 July 2 Was in the Mass USNR as Lieutenant (flag at grave) S:11

Davidson, Ira A - Died 1986 Born 1903 (also has West Barnstable Fire Dept plaque) With Emil H Davidson S:20

Davidson, Wiley Hilton - Died 1976 Jan 8 Born 1894 Nov 26 Was a Cpl in US Army during World War I S:17

Davies, Clinton A - Died 1982 Born 1931 (with wife, Marcia Crosby & others) S:19

Davies, John - Died 1984 Born 1909 (with wife, Mattie A Sturgis

Davies (Cont.)
& others) S:19

Davis, (son) - Died (no dates) Son of John & Mehitable Davis S:9

Davis, ? - Died Age 18 months, 25 days (next to Josiah Davis d1799) Son of William & Martha Davis S:9

Davis, A - Died 1864 (large crypt located at street level in a hill, large metal door, flag placed there, probably Civil War Vet or victim, large metal door) S:10

Davis, Abagail - Died 1775 Oct 3 Daughter of Jonathan & Susanna Davis (Hinckley Ceme records #10R say age was 1 year, 6 months, 32 days?) S:10

Davis, Abbie V - Died 1917 Born 1843 (with Helen A Davis & others) S:18

Davis, Abgail Mrs - Died (no date on stone) (next to Jesse & Isaac Davis) S:9

Davis, Abiah - Died 1794 Feb 9 Age 25 Wife of James Davis, the 3rd S:10R

Davis, Abigail - Died 1733 Aug 25 in her 20th yr Wife of John Davis S:9

Davis, Abigail - Died 1775 Oct 3 Daughter of Jonathan & Susanna Davis S:10+26R

Davis, Aldis N - Died 1984 Born 1897 (was a Mason) (with wife, Eleanor H Davis) S:15

Davis, Anna - Died (underground) Wife of Charles Lewis S:10

Davis, Anna - Died 1856 July 18 Age 3 months Daughter of Benjamin & Minerva Davis (between brother, Henry & James Henry Davis) S:19

Davis, Annah Mrs - Died 1830 May 8 Age 35 S:10R

Davis, Ansel Dr - Died 1830 Oct 4 Age 45 S:10R

Davis, Ansel Dr - Died 1850 Oct 1 Age 45 S:10

Davis, Asa Crocker - Died 1794 Oct 19 Age 2 years, 4 months, 15 days Son of James & Abiah

Davis (Cont.)
Davis S:10R

Davis, Barbara R - Died (still living 1991?) Born 1929 Wife of Clarence E Davis (with him & Manuel A Davis) S:20

Davis, Barnabas - Died 1799 Dec 13 in his 19th yr Son of Joseph & Mary Davis S:10+26R

Davis, Benjamin - Died 1875 Nov 13 Born 1807 May 8 (next to wife, Minerva Davis) S:19

Davis, Benjamin F - Died 1935 Feb 24 Born 1864 Aug 31 (with Harriet Sturgis, wife) S:8

Davis, Betsey - Died 1820 Dec 17 Age 41 Wife of George Davis (family all buried near each other) S:10

Davis, Catherine T Miss - Died 1825 Sept 5 in her 23rd yr Daughter of Honorable Job C & Desire Davis (next to them) S:10+26R

Davis, Charles - Died 1842 Nov 28 Age 33 (next to David Davis) S:10

Davis, Clarence E - Died 1990 Born 1923 (has 2 stones) Was a S1 in US Navy during World War II (with wife, Barbara R & uncle, Manuel A Davis) S:20

Davis, Cordelia C - Died 1936 Born 1863 Wife of George W Taylor (with him, Eleanor MT Hamilton and others on large Taylor stone) S:12

Davis, Daniel - Died 1792 Aug 8 Age 5 months 23 days Son of Honorable, John & Mercy Davis Esq S:10

Davis, Daniel - Died 1835 Oct 27 at Cambridge, Mass Born 8 May 1762 30 years, Solicitor General of the Commonwealth S:10

Davis, Daniel - Died 1843 Born 1800 (lost at sea) (listed on same stone with Henry & Datie Davis) S:8

Davis, Daniel - Died 1849 Born 1838 (on same side of stone with Daniel & Olive Davis) (listed on

136

Davis (Cont.)
    same stone with Henry & Datie
    Davis) S:8
Davis, Daniel (Honorable) - Died
    1799 April 22 in his 86th yr
    S:10R
Davis, Datie M - Died 1875/85?
    Born 1840 (buried with Henry
    Davis, husband) S:8
Davis, David - Died 1855 May 25
    (buried next to wife, Elizabeth
    Davis) S:10
Davis, Deborah - Died 1867 May 3
    Age 79 Widow of the late, George
    Davis (next to him) S:10
Davis, Deborah Mrs - Died 1813
    April 24 in her 53rd yr Wife of
    Josiah Davis (Hinckley Ceme
    records #10R say age was 53)
    S:10+26R
Davis, Desire - Died 1759 Aug in
    her 5th yr Daughter of James &
    Jane Davis S:9+26R
Davis, Desire - Died 1862 Born
    1773 Wife of Honorable, Job C
    Davis (next to him) Stone erected
    by the grandchildren (newer
    stone) S:10
Davis, Edmund G - Died 1814 Feb
    4 Age 1 year, 10 months, 8 days
    Son of Dr Ansel & Hitty Davis
    S:4
Davis, Eleanor H - Died 1973 Born
    1902 Wife of Aldis N Davis (with
    him) S:15
Davis, Elezabeth - Died 1739 June
    6 in her 59th yr Wife of Thomas
    Davis S:9
Davis, Elisha T - Died 1833 May at
    Mobile Bay, Alabama Born 1798
    Oct 28 Son of Elisha T & Ruth C
    Davis S:10
Davis, Elisha Thatcher - Died 1804
    Oct 13 Age 37 S:10
Davis, Elizabeth - Died (date not
    clear) Wife of Gershom Davis
    (Hinckley Ceme records #9R
    says death date was 1727 June
    6 in her 23rd yr) S:9
Davis, Elizabeth - Died 1724 Oct
    31 Age 17 days Daughter of
    Jonathan & Elizabeth Davis

Davis (Cont.)
    S:9R
Davis , Elizabeth - Died 1729 Nov
    28 Age 19 days Daughter of
    Jonathan & Elizabeth Davis S:9
Davis, Elizabeth - Died 1738/9 Jan
    6 in her 59th yr Wife of Simon
    Davis S:9R+26R
Davis, Elizabeth - Died 1747 June
    29 Age 11 months 24 days
    Daughter of James & Jane Davis
    S:9+26R
Davis, Elizabeth - Died 1816 Aug
    27 Age 13 months Daughter of
    Job C & Desire Davis (next to
    them) S:10
Davis, Elizabeth Mrs - Died 1733
    Sept 14 Age 32 Wife of Jonathan
    Davis S:9R
Davis, Elizabeth Mrs - Died 1860
    Nov 26 Age 86 Widow of the late
    David Davis (buried next to him)
    S:10
Davis, Emma A - Died 1933 Born
    1843 (also Henry Davis, wife
    listed on same stone) S:8
Davis, Ernest L - Died 1881 Born
    1856 (son of Henry & Datie
    Davis, on same stone) S:8
Davis, Eveline - Died 1857 Born
    1856 Daughter of Eveline &
    Frederick (on same stone) S:11
Davis, Eveline - Died 1910 Born
    1830 (a very large stone located
    in middle of cemetery) S:11
Davis, Eveline P - Died 1910 Born
    1880 (with Eveline S Davis &
    others) S:11
Davis, Eveline S - Died 1857 Born
    1856 (with Frederick W Davis &
    others) S:11
Davis, Experience - Died 1897 May
    5 Born 1810 June 25 Wife of
    Handy Harris MD S:10
Davis, Florence A - Died 1931 Born
    1872 (buried with Herbert &
    Claribel Wright) S:8
Davis, Frank E - Died 1905 Born
    1873 (with William G Davis &
    others) S:18
Davis, Frederick S (or C) - Died
    1896 Born 1822 (with Eveline P

Davis (Cont.)
Davis & others) S:11

Davis, Frederick W - Died 1933 Born 1858 Son of Frederick & Eveline Davis (on same stone) (with Susie G Davis & others) S:11

Davis, Gashum (Deacon) - Died 1790 April 29 in his 87th yr S:10R

Davis, George - Died 1847 Nov 9 Age 69 S:10+26R

Davis, George H - Died (still living 1991?) Born 1896 (listed with Elvia Clough, wife) S:14

Davis, George J - Died 1931 Born 1916 S:31

Davis, George L - Died 1812 Feb 23 Age 1 Son of George & Betsey Davis (near them) S:10

Davis, George R - Died 1957 Born 1931 (with Susan B Davis) S:12

Davis, George R - Died 1957 Born 1931 (with Riley Davis) S:12

Davis, Hannah - Died 1729 Dec 20 Age 5 months, 13 days Daughter of James & Thankfull Davis S:5

Davis, Hannah - Died 1739 May 3 in her 69th yr (next to Joseph Davis) S:9+26R

Davis, Hannah - Died 1888 Jan 4 Age 80 years, 9 months, 21 days Wife of Isaac Davis (possibly attached to her stone, but stone is gone from vandals) S:19

Davis, Harriett W - Died 1955 Born 1890 Stone says,"Mother" (next to Hartley R Davis) S:17

Davis, Hartley R - Died (no dates) Stone says,"In memory of him, Sportsman of Cape Cod" (next to Harriett W Davis) S:17

Davis, Helen A - Died 1866 Born 1865 (with William R Davis & others) S:18

Davis, Henrietta - Died 1836 Born 1836 (on same side of large stone with Daniel & Olive Davis) (listed on Henry & Datie Davis stone) S:8

Davis, Henrietta - Died 1849 Born 1843 (stone is perpetual care)

Davis (Cont.)
(buried with Daniel & Olive Davis & others) S:8

Davis, Henry - Died 1857 Oct 13 Age 4 years, 23 days (stone is down) Son of Benjamin & Minerva Davis (between mother & sister, Anna Davis) S:19

Davis, Henry L - Died 1899 Born 1837 (very large stone with many on it) (buried with Datie M Davis, his wife) S:8

Davis, Hetty Miss - Died 186? April 10 Born 1779 Oct 13 Stone says, "Gone Home" (stone is broken at base laying on ground) S:10

Davis, Isaac - Died (no date) Son of John & Mehitable Davis (Hinckley Ceme records #9R say death was 1724 Aug 23 age 20 days) S:9

Davis, Isaac - Died (stone is gone and is part of wifes, stone, Hannah Davis, this is only a guess that Isaac is here with her) S:19

Davis, Isaac - Died 1727 Nov 2 Age 1 year, 8 months Son of John & Mehetable Davis S:9R

Davis, Isaac - Died 1804 Aug Age 40 Stone erected by his children S:10

Davis, James - Died 1745 Oct 6 in his 46th yr S:9R+26R

Davis, James - Died 1767 April 22 in his 3rd yr Son of James & Jane Davis S:9R+26R

Davis, James - Died 1796 May 9 in his 69th yr S:10R+26R

Davis, James - Died 1821 Jan 22 Age 78 S:10

Davis, James Henry - Died 1853 Dec 14 Age 17 years, 1 month, 26 days (next to Anna Davis) S:19

Davis, James Jr - Died 1798 Sept 16 Age 31 S:10

Davis, James Newton Cannon - Died 1826 Oct 22 Age 6 weeks, 2 days Son of Lothrop & Harriet Davis S:10R

Davis, Jane C - Died 1812 Jan 10 Age 13 months,6 days Daughter of Job C & Desire Davis (next to them) S:10

Davis, Jane Mrs - Died 1766 Nov 27 in her 67th yr Widow of Deacon Robert Davis S:9R+26R

Davis, Jenette - Died 1826 June 2 Age 15 years or 15 years Daughter of Ansel Davis S:10R

Davis, Jesse - Died 1724 Oct 28 Age 2 mos 25 days Son of John & Mehitable Davis S:9+26R

Davis, Job C (Honorable) - Died 1827 Oct 17 Age 56 S:10

Davis, John - Died 1739 Nov 29 (Hinckley Ceme records #9R say died in his 59th yr) S:9+26R

Davis, John - Died 1863 (?) Mar 19 Age 34 Son of Joseph A & Phebe Davis (in Davis Plot with metal fence around it on hill near the street) S:10

Davis, John (Honorable) - Died 1825 Mar 27 in his 81st yr (he held many important public offices) (stone is a large monument) S:10+26R

Davis, Jonathan - Died 1729 Nov 7 in his 3rd yr Son of Jonathan & Elizabeth Davis S:9+26R

Davis, Jonathan - Died 1840 Sept 22 in his 91st yr S:9+26R

Davis, Joseph - Died 1735 Aug 10 in his 71st yr S:9+26R

Davis, Joseph - Died 1745 Dec 30 in his 48th yr S:9R+26R

Davis, Joseph - Died 1804 Feb 12 Age 71 S:10

Davis, Joseph A - Died 1877 Mar 22 Age 73 (in Davis plot) S:10

Davis, Joseph S - Died 1963 Born 1885 (with Mary Davis) S:16

Davis, Joshia - Died 1776 June 29 Age 12 years, 9 months (noted as Obit) Son of Solomon & Elizabeth Davis S:9

Davis, Josiah - Died 1736 April 15 Born 1722 Feb 19 Son of John Davis Esq S:9R

Davis, Josiah - Died 1799 Son of John Davis S:9

Davis, June H - Died (still living 1991?) Born 1930 (listed with Manuel Davis) S:20

Davis, L - Died 1862 (possibly Civil War Casualty?) Large crypt at street level with large metal door dug into a hill S:8

Davis, Lothrope - Died 1839 April 29 Age 9 Son of Elisha T & Ruth Davis S:10

Davis, Louisa - Died 1891 Born 1816 Daughter of Ebenezer & Phoebe Bacon (buried in Bacon family plot) S:9

Davis, Louisa A - Died 1814 Aug 6 Age 6 years, 7 months Daughter of Dr Ansel & Hitty Davis S:4

Davis, Louisa B - Died 1887 Nov 17 Age 44 years, 9 months, 17 days Wife of Prentiss H Davis (next to him) S:19

Davis, Louisa Miss - Died 1803 March 5 Age 10 years Daughter of Elisha Thatcher Davis & Ruthy Crocker Davis S:10

Davis, Lucern Mrs - Died 1775 April 15 Age 37 Wife of Joseph Davis S:10

Davis, Lucernia ? - Died 1775 Sept 25 Daughter of Joseph Davis S:10

Davis, Lydia - Died 1811 (?) Jan 24 Age 23 (stone worn) Daughter of Josiah & Deborah Davis S:10

Davis, Lydia Mrs - Died 1763 Dec 12 in her 55th yr Daughter of Joseph & Hannah Davis S:9R+26R

Davis, Manuel A - Died 1984 Born 1889 (has undertaker plaque also) Uncle of Clarence E Davis (with him & Barbara R Davis) S:20

Davis, Manuel H - Died 1987 Born 1921 (with June Davis) S:20

Davis, Martha - Died 1761 May 17 Age 18 months, 25 days Daughter of William & Martha Davis S:9R

Davis, Martha - Died 1773 (Hinckley Ceme records say death on 5 Jan age 47) Widow of Capt

Davis (Cont.)

William Davis S:9

Davis, Mary - Died 1756 March 31 in her 53rd yr Wife of Gershom Davis S:9+26R

Davis, Mary - Died 1824 April 13 in her 84th yr Widow of Joseph Davis (located at Cobb Hill East Cemetery)(Goodspeed or Meeting House Hill East) S:26R

Davis, Mary - Died 1849 April 9 Age 82 Widow of James Davis Jr (buried next to him) S:10

Davis, Mary - Died 1911 Born 1831 Wife of Paul Maraspin (buried next to him) S:10

Davis, Mary - Died 1983 Born 1888 (with Joseph S Davis) S:16

Davis, Mary Annie - Died 1898 Oct 24 Born 1846 July 12 Wife of Afred Crocker (buried next to him) S:10

Davis, Mary F Miss - Died 1823 Aug 30 in her 20th yr Daughter of George & Betsey Davis (next to father) S:10+26R

Davis, Mary Freeman - Died 1917 Dec 16 Age 86 years, 4 months, 9 days Wife of Otis Hinckley (next to him) S:19

Davis, Mehetable - Died 1760 June 14 in her 42nd yr Wife of Daniel Davis S:9R+26R

Davis, Mehitable - Died 1803 Oct 10 Age 88 Widow of Honorable Daniel Davis Esq S:10

Davis, Mehitable - Died 1846 Sept 18 Age 58 Widow of Dr Ansel Davis (buried next to him) S:10

Davis, Mercy - Died 1796 Dec 12 in her 36th yr 2nd Wife of Joseph Davis S:10+26R

Davis, Mercy Mrs - Died 1832 Oct 29 Relict of Honorable, John Davis Esq S:10

Davis, Minerva - Died 1903 April 5 Born 1812 June 2 Wife of Benjamin Davis (next to him & son, Henry Davis) S:19

Davis, Nellie M - Died 1948 Born 1893 S:16

Davis, Olive D - Died 1870 Born

Davis (Cont.)

1806 (listed on same side of stone with Daniel Davis) (on same stone with Henry & Datie Davis) S:8

Davis, Patience - Died 1759 May 12 in her 25th yr Wife of Benjamin Davis S:11+26R

Davis, Patience Mrs - Died 1739 or 59 May 12 Wife of Benjamin Davis S:11

Davis, Phebe - Died 1874 Jan 6 Age 68 years 6 months Wife of Joseph A Davis (next to him in Davis plot) S:10

Davis, Phyllis M - Died 1956 Born 1907 (buried with Rosa & Orren Kelley & family) S:8

Davis, Placide - Died (no date) Born 1882 (listed with Edward C Williams) S:17

Davis, Prentiss H - Died 1889 May 13 Age 47 years, 10 months Was a Private in CoH, 24th Regiment MVM (also has plaque that says, 1861-65) (next to wife, Louisa B Davis) S:19

Davis, Priscilla - Died 1751 April 24 in her 42nd yr Wife of Capt Simon Davis (next to him) S:3R

Davis, Rebecca N - Died 1863 Jan 16 Age 44 years, 6 months S:4

Davis, Rebecka - Died 1769 (Hinckley Ceme records #9R say death was 28 Nov Age 65 years, 6 months) Wife of Stephen Davis S:9

Davis, Reliance Mrs - Died 1817 April 22 Age 67 Wife of James Davis S:10

Davis, Riley E - Died 1976 Born 1899 (with Susan B Davis) S:12

Davis, Robert - Died 1738 Dec 3 in his 7th yr Son of Gershom & Mary Davis S:9+26R

Davis, Robert - Died 1765 June 1 in his 70th yr Was Deacon of the East Church in Barnstable for nearly 27 years S:9R+26R

Davis, Robert - Died 1771 Aug 30 Age in his 12th yr Son of James & Jane Davis S:9R+26R

Davis, Robert E - Died 1937 Born 1887 Member of the Barnstable Fire Dept (flag at stone) S:11

Davis, Robert O - Died 1971 Born 1928 (with Susan & George Davis) S:12

Davis, Sally Mrs - Died 1807 March 17 Age 13 Daughter of Honorable John Davis Esq & Mercy Davis S:10

Davis, Shirley - Died 1872 Born 1868 (daughter of Henry & Datie Davis, on same stone) S:8

Davis, Shubel - Died 1745 June 27 in the 61st yr S:3

Davis, Simon - Died 1755 April 10 in his 72nd yr (next to wife Pricilla) S:3R

Davis, Stephen - Died 1757 Dec 7 in his 64th yr S:3

Davis, Stephen - Died 1782 Jan 4 in his 82nd yr S:9

Davis, Stephen Jr - Died 1777 Dec 18 Age 39 S:3

Davis, Susan B - Died 1961 Born 1897 (with George R Davis & Riley Davis) S:12

Davis, Susannah - Died 1841 Sept 26 in her 92nd yr Widow of Jonathan Davis S:9

Davis, Susie C - Died 1940 Born 1860 Daughter of Eveline & Frederick Davis (on same stone) S:11

Davis, Susie G - Died 1946 Born 1860 (with Frederick W Davis & others) S:11

Davis, Synthia Mrs - Died (no dates) Daughter of Joseph & Mercy Davis S:10

Davis, Thankful - Died 1745 Aug 24 in her 36th yr Wife of James Davis S:9R+26R

Davis, Thomas - Died 1792 Feb 24 Age 10 days Son of Honorable, John & Mercy Davis Esq S:10

Davis, Timothy - Died 1733 Nov 26 (next to John Davis who died 1739) (Hinckley Ceme records #9R say death was 1753 age 8 months, 23 days) S:9

Davis, Timothy - Died 1874 April 9

Davis (Cont.)
at New York City Born 1792 Oct 1 (on same stone with Elisha T Davis) S:10

Davis, William G - Died 1908 Born 1842 (with Abbie V Davis & others) S:18

Davis, William R - Died 1905 Born 1875 (with Frank E Davis & others) S:18

Davy, Eleanor E - Died 1985 Born 1890 S:15

Day, Mary H - Died 1903 May 7 Born 1864 Jan 22 S:11

Day, Thomas C - Died 1905 April 27 Born 1856 April 20 S:11

Day, Thomas Chadwick Jr - Died 1905 Aug 17 Born 1886 June 24 S:11

Day, Vincent Francis - Died 1985 Feb 5 Born 1898 May 23 S:16

De Hall, Osceoloa - Died 1980 Born 1899 (with John P Harris) S:17

De Veer, Flossie V - Died 1977 Born 1888 (with Harold W De Veer) S:14

De Veer, Harold W - Died 1969 Born 1890 (with Flossie V De Veer) S:14

DeAdder, Arland W - Died (still living 1991?) Born 1917 Stone says,"Son" (with Minnie F & next to Robert W DeAdder) S:19

DeAdder, Minnie F - Died (still living 1991?) Born 1892 Stone saus,"Mother" (with Arland W & next to Robert W DeAdder) S:19

DeAdder, Robert W - Died 1962 Aug 23 Born 1897 Jan 17 From Massachusetts, was Private in Co K, 2 inf NG during World War I (next to Minnie & Arland DeAdder) S:19

DeAmaril, Corillia - Died (no dates) Born 1848 (with Asa Matthews & others) S:21

Dean, Genevieve S - Died 1979 Born 1918 S:20

Debitetto, Angelo - Died 1982 Born 1895 (has two stones) Was a Pvt in US Army during World War I S:15

141

Decker, Eva K - Died 1969 Born 1897 Wife of Lambert Decker (with him) S:16

Decker, Lambert J - Died 1981 Born 1898 (with wife, Eva K Decker) S:16

Decoteau, Florence M - Died 1974 Born 1900 (with Henry D Decoteau) S:16

Decoteau, Henry D - Died 1974 Aug 31 Born 1899 July 14 Was a Sea in US Navy (with Florence M Decoteau) S:16

Deehr (?), James McDonoth (?) - Died 1822 Oct 1 Age 9 or 19 (stone not clear, badly worn) S:10

Degnan, Mary E - Died 1967 Born 1881 S:16

DeGrace, Annette M - Died 1987 Born 1895 (with John DeGrace Sr) S:18

DeGrace, Benjamin Sr - Died 1984 Born 1886 Stone says, "Loving Memories" (next to Maria A DeGrace) S:15

DeGrace, Isaac - Died 1928 Born 1894 (next to Leander & Annette DeGrace) S:18

DeGrace, John Sr - Died 1984 Born 1894 (with Annette M DeGrace) S:18

DeGrace, Leander F - Died 1956 Sept 8 Born 1918 Dec 27 From Massachusetts, was a TEC 167, CML Smoke Genr Co during World War S:18

DeGrace, Maria A - Died 1971 Born 1890 (with Benjamin DeGrace Sr) S:15

Deleo, Henry F - Died 1967 Born 1893 Stone says, "Father" (with Ida M Deleo) S:15

Deleo, Ida M - Died 1978 Born 1895 Stone says, "Mother" (with Henry F Deleo) S:15

Delomba, Julio - Died 1982 Born 1897 S:15

Delopadua, Rita B - Died 1967 Born 1883 (next to Vass U Delopadua) S:13

Delopadua, Vass U - Died 1971

Delopadua (Cont.) Born 1889 (next to Rita B Delopadua) S:13

Delp, Clarence E - Died 1979 Aug 12 Born 1893 Sept 8 (has 2 stones) Was a CWO in US Army during World War I & II (with wife, Linda K Delp) S:16

Delp, Linda K - Died (still living 1991?) Born 1898 Wife of Clarence E Delp (listed with him) S:16

DeMarco, Albert - Died 1978 Born 1915 (with Alfonso DeMarco) S:16

DeMarco, Alfonso - Died 1961 Born 1872 (with Albert DeMarco) S:16

DeMarco, Lyn Kearney - Died 1985 Born 1946 (large rock marked "Kearney") Stone says, "If love could only have saved you, you never would have died" S:20

Demartino, Alma J - Died 1980 Born 1916 (with Anthony M Demartino) S:20

Demartino, Anthony M - Died 1990 Born 1907 (with Alma J Demartino) S:20

DeMello, Mary L - Died 1943 Born 1897 S:16

Demelo, Diolinda - Died 1975 Born 1903 (with Manuel P Demelo) S:16

Demelo, Jose E - Died 1969 Born 1899 S:16

Demelo, Manuel P - Died 1970 Born 1894 (with Diolinda Demelo) S:16

Demone, Emily M - Died (still living 1991?) Born 1904 (listed with Urban E Demone) S:15

Demone, Urban E - Died 1980 Born 1894 (with Emily M Demone) S:15

Demore, Leman R - Died 1966 Born 1890 (with Sadie L Demore) S:15

Demore, Sadie L - Died 1987 Born 1891 (with Leman R Demore) S:15

Dempsey, J Walter - Died 1983 Jan 28 Born 1894 Dec 14 Was a

Dempsey (Cont.)
SK2 in US Navy during World War I S:15

Dennis, Gerald M - Died 1979 Born 1897 (with Jennie K Dennis) S·15

Dennis, Jennie K - Died (still living 1991?) Born 1899 (listed with Gerald M Dennis) S:15

DeRoza, Emma - Died 1916 Born 1876 S:18

Derwin, Mary M - Died 1982 Dec 25 Born 1921 July 27 Wife of Malcolm Adams (with him) S:20

Desmond, Ellen J - Died 1980 Born 1900 (with Richard Desmond) S:16

Desmond, Richard - Died (still living 1991?) Born 1900 (listed with Ellen J Desmond) S:16

Devanney, Yvonne H - Died 1973 Born 1922 (stone says, "daughter"?) S:31

Devaughan, Julie V - Died 1968 June 30 Age 6 days S:20

Deveney, Edward P - Died 1989 Sept 25 Born 1907 Aug 18 S:19

Devine, Kathleen - Died 1989 Born 1926 (A rock stone) S:20

Deware, Bertram E - Died 1975 Born 1898 S:18

Dewey, Marjorie - Died 1978 Born 1879 (with William Gibbons Morse) S:14

Dewire, Thomas A (Tad) IV - Died 1981 Sept 26 Born 1957 Oct 15 Son of Thomas A Dewire III (with him) S:20

Dewire, Thomas A III - Died 1987 March 13 Born 1927 Aug 29 (with son, Thomas A Dewire IV) S:20

DeWitt, Earle M - Died 1918 Born 1885 Son of Edgar & Lillie DeWitt (with them & others on large DeWitt stone) S:12

DeWitt, Edgar W - Died 1884 Born 1847 (large DeWitt stone) (with Lillie F DeWitt & others) S:12

DeWitt, Ernest W - Died 1971 Born 1885 (with Sarah & Earle DeWitt & others on large DeWitt stone)

DeWitt (Cont.)
S:12

DeWitt, Freeman H - Died 1896 Born 1881 Son of Edgar & Lillie DeWitt (with them & others on large DeWitt stone) S:12

DeWitt, Lillie F - Died 1934 Born 1857 Wife of Edgar W DeWitt (with him & others on large DeWitt stone) S:12

DeWitt, Sarah H - Died 1973 Born 1892 Wife of Earle M DeWitt (with him & others on large DeWitt stone) S:12

Dexter, John - Died 1722 Jan 12 or 13 Age 69 S:11

Dexter, John - Died 1829 Jan 13 (row cannot be read) in his 69th yr S:11R+26R

Dexter, Rebecca - Died 1815/18 ? Sept 1 (stone badly worn) Widow of John Dexter (buried next to him) S:11

Dexter, Rebecca - Died 1848 located in row 1 S:11R

Dexter, Rosella A - Died 1879 Oct 1 Age 35 Wife of Capt Levi Dexter S:14

Diamond, Martha Amy - Died 1971 Born (no date) Stone says, "Grandmom" S:18

Dian, Edith Allen - Died 1953 Born 1870 (next to Frank D Allen) S:12

Diaz, Vera Baldwin - Died (no dates) (listed with Margaret May Baldwin) S:18

Dickey, Howard A - Died 1962 May 24 Born 1887 April 19 (with Martha S Dickey) S:20

Dickey, Martha S - Died 1983 June 20 Born 1899 Oct 21 (With Howard A Dickey) S:20

Diggins, John P - Died 1969 Born 1879 (with Marion H Diggins) S:15

Diggins, Marion H - Died 1981 Born 1894 (with John P Diggins) S:15

Diggs, Craig Wayne - Died 1975 Born 1956 S:13

Dight, Robert F - Died 1939 Born

Dight (Cont.)
1860 (with wife, Martha Roberts) S:14

Dilger, Nell - Died 1966 Born 1892 (next to husband, Amedee Tetrault) S:15

Dill, Charles O - Died 1924 Born 1889 S:21

Dill, Frederick S S - Died 1941 Born 1878 (with Beatrice Cowan Dill Crosby) S:12

Dimery, Mabel G - Died 1970 Born 1887 Wife of Raymond Neil (with him & Donald & Douglas Neil) S:19

Dimmock, Charles - Died 1832 Sept 8 in his 76th yr S:10+26R

Dimmock, Deborah Mrs - Died 1826 Sept 7 in her 61st yr Wife of Charles Dimmock (buried next to him) S:10+26R

Dimmock, Hannah - Died 1755 Oct 5 Widow of Capt Edward Dimmock (Hinckley Ceme records #9R says died in his 55th yr) S:9+26R

Dimmock, Ruth H - Died 1887 Sept 5 Age 76 years,4 months S:10

Dimmock, Shubal - Died 1728 Dec 18 Age 55 (Hinkley reference to other sources - not off stone) S:11R+26R

Dimmock, Thomas - Died 1796 Dec 27 Age 2 years, 10 months Son of Edward & Hannah Dimmock (Hinckley Ceme records #9R say death date was 1726/7 Jan 27) S:9+26R

Dimmock, Thomas - Died 1829 Nov 22 Age 8 months Son of Elliah I & Sarah Dimmock S:10

Dimock, David (Capt) - Died 1755 Aboard (ship)? Age 35 (on same stone with Thankful Dimock) S:10

Dimock, Edward - Died 1726/7 May Age 10 months Son of Edward & Hannah Dimock S:9+26R

Dimock, Elizabeth Mrs - Died 1811 Oct 17 Age 80 Relict of Thomas

Dimock (Cont.)
Dimock (buried next to him) S:10

Dimock, Mehetable - Died 1725 Dec 27 Age 1 year, 8 months Daughter of Samuel & Hannah Dimock S:9R

Dimock, Ruthy Burrill - Died 1801 Jan 25 Age 9 years, 5 months Daughter of Charles & Deborah Dimock S:10

Dimock, Tabitha Mrs - Died 1727 July 24 in her 57th yr Widow of Shubal Dimock S:11R+26R

Dimock, Thankful Died 1807 Nov 31 Age 83 (on same stone with - Capt David Dimock) S:10

Dimock, Thomas - Died 1806 Sept 19 Age 79 (buried next to wife, Elizabeth Dimock) S:10

Dincley, Alonzo D - Died 1911 May 18 Born 1856 Aug 14 (stone is down) S:21

Dineen, Annie M - Died 1891 Born 1867 (with Timothy W Dineen & others) S:31

Dineen, Catherine - Died 1925 Born 1860 (with Elizabeth A Dineen & others) S:31

Dineen, Cornelius - Died 1884 Born 1812 (with Mary Dineen & others) S:31

Dineen, Cornelius - Died 1914 Born 1823 S:31

Dineen, Elizabeth A - Died 1871 Born 1848 (with Timothy W Dineen & others) S:31

Dineen, Henry M - Died 1884 Born 1865 (with Annie M Dineen & others) S:31

Dineen, Julia E - Died 1890 Born 1863 (with Henry M Dineen & others) S:31

Dineen, Mary - Died 1914 Born 1823 (with Catherine Dineen & others) S:20

Dineen, Timothy W - Died 1878 Born 1857 (with Julia E Dineen & others) S:31

Diven, Abbie N - Died 1974 Born 1886 (with Lester W Nickerson) S:14

144

Dixon, Charles C - Died 1961 Born 1887 (next to Laura B Dixon) S:11

Dixon, Fred S - Died 1972 Feb 5 Born 1896 June 17 From Massachusetts, was Pvt in US Army during World War I (next to Herbert & Vernice Dixon) S:19

Dixon, Harriette M - Died 1952 Born 1884 (next to Richard F Dixon) S:19

Dixon, Herbert R - Died (still living 1990?) Born 1905 (listed with Vernice Dixon & next to Fred Dixon) S:19

Dixon, John - Died 1917 Born 1852 (with William Dixon & next to Rev Sarah A Dixon Phd) S:19

Dixon, Joice - Died 1887 June 30 Age 60 years, 11 months Stone says, "Mother" Wife of William Dixon (between two William Dixon's) S:19

Dixon, Katharyn H - Died 1968 Born 1907 (with Melville F Dixon) S:11

Dixon, Laura B - Died (still living 1991?) Born 1889 Wife of Charles C Dixon (next to him) S:11

Dixon, Lizzie H - Died 1929 Aug 17 Age 90 years, 5 months, 25 days Wife of Charles Floyd (with him & Charles H Floyd) S:19

Dixon, Melville F - Died 1979 Born 1909 (with Katharyn H Dixon) S:11

Dixon, Richard F - Died 1939 Born 1877 He was a Mason (next to Harriette M Dixon) S:19

Dixon, Sarah A (Rev) (Phd) - Died 1939 Nov 20 Born 1866 Oct 15 (next to Thomas H Dixon) S:19

Dixon, Thomas H - Died 1958 Born 1890 (next to Rev Sarah A Dixon Phd) S:19

Dixon, Vernice J - Died 1988 Born 1905 (with Herbert Dixon & next to Fred Dixon) S:19

Dixon, William - Died 1921 Born 1826 Was in Co E, 40th Reg, Massachusetts Volunteers,

Dixon (Cont.) 1861-65 (Veteran star there too) (with John Dixon & next to Joice Dixon) S:19

Dixon, William A - Died 1915 Born 1855 (this is a stone marker covered with small rocks cemented all over it) (next to Joice Dixon & William Dixon) S:19

Doane, Barbara - Died 1889 Dec 10 Born 1827 Mar 20 Wife of Eliphalet Doane S:7

Doane, Bethia H - Died (date not clear) Age 71 Wife of Joseph Doane S:7

Doane, Caroline L - Died 1866 Jan 27 Age 42 years, 11 months, 7 days Wife of George W Doane MD S:9R

Doane, Caroline L - Died 1886 Born 1823 (with George & William G Doane & others) S:18

Doane, Carrie - Died 1856 Born 1854 Stone says,"Little Carrie" (with Kies Doane & Catherine Hinckley & others) S:18

Doane, Chilion F - Died 1896 Born 1846 (with wife, Miriam D Doane) S:18

Doane, Eliphalet - Died 1864 July 20 in the 39th yr (died at Petersburg) S:7

Doane, Eliza A - Died 1889 June Oct Age 59 years, 9 months Wife of Simeon Doane (buried next to him) S:6

Doane, Elizabeth - Died 1842 Jan 16 Age 74 Widow of Hezekiah (next to him) S:10

Doane, Ella P - Died 1874 Born 1852 (with Caroline & Isaac Doane & others) S:18

Doane, Ella T - Died 1874 April 11 Age 22 years, 2 months S:9R

Doane, Eva Marsters - Died 1958 Born 1911 S:20

Doane, George O - Died 1856 Born 1855 (with Caroline & Isaac Doane & others) S:9

Doane, George W - Died 1905 Born 1824 (with Louisa J Doane & others) S:18

Doane, Hezekiah - Died 1832 Sept 18 in the 20th yr Died at sea (listed on James G Doane stone) S:10+26R

Doane, Hezekiah - Died 1834 May 6 in the 67th yr S:10+26R

Doane, Isaac C - Died 1864 Born 1859 (with Ella & Caroline Doane & others) S:9

Doane, James G - Died 1832 July 15 Age 30 S:10

Doane, Kies - Died 1895 Born 1812 (with Chilion & Miriam Doane) (also with wife Catherine Hinckley & Carrie Doane) S:18

Doane, Louisa J - Died 1903 Born 1834 (with George & Susan Doane & others) S:18

Doane, Miriam D - Died (no dates) Wife of Chilion Doan (listed with him & Kies Doane) S:18

Doane, Robert H - Died 1939 Born 1896 (with Robert M Doane) S:14

Doane, Robert M - Died 1937 Born 1867 (with Robert H Doane) S:14

Doane, Simeon - Died 1880 Mar 24 Age 66 years, 4 months (wife, Eliza A Doane buried next to him) S:6

Doane, Susan P (or T) - Died 1899 Born 1836 (with George & Caroline Doane & others) S:9

Doane, William G (or C) - Died 1850 Born 1849 (with Caroline & George Doane & others) S:9

Dobson, Harriet N - Died 1913 Born 1827 (with Job Dobson) S:12

Dobson, Job - Died 1913 Born 1833 (with Harriet N Dobson) S:12

Dodge, Charles S - Died (no dates) (with wife, Alice M Mooney) S:20

Dodge, Grace H - Died 1975 Jan 7 Born 1894 June 17 (with Edwin S Carr & others) S:18

Dodge, John R - Died 1960 Aug 27 Born 1889 Dec 17 (with Grace H Dodge & others) S:18

Dodge, Walter - Died 1903 Born 1881 (large metal hollow marker

Dodge (Cont.) with an anchor at the top) (with Herbert W Adams) S:12

Doe, Genevieve H - Died 1929 Born 1905 (with William H Peak & others) S:18

Doerfler, William E - Died 1974 Aug 10 Born 1894 March 31 Stone says, "Father" S:15

Doherty, James - Died 1896 Born 1818 (next to Margaret Doherty) S:31

Doherty, James H - Died 1949 Born 1881 (with Mary E Doherty) S:16

Doherty, Margaret - Died 1900 Born 1817 (between James & Mary A Doherty) S:31

Doherty, Mary A - Died 1913 July 10 Born 1857 May 13 (next to James & Margaret Doherty) S:31

Doherty, Mary E - Died 1950 Born 1882 (with James H Doherty) S:16

Dolan, Rose M - Died 1965 Born 1885 S:15

Dolby, George - Died 1883 July 27 Age 74 years, 7 months (next to Mary J & George E Dolby) S:19

Dolby, George E - Died 1932 Born 1853 (next to George & Mary J Dolby) S:19

Dolby, Mary J - Died 1883 Nov 28 Age 65 Wife of George Dolby (next to him & George E Dolby) S:19

Dolliver, Marjorie I - Died 1968 Born 1900 Wife of Warren G Ryder (with him & Charles Ryder & Lucretia Hallett) S:19

Donaghy, Mary E - Died 1963 Born 1884 Wife of James Ensor (with him & Ernest R Smith) S:13

Donahue, Mary - Died (no dates) Wife of William Maher (with him & Michael W Maher & others) S:31

Donahue, William J - Died 1985 Born 1897 (with Adna G Donahue) S:16

Donahue Jones Annie J - Died 1987 Born 1895 S:16

Donald, John Jr - Died 1949 Born 1917 (next to Lydia Soares Donald) S:12

Donald, Lydia Soares - Died 1951 Born 1925 (next to John Donald Jr) S:12

Doncan, Jane - Died 1730 Aug 7 Daughter of John & Lydia Doncan (Hinckley Ceme records #9R says died in her 6th yr) S:9+26R

Doncan, John - Died 1729 July 17 Age 8 years, 5 months Son of John & Lydia Doncan S:9R

Dondale, Abbie B - Died 1969 Born 1886 (with husband, William Anderson) S:15

Donlay, Grace A - Died 1962 Born 1889 (with John F Donlay) S:16

Donlay, John F - Died 1977 Born 1894 (with Grace A Donlay) S:16

Donnell, Jennie - Died 1964 Born 1887 (with Samuel C Donnell, husband) S:15

Donnell, Samuel C - Died 1983 Born 1888 (with wife, Jennie Donnell) S:15

Donnelly, Bernard P - Died 1977 Born 1898 S:15

Donohue, Edna G - Died 1962 Born 1891 (with William J Donohue) S:16

Donovan, Frederick W - Died 1985 Born 1899 (with Magdalene D Donovan) S:15

Donovan, Magdalene D - Died 1990 Born 1908 (with Frederick W Donovan) S:15

Doolittle, Elizabeth C - Died 1921 Born 1857 Stone says, "Our sister" S:12

Doran, Thomas O - Died 1961 Aug 25 Born 1893 Aug 29 From Massachusetts, was PFC in Btry A, 22nd Field Artillery during World War I S:16

Dorbek, Alfred - Died (still living 1991?) Born 1903 (listed with Maria Dorbek) S:17

Dorbek, Maria - Died 1978 Born 1900 (with Alfred Dorbek) S:17

Dore, Grace E - Died (still living

Dore (Cont.) 1991?) Born 1902 (with Stanley M Dore) S:19

Dore, Stanley M - Died 1987 Born 1898 (has 2 stones and a plaque) Was a Private in US Army during World War I (with Grace E Dore) S:19

Dorkins, Evan Edward - Died (still living 1991?) Born 1916 Dec 10 (family crest on stone) (with Neda & Ted Dorkins) S:11

Dorkins, Neda - Died (no info) (family crest on stone) (with Evan & Ted Dorkins) S:11

Dorkins, Ted - Died (no info) (family crest on top of stone) (with Neda Dorkins) S:11

Dorkins, Vernada Louise - Died 1984 Jan 12 Born 1920 Feb 19 (family crest on stone) (with Evan, Neda & Ted Dorkins) S:11

Dorsey, Clarence - Died (no dates) Born 1883 (with Elizabeth Dorsey) S:18

Dorsey, Elizabeth - Died 1962 Born 1888 (with Clarence Dorsey) S:18

Dorsey, Isabel - Died 1962 Born 1865 (fenced in Lovell plot) Wife of Grafton Duvall Dorsey & daughter of Hallett Lovell who was the son of George Lovell S:12

Dorstrom, Charles O - Died 1953 Born 1864 (with Lizzie C Dorstrom) S:18

Dorstrom, Lizzie C - Died 1924 Born 1861 (stone leaning towards pond in back of cem) (with Charles O Dorstrom) S:18

Dottridge, Abigail - Died 1816 July ? Age 11 ? (info on top of stone only) (next to Freeman Chase) S:14

Dottridge, Abigail - Buried 1848 Oct 30 S:15R

Dottridge, Abigail M - Died (no date or underground) Buried 1851 Daughter of Samuel K & Caroline E Dottridge (next to them) (burial date from Old Mosswood ceme records) S:14

Dottridge, Arabella M - Died 1900 Feb 27 Born 1843 March 12 (next to Abigail M Dottridge) S:14

Dottridge, Bennett W - Died 1932 Born 1843 (with wife, Mary F Dottridge) S:14

Dottridge, Betsey B - Died 1933 Born 1849 (with Mary & Bennett Dottridge) S:14

Dottridge, Caroline E - Died 1852 Sept 16 Age 41 Wife of Samuel K Dottridge (next to him) S:14

Dottridge, Elizabeth C - Buried 1935 Grave location is section 7, lot 9, grave 4 S:15R

Dottridge, Ernest O - Died 1948 Born 1874 (he was a Mason) (next to wife, Cora L Crosby) S:14

Dottridge, Ernest O Jr - Died 1976 March 6 Born 1899 May 26 Was Sea 2 in US Navy during World War I (next to Lila Belle Childs Dottridge) S:14

Dottridge, Esther B - Died 1981 Born 1891 (with Howard Dottridge & Elizabeth Collins) S:14

Dottridge, Grace - Died 1963 Born 1886 (with John F Dottridge) S:14

Dottridge, Harriet N - Died 1906 Born 1822 (with John Dottridge) S:14

Dottridge, Howard A - Died 1924 Born 1854 (with wife, Elizabeth A Collins) S:14

Dottridge, John - Died 1889 Born 1816 (with Harriet N Dottridge) S:14

Dottridge, John F - Died 1898 Born 1880 (with Howard Dottridge & Elizabeth Collins) S:14

Dottridge, Lila Belle Childs - Died 1990 Aug 18 Born 1893 Sept 17 (next to Ernest O Dottridge Jr) S:14

Dottridge, Mary F - Died c1889 Born 1868 Aug 2 Age 21 years,8 months Wife of Bennett Dottridge (with him) (burial records at Mosswood office say that it

Dottridge (Cont.) was 1868?) S:14

Dottridge, Oliver N - Died 1859 Born 1851 (with John & Harriet Dottridge) S:14

Dottridge, Oliver N - Died 1895 Jan 14 Born 1873 Mar 13 Stone says,"Our darling Ollie, how we loved him" (next to Mary, Bennett & Betsey Dottridge) S:14

Dottridge, Robert P - Died 1909 Born 1893 (with Howard Dottridge & Elizabeth Collins) S:14

Dottridge, Samuel B - Buried 1846 Sept 3 S:15R

Dottridge, Samuel B - Died 21/24th Aug (stone worn badly) (next to Abigail Dottridge who died 1816)(name furnished by Jim Gould of Cotuit) S:14

Dottridge, Samuel K - Died 1854 July 7 Age 43 years, 17 days (next to wife, Caroline E Dottridge) S:14

Doty, Eva M - Died 1957 Born 1875 Wife of Harrison Doty (with him & Gladys E Doty & others) S:18

Doty, Gladys E - Died 1967 Born 1907 (with Nelson Bacon & others) S:18

Doty, Harroson D - Died 1946 Born 1873 (with wife, Eva M Doty & others) S:18

Doubtfire, Charles E - Died 1969 Born 1881 (with Augusta Persson, wife) S:8

Doughty, Dorothy C - Died 1981 Born 1906 (with Irving W Doughty) S:18

Doughty, Irving W - Died 1952 Born 1898 (with Dorothy C Doughty) S:18

Douglas, Mildred L - Died 1923 Born 1903 (listed on back of stone of James J Needham d1857) S:8

Douglass, Dorothy H - Died 1987 Born 1899 (with Kenneth R Douglass) S:15

Douglass, Kenneth R - Died 1983 Born 1894 (with Dorothy H

148

Douglass (Cont.)
Douglass) S:15

Douglass, Lydia H - Died 1925 May 1 Born 1859 Dec 26 S:8

Dowd, Arthur H - Died 1944 Born 1872 (with wife, Susan Dowd) S:18

Dowd, Susan W - Died 1961 Born 1870 Wife of Sylvester Marchant & Arthur Dowd (with them) S:18

Downey, Joseph L - Died 1973 Aug 1 Born 1895 Dec 31 S:15

Downing, Anne O'Connell - Died (still living 1991?) Born 1897 Oct 12 (listed with Dr John Godwin Downing) S:16

Downing, John Godwin Dr - Died 1976 April 24 Born 1890 June 22 (has 2 stones) Was a Lt in US Army MD (with Anne O'Connell Downing) S:16

Downing, Motimer Rev - Died 1942 Born 1863 Pastor of Saint Frances Xavier Catholic Church from 1913 - 1942 S:16

Downs, Lucy Mrs - Died 1852 Dec 5 Age 76 Widow of Samuel Downs S:10

Doyle, Mary T - Died 1949 Born 1881 Wife of William J Nelson (with him) S:19

Drehr, James McDonsh - Died 1822 Oct 4 Age 9 S:11R

Drew, Bessie E - Died 1950 Born 1868 (with William L Drew Jr & Sr & Lillian W Drew) S:18

Drew, Carl M - Died 1967 Born 1885 (with Mary A Drew) S:18

Drew, Carrie B - Died 1913 Born 1837 (with Etta & Ralph Hoxie) S:14

Drew, Charlotte A - Died 1929 Born 1861 (with Myron E Drew & next to George Earl Drew) S:18

Drew, Earl W - Died 187? Dec 29 Age 4 Son of JW & EL Drew (next to Joseph W Drew & others) S:18

Drew, Emma Isabel - Died 1850 July 9 Age 19 Daughter of JW & MP Drew (next to Earl W Drew & others) S:18

Drew, Emma L - Died 1904 April 14 Born 1834 April 8 (next to Holman H Drew & others & with Emma Isabel Drew) S:18

Drew, Flora B - Died 1962 Born 1874 Wife of Marshall Hinckley (with him) S:18

Drew, George Earl - Died 1911 Born 1890 Stone says, "Our dear boy" (next to Myron & Charlotte Drew) S:18

Drew, Harold McIntyre - Died 1989 Born 1921 Stone says,"Beloved Husband" (next to Suzanne Rossire Drew) S:20

Drew, Harry T - Died 1941 Born 1888 (with wife, Mary J Drew) S:18

Drew, Holman H - Died 1889 June 1 Age 57 (next to Mary M Drew & others) S:18

Drew, Ithel M - Died 1953 Born 1895 (with Ella Drew Hart & Edward West Hart) S:18

Drew, Joseph W - Died 1909 May 27 Born 1826 March 10 (next to Emma L Drew & others) S:18

Drew, Lillian W - Died 1965 Born 1890 (with William Jr & Sr & Bessie Drew) S:18

Drew, Mary - Died (no dates) (with William Drew & others) S:18

Drew, Mary A - Died 1942 Born 1894 (with Carl M Drew & next to Mary J & Harry Drew) S:18

Drew, Mary J - Died 1971 Born 1892 Wife of Harry T Drew (with him) S:18

Drew, Mary M - Died 1891 Jan 5 Age 86 (next to Emma Isabel Drew & others) S:18

Drew, Mary Snow - Died 1936 Born 1849 (with Mary Drew & others) S:18

Drew, Myron E - Died 1929 Born 1855 (with Charlotte A Drew) S:18

Drew, Olive E - Died 1917 Born 1830 Stone says, "Mother" (next to William Drew) S:18

Drew, Samuel HD - Died 1966 Born 1874 (with wife, Charlotte

149

Drew (Cont.)
Albert & others) S:18

Drew, Suzanne Rossire - Died 1979 Born 1954 Stone says "Beloved daughter" (next to Harold McIntyre Drew) S:20

Drew, Theodore F - Died 1929 Born 1845 (with Mary Snow Drew & others) S:18

Drew, William - Died (no dates) (with Samuel HD Drew & others) S:18

Drew, William L - Died 1921 Born 1866 (with Bessie E Drew & others) S:18

Drew, William L Jr - Died 1925 Born 1887 (with William Sr & Lillian & Bessie Drew) S:18

Drinkwater, Evelyn R - Died (still living 1991?) Born 1918 (listed with George Drinkwater) S:20

Drinkwater, George G - Died 1987 Born 1916 (with Evelyn R Drinkwater) S:20

Drinkwater, Harry - Died 1961 Born 1881 (with wife, Mildred Taylor Drinkwater & others on large Taylor stone) S:12

Drinkwater, Harry C - Died 1964 Born 1900 (with wife, Sarah H Drinkwater) S:15

Drinkwater, Mildred Taylor - Died 1961 Born 1887 Wife of Harry Drinkwater (with him & Maude McCray & others on large Taylor stone) S:12

Drinkwater, Sarah H - Died 1987 Born 1903 Wife of Harry C Drinkwater (with him) S:15

Driscoll, Mary J - Died 1962 Sept 25 Born 1892 March 19 Wife of Thomas A Driscoll (next to him) S:14

Driscoll, Stella T - Died 1913 Born 1850 S:12

Driscoll, Thomas A - Died 1985 March 15 Born 1890 Oct 31 (with Mary J Discoll) S:14

Driscott, Cornelius A - Died 1954 Born 1864 S:12

Drisko, Christine Smith - Died 1961 Born 1900 (with Charles

Drisko (Cont.)
Smith & George Johnson) S:18

Drody, Belinda - Died 1853 June 29 Age 54 Wife of Allen G Drody S:21

Drody, Margerat Allen - Died 1824 Aug 18 Age 5 months Daughter of Allen & Priscilla P Drody S:4

Drody, Mary - Died 1817 Apl 20 Age 24 years, 7 months Wife of Allen G Drody S:4

Drury, Bertha M - Died 1976 Born 1893 (with husband, Carl K Drury) S:15

Drury, Carl K - Died 1973 Born 1898 (with Bertha M Drury) S:15

Duarte, John N - Died 1949 Born 1873 (with Mary G Duarte) S:16

Duarte, John N Jr - Died 1985 Born 1899 (with Julia E Duarte) S:14

Duarte, Joseph - Died 1974 Born 1897 (with Louisa Duarte) S:16

Duarte, Julia E - Died 1962 Born 1903 (with John N Duarte) S:14

Duarte, Louisa - Died 1983 Born 1896 (with Joseph Duarte) S:16

Duarte, Mary G - Died 1954 Born 1874 (with John N Duarte) S:16

Dudley, Elizabeth - Died 1862 July 10 Age 26 years, 9 months Stone says, "leaving husband & mother dear, a widowed mother called to resign the loss of a family of nine" Wife of James T Dudley S:11R

Dudley, Lizzie C - Died 1862 July 10 Age 26 years, 9 months Wife of James T Dudley S:11

Duff, Bridget E - Died 1893 May 18 Age 32 years, 9 months, 28 days Daughter of John & Bridget Duff S:2

Duffin, Arthur J - Died 1951 Born 1886 (with Jessie A Duffin) S:12

Duffin, Jessie A - Died 1960 Born 1888 Wife of Arthur Duffin (with him) S:12

Duffy, Bridget - Died 1898 Nov 27 Age 78 Wife of John Duffy (next to him) S:31

Duffy, Bridget E - Died 1893 May

150

Duffy (Cont.)
18 Age 32 years, 9 months, 29
days Daughter of John & Bridget
Duffy (next to them & James
Duffy) S:31

Duffy, Helen E - Died 1987 Born
1897 (with Leo P & Thomas S
Duffy) S:15

Duffy, James - Died 1872 Nov 30
Age 24 Lost at sea on his passage from Boston to Savannah
(next to Margaret Duffy) S:31

Duffy, John - Died 1892 Nov 25/26
Age 73 years,4 months, 13 days
(next to Bridget Duffy, wife) S:31

Duffy, John - Died 1918 Born 1857
(next to John Lynch) S:31

Duffy, Josephine I - Died 1983
Born 1888 S:15

Duffy, Leo P - Died 1930 Born
1895 (with Helen E Duffy) S:15

Duffy, Margaret - Died 1924 June
2 in her 68th yr (next to Bridget
E Duffy) S:31

Duffy, Thomas S - Died 1989 Born
1928 (with Helen & Leo Duffy)
S:15

Dugener, Paul H - Died 1989 Born
1959 S:20

Dumas, Charles - Died 1975 Born
1886 (with Florence M Dumas)
S:15

Dumas, Eva M - Died 1962 Born
1895 Wife of Ovide Dumas (with
him) S:16

Dumas, Florence M - Died 1964
Born 1891 (next to Charles
Dumas) S:15

Dumas, Ovida A - Died 1980 Born
1894 (with wife, Eva M Dumas)
S:16

Dunbar, Blanche R - Died 1980
Born 1891 (with Joseph Burlingame & Inez Garder) S:14

Dunbar, Edith A - Died 1960 Born
1886 Wife of Henry L Dunbar
(with him) S:14

Dunbar, Frederick W - Died 1938
Feb 22 Born 1864 Dec 22 (this is
a large stone with hedges all
around it, with Josephine Isadore Dunbar) S:11

Dunbar, Henry L - Died 1966 Born
1890 (with wife, Edith A Dunbar)
S:14

Dunbar, James - Died 1882 Feb 8
Age 66 years, 3 months, 7 days
(next to Martha B Dunbar) S:21

Dunbar, Josephine Isadore - Died
1905 April 19 Born 1897 July 5
(on same large stone with Frederick W Dunbar, hedges all
around stone) S:11

Dunbar, Louise - Died 1965 April
10 Born 1875 Aug 4 Wife of
John Loring Glover (next to her)
S:14

Dunbar, Martha B - Died 1867
March 20 Age 61 years, 5
months, 7 days Stone says,
"Mother" Wife of James Dunbar
(next to a James Dunbar) S:21

Dunning, Mae Bradford - Died
1972 Born 1900 (next to William
& Rose Dunning) S:14

Dunning, Rose Morse - Died 1943
April 14 Born 1871 July 4 (with
William Bailey Dunning) S:14

Dunning, William Bailey - Died
1959 July 21 Born 1874 April
11 (with Rose Morse Dunning)
S:14

Dupuis, Mary E - Died 1965 Born
1889 (with Napoleon J Dupuis)
S:16

Dupuis, Napoleon J - Died 1963
Aug 21 Born 1889 or 1880 Oct 7
From Massachusetts, was PFC
in US Army during World War I
(with Mary E Dupuis) S:16

Duquette, Ann V - Died 1947 Born
1872 (with Horatio L Duquette)
S:16

Duquette, Horatio L - Died 1946
Born 1898 (with Ann V Du-
quette) S:16

Durant, Anna T - Died 1972 Aug 25
Born 1898 May 31 (next to
Wesley H Durant Sr) S:15

Durant, Wesley H Sr - Died 1981
Jan 19 Born 1898 June 18 Was
PFC in US Army during World
War I (next to Anna T Durant)
S:15

Durell, Charles P - Died 1956 June 30 Born 1883 Sept 24 (with wife, Mildred H Durell) S:14

Durell, Mildred H - Died 1952 July 21 Born 1887 Sept 4 (with Charles P Durell, husband) S:14

Durgin, Thomas G - Died 1973 Born 1891 S:17

Durning, Hugh M - Died 1979 Born 1896 S:16

Dutra, Avelino - Died 1979 Born 1894 (with Mary R & Joseph Dutra) S:16

Dutra, Joseph - Died 1949 Born 1888 (with Mary & Avelino Dutra) S:16

Dutra, Mary R - Died (still living 1991?) Born 1915 (with Avelino & Joseph Dutra) S:16

Dutton, Donald - Died 1976 Born 1903 He was a PFC in US Army during World War II S:11

Dutton, Florence R - Died (still living 1991?) Born 1904 (listed with Thomas A Dutton) S:15

Dutton, Thomas A - Died 1984 Born 1895 (with Florence R Dutton) S:15

Duxbury, Gertrude M - Died 1979 Born 1887 (with Thomas S Duxbury) S:15

Duxbury, Thomas S - Died 1966 Born 1879 (next to Gertrude M Duxbury) S:15

Dwyer, Herbert J - Died 1963 Born 1911 S:20

Dwyer, John J - Died 1927 Born 1860 (with Hallett Hamblin & others) S:18

Dyer, Arthur E - Died 1954 Born 1874 at Cape Roller, Maine A rock stone Son of Benjamin & Eliza Dyer (next to Clara F Dyer, wife) S:14

Dyer, Clara F - Died 1952 Born 1875 at Cotuit, Massacusetts Rock stone Wife of Arthur E Dyer & Daughter of Capt Frank Coleman (next to Arthur E Dyer, husband) S:14

Dyer, Ethel E - Died 1971 Born 1902 (with Harold E Dyer) S:19

Dyer, Harold E - Died 1972 Born 1900 Stone says,"DMD" (with Ethel E Dyer) S:19

Dymza, Edmund Z - Died 1973 Born 1900 (with Felicia A Banas MD) S:16

Earle, Charles W - Died 1990 Born 1900 Was Pvt in US Army during World War I S:15

Earle, Lillian - Died 1944 Born 1876 Wife of Robert Gill (with him) S:16

Easterbrook, Abigail - Died 1794 Oct 9 in her 66th yr Wife of Capt John Easterbrook (located at Lothrop's Hill) S:26R

Easterbrook, Albert - Died 1882 Nov 12 Age 73 years, 4 months (next to wife, Mary B Easterbrook) S:19

Easterbrook, Albert A - Died 1874 Oct 1 Age 3 years, 4 months Son of John W & Mary A Easterbrook (with them & others) S:19

Easterbrook, Frances Oliver - Died 1948 Born 1888 Wife of Howard Smith Sturgis (with him & Lt Col Russell B Sturgis) S:19

Easterbrook, Frank B - Died 1903 March 15 Born 1846 Aug 17 (next to Olive E Easterbrook) S:19

Easterbrook, John - Died 1853 Feb 15 Age 56 (with wifes, Sabra & Lucy H Easterbrook & others) S:19

Easterbrook, John (Capt) - Died 1802 July 1 in his 76th yr (located at Lothrop's Hill) S:26R

Easterbrook, John (Capt) - Died 1836 June 8 Age 74 S:10

Easterbrook, John K - Died 1815 Aug 8 Age 14 Died at sea (possible son of Capt Joseph & Mercy Easterbrook, on same stone with Nabby Easterbrook) S:10

Easterbrook, John W - Died 1875 March 18 Age 35 years, 7 months Lost at sea (with Mary A Easterbrook & others) S:19

Easterbrook, Joseph (Capt) - Died 1807 June 22 in his 39th yr

Easterbrook (Cont.)
S:10

Easterbrook, Lucy H - Died 1875
Nov 12 Age 63 years, 6 months
Wife of John Easterbrook (with
him & Albert A Easterbrook &
others) S:19

Easterbrook, Mary - Died 1883
April 14 Age 32 years, 6 months
Daughter of Albert & Mary B
Easterbrook (next to them) S:19

Easterbrook, Mary - Died 22nd of
Sept (year not clear) Age 88 ?
Wife of Samuel Easterbrook S:10

Easterbrook, Mary A - Died 1875
March 18 Age 28 Lost at sea
(with John W Easterbrook &
John (d1853) Easterbrook &
others) S:19

Easterbrook, Mary A - Died 1899
Born 1846 (with Thomas S
Easterbrook) S:19

Easterbrook, Mary B - Died 1891
Jan 6 Age 79 years, 1 months
Wife of Albert Easterbrook (next
to him & Mary Easterbrook) S:19

Easterbrook, Nabby - Died 1812
April 27 Age 17 Daughter of
Capt Joseph & Mercy Easter-
brook (with John K Easterbrook)
S:10

Easterbrook, Olive E - Died 1920
Feb 11 Born 1853 Feb 27 (next to
husband Frank & son, Willie
Easterbrook) S:19

Easterbrook, Rebecca - Died 1839
Oct 17 Age 75 Widow of Capt
John Easterbrook S:10

Easterbrook, Rebecca - Died 1851
Sept 30 Born 1800 June 27
Stone says, "Our Mother" Wife of
Timothy Swinerton (next to him)
S:10

Easterbrook, Rebecca - Died 1879
Aug 21 Age 48 years, 4 months,
20 days Stone says, "Mother"
Wife of George G Smith (with
daughter, Lucy J Sowle) S:19

Easterbrook, Roland Long - Died
1963 May 23 at Maui, Hawaii
Born 1913 Nov 16 at Carleton,
Nebraska (stone is a rock) (with

Easterbrook (Cont.)
Frances Ruth Hawkins) S:19

Easterbrook, Ruth - Died 1861 Nov
27 Wife of David Bursley (in
Bursley plot) S:10

Easterbrook, Sabra - Died 1835
Sept 19 Age 30 years, 3 months
Wife of John Easterbrook (with
him & Lucy H Easterbrook &
others) S:19

Easterbrook, Samuel (Capt) - Died
1811 March 3 Age (in 40's)
(stone in bad shape) S:10

Easterbrook, Thomas S - Died
1888 June 27 Age 43 years, 3
months (with Mary A Easterbrook) S:19

Easterbrook, William Lincoln -
Died 1875 March 18 Age 1 year,
5 months Lost at sea (with
parents) Son of John W & Mary
A Easterbrook (listed with them
& others) S:19

Easterbrook, Willie L - Died 1876
May 7 Age 7 months, 9 days Son
of Francis & Olive Easterbrook
(next to them) S:19

Eastman, Donald B - Died 1970
Born 1889 (next to wife, Katherine R Eastman) S:15

Eastman, Katherine R - Died 1984
Born 1896 (next to husband,
Donald B Eastman) S:15

Eastwood, Edmund C - Died 1966
April 6 Born 1896 March 1 From
Massachusetts & was a CPL in
HG Co307 Field Artillery during
World War I S:15

Eaton, Josephine J - Died 1979
Born 1886 (with Orin W Eaton)
S:16

Eaton, Orin W - Died 1960 Born
1884 (next to Josephine J Eaton)
S:16

Echteler, Anna T - Died 1984 Born
1904 (with Emil M Echteler)
S:16

Echteler, Emil M - Died 1978 Born
1899 (has 2 stones) Was a Sgt in
US Marine Corps (with Anna T
Echteler) S:16

Edgerly, Ada A - Died (still living?)

Edgerly (Cont.)
Born 1905 (listed with Carl F
Edgerly) S:12
Edgerly, Carl F - Died 1948 Born
1903 (with ada A Edgerly) S:12
Edson, Betsey S - Died 1841 Dec
20 Age 28 years, 23 days Wife of
Daniel Edson (next to him) S:11
Edson, Daniel - Died 1843 March
14 Age 31 S:11
Edson, Jane E - Died 1907 Born
1820 Wife of Nathan Edson (next
to him) S:19
Edson, Myra C - Died 1937 Born
1862 Wife of Alonzo Savery (with
him) S:14
Edson, Nathan - Died 1895 Born
1817 (next to wife, Jane E
Edson) S:19
Edwards, Arthur H - Died (still
living 1991?) Born 1936 (with
Cynthia Ann Edwards) S:20
Edwards, Basil Duke Jr - Died
1988 Born 1918 (next to Thomas
Day Edwards) S:11
Edwards, Cynthia Ann - Died 1980
Born 1939 (with Arthur H) S:20
Edwards, Thomas Day - Died 1987
June 1 Born 1931 July 20 (next
to Basil Duke Edwards Jr) S:11
Eldredge, Bethia - Died 1849 in
her 77th yr S:4
Eldredge, Charles M - Died 1953
June 27 Born 1894 Sept 24
From Massachusetts, was Pvt in
1st Co, 151 Depot Brig during
World War I (next to Genieve A
Eldredge) S:16
Eldredge, Ezra - Died 1846 May 1
Age 74 years, 8 months S:4
Eldredge, Genieve A - Died 1971
Dec 16 Born 1896 March 18 (next
to Charles M Eldredge) S:16
Eldredge, Isadore J - Died 1938
Born 1876 (with Raymond E
Eldredge & others) S:18
Eldredge, Jeremiah - Died 1863
Oct 15 in his 75th yr S:4
Eldredge, Phebe - Died 18?, Oct 1
Wife of Jeremiah Eldredge S:4
Eldredge, Raymond E - Died 1938
Born 1907 (with William C

Eldredge (Cont.)
Eldredge & others) S:18
Eldredge, William C - Died 1927
Born 1878 (with Isadore J
Eldredge & others) S:18
Eldridge, Adelaide R - Died 1884
Jan 12 Born 1839 Nov 26 Stone
says,"Mother" (next to Simeon
Eldridge) S:21
Eldridge, Alden B - Died 1874 July
9 Born 1822 June 5 (next to
son, Joseph Eldridge) S:21
Eldridge, Alice Irene - Died 1946
Born 1868 (with Rebecca Crow-
ell Crocker & next to Clarence
Crocker Eldridge) S:18
Eldridge, Ambrose - Died 1853
June 28 Age 21 years, 8 months
at Crontadt, Russia Son of David
& Jemima Eldridge (his stone is
next to them) S:19
Eldridge, Annie M - Died 1933 or
1938? Born 1857 (next to Rose
G Eldridge) S:31
Eldridge, Betsey - Died 1862 Feb 5
Age 75 Wife of Jeremiah Eldridge
S:21
Eldridge, Charles - Died 1953 Born
1884 (with Jeannett E Shepherd)
S:18
Eldridge, Charles H - Died 1926
Born 1861 (with Ebenezer &
Martha Eldridge) S:21
Eldridge, Clarence Alton - Died
1942 Born 1869 (with Alice Irene
Eldridge & others) S:18
Eldridge, Clarence Crocker - Died
1975 Born 1893 (with Marion
Hills Eldridge) S:18
Eldridge, Clarence F - Died 1903
Born 1844 (with Lucinda W
Eldridge & others) S:18
Eldridge, David - Died 1888 Feb 12
Age 84 years, 8 months, 8 days
(next to Jemima Eldridge, wife)
S:19
Eldridge, David Kenneth - Died
1979 Oct 9 Born 1953 May 21
(Eldridge plot) (with Kenneth G
Eldridge & others) S:20
Eldridge, E H - Died 1841 (in large
crypt at street level with other

Eldridge (Cont.)
Eldridge's) S:10

Eldridge, Ebenezer - Died 1864 May 12 Born 1825 March 14 Was in Company E, 58th Regiment in Massachusetts Volunteers (with Martha Eldridge & Cornelia Buck) S:21

Eldridge, Edward T - Died 1880 Dec 31 Age 21 years, 11 months, 18 days Son of Thomas R & Elizabeth E Eldridge (next to mother) S:18

Eldridge, Elizabeth E - Died 1899 Nov 30 Age 61 years 10 months 15 days Wife of Thomas R Eldridge (next to him) S:18

Eldridge, Ethel M - Died 1946 Born 1880 S:12

Eldridge, Frank H - Died 1883 Aug 5 Age 21 years, 11 months, 20 days Son of Thomas R & Elizabeth E Eldridge (next to Edward T Eldridge) S:18

Eldridge, Frank O - Died (no date) Born 1877 Son of Joseph & Lucy Eldridge (listed with them) S:18

Eldridge, Gertrude M - Died 1926 Feb 7 Born 1888 Dec 9 (with Matthias P Slavin & others) S:31

Eldridge, Hillary M - Died 1978 July 7 Born 1978 July 3 Daughter of ? S:11

Eldridge, JP - Died 1859 Located at street level in large crypt dug into hill Doorway sealed in rock & cement Buried with M Eldridge S:10

Eldridge, Jane Mrs - Died 1833 April 9 Age 30 Wife of Capt Ezra Eldridge S:21

Eldridge, Jemima - Died 1873 Aug 19 Age 69 years, 8 months Wife of David Eldridge (next to him & son, Ambrose) S:19

Eldridge, Joseph - Died 1861 Sept 10 Age 17 years, 10 months, 18 days Eldest son of Alden B & Maria G Eldridge (next to father) S:21

Eldridge, Joseph W - Died 1936 Born 1849 (with Lucy E

Eldridge (Cont.)
Eldridge) S:18

Eldridge, Kenneth Gordon - Died 1990 Born 1924 June 8 (Eldridge plot) Was a SC2 in US Navy during World War II (with Olivia Joyce Eldridge & David Kenneth Eldridge & others) S:20

Eldridge, L May - Died 1936 Born 1861 (with Warnie B Eldgridge & others) S:18

Eldridge, Laura Prescott - Died 1921 Nov 20 Born 1854 Mar 8 S:11

Eldridge, Louisa A - Died 1930 Born 1840 (with Truman D Eldridge & next to David Eldridge) S:19

Eldridge, Lucinda W - Died 1874 Born 1847 (with L May Eldridge & others) S:18

Eldridge, Lucy E - Died 1932 Born 1851 (with Joseph W Eldridge) S:18

Eldridge, M - Died 1859 (large crypt at street level dug into a hill, doorway sealed in rock & cement, buried with JP Eldridge) S:10

Eldridge, Marion Hills - Died (no date) Born 1894 (with Clarence Crocker Eldridge & next to Miriam Eldridge) S:18

Eldridge, Martha J - Died 1881 April 19 Born 1825 April 4 (with Ebenezer Eldridge & Cornelia Buck) S:21

Eldridge, Mary E - Died 1939 Born 1842 S:17

Eldridge, Mary M - Died 1942 Born 1890 Wife of Frank Eldridge (listed with him) S:18

Eldridge, Mary S - Died 1953 Born 1880 Wife of Benjamin F Crosby (with him) S:14

Eldridge, Mehitable H - Died 1880 March 13 Age 55 Wife of Richard Eldridge (next to him) S:18

Eldridge, Melenda - Died 1883 July 30 Age 87 Widow of Jonathan Eldridge (next to Mehitable & Richard Eldridge) S:18

Eldridge, Miriam - Died 1939 June 13 Born 1898 July 12 S:10

El-dridge, Olivia Joyce - Died 1921 May 7 (Eldridge plot) (with Kenneth Gordon Eldridge & others) S:20

Eldridge, Richard - Died 1890 April 18 Age 74 (with wife, Mehitable H Eldridge) S:18

Eldridge, Rose G - Died 1939 Born 1892 (next to Annie M Eldridge) S:31

Eldridge, Simeon - Died 1919 Oct 6 Born 1835 Aug 9 Stone says, "Father" (next to Adelaide R Eldridge) S:21

Eldridge, Susan - Died (no date) Born 1853 (with James W Macy) S:18

Eldridge, Susan Caroline - Died 1861 July 21 Age 22 years, 5 months Wife of Joshua Eldridge (stone broken at base, laying on the ground) S:11

Eldridge, Thomas R - Died 1873 June 20 Age 38 years, 10 months, 13 days Was in Co E, 5th Reg in Massachusetts Volunteers Militia (next to wife, Elizabeth E Eldridge) S:18

Eldridge, Truman D - Died 1896 Born 1833 (with Louisa A El-dridge) S:19

Eldridge, W - Died 1841 (in large crypt with other Eldridge's at street level) S:10

Eldridge, Warnie B - Died 1874 Born 1873 (with Clarence F Eldridge & others) S:18

Eldridge, William C - Died 1923 Born 1871 Son of Joseph & Lucy Eldridge (with them) S:18

Eliot, Edward C - Died 1989 Sept 17 Born 1926 May 2 Was a LCDR in US Navy (Next to Lois Eliot) S:20

Eliot, Lois Ellgner - Died 1988 Feb 27 Born 1926 March 17 Stone says,"Beloved wife & mother" (next to Edward Eliot) S:20

Elkin, Charlotte G - Died 1986 Born 1887 (99 years old at

Elkin (Cont.)
death) (wife of Frank L Elkin, with him) (Mosswood ceme records say she died in 1983 at age 94?) S:15

Elkin, Frank L - Died 1986 Born 1887 (101 years old at death) (with wife, Charlotte G Elkin) (Mosswood ceme records say her age was 99?) S:15

Ellgner, Edward Linclon - Died 1975 March 3 Born 1889 Nov 19 S:20

Elliot, I Fenno - Died 1948 Born 1873 (with Maud Case Elliot & others) S:18

Elliot, Maud Case - Died 1945 Born 1883 (with I Fenno Elliot & Mary Elizabeth Case & others) S:18

Elliott, Eileen G - Died 1985 Born 1898 (listed with W Scott Elliott) S:15

Elliott, Robert S - Died 1979 Born 1898 (with wife, Catherine M Danaher) S:16

Elliott, W Scott - Died (still living 1991?) Born 1900 (with Eileen G Elliott) S:15

Ellis, ? - Died 1855? (small stone, badly worn) (first name has 5 letters) (between Josephine D Washington & Joseph Mitchell) S:18

Ellis, Abbie - Died 1886 Sept Born 1833 Dec 19 (with Charles Ellis) S:12

Ellis, Abbie Webster - Died 1956 June 14 Born 1866 Dec 11 Wife of John Fish (with him) S:14

Ellis, Bertha M - Died 1964 Born 1887 (with Isaiah F Ellis & others) S:19

Ellis, Charles - Died 1895 Feb 9 Born 1830 Sept 4 (with Abbie Ellis) S:12

Ellis, DeLaurier Louise G - Died 1956 March 27 Born 1898 Sept 27 at Prince Edward Island, Canada S:20

Ellis, Eudoram - Died 1882 April 5 Born 1861 July 13 Daughter of

Ellis (Cont.)
Charles & Abbie Ellis S:12

Ellis, Isaiah F - Died 1969 Born
1883 (with Bertha Ellis &
Charles & C Marion Stansifer)
S:19

Ellis, James - Died 1893 Aug 26
Born 1829 Sept 29 (with Mary R
Ellis & others) S:21

Ellis, James R - Died 1864 Sept 11
Born 1857 Jan 28 (with Joseph
A Ellis & others) S:21

Ellis, Joseph A - Died 1860 March
25 Born 1859 March 3 (with
James Ellis & others) S:21

Ellis, Marjorie O - Died 1930 Born
1924 (with Mary J & Otis Ellis)
S:19

Ellis, Mary J - Died (still living
1991?) Born 1899 (with Otis &
Marjorie Ellis) S:19

Ellis, Mary R - Died 1894 Sept 13
Born 1834 March 6 (with James
R Ellis & others) S:21

Ellis, Otis D - Died 1983 Born 1899
(also has Barnstable Fire Dept
plaque) (with Mary J & Marjorie
O Ellis) S:19

Ellis, Paul - Died 1967 July 7 Born
1900 April 12 From Massachusetts, was Pvt in US Army during
World War I S:17

Ellman, George - Died 1973 Aug 4
Born 1896 Jan 28 (Jewish sec-
tion) From Massachusetts, was
Cpl in US Army during World
War I S:15

Elson(?), Annie M - Died 1875 Jan
9 Age 31 years, 7 months, 20
days (stone down from vandals)
(next to Hannah Bishop Coffin)
S:18

Emberg, Albin - Died 1972 Born
1883 (with Ellen C Emberg) S:15

Emberg, Ellen C - Died 1990 Born
1892 (with Albin Emberg) S:15

Emberg, Ernest S - Died 1974 Born
1879 (next to Albin & Ellen
Emberg) S:15

Emerson, George Weston - Died
1918 Dec 30 Born 1845 Dec 28
(with Herbert Watson Emerson

Emerson (Cont.)
& others) S:18

Emerson, Herbert Watson - Died
1877 Oct 15 Born 1871 Feb 14
(a metal marker) (with Nathaniel
Waldo Emerson & others) S:18

Emerson, Horace Allen - Died 1918
Oct 20 Born 1890 April 28 (with
Sarah H Emerson & others) S:18

Emerson, Nathaniel Waldo - Died
1892 May 13 Born 1885 Feb 1
(with Horace Allen Emerson &
others) S:18

Emerson, Rufus - Died 1884 Born
1847 (buried with Enuice &
Nelson Phinney & others) S:8

Emerson, Sarah H - Died 1911
June 18 Born 1848 Oct 19 Wife
of George Emerson (with Nathaniel Waldo Emerson & others) S:18

Emerton, Blanche - Died 1953
Born 1884 Wife of Harry C
Crocker (next to him) S:11

Emery, Hannah K - Died 1842
(listed on Heywood family stone)
S:11

Emery, John H - Died 1969 Born
1894 (with Marie D Emery) S:19

Emery, Marie D - Died 1987 Born
1897 (with John H Emery) S:19

Emrich, Herman G Jr - Died 1991
Born 1914 S:13

Engel, William E - Died 1977 April
17 Born 1895 Dec 9 S:15

Enos, Angie A - Died 1946 Born
1875 (with Frank S Enos) S:16

Enos, Frances A - Died 1975 Born
1896 Wife of Clarence Anderson
(with him) S:19

Enos, Frank S - Died 1940 Born
1872 (with Angie A Enos) S:16

Enos, Manuel - Died 1964 Born
1884 (with Sylvia Enos) S:15

Enos, Manuel T - Died 1944 Born
1856 (with wife, Mary G Enos &
others) S:31

Enos, Mary F - Died 1991 Born
1908 (with Frank A Clark &
others) S:18

Enos, Mary G - Died 1937 Born
1863 Wife of Manuel T Enos

Enos (Cont.)
(with him & Frances Anderson & others) S:31

Enos, Sylvia - Died 1978 Born 1895 (with Manuel Enos) S:15

Ensor, James - Died 1962 Born 1884 (with Mary E Donaghy) S:13

Entin, Edith Z - Died 1982 Mar 29 Born 1900 April 21 (Jewish section) (next to Zelek Entin) S:15

Entin, Zelek M - Died 1955 Mar 2 Born 1896 Mar 4 (Jewish section) (next to Edith Z Entin) (Mosswood ceme records say death date was 1985 age 88?) S:15

Erat, Julius - Died 1983 Born 1901 (with Muriel Erat) S:19

Erat, Muriel - Died (still living 1991?) Born 1916 (listed with Julius Erat) S:19

Erickson, Christina H - Died 1978 Born 1906 Wife of Eric O Erickson (with him) S:15

Erickson, Eric O - Died 1970 Born 1899 (with wife, Christina H Erickson) S:15

Erickson, Henry W - Died 1963 Nov 24 Born 1898 Oct 8 From District of Columbia, was Capt in US Marines Corps during World War II (next to Marion C Erickson) S:20

Erickson, Marion C - Died 1988 Born 1903 (next to Henry W Erickson) S:20

Erwin, James A - Died 1976 Born 1892 (with Teresa L Erwin) S:15

Erwin, Teresa L - Died 1977 Born 1893 (with James A Erwin) S:15

Espar, Emma D - Died 1973 Born 1900 (with James E Espar) S:15

Espar, James E - Died (still living 1991?) Born 1907 (listed with Emma D Espar) S:15

Ethier, Antoinette Storm - Died 1970 Born 1895 S:18

Euer, (Ewer) Eleazer - Died 1797 Nov 2 Age 47 S:10

Euer, (Ewer) Sarah - Died 1812 Jan

Euer (Cont.)
27 Age 74 Widow of ? S:10

Eurer, (Ewer) (male) - Died Son of Eleazer & Abagail Euer S:10

Evans, Edgar Robert - Died 1921 Born 1861 (with wife, Ida May Savery) S:12

Evans, Frederick R - Died 1962 Born 1897 (with Gertrude H Evans) S:14

Evans, Gertrude H - Died (still living 1991?) Born 1893 (listed with Frederick R Evans) S:14

Evans, Isaac Milton - Died 1965 Sept 16 Born 1898 Feb 8 From Massachusetts, was Cpl in US Army during World War I S:17

Evans, Mabel - Died 1964 Born 1879 Wife of Richard Freeman Robbins (with him) S:12

Evans, Mary Lewis - Died 1954 March 10 Born 1880 Sept 4 Wife of Sidney Alexander Kirkman (with him) S:14

Evans, Robert - Died 1881 Sept 24 Born 1794 in Ireland (with Frastus Baker) S:12

Evans, Shirley Savery - Died 1965 Sept 19 Born 1892 May 9 (has metal American Legion Star in ground next to stone) (with Maude Ethel Pierce) S:12

Evans, Sol - Died 1973 Sept 16 Born 1885 Mar 15 (Jewish section) S:15

Ewer, Abigail G - Died 1805 Oct 28 in her 23rd yr Wife of Barnabas Ewer (located at Lothrop's Hill) S:26R

Ewer, Benjamin - Died 1792 May 20 in his 71st yr S:5

Ewer, Benjamin - Died 1893 Oct 11 Born 1805 Aug 21 S:5

Ewer, Edgar - Died 1875 Born 1850 S:5

Ewer, Eleazer - Died 1797 Nov 2 in his 47th yr (located at Lothrop's Hill) S:26R

Ewer, Elizabeth Mrs - Died 1820 Oct 29 in her 37th yr Daughter of Charles & Deborah Dimmock S:10+26R

Ewer, Hannah - Died 1801 April 23 Age 71 Widow of Benjamin Ewer S:5R

Ewer, Hannah - Died 1836 Nov 17 in her 49th yr Wife of Isaac Ewer S:12+12R

Ewer, Hannah - Died 1864 July 15 Age 60 years, 10 months Daughter of Pegleg & Mehetable Ewer S:5

Ewer, Henry - Died 1863 Dec 22 Born 1844 Dec 3 Was a member of Company F, 24th Massachusetts Volunteers S:10

Ewer, Horace S - Died 1855 Feb 29 Born 1854 Sept 29 (with Howard C Ewer) S:10

Ewer, Howard C - Died 1852 April 6 Born 1852 Jan 6 (with Horace Ewer) S:10

Ewer, Isaac - Died 1794 July 22 in his 18th yr Son of Eleazer and Abigail Ewer (located at Lothrop's Hill) S:26R

Ewer, Isaac - Died 1859 Dec 10 Age 96 years, 6 months, 3 days (with Mary Ewer) S:12

Ewer, Isaac Parker - Died 1826 Oct 17 Age 2 years, 8 months (with Mercy Ewer) S:12

Ewer, John Churchill - Died 1798 Sept 1 Age 2 days (with Mary & Isaac Ewer) S:12

Ewer, Lydia - Died 1794 July 26 in her 5th yr Daughter of Eleazer and Abigail Ewer (located at Lothrop's Hill) S:26R

Ewer, Mary - Died 1800 Nov 2 at Edgartown, Martha's Vineyard, Mass Age 25 (with Isaac Ewer) S:12

Ewer, Mehetable - Died 1874 Dec 4 Age 90 years, 9 months, 20 days Wife of Pegleg Ewer S:5

Ewer, Mercy - Died 1831 Oct 4 Age 50 Wife of Isaac Ewer (with Isaac Parker Ewer) S:12

Ewer, Paully - Age 5 months (on same stone with mother, Paully C Ewer, daughter of HP Ewer) S:10

Ewer, Paully C - Died 1841 June 7

Ewer (Cont.)
Age 24 Wife of Henry Ewer (on same stone with Paully Ewer) (daughter?) S:10

Ewer, Peleg - Died 1836 Mar 31 in his 84th yr (buried next to Mehetable Ewer-wife) S:5

Ewer, Polly C - Died 1841 Age 5 months Daughter of Henry & Polly C Ewer S:10

Ewer, Polly C - Died 1841 June 11 Age 24 Wife of Henry Ewer With Polly C Ewer, daughter S:10

Ewer, Sally Otis - Died 1887 Sept 22 Born 1811 June 12 Wife of Benjamin Ewer S:5

Ewer, Susan - Died 1816 Feb 27 in her 27th yr Wife of Ansel Ewer S:10

Ewery (Every?), Hannah K - Died 1842 (located at Lothrop's Hill) S:26R

Exman, Eugene - Died 1975 Born 1900 (next to wife, Gladys Miller) S:11

Exum, Josephine C - Died 1960 Born 1879 S:17

Eyre, Florence B - Died 1976 Born 1881 (with John H Eyre) S:18

Eyre, Jane Leech - Died 1935 Born 1851 (with Sarah E Eyre & others) S:18

Eyre, John H - Died 1974 Born 1882 (with Florence B Eyre) S:18

Eyre, Joseph - Died 1928 Born 1907 (with Florence B Eyre) S:18

Eyre, Sarah E - Died 1934 Born 1860 (with Joseph Eyre & others) S:18

Faber, Charles F - Died 1972 Born 1906 (with Marjorie H Faber) S:17

Faber, Marjorie H - Died 1983 Born 1900 (with Charles F Faber) S:17

Fairfield, Isaac P - Died 1878 May 9 Age 72 years, 11 months (with Mary B Fairfield & others) S:18

Fairfield, Mary B - Died 1887 July 25 Age 66 years, 9 months (with Joseph Russell Hall & others) S:18

Fairgrieve, John - Died 1850 April 11 Born 1847 Dec 21 S:9

Falvey, Mary Alice - Died 1956 Born 1879 (large stone cross) (with Mary Julia Falvey & Mary Gertrude McKaig) S:16

Falvey, Mary Julia - Died 1945 Born 1888 (large stone cross) (with Mary Gertrude McKaig & Mary Alice Falvey) S:16

Farnsworth, (infant) - Died 1847 June Age 6 days Son of Abram & Verlina Farnsworth (next to mother) S:21

Farnsworth, Verlina Mrs - Died 1847 Oct 7 Age 25 years, 11 months Wife of Abram Farnsworth (next to infant Farnsworth) S:21

Farnum, Charles G - Died 1869 June 15 Age 48 years, 10 months, 24 days Listed that he was in Third Massachusetts Light Battery and was a Civil War Veteran (Hinckley Ceme records #5R say death year was 1867) S:5

Farnum, Charles Prince - Died 1892 Feb 19 Born 1846 Oct 27 S:5

Farnum, George C - Died 1859 July 3 Born 1856 June 6 Son of Charles G Farnum S:5

Farnum, Georgianna - Died 1868 Mar 3 Born 1859 Apr 17 Daughter of Charles G Farnum S:5

Farnum, Herbert B - Died Son Charles P Harriet Farnum (Hinckley Ceme records #5R say death date was 1877 June 30 age 6 years, 1 month, 27 days) S:5

Farnum, Mary P - Died 1874 Sept 9 Born 1827 Mar 7 Wife of Charles Farnum (buried next to him) S:5

Farquhar, Charles L - Died 1973 Nov 5 Born 1899 July 26 From Massachusetts, was Pvt in US Army during World War I S:17

Farrell, Alice T - Died 1984 Born 1888 Stone says,"Mother" (with son, John F Farrell) S:15

Farrell, John F - Died (still living 1991?) Born 1914 (listed with mother, Alice T Farrell) S:15

Farren, Blanche L - Died 1966 Born 1881 (next to Francis P Farren) S:17

Farren, Francis P - Died 1963 Born 1873 (with Blanche L Farren) S:17

Farris, Jeremiah (Capt) - Died 1818 Sept Age 46 at sea (listed on Lydia Bourne's stone) S:10

Farris, Olive Mrs - Died 1878 June 7 Born 1805 Oct 28 Widow of Washington Farris (buried next to him) S:10

Farris, Washington (Capt) - Died 1861 Nov 7 Born 1796 Oct 25 An honest man S:10

Faulmann, Charles J - Died (still living 1991?) Born 1897 Oct 24 (listed with Irene D Faulmann) S:15

Faulmann, Irene D - Died 1982 June 9 Born 1901 Oct 23 (listed with Charles J Faulmann) S:15

Fawcett, Annie M - Died 1948 Born 1872 (with James C Fawcett & others) S:16

Fawcett, Dorothy V - Died 1988 Born 1898 (with Annie M Fawcett & others) S:16

Fawcett, Harold H - Died (still living 1990) Born 1906 (with Mildred F Fawcett) S:11

Fawcett, James C - Died 1956 Born 1869 (with Annie M Fawcett & others) S:16

Fawcett, Margaret M - Died 1980 Born 1895 (with Annie M Fawcett & others) S:16

Fawcett, Mildred F - Died (still living 1990) Born 1907 (with Harold H Fawcett) S:11

Fay, Carol - Died 1985 Born 1934 (with Frederick & Harriette Sherwood) S:20

Fay, Florence M - Died 1975 Aug 4 Born 1895 Feb 6 S:15

Fay, May C - Died 1969 Born 1887 S:11

Featherstone, Margerite (Guerite)

160

Featherstone (Cont.)

A - Died 1972 April 14 Born 1918 April 16 From Massachusetts, was a Sergeant in Army Air Forces during World War II (next to Yvonne H Devanney) S:31

Fekkes, Dorothy - Died (still living 1991?) Born 1902 (a rock stone) (listed with Harry Fekkes) S:20

Fekkes, Harry - Died 1987 Born 1898 (a rock stone) (has 2 stones) Was a Cpl in US Army during World War II (with Dorothy Fekkes) S:20

Felker, William S - Died 1845 March 24 Age 31 Died at sea (with Polly Burlingame) S:14

Fellows, Henry J - Died 1966 Born 1900 S:15

Fermino, Jose J - Died 1987 Born 1887 (listed with Martha M Fermino) S:16

Fermino, Martha M - Died (still living 1991?) Born 1906 (listed with Jose J Fermino) S:16

Fernald, Eliza F - Died 1914 Dec 16 Born 1832 Aug 5 Wife of Frederick W Coleman S:8

Fernald, Margaret M - Died (still living 1990 ?) Born 1889 (on same stone with Arthur Grinnell Rotch) S:11

Fernandes, Conrad - Died 1962 Born 1875 (with wife, Mary Roderick) S:16

Fessemdem,(?) Louisa Green - Died 1903 or 8 Born 1835 (stone worn & in Bursley plot) S:10

Fessenden, Mary - Died 1858 Oct 26 Born 1782 June 18 S:6

Field, Arabella C - Died 1893 Feb 13 Born 1862 Feb 4 (with Edward & Bessie Field) S:18

Field, Bessie H - Died 1948 March 4 Born 1869 March 18 (with Edward & Arabella Field) S:18

Field, Donald H - Died 1988 Born 1916 (also has Veteran plaque) Was a Pvt in US Army during World War II (next to Nancy E Field) S:20

Field, Dorothy N - Died (still living 1991?) Born no date) (listed with Marshall J Field) S:19

Field, Edward E - Died 1912 Sept 25 Born 1861 June 20 (with Bessie & Arabella Field) S:18

Field, Harvey John - Died 1955 Jan 6 Born 1892 Aug 31 From Massachusetts, was a Pvt in CoL, 103 Inf, 26 Div during World War I (next to Nancy E Field) S:20

Field, Helen M - Died 1958 Born 1873 (with Dora P Bearse) S:18

Field, Marshall J - Died 1982 Born 1907 (with Dorothy N Field) S:19

Field, Mary E - Died 1985 Sept 8 Born 1888 April 9 (next to Merrill H Field) S:15

Field, Merrill H - Died 1968 Feb 19 Born 1887 April 30 From Massachusetts, was E1 in USNRF during World War I (next to Mary E Field) S:15

Field, Nancy E - Died 1971 Dec 28 Born 1892 March 26 (Next to Harvey John Field) S:20

Fields, Douglas W - Died 1972 June 23 Born 1898 April 3 From Massachusetts, was a Private in 503rd AERO Sq during World War I S:15

Fieux, Robert E - Died 1991 Born 1919 Was a 1st Lt in US Army during World War I S:20

Finn, Mary G - Died 1989 Born 1897 (with Matthew C Finn) S:16

Finn, Matthew C - Died 1961 Born 1892 (with Mary G Finn) S:16

Finnegan, Joseph W - Died 1930 July 8 Born 1910 Oct 23 S:31

Finnell, Margaret - Died 1901 Sept 30 Born 1827 March 27 S:20

Fish, (baby) - Died 1888 May 3 Born 1888 Apr 28 S:5

Fish, (child) - Died 1830 Oct 11 Age 8 days Son of Henry & Lydia Fish (stone hard to read) S:5

Fish, Almira S - Died 1849 Sept 3 Age 2 years, 3 months Daughter of Elisha & Mary A Fish S:5R

Fish, Almira T - Died 1850 Oct 14 Age 8 days Daughter of Henry W & Lydia F Fish S:5R

Fish, Amelia S - Died 1849 Sept 3 Age 2 years, 3 months Daughter of Elisha & Mary Fish S:5

Fish, Ann - Died 1902 Dec 15 Age 87 (plot fenced in) (with Heman Fish & others) S:19

Fish, Bathsheba - Died 1836 Nov 15 Age 33 Wife of Franklin Fish S:10

Fish, Bessie - Died 1898 Born 1848 (with James A Fish Jr & others) S:14

Fish, Betsey F - Died 1891 Nov 28 Born 1819 July 1 Wife of David Fish S:7

Fish, Caroline - Died 1902 Born 1813 (with James A Fish) (Mosswood ceme records say she was the wife of James Fish Sr) S:14

Fish, Charles H - Died 1948 Born 1882 (with wife, Fannie E Fish & Lois Keenan) S:18

Fish, Charlotte W - Died 1895 Mar 9 Born 1829 Oct 14 S:5

Fish, Cynthia - Died 1819 Apr 23 Age 4 months, 11 days Daughter of Harrison & Charlotte Fish (all buried next to each other) S:5

Fish, Cynthia - Died 1875 Feb 12 Age 82 S:5R

Fish, Cyrus B - Died 1865 Born 1844 Jan 5 Son of David & Betsey Fish S:7

Fish, David - Died 1870 July 11 (died in rebel prison at Florence, South Carolina)(there is a question to his death date - It was five years after the war?) Born 1806 Sept 16 He served in Corp Co E, 40 Reg Mass Vol Son of David & Betsey F Fish S:7

Fish, Edwin - Died 1877 May 21 Age 61 years, 1 month, 10 days S:5

Fish, Elisha - Died 1853 Apr 28 Age 36 years, 6 months (died at Inagus) S:5

Fish, Elsie M - Died 1963 Born

Fish (Cont.) 1893 Daughter of Horton & Elizabeth Reynolds (with them) S:14

Fish, Elwood G - Died 1906 Born 1875 (with Elisha Robbins) S:14

Fish, Fannie E - Died 1966 Born 1889 Wife of Charles Fish (with him & Lois Keenan) S:18

Fish, Hannah - Died 1832 Jan 11 Age 6 months, 5 days Daughter of Osborn & Rhoda B Fish (on same stone with Stephen P Fish & others) S:8

Fish, Harriet B - Died 1835 Jan 18 Age 20 months S:10

Fish, Harrison - Died 1894 Feb 21 Born 1818 May 8 S:5

Fish, Heman - Died 1844 Oct 11 Age 78 (buried next to wife, Mary Fish) S:10

Fish, Heman - Died 1887 Sept 1 Age 80 (plot fenced in) (with wife, Ann Fish & son, Nathaniel Fish) S:19

Fish, Heman C - Died 1885 Aug 15 Age 52 years, 5 months S:5

Fish, Henrietta - Died 1853 Apr 25 Age 17 months Daughter of Henry & Lydia Fish S:5

Fish, Henry W - Died 1900 Aug 4 Age 79 years, 11 months S:5

Fish, Isaac - Died 1888 Jan 29 Age 96 years, 6 months S:5

Fish, James - Died 1858(?) Nov 21 Age 73 years, 10 months (not clear) (next to Thankful Fish, whose stone is down) S:14

Fish, James A - Died 1900 Born 1811 (with Caroline Fish) S:14

Fish, James A Jr - Died 1934 Born 1848 (with James A & Caroline Fish) S:14

Fish, Jemima - Died 1810 May 1 Age 72 years, 8 months Wife of Josiah Fish (Hinckley Ceme records #5R say death year was 1840) S:5

Fish, John Milton - Died 1953 Feb 4 Born 1864 June 26 (next to Lemuel Gordon Fish) S:14

Fish, Josiah - Died 1848 June 22

Fish (Cont.)

Age 85 years, 2 months Widow of Jedidiah Jones S:5

Fish, Josiah (Capt) - Died 1866 Dec 10 Born 1803 Sept 21 S:5

Fish, Josiah C (Corp) - Died 1863 Nov 7 at Rappahannock Station Was in Company F, 6th Regiment (Maine or Mass) Volunteers Born 1841 Feb 11 S:5R

Fish, Lemuel Gordon - Died 1967 Dec 22 Born 1889 Nov 7 (next to John Milton Fish) S:14

Fish, Lizzie T - Died 1894 Aug 17 Born 1846 Nov 14 S:5

Fish, Louisa - Died (no dates or info but located next to Bessie. both stones are very small with a lamb on each, they are located just in back of the Fish family stone?) S:8

Fish, Lydia - Died 1863 Mar 4 Age 74 years, 11 months Wife of Reuben Fish & daughter of Prince Hinckley S:5

Fish, Lydia F - Died 1884 Feb 29 Age 55 years, 7 months Wife of Henry Fish S:5

Fish, Lydia S - Died 1900 Jan 2 Age 51 years, 11 months S:5

Fish, Mary - Died 1798 Feb 6 in her 63rd yr Wife of Reuben Fish (buried next to him) S:5

Fish, Mary Ann - Died 1871 Sept 27 Age 51 Daughter of Reuben & Lydia Fish & wife of Ellis Jenkins S:5R

Fish, Mary E - Died 1877 Born 1877 (with James A Fish Jr & others) S:14

Fish, Mary Mrs - Died 1855 Mar 8 Age 78 Widow of Heman Fish (buried next to him) S:10

Fish, Mildred Louise - Died 1890 Dec 24 Born 1890 July 21 S:5

Fish, Nason - Died 1868 Oct 28 in his 58th yr S:5

Fish, Nathaniel G - Died 1851 Feb 16 Age 10 years, 10 months (plot fenced in) Son of Heman & Ann Fish (with them & others) S:19

Fish, Nina R - Died 1891 Born

Fish (Cont.)

1883 S:5

Fish, Orborn - Died 1882 July 22 Age 83 years, 5 months, 16 days (buried next to wife, Rhoda B Fish) S:8

Fish, Phineas - Died 1854 June 16 at Cotuit Born 30 Jan 1785 at Sandwich Graduated at Harvard College 1807, ordained at Mashpee 18 Sept 11 Stone says, "An honored minister of Christ for many years, a faithful and devoted missionary of the Society For The Propagation Of The Gospel among the Indians - Erected by the Society" S:14

Fish, Preston Hayes - Died 1974 Born 1897 S:14

Fish, Rebecca B Mrs - Died 1876 Mar 16 Age 77 S:10

Fish, Reuben - Died 1809 Aug 25 in his 72nd yr (buried next to Mary Fish-wife) S:5

Fish, Reuben - Died 1886 June 10 in his 63rd yr S:5

Fish, Reuben (Capt) - Died 1854 May 16 in his 84th yr S:5

Fish, Rhoda B - Died 1846 June 19 in her 40th yr Wife of Orsmound Fish (stone had this spelling but other stones of family members had Osborn)(buried next to him) S:8

Fish, Ruth - Died 1879 May 1 Born 1803 Feb 12 S:5

Fish, Stephen P - Died 1834 Jan 22 Age 1 Son of Osbornd & Rhoda B Fish (on same stone with Hannah Fish & others) S:8

Fish, Susan A - Died 1884 May 28 Age 62 years, 3 months, 3 days Wife of Edwin Fish S:5

Fish, Temperance - Died 1802 Aug 23 Age 26 Wife of Ansel Fish S:7

Fish, Thankful - Died 179? Apr (stone not clear) Wife of Josiah Fish S:5

Fish, Thankful - Died 1875 Feb 11 Age 89 years, 10 months (stone is down) (next to James Fish) S:14

Fish,(?) Bessie A - Died (no dates or info but with other stone that says Louisa, both have lambs on top and located just in back of the Fish family stone? (buried 1898, wife of James Fish Jr, which this info is from the Mosswood ceme records) S:8

Fisher, (infant) - Died 1927 Born 1927 (Ames stone) (with Samuel & Mother Ames & others) S:12

Fisher, Alice Coleman - Died 1919 Born 1883 Wife of Rev C Howard Taylor S:14

Fisher, Arthur J - Died 1972 Born 1884 (with Florence C Fisher) S:16

Fisher, Basil - Buried 1957 (not sure if in cemetery 15 or 14?) S:15R

Fisher, Belle S - Died 1937 Born 1861 (with H Leston Fisher) S:14

Fisher, Christie A Died 1978 Born 1891 (Ames stone) (with Samuel & Mother Ames & others) S:12

Fisher, Clara C - Died 1905 Born 1842 (with Jarvis R Fisher) S:14

Fisher, Daisy Chatfield - Died 1958 Oct 6 Born 1865 July 25 (with Alton G Churbuck) S:14

Fisher, Drusilla - Died 1925 Jan 24 Born 1837 July 11 (with Horace G Fisher) S:14

Fisher, Edna L - Died 1966 Born 1891 (next to Victor J Fisher) S:15

Fisher, Edson E - Died 1949 Born 1865 (with wife, Eleanor C Lumbert) S:14

Fisher, Edward - Died 1885 Born 1884 (listed on Paine, Titcomb & Brown stone) S:11

Fisher, Emeline - Died 1921 Born 1837 (with Hervey W Fisher) S:14

Fisher, Emma E - Died 1890 Born 1863 (with Hervey & Emeline Fisher) S:14

Fisher, Evander D - Died 1878 May 25 Age 75 years, 5 months (with Mary M Fisher) S:11

Fisher, Florence C - Died (still

Fisher (Cont.) living 1991?) Born 1886 (listed with Arthur J Fisher) S:16

Fisher, George - Died 1887 Nov 1 Born 1817 Oct 18 (with Maria Otis) S:13

Fisher, H Leston - Died 1905 Born 1849 (with Belle S Fisher) S:14

Fisher, Hervey W - Died 1893 Born 1831 (with Emeline Fisher) S:14

Fisher, Horace G - Died 1910 Sept 18 Born 1834 June 19 (with Drusilla Fisher) S:14

Fisher, Irving H - Died 1980 Dec 12 Born 1916 July 10 Was a TEC in US Army during World War II S:11

Fisher, Isaiah Warren (Capt) - Died 1924 Born 1845 (with Priscilla Morris Fisher) S:14

Fisher, Jarvis R - Died 1920 Born 1837 (with Clara C Fisher) S:14

Fisher, John A - Died 1898 June 24 Born 1861 March 7 (with Alton G Churbuck) S:14

Fisher, Louise A - Buried 1956 Located in section S, lot 6, grave 3 S:14R

Fisher, Mary - Died 1933 Born 1852 Wife of Edward Titcomb (listed on Paine, Titcomb & Brown stone) S:11

Fisher, Mary M - Died 1876 Feb 27 Age 72 years, 10 months Wife of Evander Fisher (with him) S:11

Fisher, N A - Died (no information listed) US Navy (stone is very small & old) S:14

Fisher, Priscilla Morris - Died 1924 Born 1846 (with Capt Isaiah W Fisher) S:14

Fisher, Rhoda C - Died 1903 Sept 23 Born 1819 Dec 1 (stone is down) (with William C Fisher) S:14

Fisher, Robert S - Died 1935 Born 1920 (Ames stone) (with Samuel & Mother Ames & others) S:12

Fisher, Thomas Chatfield - Died 1956 Jan 29 Born 1889 Sept 21 (with Alton Churbuck) S:14

Fisher, Victor J - Died 1981 Born

Fisher (Cont.)
1896 Was in Surf US Coast Guard during World War I (next to Edna L Fisher) S:15

Fisher, William C - Died 1893 Feb 4 Born 1813 Sept 11 (stone is down) (with Rhoda C Fisher) S:14

Fisher, William H - Died 1945 Born 1892 (Ames stone) (with Samuel & Mother Ames & others) S:12

Fisk, Saimi M - Died 1979 Born 1898 Wife of Samuel Johnson (with him) S:20

Fitzgeral, William L - Died 1957 Born 1878 (with Bertha M Clarkin) S:15

Fitzgerald, Agnes M - Died 1983 Born 1895 Wife of Redmond J Fitzgerald (with him) S:14

Fitzgerald, Ann Louise - Died 1982 Born 1900 (with Bernard A Fitzgerald) S:15

Fitzgerald, Bernard A - Died 1984 Born 1898 (with Ann L Fitzgerald) S:15

Fitzgerald, Redmond J - Died 1964 Dec 6 Born 1894 March 10 From Massachusetts & in MUSI USNRF during World War I (with wife, Agnes M Fitzgerald) S:14

Fitzpatrick, Alice M - Died 1960 Born 1901 (with P Neil Fitzpatrick) S:16

Fitzpatrick, P Neil - Died 1963 Born 1894 (with Alice M Fitzpatrick) S:16

Fitzsimons, Mary M - Died 1908 Born 1868 (with Richard Fitzsimons) S:31

Fitzsimons, Richard - Died 1908 (with Mary M Fitzsimons) S:31

Flagler, Lyla D - Died 1983 Born 1882 S:15

Flaherty, Grace - Died 1984 June 23 Born 1899 Jan 20 Wife of Leon M Flaherty (next to him) S:15

Flaherty, Leo M - Died 1967 July 6 Born 1902 Sept 24 From Massachusetts, was CSK in USNR during World War II (next to

Flaherty (Cont.)
wife, Grace Flaherty) S:15

Flanders, Edwin D Jr - Died 1964 Jan 17 Born 1890 Aug 23 (has 2 stones) From Massachusetts, was MUS1 in USNR during World War II With Minnie E Flanders) S:17

Flanders, Minnie E - Died 1991 Born 1898 (with Edwin D Flanders Jr) S:17

Flannigan, Clementine F - Died 1968 Born 1881 Wife of James P Flannigan (next to him) S:14

Flanningan, James P - Died 1955 Born 1874 (next to wife, Clementine F Flannigan) S:14

Fletcher, Elizabeth A - Died 1862 Jan 6 Age 23 years, 8 months (called Lizzie) Wife of William Fletcher (next to Elizabeth A Fletcher) S:21

Fletcher, Elizabeth A - Died 1870 May or March Age 8 months, 4 days? (stone not clear and cracked in half) Daughter of Elizabeth Fletcher & William Small (next to mother) Stone says,"Gone home to rest" S:21

Fletcher, Henrietta Rosella - Died 1926 Jan 26 Born 1857 May 23 (buried with Frank Scudder Bearse, her husband) S:8

Fleury (Pleury?), Adele - Died 1929 Born 1927 S:31

Flewelling, Florence L - Died 1968 Born 1886 Buried 1969 April 2?) (with Margaret Landers) (Mosswood ceme records had the above burial record?) S:14

Flexon, Minnie M - Died 1976 Born 1883 (with Rosamond M Johnstone Murray) S:18

Flinn, Kathleen E - Died (still living 1991?) Born 1910 (listed with William J Flinn) S:16

Flinn, William J - Died 1988 Born 1900 (listed with Kathleen E Flinn) S:16

Flores, Manuel J - Died 1939 Born 1861 (with wife, Mary C Flores) S:16

Flores, Mary C - Died 1950 Born 1875 Wife of Manuel J Flores (with him) S:16

Floyd, Charles - Died 1863 July 27 Age 31 years, 4 months, 23 days Lost at sea (listed with Lizzie H Dixon & Charles Floyd) S:19

Floyd, Charles H - Died 1884 Oct 13 Age 24 years, 3 months, 18 days Son of Charles Floyd & Lizzie Dixon (with him) S:19

Flynn, Ellen Murray - Died 1962 Born 1875 (with James R Hargreaves) (others with later dates listed on stone) S:14

Foerste, Charles H - Died 1977 Born 1895 (has 2 stones) Was Pl Sgt in US Marine Corps during World War I & II (with wife, Una·S Foerste) S:15

Foerste, Una S - Died 1990 Born 1897 (107 years old at death) (with husband, Charles H Foerste) S:15

Foerster, Charles H - Buried 1977 March 8 Age 81 S:15R

Foertsch, Cheryl Anna - Died 1972 April 5 Born 1951 Nov 23 Stone says,"In memory of Sherry" S:20

Foley, Edward H - Died 1964 April 23 Born 1891 Sept 10 From Massachusetts, was Private in 7th Co, 151 Depot Brigade during World War I S:14

Foley, Gertrude M - Died 1988 Mar 1 Born 1898 June 12 S:14

Foley, Margaret E - Died 1954 Born 1887 Wife of Timothy S O'Shea (with him & Mary Foley & others) S:16

Foley, Marion E (Capt) - Died 1971 March 4 Born 1900 April 7 (has 2 stones) (also with Major Gertrude A Wilson) From Massachusetts, was in the Army Nurse Corps during World War II S:16

Foley, Mary - Died 1953 Born 1889 Wife of Frank D Brogan (with her & Margaret Foley & others) S:16

Folger, Ann A - Died 1849 Dec 16 in her 34th yr Wife of George Folger S:5

Folger, Cynthia - Died 1908 Born 1821 (next to Lorenzo B Folger) S:14

Folger, Joseph - Died 1911 Born 1821 (next to Cynthia Folger) S:14

Folger, Joseph B - Died 1923 Born 1848 (with wife, Mary Elizabeth Folger) S:14

Folger, Lorenzo B - Died 1877 Dec 18 Born 1850 March 16 (next to Cynthia Folger) S:14

Folger, Mary Elizabeth - Died 1944 Born 1863 (with husband, Joseph B Folger) S:14

Fontneau, Richard Thomas - Died 1982 Oct 4 Born 1943 April 11 S:19

Foote, James Harold - Died 1923 March 26 Born 1922 Oct 25 (with Manuel T Enos & others) S:31

Ford, Annie V G - Died 1945 Born 1865 Wife of Rev Herbert Ford (buried next to him) S:8

Ford, Betsey H - Died 1862 July 18 in her 74th yr Wife of Oliver Ford S:4

Ford, Clement - Died 1886 Born 1829 (with Mary Mitchell Ford) S:18

Ford, George E - Died 1943 Born 1868 S:18

Ford, Herbert (Rev) - Died 1932 Born 1860 (buried next to wife, Annie VG Ford) S:8

Ford, Lydia - Died 1836 Oct 29 in her 38th yr Wife of Dr Oliver Ford S:4

Ford, Mary Mitchell - Died 1929 Born 1844 (with Clement Ford) S:18

Ford, Oliver - Died 1865 Sept 25 in his 78th yr S:4

Ford, Phoebe A - Died 1968 Born 1888 (near Bessie B Bell) S:13

Forest, Lewellyn - Died 1909 Born 1892 (with Alice & Wesley Wright) S:14

Forstrom, Fiina C - Died 1963 Born 1884 (next to George Forstrom) S:17

Forstrom, George - Died 1969 Born 1888 (next to Fiina C Forstrom) S:17

Fortes, Jessie - Died 1954 Born 1889 (flat stone covered over with grass) (next to Manuel Fortes) S:16

Fortes, Manuel - Died 1966 Born 1894 (flat stone covered over with grass) (next to Jessie Fortes) S:16

Fossett, Thomas W'd Dr - Died ? Born 1813 Age 80 "I am over 80 years old" 9th son of Obil Fossett, grandson of John & great, great grandson of Patrick of Ireland John's mother was Scotch I have practiced on Eclectic system in Massachusetts, Ohio, Michigan for over 50 years & never lost that number Patients S:10

Foster, Catherine C - Died 1963 Born 1907 (listed with husband, Anthony Nicholas) S:15

Foster, Denis - Died 1760 May 1 Son of John & Meriam Foster S:5

Foster, Edgar William - Died 1963 Jan 29 Born 1898 April 22 From Massachusetts, was a S2 in USNRF during World War I S:17

Foster, Eliza - Died 1890 Nov 10 Age 68 years, 6 months Wife of Capt Heman Foster (buried next to him) S:9

Foster, Hellen V - Died 1990 July 4 Born 1900 June 8 Wife of Thomas Quinn Jr (listed with to her) S:15

Foster, Heman (Capt) - Died 1867 Feb 20 Age 54 years, 3 months S:9

Foster, Lovenia G - Died 1949 Born 1878 (next to Sumner D Foster) S:12

Foster, Nabbey - Died 1794 June 9 Daughter of Nathan & Mercy Foster S:5

Foster, Sumner D - Died 1945 Born 1902 (next to Lovenia G Foster) S:12

Foster, Winnifred - Died 1956 May 8 Born 1861 May 2 Stone says,"Our beloved mother is home with her brothers & sisters" S:14

Fowler, Emma F - Died 1902 Aug 21 Age 57 (with William Fowler & next to Ernest Fowler, flat stone with no dates) S:21

Fowler, Ernest - Died (no dates, flat stone) (next to William & Emma Fowler) S:21

Fowler, Ernest F - Died 1910 Aug 21 Born 1893 June 29 (with Lillian & William Fowler) S:21

Fowler, Lillian L - Died 1908 Dec 30 Born 1875 July 20 (with Ernest & William Fowler) S:21

Fowler, Richard E - Died 1981 Born 1924 He was in the US Navy (flag at stone) S:11

Fowler, William - Died 1886 Sept 25 Age 50 years, 7 months (with Emma F Fowler) S:21

Fowler, William F - Died 1889 Sept 18 Born 1866 Sept 23 (with Lillian L Fowler) S:21

Fox, Harriet Louise - Died 1980 Born 1876 S:15

Fox, Margaret - Died 1945 June in New York City Born in Ireland (located in Crocker plot) Stone says "A Faithful Freind" S:10

Fozzard, James Thomas - Died 1976 April 8 Born 1894 May 3 Was MM2 in US Navy during World War I S:17

Francis, Amelia M - Died (still living 1991?) Born 1901 (listed with Sylvester F Francis) S:16

Francis, Hannah - Died 18?? July 13 (stone is white, about 4 feet tall & badly worn) S:10

Francis, Sylvester F - Died 1960 Born 1900 (with Amelia M Francis) S:16

Francke, Emily S - Died 1990 Born 1900 (with F William Francke Jr) S:15

Francke, F William Jr - Died 1975 Born 1896 (with Emily S Francke) S:15

Franco, Maurice - Died 1967 Born 1891 Stone says,"Chacun son Tour Chacun son Heure Marcelle" S:15

Franklin, Nellie - Died 1863 June 22 Born 1862 Sept 29 (stone says "Little Nellie" S:8

Fraser, Carl A - Died 1990 May 7 Born 1904 June 24 Was a Lt Col in US Army during World War II & Korea (next to Evelyn M (Orde) Fraser) S:19

Fraser, David - Died 1949 Born 1870 (with Marjorie Fraser) S:12

Fraser, Evelyn M (Orde) - Died 1990 Nov 22 Born 1905 Aug 6 (next to Carl A Fraser) S:19

Fraser, Harold I - Died 1968 Oct 27 Born 1896 July 2 From Massachusetts, was AR2 in USNR during World War I S:17

Fraser, Julia Lissa - Died 1982 Aug 17 Born 1899 Feb 24 (next to Ronald M Fraser) S:14

Fraser, Laura B - Died 1982 Born 1898 (with Malcolm L Fraser) S:15

Fraser, Malcolm L - Died 1967 Born 1898 (with Laura B Fraser) S:15

Fraser, Marion - Died 1988 Born 1897 (with husband, Ebenezer Erskine Harvey) S:15

Fraser, Marjorie - Died 1934 Born 1877 Wife of David Fraser (with him) S:12

Fraser, Ronald M - Died 1970 April 14 Born 1896 March 18 From Massachusetts, was a Y3 in USNRF during World War I (with Julia Lissa Fraser) S:14

Fraters, Mary - Died 1928 Born 1871 S:31

Fratus, Clara M - Died 1957 Born 1893 Wife of William B Fratus (with him) S:16

Fratus, William B - Died 1939 Born 1887 (with wife, Clara M Fratus) S:16

Frazel, Christopher John - Died 1968 Aug 23 Born 1968 June 26 Stone says,"Our littlest angel"

Frazel (Cont.) S:13

Frazel, Doris E - Died 1981 Mar 3 Born 1914 Dec 28 "My Beloved" (in Marshall plot) S:11

Frazel, Hugh S Sr - Died 1972 Jan 27 Born 1910 May 25 (in Marshall plot) S:11

Frazier, Frank M - Died 1936 Born 1877 (with wife, Rose D Frazier) S:14

Frazier, Gabriel Roland - Died 1955 Feb 12 Born 1895 Aug 21 (next to Joseph Frazier Jr) S:12

Frazier, John E - Died 1932 Born 1862 (with Mary E Frazier) S:14

Frazier, Joseph Jr - Died 1958 Oct 8 Born 1901 Oct 8 Was a Private from Massachusetts in US Army during World War II S:12

Frazier, Manuel E - Died 1979 Born 1896 Was a Private in US Army during World War I (next to Mary L Frazier) S:16

Frazier, Mary E - Died 1962 Born 1877 (with John E Frazier) S:14

Frazier, Rose D - Died 1934 Born 1881 Wife of Frank M Frazier (with him) Stone also says, "Infants" (there must be more than one child buried with them) S:14

Fred, HR Bassett - Died 1918 Born 1884 (with Alfred S Johnston & others) S:18

Freeman, Anna B - Died 1977 Born 1898 (with Charles F Freeman) S:17

Freeman, Ansel - Died 1835 Feb 27 Age 30 S:10

Freeman, Bithiah Mrs - Died 1788 Oct 3 Age 32 Wife of James P Freeman S:10

Freeman, Charles F - Died 1989 Born 1894 (with Anna B Freeman) S:17

Freeman, Eliza - Died (stone broken) (next to husband, Simeon Freeman) (she is listed as his wife) S:4

Freeman, Harriot - Died 1942 Feb 15 Born 1855 Jan 10 (buried

Freeman (Cont.)
    with Charles Austin Groves,
    husband) S:8
Freeman, L Warren - Died 1835
    Jan 2 Age 10 Son of Warren &
    Sarah Freeman (with Warren
    Freeman, d1826) S:10
Freeman, Mercy - Died 1815 Aug
    31 in her 66th yr Daughter of
    Maj Gideon Freeman S:7
Freeman, Nathaniel - Died 1728
    April 8 Born 1728 March 31 Son
    of Capt Nathaniel & Mary
    Freeman S:11R
Freeman, Warren - Died 1826 Mar
    8 Age 26 Lost at sea (on same
    stone with Warren Freeman
    d1835) S:10
French, Isabella G - Died 1894
    June 11 Born 1848 May 20 S:9
French, Robert Elam - Died 1973
    Oct 28 Born 1893 Aug 10 Was
    from Massachusetts and was in
    CM3 US Navy during World War
    1 (has a veteran star at grave
    too) S:13
French, Sally Turpin - Died 1988
    June 3 Born 1920 April 13 (with
    Bertrand Carr Jr who is still
    living 1990) (in Turpin plot) S:11
Frost, Arabelle F - Died 1953 Born
    1882 (with Caroline & Maurice
    Frost & others) S:18
Frost, Caroline W - Died 1906 Aug
    13 Born 1846 June 22 (with
    George Frost & others) S:18
Frost, Elvira B - Died 1880 Born
    1815 (with Milton P Frost &
    others) S:18
Frost, George W - Died 1906 Oct 4
    Born 1845 Aug 8 (next to Maude
    Frost & Caroline Frost) S:18
Frost, Harriet J - Died 1929 Born
    1858 (with Willie ?(Frost?) &
    others) S:18
Frost, Ida D - Died 1921 Born 1849
    (with Vida D Frost & others)
    S:18
Frost, John H - Died 1881 Born
    1812 (with Elvira B Frost &
    others) S:18
Frost, John H - Died 1917 Born

Frost (Cont.)
    1843 (with Ida D Frost & others)
    S:18
Frost, Maude A - Died 1923 Born
    1875 (next to George W Frost &
    with William Linnell & others)
    S:18
Frost, Maurice L - Died 1929 Born
    1880 (with Arabelle F Frost &
    others) S:18
Frost, Milton P - Died 1858 Born
    1849 (with Harriet J Frost &
    others) S:18
Frost, Vida D - Died 1878 Born
    1876 (with Samuel Pitcher &
    others) S:18
Frost, W Wallace - Died 1907 May
    7 Born 1841 June 29 (with
    Josephine GE Howe & others)
    S:18
Frost, Willie - Died (dates & stone
    not clear) (Between Harriet J
    Frost, but closer to Joseph &
    Elizabeth Coffin?) (not sure of
    last name?) S:18
Frost, Zena - Died 1880 May 9
    Born 1880 Jan 25 Daughter to
    W Wallace Frost & Josephine
    Howe (with them) S:18
Fulcher, A Frank - Died 1972 Born
    1897 (next to Emmie & Edgar
    Fulcher) S:21
Fulcher, Edgar S - Died 1947 Born
    1931 (with A Frank Fulcher)
    S:21
Fulcher, Emmie L - Died 1979
    Born 1898 (next to A Frank
    Fulcher) S:21
Fuller, ? - Died 1732 Jan ? (stone
    not clear) (buried between
    Thankfull Fuller & MJR Micha
    Hamlin) S:5
Fuller, Abagail - Died 1775 Jan 20
    in her 23rd yr S:7
Fuller, Abigail - Died 1845 July 18
    Born 1799 Oct 23 ? Wife of
    James H Fuller (buried next to
    him) S:5
Fuller, Abram - Died 1883 Feb 10
    in his 86th yr S:5
Fuller, Abram - Died 1893 May 1
    Born 1819 Aug 11 S:7

Fuller, Adeline F - Died 1843 Born 1828 (with John B Fuller) S:14

Fuller, Alice L - Died 1953 Born 1867 (large stone that says Fuller) (buried with Prince A Fuller & others with later dates, possibly children: Rebecca E, Irving H, Prince A Jr & his wife Stella W) S:8

Fuller, Annie G - Died 1875 Dec 24 Born 1872 July 2 (with Hersehel Fuller & others on large Fuller stone) S:12

Fuller, Ansel B - Died 1892 Born 1808 S:7

Fuller, Bathsheisa - Died 1749 June in the 23rd yr S:5

Fuller, Benjamin - Died (stone not clear, but stones around him dated mid-1800's) S:3

Fuller, Benjamin (Capt) - Died 1854 June 5 Age 77 years, 10 months, 8 days S:5R

Fuller, Bethiah - Died 1737 July 1 in her 26th yr Daughter of Joseph Fuller S:5

Fuller, C Wesson - Died 1983 Born 1894 S:18

Fuller, Charles F - Died 1936 Born 1861 S:14

Fuller, Clifton M - Died 1946 Born 1867 (with Mina J Fuller & others) S:18

Fuller, Daniel - Died 1886 Born 1793 (with Adeline F Fuller & his wife, Mehitable S Jones) S:14

Fuller, David - Died 1854 Born 1795 (with Olive B Fuller) S:12

Fuller, David - Died Nov 14 (year not clear on stone) Son of Matthias 1772 Age 1 year, 3 months, 26 days) S:5

Fuller, David B - Died 1916 Born 1841 Has a veteran star post that says, "1861-65 & FLT #139" (with Eunice S Fuller) S:12

Fuller, Eben W - Died 1887 Jan 25 Age 54 years, 3 months S:5

Fuller, Edith Leb - Died 1972 Born 1883 (next to Leon C Fuller) S:15

Fuller, Edmund D - Died 1972

Fuller (Cont.)
Born 1873 (with Mary A Fuller) S:16

Fuller, Edna A - Died 1960 Born 1876 (with Clifton Fuller & others) S:18

Fuller, Edward H - Died 1935 Born 1852 (with Izetta A Fuller) S:18

Fuller, Edwin (Capt) - Died 1884 Nov 18 Age 53 Born 1831 A victim of the wreck of the City of Columbus at Gay Head, Martha's Vineyard, Massachusetts S:7

Fuller, Eliza - Died 1848 Feb 18 Age 55 years, 3 months Wife of William Fuller (buried next to her husband) S:3+3R

Fuller, Elizabeth - Died 1732/3 Jan Age 27 S:5R

Fuller, Eloise B - Died 1860 Oct 6 in her 26th yr Wife of Edwin Fuller S:7

Fuller, Emily SG - Died 1927 Jan 25 Born 1846 Sept 8 (with Hon Zeno Scudder & others on large Fuller stone) S:12

Fuller, Emma E - Died 1890 Born 1869 Daughter of Capt Edwin Fuller & Emily Stearns (with her) S:14

Fuller, Esther Phinney - Buried 1906, grave 12 S:15R

Fuller, Eunice S - Died 1919 Born 1844 (with David Fuller & others) S:12

Fuller, Eunice T - Died 1923 May 9 Born 1831 Nov 4 S:7

Fuller, Everett F - Died 1955 Born 1875 (with wife, Frances H Lovell) S:13

Fuller, George B - Died 1937 Born 1868 (with David Fuller & others) S:12

Fuller, George F - Died 1947 Dec 8 Born 1869 Nov 1 (with Capt George N Fuller & others) S:14

Fuller, George N (Capt) - Died 1920 Born 1836 (large Fuller stone) Veteran star, 1861-65 (with Esther F Phinney & others) S:14

Fuller, Grafton Phinney - Died

Fuller (Cont.)
1888/9 May 28 Born 1869 Nov
1 (with Capt George N Fuller &
others) S:14

Fuller, Henry Alton - Died 1930
April 16 Born 1859 Sept 22
(with Capt George N Fuller &
others) S:14

Fuller, Henry Gildersleeve - Died
1928 July 5 Born 1874 Feb 4
(on large Fuller stone with Annie
G Fuller & others) S:12

Fuller, Hershehel - Died 1905 Nov
24 Born 1839 Mar 29 (with
Emily SG Fuller & others on
large Fuller stone) S:12

Fuller, Izetta A - Died 1931 Born
1853 (with Edward Fuller &
others) S:18

Fuller, Jahial - Died 1843 Sept 13
Son of Stephen 6 Mercy Fuller
(Hinckley Ceme records #5R say
death date was 1845 age 64
years, 16 months) S:5

Fuller, James H Mr - Died 1826
Nov 6 in his 29th yr S:5

Fuller, Joanna - Died 1766 Apr 13
in her 77th yr Widow of Joseph
Fuller S:5

Fuller, John - Died 1732 July 24
Age 45 (Hinckley Ceme records
#5R say death was on 17 Oct
age 27) S:5

Fuller, John - Died 1739 Oct 17
(buried next to Capt Thomas
Fuller) S:5

Fuller, John B - Died 1860 Born
1851 (with Adeline F Fuller) S:14

Fuller, John Lieut - Died 1739 July
24 (Hinckley Ceme records #5R
say death date was 1732 age 43
and he was the son of John
Fuller) S:5

Fuller, Joseph - Died 1745 Sept 4
in his 63rd yr S:5

Fuller, Joseph - Died 1890 Born
1800 S:7

Fuller, Joseph C - Died 1880 Born
1815 S:7

Fuller, Lavinia - Died 1849 Born
1848 (next to Lucius Fuller) S:12

Fuller, Leon C - Died 1973 Born

Fuller (Cont.)
1888 (next to Edith Leb Fuller)
S:15

Fuller, Lizzie H Died 1875 Oct 30
Age 52 years, 2 months Born
Daughter of Abram & Lucy
Fuller S:5

Fuller, Lucius - Died 1855 Born
1852 (next to Lavinia Fuller)
S:12

Fuller, Lucy - Died 1875 Oct 17 in
her 80th yr, 5 months Wife of
Abram Fuller S:5

Fuller, Martha A - Died 1924 Born
1832 Wife of Virgil B Collins
(with him) S:14

Fuller, Martha Ann - Died 1811
June 21 Age 11 years, 5 months,
8 days Daughter of Capt David
& Olive P Fuller (next to Willie
Fuller) S:12

Fuller, Mary A - Died 1952 Born
1870 (with Edmund D Fuller)
S:16

Fuller, Mary C - Died 1929 Born
1867 (with Gilbert & Phebe &
Isabelle Crocker) S:14

Fuller, Mary H - Died 1908 Jan 24
Born 1857 Nov Wife of Capt
William Sturgis (listed with her)
S:14

Fuller, Mercy H - Died 1901 Born
1816 S:5

Fuller, Meriah - Died 1772 Apr 9 in
her 19th yr S:7

Fuller, Mina J - Died 1946 Born
1883 (with Izetta Fuller & others) S:18

Fuller, Naomi Porter - Died 1868
May 16 Born 1865 Nov 4 (with
Capt George N Fuller & others)
S:14

Fuller, Olive B - Died 1900 Born
1813 (with David Fuller) S:12

Fuller, Olive B - Died 1939 Born
1872 (with David Fuller & others) S:12

Fuller, Prince A - Died 1928 Born
1853 (large stone that says
Fuller) (buried with Alice L Fuller) S:8

Fuller, Rebekah - Died 1732 July

Fuller (Cont.)
30 Age 22 years, 1 month S:5R

Fuller, Robert R - Died 1913 Born 1839 (with Daniel Fuller & Mehitable Jones) (Mosswood ceme records say burial was in 1916?) S:14

Fuller, Sarah A - Died 1873 Born 1832 S:7

Fuller, Sophia C - Died 1866 Born 1805 S:7

Fuller, Sophia C - Died 1903 Born 1812 S:7

Fuller, Stephen B - Died 1890 Born 1812 S:5

Fuller, Thankfull - Died 1728 July 5 in her 19th yr S:5

Fuller, Thomas Died 1779 Sept 30 Age 1 year, 3 months, 25 days Son of Lemuel & Abigail Fuller S:5R

Fuller, Thomas (Capt) - Died 1719 Nov 2 in his 58th yr S:5

Fuller, Walter I - Died 1970 Born 1882 (with Esther Crocker) S:12

Fuller, Walter I Jr - Died 1980 Born 1915 (with Walter Fuller Sr & Esther Crocker) S:12

Fuller, William - Died 1875 Feb 10 Age 87 yrs 3 mos (next to wife, Eliza) S:3R

Fuller, William H (Billy) - Died 1879 Dec 4 Age 32 (A Navy anchor on stone) S:12

Fuller, Willie - Died 1845 Born 1843 (next to Lavinia Fuller) S:12

Fulton, Edith M - Died 1916 Born 1874 Stone says "Sweetheart" Wife of James M Fulton S:11

Fulton, Ellen - Died 1968 Born 1884 Wife of Robert McNutt (next to him) S:14

Funston, Laura - Died 1962 Born 1876 (with Luther H Sears Jr & Carl Sears & others) S:18

G W H, - Died (nothing else on stone) S:21

Gadsae, ? - Died 1943? Born 1875 (stone worn) (next to Arthur & Florence Gadsae) S:17

Gadsae, Arthur Garfield - Died

Gadsae (Cont.)
1881 Aug 13 in Wellesley, Massachusetts (stone down & broken) (between ? & Florence Gadsae) S:17

Gadsae, Florence Ogden - Died 1885 July 22 (stone worn) (next to Arthur Garfield Gadsae) S:17

Gage, (infant) - Died 1811 Mar 2 Born 1811 Mar 2 Son of Joseph & Abagail Gage S:4

Gage, Abagail - Died 1858 Mar 20 in her 84th yr (Relict) Wife of Joseph Gage S:4

Gage, Abby - Died 1898 Sept 27 Born 1812 May 12 Daughter of Joseph & Abagail Gage S:4

Gage, Abigail - Died 1803 Feb 10 Wife of Lot Gage S:1

Gage, Abigail - Daughter of ?? (stone not clear, she is between Gage's) S:4

Gage, Adam Joseph - Died 1960 Nov 14 Born 1892 Oct 23 From Massachusetts, was Sgt in CoA, 353 MGBN, 95BH during World War I (next to Mary E Gage) S:16

Gage, Agnes M - Died 1987 Born 1898 S:15

Gage, Charles - Died 1822 Oct 20 in his 16th yr (died in Boston, Mass) Son of Zenas & Lydia Gage S:4

Gage, Cordelia - Died 1847 June 17 Age 9 months Daughter of Leander & Rhoda M Age S:4

Gage, Desih H - Died 1878 Sept 2 Born 1819 Nov 11 S:4

Gage, Ellen T - Died 1888 March 17 Age 52 years, 8 months, 11 days Wife of William L Gage (next to him) S:18

Gage, Emma F - Died 1886 Aug 16 Age 31 years, 5 months S:21

Gage, Florence - Died 1879 June 17 Age 15 years, 3 months Daughter of William L & Ellen T Gage (next to them) S:18

Gage, Frederick A - Buried 1983 June 18 Age S:15R

Gage, Irene M - Died 1846 Oct 1 Age 4 years, 2 months Daughter

Gage (Cont.)
of Leander & Rhoda Gage S:4

Gage, Joseph - Died 1842 Nov 16 in his 75th yr S:4

Gage, Leander - Died 1846 Oct 4 Age 37 years, 6 months S:4

Gage, Lot (Capt) - Died 1791 May 24 in his 71st yr Possible wife was Abigail Gage S:1

Gage, Lydia - Died 1836 Nov 8 in her 69th yr Wife of Zenas Gage S:4

Gage, Mary E - Died 1980 March 26 Born 1897 Aug 15 (next to Adam Joseph Gage) S:16

Gage, Mary Gage - Died 1824 Sept 26 Age 18 months, 17 days Daughter of Lot & Hannah Gage S:4

Gage, Nathaniel (Capt) - Died 1824 Mar 7 in his 64th yr S:4

Gage, Rhoda M - Died 1901 Jan 5 S:4

Gage, Robert O - Died 185? July 11 Born 1822 (stone not clear) (Hinckley Ceme records #5R say death date was 1857 July 14 and the birth was 1827) S:5

Gage, Thankful - Died 1824 Nov 23 in her 60th yr Widow of Capt Nathaniel Gage S:4

Gage, Thomas - Died 1828 July 24 in his 22nd yr (died in Boston, Mass) Son of Zenas & Lydia Gage S:4

Gage, Thomas T - Died 1869 June 10 Born 1847 Apl 11 S:4

Gage, William L (Capt) - Died 1873 March 9 Age 36 years, 6 months, 12 days (stone vandalized) (next to wife, Ellen T Gage) S:18

Gage, Zenas - Died 1850 Oct 28 Died at Sacramento City, California (was he looking for gold? Gold rush was 1849) S:4

Gage, Zenas - Died 1855 Jan 29 Age 96 years, 5 months, 8 days S:4

Gagglano, Antonio - Died 1977 Born 1886 S:17

Galahan, Katheryn F Alheit - Died

Galahan (Cont.)
1982 Born 1891 S:15

Gallagher, David Warner - Died 1952 April 28 Born 1952 Feb 28 (next to Richard Sears Gallagher) S:11

Gallagher, John - Died 1966 Born 1876 (with wife, Julia Gallagher) S:16

Gallagher, John J Sr - Died 1977 Born 1899 Was a Private in US Army during World War I S:15

Gallagher, Julia - Died 1958 Born 1873 Wife of John Gallagher (with him) S:16

Gallagher, Richard Sears - Died 1976 Mar 2 Born 1915 Jan 7 1st Lieutenant, US army in World War II (plaque & flag at grave) He was Deputy Chief of Barnstable Fire Dept S:11

Gallagher, Rita M - Buried 1985 Dec 19 Age 89 S:15R

Gallant, Ferdinand J - Died 1967 Mar 12 Born 1892 May 12 From Massachusetts, was a Major in US Army during World War I & II S:15

Gallerani, Carlo - Died 1957 Born 1893 S:16

Gambino, Mary V - Buried 1981 Feb 11 Age 83 S:15R

Gambino, Thomas A - Died 1970 Born 1885 (with Mary V Gambino) S:15

Ganet, (Baby) - Died (no dates) (child of B Charles & Lila Ganet) (next to them) S:18

Ganet, B Charles - Died 1918 Sept 13 Born 1872 Aug 3 (next to Lila L Ganet) S:18

Ganet, Lila L - Died 1932 Feb 7 Born 1881 May 26 (next to B Charles & Baby Ganet) S:18

Gannon, Edward - Died 1874 Born 1837 (with Susan C Gannon) S:19

Gannon, Susan C - Died 1901 Born 1838 (with Edward Gannon) S:19

Garder, Inez I - Died 1975 Born 1889 (with Joseph H

Garder (Cont.)
Burlingame) S:14

Gardner, Andrew - Died 1872 Feb 14 in his 75th yr S:3

Gardner, Andrew B - Died 1920 Born 1833 (buried with wife, Mary E Gardner) S:8

Gardner, Anna H - Died 1972 Born 1886 (with Clarence W Mason) S:11

Gardner, Anne D Haslam - Died 1927 Jan 20 Born 1914 Mar 5 (next to Joseph Harry Haslam Jr) S:11

Gardner, Annie Bowes - Died 1881 Born 1851 (with Mark & Elizabeth Gardner) S:31

Gardner, Charles F - Died 1978 Born 1897 (with Margaret I Gardner) S:15

Gardner, David - Died 1880 Jan 5 Age 73 years, 8 months (next to wife, Mercy Gardner) S:14

Gardner, Elizabeth - Died 1886 Born 1872 (with Annie & Mark Gardner) S:31

Gardner, Elsie Rawson - Died 1948 Born 1884 (with Cora A Hallett & others) S:12

Gardner, Henry J - Died 1875 Apr 3 Born 1858 Aug 14 S:5

Gardner, Joseph W - Died 1924 Feb 3 Born 1851 Jan 19 (with Sarah B Gardner & Mary J Coleman & others) S:18

Gardner, Margaret I - Died 1968 Born 1899 (with Charles F Gardner) S:15

Gardner, Mark - Died 1878 Born 1850 (with Annie & Elizabeth Gardner) S:31

Gardner, Mary E - Died 1943 Born 1847 Wife of Andrew Gardner (buried next to him) S:8

Gardner, Mercy - Died 1876 May 11? Age 66 years, 4 months?, 2 days Wife of David Gardner (next to him) S:14

Gardner, Olive - Died 1835 June 15 in her 31st yr Wife of Andrew Gardner S:3

Gardner, Olive P - Died 1840 Oct

Gardner (Cont.)
26 Age 3 years, 3 months Daughter of Andrew & Mary Gardner (stone missing to the left of her) S:3+3R

Gardner, Sarah A - Died 1956 Born 1891 (located near pond in back of cemetery next to Ella F Sturges) S:18

Gardner, Sarah B - Died 1908 May 3 Born 1849 June 22 (with Joseph W Gardner & others) S:18

Garfield, Leon B - Died 1970 Born 1893 (next to Ragnhild S Garfield) S:15

Garfield, Ragnhild S - Died 1968 Born 1895 (next to Leon B Garfield) S:15

Garland, Edith Davis - Died 1981 Jan 2 Born 1897 Oct 6 (next to Gordon C Garland) S:17

Garland, Gordon C - Died 1969 Jan 10 Born 1894 Dec 15 From Massachusetts, was CMM in USNRF during World War I (next to Edith Davis Garland) S:17

Garouffs, George P - Died 1965 Born 1896 S:15

Garrett, Andrew Maj - Died 1835 Jan 4 in his 80th yr (Hinckley Ceme records #5R say he was a soldier in the Revolution, a true patriot and an amiable man) S:5

Garrett, Elizabeth Miss - Died 1818 Feb 27 in her 31st yr Daughter of Andrew & Olive Garrett S:5

Garrett, Lucy Mrs - Died (dates buried) Relic of Capt Andrew Garrett (destroyed stone next to her) (Hinckley Ceme records say death was 1780 July 20 age 52) S:11

Garrett, Margaret Ellen - Died 1962 Born 1880 S:11

Garrett, Mary - Died 1776 located in row 3 S:11R

Garrett, Olive - Died 1831 May 7 in her 71st yr Wife of Maj Andrew Garrett S:5

Garrit, Temperance Mrs - Died 1759 Sept 5 in her 27th yr Wife

Garrit (Cont.)
of Andrew Garrit S:9R+26R

Gasley, Hannah Miss - Died 1825 Dec 20 Age 74 S:10

Gass, Annabelle - Died 1949 Born 1863 (with John F Bell) S:13

Gass, James Augustus - Died 1965 Dec 30 Born 1894 Mar 3 From Massachusetts, was Sgt in Hq Det 12, Tn Hq & MP during World War I S:15

Gath, Doris - Died 1975 Born 1897 (with Hubert Gath) S:15

Gath, Hubert - Died 1977 Born 1892 (with Doris Gath) S:15

Geddes, Julia - Died 1882 Aug 30 Age 22 at Cotuit, Massachusetts Born at Truro, Nova Scotia, Canada S:14

Geissele, Hugo C - Died 1988 Born 1895 (listed with Dorothea M Volkheimer) S:16

Gennaco, Esther M - Died 1973 Born 1890 (with Meric E Gennaco) S:15

Gennaco, Meric E - Died 1968 Born 1890 (with Esther M Gennaco) S:15

Genrichowitch, Georgij - Died 1969 May 23 Born 1887 April 11 Stone says,"HA BYAET BOJIR TBOJ" (with Nadeschda Iwanowna) S:17

George, Anthony Jr - Died 1962 April 21 Born 1899 Mar 18 Was a F3 in US Navy during World War I (flag at stone) (with Helen E George) S:11

George, Antone R or P(?) - Died 1921 Born 1857 (with Mary A George & others) S:31

George, Helen E - Died 1990 Born 1902 (with Anthony George Jr) S:11

George, Mary A - Died 1920 Born 1860 (with Manuel Gonsalves & others) S:31

Germani, George - Died 1984 Born 1899 (with Mary T Germani) S:15

Germani, Mary T - Died 1985 Born 1900 (with George Germani)

Germani (Cont.)
S:15

Gerrard, Edythe Silver - Died 1981 Born 1893 S:15

Gerry, Martha Bingham - Died (no information listed) (next to Francis J Bingham) S:13

Gibbons, Lucy - Died 1936 July 13 Born 1839 Oct 30 Wife of James Herbert Morse (with him) S:14

Gibson, Margaret E - Died (still living 1991?) Born 1928 Wife of Russell A Gibson (listed with him) S:19

Gibson, Russell A - Died 1988 Born 1925 Married 22 March 1952, 36 years of love & happiness (Listed with wife, Margaret E Gibson) S:19

Gifford, Charles L - Died 1947 Born 1871 He served in United States House of Representitives 1922- 1947 (with wife Fannie H Handy) S:14

Gifford, Edith W - Died 1966 Born 1884 (with James F Gifford) S:17

Gifford, Edward - Died 1900 Born 1820 (with Herbert Gifford & others) S:14

Gifford, Elsie C - Died 1890 Born 1886 (with Ezra Gifford) S:14

Gifford, Ethel H - Died 1893 Born 1880 (with Harrie Gifford) S:14

Gifford, Ezra J - Died 1940 Born 1856 (with Sarah R Gifford) S:14

Gifford, F Maynard Jr - Died 1978 Born 1900 S:14

Gifford, Fannie H - Buried 1951 Located in section 7, lot 7, grave 5 S:15R

Gifford, Florence S - Died 1975 Born 1897 Wife of Howard P Claussen (with him) S:14

Gifford, Franklin M - Died 1951 Born 1876 (with Ruth B Gifford) S:14

Gifford, H Merrill - Died 1900 Born 1886 (with Harrie Gifford) S:14

Gifford, Harrie J - Died 1919 Born 1860 (with Amie H Sturges) S:14

Gifford, Harriet M - Died (still living 1991?) Born 1894 (listed with

Gifford (Cont.)

Roger G Gifford) S:17

Gifford, Herbert - Died 1921 Born 1858 (with Ruth G Gifford & others) S:14

Gifford, Herbert F - Died 1858 Born 1850 (with Ruth Crocker) S:14

Gifford, Horace T - Died 1865 Born 1844 (with Herbert F Gifford & Ruth Crocker) S:14

Gifford, Horace T - Buried 1968 May 25 Located in section 5, lot 25, grave 4 S:15R

Gifford, James F - Died 1939 Born 1877 (with Edith W Gifford) S:17

Gifford, Jennie L - Died 1960 Born 1885 (with William E Gifford) S:14

Gifford, Jennie M - Died 1950 Born 1877 (with Ruth & Franklin Gifford) (Old Mosswood ceme records say buried 1960, age 73?) S:14

Gifford, Lorenzo T - Died 1952 Born 1878 (with wife, Nora Pierce) S:14

Gifford, Marion C - Died 1902 Born 1825 (with Edward Gifford & others) S:14

Gifford, Mary A - Died 1919 Born 1842 (with William C Gifford) S:14

Gifford, Mary A - Buried 1967 Sept 21 Located in section 7, lot 16, grave 7 S:15R

Gifford, Mary J - Died 1865 Born 1846 (with Horace T Gifford) S:14

Gifford, Milton F - Died 1934 Born 1892 S:14

Gifford, Minna H - Died 1903 Born 1894 (with Ezra Gifford) S:14

Gifford, Mirrill H - Buried 1900 Located in section J, lot 4, grave 2 S:15R

Gifford, Nora P - Buried 1973 Feb 18 Located in section S, lot ?, grave 2 S:14R

Gifford, Roger G - Died 1964 Born 1905 (listed with Harriet M Gifford) S:17

Gifford, Ruth B - Died 1911 Born 1876 (with Franklin M Gifford) S:14

Gifford, Ruth G - Died 1865 Born 1853 (with Mary J Gifford & others) S:14

Gifford, Sarah R - Died 1936 Born 1856 (with Ezra J Gifford) S:14

Gifford, W Maynard - Died 1915 Born 1897 (with Nora Pierce & Lorenzo Gifford) S:14

Gifford, William C - Died 1928 Born 1843 (with Mary A Gifford) S:14

Gifford, William E - Died 1930 Born 1869 (with Jennie L Gifford) S:14

Gilbert, Pauline H - Died 1976 Born 1893 S:14

Giles, Charles E - Died 1968 Born 1885 (with Susan M Giles) S:20

Giles, Susan M - Died 1977 Born 1893 (with Charles Giles) S:20

Giles, Virginia - Died 1987 Aug 3 Born 1908 May 12 (next to Earle M Chapman) S:13

Gill, Anna H - Died 1963 Born 1898 S:14

Gill, John - Died 1947 Born 1900 S:18

Gill, Robert - Died 1943 Born 1875 (with wife, Lillian Earle) S:16

Gillies, Dorcas W - Died 1986 Born 1900 S:15

Gillis, Helen W - Died 1954 Born 1896 S:18

Gilmore, Margaret A - Died 1937 May 12 Born 1856 Dec 12 Wife of William Gilmore (with him & Agnes B McKay) S:31

Gilmore, Nancy - Died (no death recorded) Born in Derry Cerre, County Derry, Ireland Wife of Robert Evans & others S:12

Gilmore, William - Died 1912 June 26 Born 1856 Aug 5 (with wife, Margaret A Gilmore & with Agnes B McKay) S:31

Gilpatrick, Virginia Prentice - Died 1986 April 1 Born 1910 May 2 S:13

Gipps, Gladys - Died 1967 Born

Gipps (Cont.)
1915 S:13

Girard, Grace Terry - Died 1971 Born 1881 (with William F Girard) S:19

Girard, Williad F - Died 1942 Born 1877 (with Grace Terry Girard) S:19

Giroux, Mary Alice - Died 1972 Born 1887 S:16

Glancy, Frances A - Died 1951 Born 1867 (with Jane E Schwab) S:16

Gleason, Alma P - Died (still living 1991?) Born 1901 (listed with Francis R Gleason) S:15

Gleason, Catherine - Died 1904 Born 1833 Wife of Patrick Gleason (with him & Edward F Gleason MD & others) S:31

Gleason, Catherine R - Died (no dates) (with Patrick & Catherine Gleason & others) S:31

Gleason, Edward F (MD) - Died 1944 Born 1868 (with wife, Hattie C Gleason & others) S:31

Gleason, Francis R - Died 1978 Born 1898 (with Alma P Gleason) S:15

Gleason, Hattie C - Died (no dates) Wife of Edward F Gleason MD (with him & James E Odell & others) S:31

Gleason, Patrick - Died 1892 Born 1826 (with wife, Catherine Gleason & others) S:31

Glover, Alice Louise - Died 1962 Born 1875 (with Herbert Ernest Glover) S:14

Glover, Herbert Ernest - Died 1949 Born 1870 (with Alice Louise Glover) S:14

Glover, John Loring - Died 1958 Jan 15 Born 1872 Jan 26 (next to Louise Dunbar, wife) S:14

Glover, John Loring Jr - Buried 1907 Located in section C, lot 6, grave 7B S:14R

Glover, Mary - Died 1942 Mar 13 Born 1852 Mar 16 Daughter of Lothrop & Mercy Hinckley S:11

Glover, Orna C - Died 1975 Born

Glover (Cont.)
1895 (next to husband, Theodore W Glover) S:15

Glover, Theodore W - Died (still living 1991?) Born 1894 (next to wife, Orna C Glover) S:15

Glydon, Francis Xavier - Died 1987 Feb 13 Born 1950 Dec 12 S:20

Godd, Arron C - Died 1940 Born 1870 (with Mary T Jey) S:13

Godoy, Jose Antonio - Died 1972 Born 1887 (with Marion Baker, his wife) S:18

Godwin, Mary E - Died 1890 Apl 26 in her 48th yr Wife of Orin M Godwin and formerly the wife of George Crowell (his stone is next to hers) S:4

Goff, (Baby) - Died 1946 Sept 9 Born 1946 Sept 8 (between Anna L Williams & Louis Palumbo) S:13

Goff, James A - Died (still living) Born 1941 Sept 16 (with Gail D Smith) S:12

Goff, James S Col - Died 1980 Feb 5 Born 1910 April 21 (with Evelyn C William) S:12

Goffe, Mary Josephine - Died 1925 May 28 Born 1854 Jan 7 (next to Helen Goffe Pfister) S:8

Gomes, Anothny S - Died 1959 Born 1891 (with John S Gomes) S:16

Gomes, Benaldina L - Died 1977 April 29 Born 1885 Sept 15 S:17

Gomes, Emanuel N or A(?) - Died 1977 Born 1885 (with Gideon Gomes & others) S:31

Gomes, Gideon - Died 1934 Born 1858 (with wife, Marion Gomes & others) S:31

Gomes, John - Died 1924 Born 1896 (with Mary Gomes Barboza & others) S:31

Gomes, John S - Died 1954 Born 1878 (with Anthony S Gomes) S:16

Gomes, Joseph V - Died 1979 Sept 9 Born 1894 April 25 He was a Private in US Army during World War I S:13

Gomes, Leonard John - Died 1951 Born 1885 (with Mary Louise Gomes) S:18

Gomes, Manuel - Died 1980 Born 1894 S:15

Gomes, Marion - Died 1951 Born 1868/9 Wife of Gideon Gomes (with him & John Gomes & others) S:31

Gomes, Mary Louise - Died 1950 Born 1876 (with Leonard John Gomes) S:18

Gomes, Mary O'Conner - Died 1921 Born 1882 (with Emanuel N Gomes & others) S:31

Gonsalves, Candida Lopes - Died 1971 April 26 Born 1887 July 5 S:16

Gonsalves, Manuel - Died 1955 Born 1879 (with Mary Gonsalves & others) S:31

Gonsalves, Mary - Died 1926 Born 1883 (with Manuel Gonsalves & Dorothy Sullivan & others) S:31

Gonzales, H Marie - Died 1965 Born 1890 (buried with Wilhelmina Benttinnen) S:8

Goodale, Raymond H (MD) - Died 1989 Born 1898 Was Capt in US Navy during World War I S:15

Goodall, Cecil B - Died 1951 Born 1897 (he was a Mason) (next to Merton K Goodall) S:14

Goodall, Merton K - Died 1979 Born 1900 Was BUGZ in US Army during World War I (next to Cecil B Goodall) S:14

Goode, Annie V - Died 1962 Born 1869 Stone says, "Mother" S:16

Goodrich, Leonard E - Died 1895 Born 1852 (with Lizzie A Coleman & others) S:18

Goodspeed, (infant) - Died 1903 Born ? Son of Addie & Walter Goodspeed (with them) S:14

Goodspeed, (son) - Died 1823 Born 1823 (on large family stone with James Goodspeed & others) S:12

Goodspeed, A - Died (foot stone only, no last name, but next to Lydia B Goodspeed, no dates) S:21

Goodspeed, Abigail - Died 1777 May 3 in her 55th yr Wife of Joseph Goodspeed S:7

Goodspeed, Abigail - Died 1805 July 7 in her 75th yr Wife of Seth Goodspeed (buried next to him) S:7

Goodspeed, Abigail - Died 1851 Dec 29 in her 79th yr Wife of Asa Goodspeed S:7

Goodspeed, Abisher - Died 1873 Apr 14 Age 67 years, 6 months, 20 days S:7

Goodspeed, Addie Lena Leslie - Died 1947 Born 1882 Wife of Walter C Goodspeed (with him) S:14

Goodspeed, Allen - Died 1831 Jan 7 Age 62 years, 2 days S:7

Goodspeed, Allen - Died 1839 May 10 in his 33rd yr S:7

Goodspeed, Almon - Died 1839 Feb 19 in his 67th yr (buried next to wife, Rebecca Goodspeed) S:5

Goodspeed, Asa - Died 1857 Mar 5 in his 88th yr S:7

Goodspeed, Benjamin F - Died 1835 June 30 Age 1 year, 7 days Son of Charles & Sarah Goodspeed (with them & Galen Goodspeed & others) S:18

Goodspeed, Catherine B - Died 1901 Born 1840 Wife of Charles F Goodspeed (next to him) S:12

Goodspeed, Cecil L - Died (Still living 1991?) Born 1896 July 28 (with Leslie E Goodspeed) S:12

Goodspeed, Charles - Died 1852 Born 1804 S:7

Goodspeed, Charles - Died 1878 Born 1836 S:7

Goodspeed, Charles - Died 1888 Dec 4 Age 30 Son of Charles & Sarah Goodspeed (with them & others) S:18

Goodspeed, Charles - Died 1888 Oct 4 Age 84 years, 4 months, 12 days (with wife, Sarah D Goodspeed & others) S:18

Goodspeed, Charles F - Died 1874 Born 1840 (a metal marker) (with Catherine B Goodspeed)

Goodspeed (Cont.)
S:12

Goodspeed, Charles MD - Died 184? March 29 Age 78 years (stone worn & broken) (next to wife, Deidama Goodspeed) S:21

Goodspeed, Charles P - Died 1907 Feb 22 Born 1839 Nov 15 Son of Charles & Sarah Goodspeed (with them & Charles Goodspeed d1888 & others) S:18

Goodspeed, Clara - Died 1855 Born 1855 (on large family stone with others) S:12

Goodspeed, Clarissa - Died 1881 Born 1801 (large family stone with others) S:12

Goodspeed, Deborah Mrs - Died 1801 24th (month not listed) Age 32 S:5R

Goodspeed, Deidama? - Died 1852 or 1832 June 2 Age 30 or 70? (stone not clear, worn) Daughter of Charles Goodspeed MD (next to him) S:21

Goodspeed, Elias S - Died 1840 May 2 Age 2 years, 6 months, 5 days Son of Phileman & Priscilla Goodspeed (next to sister, Lucila A Goodspeed) S:14

Goodspeed, Eliphalet - Died 1866 Feb 25 Age 63 S:4

Goodspeed, Eliza - Died 1855, 18th (stone is cemented into wall of Goodspeed plot at street level) (with Eliza L or A Goodspeed) S:12

Goodspeed, Eliza A - Died 1919 Born 1838 (on large family stone with others) S:12

Goodspeed, Eliza L or A - Died 1859 Mar 15 Age 24 (stone cemented into wall of Goodspeed plot at street level) (with Eliza Goodspeed also listed on large Family stone) S:12

Goodspeed, Ella A - Died 1941 Born 1847 Wife of William H Goodspeed (with him & William C & Hattie S Goodspeed) S:18

Goodspeed, Ella B - Died 1912 Born 1884 (next to Walter &

Goodspeed (Cont.)
Addie Goodspeed) S:14

Goodspeed, Ella M - Died 1902 Born 1853 (with husband, Howard G Goodspeed) S:14

Goodspeed, Ellen D - Died 1985 Feb 26 Born 1896 June 23 Wife of Cecil L Goodspeed (with him) S:12

Goodspeed, Frank - Died 1858 Born 1835 (large family stone with others) S:12

Goodspeed, Galen - Died 1846 Sept 14 Age 1 year, 3 months, 5 days Son of Charles & Sarah Goodspeed (with them & William D Watts & others) S:18

Goodspeed, George Franklin - Died 1856 Nov 23 Age 1 year, 6 months Son of LL & Mary M Goodspeed S:5R

Goodspeed, George N - Died 1890 Born 1825 S:7

Goodspeed, Georgie - Died 1856 Nov 23 Age 1 year, 6 months Son of L & Mary Goodspeed S:5

Goodspeed, Hannah - Died 1840 Sept 21 in her 52nd yr Widow of Allen Goodspeed (buried next to him) S:7

Goodspeed, Harriet - Died 1867 Nov 4 in her 59th yr Daughter of Asa & Abigail Goodspeed S:7

Goodspeed, Hattie S - Died 1879 Born 1868 (with William H & C & Ella Goodspeed) S:18

Goodspeed, Henry C - Died 1895 Jan 20 Born 1835 July 28 Son of Charles & Sarah Goodspeed (with them & Charles P Goodspeed & others) S:18

Goodspeed, Henry J C - Died 1875 Apr 13 Age 18 years, 7 months, 20 days Son of LL & Mary M Goodspeed S:5

Goodspeed, Horace - Died 1874 Born 1827 S:7

Goodspeed, Howard G (or C) - Died 1914 Born 1856 (with wife, Ella M Goodspeed) S:14

Goodspeed, Jabez Dea - Died 1824 Feb 20 in his 86th yr He was the

Goodspeed (Cont.)
Deacon for 27 years, lived in town 64 years S:5

Goodspeed, James - Died 1902 Born 1832 (on large family stone with others) S:12

Goodspeed, John - Died 1786 Aug 26 (buried next to Mercy Goodspeed - wife) S:5

Goodspeed, Joseph - Died 1841 Nov 26 in his 52nd yr S:7

Goodspeed, Leslie E - Died 1901 Oct 10 Born 1874 Feb 18 (with Cecil L Goodspeed) S:12

Goodspeed, Levi L - Died 1879 Nov 7 Born 1822 June 11 S:5

Goodspeed, Lizzie - Died 1881 Born 1857 (on large family stone with others) S:12

Goodspeed, Louise - Died 1871 Feb 25 Age 4 years, 8 months Daughter of Henry & LH Goodspeed (stone says,"Always Loved") S:13

Goodspeed, Lucila A - Died 1847 Dec Age 19 months (stone worn) Daughter of Phileman & Priscilla Goodspeed (next to mother) S:14

Goodspeed, Lucilla - Died 1909 Born 1855 (with William & Susan Goodspeed) S:14

Goodspeed, Lydia B - Died 1850 Nov 18 Age 30 (next to A Goodspeed) S:21

Goodspeed, Martha - Died 1776 May 13 Age 3 years, 3 months Daughter of Edward & Judie Goodspeed S:5R

Goodspeed, Mary A - Died (date not clear) Wife of George Goodspeed S:7

Goodspeed, Mercy - Died 1793 May 19 in her 72nd yr Relict of John Goodspeed S:5

Goodspeed, Mercy - Died 1819 June 13 Age 4 years, 2 months Daughter of Almon 6 Rebekah Goodspeed (Hinckley Ceme records #5R say death year was 1812) S:5

Goodspeed, Minnie F - Died 1870 June 1 Born 1870 17 (with

Goodspeed (Cont.)
Charles F & Catherine B Goodspeed) S:12

Goodspeed, Nathan Bodfish - Died 1778 Apr 24 Age 1 year, 6 months Son of Joseph & Hannah Goodspeed (buried next to parents) S:7

Goodspeed, Orinda - Died 1900 Feb 6 Born 1825 Nov 4 S:5

Goodspeed, Priscilla S - Died 1850 Jan 8 Age 36 years, 8 days Wife of Phileman Goodspeed (next to daughter, Lucila A Goodspeed) S:14

Goodspeed, Puella - Died June 17 ? Wife of Thomas Goodspeed S:1

Goodspeed, Rebecca - Died 1866 Apr 3 Age 82 years, 2 months Widow of Almon Goodspeed S:5

Goodspeed, Ruth - Died 1854 July 29 in her 86th yr Widow of Allen Goodspeed S:7

Goodspeed, Sarah - Died 1766 July or Sept 25 Age 7 Daughter of John & Mercy Goodspeed (Hinckley Ceme records #5R say death day was the 23rd) S:5

Goodspeed, Sarah D - Died 1877 March 22 Age 59 years, 6 months, 12 days Wife of Charles Goodspeed (with him & Benjamin F Goodspeed, their son & others) S:18

Goodspeed, Seth - Died 1810 Mar 26 in his 82nd yr Wife was Abigail Goodspeed (buried next to him) S:7

Goodspeed, Seth - Died 1871 Born 1795 (with Clarissa Goodspeed on large family stone) S:12

Goodspeed, Solomon - Died 1777 July 7 in his 15th yr Son of Jabez & Margaret Goodspeed (buried next to Abraham ? who died the same day possibly battle?) S:7

Goodspeed, Sophronia Marston - Died 1892 Born 1803 S:7

Goodspeed, Susan L - Died 1895 Born 1811 Wife of William R Goodspeed (with him) S:14

Goodspeed, Susan L - Died 1932 Born 1839 (with William & Susan Goodspeed) S:14

Goodspeed, Susanna - Died 1773 July 10 in her 29th yr Wife of Thomas Goodspeed S:10+26R

Goodspeed, Thomas - Died 1773 Aug 7 in his 52nd yr (buried next to wife, Susanna Goodspeed) S:10+26R

Goodspeed, Walter Clifton - Died 1915 Born 1877 (with Addie Lena Leslie Goodspeed) S:14

Goodspeed, William R - Died 1893 Born 1810 (with wife, Susan L Goodspeed) S:14

Goodspeed, William C - Died 1873 Born 1870 (with Hattie S Goodspeed & others) S:18

Goodspeed, William H - Died 1920 Born 1842 (with wife, Ella A Goodspeed & others) S:18

Goodspeed, William R - Died 1905 Born 1852 (with William & Susan Goodspeed) S:14

Goodspeed, Zilpha - Died (date not clear) Wife of Joseph Goodspeed S:7

Goodwin, Mary - Died 1949 Born 1875 S:16

Goodwin, Maud Isabel - Died 1939 Born 1867 Wife of Francis L Maras pin (next to him) S:11

Googins, Clarissa - Died 1884 April 26 in South Boston Age 58 years, 5 months (with William K Googins) S:18

Googins, William K - Died 1889 Dec 4 Age 67 years, 2 months (with Clarissa Googins) S:18

Gordon, Frances - Died 1951 Mar 10 Born 1861 Mar 29 Wife of George L Kittredge (next to him) S:11

Gordon, William - Died 1981 Born 1898 Stone says,"Father" S:15

Gorham, ? Mrs - Died 1778 June 28 Wife of Shubael Gorham S:10

Gorham, ? - Died 1758 Aug 26 Age 20 (stone worn bad) Wife of George Gorham S:11

Gorham, Abagail - Died 1765 Aug 3

Gorham (Cont.)
in her 34th yr Wife of Prince Gorham S:9

Gorham, Abby T - Died 1869 May 18 Age 71 S:10

Gorham, Abigail - Died (no dates, but near Capt Samuel Gorham grave) S:10

Gorham, Abigail - Died 1765 Aug 3 in her 34th yr Wife of Mr Prince Gorham (located at Cobb Hill Cemetery East)(Goodspeed or Meeting House Hill East) S:26R

Gorham, Abigail - Died 1773 ? Feb (stone not clear) Wife of David Gorham S:10

Gorham, Abigail - Died 1820 Sept 19 ? Age 37 or 57? Wife of Edward Gorham (stone is broken in half, laying on the ground Located next to Edward Gorham) S:10

Gorham, Abigail - Died 1841 Jan 30 Born 1772 Age 69 Widow of Joseph Gorham ? (next to him & other wife, Thankful Gorham, d1844?) S:11

Gorham, Ann D - Died 1889 Born 1806 Wife of Joseph Allyn (with him) S:11

Gorham, Anna - Died (stone worn away next to Elizabeth Gorham who was the wife of David Gorham) S:10

Gorham, Anna - Died 1738 March 18 Age 2 years, 7 months, 25 days Daughter of John & Elizabeth Gorham S:9R

Gorham, Anna - Died 1792 April 21 in her 74th yr Wife of Hezekiah Gorham (buried next to him) S:10+26R

Gorham, Anna - Died 1796 Oct 13 in her 68th yr Wife of Nathaniel Gorham (located at Lothrop's Hill) S:26R

Gorham, Anna - Died 1811 Oct 29 Age 64 Wife of Silvanus Gorham (buried next to him) S:10

Gorham, Belina - Died 1866 July 27 Born 1809 April 1 (with Lot Gorham) S:11

Gorham, Benjamin (Capt) - Died 1788 April 22 Age 73 (next to wife, Mary Gorham d17??) S:11

Gorham, Benjamin (Capt) - Died 1798 Aug 28 Age 53 S:11

Gorham, Beriah - Died (no date or location) S:11R

Gorham, Bethiah - Died 1768 Dec 7 in her 73rd yr Widow of ? (Hinckley Ceme records #9R say death date was 11 Jan and that her husbands name was Job) S:9+26R

Gorham, Bethrah - Died (no date or location) S:11R

Gorham, Betsey - Died 1799 Sept 25 in her 17th yr Daughter of Silvanus & Anna Gorham (on same stone with Isiah Gorham) . S:10+26R

Gorham, Caroline - Died 1875 April 25 Age 83 years, 5 or 8 months S:10

Gorham, D L - Says "Little Sister" (no other markings, located along back road near metal fence) S:10

Gorham, David (Esquire) - Died 1786 Jan 2 in his 74th yr (stone very badly worn) (buried next to wife Hannah Gorham) S:10+26R

Gorham, Deborah - Died 14 months, 27 days (no year noted, stone worn) Daughter of Benjamin & Mary Gorham S:11

Gorham, Deborah - Died 1745 7th Age 14 months, 23 days (stone worn) Daughter of Benjamin & Mary Gorham (Hinckley Ceme records #11R say death was 1745 Oct 1 age 14 months, 25 days) S:11+26R

Gorham, Deborah - Died 1780 located in row 3 or 8 (not clear) S:11R

Gorham, Deborah - Died 1818 May 2 Age 72 Widow of Benjamin Gorham (next to Capt Ben Gorham, d1798) Relict of Josiah Crocker S:11

Gorham, Deborah L - Died 1843 May 2 Age 16 S:10

Gorham, Desire - Died 1786 Dec 15 in her 31st yr Consort to Sturgis Gorham Esq & daughter to Captain William Taylor S:11+26R

Gorham, Desire - Died 1813 Aug 20 in her 73rd yr Relict of Capt Prince Gorham S:9+26R

Gorham, Ebenezer - Died 1801 June 5 in his 28th yr (on same stone with Betsey & Isiah Gorham) S:10+26R

Gorham, Ebenezer - Died Nov?-? (stone not clear) (next to wife, Temperence Gorham) (Hinckley Ceme records #9R says death was 1776 Nov 10 at age 83rd yr) S:9+26R

Gorham, Edward - Died 1793 Oct 24 Age 9 Son of Sturgis & Desire Gorham S:11R

Gorham, Edward - Died 1822 Sept 19 Age 60 (located next to wife, Abigail Gorham) S:10

Gorham, Edward - Died 1922 Sept 9 Age 69 S:10

Gorham, Edward Sturgis - Died 1775 Feb 7 Age 10 months, 14 days Son of Sturgis & Phebe Gorham (Hinckley Ceme records #11R says death year was 1782 at age 9 years) S:11

Gorham, Edward Sturgis - Died 1789 June 4 Age 2 or 9 years, 6 months, 6 days Son of Sturgis & Desire Gorham S:11

Gorham, Edwrad Sturgis - Died 1773 Feb 7 Age 10 months, 4 days Son of Sturgis & Phebe Gorham S:11

Gorham, Elizabeth - Died 1759 Oct 2 Age 22 years, 1 month Daughter of David & Abigail Gorham Esq S:9R

Gorham, Elizabeth - Died 1784 March 29 Wife of David Gorham S:10

Gorham, Elizabeth - Died 1789 located in row 3 S:11R

Gorham, Frederic - Died 1889 Nov 3 Age 82 years, 11 months (next to wife, Lydia Gorham) S:19

Gorham, Frederic S - Died 1866
Born 1863 Son of Sumner &
Ellen Gorham S:19

Gorham, George - Died 1839 Oct 8
S:10

Gorham, George P - Died 1889
April Born 1858 Feb S:11

Gorham, Gordelia - Died 1919 Nov
11 Age 93 Wife of George Phinney (next to him & daughter,
Mary Phinney) S:19

Gorham, Hannah - Died 1727 Feb
in her 75th yr Wife of James
Gorham (Hinckley Ceme records
#11R says death day was the
13th) S:11+26R

Gorham, Hannah - Died 1810 Oct
2 in her 80th yr Widow of David
Gorham Esq (buried next to him)
S:10+26R

Gorham, Hannah - Died 1879 Aug
17 Age 85 years, 9 months (plot
fenced in) Wife of Nathaniel
Gorham (with him & Ann Fish &
others) S:19

Gorham, Helen O - Died 1957 Born
1877 (with Rufus C Gorham)
S:18

Gorham, Henry - Died 1816 Nov 7
Age 2 Son of Silvanus & Lydia
Gorham S:10

Gorham, Hezekiah Mr - Died 1778
Nov 30 in his 67th yr (stone not
clear) S:10+26R

Gorham, Isaac (Capt) - Died 1871
located in row 16 (opp) (not sure
if same as Capt Isaac d 1874)
S:11R

Gorham, Isaac (Capt) - Died 1874
April 23 Age 73 yrs 2 mos (wife,
Sophia next to him, d1902) S:11

Gorham, Isiah - Died 1799 Jan 19
Age 24 (on same stone with
Betsey & Ebenezer Gorham)
S:10

Gorham, James - Died 1707 Nov
18 in his 58th yr S:11+26R

Gorham, James - Died 1718 Sept
10 in his 49th yr (Hinckley Ceme
records #9R say he died in his
42nd yr) S:9+26R

Gorham, Job (Capt) - Died 1804

Gorham (Cont.)
Feb Wrecked at sea Age 49
(listed with wife, Rebeccah
Gorham Erected by son, Job
Gorham) S:10

Gorham, John - Died 1824 Oct 11
Age 41 S:10

Gorham, John - Died 1866 Oct 9
Age 76 (next to wife, Sally
Diane? Gorham) S:19

Gorham, John (Esquire) - Died
1769 Oct 4 Age 82 S:11

Gorham, John Col Esq - Died 1715
Nov 11 in his 65th yr (buried
next to wife, Mary Gorham,
d1732) S:9+26R

Gorham, John Esq - Died 1769 Oct
4 Age 82 S:11

Gorham, Johny - Died (dates worn
off, several other stones worn off
next to this one) Son of John &
Hannah Gorham S:11

Gorham, Joseph - Died 1881 Aug 8
Age 78 (stone worn) (stone next
to him is down and cannot be
read) S:11

Gorham, Joseph E - Died 1844
location not listed) S:11R

Gorham, Josiah - Died 1829 May
11 in his 70th yr S:11

Gorham, Lewis - Died 1821 Jan 16
Born 1752 Nov 11 (no stone,
just metal post with statistics on
it, was revolutionary war soldier,
plaque is from RevWar society)
S:11

Gorham, Lot - Died 1887 May 9
Born 1803 July 30 (with Belina
Gorham) S:11

Gorham, Lot E - Died 1927 Born
1841 (with Mary H Gorham)
S:21

Gorham, Lucietia T - Died 1864
Jan 25 Age 73 S:10

Gorham, Lydia - Died 1904 April
30 Age 95 years, 9 months Wife
of Frederic Gorham (next to him)
S:19

Gorham, Martha A - Died 1920
Born 1829 (next to Sumner P
Gorham) S:19

Gorham, Martha Mrs - Died 1859

Gorham (Cont.)
Feb 20 Age 54 Widow of John Gorham (buried next to him) S:10

Gorham, Mary - Died (no dates) located in row 2 S:11R

Gorham, Mary - Died 1732 April 1 Consort to Col John Gorham (buried next to him) S:9

Gorham, Mary - Died 1738 Jan 27 Age 4 years, 1 month, 27 days Daughter of John & Elizabeth Gorham S:9R

Gorham, Mary - Died 1741 Feb 10 in his 25th yr Wife of Isaac Gorham S:9R+26R

Gorham, Mary - Died 1778 June 28 Age 92 Relict of Hon Shubal Gorham Esq (located at Lothrop's Hill) S:26R

Gorham, Mary - Died 1857 April 27 Age 85 Wife of George Gorham S:10

Gorham, Mary - Died 1877 Dec 14 Born 1793 June 28 Wife of Willard Crocker S:5

Gorham, Mary - Died 1904 Oct 29 Age 74 years, 5 months, 14 days Daughter of Capt Joseph Parker & wife of F B Goss S:9

Gorham, Mary - Died April 9 (no date) Relict of Capt Benjamin Gorham S:11

Gorham, Mary H - Died 1923 Born 1841 (with Lot E Groham) S:21

Gorham, Mary Mrs - Died 17?? April 20 Relict of Capt Benjamin Gorham (next to him) S:11

Gorham, Mary Prentice - Died 1780 July 8 Age 26 A sincere Christian affectionate companion & agreeable friend Wife of William Pretice & daughter of David Gorham S:10

Gorham, Mehitable Mrs - Died 1788 Dec 26 Age 43 Wife of Capt Benjamin Gorham (d1798) (next to him) S:11

Gorham, Nancy - Died 1766 July 18 Age 10 months,14 days Daughter of Sturgis & Phebe Gorham S:11

Gorham, Nathaniel - Died 1876 July 6 Age 86 years, 9 months (plot fenced in) (with wife, Hannah Gorham & others) S:19

Gorham, Phebe - Died 1780 located in row 1 S:11R

Gorham, Phebe - Died 1820 ? Wife of George Gorham S:11

Gorham, Phebe Mrs - Died 1775 Nov 7 Age 32 Daughter to Capt William Taylor Consort to Capt Sturgis Gorham Stone says, "She lived a dutiful child, virtuous wife, a tender parent, a faithful friend, a pious christian and died" S:11

Gorham, Phebe Taylor Died 1783 Feb 12 Age 16 months, 13 days Daughter of Sturgis & Desire Gorham S:11

Gorham, Prudence - Died 17?? May 26 Age 26 Wife of John Gorham Esq (buried next to him, her stone not very clear) S:11

Gorham, Prudence - Died 1811 located in row 15 S:11R

Gorham, Prudence - Died 1844 S:11R

Gorham, Prudence G - Died 1844 May 9 Age 33 Born 1808 Dec Wife of Joseph F Gorham S:11R

Gorham, Rachel - Died 1808 Oct 29 in her 59th yr Wife of James Gorham S:10+26R

Gorham, Rebeccah - Died 1840 May 4 Age 74 Widow of Capt Job Gorham who was wrecked at sea Feb 1804 S:10

Gorham, Rose Anet - Died 1829 located in row 16 (opp) (could be same as Rose Ann d1827?) S:11R

Gorham, Rose Ann - Died 1829 July 10 Age 2 years, 9 months Daughter of Isaac & Sophia Gorham (next to mother) S:11

Gorham, Rufus (Capt) - Died 1860 Mar 4 Age 43 years 8 months S:10

Gorham, Rufus C - Died 1957 Born 1873 (with Helen O Gorham) S:18

Gorham, Sally - Died 1878 June 4 Age 85 Wife of Barnabas Hinckley (next to him) S:11

Gorham, Sally? Diane - Died 1848? April 15 Age 49 years (stone worn) Widow of John Gorham (next to him) S:19

Gorham, Sarah - Died 1880 Feb 9 Age 80 years, 7 months, 28 days at Roxbury, Mass Wife of David P Lewis (buried next to him) S:10

Gorham, Shuball - Died 1748 Dec 22 Age 2 years, 10 months Son of David & Abigail Gorham Esq S:9R

Gorham, Silvanus - Died 1805 May 29 in his 58th yr S:10+26R

Gorham, Sophia - Died 1902 Sept 11 Born 1806 Nov 7 Wife of Isaac Gorham (next to him, d1874) S:11

Gorham, Sturgis - Died 1793 located in row 3 S:11R

Gorham, Sturgis (Esquire) - Died 1795 April 26 in his 53rd yr S:11+26R

Gorham, Sumner P - Died 1917 Born 1835 (with wife, Ellen A Swinerton) S:19

Gorham, Susan A - Died 1910 Born 1825 Wife of Warren Ryder (with him & Caroline & Horace Ryder) S:19

Gorham, Susanna - Died 1738 March 16 Age 5 years, 3 months, 23 days Daughter of John & Elizabeth Gorham S:9R

Gorham, Sylvanus - Died 1803 May 29 Age 58 S:10

Gorham, Temperance - Died 1875 located in row 18 S:11R

Gorham, Temperance - Died 1875 Sept Age 68 years, 1 month Wife of Joseph F Gorham S:11R

Gorham, Temperence - Died 1767 Feb 21 Wife of Ebenezer Gorham (buried next to him) (Hinckley Ceme records #9R say died in her 62nd yr) S:9+26R

Gorham, Thankful - Died 1844 ? May Born 1808 Dec Age 33 Wife

Gorham (Cont.) of Joseph Gorham, d1881? (next to him) S:11

Gorham, William Taylor - Died May (underground) Son of Sturgis & Phebe Gorham (Hinckley Ceme records #11R say death was 1790 May 8 in his 15th yr) S:11+26R

Gorham,(?) ? - Died 1808 Oct 1 Age 14 months, 6 days (stone not clear) Daughter of Benjamin & Nabby (next to Thomas Harris, tall monument in front of cemetery to the left) (also next to Deborah & Capt Benjamin Gorham d1798) S:11

Gorham, ? - Mrs Died 1778 June 28 Wife of Shubael Gorham S:10

Goss, Edna Damaris Baker - Died 1936 Born 1849 (on large Goss stone) S:11

Goss, Emma Matthews - Died 1932 Born 1871 (with Hettie Gray) S:18

Goss, Frank Percy - Died 1926 Born 1852 (with Hettie Gray) S:18

Goss, Franklin - Died 1886 April 18 Age 74 years, 9 months, 1 day S:9

Goss, George R - Died 1886 Oct 10 Born 1872 April 10 S:9

Goss, Gussie M - Died 1958 Born 1873 Wife of John Pope (buried with him in Guest plot) S:8

Goss, Hettie Gray - Died 1912 Born 1854 (with Frank Percy Goss & others) S:18

Goss, Lillie S - Died 1892 March 19 Born 1803 July 22 Married to WJ Brooks S:9

Goss, William Freeman Myrick - Died 1928 Born 1859 (On Goss stone) S:11

Gott, Elizabeth E - Died 1979 Born 1895 Wife of Roger T Gott Sr (with him) S:14

Gott, Roger T Sr - Died 1984 Born 1891 Was in CCM, US Navy during World War I (next to wife, Elizabeth E Gott) S:14

Gould, Martha - Died 1880 Aug 7 Age 64 years, 5 months Formerly the wife of Benjamin E Gould S:21

Goulding, Joseph E - Died 1984 Born 1914 S:18

Gourdin, Edward O - Died 1966 July 21 Born 1897 Aug 10 He was a Brig General in US Army & Justice of Superior Court S:15

Gourdin, Ida I - Died 1984 Born 1890 (undertaker plaque only) S:15

Goutal, Suzanne J - Died 1961 Born 1902 S:13

Govoni, Dalmina - Died 1960 Born 1887 (with Joseph Govoni) S:16

Govoni, Joseph - Died 1960 Born 1887 (with Dalmina Govoni) S:16

Grace, Ella V - Died 1968 Born 1884 (with Moses A Grace) S:18

Grace, Moses A - Died 1966 Born 1880 (with Ella V Grace) S:18

Gracia, Joseph F - Died 1968 Born 1895 (with Palmeida Gracia) S:14

Gracia, Palmeida - Died (still living 1991?) Born 1896 (listed with Joseph F Gracia & Irene G Perry) S:14

Gracia, Rose M - Died 1937 Born 1851 S:16

Graham, Florence Tomlinson - Died 1967 Born 1880 (with James Graham 6 Florence Clouter) S:14

Graham, James R - Died 1964 Born 1898 (with wife, Florence B Clouter) S:14

Grammaticas, Euthymios P - Died 1985 Born 1894 (with Thalia Grammaticas) S:15

Grammaticas, Thalia - Died 1975 Born 1901 (with Euthymios P Grammaticas) S:15

Grant, Chester Noble - Died 1967 Born 1883 S:17

Grant, Donald H - Died (still living 1990) Born 1903 (with Mary C Grant) S:11

Grant, Evelyn - Died (still living 1991?) Born 1900 March 30

Grant (Cont.) (listed with Paul E Johnson) S:15

Grant, Gladys L - Died 1975 Born 1908 (with Mary S & Donald H Grant) S:11

Grant, Mary S - Died 1959 Born 1894 (with Donald H Grant) S:11

Grauer, Albert - Died 1962 Born 1889 (with wife, Rebecca C Grauer) S:14

Grauer, Rebecca C - Died 1972 Born 1893 Wife of Albert Grauer (with him) S:14

Gray, Abby G - Died 1891 Dec 29 Born 1813 Sept 27 (next to John Gray) S:9

Gray, Agnes - Died 1955 Born 1879 Wife of Briah A Connor (with him & others in plot) S:11

Gray, Alton - Died 1924 Born 1856 (with Georgianna Gray & others) S:18

Gray, Ancenette C - Died 1923 Jan 5 Born 1846 Oct 7 (with Ethel Gray & others) S:18

Gray, Bertha C - Died 1955 Born 1875 Wife of Julius A Walley (with him) S:18

Gray, Charles - Died 1883 Aug 22 Age 76 years, 7 months, 11 days (buried next to wife, Rebecca Gray) S:5

Gray, Charles I - Died 1926 Born 1889 (with Alton Gray & others) S:18

Gray, Cora W - Died 1924 Oct 28 Born 1884 Dec 6 (with Nellie Gray & others) S:18

Gray, Elisa - Died 1776 Feb ? 16 (Hinckley Ceme records #11R say death was on the 13th in her 32nd yr) S:11+26R

Gray, Elisha Jr (?) - Died 1776 Dec 16 Age 39 S:11

Gray, Ellwood - Died (no dates) (with Florence Gray & others) S:18

Gray, Ernest - Died 1894 Born 1893 (with Alton Gray & others) S:18

Gray, Ethel H - Died 1894 Nov 17

Gray (Cont.)

Born 1890 Feb 26 (with Cora Gray & others) S:18

Gray, Florence - Died (no dates) (listed with Winona Gray & others) S:18

Gray, Florence J - Died (no dates, metal marker) 7 years, 11 months, 27 days S:21

Gray, Georgianna - Died 1940 Born 1851 (with Alton Gray & others) S:18

Gray, Hannah (?) - Died 1765 Age 60 (worn) Widow of Elisha (next to him) (stone next to her has worn front and cannot read) S:11

Gray, Harriet G - Died 1897 March 29 Born 1819 July 22 Stone says, "Mother" (with Thomas Gray) S:18

Gray, Henry W - Died 1926 April 3 Born 1843 Aug 19 (with Ancenette Gray & others) S:18

Gray, John - Died 1897 Born 1817 (next to Abby G Gray) S:9

Gray, Joseph - Died (no date listed) Died at Saint Croix in Westinges in his 21st year (listed on same slate with William Gray who died 1795 Dec 16 in his 24 year) S:11R

Gray, Marion - Died 1940 Born 1888 (with Henry Gray & others) S:18

Gray, Nellie G - Died 1926 March 24 Born 1867 Oct 19 (with Marion Gray & others) S:18

Gray, Rebecca - Died 1879 Aug 4 Age 69 years, 6 months Wife of Charles Gray S:5

Gray, Ruthy Mrs - Died 1810 Feb 20 in her 48th yr Wife of Capt Thomas Gray (next to him) S:10 +26R

Gray, Samuel - Died 1806 Oct 29 in his 34th yr S:10+26R

Gray, Susan - Died 1768 Dec 19 Age 66 Widow of Elisa Gray (Hinkley records say she died in the 60th yr) (stone next to her is broken Only inscription is "in

Gray (Cont.)

the 65th year of his age") S:11 +26R

Gray, Temy Mrs - Died 1806 Oct 10 in her 28th yr Wife of Samuel Gray S:10+26R

Gray, Thomas - Died 1892 July 4 Born 1820 Jan 28 Stone says, "Father" (with Harriet G Gray) S:18

Gray, Thomas (Capt) - Died 1811 Sept 25 in his 45th yr S:10+26R

Gray, William - Died 1795 Dec 16 in his 24th yr (with Joseph Gray who died at Saint Croix) S:11R +26R

Gray, William D - Died 1818 Age 25 Lost at sea in autumn of 1818 on the Schooner, Reporter on its passage from Fredericksburg to Boston S:10

Gray, Winona - Died (no dates) (listed with Hervey E Luce & others) S:18

Green, (still born) - Died (no date) Baby of Rev Joseph & Hannah Green S:9

Green, Abigail - Died 1799 Oct 26 in her 38th yr Wife of Joseph Green and Daughter of Samuel Crocker (located at Lothrop's Hill) S:26R

Green, Arthur F - Died 1867 May 4 in his 48th yr (lost at sea) S:7

Green, Elizabeth - Died 1782 March 28 in her 47th yr Wife of John Green (located at Lothrop's Hill) S:26R

Green, Elizabeth - Died 1818 Mar 3 Age 20 days (underground - small stone) Daughter of Isaiah & Louisa Green S:10+26R

Green, Florence H - Died 1971 Born 1898 S:16

Green, Hannah - Died 1745 July 7 Age 1 month, 1 day Daughter of Rev Joseph & Hannah Green S:9R

Green, Hannah - Died 1745 June 6 in her 38th yr Consort of Rev Joseph Green (next to him) S:11 +26R

Green, Hannah - Died 1877 Aug 7 in her 80th yr Wife of David Green (buried next to him) S:7

Green, Huldah D - Died 1869 May 17 in her 42nd yr Widow (there is a marker next to her of Arthur Green who probably was her husband) S:7

Green, James - Died 1798 July 11 in his 28th yr at sea (located at Lothrop's Hill) S:26R

Green, John - Died 1800 June 15 in his 68th yr (located at Lothrop's Hill) S:26R

Green, John - Died 1804 Aug 28 in his 38th yr (located at Lothrop's Hill) S:26R

Green, Joseph - Died (stone worn) (next to Hannah Green) S:11

Green, Joseph (Capt) - Died 1790 located in row 8 (could be the same as Joseph, stone worn but next to Hannah Green) S:11R

Green, Joseph (Capt) - Died 1798 Feb 9 in his 42nd yr S:11R+26R

Green, Joseph Rev - Died 1770 Oct 4 Born 1701 June 21 Graduated from Harvard, 1720, ordained 1725 May 12 S:11R

Green, Martha Mrs - Died 1791 Jan 24 in her 61st yr (stone next to her, cannot read) Daughter of Rev Joseph & Hannah Green S:11+26R

Green, Mary - Died 1760 July 23 Relict of Joseph Green (Hinckley Ceme records #5R says Age was 84 and husband was from Boston) S:5

Green, Rita - Died 1981 Born 1897 (undertaker plaque) S:18

Green, Rollan Alvin - Died 1957 Born 1875 (next to Rose Zelinda Green) S:14

Green, Rose Zelinda - Died 1951 Born 1878 (next to Rollan Alvin Green) S:14

Greene, Arabella F - Died 1956 Born 1863 (next to Joseph Greene) S:18

Greene, Charles A - Died 1845 Sept 3 Age 13 months, 5 days Son of

Greene (Cont.)
Charles G & Nancy F Greene S:7

Greene, David - Died 1858 Oct 16 in his 67th yr (buried next to wife, Hannah Green) S:7

Greene, David - Died 1964 Born 1893 (with Goldie M Greene) S:18

Greene, Dorcash - Died 1892 June 27 Born 1844 Feb 1 Wife of George A Greene (next to Susan Greene) S:13

Greene, Edward S - Died 1928 Born 1882 (next to Joseph Greene) S:18

Greene, Goldie M - Died 1947 Born 1885 or 1884 (has 2 stones, one says 1884) (with David Greene) S:18

Greene, Joseph - Died 1908 Born 1840 (next to Edward S Greene) S:18

Greene, Joseph - Died 1961 Sept 12 Born 1886 Jan 5 From Massachusetts, was F1, USNRF during World War I (next to Thomas H Greene) S:18

Greene, Kenneth Dorchester - Died (still living 1990) Born 1904 (with Mamie S Polto, wife) S:11

Greene, Richard Thurston - Died 1949 Born 1867 (buried with Charlotte Louise Berry) S:8

Greene, Susan T - Died 1907 March 8 Born 1875 Feb 28 Stone says, "Sister" (next to Dorcash Greene) S:13

Greene, Thomas H - Died 1980 Born 1891 Was WRSTD in US Navy during World War I (next to Bessie M Walton) S:18

Greenwood, Charles S - Died 1949 Born 1877 (with E Katherine Greenwood) S:14

Greenwood, E Katherine - Died 1965 Born 1878 (with Charles S Greenwood) S:14

Greenwood, Elsie R - Died 1950 Born 1884 (with Lillian A Greenwood) S:16

Greenwood, Helen H - Died 1980 Born 1886 (with Lillian & Elsie

Greenwood (Cont.)
Greenwood) S:16

Greenwood, Lillian A - Died 1955 Born 1882 (with Elsie R Greenwood) S:16

Greer, Louise M - Died (still living 1990) Born 1906 (next to Richard W Greer) S:11

Greer, Richard W - Died 1980 Born 1901 (next to Louise M Greer) S:11

Gregson, George E - Died 1976 Born 1897 (with Mary J Gregson) S:15

Gregson, Mary J - Died 1984 Born 1898 (with George E Gregson) S:15

Grew, David Davis - Died 1958 April 21 Born 1891 March 21 Was from Massachusetts, was SFC in US Army during World War I S:18

Grey, Elisha - Died 1776 located in row 3 S:11R

Grey, Susana - Died 1768 located in row 3 S:11R

Griffin, Anne E - Died 1975 Born 1914 Wife of Edward O Griffin (with him) S:11

Griffin, Edward O - Died 1971 Born 1905 (with wife, Anne E Griffin) S:11

Griffin, Lilian May Johnson - Died (still living 1990) Born 1903 May 26 S:11

Griffin, Sidney - Died 1967 May 19 Born 1896 Nov 10 (rock with 1917-18 World War 1 engraving on it) Was Sargeant in 2nd Div AEF, World War 1 S:11

Grigson, Bertha W - Died 1950 Born 1868 (with John A Grigson) S:14

Grigson, John A - Died 1948 Born 1869 (with Bertha W Grigson) S:14

Grondin, Mary M - Died 1977 Born 1899 (with George W Brewster & others) S:14

Gronlund, Hanna H - Died 1963 Born 1885 S:20

Grouchey, Rose M - Died 1962

Grouchey (Cont.)
Born 1878 Stone says, "Mother" S:16

Groves, Charles Austin - Died 1942 Aug 16 Born 1850 Dec 8 (buried with Harriot Freeman, wife) S:8

Groves, Edith F - Died 1971 Born 1882 wife of George Howes, husband (buried with him) S:8

Groves, Janet M - Died 1967 Born 1881 S:17

Grundell, Anna Josephine - Died 1968 Born 1895 Wife of John B Souza (with him) S:12

Guest, George H - Died 1934 Born 1861 (buried with Lucie A Pope, wife) S:8

Guest, Pauline L - Died 1985 Born 1891 Wife of Robert G Guest (buried with him) S:8

Guest, Robert G - Died 1969 Born 1892 (buried with family) S:8

Guest, Robert G Jr - Died 1976 Born 1918 (buried with family) S:8

Gulachenski, Julia - Died 1976 Born 1894 (with Michael Gulachenski) S:16

Gulachenski, Michael - Died 1961 Born 1890 (with Julia Gulachenski) S:16

Gunderson, Mercy T - Died 1896 Jan 10 Wife of Gregory Gunderson S:7

Gunnitt, Bridget - Died 1862 Feb 8 Age 52 (stone worn) S:14

Gustafson, Isabelle - Died 1918 Born 1890 (with Alonzo S Williams & John W Williams & others) S:13

Gustafson, Sophie - Died 1961 Born 1882 S:11

Gutgsell, Alice G - Died 1947 Born 1902 (with James R Graham) S:14

Gyder, Eugenia D - Died 1950 Born 1889 (with Charles Crowell & Albert Kelley & others) S:19

Gymer, Gladys W - Died 1970 Born 1893 S:15

H B F, - Died 1835 (very small stone located between Mary

H B F (Cont.)
Lothrop and Harriet B Fish) S:10

Hadaway, Benjamin - Died 1851 Apr 27 Age 76 years, 8 months, 15 days S:5

Hadsell, Esther B - Died 1986 Born 1890 Age 95 (age from the Mosswood ceme records) (with Irving W Hadsell) S:15

Hadsell, Irving W - Died 1967 Born 1893 (with Esther B Hadsell) S:15

Hageman, L Coulson - Died 1989 Born 1916 (he was a Mason) (next to Cleone C Post & others) S:18

Hakkarainen, Eva N - Died 1922 Born 1883 From Finland S:18

Hale, Charles E - Died 1871 Nov 25 Age 19 years, 6 months Son of Eldridge G & Lucy H Hale S:5

Halett, Rowland - Died 1816 Aug 10 Age 74 S:1

Haley, Francis T - Died 1966 April 2 Born 1890 Aug 23 From Massachusetts & was an S2 in USNRF during World War I S:15

Hall, (?) Hannah - Died 1762 Age 25 (stone very bad condition) Daughter of ? & Thankful Hall S:11

Hall, Agnes V - Died 1991 Born 1904 (listed on undertaker plaque, not on stone yet) (with Walter Turnbull Hall) S:15

Hall, Andrew P - Died (still living) Born 1917 (with Charles & Helen Hall) S:12

Hall, Azor D - Died 1930 Born 1850 (flat stone in ground, sinking into grass) (next to Ida M Hall) S:12

Hall, Bartlett - Died 1824 Age 20 Died in Galan (on stone with Edward Hall & others) S:10

Hall, Bartlett - Died 1849 May 15 Age 21 years 2 months (on same stone with Oliver Hall & others) S:10

Hall, Bethia HB - Died 1940 Jan 15 Born 1857 Sept 6 (with Russell DF Hall & others) S:18

Hall, Charles A - Died 1971 Born 1874 (next to Ethel M Hall) S:12

Hall, Charles P - Died 1956 Born 1879 (with Helen S Hall) S:12

Hall, Cyda Gundersen - Died 1984 Born 1891 (with William L Hall) S:14

Hall, Daniel - Died 1779 Feb 21 Age 10 months Son of Daniel & Mehetable Hall S:9R

Hall, Edward - Died 1825 Age 7 Son of Ezekial & Susan Hall (on stone with Lucy Hall & others) S:10

Hall, Edward Bartlett - Died 1825 ? Age 1 year 5 months Son of Ezekial & Susan Hall (on stone with Lucy Hall and others) S:10

Hall, Eliza - Died 1874 Mar 8 in her 69th yr Wife of John W Scudder (buried next to him) S:8

Hall, Elizabeth - Died 1871 July 16 Age 76 S:10

Hall, Elizabeth - Died 1922 Born 1872 S:11

Hall, Erwin Albert - Died 1943 Born 1854 (with Ellen McKean Judson, his wife) S:11

Hall, Ethel M - Died 1955 Born 1875 (next to Ida M Hall) S:12

Hall, Ezekial - Died 1857 Mar 12 Age 79 years 1 month (next to wife, Susannah Hall) S:10

Hall, Florence P - Died 1981 Born 1892 S:15

Hall, Frank W - Died 1965 June 2 Born 1891 July 29 From Massachusetts, was Cpl in CoE, 401 Telegraph Bn, during World War I (next to Lillian Wheeler Hall) S:15

Hall, Gorham - Died 1830 Nov 21 Age 58 at Boston S:10

Hall, Gyda G - Buried 1986 July 28 Age 92 Located in section D, lot 16, grave 5 S:14R

Hall, Helen S - Died 1970 Born 1892 Wife of Chales Hall (with him) S:12

Hall, Ida M - Died 1939 Born 1853 (flat stone in ground, also worn) (next to Azor D Hall) S:12

Hall, Jean H - Died (still living) Born 1920 (with Charles & Helen Hall) S:12

Hall, John T - Died 1905 (listed on Heywood family stone) S:11

Hall, Joseph R - Died 1892 April 9 Born 1821 Aug 9 (with Maria J Hall & others) S:18

Hall, Joseph Russell - Died 1963 Born 1882 Stone says, "Knights of Columbus" (with Percy Bassett Hall & others) S:18

Hall, Joseph T - Died 1909 Nov 22 Born 1850 Nov 20 (with Bethia HB Hall & others) S:18

Hall, Judith Sylvester - Died (still living 1990) Born 1934 (large Chase grinding wheel stone for marker) S:11

Hall, Julia Harding - Died 1975 Born 1883 Wife of Frances Fessenben Chase (with him & others) S:11

Hall, Lillian Wheeler - Died 1984 Born 1894 (next to Frank W Hall) S:15

Hall, Lucy - Died 1823 Age 1 year 6 months Daughter of Ezekial & Susan Hall S:10

Hall, Maria J - Died 1917 June 22 Born 1831 Oct 14 (with Joseph T Hall & others) S:18

Hall, Mary - Died 1823 or 29 ? Feb 19 at Boston Daughter of Gorham & Mary Hall S:10

Hall, Mary - Died 1856 April 5 Age 85 at East Cambridge, Mass Widow of Gorham Hall (next to him) S:10

Hall, Mary E - Died 1942 May 13 Born 1863 Aug 30 (with Maria J Hall & others) S:18

Hall, Mehitable Mrs - Died 1784 Sept 22 Age 29 Widow of Daniel Hall S:11

Hall, Oliver - Died 1848 Sept 10 Age 38 (on same stone with Philander Hall & others) S:10

Hall, Percy Bassett - Died 1969 Born 1885 (with Isaac P Fairfield & others) S:18

Hall, Philander - Died 1860 Dec 18

Hall (Cont.)
Age 53 S:10

Hall, Russell DF - Died 1935 May 23 Born 1860 Aug 22 (with Mary E Hall & others) S:18

Hall, Sarah Agnes - Died 1896 (listed on large Heywood family stone) S:11

Hall, Seth - Died 1810 Aug 4 Son of (stone not clear for father) & Sarah Hall S:3

Hall, Susan Miss - Died 1841 Dec 2 Age 28 (on stone with Bartlett Hall & others) S:10

Hall, Susannah Died 1860 Jan 13 Age 76 Wife of Ezekial Hall S:10

Hall, Walter Turnbull - Died 1970 July 27 Born 1896 Nov 4 (with Agnes V Hall) S:15

Hall, William L - Died 1956 Born 1883 (with Cyda Gundersen Hall) S:14

Hallet, Betsey S - Died 1803 Apl 16 in her 24th yr Wife of Capt Jonathan Hallet S:4

Hallet, Bullah - Died 1814 Oct 9 Age 16 months, 17 days Daughter of Capt Lot & Esther Hallet S:4

Hallet, Desire - Died 1816 Sept 8 in her 63rd yr Wife of Nathaniel Hallet S:4

Hallet, Emily - Died 1918 Born 1854 (buried with Eunice & Nelson Phinney & others) S:8

Hallet, Esther - Died 1824 June 14 in her 39th yr Wife of Capt Lot Hallet S:4

Hallet, George F - Died 1966 Sept 3 Born 1899 Nov 12 From Massachusetts, was CBM, Co ST Guard during World War I & II (next to Oliver & Marian Hallet) S:19

Hallet, Hannah - Died 1819 Mar 17 in her 38th yr Wife of Joshua Hallet S:4

Hallet, Helen J - Died 1929 Born 1898 (a small copper plaque, 4X8" next to William Hallet) S:8

Hallet, Hirahm - Died 1802 Mar 8 Age 1 year, 3 months Son of

Hallet (Cont.)
Edward & Lucinda Hallet S:4

Hallet, Hiram S - Died 1817 Aug 13 Age 8 months, 20 days Son of Sears & Sophia Hallet S:4

Hallet, Jean - Died 1799 July 20 in her 51st yr Wife of Rowland S:1

Hallet, Joseph H - Died 1861 Jan 5 Age 19 Son of Mary D & Nathaniel S Hallet (with them) S:19

Hallet, Joshua - Died 1817 Apl 22 in his 4th yr Son of Joshua & Hannah Hallet S:4

Hallet, Keziah C - Died 1822 Born 1807 Wife of William L Hallett (next to him) (this stone was in the Barnstable cemetery office until location was found on 21 Oct 1991 by this author) S:18

Hallet, Lois - Died 1805 Aug 7 in her 48th yr Wife of Capt John Hallet S:1

Hallet, Lucenda - Died 1806 July 18 in her 37th yr Wife of Edward Hallet S:4

Hallet, Lucinda - Died 1804 Oct 1 Age 1 year, 1 month, 19 days Daughter of Edward & Lucinda Hallet S:4

Hallet, Marian L - Died 1968 Born 1912 (next to Oliver W Hallet) S:19

Hallet, Mary D - Died 1876 Jan 18 Age 67 years, 1 month Wife of Nathaniel S Hallet (next to him & son, Joseph Hallet) S:19

Hallet, Mercy - Died 1770 Feb 22 in her 47th yr Wife of Jonathan Hallet S:1

Hallet, Nancy - Died 1786 Jan 20 Age 15 months Daughter of Capt John & Lois Hallet S:1

Hallet, Nathaniel - Died 1822 Nov 20 in his 75th yr S:4

Hallet, Nathaniel S - Died 1883 Feb 16 Age 79 years, 8 months (next to wife, Mary D, & son, Joseph H Hallet) S:19

Hallet, Oliver W - Died 1964 Born 1908 (next to Marian L Hallet & Yohhann Hatfield) S:19

Hallet, Rachel - Died 1776 June 20

Hallet (Cont.)
in her 26th yr Wife of John Hallet S:1

Hallet, Robert B - Died 1800 Oct 19 Age 11 months, 13 days Son of Jonathan & Betty Hallet S:4

Hallet, Samuel - Died 1802 April 17 Age 20 Son of Samuel 6 Sarah Hallet S:12

Hallet, Samuel - Died 1813 Oct 5 Age 57 S:12

Hallet, Samuel - Died 1850 Mar 1 Age 41 years, 5 months, 23 days Buried with Susan Hallet S:5

Hallet, Samuel W (Capt) - Died 1858 Jan 2 Age 30 years, 4 months S:4

Hallet, Sarah - Died 1754 July 16 Age 22 Wife of David Hallet S:1

Hallet, Sarah - Died 1824 Jan 29 Age 55 (next to Samuel Hallet) S:12

Hallet, Seth - Died 1799 June 9 in his 96th yr S:1

Hallet, Susan - Died 1842 June 10 in her 33rd yr Wife of Samuel Hallet (also buried with him) S:5

Hallet, Temprance - Died 1788 Nov 22 in her 60th yr S:1

Hallet, Thankful - Died 1862 Feb 13 Age 55 years, 9 months, 17 days Widow of Capt Warren Hallet S:4

Hallet, Thomas - Died 1773 April 12 Age 21 Months Son of John & Rachel Hallet S:1

Hallet, Warren (Capt) - Died 1865 Sept 18 Age 78 years, 9 months, 6 days S:4

Hallet, William - Died 1798 Sept 20 in his 33rd yr S:1

Hallet, William - Died 1802 Aug 26 Age 5 years, 10 months, 26 days Son of William & Jemime Hallet S:3

Hallett, (infant daughter) - Died 1835 May 25 Born 1835 Apl 11 Daughter of Samuel & Dorcas Hallett S:4

Hallett, (infant) - Died (not there) Daughter of Jonathan & Mary Hallett (next to brother, Milton B

Hallett (Cont.)
Hallett) S:21

Hallett, (infant) - Died 1810 March 12 Age 4 days (stone badly worn) Son of Benjamin & Abigail Hallett (next to them) S:12

Hallett, (infant) - Died 1834 Born 1834 Infant child of Samuel & Dorcas Hallett (last name on stone not clear) S:4

Hallett, (infant) - Died 1840 May 1, 14 days Son of Samuel & Dorcas Hallett S:4

Hallett, (infant) - Died 1852 May 6 Daughter of Alvan & Sarah Hallett S:4

Hallett, (infant) - Died 1854 Born 1854 Daughter of Samuel & Dorcas Hallett S:4

Hallett, (infant) - Died 1855 July 28 Born 1855 July 25 Son of Alvan & Sarah Hallett S:4

Hallett, ? - Died 1968 Born ? (small copper plaque next to ? Bradley & Helen J Hallet but letters all broken off plaque, RELLIC were all that was found) S:8

Hallett, A Jeannette - Died 1957 Born 1893 (with Cora A Hallett & others) S:12

Hallett, Abigail - Died 18?? Age 31 (stone is broken in half by vandals) Wife of Roland Hallett (next to him & his other wife, Cordelia Hallett) S:18

Hallett, Abigail Lovell - Died 1845 Dec 1 Age 79 Born 1765 March (stone broken at base) Wife of Benjamin Hallett (next to him) S:12

Hallett, Adeline L - Died 1900 Born 1816 (with Horace F Hallett & others) S:18

Hallett, Albert - Died 1863 Aug23 Age 23 years, 10 months, 3 days Son of Hartson & Eunice Hallett (next them & next to sister, Cornelia Hallett) S:18

Hallett, Albert C - Died 1943 Feb 19 Born 1877 April 5 (with Lottie B Hallett) S:18

Hallett, Alcott N - Died 1942 Born 1857 (with Sarah H Crosby) S:12

Hallett, Alexander C - Died 1869 March 22 Age 51 years, 7 months (next to wife, Sarah Hallett) S:21

Hallett, Alexander H - Died 1888 Dec 29 Born 1848 Aug 10 S:18

Hallett, Allen - Died 1881 Dec 28 Age 81 years, 8 months (next to wife, Relief Hallett) S:21

Hallett, Allen - Died 1895 Born 1830 (with Elsie Hallett) S:18

Hallett, Almoran - Died 1886 Dec 11 Age 82 years, 9 months (next to wife, Eliza Hallett) S:21

Hallett, Alton Sears - Died 1940 July 24 Born 1856 June 26 (with Ida May Coburn & others) S:18

Hallett, Alvin S - Died 1845 Oct 4 Age 21 months Son of Samuel & Dorcas Hallett S:4

Hallett, Amiel B - Died 1822 Nov 23 Age 2 years, 1 month, 16 days Son of Warren & Thankful Hallett S:4

Hallett, Anna R - Died 1890 Born 1847 (with Clinton F Hallett & others) S:18

Hallett, Annah D - Died 1892 Born 1830 (with Rufus G Marston & others) S:19

Hallett, Arthur C - Died 1933 Born 1874 (next to John H Hallett) S:21

Hallett, Asa - Died 1900 Apl 3 Born 1818 Jan 5 S:4

Hallett, Barbara F - Died (still living 1991?) Born 1928 June 29 (listed with Francis Holmes & others) S:19

Hallett, Benjamin - Died 1840 Dec 31 Born 1760 Jan 18 Age 90 He was a Baptist (in a large coffin crypt) "A soldier of the Revolution in his youth A christian patriaron in his age" S:12

Hallett, Benjamin - Died 1889 Born 1812 (with Adeline L Hallett & others) S:18

Hallett, Benjamin W - Died 1947

Hallett (Cont.)
Born 1866 (next to James D & Persis C Hallett) S:13

Hallett, Bertha L - Died 1941 Born 1861 (with Russell Lovell & others) S:12

Hallett, Betsey - Died 1855 Dec 5 Age 38 Wife of Reuben Hallett (next to him) S:19

Hallett, Betsey C - Died 1943 Born 1871 (with Russell Hallett) S:19

Hallett, Betsy - Died 1836 June 11 in her 36th yr Wife of Rowland Hallett S:4

Hallett, Blanche A - Died 1967 Born 1877 (next to William & Martha Hallett) S:21

Hallett, C Webster - Died 1932 Born 1860 (with wife, Cora Augusta Hallett) S:12

Hallett, CL - Died 1871 Jan 12 Age 50 Stone says,"Mother" (next to Lovica & Capt Hartson Hallett) S:21

Hallett, Charles - Died 1806 Jan 30 (rest of stone not clear) S:1

Hallett, Charles - Died 1909 Born 1833 (with Annah D Hallett & others) S:19

Hallett, Charles G - Died 1905 Born 1827 (with wife, Elvira Nickerson & Harry Azadian & others) S:19

Hallett, Charles Norman - Died 1903 Dec 18 Born 1901 Jan 19 (small lamb stone) Son of Charles & Mabel Hallett (next to Mother) S:19

Hallett, Charlotte A - Died 1943 Born 1865 (with Harold R Hallett & others) S:18

Hallett, Christiana F - Died 185? Aug 9 Age 10 years, 11 months Daughter of Jonathan & Mary Hallett (next to brother, Gorham C Hallett) S:21

Hallett, Clara J - Died 1959 March 28 Born 1858 Sept 19 (99 years old) (with Edmund Hallett & others) S:18

Hallett, Clarance F - Died 1846 Sept 16 (small stone) Son of

Hallett (Cont.)
Freeman & Lucy Hallett (next to sister, Nellie Hallett) S:21

Hallett, Clinton F - Died 1943 Born 1869 (with Charlotte A Hallett & others) S:18

Hallett, Cora Augusta - Died 1933 Born 186? Wife of C Webster Hallett (with him & others) S:12

Hallett, Cordelia - Died 1857 Jan 2 Age 39 Wife of Roland S Hallett (next to his other wife, Abigail & himself) S:18

Hallett, Cordella Mrs - Died 1842 Nov 6 Age 23 Wife of Charles G Hallett S:21

Hallett, Cornelia - Died 1843 Feb 5 Age 1 year, 2 months, 16 days Daughter of Hartson & Eunice Hallett (near them & next to Luther C Hallett) S:18

Hallett, Daniel - Died 1800 Jan 11 (stone worn & broken in half) (next to Lydia Hallett) S:12

Hallett, Daniel - Died 1824 May 8 in his 52nd yr S:4

Hallett, Daniel S - Died 1852 Sept 3 Age 50 years, 11 months (next to wife, Lydia B Hallett) S:21

Hallett, Deborah H - Died 1884 March Age 72 years, 6 months Wife of Gorham Hallett S:9R

Hallett, Debra (Debroah) H - Died 1880 Born 1847 Wife of Ansel Lothrop (on same stone) S:10

Hallett, Dorcas L - Died 1888 Apl 2 Born 1810 Nov 1 S:4

Hallett, ER - Died 1944 Born 1864 (with Helen Berry Hallett & others) S:18

Hallett, Edmund - Died 1804 May 20 in his 27th yr S:1

Hallett, Edmund - Died 1837 Jan 8 Born 1805 Sept 28 (with Polly Hallett & others) S:18

Hallett, Edward B - Died 1875 May 1 Age 44 years, 21 days S:9R

Hallett, Eldora A - Died 1941 Jan 4 Born 1849 Feb 7 (with Luther C Hallett) S:18

Hallett, Elijah B - Died 1921 Born 1837 (with Florentine Hallett &

Hallett (Cont.)
    others) S:18
Hallett, Elisa? A - Died 1840 Feb
    25 Age 5 years, 10 months
    (stone worn) Daughter of John &
    ? Hallett (next to Allen Hallett)
    S:21
Hallett, Eliza - Died 1808 Oct 24
    Age 7 years, 4 months (stone
    badly worn) Daughter of Benja-
    min & Abigail Hallett (next to
    them) S:12
Hallett, Eliza - Died 1865 July 4
    Born 1863 March 23 (small
    stone that says "Little") Daugh-
    ter of Joshua & Ellen Hallett
    (next to mother) S:21
Hallett, Eliza - Died 1879 Oct 20
    Age 74 years, 3 months Wife of
    Almoran Hallett (next to him)
    S:21
Hallett, Eliza H - Died 1857 Nov 3
    Age 9 years, 9 months, 12 days
    Daughter of Almoran & Eliza H
    Hallett (next to Leander G Hal-
    lett) S:21
Hallett, Ella F - Died 1878 Born
    1867 (with Joseph S Hallett)
    S:14
Hallett, Ellen - Died 1888 May 25
    Age 43 years, 9 months Wife of
    Joshua S Hallett (next to Eliza
    Hallett) S:21
Hallett, Ellen B - Died 1925 Born
    1856 (with Alva Thayer & others)
    S:18
Hallett, Ellis Archer - Died 1943
    May 5 (next to Joseph & Mary &
    Herbert Hallett) S:18
Hallett, Elsie A - Died 1905 Born
    1835 (with Allen Hallett) S:18
Hallett, Emeline - Died 1872 July
    20 Born 1830 Sept 26 (with
    Clara J Hallett & others) S:18
Hallett, Emily H - Died 1962 Born
    1875 (with Alcott N Hallett &
    Sarah H Crosby) S:12
Hallett, Emma IV - Died 1929 Born
    1840 (with Zenas D Basset &
    others) S:18
Hallett, Ethel M - Died 1923 Born
    1883 (with L Coulson Hageman

Hallett (Cont.)
    & others) S:18
Hallett, Etta - Died 1862 Feb 1
    Born 1861 Jan 11 (with Martha
    A Hallett & others) S:18
Hallett, Eugenia A - Died 1840
    Born 1839 (with Horace F
    (d1840) & Horace F (d1900)
    Hallett & others) S:18
Hallett, Eunice - Died 1900 April
    14 Age 81 years, 18 days (with
    Hartson Hallett) S:18
Hallett, Eunice B - Died 1830 Oct
    21 Age 32 years, 12 days Wife of
    Rodman S Hallett S:4
Hallett, Eunice M - Died 1890 Aug
    6 Age 67 years, 1 month S:2
Hallett, Eva W - Died 1928 June
    27 Born 1862 Sept 21 (next to
    Rev Horace F Hallet, possible
    husband) S:8
Hallett, Fannie F - Died 1915 Born
    1838 (with Joseph S Hallett)
    S:14
Hallett, Flora J - Died 1857 Aug 26
    Born 1856 May 2 (with Etta
    Hallett & others) S:18
Hallett, Florentine - Died 1923
    Born 1843 (with Joyce Taylor &
    others) S:18
Hallett, Frank - Died 1855 Sept 20
    Age 10 days Son of William H &
    Eliza H Hallett (next to brother,
    Willie W Hallett) S:13
Hallett, Frank P - Died 1937 Born
    1858 (with Grace B Hallett &
    others) S:18
Hallett, Franklin P - Died 1849
    Born 1847 (with William Jenkins
    & others) S:18
Hallett, Freddie N - Died 1877 Feb
    16 Age 21 years, 3 months, 7
    days Son of Nathaniel & Phebe A
    Hallett (next to sister, Hattie E
    Hallett) S:18
Hallett, Freeman - Died (died
    before 1883, stone is turned over
    onto ground, cannot turn it over
    because of its size, same style as
    wife, Lucy B Hallett who is next
    to him) (this is only a guess that
    it is him) S:21

Hallett, Freeman H - Died (dates underground) Son of Freeman & Lucy Hallett (next to them) S:21

Hallett, George A - Died 1907 Mar 18 Born 1854 Oct 15 (new cement base restored) S:12

Hallett, George H - Died 1915 Born 1820 (with Sally A Hallett & others) S:18

Hallett, George O - Died 1868 Aug 2 Age 18 years, 4 months, 17 days Son of Moses F & Eunice M Hallett S:2

Hallett, George W - Died 1901 Born 1840 (with Emma IV Hallett & others) S:18

Hallett, Gideon - Died 1892 Oct 1 Born 1817 June 12 (a large metal marker) (with Martha A Hallett & others) S:18

Hallett, Gorham (Capt) - Died 1889 Jan Born 1840 July S:11

Hallett, Gorham C - Died 1856? March 31 Age 18 years, 3 months, 11 days (stone worn) Son of Jonathan & Mary Hallett S:21

Hallett, Grace B - Died 1919 Born 1858 (with Francis P Basset & others) S:18

Hallett, Hansard - Died 1874 Jan 26 Age 78 years, 6 months (next to 2 Lydia Hallett's) S:12

Hallett, Harold R - Died 1974 Born 1894 (with Hazel E Hallett & others) S:18

Hallett, Harry H - Died 1874 Mar 20 Age 6 months Son of Capt Gorham & E J Hallett (next to father) S:11

Hallett, Hartson - Died 1902 May 9 Age 85 years, 5 months, 27 days (with Eunice Hallett) S:18

Hallett, Hartson (Capt) - Died 1867 Dec 25 Age 70 (next to wife, Lovica Hallett) S:21

Hallett, Harvey - Died 1841 Born 1797 (stone marked "Father") (buried with Nancy C Hallett) S:8

Hallett, Hattie E - Died 1878 Aug 2 Age 21 years, 11 months, 2 days Daughter of Nathaniel & Phebe

Hallett (Cont.)
A Hallett (next to brother, Nathaniel Hallett) S:18

Hallett, Hazel E - Died 1947 Born 1894 (with Walter S Hallett & others) S:18

Hallett, Hazel Foster - Died 1892 Jan 27 Born 1888 March 5 (with Roland Sears Hallett & others) S:18

Hallett, Helen - Died 1869 June 26 Born 1841 March 23 Wife of Charles H Hallett S:18

Hallett, Helen Berry - Died 1888 Aug 17 Born 1888 March 5 (with Hazel Foster Hallett & others) S:18

Hallett, Henry - Died 1824 Sept 26 Age 43 years, 3 months S:4

Hallett, Henry - Died 1905 March 6 Born 1824 Sept 3 (a metal marker with one panel missing) (with Oren & Caroline Crowell) S:18

Hallett, Henry C - Died 1916 Born 1859 (with Ellen B Hallett & others) S:18

Hallett, Herbert Henry - Died 1950 Oct 20 (next to Joseph & Mary Hallett) S:18

Hallett, Holly - Died 1859 Apl 23 Age 76 years, 10 months Widow of Joseph Hallett S:4

Hallett, Horace F - Died 1840 Born 1836 (with Eugenia A Hallett & others) S:18

Hallett, Horace F - Died 1900 Born 1846 (with Julia G Hallett & others) S:18

Hallett, Horace F - Died 1959 Born 1893 (he is listed with three other Horace's & Mary Josephine Hallett & others) S:18

Hallett, Horace F (Rev) - Died 1916 July 20 Born 1861 June 10 "He lived in a house by the side of the road and was a friend to man" S:8

Hallett, Howard - Died 1908 July 2 Born 1862? March 3 (with Capt Joshua Hallett & others) S:18

Hallett, Howard I(?) - Died 1858?

Hallett (Cont.)
Jan 29 Born 1848 Sept 19 (stone badly worn) Son of Theodore Hallett (next to him) S:18

Hallett, Ida - Died 1891 Dec 5 Born 1869 May 20 The only daughter of Edward B & Sarah E Hallett S:9R

Hallett, JP - Died (no dates) (above ground crypt) (with A Baxter) S:18

Hallett, James D - Died 1910 Dec 29 Born 1834 May 30 (with Persis C Hallett) S:13

Hallett, James Harvey - Died 1871 Born 1827 S:7

Hallett, James Harvey - Died 1973 Born 1891 (with Cora A Hallett & others) S:12

Hallett, Jamie - (small stone in back of William W Hallett & Julia Phinney Not sure if parents) S:8

Hallett, John - Died 1808 Age 3 months, 3 days Son of Henry Hallett S:1

Hallett, John (Capt) - Stone badly worn S:1

Hallett, John H - Died 1851 Apl 2 in his 35th yr Lost at sea from Glasgow to Baltimore on the ship, Bark Gov Briggs S:4

Hallett, John H - Died 1883 Born 1830 (with Susan E Hallett) S:21

Hallett, John H - Died 1902 Born 1845 (with Anna R Hallett & others) S:18

Hallett, Jonathan - Died 1911 Born 1844 (with Caroline Robinson) S:21

Hallett, Joseph H - Died 1935 Born 1872 (with Asa, Emmeline & Harry Robinson) S:21

Hallett, Joseph Lewis - Died 1911 Sept 2 Born 1841 Sept 2 (next to Mary Archer Hallett) S:18

Hallett, Joseph S - Died 1904 Born 1827 (with Ella & Fannie Hallett) S:14

Hallett, Joshua - Died 1854 May 2 in his 56th yr S:4

Hallett, Joshua (Capt) - Died 1893 Jan 31 Born 1822 April 15 (with Lucy C Hallett & others) S:18

Hallett, Josiah H - Died 1900 May 8 Born 1828 Oct 16 (with Emeline Hallett & others) S:18

Hallett, Judith A - Died 1890 Dec 2 Age 30 years, 7 months Wife of Osborne L Hallett (next to him) S:18

Hallett, Julia A - Died 1882 May 20 Age 55 years, 5 months Widow of Robert B Hallett (next to him & son, Leston B Hallett) S:21

Hallett, Julia G - Died 1934 Born 1852 (with Nina E Hallett & others) S:18

Hallett, Laura G - Died 1893 Oct 15 Born 1857 July 29 S:2

Hallett, Leander - Died 1897 Aug 17 Age 82 (next to wife, Susan S Hallett) S:19

Hallett, Leander (Capt) - Died 1850 Dec 25 Age 37 years, 3 months (top of stone is missing, also with ? Hallett who died 1845 July 3) S:21

Hallett, Leander G - Died 1858 Jan 14 Age 23 years, 1 month Son of Almoran & Eliza H Hallett (next to them) S:21

Hallett, Leston B - Died 1883 Aug 5 Age 28 years, 5 months Son of Robert & Julia Hallett (next to them) S:21

Hallett, Lillian B - Died 1909 Born 1867 (with Lincoln B Hallett) S:18

Hallett, Lincoln B - Died 1935 Born 1866 (with Lillian B Hallett) S:18

Hallett, Lot - Died (no dates) (above ground crypt next to Joseph Baxter crypt) S:18

Hallett, Lot (Capt) - Died 1825 July 2 in his 41st yr S:4

Hallett, Lottie B - Died 1933 March 29 Born 1886 Nov 26 (with Albert C Hallett) S:18

Hallett, Lovica - Died 1849 Nov 2 Age 49 Wife of Capt Hartson

Hallett (Cont.)
Hallett (next to him) S:21

Hallett, Lucretia G - Died 1952
Born 1866 Wife of Charles C
Ryder (with him & Warren G
Ryder & Marjorie I Dolliver) S:19

Hallett, Lucy - Died 1837 July 19
in her 33rd yr Wife of Watson
Hallett S:4

Hallett, Lucy B - Died 1883 June
23 Age 64 years, 6 months, 4
days Widow of Freeman Hallett
(possibly next to her) S:21

Hallett, Lucy C - Died 1913 Oct 15
Born 1831 July 19 (with son,
Willis Hallett & others) S:18

Hallett, Lucy P - Died 1968 Born
1870 Wife of Rev Elmer Newell
(buried with him & son, Freder-‐
ick) S:8

Hallett, Luther C - Died 1931 July
3 Born 1848 Oct 28 (with Eldora
A Hallett) S:18

Hallett, Lydia - Died 1842? June 2
(stone worn) (next to Lydia Hallett) S:12

Hallett, Lydia - Died 1867? June 4
(stone worn & broken at base)
(next to Daniel Hallett) S:12

Hallett, Lydia B - Died 1869 Oct 3
Age 68 Wife of Daniel S Hallett
(next to him) S:21

Hallett, Lydia B - Died 1871 July 1
Age 48 years, 4 months Wife of
Capt AS Hallett S:18

Hallett, Lydia Ella - Died 1856
Sept 16 Age 15 Months, 21 days
Daughter of AS & Lydia Hallett
S:4

Hallett, Mabel Phinney - Died 1952
Born 1864 (with Dorothy Hallett
Henry & next to Charles Norman
Hallett, son) S:19

Hallett, Maria L - Died 1905 Jan 6
Age 87 years, 7 months Wife of
Reuben Hallett (next to him)
S:19

Hallett, Martha A - Died 1881 July
9 Born 1825 Jan 7 (with Alma L
Keene & others) S:18

Hallett, Martha D - Died 1921
Born 1845 (with William W

Hallett (Cont.)
Hallett) S:21

Hallett, Martha M - Died 1894
March 24 Age 88 years, 5
months Youngest daughter of
Benjamin & Abigail Hallett (next
to them) S:12

Hallett, Mary - Died 1763 in her
63rd yr Wife of Seth Hallett S:1

Hallett, Mary Archer - Died 1898
Oct 29 Born 1848 March 23
(next to Joseph Lewis Hallett)
S:18

Hallett, Mary B - Died 1915 March
25 Born 1829 Sept 4 (with Sears
L Hallett) S:18

Hallett, Mary C - Died 1970 Born
1889 (with Vernon C Hallett)
S:15

Hallett, Mary E - Died 1857 Born
1853 (with Charles G Hallett &
others) S:19

Hallett, Mary E - Died 1858? Dec 6
Age 4 years, 8 months, 13 days
(stone worn) Daughter of Charles
& Elvira Hallett (next to them)
S:19

Hallett, Mary E - Died 1900 July
29 Born 1836 Aug 23 S:2

Hallett, Mary Josephine - Died
(still living 1991?) Born 1899
(with Horace F Hallett (d1959) &
others) S:18

Hallett, Mary S - Died 1920 Born
1834 (stone down from vadalism) (with Samuel W Hallett)
S:18

Hallett, Mary? - Died 1862 April 19
Age 19 years, 2 months (stone
worn) Wife of AS Hallett S:21

Hallett, Melinda - Died 1867 Oct
31 Age 51 years, 3 months, 13
days Wife of Asa Hallett S:4

Hallett, Mercy B - Died 1900 Born
1822 (with William Hallett &
Franklin P Hallett & others) S:18

Hallett, Milton B - Died 1839 Feb
26 Age 11 months (stone is
down) Son of Jonathan & Mary
Hallett (next to sister, Christiana
F Hallett) S:21

Hallett, Moses - Died 1892 Jan 7

Hallett (Cont.)

Age 74 years, 5 months S:2

Hallett, Nancy C - Died 1868 Born 1798 (stone says, "Mother) (buried with husband, Harvey Hallett) S:8

Hallett, Nathaniel - Died 1875 (stone small & not clear) Son of Nathaniel & ? Hallett (next to sister, Hattie E Hallett) S:18

Hallett, Nellie - Died (dates underground) Daughter of Freeman & Lucy Hallett (next to brother, Freeman H Hallett) S:21

Hallett, Nelson B - Died 1900 Oct 12 Born 1832 Aug 23 S:2

Hallett, Nina E - Died 1877 Born 1876 (with Horace F(d1959) Hallett & others) S:18

Hallett, Olive Mrs - Died (dates broken off) (stone is down & worn) Wife of Leander Hallett S:21

Hallett, Osborne L - Died 1921 May 9 Age 63 years, 6 months (stone face chipped) (next to wife, Judith A Hallett) S:18

Hallett, Patience - Died 1868 Dec 31 Age 85 years, 9 months, 19 days Wife of Joshua Hallett S:4

Hallett, Persis - Died 1868 Dec 11 (stone is broken off base) Wife of Samuel Waitt S:12

Hallett, Persis C - Died 1907 Aug 1 Born 1839 Feb 10 (with James D Hallett) S:13

Hallett, Phebe Mrs - Died 1851 July 6 Age 76 years, 3 months Widow of Daniel Hallett (next to Mrs Olive Hallett) S:21

Hallett, Polly Died 1846 Sept 24 Born 1803 Nov 27 (with Clara J Hallett & others) S:18

Hallett, Polly - Died 1865 June 20 Age 75 years, 9 months Widow of Henry Hallett S:4

Hallett, Relief - Died 1871 Oct 8 Age 65 (stone broken off at base) Wife of Allen Hallett (next to him) S:21

Hallett, Reuben - Died 1894 March 18 Age 78 (between wifes, Maria

Hallett (Cont.)

L & Betsey Hallett) S:19

Hallett, Richard - Died 1868 Sept 11 Born 1866 July 7 Son of Joshua & Ellen Hallett (next to Ellen & Eliza Hallett) S:21

Hallett, Robert B (Capt) - Died 1865 Dec 24 Age 37 (stone cracked) (next to wife, Julia A Hallett) S:21

Hallett, Rodman S - Died 1866 Aug 11 in his 44th yr S:4

Hallett, Rodman S - Died 1873 Oct 9 Age 18 years, 9 months Son of Alexander & Sarah Hallett S:21

Hallett, Roland Sears - Died 1892 Feb 10 Born 1891 Oct 26 (with Helen Derry Hallett & others) S:18

Hallett, Roland Sears - Died 1894 Nov 6 Born 1809 Nov 4 (next to both wifes, Abigail & Cordelia Hallett) S:18

Hallett, Rowland - Died 1855 June 6 in his 81st yr S:4

Hallett, Russell - Died 1957 Born 1874 (with Betsey C Hallett) S:19

Hallett, Sally - Died 1851 July 24 in her 41st yr Wife of Alvan S Hallett S:4

Hallett, Sally A - Died 1916 Born 1824 (with Nellie C Sears & others) S:18

Hallett, Sally S - Died 1852 June 6 Age 21 years, 7 months, 18? days S:21

Hallett, Samuel W - Died 1880 Born 1831 (stone down from vadalism) (with Mary S Hallett) S:18

Hallett, Samuel W - Died 1929 Born 1858 Stone says, "VERIMAS" (next to Samuel W & Mary S Hallett) (possibly parents?) S:18

Hallett, Sarah - Died 1880 Jan 10 Age 60 (stone down & broken) Wife of Alexander C Hallett (next to him) S:21

Hallett, Sarah - Died 1960 Born 1863 (next to Hallett Boult) S:12

Hallett, Sarah Augusta - Died 1853 Aug 30 Age 3 years, 2 months Daughter of John H & Sophronia B Hallett S:4

Hallett, Sears L - Died 1901 March 8 Born 1824 Nov 27 (with Mary B Hallett) S:18

Hallett, Seth - Died 1737 May in his 59th yr S:1

Hallett, Seth - Died 1850 Aug 16 Born 1839 May 22 (next to sister, Sarah Spear & parents, Seth & Sophia Hallett) S:21

Hallett, Seth - Died 1863 Nov 11 Age 64 years (next to wife, Sophia B Hallett) S:21

Hallett, Sophia B - Died 1884 Age 84 years, 8 months, 7 days Born 1799 (next to husband, Seth Hallett, d1863) S:21

Hallett, Susan A - Died 1853 July 15 Age 8 years, 12 days Daughter of Leander & Susan Hallett (next to them) S:19

Hallett, Susan Crocker - Died 1884 Born 1840 Wife of Francis Hallett S:9R

Hallett, Susan E - Died 1928 Born 1845 (with John H Hallett) S:21

Hallett, Susan Frances - Died 1849 March 10 Age 5 months Daughter of Gorham & Deborah H Hallett S:9R

Hallett, Susan S - Died 1892 July 14 Age 73 years, 6 months (stone is off its base but in the ground) Wife of Leander Hallett (next to him) S:19

Hallett, Theadore - Died 1817 June 28 Age 29? (stone worn bad) (next to Daniel Hallett) S:12

Hallett, Theodore - Died 1873 Oct 2 Age 47 (part of stone under ground) (next to son, Howard I Hallett) S:18

Hallett, Theodore B - Died 1906 Nov 5 Born 1854 Oct 29 S:13

Hallett, Vernon C - Died 1972 Born 1883 (with Mary C Hallett) S:15

Hallett, WB - Died 1929 Born 1858 (with ER Hallett & others) S:18

Hallett, Walter S - Died 1982 Born

Hallett (Cont.)
1895 (has two stones) Was a Corporal in US Army during World War I (with Charlotte A Hallett & others) S:18

Hallett, Warren - Died 1848 Apl 29 Age 4 years, 4 months, 15 days Son of John H & Sophronia B Hallett S:4

Hallett, Warren (Capt) Jr - Died 1810 Feb in his 24th yr (lost at sea) S:4

Hallett, Watson - Died 1842 Apl 25 in his 39th yr S:4

Hallett, Watson - Died 1842 Oct 16 Age 13 months, 14 days Son of Watson & Mary Hallett (recorded, Walson?, could have been a recording error?) S:4

Hallett, William - Died 1802 Aug 26 Age 5 yrs 10 mos 26 days Son of William and Jemine Hallett S:3R

Hallett, William A - Died 1900 Born 1819 (with Mercy B Hallett & others) S:18

Hallett, William A - Died 1930 Born 1844 (with Sally A Hallett & others) S:18

Hallett, William F - Died 1939 Born 1863 (stone is a small flat copper plaque that measures 4X8 inches) S:8

Hallett, William Hamilton - Died 1896 Born 1848 S:18

Hallett, William L - Died 1872 March 5 Age 67 years, 4 months, 20 days (stone next to him is gone, but has same style base A wife?)(on 21 Oct 1991, I located his wife's stone which was in the Mosswood cemetery waiting for my help to find it) S:18

Hallett, William W - Died 1863 Jan 3 (?) Age 33 years, 8 days (stone says,"Lost at Sea") (stone worn badly) S:13

Hallett, William W - Died 1906 Born 1835 (buried with Julia F Phinney) (two small stones in back that say, Willie & Jamie,

Hallett (Cont.)
possibly children?) S:8

Hallett, William W - Died 1924 Born 1868 (with Martha D Hallett & next to Blanche A Hallett) S:21

Hallett, Willie - Died (small stone in back of William W Hallett & Julia Phinney Not sure if he is son of theirs) S:8

Hallett, Willie W - Died 1863 March 18 Age 6 months, 18 days Son of William & Eliza H Hallett (next to father's stone) S:13

Hallett, Willis - Died 1873 Dec 5 Born 1855 Oct 31 Son of Joshua & Lucy Hallett (with them & Howard Hallett) S:18

Hallett, Zenas DB - Died 1940 Born 1867 (with Zenas D Basset & others) S:18

Hallett,? - Died 1845 July 3 Age 37 years, 8 months (top of stone broken off) (possible wife of Capt Leander Hallett who is next to him) S:21

Hallinan, Mary H - Died 1966 Born 1891 S:16

Halloran, Estella M - Died 1925 Born 1893 (with Herbert & Patrick Halloran) S:31

Halloran, Herbert - Died 1925 Born 1920 (with Estella & Patrick Halloran) S:31

Halloran, Patrick J - Died 1932 Born 1887 (with Herbert & Estella Halloran) S:31

Halme, Esa - Died 1978 Born 1901 (with Sivia Halme) S:20

Halme, Sivia - Died 1984 Born 1904 (with Esa Halme) S:20

Ham, Hannah - Died (no dates) located in row 3 S:11R

Hamalainen, Kauko A - Died 1965 Dec 7 Born 1920 April 24 From Massachusetts, was Cpl in CoB, 254th Eng BN during World War II S:20

Hamblen, Abigail - Died 1858 July 6 Born 1771 Nov 7 Widow of Lewis Hamblen (buried next to him) S:7

Hamblen, Barnbas (Barnadas) - Died 1826 Dec 21 Age 27 years, 7 months S:7

Hamblen, Deborah - Died 1786 Nov 10 in her 66th yr Wife of Capt Josiah Hamblen S:3

Hamblen, Elkanah - Died 1750 Apr 19 in his 10th yr Son of Ruden Hamblen S:5

Hamblen, Joel - Died 1888 July 9 Age 79 years, 6 months, 7 days (buried next to wife, Phebe) S:7

Hamblen, John - Died 1855 June 21 Age 26 years, 2 months, 3 days (died in Australia) S:7

Hamblen, Jonathan - Died 1743 June 22 in his 74th yr (next to Ester Hamblen, his wife) S:3R

Hamblen, Lewis - Died 1838 Nov 22 Age 69 years, 11 months S:7

Hamblen, Melissa J - Died 1929 Born 1848 (buried with Philander Crosby & many others on this large stone, also with later dates) S:8

Hamblen, Olive - Died 1838 Apr 13 Age 30 years, 8 months Born 1807 Aug 12 Wife of Reuben Hamblen S:7

Hamblen, Phebe - Died 1864 Mar 3 Age 55 years, 8 months, 9 days Wife of Joel Hamblen S:7

Hamblen, Sarah - Died 1773 Nov 6 in her 67th yr Widow of Seth Hamblen (stone is not clear for last name but buried next to Seth Hamblen) S:5

Hamblen, Seth (Lieut) - Died 1771 May 16 in his 64th yr S:5

Hamblen, Sophia - Died 1901 May 21 Age 86 years, 8 months Wife of Joel Hamblen S:7

Hamblin, Adeline A - Died 1870 Age 6 months S:7

Hamblin, Adresta G - Died 1882 June 26 Age 42 years, 4 months, 10 days S:14

Hamblin, Alonzo P - Died 1925 Born 1859 (with Celia E Hamblin) S:18

Hamblin, Amanda - Died 1890 May 13 Age 79 years, 4 months, 16

Hamblin (Cont.)

days Wife of William Hamblin S:4

Hamblin, Bethiah B - Died 1881 Born 1811 S:5

Hamblin, Calvin - Died 1898 Born 1812 S:7

Hamblin, Caroline - Died 1895 May 13 Age 80 years, 8 months S:7

Hamblin, Catherine - Died 1863 Born 1817 (with Capt Simeon & Nancy Hamblin) S:18

Hamblin, Celia E - Died 1946 Born 1864 (with Alonzo & Lila Hamblin) S:18

Hamblin, Charlie Franklin - Died 1870 Oct 5 Born 1865 Apr 29 Son of George W & Chloe J Hamblin S:8

Hamblin, Charlotte D - Died (no dates) (with George Lewis & others) S:18

Hamblin, Chloe J - Died 1880 Feb 17 Born 1830? Feb 19 (stone not clear) Stone says, "Mother" Wife of George W Hamblin (buried next to him) S:8

Hamblin, Christina L - Died 1921 Born 1841 (with Sylvanus S Hamblin & Eliza M Jones) S:21

Hamblin, Cynthia F - Died 1887 Oct 17 Age 72 years, 3 months, 25 days Wife of Ellis Hamblin S:7

Hamblin, Cyrils S - Died 1955 Born 1898 (with David & Mary Hamblin) S:14

Hamblin, David E - Died 1942 Born 1871 (with wife, Mary C Hamblin) S:14

Hamblin, Edmund H - Died 1911 Born 1837 (entire family buried around him) S:7

Hamblin, Edward F - Died 1928 Born 1846 (with Charlotte D Hamblin & others) S:18

Hamblin, Eliza J - Died 1860 Aug 31 Born 1840 Dec 24 Daughter of Luther & Caroline Hamblin S:7

Hamblin, Eliza P - Died 1929 April 13 Born 1832 May 5 (stone

Hamblin (Cont.)

down from vandals) (next to another stone down but cannot read) (stone after this one is Willis E Crowell MD) S:18

Hamblin, Elizabeth H - Died 1944 Born 1870 (with William H Hamblin & others) S:18

Hamblin, Ella D - Died 1931 Born 1857 (buried with Theodore V West, husband) S:8

Hamblin, Ellis - Died 1871 Apr 26 Age 64 years, 9 months (buried next to wife, Cynthia) S:7

Hamblin, Elvin - Died 1876 Born 1794 S:4

Hamblin, Emily Vernon - Died 1865 July 7 Age 3 years, 7 months Daughter of Daniel W & Ann? S Hamblin S:5R

Hamblen, Ester - Died 1746 Sept in her 69th yr S:3+3R

Hamblin, Eugene - Died 1874 Aug 19 Age 3 years, 11 months Son of Edmund & Rose e Hamblin S:7

Hamblin, Evelina G - Died 1875 Nov 6 Age 49 years, 2 months, 3 days (base of stone cracked) Wife of Hiram Hamblin (next to Harriet A Hamblin) S:18

Hamblin, Everett W - Died 1888 Born 1884 (with Ellen K Haskins & Roscoe Hamblin & others) S:18

Hamblin, Freeman H - Died 1890 Born 1839 S:7

Hamblin, George W (Capt) - Died 1909 Oct 30 Born 1826 Sept 13 Stone says, "Father" (buried next to wife, Chloe J Hamblin) S:8

Hamblin, Grenville F - Died 1846 Sept 17 Age 21 months, 26 days Son of Josiah & Cynthia F Hamblin S:7

Hamblin, Hallett - Died 1911 Born 1828 (with Harriet H Hamblin & others) S:18

Hamblin, Hannah M - Died 1897 Oct 8 in her 68th yr S:5

Hamblin, Harold B - Died 1888 Born 1885 (with Roscoe Hamblin

Hamblin (Cont.)
& Ellen Haskins & others) S:18

Hamblin, Harriet A - Died 1939 Born 1848 Wife of Osmond W Bearse (with him) S:18

Hamblin, Harriet H - Died 1912 Born 1840 (with Harriet M Hamblin & others) S:18

Hamblin, Harriet M - Died 1895 Born 1895 (with Elizabeth H Hamblin & others) S:18

Hamblin, Jacob PH - Died 1955 Born 1873 (with Mary E Hamblin) S:18

Hamblin, James H - Died 1867 Born 1850 S:7

Hamblin, James H - Died 1895 Born 1866 Son of Freeman & Lydia Hamblin S:7

Hamblin, Jane - Died 1882 Born 1807 S:4

Hamblin, John - Died 1863 Apr 25 Age 89 years, 2 months S:7

Hamblin, Joseph H - Died 1873 Jan 1 in his 46th yr S:5

Hamblin, Josiah (Capt) - Died 1789 Mar 1 in his 69th yr Wife was Deborah S:3

Hamblin, Laura A - Died 1843 May 17 Age 35 years, 4 months Wife of Stephen Hamblin S:7

Hamblin, Laura A - Died 1853 Born 1818 S:7

Hamblin, Lewis - Died 1888 Sept 12 Age 87 years, 11 months, 5 days S:7

Hamblin, Lila M - Died 1963 Born 1885 Daughter of Alonzo & Celia Hamblin (with them) S:18

Hamblin, Lucy - Died 1880 Dec 8 Age 71 years, 6 months S:7

Hamblin, Luther - Died 1888 Feb 29 Age 77 years, 11 months, 2 days S:7

Hamblin, Lydia T - Died 1905 Born 1839 S:7

Hamblin, Madeline N - Died 1982 Born 1891 (with Roscoe Hamblin & Ellen Haskins) S:18

Hamblin, Marjorie J - Died (still living 1991?) Born 1904 (with John J Dwyer & others) S:18

Hamblin, Mary B - Died 1891 Born 1818 S:7

Hamblin, Mary C - Died 1947 Born 1877 Wife of David E Hamblin (with him) S:14

Hamblin, Mary E - Died 1944 Born 1874 (with Jacob Hamblin) S:18

Hamblin, Maude Crocker - Died 1950 April 23 Born 1878 Sept 28 (with Wendell Parker Hamblin) S:14

Hamblin, Mercy - Died 1789 Aug 4 in her 35th yr Daughter of Capt Josiah & Deborah Hamblin S:3

Hamblin, Mercy - Died 1879 Born 1816 S:7

Hamblin, Milton - Died 1882 Mar 31 Age 16 years, 7 months Son of Edmund & Rose E Hamblin S:7

Hamblin, Nancy - Died 1837 Born 1814 (with Capt Simeon & Catherine Hamblin) S:18

Hamblin, Nannie V - Died 1989 Born 1890 (with David & Mary Hamblin) S:14

Hamblin, Nathan - Died 1888 Born 1807 S:5

Hamblin, Rachel - Died 1848 Oct 9 Age 83 years, 1 month S:7

Hamblin, Roscoe W - Died 1945 Born 1854 (with wife, Ellen K Haskins) S:18

Hamblin, Rose E - Died 1904 Born 1844 Wife of Edmund Hamblin (buried next to him) S:7

Hamblin, Shubael - Died 1846 Aug 14 in his 80th yr S:7

Hamblin, Shubael - Died 1871 Oct 21 Age 27 years, 2 months, 23 days Son of Joel & Phebe Hamblin S:7

Hamblin, Simeon (Capt) - Died 1892 Born 1807 (with Nancy & Catherine Hamblin) S:18

Hamblin, Stephen - Died 1892 Born 1814 S:7

Hamblin, Stephen C - Died 1881 Sept 21 in his 30th yr S:7

Hamblin, Stewart W - Died 1972 Sept 8 Born 1894 June 14 From Massachusetts, was Bugler in

Hamblin (Cont.)
US Army during World War I)
(next to Hallett Hamblin) S:18

Hamblin, Sylvanus S - Died 1907
Born 1836 (with Christina L
Hamblin & Eliza M Jones) S:21

Hamblin, Thankful - Died 1934
Born 1846 Wife of Granville
Ames (with him) S:13

Hamblin, Walter C - Died 1865
Sept 18 Son of Joseph &
Hannah M Hamblin S:5

Hamblin, Warren B - Died 1904
Born 1854 S:7

Hamblin, Wendell Parker - Died
1928 June 1 Born 1878 July 18
(with Maude Crocker Hamblin)
S:14

Hamblin, William - Died 1893 May·
26 Age 80 years, 11 months, 13
days S:4

Hamblin, William H - Died 1954
Born 1868 (with Marjorie J
Hamblin & others) S:18

Hamilton, Eleanor MT - Died 1936
Born 1903 Daughter of George
W Taylor & Cordelia C Davis
(with them & Elmer B Taylor &
others - large Taylor stone) S:12

Hamister, Lee Capen - Died 1981
July 1 Born 1898 Dec 3 (next to
Waldemar O Hamister) (middle
name from Mosswood cemetery
records) S:15

Hamister, Waldemar O - Died 1974
Dec 3 Born 1894 Sept 23 (next
to Lee C Hamister) S:15

Hamlen, (child) - Died 1760's July
3 Age 9 months Child of Seth &
Cloe Hamlen Jr S:5

Hamlen, Abagail - Died 1820 Apr
28 in her 76th yr Wife of Micah
(buried next to him) S:5

Hamlen, Benjamin - Died 17?? Jan
23 Age 31 (stone not clear)
(Hinckley Ceme records #5R say
death was 1732/3) S:5

Hamlen, Consider - Died 1769 July
3 Age 9 months, 11 days Son of
Seth & Chloe Hamlen S:5R

Hamlen, David - Died 1772/3 Nov
4 (Hinckley Ceme records #5R

Hamlen (Cont.)
says age was 25) S:5

Hamlen, Ebenezer - Died 1765 July
18 Age 4 years, 7 months, 9
days Son of Ebenezer & Joanna
Hamlen (top of stone broken)
S:11

Hamlen, Hannah - Died 1735 Nov
(stone not clear) S:5

Hamlen, Hannah - Died 1806 Mar
14 in her 90th yr Wife & Widow
of Joseph Hamlen, Jr S:5

Hamlen, Joanna - Died 1790 May
9 Age 71 Wife of Deacon, Ebenezer Hamlen (next to son,
Ebenezer) S:11

Hamlen, Job - Died Sept 28 (stone
not clear) (Hinckley Ceme records #5R say death was 1732
age 22) S:5

Hamlen, John - Died 1766 Aug 27
in his 86th yr S:5

Hamlen, John - Died 1767 Aug 8
Age 53 S:5R

Hamlen, Jonah - Died Mid-1700's?
June 22 Stone not clear S:3

Hamlen, Joseph - Died 1766 Aug
27 Age 86 S:5R

Hamlen, Joseph - Died 1768 July 8
in his 83rd yr S:5

Hamlen, Joseph - Died 1860 Nov 8
Age 88 years, 11 months S:5

Hamlen, Martha - Died 1735 or 56
? Dec 20 Age 41 Wife of Sout ?
Hworth Hamlin(not clear)
(Hinckley Ceme records #5R
says death was 1756 Sept 20
and that husbands name was
Southworth) S:5

Hamlen, Martha AL - Died 1819
Dec 22 Age 4 years, 2 months
Daughter of Joseph & Zerviah
Hamlen S:5

Hamlen, Mary - Died 1715 April 19
in her 73rd yr Wife of James
Hamlen S:11R+26R

Hamlen, Ruth - Died 1809 Feb 21
in her 64th yr Widow of Shubel
Hamlen S:7

Hamlen, Sarah - Died 1773 Nov 6
Age 67 Widow of Lt Seth Hamlen
S:5R

204

Hamlen, Shubel - Died 1776 Apr 12 in his 52nd yr S:7

Hamlen, Southworth - Died 1700's Age 45 Buried next to John Hamlen d1766 (Hinckley Ceme records say death was 13 Jan 1776) S:5

Hamlen, Temperance - Died 1775 Sept 17 Age 1 year, 10 months Daughter of Capt Micah & Abigail Hamlen S:5R

Hamlen, Wendell - Died 1837 Nov 15 in his 38th yr S:5

Hamlen, Zerviah - Died 1837 Nov 25 in her 62nd yr Wife of Joseph Hamlen (buried next to him) S:5

Hamlin, Cynthia F - Died 1890 Feb 12 Age 79 years, 4 months Wife of Josiah Hamlin (buried next to him) S:7

Hamlin, Hopfull - Died 1806 May 20 in the 33rd yr S:7

Hamlin, Horace L - Died 1866 Sept 14 Age 24 years, 11 months S:5

Hamlin, James - Died 1830 Dec 7 in his 20th yr (on same stone with Joseph Hamlin d1821) S:5

Hamlin, Jeannette W - Died 1963 Born 1871 Wife of Joseph Hamlin (listed with her) S:14

Hamlin, Joseph - Died 1821 Age 19 who died in South America (on same stone with James C Hamlin) S:5

Hamlin, Joseph - Died 1860 Nov 8 Age 88 years, 11 months S:5R

Hamlin, Joseph W - Died (no date) Born 1876 (listed with wife, Jeannette W Hamlin) S:14

Hamlin, Josiah - Died 1873 Jan 6 Age 63 years, 3 months S:7

Hamlin, Mary - Died 1714 located in row 17 S:11R

Hamlin, Mary - Died 1715 April 10 in her 73rd yr Wife to James Hamlin S:26R

Hamlin, Micha MJR - Died 1814 June 6 Age 73 (Hinckley Ceme records #5R say name is Micah) S:5

Hamlin, Susannah - Died 1727 Aug 9 in her 74th yr Wife of

Hamlin (Cont.)
Bartholimu Hamlin S:5

Hammill, Frances E - Died 1977 Born 1902 (with John C Hammill) S:16

Hammill, John C - Died 1970 Born 1900 (with Frances E Hammill) S:16

Hammond, Alice M - Died 1967 Born 1894 (undertaker plaque only) S:17

Hammond, Almira P - Died 1846 April 4 Age 2 Daughter of Clark & Francis Hammond S:10

Hammond, Esther B - Died 1983 Born 1897 Wife of Garry Pierce (with him) S:14

Hammond, J Frederick - Died 1928 Born 1848 (buried with Marifita I Hammond) S:8

Hammond, James Henry - Died 1839 Nov 12 Age 4 Son of Clark & Francis Hammond S:10

Hammond, Marifita I - Died (no death date listed, is she buried there?) Born 1847 (listed on same stone with J Frederick Hammond) S:8

Handren, James - Died 1896 Born 1834 (with Mary J Handren) S:14

Handren, Mary J - Died 1931 Born 1837 (with James Handren) S:14

Handy, Abagail G - Died 1925 Born 1837 (with Richard S Handy) S:14

Handy, Alice L - Died 1826 Born 1855 (with Seth & Cynthia L Coleman) S:14

Handy, Alice Saalfield - Died 1980 Dec 11 Born 1897 Jan 16 (Rock marker with plaque) Stone says,"At last amen, the lovers are back together again" (with Edward Otis Handy & next to Edward Adino Handy) S:19

Handy, Anna A - Died 184? Feb 28 Age 24 years, 7 months Wife of Hervy W Handy (Hinckley Ceme records #5R say death was 1840 age 24 years 3 months) S:5

Handy, Anne A - Died 1892 July 10

Handy (Cont.)
Born 1842 June 15 Wife of Rev
Charles N Hinckley S:5

Handy, Annie I - Died 1914 Born
1851 (next to Mary I Handy)
S:19

Handy, Archie D - Died 1875 Born
1875 (with James & Mary
Handy) S:14

Handy, Asa S - Died 1825 Sept 26
Age 3 years Son of Job & Lydia
Handy (next to mother) S:14

Handy, Asa S - Died 1830 Born
1830 Son of Richard & Rebecca
Handy (with them) S:14

Handy, Asa S (2nd) - Died 1843
Born 1841 Son of Richard &
Rebecca Handy (with them) S:14

Handy, Azubah Mrs - Died 1819 .
March 15 Age 45 Wife of Bethuel
G Handy (next to Bethuel) S:14

Handy, Benjamin F - Died 1850
Dec 15 Age 30 years, 1 months,
15 days S:4

Handy, Benjamin F - Died 1859
Born 1829 (stone says, "Father")
(buried next to Margaret S
Handy, wife) S:8

Handy, Bethuel G - Died 1825 April
17 Age 1 year, 3 months, ? days
Son of Bethuel G & Mary Handy
(next to Job Handy) (a small
stone is also next to him, but
broken down) S:14

Handy, Bethuel G - Died 1856 Nov
31 Age 77 years, 7 months, 21
days (next to wife, Mary Handy)
S:14

Handy, Betsey - Died 1816 Apr 3 in
her 27th yr Wife of Micajah
Handy S:7

Handy, Caroline C - Died 1845
Born 1843 Daughter of Richard
& Rebecca Handy (with them)
S:14

Handy, Charlotte M - Died 1838
Born 1833 Daughter of Richard &
Rebecca Handy (with them) S:14

Handy, Clarinda J - Died 1879 Feb
8 Born 1851 Aug 31 Wife of
Azariah P Jones S:5

Handy, Cynthia L - Died 1877 Born

Handy (Cont.)
1843 (with Seth, Alice & Cynthia
L Coleman) S:14

Handy, Daniel Harvey - Died 1894
April 11 Born 1863 Aug 30 (with
Maria Handy & others) S:14

Handy, Deborah C - Died 1909
May 31 S:5

Handy, Edith N - Died 1876 Aug 28
Age 24 years, 4 months (stone
worn) Wife of Charles Handy
(with Allen Howes & others) S:19

Handy, Edmund C - Buried 1946
Located in section 7, lot 2, grave
3 S:15R

Handy, Edward Adino - Died 1907
Nov 21 at Chicago, Ill Born 1855
April 4 at Barnstable, Mass (rock
marker) (next to Edward Otis &
Alice Saalfield Handy) S:19

Handy, Edward Otis - Died 1956
April 28 Born 1894 March 19
(rock marker & plaque) (with
Alice Saalfield Handy) S:19

Handy, Eleanor - Died 1917 Born
1848 (with James & Mary
Handy) S:14

Handy, Eliza M - Buried 1905
Located in section O, lot 19,
grave 3 S:14R

Handy, Ella M - Buried 1945
Located in section 7, lot 2, grave
4 S:15R

Handy, Eunice - Died 1810 Jan 16
Age 4 years, 21 days Daughter of
Josiah & Caroline Handy (next
to brother, Job S Handy) S:14

Handy, Fannie H - Died 1951 Born
1871 Wife of Rep Charles L
Gifford (with him) S:14

Handy, Grisyld A - Buried 1845
March 31 Located in section R,
lot 36, grave 4 S:14R

Handy, Hatsel K (Capt) - Died 1851
Oct 12 Age 62 years, 1 months,
6 days S:4

Handy, Hervey W - Died 1879 Aug
11 Age 68 years, 8 months S:5

Handy, Hubert L - Died 1902 Born
1892 (with James & Mary
Handy) S:14

Handy, James H - Died 1854 July

Handy (Cont.)
29 Age 51 years, 7 months (with Mary Ann Handy & the Swan's) S:14

Handy, James H - Died 1923 Born 1837 (with Mary A Handy) S:14

Handy, Job - Died 1854 Sept 29 Age 67 years, 6 days (next to Job Handy) S:14

Handy, Job S - Died 1810 Jan 18 Age 7 years, 7 months Son of Josiah & Caroline Handy (next to possible brother, Josiah G Handy) S:14

Handy, Job W (Capt) - Died 1874 April 12 Age 50 years, 4 months (next to wife, Rebecca Otis) S:19

Handy, John M - Buried 1889 Located in section O, lot 19, grave 2 S:14R

Handy, Josiah G - Died 1841 Dec 6 Age 31 (next to Job & Eunice Handy) S:14

Handy, Lawson E - Died 1848 Aug 23 Age 2 years, 3 months Son of James H & Mary A Handy (with them & the Swan's) S:14

Handy, Lillian R - Died 1929 Born 1857 Wife of James H Burlingame (with him) S:14

Handy, Lydia - Died 1850 Feb 7 Age 63 years, 6 months, 23 days Wife of Job Handy (next to him) S:14

Handy, Margaret S - Died 1919 Born 1832 Stone says "Mother" (buried with Benjamin F Handy) S:8

Handy, Maria - Died 1936 Nov 29 Born 1868 April 11 (with Daniel Harvey Handy) S:14

Handy, Martha S - Died 1822 Aug 1 Age 2 Daughter of (possibly) Job & Lydia Handy (next to Lydia & brother, Asa S Handy) S:14

Handy, Mary - Died 1855 Sept 27 Age 62 years, 9 months, 7 days Wife of Bethuel G Handy (next to him) S:14

Handy, Mary A - Died 1869 Born 1839 (with James H Handy) S:14

Handy, Mary Ann - Died 1902 Sept 17 Born 1809 Dec 18 Stone says, "Passed on" (with Susan, Vanlentine, Henry & Horace Swan & others) S:14

Handy, Mary E - Died 1938? Born 1873 (next to Annie I Handy) S:19

Handy, Olive P - Died 1906 May 24 Born 1841 Feb 25 (with Solon L Handy) S:18

Handy, Percy L - Died 1965 Born 1888 S:14

Handy, Richard S - Died 1856 Born 1808 (with Lillian R Handy Her father?)(also with wife, Rebecca H Nickerson) S:14

Handy, Richard S - Died 1920 Born 1835 (with Abagail G Handy) S:14

Handy, Robert C (or G) - Died 1905 May 16 Born 1843 Sept 17 S:14

Handy, Ruth - Died 1859 Dec 15 Age 95 Widow of Levi Handy S:4

Handy, Sarah - Died 1860 Feb 1 Age 68 years, 5 months Widow of Hatsel Handy S:4

Handy, Seth N - Died 1929 Born 1838 (with Cynthia L Handy) S:14

Handy, Solon L - Died 1902 April 16 Born 1829 Oct 16 (with Olive P Handy) S:18

Handy, Syrenia C - Died 1838 Aug 1838 Age 18 years, 5 months, 9 days Wife of Calveant Handy S:14

Handy, William S - Died 1853/8 June 2 Son of Benjamin & Margaret Handy S:4

Hanes, Edmund - Died 1762 located in row 6 S:11R

Hanff, David Maurice - Died 1978 Born 1888 (with Bessie Bartlett) S:15

Hanigan, Loretta A - Died 1986 Born 1897 (next to Marion A Hanigan) S:15

Hanigan, Marion A - Died 1974 Born 1899 (next to Loretta A Hanigan) S:15

Hanlon, John - Died 1950 Born

Hanlon (Cont.)
1873 (with wife, Margaret Hanlon) S:16

Hanlon, Margaret - Died 1941 Born 1874 Wife of John Hanlon (with him & Mary Mollie O'Brien) S:16

Hanni, Frieda H - Died (still living 1991?) Born 1899 Wife of Edward Landers (2nd wife) (with him) S:14

Hansberry, Abigail M - Died 1930 Born 1872 (between John J & Thomas J Hansberry) S:31

Hansberry, John J - Died 1940 Born 1864 (next to Abigail & Thomas Hansberry) S:31

Hansberry, Thomas J - Died 1919 Born 1898 (next to John & Abigail Hansberry) S:31

Hansell, Mary E - Died 1979 Born 1897 Wife of William J Hansell (with him) S:16

Hansell, William J - Died 1939 Born 1898 (with wife, Mary E Hansell) S:16

Hanson, Clarence F - Died (still living 1991?) Born 1892 (listed with Josephine V Hanson) S:16

Hanson, Ellen Weston - Died 1944 Born 1871 S:16

Hanson, Florence - Died 1954 Born 1892 Wife of Earle Rexford Avery (with him) S:18

Hanson, Josephine V - Died (still living 1991?) Born 1894 (listed with Clarence F Hanson) S:16

Harden, Octavia - Died 1866 May 31 Age 54 years, 10 months, 13 days S:4

Harding, Alice G - Died 1913 Born 1838 (on large Hudson & Hinckley stone) S:11

Harding, Dora J - Died 1971 Born 1899 S:15

Harding, Edward M - Died 1938 Born 1868 (on large Hudson & Hinckley stone) S:11

Harding, Evelyn - Died 1969 Born 1907 S:12

Hardy, Annie R - Died 1924 Born 1848 (with Ruth M Hubly & others) S:18

Hargreaves, Edna R - Died 1973 Born 1893 (with James R Hargreaves) S:14

Hargreaves, James R - Died 1962 Born 1894 He was a Mason (with Ellen Murray Flynn & others) S:14

Harlow, Abbott FL - Died 1975 Born 1888 (on mort plaque in ground) He was a Mason (with Elizabeth M Harlow) S:14

Harlow, Adelaide F - Died 1942 Born 1869 (next to William G Harlow) S:14

Harlow, Agnes A - Died 1974 Born 1893 (next to John P Harlow) S:14

Harlow, Agnes J - Died (no info) (with Abbott FL Harlow & others) S:14

Harlow, Andrew Jason - Died 1954 Born 1891 Was a Private in US Army during World War I Has Veteran star at grave (next to Charles O Harlow) S:14

Harlow, Bridget - Died 1973 Born 1895 (with Oliver Harlow) S:14

Harlow, Carleton T - Died 1918 Aug 9 Age 29 years, 5 months Was in Machine Gun Company, 59th Infantry Killed in France during World War I (with Wallie F Harlow) S:14

Harlow, Catherine - Died 1941 Born 1885 (with Granville T Harlow) S:12

Harlow, Charles O - Died 1951 Born 1868 (with wife, Ellen M Harlow) S:14

Harlow, Chester M - (no info) (with Agnes J Harlow & others) S:14

Harlow, Clara - Died 1906 Born 1899 (with Ernest S Harlow) S:14

Harlow, Doris Eldridge - Died 1985 Born 1917 (with Granville & Catherine Harlow) (wife of Granville) S:12

Harlow, Elijah P - Died (no info) (with Elizabeth A Harlow) S:14

Harlow, Elizabeth A - Died (no info) Buried 11 Oct 1981 Age 87

Harlow (Cont.)

(burial record & age from Moss wood ceme record)(with Chester M Harlow & others) S:14

Harlow, Elizabeth M - Died (no info) (with Abbott FL Harlow & others) S:14

Harlow, Ellen M - Died 1959 Born 1870 Wife of Charles O Harlow (next to him) S:14

Harlow, Emma H - Buried 1914 Located in section S, lot 9, grave 5 S:14R

Harlow, Ernest S - Died 1929 Born 1874 (with Marietta G Harlow) S:14

Harlow, Granville T - Died (still living) Born 1905 (with Catherine & Doris Harlow) S:12

Harlow, Horace W - Died 1967 Born 1891 S:14

Harlow, John J - Died 1922 Born 1833 (with Susan P Harlow) S:14

Harlow, John P - Died 1981 Born 1895 (next to Agnes Harlow) S:14

Harlow, Josephine F - Died 1937 Born 1859 (with Wallie F Harlow) S:14

Harlow, Laura C - Died 1928 Born 1881 Wife of Louis Clarner Jr (with him) S:14

Harlow, Lillie M - Died 1943 Born 1866 (with Wallie F Harlow) S:14

Harlow, Lydia E - Died 1952 Born 1863 (next to Martha P Harlow) S:14

Harlow, Marietta G - Died 1958 Born 1873 (with Ernest S Harlow) S:14

Harlow, Marjorie - Buried 1906 Located in section S, lot 19, grave 1 S:14R

Harlow, Martha P - Died 1888 Born 1877 (next to Lydia E Harlow) S:14

Harlow, Oliver - Died 1957 Born 1882 (with Bridget Harlow) S:14

Harlow, Roland T - Buried 1909 Located in section S, lot 9, grave 6 S:14R

Harlow, Seaver R - Died 1988 Born

Harlow (Cont.)

1900 Was ACM2 in US Navy during World War I (next to William & Adelaide Harlow) S:14

Harlow, Susan P - Died 1928 Born 1838 (with John J Harlow) S:14

Harlow, Temple P - Died 1880 June 25 Born 1844 Feb 28 Wife of Elias Burrows (with him) S:14

Harlow, Wallie F - Died 1957 Born 1856 (with Josephine F Harlow) S:14

Harlow, William G - Died 1939 Born 1864 (next to Adelaide F Harlow) S:14

Harold, J - Died 1941 Born 1886 (with Joseph Burlingame & Inez Garder) S:14

Harper, Albert Edward - Died 1982 Born 1899 (undertaker plaque only) Buried in section 10, lot 57, grave 1 (from Mosswood ceme records) S:15

Harper, Sally E - Died 1935 Born 1868 (with William S Harper) S:31

Harper, William S - Died 1924 Born 1857 (with Sally E Harper) S:31

Harrington, Lydia - Died 1843 April 14 Age 52 Wife of Elias Harrington S:11

Harris, (infant) - Died (dates underground) Child of Washington & Sally Harris (on same stone with mother) S:10

Harris, Anna - Died 1855 Jan 12 Age 79 years, 9 months (on large stone with Thomas Harris & others) S:11

Harris, Anstis L - Died 1914 Aug 4 Born 1850 Oct 18 (next to Marcus N Harris) S:11

Harris, Caroline G - Died 1966 Born 1881 (next to Charles E Harris) S:18

Harris, Charles E - Buried 1976 July 24 Located in section 6, lot ?, grave 9 S:15R

Harris, Charles E (MD) - Died 1947 Born 1868 (next to Caroline G Harris) S:18

Harris, Frank E - Died 1977 Born

Harris (Cont.)
1898 Stone says,"Husband" (with wife, Mary G Harris) S:14

Harris, Henrietta - Died 1826 Dec 27 Age 5 weeks, 4 days Daughter of Thomas & Mehitable Harris S:11

Harris, Ina Winifred - Died 1911 June 22 Born 1875 May 14 (on large Whelden stone in middle of cemetery with others) S:11

Harris, John P - Died 1971 Born 1889 (with Osceoloa de Hall) S:17

Harris, Marcus N - Died 1942 Dec 28 Born 1848 Sept 19 S:11

Harris, Mary G - Died 1989 Born 1902 Stone says, "Wife" (with husband, Frank E Harris) S:14

Harris, Mehible - Died 1890 July 8 Age 83 years, 1 month Wife of Thomas Harris (on same stone with him & others) S:11

Harris, Mehitable - Died 1830 July 8 Age 83 years, 1 month Wife of Capt Thomas Harris S:11

Harris, Richard L - Died 1986 Born 1900 S:17

Harris, Sally - Died 1822 Mar 16 Age 31 ? Wife of Capt Washington Harris (on same stone with infant child) S:10

Harris, Thomas - Died 1803 Feb 10 Age 28 (on with others on large tall stone) S:11

Harris, Thomas - Died 1889 March 12 Age 86, 3 months (on same stone with Thomas Harris & others) S:11

Harris, Thomas (Capt) - Died 1889 Mar 22 Age 86 years, 3 months (with Mehitable Harris) S:11

Harry, Priscilla - Died 1845 Sept 19 Born 1789 April 7 Widow of John Harry S:5

Hart, CC - Died (no dates) (small stone) Was in CoD, Massachusetts 45th Inf (next to Frederick M Hart) S:18

Hart, Edward West - Died 1977 Born 1892 (with Ithel Drew & Ella Hart) S:18

Hart, Elizabeth S - Died 1941 Born 1868 (with William m Hart) S:18

Hart, Ella Drew - Died 1967 Born 1894 (with Ithel Drew & Edward Hart) S:18

Hart, Frederick M - Died 1916 Born 1888 (Was a Mason) (with George F Hart) S:18

Hart, George F - Died 1930 Born 1857 (with Frederick & Mary Hart) S:18

Hart, Mary A - Died 1914 Born 1831 (small stone) (next to CC Hart) S:18

Hart, Mary R - Died (no dates) (listed with George & Frederick Hart) S:18

Hart, William M - Died 1940 Born 1867 (with Elizabeth S Hart) S:18

Hartford, Helen C - Died 1967 Born 1885 S:18

Hartwell, Billie O - Died 1978 Born 1916 Wife of Glenn Hartwell (with him & Mary S Hartwell & others) S:20

Hartwell, Charles - Died 1922 Born 1849 (with Sarah F Hartwell, wife) S:11

Hartwell, Edwin S - Died 1982 Born 1891 (with wife, Mary S Hartwell & others) S:20

Hartwell, Glenn W - Died (still living 1991?) Born 1917 (with wife, Billie O Hartwell & others) S:20

Hartwell, Mary S - Died 1954 Born 1892 Wife of Edwin Hartwell (with him & Mary Ann Horn & others) S:20

Hartwell, Mildred M - Died 1951 Born 1882 S:11

Hartwell, Sarah F - Died 1934 Born 1848 Wife of Charles Hartwell (next to him) S:11

Harvey, Ebenezer Erskine - Died 1964 Born 1894 (with wife, Marion Fraser) S:15

Hasckel, David - Died 1986 Born 1898 (Jewish section) (with Dora G Hasckel) S:15

Hasckel, Dora G - Died 1987 Born

Hasckel (Cont.)
1902 (Jewish section) (with
David Hasckel) S:15

Haskell, Beatrice - Died 1972 Born
1886 Wife of John W Vallis (next
to him) S:11

Haskell, George - Died 1939 Born
1867 (1 large Haskell stone)
(buried with Rosetta J & Marcus
M Haskell) S:8

Haskell, Marcus M - Died 1925 Oct
29 Born 1843 Feb 12 Medal of
honor, Serg Co C 35th Massachusetts Inf in Civil War (listed
on large stone with Rosetta J &
George m Haskell) S:8

Haskell, Rosetta J - Died 1923
Born 1846 (listed on stone with
Marcus M & George M Haskell)
S:8

Haskins, Ellen K - Died 1930 Born
1851 Wife of Roscoe W Hamblin
(with him) S:18

Haskins, Florence - Died 1982
Born 1890 Wife of Bertram F
Ryder (with him) S:14

Haskins, Grace C - Died 1939 Born
1863 (next to Solomon F Haskins) S:14

Haskins, Henry S - Died 1959 Born
1883 (next to Olive H Haskins)
S:14

Haskins, Olive H - Died 1960 Born
1888 (next to Solomon F Haskins) S:14

Haskins, Solomon F - Died 1928
Born 1858 (next to Grace C
Haskins) S:14

Haslam, Joseph Harry Jr - Died
1953 Dec 3 Born 1907 Nov 22
From Mass and was a Staff Sgt
in 211, Base Unit AAF during
World War II (next to Anne D
Haslam Gardner) S:11

Hassett, Jeanette G - Died 1950
Born 1906 (with Joseph Hassett)
S:16

Hassett, Joseph - Died (still living
1991?) Born 1900 (with Jeanette
G Hassett) S:16

Hassett, Joseph - Died 1981 Born
1900 Was S2 in US Navy during

Hassett (Cont.)
World War I S:15

Hastings, Martha M - Died 1983
Nov 9 Born 1899 May 1 (with
Walter S Hastings) S:18

Hastings, Walter S - Died 1978
Sept 5 Born 1891 Dec 20 Was a
Corporal in US Army during
World War I (next to Martha M
Hastings) S:18

Hatch, Abigail - Died 1811 located
in row 18 S:11R

Hatch, Abigail - Died 1841 Jan 30
Age 69 Born 1772 Widow of
Gorham Hatch S:11R

Hatch, Abigail Miss - Died 1829
Nov 7 Age 28 S:11

Hatch, Ida M - Died 1928 Born
1849 Wife of Joseph Phinney
(with him & daughter Agnes
Smith) S:18

Hatch, Jabez - Died (stone worn
bad, possibly dated 1600's) (next
to Elizabeth Lathrop, d1694)
S:11

Hatch, Jabez - Died 1757/8 Feb 15
in his 21st yr S:11R+26R

Hatch, Jabez - Died 1757 located
in row 17 (could be the same as
Jabez which is listed with stone
worn bad) S:11R

Hatch, Olive Dexter - Died 1987
Born 1902 S:12

Hatfield, Yohhann (Hans) - Died
1982 Aug 24 Born 1976 March
10 Stone says, "Mama & Papa's
Boy" (with Oliver & Marian
Hallet plot) (there is a small red
racing car left at his grave) S:19

Hathaway, (unnamed) - Died 1821
Feb 12 Wife of James Hathaway
S:26R

Hathaway, Benjamin - Died 1838
Oct 2 Age 74 S:26R

Hathaway, Daniel - Died 1922
Born 1849 (next to Mary S
Hathaway) S:18

Hathaway, Eleanor V - Died 1975
Born 1922 Wife of Herbert
Sunderman (listed with him &
Beth & Rebecca Sunderman)
S:20

Hathaway, James - Died 1827 July 25 Age 94 S:26R

Hathaway, James O - Died 1900 Born 1823 (next to Mary S Hathaway) S:18

Hathaway, Lot - Died 1799 Jan 2 in his 10th yr Son of Benjamin and Temperance Hathaway (located at Lothrop's Hill) S:26R

Hathaway, Mary S - Died 1887 Born 1823 (next to Daniel Hathaway) S:18

Hathaway, Oliver - Died 1799 Jan 2 in his 6th yr Son of Benjamin and Temperance Hathaway S:26R

Hathaway, Temperance - Died 1837 Nov 22 Age 71 Wife of Benjamin Hathaway S:26R

Hathway, Hannah S - Died 1840 Feb 20 Age 5 years, 3 months Daughter of Prince & Hope Hathway S:4

Hausberry, James J - Died 1964 Jan 6 Born 1894 Sept 4 From Massachusetts, was PFC in 302 Repair Unit, MTC during World War I S:15

Havlin, John F Lt Col - Died 1944 Jan 21 (with Mary Z Havlin) S:16

Havlin, Mary Z - Died 1975 Born 1885 (with LtCol John F Havlin) S:16

Hawes, Bess - Died 1889 Age 3 months (next to Lot E & Mary Hawes) S:19

Hawes, Edmund - Died 1762 May 11 in his 63rd yr (next to Mary Hawes, wife) (Hinckley Ceme records #11R says death was 1762 May 11) S:11+26R

Hawes, Edward Everett (MD) - Died 1944 Born 1862 (with wife, Emily Crowell Hawes & others) S:18

Hawes, Emily Crowell - Died 1938 Born 1863 Wife of Edward Everett Hawes MD (with him & Everett C Hawes & others) S:18

Hawes, Everett Crowell - Died 1894 Born 1894 (with Emily Hawes &

Hawes (Cont.)
Elkanah Crowell & others) S:18

Hawes, George L - Died 1888 Born 1824 (with Charles & Sarah Welch & others) S:18

Hawes, Hannah - Died 1762 Aug 7 in her 25th yr Daughter of Thomas & Thankful Hawes S:11R+26R

Hawes, Jacob - Died 1840 Born 1797 (with Charles Welch & Sylvia Hawes & others) S:18

Hawes, Katharine S - Died 1903 Born 1863 Wife of Arthur M Coville (with him) S:19

Hawes, Lot E - Died 1934 Born 1865? (Stone worn) (Between Mary & Bess Hawes) S:19

Hawes, Mary - Died 1754 Feb 25 Daughter of Edmund & Mary Hawes (Hinckley Ceme records #11R say died in her 19th yr) S:11+26R

Hawes, Mary - Died 1775 ? 19th in her 75th yr (stone on the ground) Widow of Edmund Hawes (next to him) (Hinckley Ceme records #11R say death was 1775 June age 75) S:11+26R

Hawes, Mary D - Died 1938 Born 1860 (next to Lot E Hawes) S:19

Hawes, Prentiss - Died 1887 Aug 17 Born 1825 March 7 (with Susan O Hawes) S:19

Hawes, Sarah - Died 1754 June 12 in her 22nd yr Daughter of Edmund & Mary Hawes S:11R+26R

Hawes, Susan O - Died 1923 Feb 5 Born 1832 May 28 (with Prentiss Hawes) S:19

Hawes, Sylvia - Died 1886 Born 1798 (with Charles Welch & William P Hawes & others) S:18

Hawes, William P - Died 1833 Born 1830 (with Charles Welch & Sylvia Hawes & others) S:18

Hawkins, Frances Ruth - Died 1983 June 26 at Dennis, Massachusetts Born 1906 Dec 25 at St Joseph, Missouri (marker is a

Hawkins (Cont.)
rock) (with Roland Long Easterbrook) S:19

Hawkins, Jack Bernard - Died
1949 Born 1904 S:12

Hawley, Elizabeth - Died 1797 Aug
7 in her 70th yr 2nd wife to
Gideon Hawley S:7

Hawley, Gideon (Esq) - Died 1851
May 4 in his 84th yr S:7

Hawley, Gideon (Rev) - Died 1807
Oct 3 Born 1727 Nov 5 at Strat-
ford, Connecticut (buried next to
children) S:7

Hawley, James (Rev) - Died 1800
Oct 8 in his 30th yr Son of Rev
Gideon Hawley S:7

Hawley, Lucy - Died 1777 Dec 25
in her 50th yr Wife of Rev
Gideon Hawley & daughter of
Rev B Fessenden S:7

Hawley, Lucy Miss - Died 1837 Mar
20 in her 72nd yr Daughter of
Rev Gideon Hawley S:7

Hawley, Zerviah - Died 1839 Apr
20 in her 58th yr Wife of Gideon
Hawley Esq S:7

Hayden, Ann F - Died 1958 Born
1877 Wife of William Hayden
(with him) S:16

Hayden, William - Died 1962 Born
1872 (with wife, Ann F Hayden)
S:16

Haydon, Nan B - Died (still living
1991?) Born 1897 (listed with
Richard Haydon) S:20

Haydon, Richard HD - Died 1972
March 17 Born 1899 April 17
From Massachusetts, was PFC
in US Army during World War I
S:20

Hayes, James (Capt) - Died 1813
Apr 29 in his 70th yr S:5

Haymaker, Marion - Died 1975
Born 1896 (undertaker plaque
only) S:17

Hayward, Catherine Davenport -
Died 1923 Oct 11 at Boston
Born 1833 Sept 26 at Boston
Wife of Samuel Savage (in
Bowles plot) S:10

Hazelton, Betsey - Died 1915 Born

Hazelton (Cont.)
1839 (with Henrietta Hazelton &
others) S:18

Hazelton, Donald R - Died 1983
Born 1928 He was a PFC in US
Army S:19

Hazelton, Frederick E - Died 1976
Born 1911 (with Lillian & James
Hazelton) S:18

Hazelton, Henrietta - Died 1876
Born 1863 (with Mary L Hazelton & others) S:18

Hazelton, Henry - Died 1905 Born
1840 Also plaque that
reads,"IORM Iyanough Tribe
#147 Hyannis" (with Betsey
Hazelton & others) S:18

Hazelton, James B - Died 1941
Born 1876 (with Lillian & Freder
Hazelton) S:18

Hazelton, Lillian K - Died 1950
Born 1889 (with James & Frederick Hazelton) S:18

Hazelton, Mary L - Died 1886 Born
1866 (with Henry Hazelton &
others) S:18

Hazelton, Nellie Henderson - Died
1912 Born 1889 (next to Henry
Hazelton & others) S:18

Healey, (a son) - Died 1860 July 17
Born 1860 July 4 (on same
stone with mother, Eliza G
Healy)(see mothers stone for
inscription) S:26R

Healey, Eliza G - Died 1860 Aug 25
Age 19 yrs 9 mos (on same stone
with a son d 17 July 1860)
Stone says "Why do we mourn
for dying friends, or shake at
deaths alarms, Tis but the voice
that news sends, To call them to
his arms" (footnote - E.G.H.)
S:26R

Healy, Leonard G - Died 1966 Born
1900 S:16

Heaman, Charles F - Died 1968
July 20 Born 1898 July 30 From
Massachusetts & was a Wagoner
in Battery B, 51st Coast Artillery
during World War I (next to Viola
Heaman Ruedy) S:15

Heard, Elspeth M - Died 1967 Born

Heard (Cont.)
1889 S:17

Hearn, Esther M - Died 1974 Born 1893 (with Hubert F Hearn) S:16

Hearn, Hubert F - Died 1947 Born 1895 (with Esther M Hearn) S:16

Hebditch, Frederick R - Died 1962 Nov 19 Born 1893 Nov 19 From Massachusetts, was a E2 in USNRF during World War I S:17

Hedee, Rebecca - Died 1872 April 1 Born 1831 Aug 2 Stone says,"Sister" (a small stone) Wife of Sellick & Sally Hedee S:19

Hedee, Sally E - Died 1868 Dec 22 Age 74 years, 6 months Stone says,"Mother" (a small stone) Wife of Sillek Hedee S:19

Hedge, Amelia M - Died 1903 May 22 Age 61 years, 6 months Wife of Isaac G Hedge (next to him) S:19

Hedge, Charles H - Died 1949 Born 1873 (with Lillian E Hedge) S:19

Hedge, Charles W - Died 1906 Born 1837 (with Hannah S Hedge) S:19

Hedge, Charlie - Died 1873 (small lamb stone) Age ? years, ? months, 2 days (stone not clear) (next to Amelia M Hedge) S:19

Hedge, David E - Died 1817 Nov 21 Age 4 mos Son of Sellik & Sally Hedge S:10+26R

Hedge, Eleanor - Died 1821 April 20 Age 6 months Daughter of Sellick & Sally Hedge S:10

Hedge, Elizabeth - Died 1827 Aug 15 Age 6 weeks Daughter of Sellik & Sally Hedge (on same stone with John Hedge, brother) S:10

Hedge, Hannah S - Died 1928 Born 1845 (with Charles W Hedge) S:19

Hedge, Isaac G - Died 1910 Feb 3 Born 1829 May 13 (next to wife, Amelia M Hedge) S:19

Hedge, John E - Died 1831 Aug 2 Son of Sellik & Sally Hedge (on same stone with Elizabeth, sister) S:10

Hedge, Lillian E - Died 1952 Born 1874 (with Charles H Hedge) S:19

Hedge, Mary Lee - Died 1841 Dec 5 Age 7 (stone flat on ground, broken off at base) Daughter of Sillek & Sally Hedge S:10

Hedge, Rebecca D - Died 1831 Feb 18 Age 18 mos (dates underground, stone in bad shape) Daughter of Sellik & Sally Hedge S:10+26R

Hedge, Sally T - Died 1844 Feb 27 Age 25 Daughter of Sellik & Sally Hedge S:10

Hedlund, Christina S - Died 1964 Born 1894 (buried with Thure Hedlund) S:8

Hedlund, Thure A - Died 1952 Born 1869 (buried with Christina S Hedlund) S:8

Hedman, Alma - Died 1977 Born 1883 Stone says,"AVTI" S:20

Hefler, Caroline G - Died 1920 Born 1892 (with Thomas, Harriet & Ella Nickerson & others) S:18

Heinonen, Ellen - Died 1985 Born 1891 Wife of Emil Heinonen (with him) S:20

Heinonen, Emil - Died 1962 Born 1880 (with wife, Ellen Heinonen) S:20

Heisler, Charles L - Died 1988 Born 1894 (a rock stone) (has 2 stones) Was a 1st Lt in US Army during World War I (listed with Lillian Heisler) S:20

Heisler, Lillian (Billie) - Died (still living 1991?) Born 1903 (listed with Charles Heisler) S:20

Hellberg, Edith M - Died 1987 Born 1892 (with Oscar W Hellberg) S:18

Hellberg, Oscar W - Died 1954 Born 1893 (with Edith M Hellberg) S:18

Heller, Hortense M - Died 1926 Born 1873 Wife of Edward Crocker (with him) S:12

Hemm, Hilda - Died 1968 Born 1896 (with John & Laila Hemm)

Hemm (Cont.)
S:18

Hemm, John F - Died 1941 Born
1891 (with Hilda & Laila Hemm)
S:18

Hemm, Laila - Died 1968 Born
1931 (with Hilda & John Hemm)
S:18

Henderson, Anna M - Died 1932
Born 1859 (Henderson plot)
(with James & Mattie Henderson
& others) S:18

Henderson, Charles A - Died 1926
Born 1868 S:18

Henderson, James M - Died 1925
Born 1891 (with Mary E Henderson) S:18

Henderson, Mary E - Died 1979
Born 1894 (with James M
Henderson) S:18

Henderson, Mattie May - Died
1942 Born 1879 (Henderson
plot) (with Anna M Henderson &
others) S:18

Hendrickson, Mary A - Died 1980
Born 1892 S:15

Hendrickson, Mildred Davis -
Buried 1980 Jan 10 Age 87
Located in section 10, lot 42,
grave 1 S:15R

Hendrix, Olin C MD - Died 1986
Oct 23 Born 1900 Dec 18 Was a
Captain in US Navy during
World War II (has 2 stones) S:15

Henerdson, James T - Died 1920
Born 1856 (Henderson plot)
(with Anna M Henderson &
others) S:18

Hennessy, Elizabeth L - Died (no
dates listed) (listed with William
C Hennessy) S:16

Hennessy, John P - Died 1959
Born 1881 (with Mary Agnes
Hennessy) S:16

Hennessy, Mary Agnes - Died 1986
Born 1896 (with John P Hennessy) S:16

Hennessy, William C - Died 1949
Born 1884 (Elizabeth L Hennessy listed with him) S:16

Henry, Dorothy Hallett - Died 1966
Born 1906 (with Mabel Phinney

Henry (Cont.)
Hallett & next to Charles N
Hallett) S:19

Henton, Amanda E - Died 1871
June 27 Age 38 years, 9 months,
10 days Wife of Stephen Henton
& only daughter of Albert &
Elizabeth Chase (next to parents) S:18

Herrmann, Dorothy - Died (still
living in 1990?) Born 1936 June
18 S:11

Herron, John William - Died 1974
Feb 26 Born 1901 Jan 7 (with
Dorothy Blodgett) S:13

Herse, Joseph - Died 1751 April 26
in hid 43rd yr S:1

Hersey, Abner Dr - Died 1787 Jan
9 (buried next to wife Hannah
Hersey) (Hinckley Ceme records
#9R say died in his 66th yr) S:9
+26R

Hersey, Hannah - Died 1794 June
10 in her 71st yr Wife of Dr
Abner Hersey S:9+26R

Hersey, James Doc - Died 1741
July 29 in his 25th yr S:9+26R

Hersey, Lydia - Died 1740 Nov 19
Age 22 years, 4 months Wife of
Doc James Hersey S:9

Hersey, Mary - Died 1756 Sept 1
Age 6 years, 7 months, 2 days
Daughter of Dr Abner & Hannah
Hersey S:9R

Heywood, Augusta - Died 1885
(listed on Heywood family stone)
(Hinckley Ceme records #11R
says age was 53) S:11

Heywood, Hannah E - Died 1912
(listed on Heywood family stone)
S:11

Heywood, Nancy G - Died 1865
Wife of Reuben Heywood (listed
on large family stone with others)(Hinckley Ceme records
#11R say age was 70) S:11

Heywood, Reuben - Died 1876
(large family stone with others)
(Hinckley Ceme records #11R
say age was 83) S:11

Hibbert, George E - Died 1981
Born 1882 (with Lelia Hibbert)

Hibbert (Cont.)
S:18
Hibbert, Lelia - Died 1982 Born 1887 (with George Hibbert) S:18
Hickey, Birja C - Died 1946 Born 1888 (with Wallace Ryder & Laura Clayton) S:14
Hicks, Margaret - Died (still living 1990) Born 1921 Wife of George Linthwaite (next to him) S:11
Higby, Lois - Died (still living 1991?) Born 1934 (With Dana Lee Milstead & Centry Allen Milstead Jr) S:20
Higgins, Benjamin - Died 1814 Sept 25 drowned in his 34th yr He was from Orleans, Mass S:11+26R
Higgins, Mae Kelley - Died 1978 Born 1883 (next to Charlie Kelley, Edwin & Emma Kelley) S:18
Hiles, Emily F - Died 1968 Born 1894 Wife of Marshall W(?) Robbins (with him) S:14
Hill, Amelia - Died 1971 Born 1891 S:18
Hill, Edward - Died 1949 Born 1895 (with Oscar A Hill) S:18
Hill, Helen FW - Died 1941 Feb 28 Born 1860 April 1 wife of Elisha Worrell (buried with him) S:8
Hill, Isabella B - Died 1881 Aug 1 Born 1841 Oct 11 Wife of William G Hill (Hinckley Ceme records #5R say death was 1884 and birth was 1844) S:5
Hill, James - Died 1941 Born 1859 (buried with Carrie M Coleman in Lowry plot) S:8
Hill, Kenneth V - Died 1980 Born 1899 (with Laveta Hill) S:20
Hill, Laveta M - Died (still living 1991?) Born 1919 (listed with Kenneth Hill) S:20
Hill, Oscar A - Died 1951 Born 1887 (with Edward Hill) S:18
Hillard, Sally H - Died 1882 Born 1787 (buried with Azuba S Bearse) S:8
Hiller, Virginia B - Died 1967 Born 1889 S:18

Hilliard, Bertha M - Died 1991 March 26 Born 1897 Feb 27 (With Charles F Hilliard) S:20
Hilliard, Charles F - Died 1977 March 18 Born 1904 Jan 8 (With Bertha Hilliard) S:20
Hinckley, (?) - Died 1808 ? 13th Age 22 (buried next to Eleaza May) S:11
Hinckley, (daughter) - Died 1755/85 ? Nov (stone badly worn) Daughter of Ebenezer Hinckley ? S:11
Hinckley, (daughter) - Died 1785 ? Nov (stone not very clear) (possibly says, daughter of Ebenezer Hinckley) S:11
Hinckley, (female) - Died 181? Age 19 (stone down, face gone) Daughter of Nymphas & Chloe Hinckley S:12
Hinckley, (female) - Died 1823 Sept 23 Age 7 days (very small stone & worn) Daughter of Oliver & Louisa Hinckley S:12
Hinckley, (infant) - Died 1805 June 28 Age 7 days Son of Chipman & Olive Hinckley S:7
Hinckley, (stillborn) - Died 1759 Child of Nathaniel & Desire Hinckley S:5R
Hinckley, ? - Died 1811 July 25 Age 2 days Son of Chipman & Olive Hinckley S:7
Hinckley, ? - Died (stone is destroyed) (stone located in back of Crocker & Caroline Hinckley) S:8
Hinckley, ? - Died 1808 13th ? Age 22 (stone broken in half) (next to Joseph Allyn d1871) S:11
Hinckley, ? (female) - Died 1776 Sept 25 Wife of John Hinckley, d1835 (next to him) (stone has an Acorn on top of it) S:11
Hinckley, ? - Died 1904 (cannot read month) 11th Born 1813 (top of stone broken off) (next to Caroline Hinckley) S:21
Hinckley, Abagail - Died 1877 Jan 17 Age 90 years, 4 months, 28 days Wife of Chipman Hinckley S:7

Hinckley, Abba S - Died 1856 May 27 Age 30 Wife of Thatcher (Thacher) Hinckley (next to him) S:21

Hinckley, Abbie C - Died 1892 Dec 14 Born 1843 Dec 17 S:18

Hinckley, Abbie L - Died 1923 Born 1835 (with Lothrop Hinckley & others) S:10

Hinckley, Abby - Died 1874 Feb 22 Age 47 yrs 6 mos 15 days Born 1826 Aug 7 Wife of ? (maybe Josiah Hinckley) (large dark Hinckley stone with Gustavus A Hinckley & others) S:11+26R

Hinckley, Abby H - Died 1848 May 10 Born 1822 (on stone with Henry W Stimson & others) (wife of John W. Hinckley MD of Boston) S:11+26R

Hinckley, Abica? - Died 1853 July 1 Daughter of Adino & Elizabeth Hinckley S:10

Hinckley, Abigail - Died 1757 Oct 14 Daughter of Benjamin & Lydia Hinckley S:3

Hinckley, Abigail - Died 1854 Nov 13 Age 51 Wife of Zenas Hinckley S:7

Hinckley, Abigail - Died 1865 Sept 3 Age 60 years, 11 months, 5 days Wife of Heman Hinckley (next to him) S:13

Hinckley, Abraham - Died 1880 Jan 31 Age 91 years, 11 months S:9R

Hinckley, Ada F - Died 1957 Jan 26 Born 1864 Sept 30 (possible daughter to Josiah & Abby Hinckley) (large Hinckley stone, dark, with Gustavus A Hinckley & others) S:11

Hinckley, Adeline - Died 1891 Feb 27 Born 1819 Nov 27 Wife of Benjamin Hinckley (next to him) S:11

Hinckley, Adino - Died 179? (stone broken off info from foot stone) (Hinckley Ceme records #11R say death was 1793 Feb 5 in his 58th yr) S:11+26R

Hinckley, Adino - Died 1848 Dec

Hinckley (Cont.) 29 Age 80 S:10

Hinckley, Albert L - Died 1921 Born 1878 (with Mona B Hinckley) S:12

Hinckley, Albert L - Buried 1979 April 6 Located in section 3, lot 3, grave 1 S:15R

Hinckley, Albert M - Died (still living 1991?) Born 1921 (listed with Walton Hinckley) S:13

Hinckley, Alice Augusta - Died (date broken off stone) (stone has been cemmented back on base, was broken) Daughter of Rev Edward B Hinckley S:12

Hinckley, Alice L - Died 1964 Born 1872 (with Arthur E Hinckley) S:18

Hinckley, Alice Mrs - Died 1847 Sept 24 in her 74th yr Wife of Robinson T Hinckley (next to him) S:11+26R

Hinckley, Allen Carter - Died 1954 Jan 28 Born 1877 Oct 11 Son of FA & EC Hinckley (on same stone with Elizabeth S Hinckley & others A very large stone in middle of cemetery) S:10

Hinckley, Allen Crosby - Died 1944 Born 1858 S:8

Hinckley, Allen Howes - Died 1958 Born 1884 (listed on large family stone with John & Rebecca Hinckley & others) S:11

Hinckley, Alpheus - Died 1808 Feb 20 in his 27th yr S:7

Hinckley, Alvin - Died 1856 Feb 19 in his 70th yr S:7

Hinckley, Ann - Died 1837 Oct 2 Age 17 years, 5 months, 22 days Daughter of Alvin & Polly Hinckley S:7

Hinckley, Ann - Died 1878 Oct 24 in her 80th yr S:6

Hinckley, Ann Nye - Died 1907 Oct 24 Age 71 years, 8 months (on same stone with Ralph Sheldon Barrow & others) S:11

Hinckley, Anna - Died 1815 Apr 7 in her 34th yr Daughter of Enoch & Marcy Hinckley S:7

Hinckley, Anna Allyn - Died 1892
Nov 14 Born 1817 Oct 6 Stone
says, "At Rest" S:11

Hinckley, Annie B - Died 1934
Born 1853 Daughter of John &
Rebecca Hinckley (listed on
family stone with them & others)
S:11

Hinckley, Annie Gorham - Died
1944 Born 1881 (with Frank H
Hinckley & others) S:19

Hinckley, Arthur E - Died 1903
Born 1876 (with Alice L Hinckley) S:18

Hinckley, Asa - Died 1835 May 5
Age 2 years, 11 months, 5 days
Son (buried next to Asa &
Hannah Hinckley) S:7

Hinckley, Asa - Died 1848 Oct 16
in his 79th yr S:7

Hinckley, Barnabas - Died 1852
Jan 3 Age 67 years 7 months
(between wifes, Rebecah Hinckley & Sally Gorham) S:11

Hinckley, Beatrice Jey - Died 1977
Born 1894 Wife of George C
Burlingame (with him) S:14

Hinckley, Beihiah - Died 1820 Jan
7 in her 55th yr Wife of Deacon
Silvanus Hinckley S:3

Hinckley, Benjamin - Died 1765
April 15 in his 38th yr S:3

Hinckley, Benjamin - Died 1872
April 10 Age 90 years, 10
months S:10

Hinckley, Benjamin - Died 1888
Sept 16 Born 1814 Dec 29 (next
to Herbert A Hinckley) S:11

Hinckley, Benjamin F - Died 1901
March 13 (?) Age 77 (next to
wife, Emeline Hinckley) S:13

Hinckley, Bennie - Died 1893 Aug
5 Born 1892 Sept 9 (small stone
under tree) Son of William &
Carrie A Hinckley S:19

Hinckley, Bertie - Died (not
clear)(not sure of last name?)
(between Ophelia & Wilfred N
Hinckley) S:21

Hinckley, Bessie Frances - Died
1938 July 18 Born 1867 Feb 18
Wife of Myron (buried with him)

Hinckley (Cont.)
S:8

Hinckley, Bethia(Bethiah?) - Died
1909 Jan 16 Age 83 years, 10
months S:10

Hinckley, Bethiah - Died 1734 (no
location) S:11R

Hinckley, Bethiah - Died 1773 Feb
23 Age 28 Daughter of John &
Bethiah Hinckley (Hinckley
Ceme records #11R say death
was 1775) S:11

Hinckley, Bethiah - Died 1783 Dec
15 Age 1 month Daughter of
John & Lydia Hinckley S:11

Hinckley, Bethiah - Died 1788 Aug
29 in her 64th yr Widow of John
Hinckley S:11R+26R

Hinckley, Bethiah - Died 1813
Sept 15 Age 26 Wife of Benjamin
Hinckley (next to her is a tree
trunk cut off at the ground, but
had managed to grow over a
marker completely, on over side
is another wife of Ben, is it Ben?)
S:10

Hinckley, Bethiah Mrs - Died 1760
March 31 in her 56th yr Wife of
Deacon John Hinckley
S:11R+26R

Hinckley, Bethiah Mrs - Died 1777
located in row 13 S:11R

Hinckley, Bethiea - Died 1715
April 20 Age About 42 (stone is
leaning) (Hinckley Ceme records
#11R say day was the 2nd) S:11

Hinckley, Betiha ? - Died 1909 Jan
16 Age 83 years, 10 months
S:10

Hinckley, Betsey - Died (underground) Daughter of Joshua
Joshua & Betsey Hinckley (next
to mother) S:10

Hinckley, Betsey - Died 1795 Nov
27 Age 5 weeks, 6 days Daughter of Josiah & Desire Hinckley
S:10

Hinckley, Betsey - Died 1811 Aug
7 in her 24th yr Wife of Edmund
Hinckley S:7

Hinckley, Betsey - Died 1830 April
3 Age 47 Widow of Joshua

Hinckley (Cont.)

Hinckley (next to him) S:10

Hinckley, Betsey - Died 1847 Nov 30 Born 1813 Mar 7 Wife of Nathaniel Hinckley (buried next to him) S:7

Hinckley, Betsey - Died 1867 Sept 16 Age 75 years, 8 months, 11 days Wife of Abraham Hinckley S:9R

Hinckley, Betsey B - Died 1855 July 8 Age 32 Died of fatal disease of consumption Wife of Capt Marshall Hinckley (with him) S:21

Hinckley, Betsey H - Died 1866 Aug 9 Age 17 yrs 6 mos Daughter of John & Rebecca Hinckley (with others on family stone) S:11+26R

Hinckley, Betsey S - Died (underground - small stone) Daughter of John & Betsey Hinckley S:10

Hinckley, Betsey S - Died 1915 Jan 11 Born 1840 Dec 27 Wife of Marshall Hinckley (with him) S:21

Hinckley, C Stuart - Died (still living 1991?) Born 1918 (a rock stone) (with John Howland Crocker & Mary Hinckley) S:20

Hinckley, Caroline - Died 1817 Dec 16 Age 21 Wife of Isaac Hinckley (next to him, d1850) S:11

Hinckley, Caroline - Died 1830 Oct 14 Age 27 Wife of Warren Hinckley Jr S:1

Hinckley, Caroline - Died 1835 Sept 29 Age 39 Wife of Eli Hinckley (next to him) S:21

Hinckley, Caroline - Died 1874 Nov 24 Age 65 (buried next to Crocker Hinckley, husband) S:8

Hinckley, Caroline D - Died 1853 Oct 30 Age 23 years, 9 months, 3 days Wife of William Hinckley S:10

Hinckley, Caroline Miss - Died 1819 Sept 15 Age 26 Daughter of Isaac & Nancy Hinckley S:11

Hinckley, Caroline Miss - Died 1849 Sept 15 Age 26 Daughter

Hinckley (Cont.)

of Isaac & Nancy Hinckley S:11R

Hinckley, Caroline S - Died 1902 Born 1829 (with Warren T Hinckley & others) S:18

Hinckley, Catherine - Died 1857 Born 1825 Wife of Kies Doane (with him & Carrie Doane & others) S:18

Hinckley, Charles - Died 1820 Jan 21 Age 23 years, 6 months S:7

Hinckley, Charles - Died 1874 Jan 15 Age 84 years, 11 months (next to wife, Gemimah (Jemimah) Hinckley, d1821) (Hinckley Ceme records #11R say age was 84) S:11+26R

Hinckley, Charles E - Died 1923 Born 1858 S:7

Hinckley, Charles H - Died 1891 Nov 12 Born 1812 June 9 S:11

Hinckley, Charles N Rev - Died 1917 Sept 30 Born 1829 July 2 S:5

Hinckley, Charles W - Died 1898 Born 1837 (with Elizabeth C Baxter & Maurice Carleton Bond) S:18

Hinckley, Charlie - Died 1858 Age 4 or 14 years (not clear) (a cross marker, broken and repaired again) (was called "little Charle") S:21

Hinckley, Chipman - Died 1858 May 7 in his 88th yr (Entire family buried next to each other) S:7

Hinckley, Chloe - Died 1849 Sept 11 Age 87 years, 6 months Widow of Nymphas Hinckley (next to him) S:12

Hinckley, Clarence - Died 1848 Oct 14 Age 11 weeks Son of Marshall & Betsey Hinckley (next to brother, Marshall Hinckley) S:21

Hinckley, Cora B - Died 1924 Born 1830 (with Washburn Hinckley) S:13

Hinckley, Cordelia - Died 1851 April 14 Age 24 years, 2 months, 12 days Daughter of Heman &

Hinckley (Cont.)
Prudence Hinckley (they are two stones away) S:13

Hinckley, Crocker - Died 1885 April 22, Age 84 years, 10 months (next to Caroline Hinckley) S:8

Hinckley, Curtis B - Died 1943 Born 1896 (Rock marker) (with wife, Emily F Hinckley) S:17

Hinckley, Curtis F - Died 1983 Born 1900 (with Virginia M Hinckley) S:13

Hinckley, Date - Died 1810 Oct 29 in her 13th yr Daughter of Levi & Sarah Hinchley S:3

Hinckley, David - Died 1863 April 24 in his 88th yr S:1

Hinckley, David L - Died (still living 1991?) Born 1933 (listed with Ralph David & Helen L Hinckley) S:13

Hinckley, Deborah - Died 1833 April 15 Born 1740 Feb 13 Widow of Jabez Hinckley (next to him) S:11

Hinckley, Deborah E - Died 1870 Sept 23 Age 21 years, 7 months Daughter of Freeman & Mehitable S Hinckley S:11

Hinckley, Desire - Died March (date under the ground) Born 1769 Dec 2 S:10

Hinckley, Desire - Died 1759 June 7 Age 40 "A stillborn child on her arm" Wife of Nathaniel Hinckley S:5R

Hinckley, Desire - Died 1911 Born 1831 (with lothrop Hinckley & others) S:10

Hinckley, Earl W - Died 1926 Born 1899 S:18

Hinckley, Ebenezer - Died 1822 Sept 5 in his 69th yr (Hinckley Ceme records #11R say death was in 1822) S:11+26R

Hinckley, Ebenezer - Died 1751 April 12 in his 66th yr S:11R+ 26R

Hinckley, Ebenezer - Died 1780 June 12 in his 68th yr (next to wife, Mehitable Hinckley) S:11+

Hinckley (Cont.)
26R

Hinckley, Edgar A - Died 1854 Feb 22 Born 1843 Nov 25 Son of Washburn & Cora Hinckley (next to them) S:13

Hinckley, Edmund - Died 1883 (month & day not clear) in his 65th yr S:7

Hinckley, Edmund C - Died 1883 Born 1816 S:7

Hinckley, Edna L - Died 1895 Jan 27 Age 85 years, 28 days (next to Leander Hinckley) S:18

Hinckley, Edward - Died 1771 May 3 Age 3 months, 4 days Son of Samuel & Keziah Hinckley S:11

Hinckley, Edward B Rev - Died 1903 Born 1826 (stone errected in 1898) S:12

Hinckley, Edward Carroll - Died 1932 Born 1866 (with Hope Norris Hinckley & others) S:18

Hinckley, Edward Osman - Died 1873 Dec 2 Born 1852 May 6 Son of Edward B & Ruth F Hinckley (next to brother, George H Hinckley) S:12

Hinckley, Eli - Died 1876 May 29 Age 81 years, 23 days (next to wife, Caroline Hinckley) S:21

Hinckley, Eli T - Died 1844 Sept6 Age 2 years, 5 months Son of Eli & Charlotte M Hinckley (next to Mary Gage Hinckley, his sister) S:21

Hinckley, Elisabeth - Died 1800 May 6 in her 66th yr Wife of Nathaniel Hinckley S:7

Hinckley, Eliza S - Died 1937 Born 1860 (buried with Capt Joseph Hinckley & wife, Julia Cornish) S:8

Hinckley, Elizabeth - Died 1872 Born 1869 (with George G Seabury & others) S:11

Hinckley, Elizabeth - Died 1776 Sept 25 in her 23rd yr Wife of John Hinckley S:11R+26R

Hinckley, Elizabeth - Died 1733 Oct 28 Age 21 Daughter of Joseph Hinckley S:5R

Hinckley, Elizabeth - Died 1767 Feb 11 Age 78 Consort of Isaac Hinckley S:5R

Hinckley, Elizabeth - Died 1776 located in row 15 S:11R

Hinckley, Elizabeth Carter - Died 1928 Jan 21 Born 1848 July 19 Wife of FA Hinckley S:10

Hinckley, Elizabeth R - Died 1849 Sept 20 Age 27 (a large space between stones, many missing markers?) Eldest daughter of Barnabas & Sally Hinckley S:11

Hinckley, Elizabeth S - Died 1963 Born 1887 Wife of Allen S Hinckley (on same stone with Allen Carter Hinckley) S:10

Hinckley, Ella V - Died 1817 July 11 Age 2 months, 11 days (next to Jennie Hinckley Boult) S:12

Hinckley, Emeline - Died 1890 June 27 Age 62 years, 6 months, 23 days Wife of Benjamin F Hinckley (next to him) S:13

Hinckley, Emily F - Died 1986 Born 1900 (Rock marker) Wife of Curtis B Hinckley (with him) S:17

Hinckley, Emma Caroline - Died (no dates) (Widow of Capt Joseph Lewis, same stone Also wife of Rev William R Joyslin, buried there on same stone) S:8

Hinckley, Enoch - Died 1842 Nov 29 in his 92nd yr S:7

Hinckley, Esther - Died 1796 March 22 Age 19 months, 4 days (this may be in error because there is a "Mrs" after her name?) S:11

Hinckley, Esther - Died 1817 Oct 24 in her 64th yr Wife of Ebenezer Hinckley S:11+26R

Hinckley, Eunice - Died 1845 Mar 6 in her 81st yr Widow of Prince Hinckley S:6

Hinckley, Eunice M - Died 1955 Born 1897 (with Harriett M Hinckley & others) S:19

Hinckley, Eunice Mrs - Died 1817 April 17 Age 36 years, 4 months, 25 days Wife to Marshall

Hinckley (Cont.)
Hinckley (next to him) S:12

Hinckley, Eva Bell - Died 1945 Born 1872 (with Ulysses G Hinckley) S:13

Hinckley, Everett H - Died 1932 Born 1875 (with Mary E Hinckley) S:18

Hinckley, Ezra - Died 1849 June 2 at Fort Kearney, Pawnee, Indian Territory Age 32 Son of Isaac & Caroline Hinckley S:11R

Hinckley, Ezra - Died 1809 Nov Age 19 yrs Son of John & Hannah Hinckley S:11+11R

Hinckley, F Howard - Died 1961 Born 1884 (was on the Barnstable Fire Department, their marker is there) S:19

Hinckley, Frank H - Died 1926 Born 1850 (with Harriett M Hinckley & others) S:19

Hinckley, Franklin - Died 1815 June 4 in his 13th yr Son of Levi & Sarah Hinckley S:3+3R

Hinckley, Franklin H - Died 1880 Sept 28 Age 7 months (small stone)(next to Joseph Hinckley) S:13

Hinckley, Fred Lincoln - Died 1895 March 29 Age 4 years, 7 months, 10 days Son of James & Martha E Hinckley (next to brother, Walton Percival Hinckley) S:19

Hinckley, Frederic - Died 1891 Dec 18 Born 1820 Nov 3 S:10

Hinckley, Frederic Allen - Died 1917 Nov 22 Born 1845 July 2 A Unitarian minister of sweetness & light S:10

Hinckley, Frederick - Died 1863 Sept 11 Age 11 years, 11 months, 17 days Son of William & ? Hinckley S:10

Hinckley, Frederick - Died 1891 Dec 18 Born 1820 Nov 3 S:10

Hinckley, Frederick Allen - Died 1917 Nov 22 Born 1845 July 2 A Unitarian minister of sweetness and light S:10

Hinckley, Freeman - Died 1812

Hinckley (Cont.)
Feb 21 in his 19th yr Son of Timothy & Jerusha Hinckley S:7

Hinckley, Freeman - Died 1808 Jan 5 Age 50 S:11

Hinckley, Freeman - Died 1877 Nov 5 Born 1810 Sept 18 Stone says, "Passed to spirit life" S:11

Hinckley, Gemimah Mrs - Died 1821 Dec 28 Age 30 Wife of Charles Hinckley, 1874 (next to him) S:11

Hinckley, George B F (AM) - Died 1888 July 8 Born 1848 Sept 2 Devoted to education of humanity & church (with Sophronia D Hinckley) S:12

Hinckley, George H - Died 1882 Oct 29 Born 1854 Aug 21 Son of Edward B & Ruth F Hinckley (next to brother, Edward O Hinckley) S:12

Hinckley, George H - Died 1891 July 2 Born 1829 Oct 28 (with Lucinda J Hinckley) S:12

Hinckley, George H - Died 1888 July 7 Born 1854 July 23 Son of George BF & Sophronia D Hinckley (his birth date could be an error because his father was born 1848?, but they died 1 day apart, he is next to parents) S:12

Hinckley, George H - Died 1871 Born 1794 (with John York & others in York plot on street) S:13

Hinckley, Georgianna J - Died 1959 Born 1864 (with Charles C Jones & others) S:19

Hinckley, Gertrude - Died 1930 Born 1843 Daughter of John & Rebecca Hinckley (on family stone with others) S:11

Hinckley, Gilbert L - Died 1937 Born 1854 (with Laura L Hinckley) S:21

Hinckley, Gloria A - Died 1904 Mar 22 Born 1818 May 8 Wife of Nelson Bearse, buried next to him S:8

Hinckley, Gustavus - Died 1870 Born 1828 (with Caroline S

Hinckley (Cont.)
Hinckley & others) S:18

Hinckley, Gustavus A - Died 1905 Born 1822 (with Lothrop Hinckley & others) Stone says, "Stone erected in memory of Lothrop John Kennedy & Abby Louisa, Gustavus Adolphus, Josiah, Desire Elizabeth in 1886 Birth, August 15 S:10

Hinckley, Gwen G - Died 1970 Born 1896 (with Leon G Hinckley) S:13

Hinckley, Hannah - Died 1792 located in row 14 S:11R

Hinckley, Hannah - Died (date not listed) Wife of Isaac Hinckley Esq S:5R

Hinckley, Hannah - Died 1779 Dec Age 34 Widow to John Hinckley S:11

Hinckley, Hannah - Died 1782 Apr in her 21st yr Daughter of Nathaniel & Elisabeth Hinckley S:7

Hinckley, Hannah - Died 1883 Oct 29 in her 76th yr Widow of Willard Hinckley S:7

Hinckley, Hannah - Died 1732 July 7 Age 18 Daughter of Joseph Hinckley S:5R

Hinckley, Hannah - Died 1810 Jan 14 Age 3 months, 28 days Daughter of Chipman & Olive Hinckley S:7

Hinckley, Hannah - Died 1879 Dec 22 in her 63rd yr Wife of David Hinckley S:1

Hinckley, Hannah - Died 1805 or 9 Aug 29 (stone worn) Daughter of John & Hannah Hinckley S:11

Hinckley, Hannah - Died 1909 located in row 14 S:11R

Hinckley, Hannah E - Died 1946 Born 1862 S:7

Hinckley, Hannah H - Died 1925 Born 1848 (with Mary Louise Hinckley & others) S:19

Hinckley, Hannah H - Died 1912 June 9 Born 1849 March 26 S:18

Hinckley, Hannah Miss - Died

Hinckley (Cont.)
1802 Aug 29 Age 16 yrs Daughter of John and Hannah Hinkley S:26R

Hinckley, Harriet - Died 1846 Nov 29 Age 17 years, 8 months Daughter of Prince H & Susan Hinckley S:11R

Hinckley, Harriet - Died 1883 Aug 12 Age 64 years, 9 months, 4 days Daughter of Prince & Theodate G Hinckley S:4

Hinckley, Harriet E - Died (no death date listed) Born 1833 Feb 8 (listed with Walton Hinckley) S:14

Hinckley, Harriet P - Died 1913 Dec 29 Born 1849 July 2 S.11

Hinckley, Harriett M - Died 1932 Born 1852 (with F Howard Hinckley & others) S:19

Hinckley, Helen L - Died 1990 Born 1908 (with Ralph David Hinckley & listing of David L Hinckley) S:13

Hinckley, Heman - Died 1874 Aug 2 Age 82 years, 2 months (between both wifes, Abigail & Prudence Hinckley) S:13

Hinckley, Henry - Died 179? located in row 1 S:11R

Hinckley, Henry - Died 1796 March 22 Age 19 months, 4 days Son of Eben & Esther Hinckley S:11R

Hinckley, Herbert A - Died 1882 Nov 4 Born 1848 Oct 6 S:11

Hinckley, Herbert L - Died 1977 Dec 21 Born 1892 Mar 7 S:15

Hinckley, Hope Norris - Died 1936 Born 1869 (with Isabel Carroll Hinckley & others) S:18

Hinckley, Horace C - Died 1862 Oct 7 Age 1 year, 4 month Son of Marshall & Maria B Hinckley (next to them) S:21

Hinckley, Horatio - Died 1842 Sept 7 Age 11 years, 7 months Son of Leander & Edna Hinckley (one stone away from them) S:18

Hinckley, Ira L - Died 1920 Born 1852 (with wife, Mary C

Hinckley (Cont.)
Hinckley) S:12

Hinckley, Isaac - Died 1783 June 8 in his 11th month Son to John and Hannah Hinkley S:26R

Hinckley, Isaac - Died 1828 Sept 30 in his 31st yr Son of Timothy & Jerutia Hinckley S:7

Hinckley, Isaac - Died 1850 Nov 17 Age 58 (next to both wifes, Nancy & Caroline) S:11

Hinckley, Isaac - Died 1762 Aug 22 Age 88 S:5R

Hinckley, Isaac - Died (date worn off) Son of Isaac & Hannah Hinckley S:11

Hinckley, Isaac Esq - Died 1802 Dec 2 in his 83rd yr Place on stone for wife Hannah, but she is not listed as died S:5

Hinckley, Isabel - Died 1880 Oct 28 Age 37 years, 3 months, 4 days Wife of S Alexander Hinckley (with him & Johnnie Hinckley & others) (there are several small stones all around her that are broken off at ground level-children?) S:18

Hinckley, Isabel - Died 1929 Oct 4 Born 1888 Sept 23 Wife of Arthur E Van Bibber (with son Arthur E Van Bibber & others) S:18

Hinckley, Isabel Carroll - Died 1911 Born 1839 (with Edward Carroll Hinckley & others) S:18

Hinckley, Isabella - Died 1862? July 5 Age 27 years, 2 months Wife of S Alexander Hinckley (with him & Isabel Hinckley, his other wife & others) S:18

Hinckley, Isaiah - Died 1781 June 20 in his 2nd yr Son of John & Lydia Hinckley S:11R+26R

Hinckley, Isaiah - Died 1860 Oct 7 Age 93 years, 11 months S:11R

Hinckley, Isaiah - Died 1841 May 2 Age 19 years, 8 months Son of Charles & Jemimah Hinckley (next to mother, d1821) (Hinckley Ceme records #11R say death year was 1841) S:11+26R

Hinckley, Isaiah - Died 1880 Dec 7 Age 93 yrs 11 mos S:11+26R

Hinckley, Jabez - Died 1817 Feb 19 Born 1740 Oct 17 (an American flag in front of stone) (next to wife, Deborah) S:11

Hinckley, James - Died 1821 Oct 14 Born 1820 June 13 Son of Josiah & Mercy C Hinckley (with Lothrop Hinckley & others) S:10

Hinckley, James A - Died 1908 Jan 6 Born 1840 Feb 3 S:11

Hinckley, James F - Died 1861 May 5 Age 26 years, 7 months S:11

Hinckley, James W - Died 1944 Born 1866 (with wife, Martha C Hinckley) S:19

Hinckley, Jemima Mrs - Died 1821 Dec 28 Age 30 Wife of Charles Hinckley S:11R

Hinckley, Jenlima - Died 1842? Mar 12 Age 7 years, 6 months S:12

Hinckley, Jennie (Buroughs?) - Died 1914 Nov 6 Born 1858 May 22 (stone says, "Heart overflowing with love, always brave, cheerful & helpful") (on same stone with Frederick Hinckley) S:10

Hinckley, Jerusha - Died 1824 Nov 6 in her 59th yr Wife of Timothy Hinckley (buried next to him) S:7

Hinckley, John - Died 1835 Oct 1 Age 87 (next to wife, Lydia d1826) S:11

Hinckley, John - Died 1886 Feb 6 Born 1821 Oct 25 S:11R

Hinckley, John - Died 1884 Born 1826 (with Mary Hinckley, wife & others) S:19

Hinckley, John - Died 1775 Mar 17 in his 58th yr (Hinckley Ceme records #11R say death year was 1775) S:11+26R

Hinckley, John - Died 1814 May 12 Age 59 S:11

Hinckley, John - Died 1888 Born 1821 (large family stone with Rebecca Hinckley and others) S:11

Hinckley, John (Deacon) - Died 1765 April 13 in his 65th yr S:11R+26R

Hinckley, John D - Died 1883 Born 1818 (With Olive F Hinckley & others) S:11

Hinckley, John E - Died 1957 Born 1889 (with Marion RF Hinckley 9 S:18

Hinckley, John Howes - Died 1852 Oct 6 Age 6 years Born 1846 Dec 7 Son of Eli & Charlotte Hinckley (next to father) S:21

Hinckley, John K - Died 1902 Born 1818 (with Lothrop Hinckley & others) S:10

Hinckley, Johnnie - Died 1868 May 7 Age 11 Son of S Alexander & Isebella Hinckley (with parents & others) S:18

Hinckley, Joseph - Died (1700's) Aug 29 (stone is in bad shape) S:10

Hinckley, Joseph - Died 1819 Sept 24 Age 17 Son of Asa & Hanna Hinckley S:7

Hinckley, Joseph - Died 29 Aug 17?? (stone in bad shape) S:10

Hinckley, Joseph - Died 1864 March 14 (?) Age 6 months (small stone) (next to Franklin H & Emeline Hinckley) S:13

Hinckley, Joseph - Died 1753 July 4 Age 82 S:5R

Hinckley, Joseph - Died 1746 April 21 Age 12 mos 11 days Son of John & Bethiah Hinckley S:11+26R

Hinckley, Joseph - Died 1746 (one has no location and the other Joseph is in row 13) S:11R

Hinckley, Joseph - Died 185? the 20th Born 1856/8 Jan 15 (stone not clear) Son of Oliver & Elizabeth Hinckley S:11

Hinckley, Joseph C - Died 1859 Feb 20 Born 1858 Jan 15 Infant son of Oliver M and Elizabeth A Hinckley S:26R

Hinckley, Joseph H (Capt) - Died 1911 Born 1829 (buried with Julia A Cornish-wife) S:8

Hinckley, Joseph W - Died 1880 Feb 13 Born 1835 Oct 27 (stone is perpetual care) (with Hannah Nickerson) S:8

Hinckley, Joshua - Died 1829 Feb 22 Age 50 S:10

Hinckley, Josiah - Died 1796 April 8 Born 1794 Aug 28 S:10

Hinckley, Josiah - Died 1794 Aug 28 Born 1796 April 8 S:10

Hinckley, Josiah - Died 1915 Oct 27 Born 1824 April 26 (large Hinckley stone with Gustavus A Hinckley & others) S:11

Hinckley, Josiah - Died 1883 Nov 28 Born 1794 Oct 24 Son of Josiah Hinckley & Desire Lothrop (with Lothrop Hinckley & others) S:10

Hinckley, Julia - Died 1835 Jan 12 Age 4 years, 9 months, 20 days Daughter of Warren & Caroline Hinckley S:1

Hinckley, Julia - Died 1785 Nov 16 Age 1 year, 3 months, 18 days Daughter of Ebenezer & Esther Hinckley S:11R+26R

Hinckley, Katherine E - Died 1961 Born 1877 (next to George BF & Sophronia D Hinckley) S:12

Hinckley, Keziah (Kezia) - Died 1821 Jan 24 in her 85th yr Relect of Capt Samuel Hinckley S:11+26R

Hinckley, Laura L - Died 1912 Born 1856 (with Gilbert L Hinckley) S:21

Hinckley, Leander - Died 1871 Aug 31 Age 61 years,2 months,15 days (next to Edna L Hinckley) S:18

Hinckley, Lena G - Died 1943 Born 1867 Wife of Fred S Parmenter (Next to him) S:11

Hinckley, Leon G - Died 1981 Born 1895 With Gwen G Hinckley Stone says, "OMI US Navy during World War 1 S:13

Hinckley, Letetia J - Died 1877 Aug 26 Born 1846 Dec 23 Eldest child of Lothrop & Mercy L Hinckley S:11

Hinckley, Levi - Died 1830 Jan 31 in his 66th yr S:3

Hinckley, Lizzie Davis - Died 1863 May 30 Age 1 year, 4 months, 25 days (A small childs stone) Daughter of Otis & Mary Hinckley (next to them) S:19

Hinckley, Lot - Died 1796 Sept 1 Age 12 Son of Nymphas & Chloe Hinckley S:12

Hinckley, Lot - Died 1839 Oct 8 Born 1838 Dec 24 Infant son of Oliver M & Elizabeth A Hinckley S:11

Hinckley, Lot - Died 1852 Sept 2 Age 70 years, 6 months, 14 days (next to wife, Rebecca Hinckley d1871) S:11+26R

Hinckley, Lot - Died 1859 (not sure if Lot d 1839 is the same) S:11R

Hinckley, Lot - Died 1886 Jan 5 Born 1797 Oct 26 (stone says, "Father" Next to Rachel Hinckley) S:12

Hinckley, Lot C - Died 1835 Oct 13 in his 22nd yr Son of Lot & Rebecca Hinckley S:11+26R

Hinckley, Lothrop - Died 1888 Sept 23 Born 1816 June 6 S:11

Hinckley, Lottie W - Died 1864 June 2 Age 20 years, 5 months ? Daughter of Prince & Susan Hinckley (Hinckley Ceme records #11R say death was 1861 age 20 years 9 months) S:11+26R

Hinckley, Louisa - Died 1881 Aug 20 Age 82 years, 10 months Wife of Oliver Hinckley (next to him) S:12

Hinckley, Lucinda J - Died 1905 Nov 2 Born 1826 Nov 8 (with George H Hinckley) S:12

Hinckley, Lucy - Died 1847, 23rd Born 1846 July 30 (stone not clear) Infant dau of Oliver M & Elizabeth A Hinckley (between brothers, Lot & Joseph) S:11

Hinckley, Lucy - Died 1845 June 1 in her 72nd yr Widow of Timothy Hinckley S:7

Hinckley, Lucy - Died 1818 July 24 (stone not clear) Dau of Adino

Hinckley (Cont.)
& Elizabeth Hinckley S:10+26R

Hinckley, Lucy Mrs - Died 1808
Jan 13 in her 22nd yr Wife of
Barnabas Hinckley S:11R+26R

Hinckley, Luther - Died 1833 Apr
21 Age 92 years, 11 months, 2
days Born 1789 May 13 (age?)
May 19 (buried next to wife,
Thankful a Hinckley) S:7

Hinckley, Lydia - Died 1826 Oct 1
in her 68th yr Wife of John
Hinckley, d1835 (next to him)
S:11+26R

Hinckley, Lydia A - Died 1909
March 18 Age 71 years, 1 month
Wife of William Hinckley (next to
him) S:10

Hinckley, Lydia C - Died 1910 July
28 Age 79 years, 4 months, 9
days S:7

Hinckley, M - Died 1839 (a large
crypt metal door & look on
street-Rt 6A) S:11

Hinckley, Mabel Ellis - Died 1891
Jan 3 Born 1873 Oct 20 Daughter of F A & E C Hinckley S:10

Hinckley, Mallie G - Died 1942
Born 1865 Wife of George G
Hinckley (with him) S:11

Hinckley, Marcy Miss - Died 1820
April 2 Age 71 S:10

Hinckley, Margaret A - Died 1930
Dec 6 Age 59 (next to Walton
Percival Hinckley) S:19

Hinckley, Margaret A - Died 1863
Sept 16 Age 65 Wife of Thomas T
Hinckley S:10

Hinckley, Maria - Died 1825 Dec 9
Age 28 days Daughter of Prince
& Theodate Hinckley S:4

Hinckley, Maria B - Died 1868 Nov
18 Age 39 years, 1 month, 16
days Wife of Marshall Hinckley
(with him) S:21

Hinckley, Marion RF - Died 1967
Born 1897 (with John E Hinckley) S:18

Hinckley, Marshall - Died 1898
April 1 Born 1818 Dec 18 (with
wives, Maria B & Betsey S &
Betsey B Hinckley) S:21

Hinckley, Marshall - Died 1846
Sept 27 Age 66 years, 4 months,
25 days S:12+12R

Hinckley, Marshall - Died 1851
Nov 1 Age 2 years, 2 months Son
of Marshall & Betsey Hinckley
(next to brother, Horace C
Hinckley) S:21

Hinckley, Marshall B - Died 1942
Born 1871 (with Flora B Drew,
his wife) S:18

Hinckley, Martha C - Died 1908
April 9 Born 1870 Oct 6 Wife of
James W Hinckley (with him)
S:19

Hinckley, Mary - Died 1825 Feb 5
in her 89th yr Widow of Timothy
Hinckley (buried next to him) S:7

Hinckley, Mary - Died (still living
1991?) Born 1914 (with C Stuart
Hinckley & John Howland
Crocker) S:20

Hinckley, Mary - Died 1738 Jan 4
in her 88th yr Wife of Samuel
Hinckley S:5

Hinckley, Mary - Died 1748 Oct 23
Age 69 Consort of Capt Joseph
S:5R

Hinckley, Mary - Died 1793 April
21 Wife of Adino Hinckley
(buried next to him) S:10

Hinckley, Mary - Died 1802 July
29 in her 38th yr Wife of Silvanus Hinckley S:3+3R

Hinckley, Mary - Died 1813? located in row 1 S:11R

Hinckley, Mary - Died 1924 Born
1908 (next to Mona B & Albert L
Hinckley) S:12

Hinckley, Mary - Died 1907 Born
1824 Wife of John Hinckley
(with him & Hannah H Hinckley
& others) S:19

Hinckley, Mary C - Died 1925 Born
1854 Wife of Ira L Hinckley (with
him) S:12

Hinckley, Mary E - Died 1938 Born
1876 (with Everett H Hinckley)
S:18

Hinckley, Mary E - Died 1951 Born
1868 Wife of Wilfred Hinckley
(with him) S:21

Hinckley, Mary F - Died 1881 Jan 25 Age 35 Wife of Alexander C Hinckley (next to Arthur E Hinckley) S:18

Hinckley, Mary Gage - Died 1862 Oct 21 Age 17 years, 8 months Daughter of Eli & Charlotte M Hinckley (next to sister, Mary Gage Hinckley, d1834) S:21

Hinckley, Mary Gage - Died 1834 July 2 Age 1 year, 10 months, 12 days Daughter of Eli & Caroline Hinckley (next to sister, Mary Gage Hinckley, d1862) S:21

Hinckley, Mary (Glove or Glow?) - Died 1703 July 29 in her 73rd yr "Here lyth ye body of the truly virtuous and praiseworthy Mrs Mary Hinckley, wife to Mr Thomas Hinckley" Noted that she was 2nd wife of Gov Thomas Hinckley (Record says that information was "gathered from said stone by Capt Mathias Hinckley after the storm of a century and a half had sent it in pieces") S:28R

Hinckley, Mary Idella - Died 1860 Dec 24 Age 11 years, 7 months, 18 days Daughter of Ira & Hannah Hinckley S:12

Hinckley, Mary L - Died 1903 Dec 20 Born 1883 Sept 12 Daughter of Ira & Mary C Hinckley (with them) S:12

Hinckley, Mary Louise - Died 1943 Born 1879 (with Annie Gorham Hinckley & others) S:19

Hinckley, Mary Miss - Died 1809 Aug 9 Age 48 S:11

Hinckley, Mary Miss - Died 1820 April 2 in her 71st yr S:26R

Hinckley, Mary Mrs - Died 1799 (stone not clear) Consort of William Hinckley (buried next to him) (Hinckley Ceme records #11R say death was Aug 11 in her 34th yr) S:11+26R

Hinckley, Mary O - Died 1807 May 22 Age 3 years, 9 months Daughter of Robinson T and

Hinckley (Cont.)
Alice Hinckley (Hinckley Cemetery records #11R say death was 1802 Jan 22 in her 4th yr) S:11+26R

Hinckley, Mary S - Died 1862 March 6 Age 33 years, 4 months, 4 days (stone worn & cracked) Wife of Thacher Hinckley (next to him) S:21

Hinckley, Mehetable - Died 1788 Aug 20 Age 64 Wife of John Hinckley (next to him, d1773) S:11

Hinckley, Mehitable Mrs - Died 1773 Nov 14 Age 50 Wife of Ebenezer Hinckley (next to him) (Hinckley Ceme records #11R says death was 1773) S:11+26R

Hinckley, Mehitable S - Died 1873 April 15 Age 57 years, 10 months Wife of Freeman Hinckley (next to him) S:11

Hinckley, Mercy - Died 1835 Mar 18 in her 78th yr Wife of Enoch Hinckley S:7

Hinckley, Mercy B - Died 1852 Feb 24 Age 63 years, 2 months, 11 days Wife of Isaiah Hinckley (Buried next to him) S:11

Hinckley, Mercy Mrs - Died 1793 Feb 19 in her 59th yr Wife of Adino (next to him) (Hinckley Ceme records #11R says death was 1793 Feb 19) S:11+26R

Hinckley, Mercy O - Died 1807 May 22 Age 3 years, 9 months Daughter of Robinson T & Alice Hinckley S:11R

Hinckley, Mercy O - Died 1879 Feb 22 Age 69 years, 1 month (with Rachel G Hinckley) S:11

Hinckley, Minerva W - Died 1847 Mar 9 Age 51 years, 2 months, 27 days Wife of Luther Hinckley S:7

Hinckley, Minerva, Frances - Died 1840 Feb 19 Age 4 years, 6 months, 23 Daughter of Luther & Minerva Hinckley S:7

Hinckley, Minnie Niles - Died 1938 Born 1863 Possible wife of Allen

Hinckley (Cont.)

Hinckley (buried next to him) S:8

Hinckley, Mona B - Died 1971 Born 1888 (with Albert L Hinckley) S:12

Hinckley, Myra B - Died 1945 Born 1858 Daughter of John & Rebecca Hinckley (listed with them on large family stone & others) S:11

Hinckley, Myron Lewis - Died 1922 Dec 19 Born 1863 May 22 (buried with Bessie Frances Hinckley, wife) S:8

Hinckley, Nancy - Died 1853 April 20 Age 23 years, 7 months (stone flat on ground) Dau of Isaac & Nancy Hinckley (next to Thomas Hinckley d16 Feb) S:11·

Hinckley, Nancy - Died 1922 Born 1841? (stone badly worn) (located between Helen Crowell & Martha Bearse) S:18

Hinckley, Nancy Mrs - Died 1849 April 2 Age 54 Wife of Isaac Hinckley (next to him, d1850) S:11

Hinckley, Nathan - Died 1857 June Born 1773 Dec S:7

Hinckley, Nathaniel - Died 1779 April 27 Age 77 S:5R

Hinckley, Nathaniel - Died 18?? Sept 13 Age 69 (entire family buried next to each other) S:7

Hinckley, Nathaniel - Died 1894 Apr 11 Born 1806 May 28 Wife was Betsey (buried next to him) S:7

Hinckley, Nymphas - Died 1832 Dec 12 Age 80 S:12

Hinckley, Nymphas - Died 1804 July 23 Age 18 Son of Nymphas & Chloe Hinckley S:12

Hinckley, Olive - Died 1865 April 3 in her 62nd yr S:1

Hinckley, Olive - Died 1817 Dec 8 Age 33 years, 9 months, 3 days Wife of Chipman Hinckley & Daughter of Jabez & Temperance Nye of Sandwich, Massachusetts S:7

Hinckley, Olive - Died 1869 Nov 15

Hinckley (Cont.)

Age 46 Wife of Timothy Hinckley & dau of Chipman & Abagail Hinckley S:7

Hinckley, Olive F - Died 1823? Born 1811 (on large Hinckley & Hudson stone) S:11

Hinckley, Olive F - Died 1929 Born 1841 (with John D Hinckley & others) S:11

Hinckley, Oliver - Died 1888 Oct 5 Age 96 years, 6 months S:12

Hinckley, Oliver P - Died 1840 Mar 20 or 30 Age 18 years, 10 months, 22 days S:12+12R

Hinckley, Ophelia - Died 1937 Born 1845 (next to Bertie Hinckley?) S:21

Hinckley, Orville - Died 1874 May 6 Age 34 Son of Nathaniel & Betsey Hinckley S:7

Hinckley, Otis - Died 1874 May 16 Age 41 years, 4 months, 11 days (next to wife, Mary Freeman Davis & daughter, Lizzie Davis Hinckley) S:19

Hinckley, Patricia L - Died 1898 Born 1916 Was Capt in US Army during World War II (next to William C Hinckley Was he the Capt???) S:11

Hinckley, Patty - Died 1819 Sept 27 Age 9 years Daughter of Asa & Susanna Hinckley S:7

Hinckley, Polly - Died 1883 Born 1799 (with Gustavus Hinckley & others) S:18

Hinckley, Polly - Died 1819 Oct 10 Age 21 Daughter of Asa & Susanna Hinckley S:7

Hinckley, Polly - Died 1830 Oct 5 in her 40th yr Wife of Luther Hinckley & daughter of Winslow & Elizabeth Marstons S:7

Hinckley, Polly - Died 1848 Sept 20 Age 57 years, 5 months, 28 days Wife of Alvin Hinckley S:7

Hinckley, Prince - Died 1849 Jan 16 Age 58 years, 9 months S:4

Hinckley, Prince - Died 1844 Nov 30 in his 85th yr S:6

Hinckley, Prince - Died 1862 Mar

Hinckley (Cont.)
20 Age 61 yrs 3 mos S:11+26R

Hinckley, Prince L - Died 1853 June 27 in his 24th yr S:4

Hinckley, Prudence - Died 1855 Nov 28 Age 63 years, 9 months, 10 days Wife of Heman Hinckley (next to him) S:13

Hinckley, Puell A - Died 1885 Born 1801 Wife of George H Hinckley (with him in York plot on street) S:13

Hinckley, Rachel - Died 1880 Mar 26 Born 1809 Jan 31 (stone says, "Mother" Next to Lot Hinckley) S:12

Hinckley, Rachel G - Died 1870 Mar 30 Age 63 yrs 3 mos (with Mercy O Hinckley) (Hinckley Ceme records #11R says death was 1870) S:11+26R

Hinckley, Ralph David - Died 1986 Born 1905 (with Helen L Hinckley) S:13

Hinckley, Rankine? - Died 1845 March 5 (stone down & worn) Son of ? (cannot read) S:21

Hinckley, Rebecah - Died 1813 Mar 30 in her 27th yr Wife of Barnabas Hinckley (next to him) S:11+26R

Hinckley, Rebecca - Died 1878 Feb 22 Age 89 Wife of Benjamin Hinckley S:10

Hinckley, Rebecca - Died 1825 (no location) S:11R

Hinckley, Rebecca - Died 1921 Born 1844 (on same stone with, Sarah T Hinckley) S:11

Hinckley, Rebecca - Died 1963 Born 1888 (listed on large family stone with John & Rebecca Hinckley & others) S:11

Hinckley, Rebecca - Died 1826 Nov 23 in her 22nd yr (stone badly overgrown with moss) Wife of Solomon Hinckley S:10+26R

Hinckley, Rebecca - Died 1890 Born 1823 April 27 Wife of John Hinckley (large family stone with Betsey H Hinckley & others) S:11

Hinckley, Rebecca C - Died 1850 Nov 5 Age 18 years, 10 months Daughter of Prince & Susan Hinckley S:11

Hinckley, Rebecca E - Died 1823 Sept 4 Age 18 Daughter of Ebenezer C & Delia Hinckley of Carmel, Maine (located at Lothrop's Hill) S:26R

Hinckley, Rebecca H - Died 1876 Born 1851 Daughter of John & Rebeeca Hinckley (on family stone with others) S:11

Hinckley, Rebecca Mrs - Died 1871 Dec 26 Age 86 years, 6 months Widow of Lot Hinckley S:11

Hinckley, Rebeckah - Died 1837 July 20 in her 29th yr Wife of Joseph Hinckley S:2

Hinckley, Rebekah - Died 1823 Sept 4 Age 18 Daughter of Ebenezer & Della Hinckley Della was from Carmel, Maine (Hinckley Ceme records #11R says death year was 1823) S:11

Hinckley, Rebh?ah ? - Died 1813 March 30 Wife of Barnabas Hinckley (buried next to him) S:11

Hinckley, Reliance - Died 1777 April 13 in her 9th yr Daughter of Silvanus & Sarah Hinckley S:3

Hinckley, Reliance Miss - Died 1836 Nov 26 in her 52nd yr Daughter of Prince & Eunice Hinckley S:6

Hinckley, Rennie - Died 1967 May 25 Born 1914 May 20 Was in Massachusetts Cap 96th Infantry during World War II S:12

Hinckley, Robinson T Mr - Died 1857 May 5 in his 83rd yr S:11 +26R

Hinckley, Ruhanah A - Died 1828 Oct 29 Age 1 year, 5 months Daughter of Benjamin & Rebecca Hinckley S:10

Hinckley, Ruhanah Mrs - Died 1822 June 30 Age 33 Wife of Benjamin Hinckley (next to overgrown marker by tree trunk,

Hinckley (Cont.)
    is it Ben?) S:10
Hinckley, Russell - Died 1817
    June 4 Age 4 years, 2 months
    Son of Chipman & Olive Hinck-
    ley S:7
Hinckley, Ruth F - Died 1882 Nov
    16 Born 1825 Nov 8 Wife of
    Edward F hinckley (next to sons,
    Edward O & George H) S:12
Hinckley, S Alexander - Died Oct
    (stone broken in half at this
    point, cannot read year) Age 69
    years, 3 months (with wife, Ora
    Adams & others) S:18
Hinckley, Sally - Died 1870 Apl 8
    Widow of Eben G Hinckley S:4
Hinckley, Sally F - Died 1869 Oct
    24 Age 59 years, 2 months Wife
    of Solomon Hinckley (next to
    him) S:19
Hinckley, Salone N - Died 1877
    Feb 11 Age 79 years, 8 months
    Wife of Charles Hinckley, d1874
    S:11
Hinckley, Samuel - Died (no date
    but located in row 4) S:11R
Hinckley, Samuel - Died 1798 Sept
    19 Son of William & Mary Hinck-
    ley S:11
Hinckley, Samuel - Died 1838 Mar
    31 in his 60th yr S:7
Hinckley, Samuel - Died 1777 Feb
    21 Son of Nathaniel & Elisabeth
    Hinckley S:7
Hinckley, Samuel - Died 1727 Jan
    2 Age 85 S:5R
Hinckley, Samuel - Died 1733 Oct
    14 Age 28 S:5R
Hinckley, Samuel - Died 1771 July
    3 Son of Samuel & Keziah
    Hinckley (Hinckley Ceme records
    #11R says age was 5 months)
    S:11
Hinckley, Samuel (Capt) - Died
    1804 Aug 24 in his 77th yr S:11
Hinckley, Sarah - Died 1802 Nov
    14 in her 81st yr Widow of
    Edmund (she is buried next to a
    Edmund but he died 1883?
    possible son?) S:7
Hinckley, Sarah - Died 1848 Apr

Hinckley (Cont.)
    11 in her 67th yr Wife of
    Zaccheus Hinckley S:7
Hinckley, Sarah - Died 1805 Feb
    23 in her 33rd yr Wife of Levi
    Hinckley S:3
Hinckley, Sarah - Died (dates not
    clear) Wife of Ebenezer Hinckley
    (Hinckley Ceme records #11R
    says death was 1737 March 21
    in her 47th yr) S:11+26R
Hinckley, Sarah - Died (stone
    down, worn & broken) Daughter
    of Prince & Susan Hinckley S:11
Hinckley, Sarah - Died 1814 June
    30 in her 83rd yr Husband or
    father of Silvanus Hinckley
    Stone has noted on it "Relict"
    S:3+3R
Hinckley, Sarah A - Died 1890 Aug
    14 Born 1823 Dec 12 (with
    Frederick Hinckley) S:10
Hinckley, Sarah T - Died 1931
    Born 1854 (on same stone with
    Rebecca Hinckley, d1921) S:11
Hinckley, Seth - Died 1887 Feb 12
    in his 80th yr S:6
Hinckley, Silvanus - Died 1799
    June 28 in his 71st yr S:3
Hinckley, Silvanus (Deacon) - Died
    1841 Aug 1 in his 85th yr S:3
Hinckley, Silvia - Died 1820 Sept
    20 in her 75th yr Widow of
    Alpheus Hinckley S:7
Hinckley, Solomen - Died 1877
    located in row 18 or 19? S:11R
Hinckley, Solomon - Died 1885
    Jan 27 Age 81 or 87? (stone
    broken in half) (next to wife,
    Sally F Hinckley) S:19
Hinckley, Sophia - Died 1879 Born
    1842 (with Godfrey Small &
    Eliza Scudder) S:13
Hinckley, Sophronia D - Died 1922
    Born 1852 Stone says,"Veritas"
    (with George BF Hinckley AM)
    S:12
Hinckley, Susan - Died 1879 Jan
    12 Age 78 years, 5 months Wife
    of Prince Hinckley (next to him)
    S:11
Hinckley, Susanna - Died 1850

Hinckley (Cont.)

Apr 25 in her 81st yr Widow of Asa Hinckley (buried next to him) S:7

Hinckley, Susanna - Died 1700's (stone in very poor condition) S:11

Hinckley, Susanna - Died 1790 Sept 26 Age 27, 5 months, 23 days Daughter of Capt Samuel & Kezia Hinckley S:11

Hinckley, Susanna Mrs - Died 1801 ? 9th (stone worn badly) (next to Mrs Sarah Hynckly) (Hinckley Ceme records #11R says death was in July at age 81) S:11+26R

Hinckley, Susannah - Died 1806 or 01 Sept 18 Age 4 years, 9 months, 3 days Daughter of Levi & Sarah Hinckley S:3+3R

Hinckley, Susannah - Died 1810 Feb 25 in her 18th yr Daughter of William & Mary Hinckley S:11+26R

Hinckley, Susannah - Died 1822 April 25 Age 15 Daughter of Levi and Marcy Hinckley S:3R

Hinckley, Sylvanus - Died 1799 June 28 in his 79th yr (next to wife, Sarah) S:3R

Hinckley, Sylvanus Alexander - Died 1828 Nov 27 Age 7 years, 4 months, 10 days Son of Eli & Caroline Hinckley S:4

Hinckley, Temperance - Died 1872 Born 1805 (with Walter F Hinckley & others) S:18

Hinckley, Temperance - Died 1835 April 22 in her 29th yr Daughter of Deacon Silvanus & Bethiah Hinckley S:3+3R

Hinckley, Temperance - Died 1776 located in row 4 S:11R

Hinckley, Temperance - Died 1766 Aug 3 Age 1 year, 5 months (stone worn) Daughter of Samuel & Keziah Hinckley (a little stone, worn next to her, cannot read) S:11+26R

Hinckley, Thacher - Died 1873 March 10 Age 62 (next to wives,

Hinckley (Cont.)

Mary S & Abba S Hinckley) S:21

Hinckley, Thankful - Died 1816 Oct 30 Age 58 Widow of John Hinckley (next to him, d1814) S:11

Hinckley, Thankful - Died 1765 Dec 12 Wife of Ebenezer Hinckley (Hinckley Ceme records #11R says death was 1763 Dec 13 in her 78th yr) S:11+26R

Hinckley, Thankful - Died 1767 located in row 3 S:11R

Hinckley, Thankful A - Died 1881 Nov 8 Age 59 years, 10 months, 28 days Wife of Luther Hinckley S:7

Hinckley, Thankful G - Died 1844 Oct 4 Age 17 years, 4 months Daughter of Eli & Caroline Hinckley (next to Eli T Hinckley her brother) S:21

Hinckley, Thankful H - Died 1882 Born 1807 (on large Hudson & Hinckley stone) S:11

Hinckley, Theadore - Died ?? June 18 (year not clear) in his 24th yr S:12R

Hinckley, Theodate - Died 1896 Feb 12 Age 75 years, 11 months, 15 days Daughter of Prince & Theodate Hinckley S:4

Hinckley, Theodate G - Died 1856 Dec 1 Age 58 years, 3 months Wife of Prince Hinckley S:4

Hinckley, Thomas - Died 1706 Age 85 Flat coffin stone above ground, erected 1829 Elected to Gov of Plymouth Colony 1658-1681 & to Governor by Sir Edmund Andros 1681 to Junction Plymouth w/Mass in 1692 S:11

Hinckley, Thomas - Died 1776 April 10 in his 59th yr S:26R

Hinckley, Thomas - Died 1857 Feb 16 Age 29 yrs 4 mos (stone broken and flat on ground) Son of Isaac & Nancy Hinckley (Hinckley Ceme records #11R say death was 1857 age 29 years, 4 months) S:11+26R

Hinckley, Thomas H - Died 1823 Feb 15 Age 2 years,5 months,4 days Son of Barnabas & Sally Hinckley S:11

Hinckley, Timothy - Died 1839 Dec 31 in is 72nd yr (buried next to wife, Jersuha Hinckley) S:7

Hinckley, Timothy - Died 1814 Mar 1 in his 76th yr S:7

Hinckley, Tryphosa F - Died 1919 Born 1827 S:7

Hinckley, Turner - Died 1889 Born 1805 (on large Hudson & Hinckley) S:11

Hinckley, Ulysses G - Died 1934 Born 1866 (with Eva Bell Hinckley) S:13

Hinckley, Vicky - Died 1817 located in row 11 S:11R

Hinckley, Vicy - Died 1862 June 3 Born 1785 Dec 5 Daughter of Jabez & Deborah Hinckley Plaque in front of stone of the Daughters of the American Revolution S:11+26R

Hinckley, Virginia M - Died 1982 Born 1907 Wife of Curtis F Hinckley (with him) S:13

Hinckley, Walter F - Died 1855 Born 1834 (with Franklin Crocker & others) S:18

Hinckley, Walton - Died (still living 1991?) Born 1910 (listed with Albert M Hinckley) S:13

Hinckley, Walton - Died 1911 Feb 18 Born 1830 Oct 8 (with Harriet E Hinckley) S:14

Hinckley, Walton Percival - Died 1899 May 27 Age 28 days Son of James & Martha E Hinckley (next to brother, Fred Lincoln Hinckley & Margaret A Hinckley) S:19

Hinckley, Warren - Died 1877 Born 1805 (with Temperance Hinckley & others) S:18

Hinckley, Warren T - Died 1875 Born 1869 (with Polly Hinckley & others) S:18

Hinckley, Washburn - Died 1909 Born 1829 (with Cora B Hinckley) S:13

Hinckley, Wendell Lewis - Died 1919 Born 1832 (with Isabel Carroll Hinckley & others) S:18

Hinckley, Wilfred N - Died 1926 Born 1870 (with wife, Mary E Hinckley) S:21

Hinckley, Willard - Died 1858 Nov 5 Age 54 years, 2 months S:7

Hinckley, William - Died 1881 Sept 1 Age 65 years, 9 months, 23 days S:10

Hinckley, William C - Died 1986 Born 1908 (next to Patricia L Hinckley) S:11

Hinckley, William Esq - Died 1801 Aug 17 Age 42 S:11R

Hinckley, William Esq - Died (stone broken and not clear Located between wife, Mary and son Samuel Hinckley) S:11

Hinckley, Willis T - Died 1848 Aug 4 Born 1847 Dec 17 Son of Thacher & Abba Hinckley (next to them) S:21

Hinckley, Zaccheus - Died 1857 Feb 12 in his 79th yr S:7

Hinckley, Zenas - Died 1803 Feb 26 Age 15 Son of Timothy & Jerusha Hinckley S:7

Hinckley, Zenas - Died 1873 Jan 27 Age 69 years, 6 months, 5 days (buried next to wife, Abigail) S:7

Hincks?, Doris N - Died 1974 Born 1897 (With Frank C Hincks?) S:20

Hincks?, Frank C - Died (still living 1991?) Born 1905 (with Doris H Hincks?) S:20

Hincks?, Linda Ann - Died 1955 Born 1953 (next to Frank C Hincks?) S:20

Hinds, Deborah F P - Died 1841 April 8 Age 19 years, 11 months Wife of Ambrose Hinds & only child to James F & Mira C Prentier S:11

Hinds, Hilbertha B - Died 1977 Born 1895 (with Hilton D Hinds) S:15

Hinds, Hilton D - Died 1967 Born 1888 (with Hilbertha B Hinds)

Hinds (Cont.)
S:15

Hines, Frances F - Died 1981 Born 1900 (with Francis J Hines) S:16

Hines, Frances J - Died 1969 Born 1902 (with Frances F Hines) S:16

Hines, John - Died 1889 Aug 23 Age 55 (next to wife, Mary A Hines) S:31

Hines, Mary A - Died 1909 Sept 11 Age 64 Wife of John Hines (next to him) S:31

Hinkle, George Allen - Died 1971 Born 1887 (with wife, Mary Agnes Hinkle) S:16

Hinkle, Mary Agnes - Died 1975 Born 1892 (with husband George Allen Hinkle) S:16

Hinkley, Desire - Died 1759 June 7 Note on stone: A still born child on her arm who died Wife of Nathan Hinkley (buried next to him) S:5

Hinkley, Eliz - Died 1733 Oct 28 in her 21st yr Daughter of Joseph & Mary Hinkley S:5

Hinkley, Elizabeth - Died 1763 Feb 11 in her 78th yr Consort to Isaac Hinkley S:5

Hinkley, Hannah - Died 1732 July 17 in her 18th yr Daughter of Joseph & Mary Hinkley S:5

Hinkley, Isaac - Died 1762 Aug 22 in his 88th yr S:5

Hinkley, Joseph - Died 1753, July 4 in his 82nd yr S:5

Hinkley, Mary - Died (date not clear) Consort & Wife of Capt Joseph (buried next to her) S:5

Hinkley, Nathan - Died 1779 Apr 27 in his 77th yr S:5

Hinkley, Samuel - Died 1727 Jan 2 in his 85th yr S:5

Hinkley, Samuel - Died 1733 Oct 14 in his 28th yr S:5

Hinkley, Susannah - Died 1822 April 25 in her 15th yr Daughter of Levi & Mercy Hinkley S:3

Hirsch, Hannah - Died 1876 Feb 28 in her 86th yr S:4

Hirsch, Sally - Died 1859 Sept 22

Hirsch (Cont.)
Age 75 years, 1 month, 6 days S:4

Hoaglund, Ingrid J - Died (still living 1991?) Born 1922 (listed with Robert G Hoaglund) S:19

Hoaglund, Robert G - Died 1980 Born 1908 (with Ingrid J Hoaglund) S:19

Hobbs, G Ward - Died 1984 Sept 24 Born 1908 Aug 6 Was a Col in US Air Force during World War II S:11

Hobson, Ellen M - Died 1967 Born 1879 (with Ezra Hobson) S:14

Hobson, Esther L - Died 1967 Born 1894 Wife of Earl W Landers (with him) S:14

Hobson, Ezra P - Died 1933 Born 1860 (with wife, Rosa J Childs) S:14

Hobson, Gladys Lovejoy - Died 1981 Born 1904 S:11

Hobson, Leslie P - Died 1934 Born 1884 (with Ezra Hobson) S:14

Hobson, Sophia C - Died 1911 Born 1886 (with Ezra Hobson) S:14

Hochberg, Sheila B - Died 1990 Born 1900 (Jewish section) S:15

Hochhauser, Frieda Green Field - Died 1983 Born 1898 (Jewish section) S:15

Hodge, Jehiel P - Died 1906 Born 1827 (DeWitt stone, one side DeWitt, other Hodges) (with Elizabeth F Hodges) S:12

Hodges, Annie A - Died 1950 Born 1860 (with Frank W Hodges) S:12

Hodges, Benjamin - Died 1807 Feb 27 Age 6 weeks Son of Haa??? & Lydia Hodges (with Joseph Hodges) S:12

Hodges, Eliza J - Died 1898 Born 1848 (with Henry Hodges) S:14

Hodges, Elizabeth F - Died 1911 Born 1829 (on Hodges stone, other side DeWitt) (with Jehiel P Hodges) S:12

Hodges, Eunice Agnes - Died 1990 Born 1889 (with Henry Hodges)

Hodges (Cont.)
S:14

Hodges, Florence M - Died 1948 Born 1884 (with William P Hodges) S:12

Hodges, Frank W - Died 1915 Born 1852 (with Annie A Hodges) S:12

Hodges, Frederick A - Died 1839 Born 1837 (with Isaac & Hannah Hodges & others) S:12

Hodges, Frederick A - Died 1848 Born 1841 (listed with Isaac & Hannah Hodges & others) S:12

Hodges, Hannah - Died 1859 Born 1801 (with Isaac Hodges & others) S:12

Hodges, Henry M - Died 1921 Born 1835 Was in Company N, 49th Massachusetts Volunteers (with Eliza J Hodges) S:14

Hodges, Isaac - Died 1879 Born 1796 (with Hannah Hodges & others) S:12

Hodges, Isaac Jr - Died 1861 Nov 17 Age 26 years, 6 months S:12

Hodges, Isaac S - Died 1834 Born 1830 (listed with Isaac & Hannah Hodges & others) S:12

Hodges, Joseph - Died 1807 Jan 20 Son of Haa?? & Lydia Hodges (with Benjamin Hodges) S:12

Hodges, Joseph P - Died 1825 Born 1823 (listed with Isaac & Hannah Hodges & others) S:12

Hodges, Judson - Died (dates not there) Son of Cromwell & Rosa P Hodges (next to mother) S:12

Hodges, Rosa P - Died 1921 Born 1859 Wife of Cromwell Hodges S:12

Hodges, Sarah A - Died 1886 April 5 Born 1807 Dec 22 (next to Henry M Hodges) S:14

Hodges, Susan - Died 1901 Born 1809 (listed with Isaac & Hannah Hodges & others) S:12

Hodges, William P - Died 1950 Born 1884 (with Florence M Hodges) S:12

Hodgkins, Elizabeth W - Died 1985 Born 1896 (with Vinton Hodgkins Sr) S:18

Hodgkins, Vinton T Sr - Died 1969 Born 1897 (he was a Mason) (with Elizabeth W Hodgkins) S:18

Hogan, Sarah E - Died 1953 Born 1886 (with Thomas A Hogan) S:16

Hogan, Thomas A - Died 1963 Born 1878 (with Sarah E Hogan) S:16

Holbrook, Hannah - Died (dates worn off) Relict of Joseph Green S:11

Holbrook, Hannah - Died 1805 located in row 10 (could be same as Hannah with dates worn off) S:11R

Holbrook, Hannah Mrs - Died 1803 Jan 29 Age 72 Widow of Ezekiel Holbrook & relict of the late Rev Joseph Green Jr S:11R

Holbrook, Naaman Mr - Died 1784 Age 25 (very small stone) S:10+ 26R

Holden, Agnes C - Died 1988 Born 1900 (with Richard Holden) S:15

Holden, Bertha A - Died 1982 Born 1897 (with Edith & Earl Holden) S:18

Holden, Earl E - Died 1949 Born 1883 (with wife, Edith & Bertha Holden) S:18

Holden, Edith C - Died 1960 Born 1878 Wife of Earl E Holden (with him & Bertha Holden) S:18

Holden, Richard - Died 1982 Born 1894 (with Agnes C Holden) S:15

Holland, James - Died 1850? April 3 Age 43 (stone worn) (next to wife, Olive H Holland) S:19

Holland, Olive H - Died 1901 Born 1844 Wife of James Holland (next to him) S:19

Hollidge, Crawford H - Died 1979 Born 1899 Col in US Air Force during World Wars I & II S:15

Holloway, Raymond D - Died 1966 Born 1889 (with wife, Ruth I Holloway) S:15

Holloway, Ruth I - Died (still living 1991?) Born 1904 (listed with husband, Raymond D Holloway) S:15

Holm, Charlotta - Died 1926 Born 1851 (with Hilma G Lawson) S:12

Holmes, Abbie A - Died 1890 Jan 21 Born 1844 July 2 S:11

Holmes, Abiah - Died 1869 Feb 4 Born 1796 July 24 Wife of Nathaniel Holmes (buried next to him) S:10

Holmes, Abigail - Died 1814 Nov 1 Age 43 Wife of Bartlet Holmes S:12

Holmes, Allen - Died 1924 Born 1884 (a rock marker) (with Cynthia Holmes & others) S:18

Holmes, Amanda K - Died 1939 Born 1867 Wife of James W Holmes (large Holmes/Nickerson stone with family) S:11

Holmes, Anna - Died 1830 May 5 Age 25 S:10

Holmes, Carrie - Died 1875 Oct 20 Born 1853 Sept 20 Daughter of William D & Sarah C Holmes S:9

Holmes, Charles - Died 1915 Born 1842 (with Lizzie E Holmes) S:18

Holmes, Charles H - Died 1872 June 17 Age 1 year, 10 months Son of WP & SL Holmes S:11R

Holmes, Charlie - Died (dates not clear) Stone says, "We loved him well" (this is a small stone) S:11

Holmes, Cynthia - Died 1900 Born 1838 (a rock marker) (with William Baxter & others) S:18

Holmes, Elisha - Died 1802 Oct 1 Age 62 (a metal brace is around stone to reinforce it) S:12

Holmes, Eliza - Died 1832 Jan 28 Age 28 Wife of Joseph Holmes (with Eliza Crocker Holmes) S:10

Holmes, Eliza Crocker - Died (underground) Daughter of Joseph & Eliza Holmes (listed with mother) S:10

Holmes, Elizabeth - Died 1834 Dec 30 Age 6 Daughter of Thomas & Polly Holmes S:11

Holmes, Eluathan ? - Died 1836 Aug 17 Age 39 Born 1797 Feb 9 S:10+26R

Holmes, Ephraim - Died 1869 Jan

Holmes (Cont.)
27 at Sacramento, California Born 1821 July 20 Son of Nathaniel & Abiah C Holmes (stone next to them) S:10

Holmes, Francis - Died 1980 Nov 4 Born 1897 Dec 8 (also has plaque of 1941-45 World War II service) (with George H Beaupre & others) S:19

Holmes, Grace - Died 1900 May 11 Born 1873 Oct 5 Daughter of William D & Sarah C Holmes S:9

Holmes, Helen C - Vanduzer Died 1971 Born 1935 S:11

Holmes, Horatio - Died 1913 Born 1840 Buried with Reanne S Holmes (same stone) S:4

Holmes, James D - Died 1853 Oct 7 Born 1852 Sept 10 Son of William D & Sarah C Holmes S:9

Holmes, James T - Died 1823 Feb 27 Age 5 months, 13 days Son of Thomas & Polly Holmes S:11

Holmes, James W - Died 1951 Born 1858 (large Holmes/Nickerson stone with family) S:11

Holmes, Lazarus - Died 1802 Sept 13 Age 39 S:12

Holmes, Lizzie E - Died 1902 Born 1846 (with Charles Holmes) S:18

Holmes, Lucy - Died 1825 Sept 24 Born 1814 Dec 9 Daughter of Nathaniel & Abiah C Holmes S:10

Holmes, Lucy - Died 1901 June 7 Born 1826 Sept 7 S:10

Holmes, Martha - Died 1817 Feb 27 Age 16 Widow of Nelson Holmes S:10

Holmes, Mary - Died 1868 Mar 8 Born 1823 Oct 1 Daughter of Nathaniel & Abiah C Holmes (buried next to them) S:10

Holmes, Nathaniel - Died 1853 Aug 15 Born 1871 Dec 6 Son of William D & Sarah C Holmes (Hinckley Ceme records #9R say death was 1873 Aug 17) S:9

Holmes, Nathaniel - Died 1869 Dec 13 Born 1783 Jan 17 S:10

Holmes, Nelson - Died 1800 Oct 29 in his 46th yr S:10+26R

Holmes, Nelson - Died 1817 Feb 27 in his 46th yr S:26R

Holmes, Parker S - Died 1987 Born 1909 (has a Barnstable Fire Dept marker also) Was a Tec 5 in US Army during World War II S:19

Holmes, Polley - Died 1797 July 23 Age 2 yrs 6 mos Daughter of Nelson and Pattey (or Polley?) Holmes S:26R

Holmes, Polly - Died 1893 Jan Born 1800 Aug Wife of Thomas Holmes (next to him) S:11

Holmes, Ralph W - Died 1972 Born 1894 S:11

Holmes, Reanne S - Died 1900 Born 1840 Buried with Horatio Holmes (same stone) S:4

Holmes, Sarah - Died 1840 Jan 2 Born 1835 Sept 24 Daughter of Nathaniel & Abiah C Holmes S:10

Holmes, Sarah L - Died 1891 April 29 Born 1832 Sept 8 Wife of William Phinney Holmes S:11

Holmes, Sarah Lizzie - Died 1890 April 18 Born 1869 Oct 22 Daughter of William D & Sarah C Holmes S:9

Holmes, Temperance - Died 1819 Oct 4 Age 23 Daughter of Bartlet & Abigail Holmes S:12

Holmes, Thomas - Died 1858 Oct 10 Age 59 years,4 months (there is another Thomas who is listed in #11 cemetery, could this be an error and they are the same person?) S:10

Holmes, Thomas - Died 1858 Oct Born 1799 June (with Polly Holmes) (another Thomas in #10, not sure if same person listed) S:11

Holmes, Thomas William - Died 1936 Born 1867 Son of SL & WP Holmes S:11

Holmes, Worthington D - Died 1825 Feb 1 Age 2 years, 6 months Son of Shubael & Lydia Holmes S:4

Holway, Betsey - Died 1822 Aug 7

Holway (Cont.)
Age 38 Wife of Lemuel Holway S:12

Holway, CB - Died 1945 Born 1867 (next to Mary W Holway) S:18

Holway, Cynthia - Died 1858 Oct 23 Age 57 years, 2 months Wife of Rev Abraham Holway S:5

Holway, Desire - Died 1869 Sept 9 Age 70 Wife of Lemuel Holway (next to him) S:18

Holway, Eddie - Died 1863 June 17 Born 1863 Jan 2 Son of Joseph W Holway? (next to CB Holway) S:18

Holway, Ellis - Died 1811 July 11 Age 5 months, 5 days Son of Lemuel & Betsey Holway S:12

Holway, Grace Bacon - Died 1925 Born 1863 S:9

Holway, IR - Died 1926 Born 1870 (with James O Holway) S:18

Holway, James O - Died 1906 Dec 28 Born 1839 June 1 (next to wife, Mary W Holway & with IR Holway) S:18

Holway, Jason - Died 1841 Sept Age 9 months Son of Joseph & Sarah Holway S:5

Holway, John A - Died 1949 Born 1865 Member of the Barnstable Fire Department (a plaque and flag at grave too)(with Etta M Brackett & Margarilla Holway) S:11

Holway, Joseph - Died 1862 Oct 17 in his 56th yr S:5

Holway, Lemuel - Died 1854 April 30 Age 70 (between wives, Desire & Millissa H Holway) S:18

Holway, Lucretia Bacon - Died 1900 Born 1830 S:9

Holway, Margrailla - Died 1989 Born 1898 (possible daughter to Etta M Brackett & John A Holway (buried with them) S:11

Holway, Martha - Died October 10 (stone not clear for year) Wife of James Holway (Hinckley Ceme records #5R say death year was 1802 age 43) S:5

Holway, Mary W - Died 1900 Jan

236

Holway (Cont.)
11 Born 1836 April 23 Wife of
James Holway (next to him) S:18

Holway, Melissa - Died 1829 June
10 in her 35th yr Wife of Lemuel
Holway S:1

Holway, Millissa H - Died 1829
June 10 Age 35 Wife of Lemuel
Holway (next to him) S:18

Holway, Sarah - Died 1897 Dec 29
Age 78 years, 6 months Born
1819 June Widow of Joseph
Holway (Hinckley Ceme records
#5R say death year was 1891)
S:5

Holway, Seth Parer - Died 1896
Born 1833 S:9

Holway, Willard Warren - Died
1911 Born 1859 S:21

Holway, ? Seth - Died (a small
white stone next to Betsey
Holway) S:12

Homan, Helen B - Died 1979 Born
1899 (with Louis V Homan) S:20

Homan, Louis V - Died 1963 Born
1892 (with Helen B Homan) S:20

Homer, Albert M - Died (no date)
Born 1859 (with Aliza B Homer
& others) S:18

Homer, Eliza B - Died 1937 Born
1862 (with Capt Joshua A Chase
& others) S:18

Hope, Henry A - Died 1990 Born
1904 (with Virginia N Hope) S:20

Hope, Virginia N - Died 1982 Born
1917 (with Henry A Hope) S:20

Hopkins, Alice - Died 1818 June 9
Age 17 months Daughter of
Joshua & Floretta Hopkins S:4

Hopkins, Caroline Dwight - Died
1881 Born 1813 (with Isabella
Piepont Hopkins & others) S:18

Hopkins, Ellen A - Died (stone
badly damaged) Daughter of
Joshua & Floretta Hopkins S:4

Hopkins, Grace H - Died 1962
Born 1883 (with Hubert B
Hopkins) S:17

Hopkins, Hattie A - Died 1954
Born 1865 Wife of Isaac T
Hopkins (with him & Edward C
Pickard) S:18

Hopkins, Hubert B - Died 1982
Born 1890 (with Grace H Hopkins) S:17

Hopkins, Isaac T - Died 1896 Born
1860 (with Hattie Hopkins &
Edward Pickard) S:18

Hopkins, Isabella Piepont - Died
1906 Born 1839 (with Caroline
Dwight Hopkins & Margarette
Dwight Ward & others) S:18

Hopkins, Joshua - Died (stone
badly damaged) Son of Joshua &
Floretta Hopkins S:4

Hopkins, Joshua - Died 1871 Dec
15 Age 51 years, 10 months S:4

Hopkins, Raymond Alton - Died
1924 Mar 6 at Barnstable, Mass
Born 1867 Feb 10 at North
Truro, Mass (his stone is a rock
with a plaque on it) S:11

Hopkins, Samuel - Died 1886 Born
1808 (with Caroline Dwight
Hopkins & others) S:18

Hopkins, William - Died 1859 Jan
3 Age 4 years, 11 months, 9
days Son of Joshua & Floretta
Hopkins S:4

Horn, Mary Ann - Died 1969 Born
1938 (with Glenn W Hartwell &
others) S:20

Horne, Bernard W - Died 1965
Born 1915 S:12

Horne, Edna B - Died 1915 Born
1879 (with Bernard W Horne)
S:12

Horne, Eric M (Ricky) - Died 1980
Aug 24 Born 1959 Dec 2 S:20

Horne, James B - Died 1947 Born
1879 (with wife, Jane E Horne)
S:16

Horne, Jane E - Died 1967 Born
1896 Wife of James Horne (with
him) S:16

Horne, R Ralph - Died 1966 April
26 Born 1900 June 23 (Hebrew
writing on stone) (Jewish section) (next to Rose E Horne) S:15

Horne, Rose E - Died 1989 May 11
Born 1899 Nov 20 (Hebrew
writing on stone) (Jewish section) (next to Ralph Horne) S:15

Horner, Helen T - Died 1975 Sept 3

Horner (Cont.)
Born 1898 April 9 (with William
M Horner) S:11

Horner, William M - Died 1973 Jan
6 Born 1889 July 13 (with Helen
T Horner) S:11

Hornig, Yvonne F - Died 1983 Born
1914 S:13

Hornor, Grace Marshall - Died
1968 Oct 24 Born 1890 May 23
(with John West Hornor) S:15

Hornor, John West - Died 1970
Mar 9 Born 1875 Oct 2 (with
Grace Marshall Hornor) S:15

Horsley, Albert E - Died 1985 Born
1902 (with Dora Horsley) S:20

Horsley, Dora E - Died 1979 Born
1894 (with Albert Horsley) S:20

Houghton, Charles - Died 1864
Nov 16 Age 2 years, 10 days Son
of Amanda Houghton S:7

House, Alice Norton - Died (no
dates) (listed with Mary Sterling
& William Sterling House) S:18

House, Mary Sterling - Died (no
dates) (listed with William Sterling & Alice Norton House) S:18

House, William Sterling - Died (no
dates) (listed with Mary Sterling
& Alice Norton House) S:18

Howard, Barbara Mitchell - Died
(still alive 1990) Born 1920 Sept
9 (listed with John Glenny
Howard Jr in Howard plot) S:11

Howard, Bessie - Died 1973 Born
1896 (with Milton Howard) S:15

Howard, Clarence Orville - Died
1920 Born 1846 (Civil War
veteran & flag also plaque on
rock) (with Lucretia Stanley
Howard) S:11

Howard, John Glenny - Died 1945
Born 1888 (in Howard plot) S:11

Howard, John Glenny Howard Jr -
Died (still alive 1990?) Born
1920 Aug 10 (with Barbara
Mitchell Howard in Howard plot)
S:11

Howard, Louis G (MD) - Died 1986
Born 1896 (undertaker plaque
only) (Mosswood ceme records
say, buried 5 Jan 1987 age 90?)

Howard (Cont.)
S:15

Howard, Lucia Seymour - Died
1879 Born 1967 (in Howard plot)
S:11

Howard, Lucretia Stanley - Died
1934 Born 1855 With Clarence
Orville Howard S:11

Howard, Mary Ann - Died 1849 Oct
5 Age 26 years, 10 months Wife
of Joseph Howard S:4

Howard, Milton - Died 1968 Born
1898 (with Bessie Howard) S:15

Howard, Ruth Garland - Died 1981
Born 1892 (in Howard plot) S:11

Howard, Sally Garland - Died 1945
Nov 14 Born 1945 Nov 13 (in
Howard plot) S:11

Howard, Willie H - Died 1860 Sept
12 Age 5 years, 6 months, 15
days Son of Joseph & Mary F
Howard S:4

Howe, Charles Lee - Died 1930
Born 1864 (buried next to Helen
G Howe) S:8

Howe, Clifford H - Died 1968 Born
1887 (with wife, Ethel M Howe &
Edward O Williams & others)
S:19

Howe, Dorothy Blanche - Died
1954 Born 1898 Wife of Davis G
Maraspin (with him) S:11

Howe, Ethel M - Died (still living
1991?) Born 1891 (100 years
old?) Wife of Clifford H Howe
(with him & Edward O Williams
& others) S:19

Howe, George Edward - Died 1948
Born 1868 (buried with Edith F
Groves, wife) S:8

Howe, Helen G - Died 1936 Born
1853 (buried next to Charles Lee
Howe) S:8

Howe, Josephine GE - Died 1913
Aug 26 Born 1843 Sept 23 (with
Zena Frost & others) S:18

Howe, Richard (PFC) - Died 1960
Born 1917 Son of Clifford &
Ethel Howe (with them &
Edward O Williams & others)
S:19

Howes, (daughter) - Died 1877 Dec

Howes (Cont.)

27 (age connot be read) Daughter of George & Amelia Howes (next to mother) S:14

Howes, Allen (Capt) - Died 1865 Oct Age 45 years, 9 months Stone says,"While passage from Havana to New York, vessel never heard from again" (with wife, Temperance Howes & others) S:19

Howes, Allen C - Died 1875 Aug 6 Age 12 years, 6 months, 6 days Son of Allen & Temperance Howes (next to them & with brother Elisha Howes & others) S:19

Howes, Alyan - Died 1870 June 17 or 11 Born 1800 Nov 27 (stone worn) (between wives, Nancy & Maria Howes) S:19

Howes, Amelia D - Died 1835 Mar 31 Born 1895 Jan 31 Wife of George E Howes (next to his stone) S:14

Howes, Bertha - Died 1890? Oct 2 (stone worn) Daughter of John & Lucy Howes) S:19

Howes, Betsy - Died 1833 Nov 13 Born 1771 Feb Wife of Reuben Howes (stone broken at base and laying on the ground) S:10

Howes, Betsey - Died 1840 June 25 in her 52nd yr Wife of Richard Howes S:6

Howes, Charles H - Died 1980 Born 1914 (on same stone with Suzanne St Coeur) S:11

Howes, Daniel - Died 1804 Feb 24 Son of Seth Howes S:10

Howes, Desire - Died 1822 Jan 11 in her 75th yr Widow of Peter Howes S:6

Howes, Elisha - Died 1848 Sept 11 Son of Allen & Temperance Howes (next to them & with Susan Ella Howes,his sister & others) S:19

Howes, Elisha - Died 1878 Feb 12 Age 51 years, 11 months (next to Helen Howes) S:19

Howes, Eliza - Died 1892 Aug 12

Howes (Cont.)

Age 83 years, 11 months, 12 days Wife of Freeman Howes S:6

Howes, Ella W - Died 1911 March 11 Born 1849 March 6 Wife of Sidney E Nickerson (next to him) S:18

Howes, Emily - Died 1885 Sept 19 Age 72 years, 3 months Wife of Dr Thomas w Fossett & 8th Daughter to Reuben Howes Stone says,"Here lies my body mouldering to clay I conversed with the spirit of the dead for 40 yras w/living" S:10

Howes, Ethel H - Died (no info) (with Josephine Howes) S:11

Howes, Florence A - Died 1963 Born 1880 S:15

Howes, Freeman - Died 1879 July 27 Age 74 years, 10 months, 21 days S:6

Howes, George E - Died 1880 Mar 4 Age 41 years, 8 months Lost at sea (listed next to wife, Amelia D Howes) S:14

Howes, George L (Capt) - Died 1936 Born 1855 (buried with Justina Howes-wife) S:8

Howes, Grace - Died 1897 Born 1852 Wife of Edwin Scudder (Phinney) (buried with Edwin, husband) S:8

Howes, Gustavus E - Died 1839 Feb 16 Age 1 year, 2 months, 27 days Son of Freeman & Eliza Howes S:6

Howes, Harriet - Died 1891 May 2 Age 72 Wife of Freeman B Howes S:10

Howes, Helen - Died 1912 Dec 8 Age 80 years, 10 months (next to Elisha Howes) S:19

Howes, Isaac - Died 1894 Feb 27 Born 1817 Sept 28 S:6

Howes, Josephine - Died 1941 Born 1913 Wife of Stephen H Howes (with Ethel H Howes) S:11

Howes, Josiah - Died 1876 May 6 in his 62nd yr S:6

Howes, Justina - Died 1903 Born

Howes (Cont.)
1857 Wife of Capt George Howes
(buried with to him) S:8

Howes, Lydia S - Died 1960 Born
1871 Wife of Braddock Coleman
(with him) S:14

Howes, Mabel - Died 1866 July 25
Age 2 months, 7 days Daughter
of George F & Amelia Howes
(with sister, Mary T Howes) S:14

Howes, Maria W - Died 1891 Jan
25 Born 1820 April 24 (area
overgrown) Wife, of Alyan Howes
(next to him) S:19

Howes, Marie E - Died 1987 Born
1911 (wooden cross with flowers
in ground next to stone) (with
Stephen H Howes) S:11

Howes, Mary Abby - Died 1842
Sept 23 Age 2 years, 6 months
Daughter of Phillip & Temper-
ance b Howes S:6

Howes, Mary G - Died 1828 April
11 Age 27 Wife of Reuben Howes
Jr S:10

Howes, Mary T - Died 1863 Oct 19
Age 2 months, 10 days Daughter
of George F & Amelia Howes
(with sister, Mabel Howes) S:14

Howes, Nancy L - Died 1869 Jan 5
Age 68 Wife of Alyan Howes
(next to him) S:19

Howes, Peter - Died 1800 Nov 27 in
his 58th yr S:6

Howes, Peter - Died 1847 Mar 13 in
his 73rd yr S:6

Howes, Philip - Died 1867 Dec 6
Age 56 years, 2 months (buried
next to wife, Temperance Howes)
S:6

Howes, Rebeckah - Died 1847 Jan
13 in her 72nd yr Wife of Peter
Howes S:6

Howes, Richard - Died 1841 Mar
20 in his 69th yr (buried next to
both wifes, Betsey, Rose) S:6

Howes, Rose - Died 1825 Oct 10 in
her 42nd yr Wife of Richard
Howes S:6+26R

Howes, Ruth - Died 1899 Sept 24
Born 1819 Oct 20 S:6

Howes, Samuel - Died 1887 May

Howes (Cont.)
20 in his 77th yr S:6

Howes, Sophia - Died 1911 July 2
Born 1842 April 29 Wife of
Henry C Lumbert (next to him)
S:18

Howes, Sophia W - Died 1843 Oct
17 in her 21st yr Wife of Freeman B Howes S:5

Howes, Stephen H - Died 1980
Born 1911 (wooden cross with
flowers in ground next to stone)
(with Marie E Howes) S:11

Howes, Susan Ella - Died 1850 Dec
6 Age 21 mos Daughter of Allen
& Temperance Howes (next to
them & with Edith N Handy &
others) S:19+26R

Howes, Temperance B - Died 1887
Dec 11 Age 66 years, 11 months,
2 days S:6

Howes, Temperance N - Died 1912
Oct 27 Age 92 years, 2 months
Wife of Capt Allen Howes (listed
with him & Thomas Smith &
others) S:19

Howlan, Isaac - Died 1700 Dec 26
in his 66th yr S:5

Howland, (dau) - Died 17?9 Age 12
hours (also with a twin) Daughter of Bo Howland (mother)
(Hinckley Ceme records #5R say
death was 1769 and born 1769
May 10, 12 hours and daughter
of Lt Ansell & Elizabeth) S:5

Howland, (dau) - Died 17?9 Age 24
hours (also a twin with her)
Daughter of Bo Howland (mother) (Hinckley Ceme records #5R
say death was 1769, born 1769
May 10 24 hours and daughter
of Lt Ansell & Elizabeth) S:5

Howland, (daughter) - Died 1807
Aug 24 Age 5 weeks Daughter of
Ansel & Mercy Howland S:5R

Howland, Abigail Thacher - Died
1779 June 30 Age 4 Daughter of
Nathaniel & Martha Howland
S:5R

Howland, Adelaide M - Died 1881
Born 1855 S:5

Howland, Anna F - Died 1887 Aug

Howland (Cont.)
18 Age 86 years, 9 months Wife of Jason Howland S:5

Howland, Anna Mrs - Died 1820 Sept 24 Age 27 She died shortly after the decease of her pious & loving husband, Capt Job P Howland, 8 May 1820 who died in Havana, Cuba age 29, leaving orphaned children S:12

Howland, Ansell (Capt) - Died 1802 Feb 23 in his 64th yr Died suddenly S:5

Howland, Ariel C - Died 1879 July 4 Age 25 years, 10 months, 4 days (with wife, Mary Ella Howland) S:14

Howland, Benjamin - Died Son of John Howland (Hinckley Ceme records #5R say death was 1770 Jan 14 age 17 months and father's name was Job) S:5

Howland, Charles N - Died 1837 Oct 10 Son of Jason & Anna F Howland (Hinckley Ceme records #5R says age was 5) S:5

Howland, Charles N - Died 1896 Mar 27 Age 58 years, 5 months S:5

Howland, Clifton - Died 1871 Aug 17 Age 7 months, 8 days Son of AJ & BF Howland S:5R

Howland, Daniel J - Died 1971 Born 1899 (with MMadeline Howland) S:16

Howland, David - Died 1873 Born 1856 S:7

Howland, Dorinda - Died 1861 Born 1818 S:7

Howland, Edwin T - Died 1918 Born 1847 S:7

Howland, Elisabeth - Died 1775 Oct 18 in her 72nd yr Widow of Jabez Howland S:5

Howland, Emeline C - Died 1913 Born 1821 (with Julius W Howland & others in Tallman plot) S:12

Howland, George L (Capt) - Died 1854 Nov 23 Age 35 Was from Cape Verde Islands (with Harriet A Howland) S:18

Howland, Hannah - Died 1773 Sept Wife of Jobe Howland (Hinckley Ceme records #5R say death was 1781 Sept 21 at age 48) S:5

Howland, Hannah - Died 1781 Sept 21 Age 48 S:5R

Howland, Harriet A - Died 1894 Jan 11 Age 73 (with Capt George L Howland) S:18

Howland, Huldah - Died 1739 Feb 23 Second wife of Job Howland S:5

Howland, Isaac - Died 1724 Dec 26 Age 65 S:5R

Howland, Jabez - Died 1765 Dec 25 in his 64th yr S:5

Howland, James - Died 1867 Apr 20 in his 88th yr S:5

Howland, James N - Died 1833 Age 33 Born 1800 S:5

Howland, Jamie - Died (stone not clear) (Hinckley Ceme records #5R say death was 1872 Aug 12 at age 10 months, 18 days and parents were JN & EP Howland) S:5

Howland, Jason - Died 1863 May 26 Age 67 years, 4 months S:5

Howland, Job P (or) R (Capt) - Died 1820 May 8 at Havana, Cuba (see wife, Anna Howland for more details) S:12

Howland, Jobe - Died 1794 May 1 in his 68th yr (Hinckley Ceme records #5R say that he was a 4th generation descendant of John Howland, pilgrim on the Mayflower) S:5

Howland, John - Died 1851 Nov 9 in his 83rd yr (family buried next to each other) S:7

Howland, John - Died 17?8 Feb 14 in his 65th yr Buried next to Mary Howland who says her husband was John (Hinckley Ceme records #5R say death was 1738 age 63) S:5

Howland, John F - Died 1884 May 3 Born 1816 May 3 Son of Job R & Anna Howland S:12

Howland, Jonathan - Died 1812 Sept 17 S:5

Howland, Joseph - Died 1897 Sept 23 Born 1819 Sept 5 in Sandwich, Mass S:5

Howland, Josiah B - Died 1825 Feb 22 Age 6 months, 10 days Son of James N & Lurana Howland S:5

Howland, Julius W - Died 1931 Born 1857 (with Beatrice B Tallman & others in Tallman plot) S:12

Howland, Lavina - Died 1830 Dec 25 in her 82nd yr (Hinckley Ceme records #5R say death was 1850 and that she was a Miss) S:5

Howland, Leah F - Died 1975 Born 1903 (next to Norris P Howland) S:20

Howland, Lulie - Died 1876 Aug 25 Age 8 months Daughter of AJ & BF Howland S:5R

Howland, Lurana - Died 1892 Born 1806 S:5

Howland, M Madeline - Died 1977 Born 1901 (with Daniel J Howland) S:16

Howland, Mabel - Died 1871 Feb 10 Age 3 days Daughter of Josiah & Lucy Howland S:5

Howland, Martha - Died 1841 Apl 13 in her 69th yr Wife of John Howland S:7

Howland, Martha - Died 1862 May 14 in her 78th yr Wife of James Howland S:5

Howland, Martha T - Died 1838 May 15 Age 30 years, 5 months, 15 days Daughter of John & Martha Howland S:7

Howland, Martha T - Died 1923 Born 1846 S:7

Howland, Mary - Died 1830 Sept 3 in her 82nd yr S:4

Howland, Mary - Died 1759 Sept 10 in her 79th yr Wife of John Howland S:5

Howland, Mary - Died 1843 May 27 Age 12 years, 10 months, 23 days Daughter of John & Martha Howland S:7

Howland, Mary - Died 1815 July 21 Widow of Zenas D Howland ?

Howland (Cont.)
(but mentions Mary Bassett/ll/) (is she the widow or daughter?) S:4

Howland, Mary Ella - Died 1879 May 31 Age 24 years, 10 months, 22 days Wife of Ariel C Howland (with him) S:14

Howland, Mary S - Died 1889 Feb 6 Age 28 years, 10 months, 3 days Daughter of Josiah & Lucy Howland S:5

Howland, Maud - Died 1893 July 30 Born 1868 Dec 14 Stone says, "Sleepin" S:12

Howland, Mercy - Died 1795 Mar 10 in her 60th yr Wife of ? (Hinckley Ceme records #5R say that her name was Marcy) S:5

Howland, Myron Poole - Died 1970 Born 1886 (with wife, Helen F Macy) S:13

Howland, Nathaniel - Died 1896 Born 1810 S:7

Howland, Norris P - Died 1970 Born 1886 (next to Leah P Howland) S:20

Howland, R - Died (stone not clear) Wife of James Howland (Hinckley Ceme records #5R say death was 1774 May 22 at Age 44 and that her first name was Rebekah) S:5

Howland, Roland - Died 1767 April 27 Age 1 year, 5 months, 15 days "Stone was given by grandfather" Son of Nathaniel & Martha Howland S:5R

Howland, Sarah B - Died 1891 Mar 22 in her 71st yr Wife of Joseph Howland S:5

Howland, Sarah N - Died 1906 Born 1824 S:5

Howland, Shadrach Nye - Died 1900 Born 1808 S:5

Howland, Shubael - Died 1737 June 17 Age 65 S:5R

Howland, Thomas T - Died 1879 Born 1825 (in Tallman plot with Emeline C Howland & others) S:12

Howland, William G - Died 1901

Howland (Cont.)
Feb 2 Age 77 years, 1 month, 7 days S:5

Howland, Zachaus - Died 1740 Oct 22 in his 28th yr S:5

Hoxie, Anson W - Died 1860 Sept 5 Age 1 year, 10 months, 18 days Son of Oliver & Lucy Hoxie (with them & others) S:21

Hoxie, Bernice L - Died (still living 1991?) Born 1905 (listed with Etta & Ralph Hoxie) S:14

Hoxie, Etta C - Died 1941 Born 1864 Wife of Everett Hoxie (with him) S:14

Hoxie, Everett L - Died 1944 Born 1869 (with wife, Etta C Hoxie) S:14

Hoxie, Lucy S - Died 1903 Aug 18 Age 71 years, 4 months (metal marker) Wife of Oliver C Hoxie (with him & others) S:21

Hoxie, Margorie L - Died 1964 Sept 28 (wife of Maurice A Hoxie) S:15

Hoxie, Maurice A - Died 1978 Oct 10 Born 1897 July 17 (he was a Mason) (with wife, Margorie L Hoxie) S:15

Hoxie, Oliver C - Died 1862 June 20 Age 8 years, 4 months, 26 days (metal marker) Son of Oliver C & Lucy S Hoxie (with them) S:21

Hoxie, Oliver C - Died 1903 Dec 22 Age 71 years, 7 months (metal marker) (with Zenas M Hoxie & others) S:21

Hoxie, Ralph B - Died 1918 Born 1893 (with Etta C Hoxie) S:14

Hoxie, Zenas H - Died 1878 Nov 4 Born 1841 Jan 30 Member of Company D, 29th Massachusetts Volunteers S:11

Hoxie, Zenas M - Died 1856 Aug 5 Age 4 months Son of Oliver & Lucy Hoxie (with them & others) S:21

Hubbart, Ruth T - Died 1942 Born 1888 Wife of Horace L Norris S:16

Hubly, Ruth M - Died 1917 Born 1896 (with Luther Sears &

Hubly (Cont.)
others) S:18

Huckings, H N - Died 1895 (a small foot marker only Regular stone is gone) (next to Joseph Huckins) S:11

Huckins, Adolphus - Died 1851 Mar 24 Age 22 at Rio Janairo, Brazil Son of Capt Joseph Huckins, d1861 (on same stone) S:11

Huckins, Adolphus - Died 1870 June 10 Age 19 years, 6 months Son of James & Mary B Huckins (next to them) S:11

Huckins, Annah H - Died 1907 Mar 24 Born 1827 Mar 25 (possible wife of Joseph Huckins, next to him) S:11

Huckins, Betsey - Died 1873 Sept 11 Age 75 Wife of Joseph Huckins, d1861 (next to him) S:11

Huckins, Caroline - Died 1795 March 31 Age 5 weeks, 4 days Daughter of Samuel & Sarah Huckins S:11R

Huckins, Caroline - Died 1796? (not sure of location) S:11R

Huckins, Emma H - Died 1918 Born 1855 Daughter of John & Rebecca Hinckley (listed on large family stone with them & others) S:11

Huckins, Hannah - Died 1696 Feb 4 Wife of Thomas Huckins (Hinckley Ceme records #11R say death was 1696 Nov 4 in her 37th yr) S:11+26R

Huckins, Hannah - Died 1802 Dec 25 Age 2 years, 10 months, 9 days Daughter of Capt Samuel & Sarah Huckins S:11R

Huckins, Hannah - Died 1802 located in enclosure area S:11R

Huckins, Harriet Newell - Died (underground) Daughter of Joseph & Rebecca Huckins (next to them) (Hinckley Ceme records #11R say death was 1825 May 5 at age 2 years, 4 months, 14 days) S:11

Huckins, Ida Burgess - Died 1907

Huckins (Cont.)
Feb 16 Born 1853 Aug 9 (two
stones down next to her due to
vandals, cannot read) (also next
to James B Huckins) S:18

Huckins, James (Capt) - Died 1880
Nov 16 Age 55 years, 8 months
(next to Mary B Huckins, d1882)
(Hinckley Ceme records #11R
say death was 1880) S:11+26R

Huckins, James B - Died 1931 May
14 Born 1848 July 6 (next to Ida
Burgess Huckins who is also
next to 2 stones that are down
due to vandals, cannot read
them) S:18

Huckins, John - Died 1791 July 27
in his 71st yr S:11+26R

Huckins, John - Died 1795 located
in enclosure area S:11R

Huckins, Joseph - Died 1774 Nov
11 in his 49th yr S:11+26R

Huckins, Joseph - Died 1889 Mar
22 Born 1821 July 12 S:11

Huckins, Joseph (Capt) - Died
1861 Oct 5 Age 75 Born 1786
July 12 (on same stone with,
Adolphus Huckins, d1851) S:11

Huckins, Lydia - Died 1802 located
in enclosure area S:11R

Huckins, Lydia Mrs - Died 1776
Jan 20 in her 41st yr Wife of
James Huckins S:11R+26R

Huckins, Mary B - Died 1882 July
23 Age 57 years, 6 months Wife
of Capt James Huckins, d188?
S:11+26R

Huckins, Mary C - Died 1898 Born
1819 S:9

Huckins, Rachel Mrs - Died 1765
March 22 Age 77 Wife of Thomas
Huckins S:11R

Huckins, Rebecca Mrs - Died 1837
Feb 12 Age 36 Born 1801 Oct 27
Wife of Capt Joseph Huckins,
d1861 (next to him) S:11

Huckins, Samuel (Capt) - Died
1824 Aug 22 in his 62nd yr
S:11R+26R

Huckins, Sarah - Died 1820 located in enclosure area S:11R

Huckins, Sarah Mrs - Died 1820

Huckins (Cont.)
Aug 23 in her 61st yr Wife of
Capt Samuel Huckins S:11R+
26R

Huckins, Thomas - Died 1794 May
6 in his 76th yr S:11+26R

Huckins, Thomas - Died 1774
March 3 Age 87 S:11R

Huckins, Thomas Mr - Died 177?
located in enclosure area S:11R

Hudson, Olive H - Died 1896 Born
1835 (on large Hudson & Hinckley stone) S:11

Hudson, William - Died 1870 Born
1833 (large Hudson & Hinckley
stone with others) S:11

Huggard, Annie Laurie - Died 1937
Born 1898 (plaque on rock
surrounded by bushes) S:12

Hughes, George P - Died 1960 Born
1882 (with Mabel Hughes) S:20

Hughes, Mabel E - Died 1960 Born
1889 (with George P Hughes)
S:20

Hughes, Philip - Died 1932 Aug 3
Born 1840 April 1 Was in
Company E, 40th Massachu-
setts Infantry (next to James R
Atwood, another military stone)
S:18

Hukins, Caroline - Died 1793 Mar
31 Age 5 weeks, 2 days Daughter to Samuel & Sarah Hukins
S:11

Hukins, Hannah - Died 1805 Dec
23 Age 2 years, 10 months, 9
days Daughter of Capt Samuel &
Sarah Hukins (next to them)
S:11

Hukins, Lydia - Died 1776 Jan 20
Age 41 Widow of James Hukins
S:11

Hukins, Rachel - Died 1763 March
22 Age 77 Wife of Thomas
Hukins (next to him) S:11

Hukins, Samuel (Capt) - Died 1824
Aug 22 Age 62 (next to wife,
Sarah Hukins) S:11

Hukins, Sarah - Died 1820 Aug 23
Age 61 Wife to Capt Samuel
Hukins S:11

Hukins, Thomas - Died 1700's?

Hukins (Cont.)
March (next to wife, Rachel Hukins) S:11

Hull, Eliza S Miss - Died 1840 Feb 25 Age 22 Daughter of Rev Salmon & Lucy Hull S:11

Hull, Fern L - Died 1878 Born 1874 (with Ulysses A Hull & others) S:14

Hull, Joseph - Died 26th (dates worn off) (stone next to him worn off) (next to Miss Eliza S Hull) S:11

Hull, Ulysses A - Died 1917 Born 1848 (with Fern L Hull & others) S:14

Humes, Adresta - Died 1910 Born 1824 (with Adresta M Humes & others) S:21

Humes, Adresta M - Died 1857 Aug 16 Born 1849 Dec 12 (with Ella B Humes & others) Daughter of Daniel & Adresta Humes S:21

Humes, Daniel - Died 1899 Feb 2 Born 1822 Feb 24 (with Adresta Humes & others) S:21

Humes, Daniel L - Died 1855 May 4 Born 1855 Feb 6 Son of Daniel & Adresta Humes (with them) S:21

Humes, Ella B - Died 1861 Nov 14 Born 1855 April 16 Daughter of Daniel & Adresta Humes (with them) S:21

Humes, Emma J - Died 1855 June 14 Born 1853 Oct 17 Daughter of Daniel & Adresta Humes (with them & Daniel L Humes & others) S:21

Humes, George L - Died 1843 SEpt 15 Born 1843 Feb 12 Son of Daniel & Adresta Humes (with them & Emma Humes & others) S:21

Humes, Sarah E - Died 1867 March 31 Born 1847 Aug 12 Daughter of Daniel & Adresta Humes (with them & George L Humes) S:21

Hunnewell, Eleanor - Died 1913 Born 1823 (with Jonas Hunnewell) S:14

Hunnewell, Ella M - Died 1951 Born 1864 Wife of A Seabury Childs (with him) S:14

Hunnewell, Ellena - Died 1867 Aug 10 Age 1 year, 6 months, 13 days Daughter of John & Eleanor Hunnewell (next to William) S:14

Hunnewell, Jonas - Died 1887 Born 1816 (with Ella M Hunnewell & A Seabury Childs) S:14

Hunnewell, William - Died 1873 July 31 Age 1 year, 9 months, 21 days Son of John & Eleanor Hunnewell (next to Ellena Hunnewell) S:14

Hunt, Eugene - Died 1960 Born 1893 S:14

Hursh, Mildred Rich - Died 1983 Born 1898 (next to Walter C Hursh) S:17

Hursh, Walter C - Died 1967 July 25 Born 1890 Dec 2 From Massachusetts, was QM2 in USNRF during World War I (next to Mildred Rich Hursh) S:17

Hurst, Annie - Died 1941 Born 1859 Wife of Samuel T Landers (with him) S:14

Hurtt, James W - Died 1961 April 8 Born 1922 April 24 Was from Massachusetts, a Corporal in 3678 QM Truck Div during World War II S:13

Hussey, Alfred Rodman Jr - Died 1964 Born 1902 Commander in USNR (flag at stone) S:11

Hussey, Alfred Rodman Rev - Died 1947 Born 1869 (with wife, Mary Lincoln Warren) S:11

Hutcheson, David W - Died 1968 Oct 20 Born 1893 March 20 From Massachusetts, was SFC in US Army during World War I (next to Katherine M Hutcheson) S:17

Hutcheson, Katherine M - Died 1969 March 25 Born 1895 March 8 (next to David W Hutcheson) S:17

Hutchins, Clara L - Died 1946 Born 1890 (with Percy C

Hutchins (Cont.)
Hutchins) S:17

Hutchins, Eugene - Died 1892 Feb 15 Age 33 S:14

Hutchins, Mary E - Died 1902 Born 1835 (with Ulysses A Hull & others) S:14

Hutchins, Palmira - Died 1985 Oct 26 Born 1913 Sept 13 (with Frank & Gregory Senteio) S:16

Hutchins, Percy C - Died 1957 Born 1904 (with Clara L Hutchins) S:17

Hutchins, Uriel M - Died 1881 Born 1830 (with Mary E Hutchins) S:14

Hutchinson, Florence Emily - Died 1959 Born 1906 Daughter of Harriet Ann Hutchinson (next to her) S:20

Hutchinson, Harriet Ann - Died 1960 Born 1883 Stone says,"Mother" (next to Florence Emily Hutchinson) S:20

Hyde, Julia - Died 1948 Born 1864 (with William Henry Kinnicutt) S:8

Hyland, Madge - Died 1970 Born 1886 S:15

Hynckly (Hinckley), Sarah Mrs - Died (worn bad) (Ebenezer shows up on stone, not sure if she is another wife of his, she is next to his wife, Thankful Hynckley) S:11

Hynkkly (Hinckley), Thankful - Died 176? Dec 17 Wife of Ebenezer Hinckley S:11

Iantuoni, Florence - Died 1983 Born 1897 (with Joseph Iantuoni) S:16

Iantuoni, Joseph - Died 1976 Born 1891 (with Florence Iantuoni) S:16

Iasigi, Oscar A - Died 1966 Born 1884 S:11

Iliffe, Carolyn L - Buried 1984 April 11 Age 85 Located in Block 4, lot 4, grave 2 S:15R

Imberg, N George - Died 1971 Born 1894 Husband of Ann Mi(?) S:16

Inman, Bessie D - Died 1981 April

Inman (Cont.)
1 Born 1892 June 15 (next to Laurence H Inman) S:17

Inman, Laurence H - Died 1962 April 20 Born 1890 Jan 8 From Massachusetts, was a Cpl in Hg Co 33 Field Artillery during World War I (next to Bessie D Inman) S:17

Isham, Chloe Mrs - Died 1840 Aug 12 Age 78 Widow of Heman Isham (next to him) S:12+12R

Isham, Heman - Died 1836 Aug 29 in his 76th yr (stone reads "Erected to the memory of") S:12

Isham, Lucy - Died 1841 Sept 5 in her 44th yr Wife of Thomas Isham (next to him) S:12+12R

Isham, Sophia - Died 1823 Jan 12 in her 34th yr Wife of Thomas Isham (next to him) S:12+12R

Isham, Thomas - Died 1869 Oct 17 Age 80 years, 11 months, 27 days S:12

Ivers, Edward E - Died (still living 1991?) Born 1900 Nov 28 (listed with Mary M Ivers) S:15

Ivers, Mary M - Died 1989 June 8 Born 1899 June 10 (with Edward E Ivers) S:15

Iwanowna, Nadeschda - Died 1962 Jan 29 Born 1892 July 26 Stone says, "HA BYAET BOJIR TBOJ" (with Georgij Genrichowitch) S:17

Jaakkola, Helvi S - Died 1988 Born 1904 (with Leo T Jaakkola) S:20

Jaakkola, Leo T - Died (still living 1991?) Born 1911 (with Helvi S Jaakkola) S:20

Jackson, Abigail - Died 1779 (stone not clear) Wife of Nathaniel Jackson (Hinckley Ceme records #5R say death was 1719 Sept 11 at age 26) S:5

Jackson, Alvina - Died 1977 Born 1978 (small plaque in ground, no stone yet) S:13

Jackson, Benjamin - Died 1790 Sept 9 Age 4 Son of Richard & Elizabeth Jackson S:10

Jackson, Elizabeth - Died 1790

Jackson (Cont.)
(stone badly damaged) Consort of Richard Jackson S:10

Jackson, Elizabeth - Died 1844 Nov 21 Born 1768 Feb 10 Wife of Thomas Sturgis (in stone coffin with children) S:10

Jackson, Elizabeth - Died 1856/66 Sept 4 Age 47 Wife of Richard Jackson S:10

Jackson, Elmer G - Died 1956 Born 1917 (with Lillian P Prentiss) S:20

Jackson, Elvira L - Died 1968 Born 1907 Wife of John R Jackson (with him) S:12

Jackson, John R - Died 1958 Born 1900 (with Elvira L Jackson, wife) S:12

Jackson, Mary Mrs - Died 1807 June 10 Age 21 Consort of Capt Joseph Jackson S:10

Jackson, Richard - Died (stone worn badly, can't be read, next to Elizabeth Jackson, his wife) S:10

Jackson, Richard - Died 1790 Sept 9 Age 4 Son of Benjamin & Elizabeth Jackson S:10

Jackson, Richard Judah - Died 1823 Jan 28 Age 44 colored (written in pencil) S:26R

Jacobs, Adeline Hallett - Died 1912 Dec 26 Born 1818 June 16 (with Gustavus N Jacobs) S:14

Jacobs, Gustavus Nelson - Died 1930 Jan 30 Born 1855 July 15 (with Howard Malcom Jacobs) S:14

Jacobs, Harriet Clementine - Died 1912 Dec 7 Born 1844 July 24 (with Gustavus N Jacobs) S:14

Jacobs, Howard Malcom - Died 1918 Aug 30 Born 1852 Nov 26 (with Gustavus Nelson Jacobs) S:14

Jacobs, Mary Louise - Died 1985 Born 1890 (undertaker plaque only) S:15

Jacobs, William B - Died 1895 Aug 22 Born 1808 Jan 9 (with Gustavus N Jacobs) S:14

Jacobsen, Drew F - Died 1984 Nov 25 Born 1908 Sept 1 Was a TEC 5 in US Army during World War II S:21

Jaggar, Abagail L - Died 1833 June 2 in her 25th yr Wife of Silvanus Jaggar (buried next to son, Chaplin Henry Jaggar) S:8

Jaggar, Chaplin Henry - Died 1833 (stone badly worn) Son of Silvanus & Abagail L Jaggar (buried next to Abagail L Jaggar, mother) S:8

Jaggar, Cyrus B - Died 1863 Apr Age 18 years, 11 months He drowned (listed with possible parents, Sylvanus & Sarah Jaggar) S:8

Jaggar, Lillie H - Died 1878 Aug 24 Age 17 years, 8 months, 9 days (buried with parents, Sylvanus & Sarah Jaggar) S:8

Jaggar, Sarah C - Died 1856? July 12 (stone not clear) Wife of Sylvanus Jaggar (buried next to him) S:8

Jaggar, Sylvanus - Died 1883 July 25 Age 83 years, 11 months, 19 days (buried between wife, Sarah C & possible son, Cyrus B Jaggar) S:8

Jalonen, Helen W - Died 1969 Born 1896 S:20

Jansson, Gustave E - Died 1970 Born 1889 (with Ruth E Jansson) S:19

Jansson, Ruth E - Died 1987 Born 1890 (with Gustave E Jansson) S:19

Jansson, Stig H - Died 1984 Born 1919 S:19

Jarry, Albert W - Died 1973 Born 1900 (with Mary C Jarry) S:16

Jarry, Mary C - Died 1985 Born 1900 (with Albert W Jarry) S:16

Jarvi, A Pauline - Died (still living 1991?) Born 1931 (with Aili & Aleksanter Jarvi) S:20

Jarvi, Aili M - Died (still living 1991?) Born 1901 (with A Pauline & Aleksanter Jarvi) S:20

Jarvi, Aleksanter - Died 1980 Born

Jarvi (Cont.)
1890 (with Aili M & A Pauline Jarvi) S:20

Jason, Alma E - Died 1973 Born 1908 (stone the same as M Joseph, Susie A & Herbert J Jason, all next to each other) S:11

Jason, Herbert J - Died 1968 Born 1906 Member of the Cape Cod Police Officials Council (grave has flag) (stone same design as M Joseph, Susie A & Alma E Jason) S:11

Jason, M Joseph - Died 1943 Born 1874 (stone same design as Susie A Jason, Herbert J & Alma E Jason) S:11

Jason, Susie A - Died 1968 Born 1877 (stone same design as M Joseph, Herbert J & Alma E Jason) S:11

Jedrey, Wayne J - Died 1973 July 23 Born 1965 Feb 9 S:20

Jenckes, Cynthia R - Died 1910 Born 1863 (with Edwin Taylor & others) S:21

Jenkens, Susan - Died 1898 Feb 28 Born 1819 Oct 28 S:5

Jenkins, Abigail - Died 1828 Oct 16 in her 71st yr Wife of Maj Nathanel Jenkins S:5

Jenkins, Asa - Died 1847 Feb 23 Age 79 years, 7 months July S:5

Jenkins, Barbara M - Died 1962 Born 1923 Daughter of Harold & Nellie Wheeler (with them) S:20

Jenkins, Barker - Died 1796 Sept 22 Age 6 Son of Nathaniel & Abigail Jenkins S:5R

Jenkins, Bethia - Died (date not clear) Wife of Joseph Jenkins (Hinckley Ceme records #5R says death was 1782 Jan 23 at age 37) S:5

Jenkins, Betsey - Died 1875 Feb 28 Born 1797 Nov 5 Wife of Nathan Jenkins S:5

Jenkins, Betsy - Died 1814 Jan 30 Age 20 or 30 Daughter of Hannaha Jenkins S:5

Jenkins, Braley - Died 1894 Mar

Jenkins (Cont.)
27 Born 1812 May 22 S:5

Jenkins, Braley (Deacon) - Died 1872 July 3 Born 1775 Feb 7 S:5

Jenkins, Charles - Died 1861 Dec 27 Age 36 years, 7 months S:5

Jenkins, Charles C - Died 1907 Jan 26 Age 92 years, 3 days S:5

Jenkins, Charlie W - Died 1866 Born 1864 (with Sarah E Jenkins & others) S:18

Jenkins, Chloe C - Died 1888 Mar 1 Age 50 years, 11 months Wife of William Jenkins (with him) S:12

Jenkins, Content W - Died 1905 Oct 14 Age 55 years, 8 months S:5

Jenkins, Crocker - Died 1796 Apl 30 Son of Prince & Lydia Jenkins (Hinckley Ceme records #5R says age was 5 months, 15 days) S:5

Jenkins, Elias - Died 1796 Sept 15 Age 10 years Son of Nathaniel & Abigail Jenkins S:5R

Jenkins, Elisha - Died 1799 Jan 2 Age 14 Son of Alvan & Mariah Jenkins S:5R

Jenkins, Eliza C - Died 1859 July 25 Born 1808 Dec 8 Wife of George Jenkins S:5

Jenkins, Elizabeth - Died 1853 Nov 1 (at New York) Age 13 years, 2 months, 4 days S:5

Jenkins, Ellis - Died 1859 Jan 23 Age 77 years, 6 months (buried next to wife Susannah Jenkins) S:5

Jenkins, Ellis - Died 1891 Dec 7 Age 74 years, 6 months S:5

Jenkins, Eunice - Died 1872 July 3 Born 1776 Aug 19 S:5

Jenkins, Fear H - Died 1896 May 24 Age 57 years, 5 months Wife of John J Jenkins S:5

Jenkins, Flora A - Died 1937 Born 1853 (with Lillie Bixby & others) S:18

Jenkins, George - Died 1861 Dec 21 Born 1805 June 10 S:5

Jenkins, George F - Died 1858 Nov 22 Born 1856 May 29 S:5

Jenkins, Hannah - Died 1806 Mar 5 in her 66th yr Wife of Joseph Jenkins S:5

Jenkins, Hannah - Died 1838 Mar 21 Age 69 years, 7 months Wife of Asa Jenkins S:5

Jenkins, Hodiah - Died 1808 May 14 in her 70th yr Wife of Simeon Jenkins S:5

Jenkins, James H - Died 1902 Born 1831 S:5

Jenkins, John - Died (no dates, but located in row 12) S:11R

Jenkins, John - Died 1736 July 8 in his 77th yr S:11R+26R

Jenkins, John - Died 1876 Born 1844 S:5

Jenkins, John J - Died 1903 Apr 13 Age 83 years, 7 months, 18 days S:5

Jenkins, Joseph - Died (no dates, but located in row 12) S:11R

Jenkins, Joseph - Died (stone not clear located between Silvanus Bodfish & Francies Barrows) (Hinckley Ceme records #5R says death was 1823 Jan 28 at age 84) S:5

Jenkins, Joseph - Died 1734 Oct 17 in his 66th yr S:5

Jenkins, Joseph - Died 1749 Jan 16 Age 47 S:5

Jenkins, Joseph - Died 1793 Oct 13 Age 3 Son of Joseph & Lydia Jenkins S:5

Jenkins, Joseph - Died 1825 Jan 28 in his 84th yr S:5

Jenkins, Joseph (Capt) - Died 1832 Nov 2 Age 62 years S:6

Jenkins, Joseph (Ensign) - Died 1743 Nov 26 in his 46th yr (church record dated 1745) S:11R+26R

Jenkins, Lemuel - Died 1842 Mar 18 Age 29 S:5

Jenkins, Lydia - Died 1795 Nov 16 Age 26 at Nantucket, Mass Wife of Prince Jenkins S:5

Jenkins, Lydia - Died 1796 Sept 29 Age 4 Daughter of Nathaniel &

Jenkins (Cont.)
Abigail Jenkins S:5R

Jenkins, Lydia - Died 1797 Jan 17 Age 3 years, 9 months (died of small pox) Daughter of Joseph & Lydia Jenkins S:6

Jenkins, Lydia - Died 1848 July 4 Age 82 years, 9 months Wife of Capt Joseph Jenkins S:6

Jenkins, Lydia C - Died 1810 Oct 25 Age 5 weeks Daughter of Prince & Anna Jenkins S:5

Jenkins, Mary Ann Fish - Died 1871 Sept 27 in her 51st yr Daughter of Reuben & Lydia Jenkins or Fish? S:5

Jenkins, Mary D - Died 1869 Aug 11 Age 65 years, 2 months Wife of Charles Jenkins S:5

Jenkins, Mary G - Died 1886 Nov 1 Age 70 years, 7 months Wife of Charles Jenkins (Hinckley Ceme records #5R says death was 1886 Nov 12 at age 78) S:5

Jenkins, Mary Miss - Died 1810 Dec 14 in her 68th yr S:5

Jenkins, Nathan - Died 1782 Nov 7 Age 48 Born 1734 (buried next to Rachel) Rachel was his wife S:5

Jenkins, Nathan - Died 1865 Nov 9 Born 1793 Dec 27 S:5

Jenkins, Nathaniel Maj - Died 1838 Nov 8 in his 79th yr (Hinckley Ceme records #5R say he was a drummer during the Revolutionary War) S:5

Jenkins, Nellie - Died 1926 April 3 Born 1870 June 3 S:12

Jenkins, Polly - Died 1876 Jan 9 Age 79 years, 6 months S:6

Jenkins, Rachel - Died 1792 Sept 16 in her 51st yr (buried next to Nathan) Widow of Nathan Jenkins S:5

Jenkins, Rachel F - Died 1872 June 6 Age 3 years, 22 days Daughter of Joseph Jenkins S:5

Jenkins, Rebecca B - Died 1881 Jan 13 Age 65 years, 4 months Wife of John J Jenkins S:5

Jenkins, Ruth J - Died 1889 Born

Jenkins (Cont.)
1839 S:5

Jenkins, Sarah - Died 1795 Oct 24 Wife of Zacheus Jenkins S:5

Jenkins, Sarah - Died 1814 Jan 25 Age 13 years, 5 months, 18 days Daughter of Perez & Sarah Jenkins S:5

Jenkins, Sarah E - Died 1920 Born 1866 (with William Jenkins & others) S:18

Jenkins, Simeon - Died 1808 Aug 19 S:5

Jenkins, Susannah - Died 1869 Mar 3 Age 86 years, 1 month Wife of Ellis Jenkins (buried next to him) S:5

Jenkins, Walley - Died 1774 Oct 3 Age 2 years, 1 month, 13 days Son of Nathaniel & Rachel Jenkins S:5R

Jenkins, William - Died 1857 Born 1855 (with Charlie W Jenkins & others) S:18

Jenkins, William - Died 1884 Nov 9 Age 51 years, 6 months (with wife, Chloe C Jenkins) S:12

Jenkins, William - Died 1933 Born 1858 (with Flora A Jenkins) S:18

Jenney, Arthur Eugene - Died 1963 May 30 Born 1870 June 15 (between Mary O & Mabel Baine Jenney) S:15

Jenney, Mabel Baine - Died 1952 Oct 25 Born 1875 Dec 25 (next to Arthur Eugene Jenney) S:15

Jenney, Mary O - Died 1978 Nov 21 Born 1898 Feb 28 Was a Nurse Director, US Phys, 1950-52 (next to Arthur Eugene Jenney) S:15

Jennings, Ellen E - Died 1891 April 10 Age 42 years, 7 months Wife of Joseph B Jennings (next to him) S:11

Jennings, Joseph B - Died 1893 Aug 10 Age 85 years, 5 months S:11

Jerauld, Annabel - Died (still alive 1990?) Born 1900 Wife of Donald Trayser (with him) S:11

Jerauld, Bruce K - Died (still living

Jerauld (Cont.)
1990?) Born 1890 (stone has flag) (with Lucile T Jerauld) S:11

Jerauld, Dennis Alfred - Died 1951 (next to Ruth F Jerauld) S:11

Jerauld, Lucile T - Died 1965 Born 1888 (stone has flag) (with Bruce K Jerauld) S:11

Jerauld, Myra E - Died 1979 Born 1894 (with Annabel Jerauld & Donald Trayser) S:11

Jerauld, Ruth F - Died 1987 Born 1927 (stone has flag) (next to Dennis Alfred Jerauld) S:11

Jey, Mary T - Died 1942 Born 1865 Wife of Arron C Godd (with him) S:13

Jincins, Mary - Died 1714 March 4 Age 55 years, 4 days S:11R

Jinkins, Mary - Died 1774 located in row 10 S:11R

Joakim, Dionysia - Died 1965 Born 1907 (with John Joakim) S:15

Joakim, John - Died 1987 Born 1897 (with Dionysia Joakim) S:15

Johnson, A Errol - Died 1962 Born 1871 (buried with George Berthole Johnson) S:8

Johnson, Agnes - Buried 1984 Oct 24 Age 89 Located in section 4, lot 109, grave 2 S:15R

Johnson, Alfred W - Died 1980 April 27 Born 1936 Oct 25 Was a AIC in US Air Force during Korea S:20

Johnson, Andrew - Died 1924 Born 1840 (with Attresta W Johnson) S:12

Johnson, Attresta W - Died 1934 Born 1847 (with Andrew Johnson) S:12

Johnson, Bertram M - Died 1987 Born 1899 (with Mildred Bassett) S:18

Johnson, Catherine Fleming - Died 1968 May 10 Born 1894 Oct 18 (with Wesley G Johnson) S:15

Johnson, Charlotte Virgina - Died 1988 Born 1910 (next to Neilo T Johnson) S:20

Johnson, Cordelia G - Died 1849

Johnson (Cont.)

Aug 14 Born 1849 May 1 Daughter of Hiram T & Charlotte H Johnson S:4

Johnson, Edith E - Died (still living 1991?) Born 1913 (listed with Eino Johnson) S:20

Johnson, Eino J - Died 1960 Born 1908 (listed with Edith E Johnson) S:20

Johnson, Eliza A - Died 1873 Dec 14 in her 63rd yr S:4

Johnson, Elizabeth - Died 1892 Born 1818 (with William Johnson & others) S:18

Johnson, Elizabeth C - Died 1912 Born 1843 (with John T Johnson & others) S:18

Johnson, Elizabeth L - Died 1960 Born 1872 (with John T Johnson & others) S:18

Johnson, Francis - Died 1850 Sept 20 Age 1 month Son of Francis & Mercy (next to them) S:21

Johnson, Francis - Died 1863 Oct 9 Age 43 years, 2 months (next to wife, Mercy & son, Francis Johnson) S:21

Johnson, George Berthole - Died 1939 Born 1865 (stone is large cross that says Johnson, located right at entrance of cemetery) S:8

Johnson, Georgia L - Died 1968 Born 1874 Wife of Charles F Smith (with him & Christine Drisko) S:18

Johnson, Gustave G - Died 1974 Born 1897 (next to Silppa Johnson) S:15

Johnson, Henry W - Died 1962 Born 1909 (next to Charlotte Virginia Johnson) S:20

Johnson, J Victor - Died 1930 Born 1895 S:18

Johnson, John T - Died 1958 Born 1879 (with Elizabeth L Johnson & others) S:18

Johnson, Joseph - Died 1898 Born 1818 (with Elizabeth Johnson & others) S:18

Johnson, Margaret C - Died 1964

Johnson (Cont.)

June 6 Born 1931 July 10 Daughter of Clara E Clagg S:11

Johnson, Martha - Died 1956 Born 1859 Stone says,"Mother" (next to William D Johnson) S:19

Johnson, Mercy H - Died 1850 Nov 2 Age 30 years, 4 months Wife of Francis Johnson (next to him & son Francis)(stone is down and broken) S:21

Johnson, Neilo T - Died 1964 May 16 Born 1915 Sept 3 From Massachusetts, Was PFC, 75 Quartermaster Co, during World War II (next to Eino J Johnson) S:20

Johnson, Paul E - Died 1974 Sept 2 Born 1898 Feb 19 (with Evelyn Grant) S:15

Johnson, Samuel S - Died 1962 Born 1889 (with wife, Saimi M Fisk) S:20

Johnson, Silppa - Died 1984 Born 1900 (undertaker plaque only) (next to Gustave G Johnson) S:15

Johnson, Wesley G - Died 1986 Feb 18 Born 1887 April 11 (with Catherine Fleming Johnson) S:15

Johnson, William - Died 1920 Born 1846 (with Elizabeth C Johnson & others) S:18

Johnson, William D - Died 1966 Born 1902 (undertaker plaque) (next to Martha Johnson) S:19

Johnston, Alfred S - Died 1950 Born 1883 (with Florence B Johnston & others) S:18

Johnston, Brent Emmet - Died 1913 Mar 17 Born 1858 Nov 18 (on Kittredge stone) S:11

Johnston, Florence B - Died 1962 Born 1887 (with Janet Bassett & others) S:18

Johnston, Milton E (MD) - Died 1979 Born 1898 Was a Capt in US Army during World War II S:15

Johnston, William - Died 1964 Born 1872 S:15

Jokela, Alma E - Died 1970 Born 1897 (next to Hilma K Jokela) S:15

Jokela, Hilma K - Died 1968 Born 1887 (next to Alma E Jokela) S:15

Jones, (infant) - Died 1839 (stone says "Infant son 1839", buried with Mallie Jones) S:6

Jones, A Ross - Died 1972 Born 1911 S:13

Jones, Abbie P - Died 1902 Jan 22 Born 1824 Jan 23 S:7

Jones, Abby F - Died 1921 Born 1841 (with Hannah R Loring, d1922) S:11

Jones, Abigail - Died 1782 Oct 30 Age 5 months, 21 days Daughter of Silvanus & Anna Jones S:5R

Jones, Abigail - Died 1809 Dec 12 Age 17 Wife of Cornelius Jones & daughter of Lemuel & Jemmia Bursley S:5

Jones, Abigail - Died 1894 Born 1808 S:7

Jones, Abner - Died 1844 Sept 9 Age 83 years, 6 months, 11 days (buried next to wife, Anna Jones) S:7

Jones, Abner A - Died 1895 Nov 4 Age 76 years, 9 months S:7

Jones, Abram C - Died 1874 Aug 11 Age 27 years, 10 months Son of David & Mary S Jones S:7

Jones, Adeline G - Died 1888 Aug 11 Age 70 years, 2 months Wife of Josiah Jones S:5

Jones, Albertina U - Died 1973 Born 1886 Wife of Chester S Jones (with him) S:11

Jones, Alexander B - Died 1890 Born 1838 Was in Company D, 45th Massachusetts Volunteers (with Eleanor F Jones & others) S:18

Jones, Alton S - Died 1919 Born 1868 S:7

Jones, Anna - Died 1835 Mar 15 Age 71 years, 5 months, 5 days Wife of Abner Jones (buried next to him) S:7

Jones, Anna E - Died 1981 Born

Jones (Cont.)
1905 (with Edwin S Jones & others) S:19

Jones, Anna Mrs - Died 1832 Sept 10 in her 81st yr Wife of Silvanus Jones S:5

Jones, Asa - Died 1860 Feb 13 Age 73 years, 4 months S:6

Jones, Asa - Died 1886 June 17 Age 71 years, 6 months S:5

Jones, Benjamin - Died 1862 Nov 15 Age 77 years, 5 months S:5

Jones, Benjamin - Died 1870 Born 1821 S:7

Jones, Benjamin - Died 1872 Age 87 years, 7 months S:7

Jones, Betsey - Died 1822 Feb 19 in her 29th yr Wife of Benjamin Jones 6 daughter of Calvin & Eunice Crocker S:5

Jones, Bettinia M - Died (still living 1991?) Born 1894 (listed with George H Jones Sr) S:18

Jones, Charles C - Died 1844 Sept 4 Age 25 S:7

Jones, Charles C - Died 1929 Born 1851 (With Hester J Jones & others) S:19

Jones, Charles C Allen - Died 1910 Jan 6 Born 1895 June 29 Son of Charles C & Hester M Jones (he has his own stone and is listed on parents stone) S:19

Jones, Charles Frank - Died 1960 Born 1881 (with Georgianna Jey Jones & others) S:19

Jones, Charles H - Died 1961 Born 1873 (mort plaque only) (next to Ethel Jones d1886) S:14

Jones, Charles M - Died 1959 Born 1859 (next to wife, Augustar Wes) S:12

Jones, Charlotte S - Died 1896 Born 1830 (buried next to Ruben Jones) S:7

Jones, Chester S - Died 1883 May 5 Age 20 years, 4 months S:6

Jones, Chester S - Died 1955 Born 1883 (with Albertina U Jones) S:11

Jones, Chloe - Died 1892 May 11 Age 76 years, 12 days S:5

Jones, Chloe B - Died 1822 July 28 Born 1818 Nov 22 Daughter of Jedediah & Hannah Jones S:7

Jones, Clara A - Died 1898 Feb 22 Born 1867 Oct 4 Wife of Leslie F Jones S:11

Jones, Clara A - Died 1936 April 2 Born 1857 Dec 17 S:21

Jones, Clarence L - Died 1899 July 30 Born 1857 Aug 12 S:14

Jones, Clarinda - Died 1849 June 4 Born 1794 Oct 22 (Hinckley Ceme records #5R say "dearest mother" and that she was the relict of Joseph L Jones) S:5

Jones, Clifford L - Died 1963 Born 1902 (with Ruth M Jones) S:13

Jones, Cornelius - Died 1795 April 7 Age 16 Son of Silvanus & Anna Jones S:5R

Jones, Cornelius - Died 1845 July 20 in his 52nd yr S:7

Jones, David - Died 1892 Jan 8 Age 68 years, 9 months S:7

Jones, David Otis - Died 1950 Born 1932 (with William A Jones Jr & others) S:19

Jones, Deborah L Hathaway - Died 1901 Sept 9 Born 1817 Aug 12 Wife of Leander Jones (buried next to him) S:6

Jones, Edmund S - Died 1979 Born 1909 (with Albertina & Chester Jones) S:11

Jones, Edwin F (Capt) - Died 1934 Born 1868 S:14

Jones, Edwin M - Died 1903 Born 1833 (with Josephine Baxter & Helen M Jones) S:14

Jones, Edwin S - Died 1930 Born 1929 (with Elvera Jones & others & next to Charles C Allen Jones) S:19

Jones, Eleanor F - Died 1927 Born 1843 (with Florence A MacDonald & others) S:18

Jones, Eleanor I - Died 1978 Born 1880 (with Eleanor F Jones & others) S:18

Jones, Eliza M - Died (no dates) Born 1847 (with Sylvanus S Hamblin & Christina L Hamblin)

Jones (Cont.) S:21

Jones, Ellery L - Died 1963 May 28 Born 1879 Sept 1 (next to Lulu Mae Jones) S:14

Jones, Ellewett - Died 1923 Born 1845 Daughter (next to Lydia C Jones) S:5

Jones, Elsie L - Died 1977 Born 1897 Wife of William A Jones (with him & David Otis Jones & others) S:19

Jones, Elvera C - Died 1924 Born 1891 (with Anna E Jones & others) S:19

Jones, Ethel G - Died 1886 June 16 Age 7 years Daughter of EP & MB (next to Charles H Jones) S:14

Jones, Eunice - Died 1870 June 24 (stone not clear on last name, but she was wife of Harvey Jones, she is also buried next to him) S:7

Jones, Francis - Died 1811 Oct 1 Age 1 year, 3 days Son of Francis & Sally Jones S:5

Jones, Francis - Died 1854 March 3 Born 1780 Oct 29 S:5R

Jones, Francis - Died 1892 Feb 1892 Age 79 years, 8 months, 4 days S:5

Jones, Frederic P - Died 1900 May 15 Born 1828 June 19 S:7

Jones, Frederick L - Died 1954 July 22 Born 1867 Aug 22 (next to Hannah R Loring & Abby F Jones) S:11

Jones, George - Died 1909 Aug 12 Born 1860 Jan 3 S:6

Jones, George H Sr - Died 1975 Born 1893 (with Bettinia M Jones) S:18

Jones, Georgianna Jey - Died 1977 Born 1883 (with Georgianna J Hinckley & others) S:19

Jones, Hannah - Died 1865 Apr 17 Age 40 years, 20 days Wife of Abner Jones S:7

Jones, Hannah - Died 1880 Feb 27 Age 86 years, 8 months S:7

Jones, Hannah - Died 1895 Aug 6

Jones (Cont.)
Age 71 years, 5 months, 17 days
S:7

Jones, Harry L - Died 1891 June 8
Age 21 years, 7 months, 22 days
Son of Leander & Temperance S
Jones S:6

Jones, Harry L - Died 1959 Born
1891 (also has a Barnstable Fire
Dept plaque) (with Elvera C
Jones & others) S:19

Jones, Harry L Jr - Died 1990 Born
1918 Was in US Navy during
World War I & he has a 1941-45
WWI plaque & he has another
plaque that says, #126 Flt S:19

Jones, Harvey - Died 1863 Nov 8
Age 67 years, 10 months, 17
days (buried next to wife, Eunice
Jones) S:7

Jones, Harvey - Died 1899 May 16
Born 1821 Nov 6 S:7

Jones, Hattie A - Died 1925 June 7
Born 1860 May 11 Wife of Isaac
Craven (same stone) S:11

Jones, Helen E - Died 1981 Born
1893 (next to William Ernest
Jones) S:13

Jones, Helen M - Died 1931 Born
1836 (with Edwin M Jones) S:14

Jones, Henry E - Died 1865 Born
1861 S:7

Jones, Herbert TW - Died 1946
Born 1885 (next to Mary A
Jones) S:19

Jones, Hester J - Died 1945 Born
1856 (with Charles Frank Jones
& others) S:19

Jones, Hezekiah - Died 1876 Aug 8
Age 49 years, 5 months, 29 days
S:7

Jones, Hiram T - Died 1878 Born
1847 (with Susan L Jones &
John & Eunice Baxter) S:14

Jones, Horace - Died 1915 Born
1826 (buried with Rosetta Jones
& others) S:8

Jones, Inez May Lucas - Died 1973
Born 1898 S:17

Jones, Isaac - Died 1809 Oct 12 in
his 90th yr (buried next to wife,
Marcy Jones) S:7

Jones, Isaac - Died 1866 Born
1801 S:7

Jones, Isabella W - Died 1915 July
30 Born 1838 May 3 S:7

Jones, Jabez C - Died 1888 Oct 20
Age 70 years, 1 month, 10 days
S:7

Jones, James H - Died 1888 Born
1836 S:5

Jones, Jane - Died 1884 Nov 21 in
her 77th yr Widow of Seth Jones
(buried next to him) S:7

Jones, Jedediah - Died 1858 Mar
19 Age 66 years, 6 months S:7

Jones, Jedidiah - Died 1840 Apr 1
Age 80 years, 6 months, 20 days
S:5

Jones, Joseph L - Died 1825 Aug
19 in Athens, Ohio Born 1789
Aug 13 Inscribed on slate, "To
memory of Mrs Clarinda Jones,
his wife" S:5R

Jones, Josiah C - Died 1902 May 1
Age 86 years, 8 months S:5

Jones, L Alexander - Died 1919
Born 1845 S:6

Jones, Leander - Died 1874 Dec 31
Born 1809 Apr 9 S:6

Jones, Lena F - Died 1887 Born
1869 S:7

Jones, Leslie F - Died 1941 June
14 Born 1849 Oct 22 (large
Jones stone) S:11

Jones, Lester B - Died 1875 Sept
29 Born 1864 Nov 30 Son of
Simeon & Mimah (Jemima)
Jones S:8

Jones, Lois - Died 1889 Born 1802
S:21

Jones, Lulu Mae - Died 1953 Born
1877 (next to Ellery L Jones)
S:14

Jones, Lydia - Died (stone not clear
for reading next to Olive Jones)
S:5

Jones, Lydia - Died 1815 Apr 15
Daughter of Abner & Anna
Jones S:7

Jones, Lydia - Died 1872 Nov 5 in
her 84th yr Daughter of Lemuel
Snow S:6

Jones, Lydia C - Died 1851 Aug 31

Jones (Cont.)
Age 12 years, 1 month Daughter of Josiah & Adaline Jones S:5

Jones, Lydia F - Died 1862 Dec 4 Age 64 years, 7 months, 22 days Daughter of Jedediah & Olive Jones S:5R

Jones, Mallie - Died 1864 Apr 19 Age 9 years, 6 months, 7 days Daughter of Leander S & Deborah L Jones S:6

Jones, Mallie - Died 1864 Apr 9 Born 1854 Oct 2 (stone says, "Infant son 1839" so there·must be a infant buried with her) S:6

Jones, Marcia A - Died 1955 Born 1928 Wife of William A Jones Jr (with him & William A Jones & others) S:19

Jones, Marcy - Died 1811 June 16 in her 86th yr Widow of Isaac Jones (buried next to him) S:7

Jones, Mary - Died 1832 Born 1795 S:7

Jones, Mary A - Died 1961 Born 1885 (next to Herbert TW Jones) S:19

Jones, Mary Abbie - Died 1887 Born 1850 S:6

Jones, Mary E - Died 1874 Oct 13 Age 81 years, 9 months Widow of Benjamin Jones (buried next to him) S:7

Jones, Mary Emily - Died 1851 May 28 Age 24 years, 8 months, 18 days Wife of Harvey Jones S:7

Jones, Mary S - Died 1884 Apr 30 Age 63 years, 3 months, 16 days Wife of David Jones S:7

Jones, Mehitable S - Buried 1881 Located in section O, lot 30, grave 2 S:14R

Jones, Mercy - Died 1813 July 28 Age 30 years, 10 months Daughter of Timothy & Hannah Jones S:7

Jones, Milton B - Buried 1921 March 23 Age 44 Located in section R, lot 15, grave 9 S:14R

Jones, Minnie E - Died 1883 Born 1862 S:7

Jones, Miriam W - Died 1962 Born 1868 S:11

Jones, Nancy M - Buried 1924 Aug 5 Located in section O, lot 6, grave 2 S:14R

Jones, Nathan - Died 1872 Oct 28 in his 81st yr S:7

Jones, Nathan Atwood - Died 1891 Born 1829 S:7

Jones, Nathaniel F - Died 1862 Aug 21 in his 33rd yr (buried next to Sadie, Horace & Rosetta Jones) S:8

Jones, Nellie W - Died 1885 Sept 27 Age 16 years, 3 months, 14 days Daughter of Thomas W & Ella Jones S:6

Jones, Olive - Died 1852 Nov 8 Age 93 years, 8 months, 12 days Widow of Jedidiah Jones S:5

Jones, Olive - Died 1907 Jan Born 1824 Oct S:6

Jones, Olive I - Died 1819 Nov 9 in her 52nd yr Wife S:5

Jones, Olive L - Died 1849 Dec 9 Age 52 Wife of Silas F Jones S:5R

Jones, Oliver B - Died 1881 Feb 26 Age 57 years, 6 months (buried next to wife, Pamelia C Jones & son, Oliver H Jones) S:8

Jones, Pamelia C - Died 1904 Feb 6 in her 80th yr Wife of Oliver B Jones (son buried next to them, Oliver H Jones b1889 d1912, was in Signal Corp World War I) S:8

Jones, Rachel - Died 1793 May 24 in her 31st yr Wife of Silvanus Jones (Hinckley Ceme records #5R says death was 1795 and that her husband was a Junior) S:5

Jones, Remember - Died 1848 Oct 2 in her 82nd yr Wife of Lot Jones S:7

Jones, Rhoda S - Died 1868 Nov 22 Age 72 years, 8 months, 8 days Wife of Nathan Jones S:7

Jones, Robert H - Died 1931 Born 1904 (next to Miriam W Jones) S:11

Jones, Robert L Sr - Died 1968 Aug 6 Born 1915 April 17 S:19

Jones, Rosetta - Died 1910 Born 1827 (buried with Sadie Jones & others) S:8

Jones, Ruben H - Died 1900 Born 1826 S:7

Jones, Ruth - Died 1896 Born 1819 (stone says, "Mother") (located next to William F Jones-husband?) S:5

Jones, Ruth M - Died (still living in 1991?) Born 1904 (listed with Clifford L Jones) S:13

Jones, Sadie - Died 1943 Born 1860 (perpetual care) (buried with Rosetta & Horace Jones) S:8

Jones, Sadie E - Died 1898 Born 1863 (stone is off the base) Wife of George W Jones S:12

Jones, Sarah - Died 1866 Feb in her 81st yr S:7

Jones, Sarah - Died 1870 Age 83 Born 1786 Wife of Francis Jones S:5

Jones, Sarah A - Died 1909 Born 1836 (buried between Thomas & Minnie E Jones) S:7

Jones, Sarah N - Died 1902 May 9 Born 1815 July 13 S:5

Jones, Seth - Died 1869 June 10 Age 66 years, 10 months (buried next to wife, Jane Jones) S:7

Jones, Seth Nye - Died 1920 Apr 16 Born 1835 Feb 19 S:7

Jones, Silas F - Died 1854 Nov 12 Age 61 years, 11 days S:5R

Jones, Silas F - Died 1903 Oct 15 (buried in California) Born 1831 June 7 S:7

Jones, Silvanus - Died 1793 Apr 7 in his 16th yr Son of Silvanus & Anna Jones S:5

Jones, Silvanus - Died 1806 March 28 Age 61 S:5R

Jones, Simeon F - Died 1909 Born 1831 (large Jones stone) S:8

Jones, Sophronia B - Died 1889 Jan 23 Age 41 years, 9 months S:6

Jones, Susan L - Died 1936 Born

Jones (Cont.)
1850 (with Hiram T Jones) S:14

Jones, Sylvester - Buried 1891 Dec 28 Located in section O, lot 6, grave 1 S:14R

Jones, Thankful - Died 1882 Nov 29 Age 76 years, 8 months S:7

Jones, Thomas - Died 1881 Born 1787 S:7

Jones, Thomas - Died 1896 Born 1823 S:7

Jones, Thomas H - Died 1897 Oct 23 Born 1807 July 31 S:6

Jones, Timothy - Died 1873 Feb 14 Age 74 years, 10 months, 22 days S:7

Jones, William - Died 1797 July 29 Son of Goodspeed & Rebekah Jones S:7

Jones, William - Died 1903 Born 1821 (with Elizabeth Crocker, possibly wife) S:8

Jones, William A - Died 1941 Born 1885 (with wife, Elsie L Jones & others) S:19

Jones, William A Jr - Died 1976 Born 1925 (also has Barnstable Fire Chief plaque at stone) (with wife, Marcia A Jones & others) S:19

Jones, William Ernest - Died 1976 April 1 Born 1888 Jan 31 Was a PFC in US Army during World War I (next to Helen E Jones) S:13

Jones, William F - Died 1915 Born 1818 (stone says,"Father")(located next to Ruth Jones-wife?) S:5

Jones, William H - Died 1935 Born 1865 (with wife, Emma F Manter) S:14

Jones, William H Jr - Died 1901 Born 1901 Son of William Jones Sr & Emma Manter (with them) S:14

Jones, Willie H - Died 1863 Born 1862 S:7

Jones, Willis C - Died 1895 Aug 19 Age 38 years, 8 months (another Willis C Jones is located next to him) S:6

Jones, Zenas - Died 1829 Apr 27

Jones (Cont.)

Age 36 years, 3 months S:7

Jordan, Marion - Died 1943 June 9 Born 1879 May 21 (with husband, William Frederick Bentinck-Smith) S:14

Jordan, Richard J - Died 1967 May 20 Born 1967 Feb 5 (a baby stone) (next to James & Esther Kurra) S:20

Jordan, William R - Died 1962 May 12 Born 1894 Sept 8 From Massachusetts, was Lt in 163 Depot Brig during World War I S:16

Joseph, Isabel L - Died 1987 Born 1924 (with Margaret F Joseph) S:31

Joseph, Margaret F - Died 1933 Born 1895 (has two stones) Stone says,"My Jesus Mercy" (with Isabel L Joseph) S:31

Josephson, Lillian M - Died 1990 Born 1913 (with Robert Josephson) S:15

Josephson, Robert - Died 1964 Born 1899 (with Lillian M Josephson) S:15

Joslin, Dorothy Bitter - Died 1985 Born 1903 (with Ellsworth Carl Joslin) S:19

Joslin, Ellsworth Carl - Died 1966 Born 1893 (with Dorothy Bitter Joslin) S:19

Joy, Harding F - Died 1929 Born 1876 (next to Janet Joy Crosby) S:12

Joyslin, William R (Rev) - Died 1922 Born 1847 (listed on same stone with wife, Emma Caroline Hinckley) S:8

Judson, Ann - Died 1910 Dec 7 Born 1827 Jan 28 Wife of Nathaniel Hinckley (buried next to him) S:7

Judson, Ellen McKean - Died 1952 Born 1862 Wife of Erwin A Hall (with him) S:11

Junevic, Anna Agnes - Died 1983 Aug 3 Born 1892 July 17 S:15

Kalas, Catherine - Died 1926 March 12 Born 1926 March 8

Kalas (Cont.)

(next to Catharine G & Christos G Bolekos) S:12

Kalas, James K - Died 1945 Born 1892 in Greece (with Mary G Bolekos) S:12

Kalweit, George H - Died 1961 Born 1916 S:20

Kaplan, Alice B - Died 1973 Born 1907 (Jewish section) (with Joseph Kaplan) S:15

Kaplan, Gertrude G - Died 1984 Sept 29 Born 1900 Jan 3 (Jewish section) S:15

Kaplan, Joseph - Died 1973 Born 1886 (Jewish section) (with Alice B Kaplan) S:15

Karram, Marguerite V - Died 1977 June 13 Born 1900 March 25 Stone says, "Mother" S:15

Kartsonis, John Paul - Died 1984 Born 1900 (above middle name from the Mosswood cemetery records) S:15

Kasetta, Frances B - Died 1990 Born 1907 (this is a small undertakers plaque only) S:13

Kasper, John M - Died 1971 Born 1890 (with wife, Anna Reedmon) S:17

Kazukynas, Victor T Sr - Died 1973 Aug 10 Born 1897 Mar 13 Was a Pvt in US Army during World War I S:15

Keane, Emma J - Died 1935 June 1 Born 1861 Oct 19 (next to Charles H Keane) S:21

Keane, Joseph J - Died 1960 Born 1892 (with Mary B Rogers) S:16

Keavy, Jean J - Died (still living 1991?) Born 1928 (listed with Scott & Samuel Keavy) S:20

Keavy, Samuel W - Died (still living 1991?) Born 1925 (listed with Jean J & Scott Keavy) S:20

Keavy, Scott R - Died 1989 Dec 7 Born 1956 Dec 9 (listed with Jean & Samuel Keavy) S:20

Keavy, Vincent DePaul - Died 1968 1900 S:16

Keck, Charles E - Died 1925 Jan 3 Born 1853 Dec 28 (has many

Keck (Cont.)

plaques from service) (cross for 1898-1902 in Phillipine Islands, Porto Rico & Cuba, was in Army United Navy, another says, FLT lOOF #119 PG LE Hawes Wankinguoah)(with Wilhelmina Dickson) S:19

Kee, Harold F - Died 1968 Born 1890 (with wife, Mildred W Kee) S:14

Kee, Mildred W - Died 1972 Born 1889 Wife of Harold W Kee (with him) S:14

Keenan, Lois F - Died 1961 Born 1881 (with Charles & Fannie Fish) S:18

Keenan, Mary C - Died 1976 Born 1896 (with William H McDevitt) S:16

Keene, Alma L - Died 1934 June 1 Born 1854 Oct 27 (with Alton C Bearse & others) S:18

Kehlenbach, Anja Sylvia Sundelin - Died 1971 Born 1923 S:20

Kelleher, George J - Died 1981 Born 1896 Was a Cpl in US Army during World War I S:15

Kelley, (infant) - Died 1883 Born 1883 (buried with Capt Hiram & Orrina Kelley) S:8

Kelley, Abigail B - Died 1910 Born 1828 (buried with David N Kelley) S:8

Kelley, Adalbert - Died 1863 Aug 29 Age 23 years 2 months (next to Cornelia Kelley) S:13

Kelley, Albert E - Died 1953 Born 1878 (with wife, Katherine F Kelley & others) S:19

Kelley, Alexander - Died 1823 July 19 Age 8 years, 6 months, 21 days Son of Arvin & Eleanor Kelley S:2

Kelley, Alexander - Died 1856 Feb in his 32nd yr (lost at sea) S:2

Kelley, Alice J - Died 1915 Born 1851 (with George F Kelley) S:19

Kelley, Arvin (Capt) - Died 1825 Oct 9 Age 43 years, 5 months S:2

Kelley, Carlton W - Died 1944 Born

Kelley (Cont.)

1903 (next to William E Kelley) S:19

Kelley, Caroline P - Died 1834 Born 1831 S:2

Kelley, Caroline P - Died 1867 Born 1834 (buried next to Caroline P Kelley who died same year she was born) S:2

Kelley, Caroline S - Died 1896 Born 1806 S:2

Kelley, Carrie M - Died 1941 Born 1874 S:8

Kelley, Charlie - Died 1878 Sept 25 Born 1875 May 1 Son of EB & EF (Edwin & Emma Kelley) (next to them) Stone says,"Our darling" (small stone) S:18

Kelley, Clement - Died 1868 Apr 12 Age 70 years, 7 months S:2

Kelley, Cornelia - Died 1846 March 29 Age 6 months 6 days (next to Adalbert Kelley) S:13

Kelley, David - Died 1861 Oct 31 Age 68 years, 5 months S:2

Kelley, David N - Died 1871 Born 1819 (buried with Abigail B Kelley) S:8

Kelley, Deborah - Died 1843 Oct 5 in his 66th yr Wife of Freeman Kelley S:2

Kelley, Deborah F - Died 1876 Oct 21 Age 70 years, 8 months Daughter of Freeman & Deborah S:2

Kelley, Eddie J - Died 1870 Feb 5 Born 1852 Oct 26 Only son of Ferdinand G & Florilla Kelley (buried next to them) S:8

Kelley, Edwin B - Died 1930 Born 1850 (with Emma F Kelley) S:18

Kelley, Eleanor - Died 1864 Apr 3 Age 76 years, 7 months, 13 days Widow of Arvin Kelley S:2

Kelley, Eliza F - Died 1892 Apr 16 in her 75th yr Widow of Nelson Kelley S:2

Kelley, Elizabeth E - Died 1934 Born 1851 Wife of Theodore Kelley (buried with him) S:8

Kelley, Ella Eliza - Died 1849 Sept 17 Born 1848 Apl 27 Daughter

Kelley (Cont.)
of Nelson & Eliza F Kelley S:4

Kelley, Ella M - Died 1931 May Born 1849 Apr 26 (Marston plot) Wife of Howard Marston, buried next to him) S:8

Kelley, Emma F - Died 1928 Born 1854 (with Edwin B Kelley & next to son, Charlie Kelley) S:18

Kelley, Esther A - Died 1986 Born 1900 Wife of Joseph A Kelley (with him) S:15

Kelley, Ferdinand G - Died 1902 July 7 Born 1818 Sept 14 (buried next to Florilla Kelley, possibly wife, stones are same design) S:8

Kelley, Florilla A - Died 1892 Dec 23 Born 1820 May 22 Stone says, Thou art gone to the home of thy rest where suffering no longer can harm you S:8

Kelley, Francis - Died 1830 June 22 Age 15 years, 1 month, 2 days (drowned from Sek Juliet(?) on the Connecticut River(stone not clear) Son of David & Patience Kelley S:2

Kelley, Freeman - Died 1848 Nov 15 Age 72 years, 9 months, 24 days S:2

Kelley, George F - Died 1915 Born 1843 (with Alice J Kelley) S:19

Kelley, Hannah - Died Age 26 when died (no year mentioned) Wife of Frank Kelley S:8

Kelley, Hannah Edwards - Died 1834 Feb 3 Age 9 months, 27 days Daughter of Jonathan & Sylvia Kelley S:2

Kelley, Henry - Died 1939 Born 1869 (with wife, Sarah Kelley) S:18

Kelley, Herbert F - Died 1916 Born 1852 (buried next to wife, Marcia A Kelley) S:8

Kelley, Herbert R - Died 1909 Born 1909 (with Albert & Katherine Kelley & Charles Crowell & Eugenia Gyder) S:19

Kelley, Hiram R (Capt) - Died 1921 Born 1848 (buried with Orrina

Kelley (Cont.)
Kelley-same stone) S:8

Kelley, Irene A - Died 1831 Aug 3 Age 4 years, 2 months, 25 days Daughter of David & Patience Kelley S:2

Kelley, Isa - Died 1859 Dec 17 Born 1854 Dec 25 (dau of Ferdinand & Florilla Our darling) (buried next to Eddie Kelley, possibly brother) Stone says, "Hold her oh father in thine arms and let her henceforth be a messenger of love between our human hearts" S:8

Kelley, James B - Died 1839 Aug 11 Age 18 years, 2 months, 14 days Son of David & Patience Kelley S:2

Kelley, James D - Died 1911 Born 1840 S:8

Kelley, Jeremiah (Rev) - Died 1873 Oct 11 Born 1797 July 26 (buried next to him, Sarah Kelley, possibly wife) S:8

Kelley, Jonathan - Died 1874 Apr 30 Age 79 years, 5 months, 6 days S:2

Kelley, Joseph E - Died 1971 Born 1896 (with wife, Esther A Kelley) S:15

Kelley, Joseph J - Buried 1983 Jan 14 Age 84 Located in section 11, lot 19, grave 1 S:15R

Kelley, Katherine F - Died 1970 Born 1882 Wife of Albert E Kelley (with him & Herbert R Kelley & others) S:19

Kelley, Kiriathian - Died 1831 Sept 15 Age 15 years, 2 months Son of David & Patience Kelley S:2

Kelley, Marcia A - Died 1935 Born 1856 Wife of Herbert Kelley (buried next to him) S:8

Kelley, Mary - Died 1876 Jan 20 Age 69 years, 3 months Wife of Clement Kelley (buried next to him) S:2

Kelley, Mary E - Died 1944 Born 1892 S:16

Kelley, Mary J - Died 1873 May 3 Age 24 years, 4 months (stone

Kelley (Cont.)
says, "Mother") S:8

Kelley, Matilda S - Died 1914 Born 1839 Dec 10 S:8

Kelley, Nelson (Capt) - Died 1875 Feb 23 Age 63 (buried next to wife, Eliza) S:2

Kelley, Orren R - Died 1893 Born 1836 (buried with Rosa C Kelley-wife-same stone) S:8

Kelley, Orren V - Died 1862 Born 1862 (one large family stone) (buried with Rosa & Orren & entire family) S:8

Kelley, Orrina M - Died 1929 Born 1857 (buried with Capt Hiram R Kelley) S:8

Kelley, Patience - Died 186? Sept (stone not clear) Age 75 Wife of David Kelley S:2

Kelley, Patience F - Died 1834 July 14 Age 6 years, 3 months, 14 days Daughter of David & Patience Kelley S:2

Kelley, Phebe A - Died 1834 July 21 Age 1 year, 10 months, 15 days Daughter of David & Patience Kelley S:2

Kelley, Phebe Ellen - Died 1842 Sept 4 Age 4 years, 7 months, 16 days Daughter of David & Patience Kelley S:2

Kelley, Prentiss - Died 1880 Born 1803 S:2

Kelley, Roland T - Died 1927 Born 1874 (with Sarah B Kelley & Lillian M Alvin & Elba D Lucas) S:18

Kelley, Rosa C - Died 1921 Born 1840 (Buried with husband, Orren R & Orren V, William Lumbert, Jennie Lumbert, Mery Lumbert, Phyllis Davis, Kenneth Clark) S:8

Kelley, Sarah B - Died 1971 Born 1879 (with Roland T Kelley) S:18

Kelley, Sarah E - Died 1890 Born 1798 (next to Rev Jeremiah Kelley) S:8

Kelley, Sarah R - Died 1848 May 30 Wife of Capt Samuel Kelley (next to Cornelia Kelley) S:13

Kelley, Sarah W - Died (no date) Born 1888 Wife of Henry Kelley (listed with him) S:18

Kelley, Sylvia - Died 1884 Sept 5 Age 82 years, 2 months, 4 days S:2

Kelley, Theodore - Died 1915 Born 1846 (buried with Elizabeth E Kelley) S:8

Kelley, William E - Died 1986 Born 1938 (next to Carlton W Kelley) S:19

Kelley, Willis L - Died 1893 June 8 Born 1872 Oct 11 S:8

Kelley, Zenas - Died 1952 Born 1872 S:18

Kelley, Zeno - Died 1866 (lost at sea) Born 1836 S:2

Kellough, Mabel L - Died 1965 Born 1884 S:20

Kelly, Abigail P - Died 1880 July 5 Age 90 years, 5 months S:7

Kelly, Annie Crocker - Died 1928 July 13 Born 1852 Jan 3 Daughter of Henry & Mary A Crocker & wife of G Wallce Kelly MD S:9

Kelly, Aubry D - Died 1981 Born 1891 Was ENS in US Navy during World War II S:15

Kelly, Hannah - Died 1810 Aug 17 in her 34th yr (stone broken) Wife of Levi Kelley (next to him) & Daughter to Solomon & Abigail Bodfish S:12+12R

Kelly, Joan - Died 1847 April 17 in her 67th yr Wife to Levi Kelley (next to him & other wives) S:12 +12R

Kelly, Katherine V - Died 1980 Born 1895 (with Walter W Kelly) S:16

Kelly, Levi - Died 1863 Mar 23 Age 83 or 88 S:12+12R

Kelly, Miriam H - Died 1970 Born 1920 S:11

Kelly, Pearl May - Died 1987 Born 1896 (with Roger T & Elizabeth E Gott) S:14

Kelly, Sally W - Died 1824 Feb 20 in her 34th yr Wife of Levi Kelley (next to him) S:12+12R

Kelly, Sarah P - Died 1878 Dec 28 Age 81 yrs 6 mos S:12+12R

Kelly, Walter W - Died 1971 Sept 29 Born 1896 Sept 30 From Massachusetts, was A5? in USNRF during World War I (with Katherine V Kelly) S:16

Kennedy, Constance H - Died 1977 Born 1895 (with Walter J Kennedy DMD) S:16

Kennedy, James H - Buried 1983 Jan 13 Age 86 Located in section 8, lot 39, grave 1 S:15R

Kennedy, John F - Died 1971 Aug 23 Born 1896 May 17 Was from Massachusetts, was a Corporal in 309th Supply Co OMC during World War I (next to Walter J Kennedy DMD) S:16

Kennedy, Rachel L - Died 1977 Born 1897 S:15

Kennedy, Virginia B - Died (still living 1991?) Born 1907 Nov 2 (with William Bearse & Delia M Bearse) S:18

Kennedy, Walter J (DMD) - Died 1973 Born 1895 (with Constance H Kennedy) S:16

Kenney, Anne C - Died 1991 Born 1931 S:20

Kenney, James F - Died 1959 Born 1871 (with wife, Georgianna Bacon) S:17

Kent, Frederick S - Died 1941 Born 1868 (a large stone with others who are recent deaths) S:8

Kent, Rebekah S - Died 1931 Born 1871 (children are listed with her which have recent dates) S:8

Kerbauch, Laura L - Died 1905 April 4 Age 84 years, 6 months S:12

Ketcham, Lucy R - Buried 1981 Aug 26 Age 83 Located in section 8, lot 96, grave 2 (near Melville K Ketcham) S:15R

Ketcham, Melville K - Buried 1981 May 11 Age 84 Located in section 8, lot 96, grave 1 (near Lucy R Ketcham) S:15R

Kettner, Florence - Died (still living 1991?) Born 1905 (listed with

Kettner (Cont.) William Kettner) S:14

Kettner, William - Died 1979 Born 1899 (with Florence Kettner) S:14

Keveney, Catherine - Died 1933 Jan 30 Born 1848 June 25 (with Michael Keveney) S:31

Keveney, Ellen J - Died 1983 Born 1903 (with John F Keveney) S:16

Keveney, John F - Died 1983 Born 1900 (with Ellen J Keveney) S:16

Keveney, Michael - Died 1903 Feb 22 Born 1825 Nov 1 (with Catherine Keveney) S:31

Keyes, Amos F - Died 1951 Born 1877 (with Clara M Keyes) S:18

Keyes, Clara M - Died 1969 Born 1878 (with Amos F Keyes & Orrin F Keyes & Dorothy C Keyes) S:18

Keyes, Dorothy C - Died 1929 Born 1901 (with Orrin F Keyes & others) S:18

Keyes, Orrin F - Died 1975 Nov 20 Born 1898 Aug 31 (has 2 stones) Was in US Army during World War I & II (with Dorothy C Keyes & Clara & Amos Keyes) S:18

Kieser, Margaret B - Died 1971 Born 1883 Wife of Philip Kieser (with him) S:18

Kieser, Philip A - Died 1935 Born 1882 (with Margaret B Kieser, his wife) S:18

Killey, Benjamin - Died 1824 Sept 29 in his 89th yr S:3+3R

Killey, Susanna - Died 1816 Dec 16 Age 79 years, 4 days Wife of Benjamin Killey S:3

Kimball, Fred M - Died 1954 Jan 9 Born 1895 Aug 17 From Massachusetts,was PFC in CoA, 101 Field Sig Bn during World War I (SS) S:17

Kincare, Grace L - Died 1986 Born 1901 (undertaker plaque only) (next to John E Kincare) S:15

Kincare, John E - Died 1976 Born 1898 Was a PFC in US Army during World War I (next to Grace L Kincare) S:15

King, Bridget T - Died 1938 Born
1872 stone says,"May her soul
rest in peace" Wife of James J
Mitchell (with him) S:31

King, Emma - Died 1875 Born
1873 Daughter of William &
Mary King (with them & others)
S:19

King, Mary A - Died 1920 Born
1850 (with husband, William
King & children, Willie A, Rosa,
Walter & others) S:19

King, Nellie M - Died 1889 Born
1871 Daughter of William &
Mary King (with them & others)
S:19

King, Rosa - Died 1882 Born 1877
Daughter of William & Mary
King (with them & Willie A King
& others) S:19

King, Walter F - Died 1882 Born
1880 Son of William & Mary
King (with them & Rosa King &
others) S:19

King, William - Died 1930 Born
1846 (with wife, Mary & Rosa
King & other children) S:19

King, Willie A - Died 1880 Born
1880 Son of William & Mary
King (with them & Walter F King
& others) S:19

Kingman, Patty - Died 1822 Jan 2
Born 1786 Jan 1 in Orleans,
Massachusetts Daughter of
Simeon Kingman Esq & Wife of
Doc Oliver Ford S:7

Kingsbury, Esther H - Died 1984
Born 1910 (with Walter E Kingsbury) S:19

Kingsbury, Walter E - Died 1976
Born1901 (with Esther H Kingsbury) S:19

Kingsley, Evelyn M - Died (still
living 1991?) Born 1918 (with
John A Kingsley) S:20

Kingsley, John A - Died 1984 Born
1919 (marker is a rock, plus he
has another stone) Was a TEC 4,
US Army during World War II
(with Evelyn M Kinsley) S:20

Kinney, (baby) - Died 1905 Born
1905 (in Kinney plot with

Kinney (Cont.)
William D Kinney & Anna L
Stevens) S:12

Kinney, Loomis S - Died 1979 Born
1906 (in Kinney plot with William D Kinney MD & Anna L
Stevens) S:12

Kinney, William D (MD) - Died
1946 Born 1873 (in Kinney plot
with Anna L Stevens, wife &
others) S:12

Kinnicutt, William Henry - Died
1954 Born 1864 (with Julia
Hyde, possibly wife) S:8

Kirk, Inez - Died (still living 1991?)
Born 1902 (with EA Leslie
Bennett) S:15

Kirkman, Sidney Alexander - Died
1956 May 10 Born 1875 May 7
(with Mary Lewis Evans) S:14

Kirkpatrick, Austin N - Died 1981
Born 1900 Was a Major in US
Army during World War II S:15

Kitchin, Gordon Graham - Died (no
dates) Stone says,"Flowers I
leave you on the grass" (with
Ruth Braodbent Kitchin) S:19

Kitchin, Ruth Broadbent - Died (no
dates) (with Gordon Graham
Kitchin) S:19

Kittredge, Dora - Died 1974 Nov 5
Born 1893 Oct 26 (on Kittredge
stone) S:11

Kittredge, Edith R - Died 1941 Aug
19 Born 1897 Feb 12 S:19

Kittredge, Edward Lyman - Died
1906 May 16 Born 1827 May 14
(a large Kittredge & Johnston
stone) S:11

Kittredge, George Lyman - Died
1941 July 23 Born 1860 Feb 28
(on Kittredge stone) S:11

Kittredge, Henry Crocker - Died
1967 Feb 19 Born 1890 Jan 4
(on Kittredge stone) S:11

Kittredge, Lucretia C - Died 1916
Oct 14 Born 1882 Oct 12 Wife of
Brent E Johnston (with him)
S:11

Kittredge, William DeWitt - Died
1903 or 8 April 15 Born 1881
Feb 14 (on Kittredge stone) S:11

262

Klimm, Joanna L - Died 1988 Born 1899 (with Capt Rasmus C Klimm) S:15

Klimm, Rasmus C (Capt) - Died 1981/ Born 1888 (with Joanna L Klimm) S:15

Knapp, Edgar L - Died 1953 Born 1884 (with Martha L Crowther & Alice L Bearse) S:17

Knight, Austin M - Died 1965 Born 1874 (with Dorothy H Knight) S:18

Knight, Dorothy H - Died 1987 Born 1904 (with Austin & Gertrude Knight) S:18

Knight, Gertrude H - Died 1950 Born 1876 (with Melvin D Knight) S:18

Knight, Ida May - Died 1957 Born 1886 S:17

Knight, Maud Chatfield - Died 1944 Nov 12 Born 1868 March 16 (with Alton Churbuck) S:14

Knight, Melvin D - Died 1960 Born 1906 (with Gertrude H Knight) S:18

Knight, Thomas H H - Died 1920 April 3 Born 1862 Feb 3 (with Alton Churbuck) S:14

Knight, Willard B - Died 1978 Nov 9 Born 1917 Feb 5 Was a TEC 5 in US Army during World War II S:11

Knoblauch, Annaliese G - Died (still living 1991?) Born 1932 (listed with Paul & Gretak Knoblauch) S:18

Knoblauch, Gretak - Died 1987 Born 1893 (with Annaliese & Paul Knoblauch) S:18

Knoblauch, Paul O - Died 1961 Born 1893 (with Gretak & Annaliese Knoblauch) S:18

Knott, Annie Tucker - Died 1938 Aug 13 Born 1871 May 20 (with Louie Ernest Knott) S:11

Knott, Louie Ernest - Died 1927 Feb 19 Born 1869 Feb 18 (with Annie Tucker Knott) S:11

Knott, Margaret Crocker - Died 1975 June 12 Born 1893 Feb 23 (with Sydney Tucker Knott) S:11

Knott, Ruth Ellen - Died 1990 Born 1927 S:11

Knott, Sydney T - Died 1979 Born 1922 (he was in the US Navy) S:11

Knott, Sydney Tucker - Died 1944 Sept 5 Born 1895 March 23 (has plaque, 1941-45 World war II & flag) (with Margaret Crocker Knott) S:11

Knott, Thomas Hoxie - Died 1956 Born 1951 (this is a small stone just in back of Ruth & Sydney Knott) S:11

Knowland, Ralph M - Died 1970 Born 1892 (with Mabel G Brinton, wife) S:17

Knowles, Barbie - Died 1862 Born 1862 (buried with Eunice & Nelson Phinney & others) S:8

Knowlton, Donald J (MD) - Died 1975 Born 1885 Was a Capt in Royal Army Med Corp 21 Feb 1917 to 28 Jan 1919 (next to Irene Jaycox Knowlton) He was in the Harvard Med unit in the British Exedi Forces S:15

Knowlton, Irene Jaycox - Died 1981 Born 1897 (next to Donald J Knowlton MD) S:15

Knox, Cynthia A - Died 1881 June 28 Born 1856 July 16 Wife of Capt John Knox (next to him) S:14

Knox, Francis E - Died 1878 April 13 Born 1877 Sept 30 (small stone cross) Daughter of John & Cynthia Knox (next to them) S:14

Knox, John (Capt) - Died 1909 Dec 9 Born 1833 June 14 (next to wife, Cynthia A Knox) S:14

Knox, M? - Died (no death date) (stone very small next to possible mother, Mary Ann Knox) S:21

Knox, Martin? - Died 185? Dec 24 (stone not clear) Son of Thomas & Mary Ann Knox (next to mother) S:21

Knox, Mary Ann - Died 1847 Feb 25 (there is a small stone next to

Knox (Cont.)
her that is not clear) Wife of Dr
Thomas P Knox S:21

Knox, Thomas P - Died (this is only
a foot stone that says only TPK,
is it Thomas P Knox?) (also next
to Martin? Knox) S:21

Knox, Thomas P Jr - Died 1847
Sept 22? Age 14 months, 7 days
Son of Thomas P & Mary Ann
Knox (next to Thomas P Knox)
S:21

Koebel, Edith - Died 1946 Born
1869 Wife of Maj Samuel Stewart (buried with him) S:8

Koenig, Charles H - Died 1970
Born 1897 (with wife, Louise S
Koenig) S:14

Koenig, Louise S - Died 1957 Born
1898 Wife of Charles H Koenig
(with him) S:14

Koenig, M Beatrice - Died 1968
Born 1895 (with Charles &
Louise Koenig) S:14

Kohler, Ethel L - Died 1987 Born
1907 (with William Kohler & Mae
& Franklin Lingham) S:19

Kohler, William E H - Died (still
living 1991?) Born 1905 (with
Ethel L Kohler & others) S:19

Kopas, John S - Died 1978 April 27
Born 1917 (next to Stephanie E
Kopas) S:11

Kopas, Stephanie E - Died (still
living 1990) Born 1920 (next to
John S Kopas) S:11

Kouthouris, George L - Died 1987
Born 1894 (with Ruth Kouthouris) S:15

Kouthouris, Ruth - Died 1977
Born 1899 (with George L
Kouthouris) S:15

Krasauskas, Ildefonsas - Died 1988
Born 1895 Stone says, "Dragu-
nevicius" S:16

Kresge, Eloise A - Died 1961 Born
1891 (with James C Kresge) S:20

Kresge, James C - Died 1958 Born
1880 (with Eloise A Kresge) S:20

Krosvik, Ole L - Died 1963 Born
1891 S:12

Kulakovs, Elisabeth - Died 1981

Kulakovs (Cont.)
Born 1891 (with Savva Kulakovs
& Edward Nelson Sr) S:17

Kulakovs, Savva - Died 1983 Born
1895 (with Elisabeth Kulakovs &
Edward B Nelson Sr) S:17

Kumpula, Carlo - Died 1953 Aug 5
Born 1895 March 17 From North
Dakota, was Pvt in 163 Depot
Brig during World War I S:20

Kunze, Donald Wayne - Died (still
living 1991?) Born 1934 Feb 6
(with George Francis Norton &
others) S:19

Kunze, William Paul - Died 1945
Sept 4 Born 1901 June 11 (with
Francis Carlton Norton & others)
S:19

Kurra, Catherine - Died 1965 Born
1880 (with Olaf E Kurra) S:15

Kurra, Esther M - Died (still living
1991?) (listed with James R
Kurra & next to Richard J
Jordan) S:20

Kurra, Heta - Died 1946 Born 1858
(buried with Olaf Kurra) S:8

Kurra, James R - Died 1986 Born
1915 (listed with Esther M Kurra
& next to Richard J Jordan) S:20

Kurra, Olaf - Died 1940 Born 1848
(buried with Heta Kurra) S:8

Kurra, Olaf E - Died 1965 Born
1887 (with Catherine Kurra)
S:15

Kurshildgen, Laura S - Died 1970
Born 1895 S:19

Kushum, Renold - Died 1967 Born
1893 (undertaker plaque only)
S:17

Kyllonen, Edwin A (Edvin?) (Pastor) - Died 1969 Born 1901 (with
wife, Gertrude M Kyllonen) S:20

Kyllonen, Gertrude M - Died (still
living 1991?) Born 1898 Wife of
Pastor, Edvin A Kyllonen (with
him) S:20

L'E Cuyer, Edmond G - Died 1986
Born 1892 (with Frances V L'E
Cuyer) S:15

L'E Cuyer, Frances V - Died 1971
Born 1898 (with Edmond G L'E
Cuyer) S:15

Lacourciere, Edna E - Died 1957 Jan 28 Born 1919 March 10 From Massachusetts, was a Capt in AF Hospital during World War II S:20

Ladd, Abby Munroe - Died 1902 Born 1820 (in Munroe plot) S:10

LaForge, Owen R - Died 1971 March 19 Born 1890 June 10 From Michigan and was in Wagoner Sup Co 39th Infantry during World War I S:15

Lagemann, (no first name) - Died (no dates) (a large rock with a whale and ship engraved on it, no names listed) S:20

Lagergren, Alfred G - Died 1985 Born 1905 (with Evelyn L Lagergren) S:12

Lagergren, Beriil L - Died 1944 Born 1897 (next to Hildur M Lagergren) S:12

Lagergren, Blanche R - Buried 1980 Dec 18 Age 89 Located in section A, lot 25, grave 10 S:14R

Lagergren, Carl L - Died 1946 Born 1873 (with Emily M Lagergren) S:12

Lagergren, Dorothy J - Died 1957 Born 1902 Stone says, "Wife" Wife of Ralph Lagergren (with him) S:12

Lagergren, Edwin C - Died 1965 June 16 Born 1898 May 2 From Massachusetts, was Private in 321 Infantry, 81 Inv Div, during World War II (with Joseph Burlingame & Inez Garder) S:14

Lagergren, Edwin C - Died 1980 Born 1921 Has military stone which says, "CCK US Marines Corps during World War II (he also has a Barnstable Police memorial plaque there) S:13

Lagergren, Emily M - Died 1953 Born 1878 (with Carl L Lagergren) S:12

Lagergren, Evelyn L - Died 1987 Born 1912 (with Alfred G Lagergren) S:12

Lagergren, Helen - Died 1928 Born 1919 (next to Oscar A Lagregren)

Lagergren (Cont.) S:12

Lagergren, Helge E - Died 1924 Born 1878 (next to Carl L Lagergren) S:12

Lagergren, Hildur M - Died 1922 Born 1900 (next to Helen Lagergren) S:12

Lagergren, Oscar A - Died 1986 Born 1908 Was in CWO, US Army in Korea S:12

Lagergren, Ralph C - Died (still living 1991?) Born 1902 (with Dorothy J Lagergren) S:12

Laha, Etta D - Died 1880 Born 1871 (with Leander B Cash & others) S:21

Laha, Isaac P - Died 1880 Born 1841 (with Etta D Laha & others) S:21

Lahteine, Adrian A - Died 1975 Nov 21 Born 1917 Nov 18 (he was a Mason) (has 2 stones) Was a Tec 5 in US Army during World War II (with Lillian Lahteine) S:20

Lahteine, Arrne O - Died 1969 Born 1915 S:20

Lahteine, Lillian A - Died (still living 1991?) Born 1918 (listed with Adrian Lahteine) S:20

Lake, Mary T - Died 1936 Born 1867 Stone says, "Mother" S:8

Lamar, Leah Sessions - Died 1960 Born 1891 (next to Mark O'Daniel Lamar) S:13

Lamar, Mark O'Daniel - Died 1975 Born 1889 (next to Leah Sessions Lamar) S:13

Lamarche, Raymah T - Died (still living 1990) Born 1936 Wife of William P Lamarche (on same stone) S:11

Lamarche, William P - Died 1968 Born 1936 (with Raymah T Lamarche) S:11

Lambert, Alma H - Died (still living 1991?) Born 1927 (listed with Gora Mauritz & others) S:20

Lambert, Francis H - Died (still living 1991?) Born 1925 (with Alma Lambert & others) S:20

Lambert, Gladys Marion - Buried 1982 Oct 9 Age 86 Located in section 8, lot 80, grave 3 S:15R

Lamondy, Ethel G - Died 1948 Born 1882 (next to George L Lamondy) S:18

Lamondy, George L - Died 1964 Nov 23 Born 1878 Oct 15 From Massachusetts, was a Corporal in Co C3 Reg Conn Inf during the Spanish American War (next to Ethel G Lamondy) S:18

Lampi, Anna A - Died 1965 Born 1884 (with Arvid Lampi) S:20

Lampi, Arvid T - Died 1959 Born 1883 (with Anna A Lampi) S:20

Lamprinos, Anastasios - Died 1968 Born 1879 S:15

Landers, Earl W - Died 1956 Born 1893 (with wife, Esther L Hobson) S:14

Landers, Edward E - Died 1938 Born 1869 (with wife, Lois B Sturgis) S:14

Landers, Hannah H - Died 1851 Aug 1 Age 22 years, 2 months Widow of Harrison Landers (buried next to him) S:7

Landers, Harrison C - Died (stone not clear) (buried next to wife, Hannah H Landers) S:7

Landers, Joseph - Died 1855 Mar 3 in his 72nd yr (buried next to wife, Tabitha Landers) S:7

Landers, Laura A - Died 1803 May 25 Born 1842 Sept 9 Wife of Elias W Burrows (with him) S:14

Landers, Lois B - Died 1925 Born 1867 (with Edward E Sturgis) S:14

Landers, Margaret (Clara) - Died 1973 Born 1888 Daughter of Samuel & Landers & Annie Hurst (with them) (Mosswood ceme records say that her first name was Clara) S:14

Landers, Samuel E - Died 1944 Born 1890 S:14

Landers, Samuel T - Died 1938 Born 1861 (with wife, Annie Hurst) S:14

Landers, Tabitha - Died 1880 Jan

Landers (Cont.)
31 Age 85 years, 5 months Wife of Joseph Landers (buried next to him) S:7

Landers, Williams H - Died 1961 Aug 22 Born 1893 May 2 From Massachusetts, was a Private in 152 Depot Brigade during World War I S:14

Landis, Mary M - Died 1987 Born 1904 in Scotland (listed with Roy H Landis) S:15

Landis, Roy H - Died (still living in 1991?) Born 1899 (with Mary M Landis) S:15

Lang, Helen K - Died (still living 1991?) Born 1900 (listed with husband, Lawrence A Lang) S:15

Lang, Ida C - Died 1959 Born 1869 (with husband, Horace W Nickerson) S:14

Lang, Lawrence A - Died 1984 Born 1901 (listed with Helen K Lang, wife) S:15

Langlands(?), Marjorie H - Died 1984 Born 1903 (this is a rock stone) S:13

Lapham, Elizabeth - Died 1891 Born 1858 S:7

Lapham, Elmer W - Died 1937 Born 1861 (with Lucy S Lapham & others) S:14

Lapham, Harriet E - Died 1930 Born 1851 Wife of Sears C Lapham S:14

Lapham, Lucy S - Died 1917 Born 1859 (with Elmer W Lapham & others) S:14

Lapham, Nancy H - Died 1935 Born 1859 Wife of Nathaniel Crocker (buried with him-same stone) S:8

Larkin, Betsey Mrs - Died 1823 Sept 3 Age 44 Widow of John Larkin S:10

Larkin, Robert B - Died 1963 Born 1916 S:11

LaRoy, Prince - Died 1825 July 27 Age 1 year, 11 months, 21 days Son of Prince & Theodate G LaRoy (on other stones these parents are Hinckley's) S:4

Larrabee, Mary L - Died 1983 Jan 26 Born 1900 May 29 (with Roger V Larrabee) S:15

Larrabee, Roger V - Died 1898 Mar 1 Born 1901 Jan 25 (with Mary L Larrabee) S:15

Larsen, Emillie - Died 1935 Born 1870 Wife of George Bain (with him) S:12

Larson, Constance S - Died 1973 Oct 5 Born 1914 Mar 17 (with George E Larson) S:11

Larson, George E - Died 1971 Aug 11 Born 1908 June 9 (with Constance S Larson) S:11

Lathrop, (Lothrop), Elizabeth - Died 1694 Nov 11 Age 2 years, 2 months (there is a small stone next to her, same age?) Daughter of John & Elizabeth Lathrop (buried next to both, John d1653) S:11

Lathrop, (Lothrop), John Rev - Died 1653 Born 1589 (below statement added later) Ancestor to Ulyses S Grant, Joseph Smith, Alvin Reed Brown Reverend of the Congregational Unitarian Church (next to Freeman Lothrop, d1600's) S:11

Lathrop, Carrie - Died 1869 Born 1867 S:5

Lathrop, John Rev - Died (erected by his descendants this is located in the back of the cemetery, it says founder 1639) (but, there is also a plaque that says 1917-18 & a flag, this pretains to WW I??) S:11

LaTouche, Hilda R - Died 1967 Born 1895 S:15

Lavell, Sabina F - Died 1942 Born 1872 Wife of Ira W Bacon (with him & Lillian L Bacon & others) S:18

Lavender, Mary - Died 1985 Born 1898 S:16

Lavers, Abby T - Died 1942 Born 1876 (next to Ruth E Lavers) S:18

Lavers, Ruth E - Died 1974 Born 1882 (next to Abby T Lavers)

Lavers (Cont.)
S:18

Law, Louse H - Died 1949 May 23 Born 1897 Feb 7 (buried with Miriam H Bearse & others) S:8

Law, Mary I - Died 1960 Born 1867 (with Annie M Fawcett & others) S:16

Lawes, Harry W - Died 1950 Born 1875 (with Harry Jr & Marisabel Lawes) S:16

Lawes, Harry W Jr - Died 1968 Born 1897 From Massachusetts, was in US Marine during World War I (with Harry W Sr & Marisabel Lawes) S:16

Lawes, Marisabel - Died 1988 Born 1894 (with Harry W Sr & Jr Lawes) S:16

Lawler, Catherine - Died 1965 Born 1894 Wife of Archer Lincoln Lumbert (with him) S:18

Lawrance, David - Died 1785 Oct 3 in his 30th yr S:10+26R

Lawrance, Lydia - Died 1783 Oct 3 Daughter of David & Sarah Lawrance (buried next to mother) S:10

Lawrence, Alwyne - Died 1961 June 8 Born 1892 May 14 (next to Anna J Lawrence) S:14

Lawrence, Anna J - Died 1983 Born 1893 (next to Alwayne Lawrence) S:14

Lawrence, Annie M - Died 1975 Born 1891 S:17

Lawrence, Henry - Died 1863 Sept 13 Age 84 years, 7 months S:5

Lawrence, Henry - Died 1869 Mar 28 Age 53 years, 10 months (Hinckley Ceme records #5R say death was 1865) S:5

Lawrence, Jason - Died 1838 Sept 11 in his 32nd yr S:5

Lawrence, John - Died 1800 Feb 13 in his 33rd yr S:1

Lawrence, Joseph - Died 1842 April 23 Age 67 (next to wife, Mercy D Lawrence) S:13

Lawrence, Louisa - Died 1860 Mar 6 in Centervelle, Mass 15 years, 4 months Born in Fathmouth,

Lawrence (Cont.)
Mass Daughter of Henry & Eunice H Lawrence S:8

Lawrence, Mary - Died 1872 Dec 11 Age 91 years, 9 months Wife of Henry Lawrence S:5

Lawrence, Melinda - Died 1849 Dec 5 Age 31 years, 8 months Wife of Leonard Chase (next to him) S:21

Lawrence, Mercy D - Died 1859 Oct 31 Age 84 years, 7 months Widow of Joseph Lawrence (next to him) S:13

Lawrence, Nancy S - Died 1849 Feb 23 Born 1825 Mar 18 (buried next to Jason Lawrence) S:5

Lawrence, Olive J - Died 1861 Nov 29 Age 42 years, 9 months (next to Mercy D Lawrence) S:13

Lawrence, Sarah - Died 1825 Feb 21 Age 76 Widow of Capt David Lawrance (buried next to him) S:10

Lawrence, Sylvester - Died 1837 Oct 24 Age 22 Died in Mississippi S:5

Lawrence, William - Died 1805 July 25 Age 36 (buried next to Lydia Lawrance) S:10

Lawson, Hilma G - Died 1925 Born 1863 (with Charlotta Holm) S:12

Lawson, Nellie - Died 1935 Born 1868 Wife of George Snyder, with him S:11

Lax, Lillian R - Died 1976 Aug 30 Born 1901 Mar 22 (Jewish section) (with Michael G Lax) S:15

Lax, Michael G - Died 1972 Oct 26 Born 1898 Nov 2 (Jewish section) (with Lillian R Lax) S:15

Layer, Ethel - Died 1974 Oct 11 Born 1895 Nov 13 (next to William Layer) S:16

Layer, William - Died 1966 April 8 Born 1896 Oct 1 From Massachusetts, was Cpl in 9 THG Bn, 3 Regiment, FARD during World War I (next to Ethel Layer) S:16

Lazar, Samuel - Died 1972 Dec 27 Born 1897 Aug 5 (Jewish

Lazar (Cont.)
section) S:15

Leadbetter, Frieda G - Died 1980 Born 1887 S:15

Leadpont, Joseph - Died 1927 Born 1884 (with Sadie Leadpont) S:13

Leadpont, Sadie - Died (no information) Wife of Joseph Leadpont (listed with him) S:13

Leander, Carl L - Died 1962 May 2 Born 1897 June 10 Was Ensign in USNRF during World War I (next to Eva Matthews & Carl T Leander Jr) S:11

Leander, Carl T Jr - Died 1967 Born 1930 (next to father, Carl L Leander) S:11

Leary, Catherine S - Died 1964 Born 1891 (with Bertha M Amirault) S:16

Leary, Daniel - Died 1887 Oct 29 Age 65 Born 1822 S:5

Leavitt, Louisa - Died 1846 Oct 8 Age 28 Wife of Peter Norris (with daughter, Willhelmina Norris) S:21

Leavitt, Sarah A - Died 1920 Born 1857 (with Erastus Webber & others) S:18

Lebel, Anna L - Died 1945 Born 1894 (with John B Lebel) S:16

Lebel, John B - Died 1954 Born 1889 (with Anna L Lebel) S:16

LeBlanc, George - Died 1911 Oct 1 Born 1879 Jan 21 (with Henriette & George LeBlanc) S:31

LeBlanc, George - Died 1955 Jan 21 Born 1873 March 4 (with wife, Henriette & son, Leo LeBlanc) S:31

LeBlanc, Henriette - Died 1911 Oct 1 Born 1879 Jan 21 Wife of George LeBlanc (with him & son, Leo LeBlanc) S:31

LeBlanc, Leo - Died 1966 Born 1908 Son of Henriette & George LeBlanc (with them) S:31

Leckie, Elizabeth Terry - Died 1969 Born 1887 (next to George & Susan Terry) S:19

Leclerc, Joseph J - Died 1960 Born

Leclerc (Cont.)

1893 (with Sadie K Leclerc) S:16

Leclerc, Sadie K - Died 1953 Born 1891 (with Joseph J Leclerc) S:16

Ledger, Annie - Died 1965 Born 1878 Wife of Walter Robinson (with him) S:19

Lee, Lillian V - Buried 1981 April 26 Age 91 Located in section 3, lot 66, grave 5 (she bought her own plot) S:15R

Leghorn, Agnes Sully - Died 1988 Born 1895 S:13

Leghorn, George Mallery - Died 1961 Born 1888 S:13

Leghorn, Suzanne - Died 1963 Aug 22 Born 1963 Aug 8 Daughter of Richard S & Camilla (Cini) Leghorn S:13

LeGrand, Nelson L - Died 1978 Born 1881 (with wife, Viola Pratt) S:17

Leland, David H - Died 1959 Born 1884 (with wife, Mary Cabral) S:14

Lelland, Mable J - Died 1905 Born 1877 Stone says, "May she rest in peace" Wife of An Lelland S:12

Lema, Mary - Died 1938 Born 1886 S:16

Lenane, Bernard M - Died 1896 July 19 Born 1895 Aug 27 Son of Martin & Maria Lenane S:20

Lenane, John - Died 1868 July 12 Age 27 (next to Mary B Lenane) S:31

Lenane, Mary B - Died 1905 Aug 23 Age 65 (next to John Lenane) S:31

Lenares, Joseph E (MD) - Died 1974 Born 1900 Stone says, "Dad" (next to Mildred F Lenares, wife) S:15

Lenares, Mildred F - Died 1980 Born 1905 Stone says, "Mom" (next to husband, Joseph E Lenares MD) S:15

Leonard, Alpha F - Died 1970 Sept 16 Born 1882 July 17 (with wife, L Estelle Leonard) S:14

Leonard, Bernice E - Died 1985

Leonard (Cont.)

Born 1898 (with Edward F Leonard) S:16

Leonard, Bessie W - Died 1935 Born 1874 (next to Minnie G Allen) S:12

Leonard, Burleigh Dalton - Died 1957 Born 1891 (with James Leonard & Lucy Crosby on Leonard stone) S:12

Leonard, Catherine White - Died 1977 Born 1905 Wife of Parker Leonard (with him & others on large Leonard stone) S:12

Leonard, Edward F - Died 1959 Born 1889 (with Bernice E Leonard) S:16

Leonard, Effie Mae - Died (still living 1991?) Born 1900 (listed with John Leonard) S:15

Leonard, Elizabeth Till - Died 1928 Feb 16 at Osterville, Mass Born 1839 May 3 in England (next to Alexander & Agnes Till) S:12

Leonard, Henry P - Died 1955 Born 1870 (on large Leonard stone with Ivy S Leonard & others) S:12

Leonard, Imogene - Died 1936 Born 1906 (also listed on large Leonard stone with Henry P Leonard and others) S:12

Leonard, Isedore - Died 1900 July 22 Age 22 years, 10 months Wife of Edward Crocker (next to him & other wife, Hortense M Heller) S:12

Leonard, Ivy S - Died 1957 Born 1878 Wife of Henry P Leonard (listed with him and others on large Leonard stone) S:12

Leonard, James Milton - Died 1944 Born 1862 (with Lucy Crosby, his wife) Leonard stone with fireman's flag S:12

Leonard, James Phinney - Died 1915 Jan 30 Born 1914 Aug 10 Son of Alpha & L Estelle Leonard (with them) S:14

Leonard, Jeffrey K - Died 1973 Born 1958 S:13

Leonard, John - Died 1972 Born

Leonard (Cont.)
1895 (with Effie Mae Leonard) S:15

Leonard, L Estelle - Died 1961 Feb 17 Born 1882 July 24 Wife of Alpha F Leonard (with him & others) S:14

Leonard, Lucian Willis - Died 1902 Born 1856 (with James Leonard & Lucy Crosby on Leonard stone) S:12

Leonard, Margerie - Died 1979 Born 1893 (with James Leonard & Lucy Crosby & others on Leonard stone) S:12

Leonard, Mercy Genieve - Died 1960 Born 1899 (with Lucy Crosby & James M Leonard on Leonard stone) S:12

Leonard, Mercy M - Died 1872 Sept 28 Age 39 Wife of Simeon L Leonard (next to him) S:13

Leonard, Parker - Died 1973 Born 1902 (listed with Catherine White Leonard & others on large Leonard stone) S:12

Leonard, Simeon L - Died 1896 Dec 20 Born 1819 March 12 (next to wife, Mercy M Leonard) Lovell, Edward M S:13

Leonard, Temperance I - Died 1850 Jan 2 Age 24 Wife of Simeon L Leonard (next to him) S:13

Leonovich, Luke J - Died 1970 Jan 21 Born 1889 Feb 6 (has 2 stones) From Massachusetts, was Pvt in 14th Co, 151 Depot Brig during World War I (with Rose B Leonovich) S:16

Leonovich, Rose B - Died 1964 April 28 Born 1896 Aug 26 (with Luke J Leonovich) S:16

Leritges, Maria - Died 1981 Born 1891 Stone says,"Mother" S:15

Lesser, Flora C - Died 1951 Born 1875 (with Frank N Lesser) S:16

Lesser, Frank N - Died 1955 Born 1873 (with Flora C Lesser) S:16

Lesser, Walter N - Died 1977 Born 1907 (with Frank & Flora Lesser) S:16

Letcher, Elnora Williams - Died

Letcher (Cont.)
1941 Born 1852 S:18

Letsche, Louis F - Died 1985 Born 1898 S:15

Lettency, Edith - Died 1879 Dec 9 Age 4 Daughter of Simeon F & Lucy E Lettency (next to brother, Willie E) S:12

Lettency, Simeon F - Died 1904 May 11 Born 1849 Nov 27 S:12

Lettency, Willie E - Died 1889 Oct 28 Age 7 years, 8 months Son of Simeon & Lucy E Lettency (next to sister, Edith) S:12

Levine, Cordelia M - Died 1959 July 5 Born 1897 June 17 (with John J Levine Sr) S:16

Levine, John J Sr - Died 1977 Born 1897 (with Cordelia M Levine) Was a S2 in US Navy during World War I S:16

Levy, Jacob - Died 1960 Sept 4 Born 1895 Oct 18 (Jewish section) (with Jeanne Levy) S:15

Levy, Jeanne - Died 1981 May 21 Born 1898 Sept 6 (Jewish section) (with Jacob Levy) S:15

Lewes, Anna or Atnah? - Died 1715 Dec 26 in her 42nd yr Wife of Ebenezer Lewes S:11 +26R

Lewes, Elizabeth Mrs - Died 1719 June 29 in her 40th yr Wife of James Lewes S:11R+26R

Lewes, Experience - Died 1749 July 24 in her 65th yr Wife of Isaac Lewes S:3R

Lewes, Johnathan - Died Age 43 Died in 1700's? S:1

Lewes, Naomi - Died 1734 June 8 in her 26th yr Wife of Jesse Lewes S:9R+26R

Lewes, Rebeckah (Rebecca) - Died 1740 July 5 in her 37th yr Wife of James Lewes (also from 9R records) S:9+26R

Lewes, Sarah - Died 1698 Mar 17 in her 63rd yr Wife of James Lewes S:11

Lewey, Rebecca J - Died 1928 Feb 1 Born 1856 Oct 6 2nd wife to Capt George Howes-stone next to him) S:8

Lewis, ?ear Mrs - Died 1758 Nov 14
in her 75th yr Widow of Nathaniel Lewis (buried next to him) S:9

Lewis, Abbie L Baker - Died 1877
May 24 Born 1830 Aug 13
Daughter of Timothy & Abigail L
Lewis Their last name could be
Baker because next to this stone
is Timothy Baker? Possibly have
married a Lewis? S:4

Lewis, Abbott W - Died 1901 April
16 Born 1848 June 15 (with M
Isabel Lewis & others) S:18

Lewis, Agnes - Died 1875 Born
1873 Daughter of Ambrose &
Belina Lewis (buried with them)
S:8

Lewis, Alice Mrs - Died 1718 Feb
22 in her 59th yr Wife of George
Lewis S:11R+26R

Lewis, Allan - Died (flat stone on
ground, says "Allan" located
near Elsie, Ida & Benjamin
Lewis Probably child of Ida &
Ben) S:8

Lewis, Ambrose - Died 1929 Born
1839 (1 large stone) (buried with
wife, Belina May Bryant) S:8

Lewis, Ann - Died 1857 July 13
Age 74 years, 5 months, 13 days
Wife of Deacon Ephraim Lewis
S:2

Lewis, Ann J - Died 1860 June 27
(in Hartford, Connecticut) Born
1832 Aug 24 (in Cornville,
Maine) Wife of J N Lewis S:2

Lewis, Anna - Died 171? located in
row 8 S:11R

Lewis, Ansel - Died 1835 Mar 26
Age 2 months, 2 days Son of
Ansel & Relief Lewis S:2

Lewis, Ansel - Died 1884 Feb 18
(stone not clear for year) Born
1810 Nov 6 (Wife, Relief buried
next to him) S:2

Lewis, Arthur F - Died 1955 Born
1879 (with H Foster Lewis &
others in Lewis plot) S:12

Lewis, Azubah - Died 1861 May 26
Age 83 years, 8 months Wife of
Jesse Lewis S:4

Lewis, Benjamin - Died 1875 May 9

Lewis (Cont.)
Born 1797 June 5 S:8

Lewis, Benjamin (DDS) - Died 1964
Born 1876 Son of Ambrose &
Belina Lewis (buried with them)
S:8

Lewis, Benjamin W Died 1844
Feb 11 Born 1824 Feb 24
(buried with Ambrose 6 Belina
Lewis) S:8

Lewis, Benjamin W (Capt) - Died
1922 Born 1846 (buried with
wife, Ida Lewis) S:8

Lewis, Bertha Sears - Died 1958
Born 1870 (with Stephen Lewis)
S:8

Lewis, Britannia J - Died 1844 Jan
21 Born 1825 Dec 9 Wife of
Benjamin Lewis (buried with
him) S:8

Lewis, Calvin J - Died 1863 Apr 19
Age 10 years, 9 months Son of
Ezra N & Elizabeth C Lewis S:6

Lewis, Caroline F - Died 1948 Born
1875 (with George D Lewis) S:12

Lewis, Carrie M - Died 1965 Born
1882 (with Edmund H Lewis)
S:12

Lewis, Catherine - Died 1815 June
8 Age 25 years, 7 months, 20
days Wife of Seth Lewis S:10

Lewis, Catherine S - Died 1896
Born 1896 (with Marietta L
Ridley & others) S:18

Lewis, Charles - Died 1881 Dec 25
Age 80 years, 11 months, 25
days S:9R

Lewis, Charles E - Died 1929 Born
1859 (next to David C Lewis)
S:12

Lewis, Charles W - Died 1873 Feb
13 Born 1813 Apr 11 Son of
Wendell & Sylvia Lewis S:2

Lewis, Charlie H - Died 1873/5?
Dec 12 Age 26 years (stone badly
worn) S:8

Lewis, Charlotte - Died 1819? Age
26? (stone badly worn) (between
Owen Crosby & (infant) Patterson) S:8

Lewis, Clifton - Died 1892 Born
1869 Son of Ambrose & Belina

Lewis (Cont.)

Lewis (buried with them) S:8

Lewis, Cora - Died 1871 Born 1854 (with Henry N & Cynthia P Lewis) S:13

Lewis, Cora A - Died 1937 Born 1860 (with H Foster Lewis & others in Lewis plot) S:12

Lewis, Cynthia - Died 1834 Dec 5 Age 26 years, 4 months Wife of Capt Joseph Lewis S:2

Lewis, Cynthia N - Died 1882 Feb 5 Age 1 year, 6 months, 2 days (next to Raymond A Lewis) S:12

Lewis, Cynthia P - Died 1861 Born 1825 (with Henry N & Cora Lewis) S:13

Lewis, D E - Died (stone is in very bad condition) (buried next to George W Lewis, son of Ephraim Lewis) S:8

Lewis, Daniel - Died 1813 April 5 Age 10 days Son of William & Sally Lewis S:10

Lewis, David - Died 1803 June 27 in his 50th yr S:10+26R

Lewis, David C - Died 1897 Born 1831 (with Mary H Lewis) S:12

Lewis, David P - Died 1850 Oct 30 ? Age 71 (buried next to wife, Sarah Gorham) S:10

Lewis, Deborah - Died 1782 Jan 28 in her 47th yr Wife of John Lewis (buried next to him) S:10+26R

Lewis, Deborah - Died 1906 May 18 Born 1822 May 7 Wife of Edward L Kittredge (with him) S:11

Lewis, Deborah L - Died 1901 Nov 2 Born 1834 Dec 9 Wife of Edmond P Lewis (next to him) S:12

Lewis, Delia M - Died 1911 Aug 15 Born 1836 Nov 25 S:2

Lewis, Desire (?) - Died 1830 Jan 13 Age 5 Daughter of David P & Hannah Lewis (next to mother) S:10

Lewis, Dorcas (Baker) Mrs - Died 1748 July 3 in her 36th yr Wife of James Lewis S:9R+26R

Lewis, Dorcas H - Died 1814 Apr 1 Wife of Capt Joseph Lewis S:2

Lewis, Dorothy - Died (date not clear) Born 1800 Apr 19 Wife of Thomas Lewis (stone broken) S:7

Lewis, Ebenezer - Died 1759 Jan 9 Age 92 yrs 7 mos 22 days located in row 8 S:11R+26R

Lewis, Edmond P - Died 1905 Dec 25 Born 1819 Nov 17 (next to Edmund H Lewis) S:12

Lewis, Edmund H - Died 1957 Born 1870 (with Carrie M Lewis) S:12

Lewis, Edvie A - Died 1929 Born 1855 (buried with George W Lewis) S:8

Lewis, Edward - Died 1833 July 16 in his 20th yr Son of Nathan & Rebecca Lewis S:10+26R

Lewis, Edward - Died 1850 June 16 in his 77th yr S:2

Lewis, Edward - Died 1876 Mar 20 Born 1813 May 17 Stone says, "Husband, Father, Friend" (buried next to Phebe C Lewis) S:8

Lewis, Ehraim - Died 1859 July 22 Age 78 years, 1 month, 22 days S:2

Lewis, Elijah - Died 1888 Mar 24 Age 87 years, 9 months (with Jane Lewis, wife) S:11

Lewis, Elijah H - Died 1880 June 16 Age 41 years, 11 months, 27 days S:2

Lewis, Elizabeth - Died 1812 Sept 21 Age 13 years, 9 months Daughter of Ephraim & Martha Lewis (buried with George W Lewis) S:8

Lewis, Elizabeth - Died 1854 Dec 20 Age 14 Daughter of Frederick & Eleanor Lewis S:9R

Lewis, Elizabeth (?) - Died 28 July ? Age 40 (stone worn) S:11

Lewis, Elizabeth C - Died 1871 July 15 Age 44 years, 5 months Wife of Ezra N Lewis S:6

Lewis, Ella S - Died 1883 Dec 13 Age 36 years, 22 days Wife of Joseph Lewis & Mother of Abbie

Lewis (Cont.)
   May Lewis S:2

Lewis, Elsie - Died (small stone that says "Elsie" located with Ida & Benjamin Lewis, possibly their child?) S:8

Lewis, Emily Frances - Died 1850 Oct 20 Age 22 years, 1 month, 3 days Wife of James Lewis S:2

Lewis, Emma W - Died 1878 Aug 2 Age 29 years, 6 months Wife of John Lewis (buried next to his stone) S:6

Lewis, Enoch - Died 1890 July 7 Born 1816 Mar 17 (buried next to possible wife, Juliet C Lewis stones the same design) S:8

Lewis, Ens E Wesley - Died 1945 Born 1923 Stone says, "In Memory of" him Was in USNR, lost in flight over Atlantic Ocean (listed next to Gertrude Bacon & her husband, William Elliott Lewis) S:18

Lewis, Ephraim - Died 1895 May 28 Born 1811 May 2 (perpetual care) Stone says, "Father" (buried next to Marie Lewis, possible wife) S:8

Lewis, Ethel F - Died 1980 Born 1906 (next to listing of Russell B Lewis) S:13

Lewis, Etta F - Died 1976 Born 1878 (with H Foster Lewis & others in Lewis plot) S:12

Lewis, Eunice B - Died 1927 Born 1846 (with Owen B Lewis) S:12

Lewis, Everett W - Died 1939 Dec 9 Born 1854 Dec 3 S:8

Lewis, Fear Mrs - Died 1758 Nov 14 in her 51st yr Widow of Nathaniel Lewis S:9R+26R

Lewis, Francis - Died 1833 July 3 Born 1830 Apr 1 Daughter of Benjamin Lewis (buried with him) S:8

Lewis, Francis N - Died 1849 Sept 23 Age 10 months, 1 day Son of James N & Emily F Lewies S:2

Lewis, Franklin Crocker - Died 1930 Feb 13 Born 1877 Feb 12 (new copper stone) For 25 years,

Lewis (Cont.)
   superinpendent of the ethical culture schools of New York City Descendant of John Howland & Elizabeth Tilley of Mayflower fame & colonial Gov Thomas Hinckley S:8

Lewis, Franklin P - Died 1933 Born 1853 (with Ida H Lewis, wife) S:18

Lewis, Frederick - Died 1877 Feb 28 Age 74 years, 5 months S:9R

Lewis, George - Died 1757 July 6 Age 53 years, 11 months, 1 day (buried next to wife, Sarah Lewis) S:9

Lewis, George - Died 1768 Nov 13 in his 96th yr (Hinckley Ceme records #11R say death was 1769) S:11+26R

Lewis, George B - Died 1932 Born 1851 (next to Gertrude H Lewis) S:18

Lewis, George D - Died 1940 Born 1870 (with Caroline F Lewis) S:12

Lewis, George L - Died 1913 Born 1826 (with Melissa Lewis) S:18

Lewis, George L - Died 1970 Born 1904 (with wife, Margaret L Lewis) S:12

Lewis, George W - Died 1812 Sept 22 Age 11 years, 5 months (buried with Elizabeth Lewis) S:8

Lewis, Gertrude H - Died 1934 Born 1865 (next to George B Lewis) S:18

Lewis, Gustavus - Died 1902 Feb 9 Born 1837 Dec 16 S:2

Lewis, H Foster - Died 1936 Born 1852 (in Lewis plot with Cora A Lewis & others) S:12

Lewis, Hannah - Died 1817 Feb 27 in her 74th yr Widow to Josiah Lewis S:26R

Lewis, Hannah - Died 1826 Dec 13 Age 6 Daughter of David P & Hannah Lewis (next to sister, Temperance Lewis) S:10

Lewis, Hannah - Died 1831 Oct 7 Age 44 Wife of David p Lewis S:10

Lewis, Hannah - Died 1858 Oct 1 Age 75 years, 10 months Widow of Edward Lewis (buried next to him) S:2

Lewis, Hannah G - Died 1907 Nov 5 Born 1843 Oct 29 Wife of Rodolphus Childs, buried with him S:8

Lewis, Henry N - Died 1906 Born 1829 (with Cynthia P Lewis & Cora Lewis) S:13

Lewis, Hepsabeth - Died 1891 Born 1811 Buried with William Lewis (Same Stone) S:4

Lewis, Ida H - Died 1931 Born 1860 Wife of Franklin P Lewis (with him) S:18

Lewis, Ida M F - Died 1940 Born 1858 (buried with husband, Capt Benjamin Lewis) (small stone in back of her says, "Elsie") S:8

Lewis, Isaac C - Died 1867 May 22 Born 1815 Jan 6 S:10

Lewis, Isabella G - Died 1905 June 3 Born 1834 Feb 5 Wife of Paul Lewis (buried next to him) S:8

Lewis, Jacob B - Died 1888 Born 1815 S:2

Lewis, James - Died 1791 Jan 8 Age 20 Son of Peter & Mehetable Lewis S:10

Lewis, James - Died 1880 Aug 10 Age 93 years, 4 months S:2

Lewis, James (Lt?) - Died 1713 Oct 4 in his 82nd yr S:11R+26R

Lewis, James N - Died 1880 June 30 Age 57 years, 6 months S:2

Lewis, Jane - Died 1877 Mar 30 Age 75 years, 2 months Wife of Elijah Lewis (next to him) S:11

Lewis, Jesse - Died 1864 Sept 2 Age 92 years, 7 months S:4

Lewis, John - Died (stone broken down) (buried next to John Lewis) d:1781 May 12 in his 50th yr S:10+26R

Lewis, John - Died 1781 May 12 Age 50 (stone broken) (buried next to another John Lewis) S:10

Lewis, John - Died 1784 May 23rd in his 21st yr (very small stone,

Lewis (Cont.)
buried in the ground) (next to John Lewis) S:10+26R

Lewis, John - Died 1816 Aug 23 Age 14 years 11 months Son of William & Olive Lewis S:10

Lewis, John H C - Died 1872 Age 31 years, 4 months (lost at sea) S:6

Lewis, John W - Died 1917 Born 1841 (with Eunice B Lewis) S:12

Lewis, Joseph - Died 1860 Mar 9 Age 81 years, 3 months, 26 days S:2

Lewis, Joseph (Capt) - Died 1896 Feb 21 Born 1810 July 10 S:2

Lewis, Joseph F (Capt) - Died 1878 Nov 7 buried at Senegal, Africa (listed on same stone with Emma Caroline Hinckley, wife) S:8

Lewis, Joseph Green - Died 1801 March 30 in his 3rd yr Son of Joseph G and Sally Lewis S:26R

Lewis, Joseph Green - Died 1806 Sept 20 in his 34th yr S:26R

Lewis, Joseph H - Died 1851 Jan 18 Age 19 years, 6 months, lost at sea S:9R

Lewis, Josiah - Died 1776 Dec 21 Age 1 yr 7 mos 7 days Son of Josiah and Hannah Lewis S:26R

Lewis, Josiah - Died 1795 Nov 15 Age 52 S:26R

Lewis, Josiah - Died 1855 July 17 Age 78 Born 1777 Sept 13 S:10

Lewis, Juliet A - Died 1917 March 21 Born 1840 Feb 4 (with William P Lewis) S:18

Lewis, Juliet C - Died 1908 Jan 8 Born 1825 Oct 27 S:8

Lewis, Laura A - Died 1895 Born 1823 (with Lot G Lewis & others) S:18

Lewis, Laura Belle - Died 1886 Born 1864 (with Lizzie L Lewis & others) S:18

Lewis, Lena - Died 1952 Born 1879 Wife of Albert Baker Wing (with him & son, Albert Baker) S:18

Lewis, Leo B - Died 1954 Jan 5 Born 1889 July 26 (with wife,

Lewis (Cont.)

Marion F Lewis) S:16

Lewis, Lillie W - Died 1958 Born 1892 Wife of Raymond J Lewis (with him) S:16

Lewis, Lizzie L - Died 1928 Born 1858 (with Laura A Lewis & others) S:18

Lewis, Lorenzo - Died 1914 Nov 8 Born 1840 Apr 20 S:6

Lewis, Lot G - Died 1916 Born 1851 (with Laura Belle Lewis & others) S:18

Lewis, Lydia G - Died 1933 Born 1843 S:21

Lewis, M C (Tina) - Died 1834 July ? Age 24 (stone bad condition) (buried next to Ephraim Lewis) S:8

Lewis, M Isabel - Died 1910 Aug 25 Born 1848 March 18 (with Willie Lewis & others) S:18

Lewis, Mabel - Died 1879 May 24 Born 1877 May 1 (with Abbott W Lewis & others) S:18

Lewis, Mabel Frances - Died 1942 Born 1868 (on family stone with others) S:11

Lewis, Maltier - Died 1814 Dec 17 Age 63 S:12

Lewis, Margaret J - Died 1924 Born 1859 Stone says, "Sister" S:12

Lewis, Margaret L - Died 1959 Born 1900 Wife of George Lewis (next to him) S:12

Lewis, Maria - Died 1896 Mar 7 Born 1811 July 26 Stone says, "Mother" (buried next to Ephraim Lewis) S:8

Lewis, Marietta - Died 1852 Jan 20 Age 6 years, 2 months Daughter of William & Hepsabeth Lewis S:4

Lewis, Marion F - Died 1980 March 26 Born 1895 Sept 14 Wife of Leo B Lewis (with him) S:16

Lewis, Martha - Died 1803 Jan 29 in her 49th yr Wife of David Lewis (buried next to him) S:10+22R

Lewis, Mary - Died 1782 Feb 8 in

Lewis (Cont.)

her 42nd yr Wife of Major George Lewis (stone worn) S:10+26R

Lewis, Mary A - Died 1878 April 26 Age 69 years, 11 months Wife of Charles Lewis S:9R

Lewis, Mary A - Died 1938 Born 1871 S:31

Lewis, Mary E - Died 1952 Born 1887 Wife of Owen Lewis (with him) S:12

Lewis, Mary Ella - Died 1917 Dec 15 Born 1852 Feb 17 S:6

Lewis, Mary H - Died 1902 Born 1824 (with David C Lewis) S:12

Lewis, Mary R - Died 1906 Dec 9 Born 1815 Feb 2? (stone not clear) (Stone says, "Mother") S:8

Lewis, Maude W - Died (still living in 1991?) Born 1906 (next to W Nason Lewis) S:12

Lewis, Mehetable - Died 1793/8 ? July 29 in her 35th yr Wife of Peter Lewis (buried next to him) S:10+26R

Lewis, Mehitable - Died 1840 Oct 14 Born 1835 Sept 21 Daughter of Benjamin Lewis (buried with him) S:8

Lewis, Mehitable - Died 1888 Aug 2 Born 1801 Mar 3 Wife of Benjamin Lewis (buried next to him) S:8

Lewis, Mehitable - Died 1894 Oct 4 Age 87 years, 9 months (next to William P Lewis & others) S:18

Lewis, Mehittable - Died 1858 Feb 21 Age 72 years, 4 months, 27 days Wife of Joseph Lewis S:2

Lewis, Melissa H - Died 1902 Born 1831 (with Edward Hamblin & others) S:18

Lewis, Mercy - Died 1740 in her 65th yr (stone worn) (Hinckley Ceme records #11R say death was 1745 Dec 7 and that her husband was James) S:11+26R

Lewis, Mercy - Died 1749 located in row 8 S:11R

Lewis, Mercy - Died 1863 Dec 18 Age 75 years, 11 months Wife of James Lewis S:2

Lewis, Mercy - Died 1896 Nov 23 Born 1817 Nov 15 Wife of Lothrop Hinckley S:11

Lewis, Myron P - Died 1895 Born 1824 (with Laura A Lewis & others) S:18

Lewis, Nabby C - Died 1804 Sept 6 Age 3 mos Daughter to Joseph G and Sarah Lewis S:26R

Lewis, Nathaniel - Died 1751 July 7 in his 44th yr S:9+26R

Lewis, OH - Died 1955 Born 1874 (with RE Lewis) S:12

Lewis, Olive H - Died 1804 Jan 27 Age 4 mos Daughter to Henry and Catherine F Lewis S:26R

Lewis, Olive Mrs - Died 1804 July 26 in her 26th yr Wife of William Lewis S:10+26R

Lewis, Owen B - Died 1936 Born 1867 (with Mary E Lewis) S:12

Lewis, Paul P - Died 1880 July 1 Born 1828 Aug 27 S:8

Lewis, Pauley - Died (date not clear) Daughter of David & Martha Lewis S:10

Lewis, Peter - Died 1793/8 ? April 10 in his 37th yr (stone cracked and deep into the ground) S:10+26R

Lewis, Phebe C - Died 1892 Dec 27 Born 1812/7? June 8 (buried next to Edward Lewis) S:8

Lewis, Polly - Died (dates not clear) Daughter of David & Martha Lewis (buried next to them) S:10

Lewis, Polly - Died 1801 Mar 23 Age 20 months Daughter of William & Olive Lewis S:10

Lewis, Polly - Died 1827 Sept 20 Age 17 Daughter of William & Sally Lewis S:10

Lewis, Polly - Died 1847 Oct 25 Age 67 Widow to Lot Lewis S:21

Lewis, Puella S - Died 1846 Sept 20 Age 27 Wife of Capt Enoch Lewis S:13

Lewis, R E - Died 1951 Born 1872 (with OH Lewis) S:12

Lewis, Raymond A - Died 1916 Born 1911 Son of EH & CM (next to Deborah L Lewis) S:12

Lewis, Raymond J - Died 1978 Born 1900 (with wife, Lillie W Lewis) S:16

Lewis, Reba Elsie - Buried 1982 Sept 18 Age 94 Located in section 8, lot 100, grave 1 S:15R

Lewis, Rebecca - Died 1734 April 10 in her 65th yr Wife of Ebenezer Lewis S:9R+26R

Lewis, Rebecca Mrs - Died 1810 Dec 25? Age 55? (stone not clear) Wife of Meltier (Maltier) Lewis (next to him) S:12

Lewis, Relief - Died 1882 Mar 1 Born 1809 Nov 3 Wife of Capt Ansel Lewis S:2

Lewis, Robert - Died 1782 Nov 14 Age 10 months Son of Major George & Mary Lewis S:10

Lewis, Russell - Died 1882 Dec 19 Age 75 or 76 years, 2 months (next to Mehitable Lewis & others) S:18

Lewis, Russell B - Died (still living 1991?) Born 1901 (listed next to Ethel F Lewis) S:13

Lewis, Sally - Died 1835 April 5 Age 50 Wife of Josiah Lewis (buried next to him) S:10

Lewis, Sarah - Died 1697/8 March 17 Age 63 Wife of James Lewis S:11R

Lewis, Sarah - Died 1735 Feb 1 in her 92nd yr in Barnstable, Massachusetts Daughter of George Lewis, first wife to James Cobb, second wife to Jonathan Sparrow of Eastham, Mass S:11R+26R

Lewis, Sarah - Died 1762 Apr 30 Age 53 yrs 2 mos Widow of George Lewis S:9+26R

Lewis, Sarah A - Died 1914 Born 1840 Wife of Seth Lewis (buried next to him) S:8

Lewis, Serephine - Died 1889 Mar 5 Born 1821 April 14 (buried next to Charlie Lewis) S:8

Lewis, Seth - Died 1910 Born 1833 S:8

Lewis, Sophia - Died 1889 Born 1834 (with Marietta L Ridley &

Lewis (Cont.)
others) S:18

Lewis, Stephen C - Died 1958 Born 1868 (buried with Cynthia & Henry Sears) S:8

Lewis, Susan - Died 1820 Aug 16 in her 63rd yr Wife of George Lewis S:4

Lewis, Susan - Died 1860 Nov 20 in her 76th yr Wife of Thomas B Lewis (buried next to him) S:6

Lewis, Susan - Died 1887 Born 1799 (with Winslow Lewis) S:18

Lewis, Susan P - Died 1848 Oct 15 Age 21 years, 8 months, 7 days Daughter of Elijah & Jane Lewis (next to her is large section of broken off markers that look like they were rocks, markings not available) S:11

Lewis, Sylvia - Died 1856 Mar 1 Born 1820 Jan 8 Wife of Wendel Lewis & daughter of Zacheus & Sally (no last name of parents listed) S:2

Lewis, Temperance - Died 1818 Feb 17 Age 11 months Daughter of David P & Hannah Lewis S:10

Lewis, Temperance - Died 1895 Born 1817 S:2

Lewis, Thankful Mrs - Died 1811 Dec 6 Age 34 Wife of Seth Lewis S:10

Lewis, Theresa D - Died 1821 Born 1875 (on same stone with Tryphosa G Lewis) S:8

Lewis, Thomas - Died 1880 Sept 21 Age 68 years, 9 months, 24 days (buried next to wife) S:7

Lewis, Thomas B - Died 1871 Dec 27 in his 78th yr (buried next to wife, Susan Lewis) S:6

Lewis, Thomas B - Died 1887 Nov 10 Age 63 years, 6 months S:6

Lewis, Thomas Percival - Died 1947 Born 1865 (large family stone with others) S:11

Lewis, Tryphosa G - Died 1920 Born 1842 (buried with Theresa D Lewis) S:8

Lewis, Vincent M - Died 1935 Born 1916 (stone is perpetual care)

Lewis (Cont.)
(with Stephen Sears) S:8

Lewis, W Nason - Died 1988 Born 1907 (next to Maude W Lewis - still living) S:12

Lewis, Walter F - Died 1957 Born 1870 (next to Maude W Lewis - still living) S:12

Lewis, Walter Mr - Died 1855 Nov 10 Age 45 at Boston S:10

Lewis, Wendell (Capt) - Died 1859 Nov 27 Age 42 years, 3 months, 16 days S:2

Lewis, William - Died 1805 Oct 21 Age 11 months, 29 days Son of Capt Jesse & Anuvah Lewis S:4

Lewis, William - Died 1835 Sept 11 Age 13 years, 22 days (drowned from Sek (Ellen? not clear), Hudson River Son of Ephrim & Anne Lewis S:2

Lewis, William - Died 1886 Born 1809 Buried with Hepsabeth Lewis (Same stone) S:4

Lewis, William D - Died Nov 16 (date underground) Born 1813 Aug 13 (Hinckley Ceme records say death was 1860) S:11+26R

Lewis, William Elliott - Died 1973 Oct 25 Born 1900 Dec 29 (has 2 stones) From Massachusetts, was LDSOMA in US Navy during World War I (with wife, Gertrude Bacon & Lillian Bacon & others) S:18

Lewis, William H - Died 1897 Born 1834 (with Sophia B Lewis & others) S:18

Lewis, William P - Died 1904 Dec 3 Born 1835 Nov 22 (with Juliet A Lewis & next to Russell & Mehitable Lewis) S:18

Lewis, Willie - Died 1874 Aug 14 Born 1874 April 21 (with Mabel Lewis & others) S:18

Lewis, Winslow - Died 1873 Born 1794 (with Susan Lewis & next to Lizzie L Lewis & others) S:18

Lewis,(Lewes) Ebenezer - Died 1759 Age 2 years, 7 months, 22 days (stone worn) (next to Anna Lewes) (Hinckley Ceme records

Lewis (Cont.)
#11R say age was 92) S:11
Libbey, Charles Henry - Died 1940 Born 1854 (next to Ella Howe Libbey) S:14
Libbey, Ella Howe - Died 1951 Born 1856 (next to Charles Henry Libbey) S:14
Libby, Albert P - Died 1927 Born 1882 (With Edith G Libby) S:11
Libby, Charles Nelson Jr - Died 1962 Oct 10 at Cummaquid, Massage 57 years,5 mon,14 days B1905 April 26 at Rockland, Mass (with wife, Grace Cynthia Anderson) Married 26 Oct 1929 (also Barnstable Fire Dept plaque) (large scalptured stone w/gold leaf "Libby" on it) S:19
Libby, Edith G - Died 1955 Born 1897 (with Albert P Libby) S:11
Libby, Jessie L - Died 1948 Born 1866 Wife of Elvin D Winchell (with him) S:19
Lightfoot, Abbie Bird - Died 1961 Born 1884 (next to Alexander Lightfoot) S:18
Lightfoot, Alexander - Died 1959 Born 1877 (next to Henry Lightfoot) S:18
Lightfoot, Henry - Died 1946 Born 1867 (next to Abbie Bird Lightfoot) S:18
Lightford, Mildred E - Died 1979 Born 1892 (next to William Lightford) S:17
Lightford, William - Died 1943 Born 1890 (next to Mildred E Lightford) S:17
Lillian, Lora - Died (still living 1991?) Born 1895 (listed with Joseph Lambert Cain) S:14
Lima, Anna M - Died 1965 Born 1893 (with Samuel Lima) S:18
Lima, Samuel T - Died 1954 Born 1895 (with Anna M Lima) S:18
Limmell, Priscilla - Died 1858 May 4 Widow of Willard Limmell S:3
Limmell, Willard - Died 1819 Dec 1 in his 29th yr S:3
Lincoln, Clark - Died 1902 Nov 11 Born 1821 Jan 1 (buried with

Lincoln (Cont.)
Elizabeth Matthews & others) S:8
Lincoln, Mary Edward - Died 1955 Aug 8 Born 1868 July 14 (buried with Mary Emeline Lincoln & others) S:8
Lincoln, Mary Emeline - Died 1868 Oct 14 Born 1868 June 14 (buried with Mary Edward Lincoln & others) S:8
Lindall, Elsa V - Died 1986 Born 1911 (with Eric B Lindall) S:19
Lindall, Eric B - Died 1979 Born 1904 (with Elsa V Lindall) S:19
Lindstrom, Edith A - Died 1975 Born 1879 Stone says, "Beloved Aunt" S:15
Linehan, John J - Died 1953 Born 1876 (with Margaret J Linehan) S:16
Linehan, Margaret J - Died 1966 Born 1879 (with John J Linehan) S:16
Linell, Dorcas - Died 1808 Nov 27 in his 85th yr Wife of Joseph Linell S:1
Linell, John - Died 1747 Feb ? Age 78 (stone is broken in half) S:11
Linell, Joseph - Died 1803 Jan 18 in his 77th yr Possible wife was Dorcas Linell S:1
Linell, Ruth - Died 1742 May 8 Age 75 Wife of John Linell S:11
Linell, Ruth Mrs - Died 1748 May 8 Age 73 Wife of John Linell S:11
Lingham, Emerson W - Died 1982 Born 1909 (with Lyda H Lingham) S:19
Lingham, Franklin W - Died 1915 Born 1863 (with Mae V Lingham & others) S:19
Lingham, Lyda H - Died (no dates) (with Emerson W Lingham) S:19
Lingham, Mae V - Died 1911 Born 1873 (with Franklin Lingham & William & Ethel Kohler) S:19
Linnel, Joseph - Died 1741 Age 4 S:1
Linnell, Abbie L - Died 1955 Born 1882 Wife of Wilton E Linnell (with him) S:14

Linnell, Abby P - Died 1851 Jan 6 Age 22 years, 10 months Wife of Orlando Linnell S:2

Linnell, Abner - Died 1837 Nov 24 in his 58th yr S:3

Linnell, Adclaide - Died 1867 Born 1845 (with Alice Linnell & others) S:18

Linnell, Adelia C - Died 1950 March 18 Born 1859 March 19 (next to Prentiss Linnell) S:21

Linnell, Alice - Died 1844 Born 1843 (with Adgar W Linnell & others) S:18

Linnell, Alice J - Died 1875 Aug 10 Age 20 years, 10 months Wife of Prentiss Linnell (next to him & Adelia C Linnell) S:21

Linnell, Almira - Died 1886 Born 1823 S:4

Linnell, Almirah - Died 1919 Born 1834 (with Alpheus Linnell) S:18

Linnell, Alpheus - Died 1912 Born 1834 (with Almirah Linnell) S:18

Linnell, Anna - Died 1782 Feb 20 in her 42nd yr Wife of James Linnell S:3

Linnell, Arabella - Died 1849 Dec 2 Daughter of Henry & Frances Linnell S:12

Linnell, Avis Willard - Died 1911 Born 1891 (with Adelaide Linnell & others) S:18

Linnell, Barzillar L - Died 1869 Apr 15 Age 48 years, 8 months S:2

Linnell, Betsey H - Died 1904 Oct 17 Born 1819 Oct 7 Stone says,"A gift from a friend" (with Isaiah B Linnell) S:21

Linnell, Caroline C - Died 1891 July 31 Born 1815 Feb 12 (with William & Euretta Linnell) S:18

Linnell, David - Died 1846 May 19 in his 75th yr S:2

Linnell, David (Capt) - Died 1879 Feb 27 Age 71 years, 1 month, 25 days S:2

Linnell, Deborah I - Died 1893 Born 1812 (with Thomas Chase & others) S:18

Linnell, Edgar W - Died 1921 Born 1849 (with Sarah E Linnell &

Linnell (Cont.)
others) S:18

Linnell, Edna Frances - Died 1872 July 18 Born 1851 Feb 26 Daughter of John & Lucy Linnell (next to brother, Wayland Linnell) S:14

Linnell, Elisha B - Died 1839 Dec 18 Age 25 S:3

Linnell, Eliza A - Died 1893 Born 1849 (with William & Isaiah Linnell) S:21

Linnell, Esther - Died 1872 July 1 b 1788 Oct 27 S:3

Linnell, Eunice - Died 1820 Dec 29 in her 24th yr Wife of Joseph Linnell S:4

Linnell, Eunice - Died 1838 Feb 20 in her 77th yr Wife of Levi Linnell S:4

Linnell, Euretta F - Died 1921 Born 1839 (with Maude Frost & Caroline & William Linnell) S:18

Linnell, Frances A - Died 1880 Dec 27 Age 59 years, 8 months, 8 days Wife of Henry S Linnell (next to him) S:12

Linnell, Hannah - Died 1773 Jan 11 in her 67th yr Wife of Samuel Linnell S:1

Linnell, Helen I - Died 1930 Born 1853 (with Julius A Linnell) S:14

Linnell, Henry S - Died 1886 Mar 28 Born 1816 Oct 2 (located between both wifes, Lucy A & Frances A linnell) S:12

Linnell, Henry Stimpson - Died 1875 Nov 23 Born 1874 May 6 Son of John W & Lucy J Linnell (next to them) S:14

Linnell, Isaiah - Died 1858 Nov 18 Age 39 years, 3 months, 16 days S:3

Linnell, Isaiah B - Died 1905 Oct 17 Born 1816 Sept 20 (with Betsey H Linnell) S:21

Linnell, Isaiah B - Died 1911 Born 1844 (with Eliza & William Linnell) S:21

Linnell, J or U - Died (only foot stone remains, but next to J L & also next to Isaiah & Betsey

Linnell (Cont.)
Linnell) (not sure if Linnell?)
S:21

Linnell, James - Died 17th
(1700's?) Stone not clear husband of Anna Linnell S:3+3R

Linnell, John - Died 1747 Feb 9 in
his 78th yr S:11R+26R

Linnell, John - Died 1747 located
in row 5 S:11R

Linnell, John - Died 1781 Jan 7 in
his 79th yr S:3

Linnell, John - Died 1787 Oct 29
in his 53rd yr S:3+3R

Linnell, John Wesley - Died 1903
Feb 28 Born 1830 April 17 Stone
says,"Father" (next to wife, Lucy
J Linnell) S:14

Linnell, Joseph - Died 1787 Aug 29
in his 44th yr S:26R

Linnell, Joseph - Died 1877 Born
1800 (with Melinda Linnell) S:18

Linnell, Joseph - Died 1903 Born
1820 (with Lilla & Susan Linnell)
S:21

Linnell, Joseph (Capt) - Died 1863
Apl 11 Age 73 years, 10 months
S:4

Linnell, Joseph H - Died 1861 Oct
7 Born 1841 July 27 Stone says,
"Passed away" (stone has cement
base added) S:12

Linnell, Josephine - Died 1896
Born 1848 (with Thomas W
Mitchell & others) S:18

Linnell, Julius A - Died 1874 Born
1850 (with Clarentine J Nickerson) S:14

Linnell, Levi - Died 1821 Mar 20 in
his 73rd yr S:4

Linnell, Lilla M - Died 1888 Feb 1
Age 24 years, 5 months (with
Joseph & Susan Linnell) S:21

Linnell, Lucy A - Died 1896 July 2
Born 1829 Sept 26 Wife of Henry
S Linnell (next to him) S:12

Linnell, Lucy J - Died 1915 April
10 Born 1830 Nov 5 Stone says,
"Mother" (with husband, John
Wesley Linnell) S:14

Linnell, Mary D - Died 1940 Born
1870 (with Sarah G Congdon)

Linnell (Cont.)
S:18

Linnell, Melinda - Died 1879 Born
1802 (with Joseph Linnell) S:18

Linnell, Mercy - Died 1842 Nov 16
in her 73rd yr Wife of David
Linnell S:2

Linnell, Mildred - Died 1988 Born
1903 Wife of Richard O'Neil (with
him & William J O'Neil & others)
S:16

Linnell, Nabby - Died 1789 Dec 6
in her 6th yr Daughter of John
& Rebecca Linnell S:3

Linnell, Orlando (Capt) - Died 1853
Oct 1 Age 30 years, 10 months
(lost from on board schooner,
River Queen bound for Rich-
mond, Virginia to Providence,
Rhode Island) S:2

Linnell, Prentiss - Died 1923
March 26 Born 1841 Aug 13
(between Alice & Adelia Linnell)
S:21

Linnell, Rodney - Died 1921 Born
1848 (with Helen I Linnell) S:14

Linnell, Ruth - Died 1748 located
in row 5 S:11R

Linnell, Ruth - Died 1773 April 28
in her 32nd yr Wife of John
Linnell S:3

Linnell, Ruth Mrs - Died 1748 May
8 in her 75th yr Wife of John
Linnell S:11R+26R

Linnell, Salome - Died 1892 Born
1814 (with Adelaide Linnell &
others) S:18

Linnell, Sarah A - Died 1888 Mar
20 Age 75 years, 5 months, 11
days, Widow of Capt David
Linnell S:2

Linnell, Sarah E - Died 1917 Born
1854 (with Avis Willard Linnell &
others) S:18

Linnell, Sophia - Died 1855 Feb 17
Age 53 years, 3 months Wife of
Thomas Linnell S:2

Linnell, Susan W - Died 1910 Born
1822 (with Lilla & Joseph Linnell) S:21

Linnell, Thomas - Died 1878 May
19 in his 81st yr S:2

Linnell, Uerburp? - Died 1853 or 55 Jan Born 1844 Jan Child of Henry & Frances Linnell S:12

Linnell, Urias C - Died 1892 Born 1812 (with Salome Linnell & others) S:18

Linnell, Wayland Meredith - Died 1865 June 27 Born 1857 Nov 8 Son of John & Lucy Linnell (next to brother, Henry S Linnell) S:14

Linnell, Willard Jr - Died 1833 Aug 6 in his 18th yr Son of Willard & Priscilla Linnell S:4

Linnell, William Albert - Died 1834 July 27 Age 2 years, 5 months Son of William & Sylvia Linnell S:4

Linnell, William E - Died 1879 May 25 Born 1806 June 14 (with Caroline C & Euretta F Linnell) S:18

Linnell, William W - Died 1876 Born 1874 (with Eliza & Isaiah Linnell) S:21

Linnell, Wilton E - Died 1963 Born 1882 (with wife, Abbie L Linnell) S:14

Linnell?, J - Died (main stone is gone, only foot stone remains with JL & next to one with J or U L) (next to Isaiah & Betsey Linnell) S:21

Linnet, Elener - Died 1816 Feb 4 in her 39th yr Wife of Josiah Linnet (she is also listed on her dau stone as Elenor Linnett) S:4

Linnett, Rebecca - Died 1806 Feb 16 Age 2 years, 3 months, 11 days Daughter of Josiah & Elenor Linnett S:4

Linthwaite, George Arthur - Died 1985 Born 1914 (with Margaret Hicks, his wife) S:11

Liszczak, Elizabeth Crocker - Died 1978 Born 1945 (next to David L Crocker) S:19

Little, Mary P - Died 1970 Born 1893 (with Robert B Little) S:15

Little, Robert B - Died 1977 Born 1891 (with Mary P Little) S:15

Livesley, Etta HC - Died 1942 Born 1871 (with Capt C Howard Allyn & others) S:18

Livesley (Cont.)
& others) S:18

Livesley, Fred B - Died (no date) Born 1882 (with Etta HC Livesley & others) S:18

Livingston, Anne Atwood - Died 1961 Born 1891 with the lord (with Benjamin Thomson Livingston) S:12

Livingston, Benjamin Thomson - Died 1948 Born 1869 A lofty soul who lavishly shared the presence of Christ (with Anne Atwood Livingston) S:12

Livingston, Deborah Knox - Died 1923 Born 1874 A soul aflame for Christ and richteousness world wide she served (with James Van Knox) S:12

Livingston, Gertrude C - Died 1988 Mar 29 Born 1892 June 1 Widow of Henry C Kittredge (next to him) S:11

Lloyd, Andrew J - Died 1962 Nov 25 Born 1893 Oct 30 From Massachusetts, was Lieutenant Col in Field Artillery during World War I & II S:14

Lockwood, Edwin G - Died 1937 Born 1843 (buried with Olive A Lockwood & others with later dates) S:8

Lockwood, Mabel V - Died 1940 Born 1872 (buried with Olive A Lockwood & many others, also with later dates) S:8

Lockwood, Olive A - Died 1918 Born 1856 (buried with Edwin G Lockwood & many others, also with later dates) S:8

Lockwood, Sarah C - Died 1968 Born 1887 (with Wray H Lockwood) S:11

Lockwood, Wray H - Died (no markings) (with Sarah C Lockwood) S:11

Lof, William J - Died 1968 Born 1893 S:20

Lofton, James R - Died 1980 Born 1927 Was a Corporal in US Army during World War II S:13

Logge, Eleanor - Died 1792 Jan 28

Logge (Cont.)
in her 75th yr Wife of John
Logge S:1

Lomas, Harriett F - Died 1952 Born
1884 (with Harry Lomas) S:12

Lomas, Harry - Died 1951 Born
1882 (with Harriett F Lomas)
S:12

Lomas, Livingston H - Died 1990
Born 1908 (with Harry & Harriett Lomas) S:12

Lomas, Ronald H - Died 1956 Born
1934 (with Harry & Harriett
Lomas) S:12

Lombard, Anna - Died 1747 May
19 in her 51st yr Wife of Capt
Samuel Lombard S:11+26R

Lombard, Benjamin - Died (small
stone, not clear) (a large tree is 4
inches from face of stone, he is
between Mrs Sarah Lumbard,
d1768 & Hannah Lumbard)
(Hinckley Ceme records #11R
say death was 1753 Jan 13 in
his 78th yr) S:11+26R

Lombard, Bethiah - Died 1753 Jan
3 in the 78th yr (next to Mrs
Sarah Lumbard d1768) S:11

Lombard, Daniel - Died 1790 July
23 in his 57th yr Possible
husband of Elisabeth Lombord
S:1

Lombard, Hannah - Died 1714
Sept 19 Age 34 Wife of Benjamin
Lombard S:11R

Lombard, Harold F Sr - Died 1985
Feb 5 Born 1898 Dec 17 Was a
Pvt in US Army during World
War I S:15

Lombard, Ichabod (Capt) - Died
1810 Feb 21 Age 64 S:1

Lombard, Jane E - Died 1894 Born
1818 Wife of Capt John K Hinckley S:10

Lombard, Joseph - Died 1747
(stone is down on the ground)
Son of Capt Samuel Lombard
(Hinckley Ceme records #11R
says death was on June 17 at in
his 26th yr) S:11+26R

Lombard, Mary Mercy - Died 1747
June 19 in her 15th yr, located

Lombard (Cont.)
in row 6 Daughter of Capt
Samuel Lombard (records also
from 11R) S:11+11R+26R

Lombard, Mercy - Died 1758 May
in her 55th yr (stone down on
the ground) Wife of Capt Mathias
Lombard S:11+26R

Lombard, Solomon - Died 1763
(stone badly worn) S:1

Lombord, Elisabeth - Died 1793
Nov 6 in her 41st yr Wife of
Daniel Lombord S:1

Lombord, Nathaniel - Died 1749
June 18 in his 71st yr S:1

Long, A Byrd - Died 1991 Born
1990 (with Beatrice L Long) S:16

Long, Arthur C - Died 1963 Born
1890 (with Eleanor F Long) S:17

Long, Beatrice L - Died 1978 Born
1899 (with A Byrd Long) S:16

Long, Edith F - Died 1972 Born
1888 (with Edwin F Long) S:18

Long, Edwin F - Died 1945 Born
1888 (with Edith F Long) S:18

Long, Eleanor F - Died 1985 Born
1890 (with Arthur C Long) S:17

Long, Herbert H Jr - Died 1970
Sept 15 Born 1897 June 3 From
Massachusetts, was a Corporal
in Motor Trans Corps during
world War I S:14

Long, Jacquelyn L - Died (still
living 1991?) Born 1933 Daughter of John Davies & Mattie
Sturgis (with them & Clinton
Davies & Marcia Crosby) S:19

Loomis, Barbara - Buried 1984
April 6 Age 93 Located in Block
11, lot 63, grave 2 (she is with
Henry Loomis) S:15R

Loomis, Henry S - Died 1989 Born
1891 (two stones) Was a 1st Lt
in US Army Air Corps during
World War I (with Barbara C
Loomis) S:15

Lopes, Eola L - Died 1970 Born
1910 (with Manuel S Lopes) S:20

Lopes, John L - Died 1862 Born
1908 (with Lucy R Lopes) S:31

Lopes, Jose D E - Died 1935 Born
1882 S:16

Lopes, Lucy R - Died 1866 (no death date) (listed with John L Lopes) S:31

Lopes, Manuel S - Died 1959 Born 1901 (with Eola L Lopes) S:20

Lopes, Marianna - Died 1978 Born 1887 (undertaker plaque) S:18

Lopes, Marie R - Died 1955 Born 1892 (with Jose DAE Lopes) S:16

Lorange, Oscar H - Died 1961 Born 1891 (with Ruth M Lorange) S:14

Lorange, Ruth M - Died 1962 Born 1899 (with Oscar H Lorange) S:14

Lord, Edwin A - Died 1970 Nov 21 Born 1897 Feb 6 From Massachusetts, was PHM3 in USNRF during World War I S:14

Loring, (an infant) - Died 1825 Dec 7 Parents were Otis & Adeline D Loring S:4

Loring, (no first name) - Died (no dates, just a flat stone marker next to another that says, Aldrich) S:21

Loring, Abby - Died (no dates listed, small stonr next to Erhraim Loring, d1866) S:11

Loring, Abigail Mrs - Died 1765 Sept 20 Age 17 years, 9 months, 4 days Wife of Elbaret (?) Loring (there are 3 very large coffin cripts on top ground, markings worn off, next to her) S:11

Loring, Ada M - Died 1868 Born 1837 Wife of Walter H Foster & daughter of Capt William Loring & Julia A Nye (buried with them) S:11

Loring, Adeline - Died 1855 June 6 Age 21 years, 9 months, 10 days Daughter of Elijah & Sarah Ann Loring S:11R

Loring, Adeline D - Died 1874 June 19 Born 1805 July 11 (stone off at base) Wife of Otis Loring (next to him) S:21

Loring, Annie N - Died 1973 Born 1901 (with Henry B Loring) S:13

Loring, Catherine R - Died 1888

Loring (Cont.)
June 16 Born 1811 June 11 S:11R

Loring, Charles Creeley - Died 1873 April 4 in Washington (DC?) Age 37 Born 1836 Feb 6 in Boston, Massachusetts Son of Edward G & Harriet B Loring (next to wife, Emma Coleman) S:14

Loring, Cora L - Died 1911 Nov 27 Born 1844 Apr 1 S:6

Loring, Cora M - Died 1871 Oct 9 Age 4 years, 3 days Daughter of Eil & Cora Loring S:6

Loring, David - Died (date not listed) Age 86 years, 6 months (stone broken in half, next to wife, Elizabeth Loring, d1863) S:11

Loring, David - Died 1777 Nov 2 in his 74th yr (stone worn badly) (next to Elpaler Loring) (Hinckley Ceme records #11R say death was on Nov 2 at age 74) S:11+ 26R

Loring, David Freeman - Died 1930 Born 1839 (with Ellen Maria Loring & others) S:19

Loring, Edward - Died 1812 Aug 29 Age 2 months Son of Edward & Phebe Loring (next to them) S:10

Loring, Edward - Died 1855 Aug 26 Age 81 S:10

Loring, Elijah - Died 1887 Oct 20 Born 1805 May 9 S:11R

Loring, Elijah L - Died 1909 Feb 14 Born 1843 Apr 22 S:6

Loring, Eliphalet - Died 1889 Mar 21 Born 1811 Apr 21 Wife was Sarah Loring (buried next to him) S:6

Loring, Eliphalet Mr - Died 1798 April 14 in his 32nd yr S:26R

Loring, Eliza A - Died 1886 Nov 27 Born 1842 Aug 24 Wife of Henry F Loring (buried next to him) S:6

Loring, Eliza Jane - Died 1802 Nov 13 Wife of Eleazer Loring S:10

Loring, Elizabeth - Died 1863 July 11 Age 71 years, 9 months Wife of David Loring (buried next to him) S:11

Loring, Ellen Maria - Died 1920 Born 1842 (with Hattie May Loring & others) S:19

Loring, Elpalet - Died 1768 May 8 in his 28th yr (this is a male person) (stone not very clear) (Hinckley Ceme records #11R says death was 1768) S:11+26R

Loring, Emma - Died 1928 July 15 Born 1845 Dec 26 Wife of Allan J Chase & daughter of Capt William Loring & Julia A Nye (on same stone) S:11

Loring, Ephraim - Died 1866 Sept 2 Age 27 years, ? months, 22 days (stone worn) Lost at sea Son of Joshua & Ella Catherine Loring (on same stone with John M Loring, d1862) S:11

Loring, Frank - Died 1915 Dec 4 Born 1822 Dec 4 S:6

Loring, Hannah - Died 1795 Sept 23 (small stone & worn) Daughter of David & Mary Loring (Hinckley Ceme records #11R say death was on Sept 23 at age 6 months, 28 days and full name was Hannah Gorham Loring) S:11+26R

Loring, Hannah R - Died 1922 Born 1847 (with Abby F Jones, d1921) S:11

Loring, Hattie May - Died 1930 Born 1868 (with Irene Freeman Loring & others) S:19

Loring, Henry B - Died 1974 Born 1888 (with Annie N Loring) S:13

Loring, Henry F - Died 1891 Dec 14 Born 1836 Oct 13 S:6

Loring, Irene Freeman - Died 1963 Born 1878 (with David Freeman Loring & others) S:19

Loring, John R - Died 1862 Aug 21 (with Ephraim Loring) (Hinckley Ceme records #11R says he drowned in Connecticut River from schooner, Juliet age was 14 years, 11 months, 14 days and middle initial may be R) S:11

Loring, Joseph G - Died 1839? June 6 Born 1814 Nov 9 (stone broken in pieces) (listed with

Loring (Cont.)
wife, Marin Loring) S:11

Loring, Joseph G Jr - Died 1878 Nov 25 Born 1849 Nov 29 (listed with Maria Elizabeth Loring, stone says,"Brother & Sister") S:11

Loring, Joshua (Capt) - Died 1850 Sept 11 Age 66, located in row 18 (next to daughter, Ruth) S:11

Loring, Julia A - Died 1853 April 18 Age 42 Wife of William Loring S:11R

Loring, Julia A - Died 1853 Age 18 yrs 10 mos Daughter of Capt William Loring & Julia A Nye (buried with them) S:11+11R

Loring, Lydia - Died 1806 Mar 26 in her 42nd yr Widow of Elpalet Loring S:4

Loring, Lydia S - Died 1893 Nov 17 Born 1839 June 7 S:10

Loring, Malvina - Died 1886 Born 1840 Wife of Joseph Foster & daughter of Capt William Loring & Julia A Nye (on same stone) S:11

Loring, Marcy - Died 1796 Sept 28 in her 24th yr Wife to Eliphalet Loring S:26R

Loring, Marcy or Mary - Died 1808 Jan 16 in her 22nd yr Wife of Joshua Loring (next to him, d1850) S:11+11R+26R

Loring, Maria Elizabeth - Died 1854 July 5 Born 1837 Sept 11 (listed with Joseph G Loring Jr, stone says,"Brother & Sister") S:11

Loring, Marin L - Died 1852? Nov 2 Born April 2 ? Wife of Joseph Loring (listed with husband, stone broken in pieces) S:11

Loring, Martha T - Died 1807 Feb 8 Age 6 months Daughter of Edward & Phebe Loring (next to them) S:10

Loring, Mary - Died 1800 Aug 17 Age 24 yrs 6 mos Daughter of Otis and Sarah Loring S:26R

Loring, Mary - Died 1808 located in row 18 S:11R

Loring, Mary Mrs - Died 1811 Mar

Loring (Cont.)
16 in her 63rd yr Widow of Otis Loring & Relict to Capt John Russell S:11

Loring, Mehitable - Died 1791 July 6 in his 21st yr Daughter to Otis and Sarah Loring S:26R

Loring, Otis - Died 1799 April 3 in his 67th yr S:26R

Loring, Otis - Died 1793 Dec 8 in his 25th yr Son of Otis and Sarah Loring S:26R

Loring, Otis - Died 1798 April 3 in his 5th yr Son of Eliphalet and Marcy Loring S:26R

Loring, Otis - Died 1859 April 9 Born 1800 Aug 11 (next to Adeline D Loring, wife) S:21

Loring, Phebe - Died 1845 Aug 28 Age 65 Wife of Edward Loring (next to him) S:10

Loring, Ruth - Died (underground) Daughter of Joshua & Elizabeth Loring (next to father, Capt Joshua, d1850) (Hinckley Ceme records #11R say death was 1816 Nov 19 age 18 years, 7 months, 20 days and born on 1835 July 9) S:11+11R

Loring, Sarah - Died 1760 May 14 in her 52nd yr Wife of David Loring (also listed in 11R records) S:11

Loring, Sarah - Died 1768 located in row 7 S:11R+26R

Loring, Sarah - Died 1785 June 23 Age 41 Wife of Otis Loring S:26R

Loring, Sarah - Died 1884 Apr 2 Born 1813 Feb 18 Wife of Eliphalet Loring (buried next to her) S:6

Loring, Sarah E - Died 1912 April 19 Born 1820 Oct 16 Widow of Joseph G Loring (next to Maria Elizabeth & Joseph G Loring Jr) S:11

Loring, Sarah H - Died 1818 July 12 Age 16 Daughter of Edward & Phebe Loring (next to family) S:10

Loring, Sarah Mrs - Died 1762 June 22 Wife of ? (stone worn)

Loring (Cont.)
(Hinckley Ceme records #11R say died in her 25th yr and wife of Otis) S:11+26R

Loring, Susie E - Died 1898 Sept 7 1875 Dec 8 Wife of Frank Loring (buried next to him) S:6

Loring, Theodore - Died 1844 June 29 Age 4 mos 29 days Born 1844 Son of Capt William Loring & Julia A Nye (buried with them) S:11+11R

Loring, William (Capt) - Died 1853 Mar 27 Age 42 (a Civil War Star plaque 1861-65) (a large family stone with others) S:11

Loring, William N - Died 1886 Born 1832 Son of Capt William Loring & Julia A Nye (on same stone) S:11

Lothrop? - Died (worn & underground) daughter of ? (next to Elizabeth Lothrop, d1747) S:11

Lothrop, (infant) - Died 1861 Jan 12 Age 4 days Daughter of Asa & Allis Lothrop S:21

Lothrop, (no name) - Died 1799 April 7 Age 9 days S:26R

Lothrop, ? - Died 1757 May 8 Age 79 Widow of Joseph Lothrop (next to him) S:11

Lothrop, ? - Died Sept (stone worn with others too, near Barnabas & Susanna Lothrop, she died 1697) S:11

Lothrop, ? - Died (stone worn down, next to Barnabas Lothrop & Susanna Lothrop she died d1697) S:11

Lothrop, A - Died 1737 May 8 Age 79 Widow of Joseph Lothrop Esq (buried next to him) S:11

Lothrop, Abigail - Died 1745 located in row 12 S:11R

Lothrop, Abigail - Died 1766 located in row 3 S:11R

Lothrop, Abigail - Died 1844 Oct 22 Age 72 Wife of Thomas Lothrop S:14

Lothrop, Abigail Mrs - Died 1715 Dec 21 Age 72 Late wife of Barnabas Lothrop Esq S:11R

Lothrop, Abigail Mrs - Died 1753 May 8 in her 79th yr Widow of Joseph Lothrop Esq S:11R+26R

Lothrop, Abner - Died 1715 located in row 16 S:11R

Lothrop, Alonzo F - Died 1915 Born 1836 (with Cynthia Lothrop & others) S:18

Lothrop, Ann - Died 1954 Born 1864 (with Benjamin Carney & others) S:18

Lothrop, Ansel - Died 1857 March 28 Born 1782 June 26 (next to Deborah Lothrop) S:19

Lothrop, Ansel D Jr - Died 1927 Born 1845 S:10

Lothrop, Barnabas - Died 1714 Dec 11 Age 20 years, 2 months, located in row 17 (Hinkley's records says death on Oct 26 1714 age 28, another says 1784) S:11R+26R

Lothrop, Barnabas - Died 1732 Oct 11 in his 70th yr, located in row 3 (Hinckley Ceme records #11R say death date was 1732) S:11+26R

Lothrop, Barnabas - Died 1808 April 6 Age 2 months Son of Josiah & Chloe Lothrop S:5R

Lothrop, Barnabas Esq - Died Oct (possibly in 1600's) (stone worn out and next too othes that cannot be read) in his 80th yr (next to possible wife, Susanna Lothrop, d1697) (Hinckley Ceme records #11R say death was 1715 on 26 Oct) S:11+26R

Lothrop, Barnabas Mr - Died 1756 April 8 Age 70 S:11R

Lothrop, Barney T - Died 1816 July 2 Age 6 weeks Son of James S & Hitty Lothrop S:10

Lothrop, Benjamin (Capt) - Died 1886 May 5 Age 41 years, 10 months S:19

Lothrop, Bethia B - Died 1874 Born 1855 (with Isa G Lothrop & others) S:18

Lothrop, Bethier - Died 1794 Oct 26 Age about 98 Wife of Barnabas Lothrop S:11

Lothrop, Carrie - Died (death not listed on stone) Born 1879 Wife of David E Seabury (on same stone) S:11

Lothrop, Chester - Died 1883 Born 1881 (with Bethia B Lothrop & others) S:18

Lothrop, Cleia A - Died 1901 Oct 14 Born 1823 July 1 (with Laura A Lothrop & others) S:18

Lothrop, Cynthia J - Died 1916 Born 1834 (with Ellsworth F Lothrop & others) S:18

Lothrop, Daniel B - Died 1863 Oct 23 Born 1844 June 23 (with James H Lothrop & others) S:18

Lothrop, David - Died 1801 March S:7

Lothrop, Deborah - Died (cannot read) (stone backed against possible husband, Ansel Lothrop) Widow of ? Lothrop S:19

Lothrop, Deborah - Died 1805 March 26 in her 41st yr Wife of John Lothrop Jr S:26R

Lothrop, Deborah - Died 1865 March 16 Age 65, 8 months S:4

Lothrop, Deborah H - Died 1880 July 18 Age 33 Wife of Ansel D Lothrop Jr S:9R

Lothrop, Ebenezer - Died 1825 Oct 21 in his 48th yr S:10+26R

Lothrop, Eliazia ? - Died 17?? April (stone very bad condition) S:11

Lothrop, Elijah (?) - Died 17?? April (stone worn bad) (next to ? Lothrop, widow of Joseph Lothrop) S:11

Lothrop, Elizabeth - Died 1795 July 25 in her 28th yr (no dates on stone) (next to Capt Isaac Lothrop) S:10+26R

Lothrop, Elizabeth - Died 1828 Jan 17 Age 22 (no dates on stone) Dau to James & Hitty Lothrop S:10+26R

Lothrop, Elizabeth - Died (not clear) S:10

Lothrop, Elizabeth - Died 1828 Dec 18 Born 1748 Mar 25 (Stone not clear) Widow to Ebenezer Lothrop S:10+26R

286

Lothrop, Elizabeth - Died 1695 Nov 11 Age 2 years, 2 months, located in row 17 Daughter of John & Elizabeth Lothrop S:11R

Lothrop, Elizabeth - Died 1747 Sept 18 in her 81st yr S:11+26R

Lothrop, Elizabeth - Died 1828 Jan 17 Age 22 Daughter of James S & Hitty lothrop S:10

Lothrop, Ella F - Died 1937 Born 1847 (with Chester Lothrop & others) S:18

Lothrop, Ellsworth F - Died 1930 Born 1861 (with Ann Lothrop & others) S:18

Lothrop, Experience - Died 1733 Dec 23 Age 55 years, 4 months, 25 days Wife of Thomas Lothrop S:9R

Lothrop, Frank G - Died 1921 April 14 Born 1857 April 29 (with Etta L Stapleton & others) S:18

Lothrop, Frederick C (Capt) - Died 1913 Born 1832 (with Isadore Lothrop & others) S:18

Lothrop, Freeman - Died Dec (could be 1600's) Age possibly 25 (stone worn very badly Next to Rev John Lathrop (Lothrop), d1653) S:11

Lothrop, Hannah - Died 1715 S:11R

Lothrop, Hannah - Died 1844 July 30 in her 67th yr (Hinckley Ceme records #5R say death date 1884) S:5

Lothrop, Henry - Died 1860 Sept 10 Born 1823 April 16 (with Joseph D & other Lothrop's) S:10

Lothrop, Hitty - Died 1834 Nov 9 Age 36 (underground) Wife of James S Lothrop (next to him) S:10+26R

Lothrop, Isa G - Died 1875 Born 1858 (with Percy Lothrop & others) S:18

Lothrop, Isaac (Capt) - Died 1835 March 11 in his 78th yr S:10+26R

Lothrop, Isabella - Died 1928 Born 1867 S:10

Lothrop, Isadore - Died 1873 Born 1835 (with Ella F Lothrop & others) S:18

Lothrop, Jabaz - Died (stone in very poor condition) S:11

Lothrop, James H - Died 1891 Sept 3 Born 1813 May 1 (with Celia A Lothrop & others) S:18

Lothrop, James S - Died 1847 Jan Born 1808 Oct 30 (on same stone with Joseph D Lothrop & others) (next to James S Lothrop) S:10

Lothrop, James S - Died 1863 Feb 11 Age 82 years,6 months S:10

Lothrop, Jamie - Died 1873 April 5 Age 7 months, 13 days Son of Ansel D Jr & Deborah H Lothrop S:9R

Lothrop, Jamie - Died 1873 Born 1868 (on same stone with Ansel Lothrop) S:10

Lothrop, John - Died (no dates, but located in row 16) S:11R

Lothrop, John - Died 1727 Sept 18 in his 85th yr (church record dated 27 Sept) S:11R+26R

Lothrop, John - Died 1876 May 26 Age 26, 4 months S:4

Lothrop, John Rev - Died 1653 Born 1584 (large plaque in front of Cemetery says, Errected in memory of him & And such first settlers who filled unmarked graves in this cemetery, Lothrop was pastor in Egerton 1611-23 and other Stats from England) S:11

Lothrop, Joseph - Died 1731 Feb 9 in his 34th yr (not sure if same as 5R Joseph Lothrop at age 24?) S:5

Lothrop, Joseph - Died 1731/2 Feb 29 Age 24 S:5R

Lothrop, Joseph - Died 1761 Mar 15 in his 29th yr S:5

Lothrop, Joseph (Esquire) - Died 1747 in his 73rd yr (stone worn) He was a judge in the Court of Commons in Barnstable county S:11+26R

Lothrop, Joseph C - Died 1842 Feb

Lothrop (Cont.)
10 Age 45 S:10

Lothrop, Joseph D - Died 1844 Dec 12 Born 1814 June 2 (with Henry Lothrop & others) S:10

Lothrop, Joseph Esq - Died 1747 Age 73 He was court justice of common pleas & supported the arm of the law and faithfully to the people S:11

Lothrop, Josiah - Died 1758 March 8 Born 1758 Feb 28 Son of Josiah & Deborah Lothrop S:5R

Lothrop, Kimble - Died 1734 Mar 29 in the 26th yr S:11+26R

Lothrop, Laura A - Died 1843 Sept 30 Born 1842 July 30 (with Daniel B Lothrop & others) S:18

Lothrop, Marcy - Died (stone worn & down) (next to Elizabeth Lothrop, d1747) S:11

Lothrop, Mary - Died 1728 June 1 Age 16 years, 11 months, 1 day Daughter of Barnabas & Elizabeth Lothrop S:11R

Lothrop, Mary - Died 1840 June ? (next to a very small stone that says,HBF) Widow of John Lothrop S:10

Lothrop, Mary - Died 1845 Aug 23 Age 84 Widow of Capt Isaac Lothrop (buried next to him) S:10

Lothrop, Meletiah - Died 1711 Feb 5 in her 66th yr S:11+26R

Lothrop, Mercy C - Died 1862 Dec 14 Born 1807 Sept 19 Wife of Oliver Chase (next to him) S:19

Lothrop, Mercy Mrs - Died 1741 July 30 in her 53rd yr S:11R+ 26R

Lothrop, Nathaniel (Capt) - Died 1807 April 14 in his 70th yr S:10+26R

Lothrop, Olive - Died 1808 Sept 30 in her 2nd yr Daughter of Capt Robert and Susanna Lothrop S:26R

Lothrop, Percy - Died 1908 Born 1877 (with Ella F Lothrop & others) S:18

Lothrop, Robert (Capt) - Died 1840

Lothrop (Cont.)
Sept 18 Age 69 S:11R

Lothrop, Ruth Hinckley - Died 1887 July 27 Born 1812 Sept 25 Wife of Ansel D Lothrop S:9R

Lothrop, Ruth Mrs - Died 1851 April 23 Age 52 Widow of Joseph C Lothrop (next to him) S:10

Lothrop, Sarah - Died 1712 May 23 in her 64th yr Wife of Meletiah Lothrop S:11R+26R

Lothrop, Sarah - Died 1723 located in row 10 S:11R

Lothrop, Sarah - Died 176? (stone worn) (next to Mary Crocker & Hannah Holbrook) S:11

Lothrop, Sarah L - Died 1889 June 19 Age 59 years, 2 months, 19 days (next to Capt Sylvester B Lothrop) S:21

Lothrop, Stephen N - Died 1812 Dec 2 Age 1 year, 6 days (buried with Abagail N Smith) Son of Ansel & Deborah Lothrop S:5

Lothrop, Susanna - Died 1697 Sep 28 Age 55 Wife of Barnabas Lothrop Esq (next to him) (Hinckley Ceme records #11R say that her grandfather was Thomas Clarke of the Mayflower) S:11

Lothrop, Susanna A - Died 1853 Oct 14 Age 83 Wife of Robert Lothrop S:11R

Lothrop, Sylvester (Capt) - Died 1899 Jan 26 Age 76 years, 4 months, 13 days (next to Sarah L Lothrop) S:21

Lothrop, Sylvester B - Died 1887 July 27 Age 24 years, 10 months, 14 days (next to Sarah L Lothrop) S:21

Lothrop, Temperance - Died 1811 July 14 Age 6 months,8 days Daughter of Ebenezer & Temperance Lothrop (next to mother) S:10

Lothrop, Temperance - Died 1837 Nov 11 Age 57 Widow of Ebenezer Lothrop (next to him) S:10

Lothrop, Temperence - Died 176? Aug 20 Age 6 years, 2 months

Lothrop (Cont.)
Daughter of Joseph & Deborah Lothrop (Hinckley Ceme records #5R say death date was 1761) S:5

Lothrop, Thankful S - Died 1843 Aug 15 Age 5 Daughter of Joseph C & Ruth Lothrop (next to them) S:10

Lothrop, Thomas - Died 1733 Dec 23 Age 55 years, 4 months, 25 days S:9

Lothrop, Willie F - Died 1881 April 24 Born 1866 Sept 23 Son of Freeman H & Hettie F Lothrop S:9R

Lothrop, Emelia H (Saunders) - Died 1839 Feb 24 Born 1813 Sept 16 Wife of Ansel D Lothrop S:9R

Lothrope, Ebenezer - Died 1815 Jan 27 Born 1743 May 15 (next to wife, Elizabeth Lothrope) S:10

Lothrope, Elizabeth - Died 1828 Dec 18 Born 1748 March 25 Widow of Ebenezer Lothrope S:10

Lothrope, James - Died 1748 April Drowned Age 46 (on same stone with Patience Lothrope) S:10

Lothrope, Joseph H - Died 1856 Aug 7 Age 30 years,11 months S:10

Lothrope, Patience - Died 1787 Jan Age 79 (on same stone with James Lothrope) S:10

Lovejoy, Anna R - Died (still living 1990?) Born 1909 (on same stone & in Lovejoy plot with Hollis C Lovejoy) S:11

Lovejoy, Florence S - Died (still living 1990?) Born 1915 (in Lovejoy plot) S:11

Lovejoy, Hollis C - Died 1987 Born 1909 (on same stone & in Lovejoy plot with Anna R Lovejoy) S:11

Lovejoy, Jean - Died (still living 1990) Born 1925 Wife of Bryce H Clowery (listed with him) S:11

Lovejoy, Kenneth A - Died 1984 Born 1912 Was a PFC in US

Lovejoy (Cont.)
Army during World War II (in Lovejoy plot) S:11

Lovejoy, William S P - Died 1943 Born 1878 (with wife, Marion E Cahoon in Lovejoy plot) S:11

Lovejoy, William S P Jr - Died 1987 Born 1905 Member of the Barnstable Fire Dept, plaque & flag (on same stone in Lovejoy plot with Florence S Lovejoy) S:11

Loveland, Gladys - Died 1988 Born 1899 (in Chesley plot with Herbert W Chesley) S:11

Lovell, (infant) - Died 1828 Oct 11, Age 9 days Son of Mary & George Lovell (with mother) S:12

Lovell, (infant) - Died 1858 Sept 9 Age 1 year, 11 months, 25 days (next to Sarah Lovell, d1858) S:12

Lovell, (son of) - Buried 1803 Sept 23 Son of Gorham & Date Lovell Esq S:4

Lovell, ? - Died 1876 (a large crypt at street level, a large stone with metal door) S:12

Lovell, Abbie C - Died 1931 Born 1873 (buried with Ploomie C Lovell & others on Isaac Crowell stone) S:8

Lovell, Abby - Died 1852 April 30 Age 31 years, 9 months Wife of Freeman Lovell (next to him) S:12

Lovell, Abby Lucinea - Died 1853 Jan 19 (stone worn) Daughter of Freeman & Abby Lovell (next to them) S:12

Lovell, Abby P - Died 1878 Born 1838 (with Cyrenius A Lovell) S:13

Lovell, Abigail F - Died 1825 Nov 12 Age 45 Wife of James Lovell (next to him) S:12

Lovell, Abigail Mrs - Died 1793 Oct 25 Age 42 (with Master, Samuel S Lovell, her son) S:12

Lovell, Abner W - Died 1892 May 30 Born 1808 Jan 19 S:4

Lovell, Abner W (Capt) - Died 1831

Lovell (Cont.)

July 2 in his 58th yr S:4

Lovell, Adeline - Died 1890 Nov 11 Age 91 Born 1799 May 28 Wife of George Lovell & daughter of Ben & Abigail Hallett S:12

Lovell, Afa - Died 1800 Sept 5 Age 27 S:12

Lovell, Alethena S - Died 1902 July 9 Born 1840 Sept 28 (with William Lovell & Arnold Bowen) S:21

Lovell, Andrew - Died 1831 Nov 6 Age 83 years, 6 months (next to wife, Temperance Lovell) S:14

Lovell, Andrew - Died 1900 Born 1813 (with Freeman & Betsey Lovell) S:14

Lovell, Anna - Died 1860 May 10 Age 15 years, 2 months, 5 days Daughter of Abner W & Temperance Lovell S:4

Lovell, Anna Mrs - Died 1793 Oct 22 Age 30 Consort to Cornelius Lovell S:12

Lovell, Asa E - Died 1886 Dec 18 Born 1821 Oct 18 (next to Ellis & Nellie Lovell) S:12

Lovell, Augusta - Died 1856 Born 1824 (with Betsey & Freeman Lovell) S:14

Lovell, Augusta - Died 1881 Born 1856 (with Freeman & Betsey Lovell) S:14

Lovell, Augusta H - Died 1930 April 15 Born 1840 Sept 7 (a dog lover) Wife of Orville D Lovell (with him & 4 dogs, Daniel, Pilot Little Pilot & Daniel in Lovell plot) S:12

Lovell, Barbara M - Died 1963 Born 1947 (with Bradford & Kathryn Lovell) S:12

Lovell, Betsey - Died 1856 Aug 12 Age 67 years, 5 months Wife of Charles Lovell (with him) S:14

Lovell, Betsey - Died 1875 Born 1790 (with Freeman Lovell) S:14

Lovell, Blanche - Died 1945 Born 1871 Wife of Robert M Daniel (with him) S:16

Lovell, Bradford - Died 1978 Born

Lovell (Cont.)

1917 (with Kathryn E Lovell) S:12

Lovell, Calvin W - Died 1876 June 13 Age 17 (next to Luther Lovell) S:14

Lovell, Caroline L - Died 1909 Born 1818 (with Freeman & Betsey Lovell) S:14

Lovell, Charles - Died 1864 May 12 Age 79 years, 5 months (next to wife, Betsey Lovell) S:14

Lovell, Charles C - Died 1896 Born 1835 (with Zenas & Lydia Lovell & others) S:12

Lovell, Charles W - Died (still living?) Born 1912 (listed with Elizabeth A Lovell) S:12

Lovell, Charles Warren - Died 1830 July 3 Age 15 Son of ? & Mercy E Lovell S:12

Lovell, Charlotte - Died 1887 Born 1846 (with Nathan P Lovell) S:18

Lovell, Chloe C - Died 1868 May 9 in her 67th yr Wife of Ezra Lovell S:7

Lovell, Christopher - Died 1838 May 6 Age 88 (listed on his stone is also, Edward S Lovell) S:12

Lovell, Clarissa - Died 1870 June 3 Age 80 years, 8 months Wife of James Lovell (next to him with other wife too) S:12

Lovell, Cordelia S - Died 1916 Born 1841 Wife of Howard Lovell (with him) S:12

Lovell, Cornelius - Died 1827 April 17 Age 71 S:12

Lovell, Cornellia M - Died 1843 Nov 11 Age 2 years, 6 months S:12

Lovell, Cyrenius A - Died 1897 Born 1833 (with Abby P Lovell) S:13

Lovell, Daniel - Died 1832 Nov 23 Age 85 (next to wife, Ollive Lovell) S:12

Lovell, Daniel - Died 1888 Jan 13 Age ? (stone worn) (next to Eliza E Lovell) S:12

Lovell, Daniel (a Dog) - Died 1902 Born 1888 (located in Lovell plot) "A gentle affectionate and

Lovell (Cont.)
faithful dog The whole broad earth around for that one heart which lead and try? bears friendship without end or bound and found the prize in you" (in plot with 3 other dogs & Orville Dewey Lovell) S:12

Lovell, Daniel (a dog) - Died 1924 Aug 1 Born 1917 March 1 "Our faithful dog an affectionate lovable companion and household pet" (in Lovell plot with 3 other dogs and Orville Dewey Lovell) S:12

Lovell, Daniel G - Died 1853 Sept 23 Born 1833 May 27 Died at San Francisco, (Ca) (next to Dorcas Lovell) S:18

Lovell, Daniel W - Died 1855 Born 1851 (with Zenas & Lydia Lovell & others) S:12

Lovell, Date - Died 1844 Mar 9 Age 75 years, 9 days Wife of Gorham Lovell Esq S:4

Lovell, David Jr - Died 1896 Nov 8 Age 72 S:14

Lovell, David Sr - Died 1858 Sept Age ? (stone not clear, next to Mary Lovell d1869) S:14

Lovell, Dorcas - Died 1882 Jan 28 Age 81 years, 2 months, 3 days (next to Daniel G Lovell) S:18

Lovell, Edgar W - Died 1929 Born 1854 (next to Mercy A Lovell) S:14

Lovell, Edward M - Died 1899 Born 1837 (with Mercy N Lovell) S:13

Lovell, Edward S - Died 1815 Aug 3 Age 14 years, 8 months, 12 days at Havana, Cuba Grandson of Christopher Lovell (listed on his stone) S:12

Lovell, Elida W - Died 1949 Born 1878 (with William Lovell) S:18

Lovell, Eliza E - Died 1892 Sept 6 Age 81 years, 2 months, 26 days Wife of Daniel Lovell (next to him) S:12

Lovell, Eliza G - Died 1893 Born 1829 (with Russell Lovell & others) S:12

Lovell, Elizabeth A - Died 1987 Born 1911 (with Charles W Lovell) S:12

Lovell, Elizabeth E - Died 1922 Born 1849 (with Freeman & Betsey Lovell) S:14

Lovell, Ella L - Died 1935 Born 1857 (with James & Lucinda Lovell & others) S:12

Lovell, Ellen A - Died 1879 June 8 Age 43 Wife of Gustavus Lovell (next to him) S:12

Lovell, Ellis B - Died 1914 Born 1863 (with Nellie W Lovell) S:12

Lovell, Ellis J - Died 1839 July 14 Born 1784 July 30 (next to Lydia G Lovell) S:12

Lovell, Emily A - Died (year not clear) Age 37 Wife of Capt Braddock Crocker (listed on same stone) S:12

Lovell, Emma Ann - Died 1849 Nov 28 Born 1846 Nov 7 Daughter of Alexander & Sally Lovell S:4

Lovell, Eunice - Died 1807 Apr 11 Age 34 Daughter of Capt Andrew Lovell S:7

Lovell, Eunice M - Died 1896 Born 1840 (with John B Lovell) S:14

Lovell, Ezra - Died 1879 May 26 Age 89 years, 8 months, 7 days S:7

Lovell, Flora - Died Age 3 (small white stone) (between Kenneth P & Lester Prince Lovell) S:12

Lovell, Frances H - Died 1955 Born 1874 Wife of Everett F Fuller (with him) S:13

Lovell, Franklyn Hallett - Died 1962 Born 1868 Son of Franklyn Hallett Lovell & grandson to George Lovell S:12

Lovell, Frederic - Died 1883 Jan 16 Age 72 (listed with Frederic A Lovell) S:18

Lovell, Frederic A - Died Lost at sea Age 20 (no dates) Son of Frederic & Lydia H Lovell (listed with Frederic Lovell) S:18

Lovell, Freeman - Died 1843 Born 1786 (with Betsey Lovell) S:14

Lovell, Freeman - Died 1877 Nov 1

Lovell (Cont.)
Age 64 S:12

Lovell, Freeman - Died 1883 Born 1842 (stone says, At Rest) S:8

Lovell, Genie M - Died 1906 Born 1847 (with James & Lucinda Lovell & others) S:12

Lovell, George - Died 1861 Nov 28 Age 74 Born 1787 July 17 (a tall monument) He was a member of the Baptist church S:12

Lovell, George Franklin - Died 1917 Jan 25 Born 1841 Jan 29 Son of Joseph & Anna Lovell (in Lovell plot with Orveille & Augusta Lovell & 4 dogs) S:12

Lovell, George Thatcher - Died 1831 April 9 Age 17 years?, 10 months, 21 days Eldest son of Capt George Lovell He was lost in disasterous wreck of the schooner, Warrier Black or Block Hawk? Capt Oliver Scudder (more written, not clear) S:12

Lovell, Gorham Esq - Died 1852 Apl 7 in his 84th yr S:4

Lovell, Gorham Jr - Died 1824 June Age 19 He was lost in the Brig Hero bound from Boston for Surinam Son of Gorham & Date Lovell Esq S:4

Lovell, Gustavus G - Died 1902 Nov 28 Age 68 Born 1834 Nov 14 Was a seaman & captain & engaged in commercial pursuits Son of George & Adeline Lovell (next to Ellen A Lovell) S:12

Lovell, Hannah - Died 1807 Feb 18 Age 81 Widow of Capt Jacob Lovell (next to him) S:12

Lovell, Hannah H - Died 1897 Oct 17 Born 1833 Oct 16 Wife of Robert H Lovell (next to him) S:12

Lovell, Harriet S - Died 1902 Born 1828 (with Freeman & Betsey Lovell) S:14

Lovell, Harrison Crocker - Died 1940 Born 1873 (in Lovell plot with Robert Winsor Lovell) S:12

Lovell, Hattie D - Died 1888 Oct 29 Born 1864 Jan 10 (on large

Lovell (Cont.)
family stone at street level with Mercy A Lovell) S:12

Lovell, Henry - Died 1858 Nov 12 Age 75 years, 1 month, 18 days (next to wife, Lydia & possible son, Henry M Lovell) S:13

Lovell, Henry A - Died 1886 Nov 2 Age 60 years, 2 months, 18 days (next to Mercy A Lovell) S:14

Lovell, Henry M - Died 1907 Feb 12 Born 1823 May 1 (next to possible parents, Henry & Lydia Lovell) S:13

Lovell, Horace - Died 1843 Aug 18 Age 21 years, 7 months, 27 days (died at sea) (listed with Zenas Lovell) S:14

Lovell, Horace S - Died 1824 Dec 21 Age 10 months, 20 days ? (stone worn) Son of George & Mary Lovell S:12

Lovell, Horace S - Died 1890 Feb 11 Age 62 years, 5 months, 4 days (next to wife, Medora M Lovell) S:12

Lovell, Howard A - Died 1854 Born 1852 (with Freeman & Betsey Lovell) S:14

Lovell, Howard M - Died 1888 Born 1842 (with wife, Cordelia S Lovell) S:12

Lovell, Isaac - Died 1824 Dec 6 Age 29 who was instantly killed on the sloop, Echo Son of Cornelius & Abigail Lovell (next to father) S:12

Lovell, Isaac - Died 1905 Dec 24 Born 1824 June 14 (on large family stone at street level with Mercy A Lovell) S:12

Lovell, Jacob - Died 1857 Oct 15 Age 55 S:12

Lovell, Jacob - Died 1897 July 5 Born 1817 June 8 (buried with Mercy C Lovell) S:8

Lovell, Jacob (Capt) - Died 1805 Nov 27 Age 82 S:12

Lovell, James - Died 1761 May 8 in his 69th yr S:1

Lovell, James - Died 1816 April 20 Age 84 S:12

292

Lovell, James - Died 1855 Oct 10 Born 1770 May 21 (next to wife, Abigail F Lovell) S:12

Lovell, James A - Died 1935 Born 1851 (with James & Lucinda Lovell & others) S:12

Lovell, James N - Died 1865 Born 1804 (with Lucinda Lovell) S:12

Lovell, Jerusha - Died 1867 Nov 9 Age 71 Wife of Robert Lovell (with him in Lovell plot) S:12

Lovell, Jesse C - Died 1876 May 14 Born 1826 July 2 S:12

Lovell, John B - Died 1877 Born 1831 (a tall monument) (with Eunice M Lovell) S:14

Lovell, John M - Died 1853 Born 1819 (with Zenas & Lydia Lovell & others) S:12

Lovell, Joshua - Died 1824 Nov 2 Age 75 S:12

Lovell, Joshua Mr - Died 1840 Sept 12 Age 47 (next to Lydia I Lovell) S:12

Lovell, Julia Adeline - Died 1845 May 5 Age 3 years, 10 months Youngest daughter of George & Adeline Lovell Stone says, "Early lost early saved" e L 12 1901 Feb 28 age 50 S:12

Lovell, Julius A - Died 1848 Born 1847 (with Freeman & Betsey Lovell) S:14

Lovell, Julius Freeman - Died 1845 Aug 19 Age 11 months Son of Freeman & Abby Lovell (next to them) S:12

Lovell, Kathryn E - Died 1952 Born 1917 (with Bradford Lovell) S:12

Lovell, Kenneth P - Died 1964 Born 1905 (next to small stone that says, "Flora Lovell age 3") S:12

Lovell, Lazarus - Died 1777 Jan 27 Age 77 S:12

Lovell, Lazarus (Capt) - Died 1808 Mar 1 Age 38 years, 11 days Died at Rio Pongo, Africa S:4

Lovell, Leander Wakefield - Died 1852 Aug 19 Age 4 months Son of Freeman & Abby Lovell (next to them) S:12

Lovell, Lester Prince - Died 1939

Lovell (Cont.) April 8 Born 1879 Aug 29 (with Minnie E Bell) S:12

Lovell, Little Pilot (a dog) - Died 1917 July 2 Born 1904 July 15 "For 12 years a loved companion & friend Gentle, faithful and brave" (in Lovell plot with 3 other dogs and Orville Dewey Lovell) S:12

Lovell, Louise Higgins - Died 1942 Born 1873 (in Lovell plot with Robert W Lovell) S:12

Lovell, Lucinda - Died 1896 Born 1805 (with James N Lovell) S:12

Lovell, Lucinda M - Died 1847 Born 1836 (with James & Lucinda Lovell & others) S:12

Lovell, Lucindia - Died 1850 Born 1825 (with Russell Lovell) S:12

Lovell, Luther - Died (no dates) (next to Mary Lovell d1869) (a stillborn) S:14

Lovell, Lydia - Died 1806 Nov 20 Daughter of Capt Andrew Lovell S:7

Lovell, Lydia - Died 1863 Aug 24 Age 74 years,8 months Wife of Henry Lovell (next to him) S:13

Lovell, Lydia - Died 1866 Born 1791 (with Zenas Lovell & others) S:12

Lovell, Lydia G - Died 1872 Mar 24 Born 1789 Aug 14 (next to Jesse C Lovell) S:12

Lovell, Lydia I Mrs - Died 1845 Mar 16 Age 47 Widow of Capt Joshua Lovell S:12

Lovell, Lydia W - Died 1903 Mar 4 Born 1815 April 5 S:12

Lovell, Mabel Bigney - Died 1988 Born 1890 Wife of Stanley P Lovell (next to him) S:12

Lovell, Martha - Died 1808 Oct 3 Age 74 Wife of James Lovell (next to him) S:12

Lovell, Martha Isabel - Died 1902 April 15 Born 1829 Feb 5 (next to Ellis B Lovell) S:12

Lovell, Mary - Died 1814 June 30 Age 54 Wife of Christopher Lovell S:12

Lovell, Mary - Died 1832 Feb 5 Age 92 Born 1740 Nov 5 Widow of Shubael Lovell S:4

Lovell, Mary - Died 1869 Nov 17 Age 86 (between Luther & David Lovell) S:14

Lovell, Mary A - Died 1921 Born 1835 (next to Abby & Cyrenius Lovell) S:13

Lovell, Mary A - Died 1943 Born 1862 Wife of Frank Phinney (buried with him & others) S:8

Lovell, Mary A - Buried 1919 Located in section S, lot 14, grave 6 S:14R

Lovell, Mary Ann - Died 1825 Apl 13 Age 24 years, 2 months Daughter of Lazarus & Sylvia Lovell S:4

Lovell, Mary Mrs - Died 1828 Oct 10 Age 57 Wife of Capt George Lovell (next to his stone and with infant Lovell) S:12

Lovell, Mary S - Died 1910 Born 1825 (with Zenas & Lydia Lovell & others) S:12

Lovell, Mary T - Died 1908 Mar 2 Born 1867 June 3 (on large family stone at street level with Mercy Lovell) S:12

Lovell, Medora M - Died 1924 Born 1837 Wife of Horace S Lovell (next to him) S:12

Lovell, Mercy (Marcy) - Died 1817 Sept 18 Age 90 Widow of Simeon Lovell S:12

Lovell, Mercy A - Died 1896 Feb 28 Age 66 years, 6 months, 23 days (next to Henry A Lovell) S:14

Lovell, Mercy A - Died 1917 Jan 6 Born 1843 Aug 3 (on large family stone at street level with Isaac Lovell) S:12

Lovell, Mercy C - Died 1911 Nov 27 Born 1820 Oct 16 Stone says, "At Rest" (buried with Jacob Lovell) S:8

Lovell, Mercy E - Died 1850 June 9 Age 37 (next to Cornellia M & Charles Warren Lovell) S:12

Lovell, Mercy N - Died 1916 Born 1837 (with Edward M Lovell)

Lovell (Cont.)
S:13

Lovell, Michall - Died 1882 Jan 27 Born 1797 May 31 at Rockingham, Vermont (next to Edgar W Lovell) S:14

Lovell, Millie - Died (no information) (a childs stone next to another Millie Lovell & Cyrenius A Lovell & Abby P Lovell) S:13

Lovell, Miriam - Died 1860 Born 1859 (with Russell Lovell & others) S:12

Lovell, Nancy J - Died 1865 ? 11th Age 12 years?, 6 months (in Lovell plot with Robert W Lovell) S:12

Lovell, Nathan P - Died 1895 Born 1844 (with Charlotte Lovell) S:18

Lovell, Nehemiah (Capt) - Died 1820 Jan 27 Age 56 S:4

Lovell, Nellie W - Died 1938 Born 1867 (with Ellis B Lovell) S:12

Lovell, Nelson A - Died 1843 Jan 10 Age 24 S:12

Lovell, Nelson O - Died 1908 Born 1850 (with Zenas & Lydia Lovell & others) S:12

Lovell, Olive C - Died 1878 July 9 Born 1800 Sept 6 S:4

Lovell, Olive Miss - Died 1796 Aug 22 Age 21 S:12

Lovell, Oliver - Died 1867 July 3 Age 4 years 8 months Son of Edward & Mercy Lovell (next to them) S:13

Lovell, Oliver S - Died 1850 June 17 Age 19 Who's death was occationed by the launching of the schooner, Elizabeth at Co?Csackie, New York on 17 June 1850 (next to Nelson A Lovell) S:12

Lovell, Ollive - Died 1812 Mar 27 Age 69 Wife of Daniel Lovell S:12

Lovell, Orville Dewey - Died 1923 Dec 17 Born 1839 May 26 "A dog lover" Son of George Lovell & Adeline Hallett (in Lovell plot with dogs, Daniel,Pilot,Little Pilot & Daniel) S:12

Lovell, Phebe - Died 1825 Aug 1

Lovell (Cont.)
Wife of Jacob Lovell (next to him)
S:12

Lovell, Pilot (My Dog) - Died 1904
July 10 Born 1897 Feb 27 Age 7
"A brave trusty protector, a faithful friend and genial companion"
(in Lovell plot with 3 other dogs
and Orville Dewey Lovell) S:12

Lovell, Ploomie C - Died 1922 Born
1841 (listed on Crosby stone
with Isaac Crowell & others) S:8

Lovell, Prudence F - Died 1883
July 29 Age 28 Wife of Warren
Lovell (1st wife) S:12

Lovell, Puella Mrs - Died 1823 Mar
18 Age 66 Wife of Joshua Lovell
S:12

Lovell, Rhoda - Died 1825 Feb 11
in her 60th yr Wife & Consort of
Capt Nehemiah Lovell S:4

Lovell, Rhoda Shaw Miss - Died
1856 Aug 10 Age 4 years, 2
months, 6 days (much written
on stone about "Little darling"
departing) S:12+12R

Lovell, Robert Dr - Died 1874 Aug
24 Age 83 (in Lovell plot with
Robert W Lovell) S:12

Lovell, Robert H - Died 1882 Oct
15 Born 1831 Oct 5 (next to
wife, Hannah H Lovell) S:12

Lovell, Robert Winsor - Died 1934
Born 1910 (in Lovell plot with
Harrison Crocker Lovell) S:12

Lovell, Russell - Died 1863 Born
1821 (with Lucindia Lovell) S:12

Lovell, Sally - Died 1836 Jan 11 in
her 79th yr (she was listed as
Miss) S:4

Lovell, Sally Payne - Died 1745
located in row 4 (not sure if
same as Sally d 1795?) S:11R

Lovell, Sally Payne Miss - Died
1795 Sept 25 in her 17th yr
S:11+26R

Lovell, Samuel S, Master - Died
1799 Aug 1799 Age 10 (with his
mother, Abigail Lovell) Son of
Christopher & Abigail Lovell
S:12

Lovell, Sarah - Died 1858 May or

Lovell (Cont.)
March 3 (face worn off stone On
street level) S:12

Lovell, Sarah E - Died 1848 Born
1843 (with Freeman & Betsey
Lovell) S:14

Lovell, Sarah H - Died 1907 Oct 8
Born 1821 Sept 20 (this is a grey
metal stone, next to her is
another stone just like it with
middle section missing, possible
husband?) S:12

Lovell, Shubael - Died 1805 Mar
31 Age 64 years, 5 months, 17
days S:4

Lovell, Simeon - Died 1810 Jan 22
Age 14 years, 10 months, 7 days
Son of Simeon & Marcy Lovell
S:12

Lovell, Simeon - Died 1832 July 7
Age 73 (next to wife, Mercy
(Marcy) Lovell) S:12

Lovell, Stanley Platt - Died 1976
Born 1890 Son of Gustavus
Lovell (with wife, Mabel Bigney
Lovell) S:12

Lovell, Susan A - Died 1883 Born
1869 (with Eunice & John B
Lovell) S:14

Lovell, Temperance - Died 1824
March 9 Age 71 Wife of Andrew
Lovell (next to him) S:14

Lovell, Temperance - Died 1862
July 15 Age 83 years, 9 months,
26 days Widow of Capt Abner W
Lovell S:4

Lovell, Velina - Died 1862 Mar 3
Age 28 years, 2 months, 27 days
Wife of James H Parker (next to
him) S:12

Lovell, Warren - Died 1923 Born
1850 (stone errected by his wife,
Prudence F Lovell) (next to him)
S:12

Lovell, William - Died 1753 April
21 in his 91st yr S:12

Lovell, William - Died 1906 Oct 17
Born 1838 Oct 18 (with Alethena
Lovell & Arnold Bowen) S:21

Lovell, William - Died 1939 Born
1873 (with Elida W Lovell) S:18

Lovell, Willis - Died 1849 Born

Lovell (Cont.)
1848 (with Russell Lovell & others) S:12

Lovell, Zenas - Died 1823 Born 1787 (with Lydia Lovell & others) S:12

Lovell, Zenas - Died 1852 Aug 25 Age 27 years, 4 months, 24 days (with Horace Lovell) S:14

Lovell, Zenas H - Died 1828 Jan 9 Age 9 months, 9 days Son of Ezra c & Chloe C Lovell S:7

Lovell, Zilpah - Died 1869 Dec 7 Age 80 years, 10 months S:12

Lowell, Edward Jackson - Died 1894 May 11 Born 1845 Oct 18 (next to wife, Elizabeth Gilbert Lowell) S:14

Lowell, Elizabeth Gilbert - Died 1904 Sept 25 Wife of Edward J Lowell (next to him) S:14

Lowis, George W - Died 1934 Born 1846 (buried with Edvie A Lewis) S:8

Lowry, Elcy Margaret - Died 1949 Born 1881 (buried with John Lowry & Mary B Mead - parents?) (other family members buried here with much later dates, they were not listed because of that) S:8

Lowry, John - Died 1920 Born 1854 (Large plot/crypt & large stone) (buried with wife, Mary B Mead & other family members) S:8

Lowry, Priscilla - Died 1982 Born 1889 (buried with John Lowry & Mary B Mead - parents?) S:8

Lowry, Robert - Died 1913 Born 1884 (buried with John Lowry & Mary Mead - parents?) S:8

Lucas, Elba D - Died 1942 Born 1859 (with Lillian M Alvin) S:18

Lucas, Moses A - Died 1978 Born 1894 (with David & Goldie Greene) S:18

Luce, Charles - Died 1890 Aug 2 Age 74 years, 10 months (with Cynthia Luce) S:18

Luce, Cynthia - Died 1902 Dec 3 Age 80 years, 10 months (with

Luce (Cont.)
Charles Luce) S:18

Luce, Hervey E - Died (no dates) (with wife, Nettie Luce & others) S:18

Luce, Mayhew A - Died 1914 Jan 11 Born 1834 Aug 23 (with Susan M Luce & others) S:18

Luce, Nettie M - Died (no dates) Wife of Hervey E Luce (listed with him & Ellwood Gray & others) S:18

Luce, Susan M - Died 1928 Aug 3 Born 1839 Nov 13 (with Horace Cobb & others) S:18

Luguer, Grace Parker - Died 1984 Born 1900 (next to Lea Shippen Luguer) S:14

Luguer, Lea Shippen - Died 1981 Born 1898 (next to Grace Parker Luguer) S:14

Luiz, Mary - Died (no date listed) Born 1875 Wife of Manuel Cabral (with him) S:14

Lumard, Parker - Died 1754 Dec 27 in his 35th yr (Parker could be his last name?) S:5

Lumbard, ? - Died (stone knocked over on ground & worn badly) S:11

Lumbard, Benjamin - Died 1753 Jan 13 in his 78th yr S:11R

Lumbard, Eliza - Died 1816 Jan Age 2 years, 1 month Daughter of Solomon & Catharine Lumbard S:1

Lumbard, Hannah - Died 1714 Sept 19 Age 34 Wife of Ben Lumbard (small stone pulled out of ground & worn off) (next to Benjamin Lombard, next to tree & ? Lumbard, stone knocked over) S:11+11R

Lumbard, Jemima - Died 1796 Dec 18 in her 47th yr Wife of Hezekiah Lumbard S:1

Lumbard, Joseph - Died 1783 Oct 14 in his 32nd yr S:3

Lumbard, Lemuel - Died 1821 May 31 in his 78th yr S:1

Lumbard, Mary - Died 1782 Sept 20 in her 52nd yr Widow of Capt

Lumbard (Cont.)

Benjamin Lumbard S:3

Lumbard, Parker - Died 1754 Dec 27 Age 35 S:5R

Lumbard, Sarah Mrs - Died 1768 Mar in her 77th yr Widow of Benjamin Lumbard (tree in front of him) (Hinckley Ceme records #11R say death was on Nov 12) S:11+26R

Lumbart, Abigail - Died 1846 April 12 Age 68 years, 6 months, 8 days S:13

Lumbart, Benjamin (Capt) - Died 1777 May 15 in his 49th yr S:3

Lumbart, Emma L - Died 1932 Born 1855 (listed on same stone with Edgar F & Isabell F Swift) S:13

Lumbart, Hannah - Died 1796 May 9 Age 61 Wife of Joshua Lumbart (next to him) S:12

Lumbart, Hannah - Died 1847 May 6 Age 45 Daughter of Simeon & Mary Lumbart (next to them) S:12

Lumbart, Joshua - Died 1807 Dec 20 Age 86 S:12

Lumbart, Joshua - Died 1881 Jan 23 Age 82 years, 8 months S:12

Lumbart, Mary - Died 1857 Oct 28 Age 83 Widow of Simeon Lumbart (next to him) S:12

Lumbart, Samuel - Died 1771 Dec Age 82 S:12

Lumbart, Sarah - Died 1881 July 5 Age 70 years, 5 months S:12

Lumbart, Simeon - Died 1850 Oct 21 Age 83 S:12

Lumbart, Thomas - Died 1863 Jan 13 Age 60 S:12

Lumbart, Timothy - Died 1808 June 1 Age 70 S:12+12R

Lumber, Betsey - Died 1885 or 88 July 31 Age 61 years, 5 months, 8 days Wife of George H Lumber(?) (stone is worn, next to John B Lovell, d1877) S:14

Lumber, Owen - Died 1805 Jan 3 Age 6 years, 6 months Son of Prince & Rebekah Lumber S:3

Lumberd, Alvah - Died 1825 Oct 29

Lumberd (Cont.)

in his 20th yr Son of Hezekiah & Anna Lumberd Anna is buried with him S:1

Lumberd, Anna - Died 1825 Sept 29 in her 58th yr Widow of Hezekiah Lumberd Buried with Alvah Lumberd S:1

Lumberd, Hezekiah (Capt) - Died 1822 Oct 19 in his 79th yr S:1

Lumbert, (infant) - Died (not marked) Baby of Benjamin & Lizzie Lumbert (buried next to them) S:8

Lumbert, Abbie - Died 1892 Born 1813 S:5

Lumbert, Adelaide W - Died 1927 Born 1846 (buried with Harrison Lumbert) S:8

Lumbert, Archer Lincoln - Died 1967 Born 1886 (with wife, Catherine Lawler) S:18

Lumbert, Benjamin F - Died 1937 Born 1850 (buried with Lizzie E Lumbert) S:8

Lumbert, Betsey B - Died 1863 Feb 23 Age 61 years, 13 days Wife of James Lumbert S:2

Lumbert, Cora W - Died 1938 Oct 28 Born 1875 Sept 3 Daughter of Henry C Lumbert & Sophia Howes (next to them) S:18

Lumbert, Daniel - Died 1900 Oct 6 Born 1832 Feb 27 (stone is knocked down) (buried between Marin Coleman & Willie Lumbert) S:8

Lumbert, Deborah F - Died 1938 Born 1847 (with Oliver C Lumbert) S:14

Lumbert, Eleanor C - Died 1961 Born 1868 Wife of Edson Fisher (with him) S:14

Lumbert, Eliza R - Died 1879 Born 1811 (with Josiah Lumbert) S:14

Lumbert, Etta F - Died 1868 Mar 14 Age 23 years, 8 months Wife of Daniel Lumbert (who is two stones away from her) Stone says, "Passed to higher life from Sandwich (Mass) (a small stone is between them which says,

Lumbert (Cont.)
"Child") S:8

Lumbert, Harrison - Died 1906 Born 1835 (buried with Adelaide W Lumbert) S:8

Lumbert, Harry F - Died 1934 Born 1866 S:8

Lumbert, Hattie Baker - Died 1916 Born 1867 Wife of Henry L Lumbert (with him) S:18

Lumbert, Henry C - Died 1925 Jan 14 Born 1836 Oct 3 (next to wife, Sophia Howes) S:18

Lumbert, Henry Lincoln - Died 1934 Born 1865 (with Hattie Baker Lumbert & next to Waldo Baker Lumbert) (Hattie is his wife) S:18

Lumbert, James - Died 1876 Apr 30 Age 73 years, 11 months S:2

Lumbert, James H - Died 1860 July 1 in his 27th yr S:2

Lumbert, Jennie R - Died (no dates) (buried with husband, William S Lumbert & Rosa & Orren Kelley family) S:8

Lumbert, John G (Capt) - Died 1889 July 27 Age 62 yesrs, 10 months, 27 days (with Prudence B Lumbert) S:18

Lumbert, Joseph - Died 1857 Apl 20 in his 75th yr S:4

Lumbert, Josiah - Died 1898 Born 1807 (with Eliza R Lumbert) S:14

Lumbert, Leonard L - Died 1881 Apr 12 Age 81 ? (stone not clear) Stone says, "Passed Away" (buried next to Mary L Lumbert) S:8

Lumbert, Lizzie E - Died 1919 Born 1855 (buried with Benjamin F Lumbert) S:8

Lumbert, Lula Sherman - Died 1929 Feb 9 Born 1885 Sept 25 (next to Emma & Charles Sherman) S:18

Lumbert, Mary L - Died 1888 Mar 9 Age 73 years, 3 months Stone says, "Passed Away" S:8

Lumbert, Mercy H - Died 1836 Aug 15 Age 7 years, 2 months

Lumbert (Cont.)
Daughter of Joseph & Polly Lumbert S:4

Lumbert, Mery R - Died 1895 Born 1894 (buried with parents, Jennie & William Lumbert & Kelley family) S:8

Lumbert, Nellie F - Died 1951 Born 1863 Wife of Harry Lumbert (buried next to him) S:8

Lumbert, Oliver C (or G) - Died 1913 Born 1847 (with Deborah F Lumbert) S:14

Lumbert, Phebe - Died 1798 Feb 9 in her 17th yr Daughter of Joseph & Sarah (stone not clear, but Lumbert's are buried nearby) S:3+3R

Lumbert, Polly - Died 1847 Mar 6 in her 50th yr Wife of Joseph Lumbert S:4

Lumbert, Prudence B - Died 1906 Jan 12 Born 1830 Oct 16 (with Capt John G Lumbert) S:18

Lumbert, Waldo Baker - Died 1950 July 13 Born 1899 April 16 (2 stones) From Massachusetts, was Sea, USNRF during World War I (next to Henry Lincoln Lumbert) S:18

Lumbert, William S - Died 1864 Jan 1 Born 1842 Mar 9 Member of Company E, 10th Regiment, Massachusetts Vol Militia Passed to the spirit land at Beaufort, South Carolina (buried next to Zimri Lumbert) S:8

Lumbert, William S - Died 1949 Born 1865 (buried with Rosa & Orren Kelley & family) S:8

Lumbert, Willie - Died (not clear) (buried next to wife, Etta F Lumbert & Daniel Lumbert) (a small stone is located between them that says "Child") S:8

Lumbert, Zimri - Died 1878 Sept 7 Age 78 years, 10 months Stone says, "Passed Away" (buried next to Mary L Lumbert) S:8

Lummus, Annie Louise Hutchison - Died 1965 Born 1888 (with Julian Louis Lummus) S:11

Lummus, Julian Louis - Died 1960 Born 1887 (next to Annie Louise Hutchison Lummus) S:11

Luoto, Ida Salmi - Died 1928 Born 1892 Wife of Lauri William Luoto (on same stone) S:11

Luoto, Lauri William - Died 1930 Born 1896 (on same stone with Ida Salmi Luoto) S:11

Lus, Dora A - Died 1968 Born 1887 (with Manuel J Lus) S:17

Lus, Manuel J - Died 1964 Born 1874 (with Dora A Lus) S:17

Lusk, George H - Died 1978 Born 1894 Was a Lt Col in US Army during World War II (next to Laura J Lusk) S:15

Lusk, Laura J - Died 1981 Born 1899 (next to George H lusk) S:15

Lynch, Carol - Died 1969 March 2 (baby) (next to Fred & Alice Nickerson) S:19

Lynch, John - Died 1906 Born 1852 (next to John Duffy) S:31

Lynch, Mary C - Died 1957 Born 1903 S:31

Lynde, Anna J - Died 1944 Born 1878 Wife of Everett Small (with him) S:12

Lyon, Neila VanBrunt - Died 1973 Mar 26 Born 1892 Aug 22 Stone says, "The Rose Lady" (with Roger Luther Lyon) S:11

Lyon, Roger Luther - Died 1964 Nov 25 Born 1889 Aug 20 Was in Mass, ensign USNRF in World War 1 (flag at stone) (with Neila VanBrunt Lyon) S:11

Maccaron, Anthony - Died 1971 Born 1887 (listed with Louise A Maccaron) S:15

Maccaron, Louise A - Died (still living in 1991?) Born 1901 (listed with Anthony Maccaron) S:15

MacCoy, Andrew Turnbull - Died 1941 Born 1866 (buried with Georgia Mary Clark) S:8

MacDonald, C Esther - Died 1976 Born 1900 (with Neil F MacDonald) S:16

MacDonald, Florence A - Died 1954 Born 1874 (with Eleanor I Jones & others) S:18

MacDonald, George W - Died 1976 Born 1910 (with Hester K MacDonald) S:20

MacDonald, Hester K - Died (still living 1991?) Born 1909 (listed with George MacDonald) S:20

MacDonald, Merle - Died (still living 1991?) Born 1898 (listed with Zenas Crocker Jr) S:14

MacDonald, Neil F - Died 1959 Born 1897 (with C Esther MacDonald) S:16

MacEacheron, Charles P - Died 1961 Born 1886 (with Mabel S Mac Eacheron) S:16

MacEacheron, Mabel S - Died 1956 Born 1886 (with Charles P Mac Eacheron) S:16

MacElhinney, Lillian M - Died 1952 Born 1869 S:18

MacEwen, Daphne L - Died 1970 Born 1895 (next to Robert M Mac Ewen) S:15

MacEwen, Robert M - Died 1989 Born 1896 He was a Mason (next to Daphne L MacEwen) S:15

MacFarlane, Alexander B - Died 1972 Born 1882 (with John D MacFarlane) S:16

MacFarlane, John D - Died 1955 Born 1879 (with Alexander B MacFarlane) S:16

MacGregor, Alfred R - Died 1967 Aug 18 Born 1879 June 25 (with wife, Anna J MacGregor) S:18

MacGregor, Anna J - Died 1952 Nov 7 Born 1882 Dec 9 Wife of Alfred MacGregor (with him) S:18

MacIsaac, Alexander - Died 1958 Born 1889 (with Genevieve M MacIsaac) S:16

MacIsaac, Genevieve M - Died 1982 Born 1902 (with Alexander MacIsaac) S:16

MacIsaac, James Angus - Died 1946 Born 1878 (with wife, Nora Manning) S:16

Mackie, Eleanor H - Died 1975

Mackie (Cont.)
Born 1907 S:18

MacLellan, Helen W - Died 1981 Dec 4 Born 1895 Feb 2 S:15

MacLeod, Marian - Died 1934 Born 1861 Wife of Lot Crocker (with him & others) S:18

MacMullen, Annie Laurie (Holt) - Died 1985 Jan 4 Born 1897 June 17 (next to Ross A MacMullen) S:13

MacMullen, Ross A - Died 1963 Dec 19 Born 1893 Feb 10 From New York and was a 2nd Lieutenant in 84th Field Artillery during World War 1 (next to Annie Laurie (Holt) MacMullen) S:13

MacNeely, Frances Dixon - Died 1983 May 23 Born 1904 March 30 (there is a stone missing next to him) S:19

MacNeill, John A - Died 1967 Born 1895 (with Neva E MacNeill) S:15

MacNeill, Neva E - Died (still living 1991?) Born 1910 (listed with John A MacNeill) S:15

MacQuade, John - Died 1951 Born 1878 (with Margaret M Mac-Quade) S:16

MacQuade, Margaret M - Died 1971 Born 1881 (with John MacQuade) S:16

Macrae, Angus H - Died 1978 Born 1892 (undertaker plaques only) (next to Ethel Macrae) S:18

Macrae, Ethel E - Died 1975 Born 1897 (undertaker plaque only) (next to Angus H Macrae) S:18

MacSwan, F B Jr ("Kirk") - Died 1956 Born 1943 (large MacSwan rock marker at foot of plot) S:11

MacSwan, Jessica D ("Jack") - Died 1985 Born 1916 (large MacSwan rock marker at foot of plot) S:11

MacSwan, John Angus - Died 1989 Born 1960 (large MacSwan rock marker at foot of plot) S:11

Macy, Eunice - Died 1879 May 19 Age 43 years, 2 months, 8 days Wife of Edwin C Macy S:5

Macy, Helen F - Died 1973 Born 1886 Wife of Myron P Howland (with him) S:13

Macy, Helen H - Died 1929 Born 1866 (with husband, Pegleg S Macy) S:13

Macy, Howard R - Died 1944 Born 1899 Son of Pegley S & Helen H Macy (next to them) S:13

Macy, James W - Died 1890 Born 1846 (with Susan Eldridge) S:18

Macy, Pegleg or Peleg S - Died 1941 Born 1859 (with wife, Helen H Macy) S:13

Macy, Robert F - Died 1900 Born 1828 S:5

Maderios, Manuel B - Died 1965 July 19 Born 1896 Oct 21 From Massachusetts, was Private in 2nd Battery FA REPL Regiment during World War I S:14

Magnenat (Magenat), Cecile M - Died 1990 Born 1897 (with Rene P Magenat (Magnenat?) S:20

Magnenat (Magenat), Rene P - Died (still living 1991?) Born 1898 (with Cecile M Magnenat) S:20

Magnuson, Alma Christina - Died 1978 Born 1884 (with Joseph Emanuel Magnuson) S:13

Magnuson, Joseph Emanuel - Died 1943 Born 1881 (with Alma Christina Magnuson) S:13

MaGuire, William Athony - Died 1965 Born 1896 S:15

Mahan, Annabel G - Died 1976 Born 1900 (with William F Mahan) S:16

Mahan, William F - Died 1990 Born 1893 (with Annabel G Mahan) S:16

Maher, Annie F - Died (no dates) Wife of Michael W Maher (with him & Thomas P Maher & others) S:31

Maher, Bridget L - Died 1915 Born 1861 Wife of John D Maher (with him & Mary A Maher & others) S:31

Maher, Edward F - Died (no dates) (listed with Mary Maher & others) S:31

300

Maher, Edward W - Died 1972 Born 1894 (next to wife, Florence Chrisholm Maher) S:16

Maher, Florence Chrisholm - Died (no dates listed) Wife of Edward Maher (next to him) S:16

Maher, Frances V - Died (still living 1991?) Born 1895 Daughter of James L Maher (with him & John D Maher & others) S:31

Maher, James L - Died 1990 Born 1893 Was a 2nd Lt in US Army during World War I (with Frances V Maher & others) S:31

Maher, John D - Died 1952 Born 1864 (with wife, Bridget L Maher & another wife, Mary A Maher & others) S:31

Maher, Joseph H - Died (no dates) (listed with William A Maher & others) S:31

Maher, Margaret E - Died (no dates) (listed with Warren A Tripp & others) S:31

Maher, Mary - Died (no dates) (listed with Joseph H Maher & others) S:31

Maher, Mary A - Died 1950 Born 1863 Wife of John D Maher (with him & James Maher & others) S:31

Maher, Michael W - Died (no dates) (listed with wife, Annie F Maher & others) S:31

Maher, Thomas P - Died (no dates) (listed with Edward F Maher & others) S:31

Maher, William - Died (no dates) (with wife, Mary Donahue & others) S:31

Maher, William A - Died (no dates) (listed with Margaret E Maher & others) S:31

Mahoney, James F - Died 1982 Born 1909 S:11

Mahoney, Mollie A - Died 1974 May 2 Born 1880 Oct 21 (with Patrick J Mahoney) S:16

Mahoney, Patrick J - Died 1954 June 15 Born 1880 April 19 (with Mollie A Mahaney) S:16

Maiellano, Francis S - Died 1969

Maiellano (Cont.) Sept 9 Born 1898 Mar 28 From Massachusetts, was Pvt Quarter Master Corps during World War I S:15

Major, James L Sr - Died 1987 Born 1898 Was a Pvt in US Army during World War I S:18

Makepeace, Edward L - Died 1884 Sept 13 Born 1864 Feb 26 S:5R

Makepeace, George O - Died 1899 May 1 Born 1859 Aug 19 S:18

Makepeace, Nellie V - Died 1948 Born 1862 Wife of Orin Nickerson (with him) S:14

Makepeace, Sarah E F - Died 1860 Dec 2 Born 1857 May 9 S:5R

Maki, Frank - Died 1970 Born 1893 (only undertaker plaque) S:20

Maki, Ida - Died 1981 Born 1896 S:20

Maki, Marie M - Died 1986 Born 1901 Stone says,"Forget-me-not" (next to Otto Maki) S:15

Maki, Otto - Died 1986 Born 1895 Was a Pvt in US Army during World War I (next to Marie M Maki) S:15

Malchman, Samuel - Died 1982 Born 1895 (Jewish section) Was a PFC in US Army during World War I S:15

Malcolm, Florence S - Died 1972 Born 1895 (with Frank E Malcolm) S:15

Malcolm, Frank E - Died 1977 Born 1893 (with Florence S Malcolm) S:15

Malone, William E - Died 1969 Born 1896 S:16

Maloney, Emma H - Died 1930 Born 1871 (with John J Maloney) S:14

Maloney, Jennie L - Died 1930 Born 1865 (with John J Maloney) S:14

Maloney, John J - Died 1930 Born 1871 (with Emma H Maloney) S:14

Mandell, Mary Hussey - Died 1986 Born 1905 (there is a US plaque,

301

Mandell (Cont.)
she is in the Hussey plot) S:11

Mann, Gladys S - Died 1983 Born 1892 (with Harold C Mann) S:18

Mann, Harold C - Died 1972 Born 1892 (with Gladys S Mann) S:18

Manni, Eleanor Waller - Died 1971 Born 1921 (with Lauri Manni & next to John Waller) S:20

Manni, Elwood E - Died 1979 March 28 Born 1927 Nov 18 (also has a West Barnstable Fire Dept plaque & flag) (next to Michele M Manni) S:20

Manni, Helvi O - Died 1958 Born 1919 (has 2 stones) (with Uno John Manni) S:20

Manni, Jeffery H - Died 1986 Born 1961 (also has a West Barnstable Fire Dept plaque & flag) (next to Uno John Manni) S:20

Manni, Lauri Victor - Died 1987 Born 1916 (with Eleanor Waller Manni) S:20

Manni, Michele M - Died 1955 Born 1954 (next to Elwood E Manni) S:20

Manni, Uno John - Died 1987 April 14 Born 1921 Dec 27 Stone says, "Mommi" Was in US Coast Guard during World War II (has 2 stones) (with Helvi O Manni) S:20

Manning, Bertha A - Died 1984 Born 1892 (undertaker plaque) S:18

Manning, George C - Died 1964 Sept 19 Born 1892 July 28 Was from Massachusetts, LRDR US Navy during World Wars, I & II S:15

Manning, Nora - Died 1955 Born 1879 Wife of James Angus MacIsaac (with him) S:16

Manssuer, Nora - Died 1985 March 14 Born 1892 Sept 29 S:20

Manter, Emma F - Died 1944 Born 1873 Wife of William H Jones(with him) S:14

Manthey, Ruth K - Died 1969 Jan 22 Born 1898 April 17 Stone says,"Nee Eriksson" S:15

Mara, S Mulcahy - Died 1983 Born 1892 S:15

Maraspin, Davis Goodwin - Died 1959 Born 1899 (with Dorothy Blanche Howe) S:11

Maraspin, Fannie A - Died 1928 Born 1853 (buried next to Sarah E Maraspin) S:10

Maraspin, Francis Lothrop - Died 1967 Born 1866 (with Maud Isabel Goodwin) S:11

Maraspin, Harriet C - Died 1876 April 25 Age 26 S:10

Maraspin, Paul - Died 1888 Born 1814 S:10

Maraspin, Sarah E - Died 1935 Born 1857 S:10

Marchant, Abbie A - Died 1920 Born 1851 (with Albert J Marchant & others) S:21

Marchant, Abby S - Died 1881 Aug 10 in her 46th yr Daughter of Freeman & Abigail Marchant S:4

Marchant, Abigail - Died 1876 May 11 in her 81st yr Widow of Freeman Marchant S:4

Marchant, Adeline - Died 1882 Nov 6 in her 65th yr S:4

Marchant, Agnes - Died 1849 Jan 16 in her 17th yr Daughter of Freeman & Abigail Marchant S:4

Marchant, Albert H - Died 1940 Born 1892 (World War I plaque) (next to Alexander & Angenora Marchant) S:21

Marchant, Albert J - Died 1870 Born 1872 (with George B Marchant & others) S:21

Marchant, Alexander - Died 1932 Born 1844 (with Angenora Marchant, wife) S:21

Marchant, Alice Arnold - Died 1975 Born 1892 (she was French) S:15

Marchant, Allen - Died 1866 March 9 Age 26 Was in 5th & 58th Regiment of Massachusetts Volunteers S:21

Marchant, Angenora - Died 1924 Born 1848 Wife of Alexander Marchant (with him & next to Albert H Marchant) S:21

Marchant, Anna - Died 1858 Dec 30 Age 75 years, 10 months S:4

Marchant, Celia F - Died 1846 Feb 15 Age 20 years, 1 months, 7 days Daughter of Crocker & Amelia Marchant S:4

Marchant, Charles B - Died 1938 Oct 15 Born 1858 Sept 19 (next to Orlando Wood Marchant) S:18

Marchant, Chester Everett - Died 1970 Born 1884 (next to Etta Carrie Marchant) S:17

Marchant, Clara Edith Marven - Died 1947 Born 1868 (stone down from vandals) Wife of Orlando Wood Marchant (with him Nelson Bursley & Edna Marven Bursley Marchant) S:18

Marchant, Content L - Died 1876 Born 1787 Wife of James Marchant S:4

Marchant, Crocker - Died 1844 Mar 10 Age 59 years, 1 month, 5 days S:4

Marchant, David S - Died 1895 or 7 Feb 15 Born 1825 Dec 25 (stone down from vandals) (with wife, Harriet S & Herbert B Marchant & others) S:18

Marchant, Eddie - Died 1860 Sept 14 Age 12 months Mentioned on mother's stone Son of David S & Elizabeth N Marchant (not sure if he is buried with her) S:4

Marchant, Edna Marven - Died 1976 Born 1901 (with Elizabeth C Marchant & others) S:18

Marchant, Edward C Delevan - Died 1839 June 27 Age 17 years, 1 month Son of Freeman & Abigail Marchant S:4

Marchant, Elizabeth C - Died 1894 Jan 18 Born 1866 Sept 8 (stone down from vandals) (stone next to her down from vandals, cannot read) (with Clara Edith Marven Marchant & others) S:18

Marchant, Elizabeth N - Died 1872 June 10 Wife of David S Marchant She died in Malden, Mass, Dau of the late Ezia Dillingham of Sandwich, Mass Mentioned

Marchant (Cont.)
also is Eddie, their son d: 1860 Sept 14 Age 12 months S:4

Marchant, Ellen D - Died 1870 Aug 2 in her 44th yr Daughter of Freeman & Abigail Marchant S:4

Marchant, Emily F - Died 1851 Nov 8 in her 22nd yr Wife of Marcus F Marchant S:4

Marchant, Emma S - Died 1914 Mar 1 Born 1854 Mar 1 S:8

Marchant, Etta Carrie - Died 1967 Born 1887 (next to Chester Everett Marchant) S:17

Marchant, Everett L - Died 1937 April 28 Born 1865 May 2 (stone down from vandals) (with Harriet S Marchant & others) S:18

Marchant, Ezra D - Died 1935 Dec 2 Born 1862 Jan 5 (with Emma A Reichert?) S:18

Marchant, Francis Freeman - Died 1825 July 31, 18 days old Son of Freeman & Abigail Marchant S:4

Marchant, Freeman Esq - Died 1866 Jan 26 in his 73rd yr S:4

Marchant, George B - Died 1879 Born 1877 (with Timothy Robbins & others) S:21

Marchant, Hannah P - Died 1845 Feb 11 in her 26th yr Wife of Henry C Marchant S:4

Marchant, Harriet S - Died 1906 March 4 Born 1837 April 29 (stone down from vandals) Wife of David S Marchant (with him & others) S:18

Marchant, Helen L - Died 1989 Aug 5 Born 1900 April 21 S:16

Marchant, Herbert B - Died 1891 March 29 Born 1860 Feb 7 (stone down from vandals) (with Everett L Marchant & others) S:18

Marchant, Irene - Died 1841 Sept 6 in her 20th yr Daughter of James & Content L Marchant S:4

Marchant, James - Died 1813 Nov 5 in his 70th yr S:1

Marchant, James Deacon - Died 1851 Born 1779 S:4

Marchant, Lemuel - Died 1926 Born 1847 (with Abbie A Marchant & others) S:21

Marchant, Lewin - Died 1898 Apl 25 Born 1815 Nov 19 S:4

Marchant, Nelson Bursley - Died 1961 Born 1898 (stone down from vandals) (with Edna Marven Marchant & others) S:18

Marchant, Orlando W - Died 1958 Jan 20 Born 1908 Aug 19 From Massachusetts, was PFC in 25 Service Group, AAF during World War II (next to Charles B Marchant) S:18

Marchant, Orlando Wood - Died 1941 Born 1862 (he was a Mason) (stone down from vandals) (with Clara Edith Marven Marchant & others) S:18

Marchant, Russell - Died 1845 Apl 8 Son of Henry C & Hannah P Marchant S:4

Marchant, Sylvester R - Died 1918 Born 1871 (with Arthur Dowd) S:18

Marchant, Theodate W - Died 1901 March 14 Age 47 years, 6 months (with Henry G Baxter) S:21

Marchant, Tirzah C - Died 1880 Oct 27 Age 90 years, 2 months S:4

Marchaud, Wilrose J - Died 1964 Aug 28 Born 1893 March 15 From Massachusetts, was Cpl in Co M, 325th Inf, 82 Div during world War II S:17

Marchent, Elisabeth - Died 1793 Sept 10 in her 81st yr S:1

Marchent, Hezekiah - Died 1792 May 9 in her 78th yr S:1

Marchetti, Cleofe - Died 1944 Born 1887 (with Ivo J Marchetti) S:16

Marchetti, Ivo J - Died 1981 Born 1887 (with Cleofe Marchetti) S:16

Marckay, James - Died (cannot read dates, stone worn bad) From Massachusetts, was in Co 65?, 40th Infantry (has Civil War star plaque, 1861-65) (not sure

Marckay (Cont.) of last name) S:19

Marckus, Charles - Died 1940 Born 1861 (buried with wife, Dorothy Marckus) S:8

Marckus, Dorothy - Died 1961 Born 1868 Wife of Charles Marckus (buried with him) S:8

Marks, Wilbert M - Died 1967 June 13 Born 1900 July 30 From Massachusetts, was S2 in US Navy during World War I S:17

Marnell, Mary G - Died 1968 Born 1886 (with William T Marnell) S:16

Marnell, William T - Died 1981 Born 1890 (with Mary G Marnell) S:16

Marney, Fraser A - Died 1956 Born 1896 (with Kenneth L Marney) S:13

Marney, Kenneth L - Died 1973 Born 1937 (also has small undertakers plaque in ground) (with Martha O Marney) S:13

Marney, Martha O - Died 1978 Born 1902 (with Fraser & Kenneth Marney) S:13

Marquette, Emma S - Died 1987 Born 1889 (with Joseph B Marquette) S:16

Marquette, Joseph B - Died 1948 Born 1887 (with Emma S Marquette) S:16

Marr, Charles Franklin - Died 1954 Born 1897 (next to Isabel Lewis Marr) S:31

Marr, Charles Franklin Jr - Died 1922 Born 1921 S:31

Marr, Isabel Lewis - Died 1992 Born 1899 (next to Charles Franklin Marr) S:31

Marrinan, John F - Died 1965 July 22 Born 1897 July 21 From Massachusetts, was CSP in USNR during World War II (also has West Barnstable Fire Dept plaque) S:20

Marshall, Isabel Souza - Died 1965 Sept Born 1893 June Wife of John M Souza & Joseph Marshall (with them both) S:14

Marshall, Joseph - Died 1972 July Born 1888 April Husband of Isabel Souza Marshall (with her) S:14

Marshall, Margaret F (Libby) - Died 1982 Born 1902 (in Marshall plot) S:11

Marston, el (?) - Died 1803 June 5 Age 7 Son of Benjamin & Eunice Marston S:7

Marston, Alice M - Died 1950 Jan 12 Born 1873 May 30 (Marston plot) (buried with Shirley Marston, husband) S:8

Marston, Allen - Died 1853 Nov 14 Age 80 years, 3 months, 11 days S:7

Marston, Allyn - Died 1758 Jan 26 Age 2 years, 3 months Born 1755 Oct 19 Son of Nymphas & Mary Marston S:5R

Marston, Almira C - Died 1905 Born 1840 Wife of Joseph Marston (with him & Jennie Marston & others) S:19

Marston, Arthur B - Died 1888 Jan 4 Age 90 years, 11 months, 2 day S:7

Marston, Benjamin - Died 1769 Mar 26 in his 76th yr (buried next to wife Lydia) S:5

Marston, Benjamin - Died 1797 Feb 8 in his 79th yr S:7

Marston, Benjamin - Died 1819 Mar 19 in his 50th yr S:7

Marston, Benjamin - Died 1877 July 2 in his 62nd yr S:7

Marston, Charles - Died 1834 Feb 11 Age 5 Son of Charles & Nancy C Marston S:7

Marston, Charles (Honorable) - Died 1866 Apr 15 Born 1792 July 21 S:7

Marston, Clement - Died 1841 Feb 22 in his 69th yr S:7

Marston, Cora J - Died 1950 Born 1874 (with Joseph Marston & others) S:19

Marston, Edward - Died 1839 Nov 12 in his 67th yr S:10+26R

Marston, Eliza - Died 1834 Feb 1 Age 11 Daughter of Charles &

Marston (Cont.)
Nancy C Marston S:7

Marston, Elizabeth - Died 1837 Aug 5 in her 72nd yr Wife of Winslow Marston (buried next to him) S:7

Marston, Elizabeth N - Died 1940 Born 1866 (with Cora J Marston & others) S:19

Marston, Elizabeth W - Died 1820 June 15 in her 20th yr Wife of Nymphas Marston S:7

Marston, Ellen - Died 1917 Sept 1 Born 1825 Mar 26 Daughter of Charles & Nancy C Marston S:7

Marston, Eunice - Died 1826 May 3 in her 55th yr Wife of Benjamin Marston (buried next to him) S:7

Marston, Eunice - Died 1834 Mar 19 Age 5 years, 8 months, 2 days Daughter of William & Minerva Marston S:7

Marston, Hannah - Died 1827 Feb 14 Age 28 years, 10 months, 26 days S:7

Marston, Hannah - Died 1860 Oct 30 Age 84 years, 7 months, 25 days S:7

Marston, Harvey - Died 1845 Dec 3 in his 45th yr (died on James River in Virginia) Son of Prince & Lydia Marston S:7

Marston, Howard - Died 1924 Apr 23 Born 1846 Oct 11 (Marston plot) (buried with wife, Ella M Kelley) S:8

Marston, Jennie W - Died 1905 Born 1876 (with Elizabeth N Marston & others) S:19

Marston, John - Died 1736 Jan 19 Age 21 S:5R

Marston, John - Died 1817 Feb 22 in his 79th yr S:10+26R

Marston, Joseph W - Died 1877 Born 1850 (with wife, Almira C Marston & others) S:19

Marston, Lydia - Died 1774 Apr 6 in her 78th yr Widow of Benjamin (buried next to him) S:5

Marston, Lydia - Died 1850 Mar 3 (died in Jerseyville Ill) Born 1775

Marston (Cont.)
Jan 10 Wife of Prince Marston
S:7

Marston, Lydia - Died 1851 Jan 9
Age 32 years,3 months,10 days
Daughter of Edward & Rhoda
Marston S:10

Marston, Lydia L - Died 1834 Feb
23 Age 21 Daughter of Allen &
Hannah Marston S:7

Marston, Malvina - Died 1875 Sept
21 Age 65 years, 21 days Wife of
Zebdial Marston (next to him)
S:14

Marston, Mary - Died 1804 May 7
in her 78th yr Widow of Nymphas Marston S:7

Marston, Mary - Died 1880 Jan 4
Age 60 years, 4 months, 19 days
Wife of William Marston S:7

Marston, Mary Mrs - Died 1816
Oct 20 in her 72 yr Wife of John
Marston (next to him) S:10+26R

Marston, Minerva - Died 1844 Oct
19 Age 38 years, 11 months, 2
days Wife of William Marston S:7

Marston, Nabby - Died 1819 Sept
14 in her 38th yr Wife of Crocker
Marston S:26R

Marston, Nancy C - Died 1845 Mar
28 Age 46 Wife of Charles Mar
ston (buried next to him) S:7

Marston, Nancy M - Died 1877 Mar
1 Age 73 years, 7 months, 16
days Wife of Arthur Marston
(buried next to him) S:7

Marston, Narry - Died 1819 Sept
Age 38 Wife of Crocker Marston
S:10

Marston, Nymphas (Honorable) -
Died 1864 May 2 Born 1788 Feb
12 Graduate from Harvard 1807
Barnstable Probate Judge 1828
Resigned in 1854 S:7

Marston, Oakes S - Died 1821 Mar
13 Age 10 months Son of
Nymphas & Elizabeth Marston
S:7

Marston, Oliver - Died (date not
clear) Son of Prince & Lydia
Marston S:7

Marston, Phebe - Died 1804 Dec 22

Marston (Cont.)
Age 5 years, 5 months, 24 days
Daughter of Winslow & Elizabeth
Marston S:7

Marston, Phebe - Died 1835 Nov 13
Age 28 years, 5 months Daugh-
ter of Prince & Lydia Marston
S:7

Marston, Prentiss - Died 1814 Nov
7 Age 19 years, 11 months, 16
days Son of Winslow & Elizabeth
Marston S:7

Marston, Prince - Died 1776 May 1
Age 40 years, 2 months S:7

Marston, Prince - Died 1857 Jan
17 Born 1773 Aug 29 S:7

Marston, Rebekah - Died 1778 May
7 Wife of Benjamin Marston S:7

Marston, Rhoda - Died 1837 Aug 5
in her 61st yr Wife of Edward
Marston (buried next to him)
S:10+26R

Marston, Rufus G - Died 1882
Born 1848 (with Mercie M
Phinney & others) S:19

Marston, Russell - Died 1907 Apr
27 Born 1816 Oct 14 (Marston
Plot) (buried with wife, Sarah
Crosby) S:8

Marston, Sally - Died 1858 Feb 25
in her 83rd yr Wife S:7

Marston, Sarah - Died 1809 Aug 5
in her 71st yr Widow of Prince
Marston S:7

Marston, Shirley - Died 1955 Feb
12 Born 1873 May 2 (Marston
plot) (buried with wife, Alice M
Marston) S:8

Marston, Susan - Died 1833 Mar
14 Age 26 years, 11 months Wife
of Edward Marston (buried one
stone away from him) S:10

Marston, Wilham B - Died 1805
April 25 Age 25 Son of Joseph &
Sarah Marston S:12

Marston, William - Died 1882 Apr
23 Age 80 years, 11 months (all
his wives & family are buried
next to each other) S:7

Marston, Winslow (Deacon) - Died
1852 Jan 6 in his 87th yr
(buried next to wife, Elizabeth

Marston (Cont.)
Marston) S:7

Marston, Zebdial S - Died 1881 April 8 Age 76 years, 5 months (next to wife, Malvina Marston) S:14

Marston, Zenas (Capt) - Died 1885 Born 1802 (with Mary Scudder) S:18

Martins, Pedro F - Died 1968 Born 1896 (undertaker plaque only) S:17

Masalskiene, Monika - Died 1978 Dec 13 Born 1891 Feb 25 in Lithuania (a small mortuary plaque says, "b1893 d1978") S:16

Mason, Clarence W - Died 1962 Born 1885 (with Anna H Gardner) S:11

Mason, Olive - Died 1986 May 22 Born 1896 Oct 1 S:15

Mason, Roy - Died 1947 Born 1907 Has an American Legion Star, ACMM, USCG S:12

Massey, Hannah B - Died 1959 Born 1883 (next to Harry D Massey) S:12

Massey, Harry D - Died 1954 Born 1882 (next to Hannah B Massey) S:12

Massicci, Alexander P - Died (still living 1991?) Born 1929 (with Marie R Massicci) S:20

Massicci, Marie R - Died 1990 Born 1921 (with Alexander Massicci) S:20

Masterton, Anne I - Died 1971 Born 1890 (with Archie Masterton) S:15

Masterton, Archie - Died 1971 Born 1888 (with Anne I Masterton) S:15

Mathews, Isiah (Capt) - Died 1803 sept 25 in his 36th yr S:10+26R

Mathewson, Ann Hendry - Died 1956 Born 1868 (a rock stone) (with Pauline Odell Mathewson & others) S:20

Mathewson, Pauline Adell - Died 1966 Born 1908 (a rock stone) (with Richard Duncan

Mathewson (Cont.)
Mathewson Jr & others) S:20

Mathewson, Richard Duncan - Died 1947 Born 1867 (a rock stone) (with Ann Hendry Mathewson & others) S:20

Mathewson, Richard Duncan Jr - Died 1975 Born 1906 (a rock stone) (with Ann Hendry Mathewson & others) S:20

Mathieson, Marcelle - Died 1990 Born 1900 S:13

Matias, Antonio B - Died 1925 Born 1844 (with Joaquina J Matias) S:31

Matias, Joaquina J - Died 1919 Born 1847 (with Antonio B Matias) S:31

Matthews, Albert S - Died 1948 May 5 Born 1881 April 29 S:11

Matthews, Asa - Died 1884 Born 1813 (with Mary J Matthews & others) S:21

Matthews, Asa W - Died 1894 Born 1852 (with Charles H Matthews & others) S:21

Matthews, Barbara H - Died 1961 Born 1909 (listed with Frederick B Matthews) S:11

Matthews, Charles B - Died 1984 Born 1912 (with Laura A Matthews) S:11

Matthews, Charles H - Died 1907 Born 1860 (with Corillia DeAmaril & others) S:21

Matthews, Doris C - Died (still living 1991?) Born 1903 (listed with Millard L Matthews) S:17

Matthews, Elizabeth - Died 1854 Aug 20 Born 1821 Apr 17 Wife of Clark Lincoln (buried with her & others) S:8

Matthews, Ellery - Died 1898 Nov 22 Born 1835 Oct 23 (next to wife, Sabra & Elmira Matthews) S:19

Matthews, Elmira E - Died 1942 June 8 Born 1865 Jan 16 (next to Sabra C Matthews) S:19

Matthews, Emily S - Died 1923 Born 1837 (with Russell Matthews) S:18

Matthews, Eva M Leander - Died 1985 Born 1908 (next to Carl L Leander) S:11

Matthews, Frederick B - Died (still living in 1990) Born 1904 (listed on same stone with Barbara H Matthews) S:11

Matthews, Laura A - Died 1989 Born 1910 (with Charles B Matthews) S:11

Matthews, Mary J - Died 1905 Born 1829 (with Asa W Matthews & others) S:21

Matthews, Millard L - Died 1974 Born 1899 (was a Mason) (listed with Doris C Matthews) S:17

Matthews, Millie - Died 1874 Aug 18 Age 1 year, 10 months, 3 days Daughter of Russell & Emily S Matthews S:9R

Matthews, Russell - Died 1892 Aug 21 Born 1838 (with Emily S Matthews) S:9

Matthews, Sabra C - Died 1908 Sept 20 Born 1838 Jan 25 Wife of Ellery Matthews (next to him) S:19

Mattos, Alvaro V - Died 1983 Born 1900 (with Mary R Mattos) S:15

Mattos, Mary R - Died 1984 Born 1901 (with Alvaro V Mattos) S:15

Mauritz, Gora M - Died 1975 Born 1902 (with Lawrence F Mauritz & others) S:20

Mauritz, Lawrence F - Died 1968 Sept 16 Born 1904 Aug 10 (has 2 stones) From Massachusetts, was Sargeant in US Army during Korea (with Francis Lambert & others) S:20

Maxwell, Janet Murray - Died 1970 Born 1930 S:13

May, Esther - Died 1799 Oct 25 in her 88th yr Relict of Mr Eleazer May S:11+26R

May, Henry O - Died 1973 Oct 30 Born 1888 June 25 From Massachusetts, was PFC in US Army during World War I S:15

McAdams, Leslie - Died 1988 Born 1935 (next to Carolyn & Louis Woodland) S:20

McAleer, Edward F - Died 1969 Born 1901 (he was a Mason) (with wife, Susan B McAleer) S:15

McAleer, Susan B - Died 1977 Born 1891 (with husband, Edward F McAleer) S:15

McArdle, Rose A - Died 1929 Born 1859 (with Frank S O'Neil & others) S:31

McBride, Mary A - Died 1954 Born 1864 Wife of Arthur McBride S:8

McCabe, Flora Carpenter - Died 1968 Born 1888 (stone down from vandals) (next to Marian Carpenter) (stone also down) S:18

McCabe, Francis E - Died 1943 Born 1876 (with Margaret G McCabe) S:31

McCabe, Margaret G - Died 1922 Born 1877 (with Francis E McCabe) S:31

McCann, Clara E - Died 1951 Born 1871 (next to Henry A McCann) S:18

McCann, Hattie D - Died 1969 Born 1893 (with John McCann) S:17

McCann, Henry A - Died 1890 Born 1845 Was in CoE, 1st Massachusetts HA (next to Clara E McCann) S:18

McCann, John - Died 1979 Born 1890/1 (has 2 stones) Was SEA in US Navy during World War I (with Hattie D McCann) S:17

McCann, Josie F - Died 1930 Born 1851 (next to Henry A McCann) S:18

McCann, Thomas - Died 1895 Born 1873 (a small stone) (next to Josie F McCann) S:18

McCarthy, Eva - Died 1889 (possible wife of James) Stone says, "Life is Eternal" (buried with James C McCarthy & others) S:8

McCarthy, James C - Died 1917 (buried with Eva McCarthy & others) S:8

McCarthy, Justin Jeremiah - Died 1976 April 8 Born 1899 Jan 25

McCarthy (Cont.)
Was a Pvt in US Army during
World War I S:15

McCarthy, Marion - Died 1985
April 21 Born 1898 Nov 2 S:15

McClelland, Alexander B - Died
1969 Born 1897 Stone says,
"Husband" (located between
Alexandria Banks & William
Price) S:15

McClusky, Ellen C - Died 1948 or
1984? (not clear) Born 1896
S:31

McCollum, Daniel C - Died 1875
Jan 28 Age 20 years, 7 months
Son of Dr Henry & Eunice H
McCollum S:7

McCollum, Eunice H - Died 1874
Aug 15 Age 47 years, 5 months
(family buried next to each
other) S:7

McCollum, Henry E - Died 1876
Oct 9 Age 31 years, 4 months
Son of Dr Henry & Eunice H
McCollum S:7

McCollum, Henry E (Dr) - Died
1867 Dec 23 Age 67 Born c1800
S:7

McCollum, Mary E - Died (date not
clear) Age 7 days Daughter of Dr
H E McCollum S:7

McCowan, Martin P - Died 1958
Born 1908 (with to Elizabeth C
Tibbetts) S:12

McCray, Maude - Died 1937 Born
1897 Wife of Elmer B Taylor
(with him & Mildred Taylor
Drinkwater & others on large
Taylor stone) S:12

McCunn, Florence V - Died 1979
Born 1887 (next to James K
McCunn) S:13

McCunn, Frances B - Died 1965
Born 1896 Wife of James K
McCunn (with him) S:13

McCunn, James K - Died 1970
Born 1904 (with wife, Frances B
McCunn) S:13

McCunn, John N - Died 1979 Born
1895 Was 2nd Lieutenant in US
Army during World War I (next
to Walter T McCunn) S:13

McCunn, Walter T - Died 1982
Born 1888 (next to John N
McCunn) S:13

McCurdy, Elsie Smith - Died 1963
Born 1885 (on family stone with
James P Smith & others) S:11

McDevitt, William H - Died 1954
Born 1893 (with Mary C Keenan)
S:16

McDonald, Elizabeth - Died 1887
July 25 Age 56 at Paris, France
(with Agnes Pollard) S:14

McDonald, Elizabeth Mae - Died
1989 Sept 19 Born 1899 Jan 8
S:15

McDonnell, John J - Died 1941
Born 1875 S:16

McDonnell, Mary - Died 1956 Born
1877 S:16

McDonogh, James Drhr (?) - Died
1822 Oct 4 Age ? S:10

McDonough, Michael J - Died 1977
Born 1898 (undertakers plaque
only) S:15

McDonough, Mary - Died 1949
Born 1876 Wife of Richard
McDonough (with him) S:31

McDonough, Richard - Died 1942
Born 1869 (with Mary Dahill &
others) S:31

McElroy, Alpha O - Died 1989
Born 1900 (with James J McElroy) S:15

McElroy, James Joseph - Died
1987 Born 1894 (middle name
from Mosswood cemetery records) (with Alpha O McElroy)
S:15

McEttrick, Ella J - Died 1941 Born
1869 (buried with Isaac &
Eleanor Crosby)(others on same
stone with later dates) S:8

McEwen, Ellsworth S - Died 1981
Born 1897 (has two stones) Was
a SN in US Navy during World
War I (with Ruth R McEwen)
S:15

McEwen, Ruth R - Died (still living
1991?) Born 1899 (listed with
Ellsworth S McEwen) S:15

McGarrell, Patrick - Died 1967
Born 1898 S:15

McGillen, Eva R - Died 1937 May 12 Born 1886 Jan 7 (with James F McGillen) S:16

McGillen, James F - Died 1956 Nov 20 Born 1888 June 14 (with Eva R McGillen) S:16

McGinlay, Catherine M - Died 1974 Born 1886 (next to John McGinlay) S:18

McGinlay, John - Died 1965 Born 1884 (next to Catherine M McGinlay) S:18

McGinn, Bertha B - Died 1970 Born 1897 S:16

McGlinchey, Sarah M - Died 1976 Born 1896 S:15

McGlothlin, Bruce - Died (still living in 1991?) Born 1959 Son of Julia McGlothlin (listed with her) S:13

McGlothlin, Julia O - Died (still living in 1991?) Born 1927 (with parents, Henry & Ada Whiteley & son, Bruce McGothlin) S:13

McGoldrick, Hugh F - Died 1965 Oct 7 Born 1900 Nov 27 From Massachusetts, was LCDR in USNR during World War II (next to wife, Mary F McGoldrick) S:15

McGoldrick, Mary F - Died 1990 Dec 14 Born 1898 March 17 (next to husband, Hugh F McGoldrick) S:15

McGrew, Stephen - Died (no dates) (with Lynda, Forrest & Mary Jane Mores) S:20

McHugh, Dorothy Hanson - Died 1964 Born 1901 (with William Thomas McHugh) S:15

McHugh, William Thomas - Died 1966 Born 1897 (with Dorothy Hanson McHugh) S:15

McInnis, Ann Hagan - Died 1975 Born 1898 (with Raymond B McInnis) S:16

McInnis, Raymond B - Died 1963 Born 1897 (with Ann Hagan McInnis) S:16

McIntyre, Emily - Died 1986 Born 1915 (no stone marker, just small grass maker) (next to William F McIntyre) S:12

McIntyre, Hazel B - Died 1965 Born 1893 (with husband, Matthew M McIntyre) S:16

McIntyre, Matthew M - Died 1954 Born 1891 (with wife, Hazel B McIntyre) S:16

McIntyre, William F - Died 1986 Born 1914 (no stone marker, just metal grass marker) (next to Emily McIntyre) S:12

McKaig, Mary Gertrude - Died 1954 Born 1880 (large stone cross) (with Mary Julia & Mary Alice Falvey) S:16

McKay, Agnes B - Died 1935 Born 1853 (with William & Margaret Gilmore) S:20

McKellar, James Archibald - Died 1975 Oct 30 Born 1890 Aug 20 S:14

McKenna, Alfred W - Died 1987 Born 1889 (listed with Arline E McKenna) S:16

McKenna, Arline E - Died (still living 1991?) Born 1903 (listed with Alfred W McKenna) S:16

McKenna, Dorothy C (or A) - Died 1985 Born 1899 (with hisband, George A McKenna) S:15

McKenna, George A - Died 1970 Born 1903 (with wife, Dorothy C McKenna) S:15

McKenzie, Albert T - Died 1982 Nov 13 Born 1914 Sept 2 Was in the US Army during World War II S:13

McKenzie, Eva - Died 1984 Born 1898 (she was called "Bommy") S:16

McKeon, Mary M - Died 1988 Born 1892 Stone says, "Mom" (with Patrick J McKeon) S:16

McKeon, Patrick J - Died 1941 Born 1884 Stone says, "Dad" (with Mary M McKeon) S:16

McKinley, Ellen - Died 1952 Born 1866 Wife of Henry T Nickerson (with him & Harold M Nickerson & others) S:21

McKinley, Mary A - Died 1950 Sept 21 Born 1857 Oct 15 Wife of Matthias P Slavin (with him &

McKinley (Cont.)
Matthias Slavin & Gertrude El
dridge) S:31

McKinley, Mary Ann - Died 1904
Feb 9 Born 1835 Oct 12 (with
Michael McKinley) S:31

McKinley, Michael - Died 1875
May 10 Born 1831 Oct 2 (with
Mary Ann McKinley) S:31

McKinnon, Gertrude Adams - Died
1990 Born 1891 Daughter of
Edson Fisher & Eleanor Lumbert
(with them) S:14

McKittrick, Harold V - Died 1977
Born 1900 S:15

McLane, Frederick S - Died 1966
Born 1891 (was a Mason) (next
to wife, Ann C Crawford) S:15

McLaughlin, Annie E - Died 1950
Born 1884 (with James F
McLaughlin) S:16

McLaughlin, James F - Died 1940
Born 1875 (with Annie E
McLaughlin) S:16

McLean, Christina - Died (still
living 1991?) Born 1899 (with
Norman McLean) S:16

McLean, Norman - Died 1987 Born
1899 (with Christina McLean)
S:16

McMakin, Annie M - Died 1911
Born 1850 Wife of John McMakin (listed on family stone) S:11

McMakin, Teresa Marie - Died
1972 Born 1955 (stone located
just in front of her could also be
for her, It says,"TESEE" - see
that listing) S:19

McNally, James F - Died 1986 Feb
4 Born 1892 Jan 10 S:16

McNerney, Alice E - Died 1985
Born 1891 S:15

McNutt, Robert R - Died 1962 Born
1877 (he was a Mason) (next to
Ellen Fulton, his wife) S:14

McPeak, Leonara - Died 1948 Born
1868 Stone says,"Mother" S:12

Meacham, Edward J - Died 1950
Born 1873 (next to Millie F
Meacham) S:14

Meacham, Millie F - Died 1957
Born 1880 (next to Edward J

Meacham (Cont.)
Meacham) S:14

Mead, Mary B - Died 1947 Born
1859 (buried in crypt with
husband, John Lowry & family)
S:8

Medeiros, Bertha - Died 1982 Born
1893 Stone says, "Wife" (next to
husband, John Medeiros & his
or her mother, Josephine M
Banks) S:15

Medeiros, Isabel C - Died 1943
Born 1882 Wife of Manuel C
Medeiros (with him) S:16

Medeiros, John - Died 1968 Born
1891 Stone says, "Husband"
(next to Josephine M Banks, his
or her mother & wife, Bertha
Medeiros) S:15

Medeiros, Manuel C - Died 1945
Born 1876 (with wife, Isabel C
Medeiros) S:16

Medeiros, Margaret J - Died 1945
Born 1862 S:16

Meechan, Harry W - Died 1975 Dec
17 Born 1896 Oct 18 Was in US
Army during World War I & II
S:15

Megathlin, Charles Walton - Died
1954 Dec 2 Born 1872 April 2
(with Louise Hulbert Megathlin)
S:18

Megathlin, Charles Walton - Died
1980 Feb 14 Born 1929 Aug 12
(with Marguerite & Mabel
Megathlin) S:18

Megathlin, Louise Hulbert - Died
1906 June 13 Born 1867 Feb 3
(with Charles Walton Megathlin
& others) S:18

Megathlin, Mabel Howard - Died
1927 Aug 14 Born 1870 Feb 27
(with Louise Hulbert Megathlin
& others) S:18

Megathlin, Marguerite Baldwin -
Died 1976 Jan 13 Born 1894
April 16 (with Mabel & Charles
W Megathlin Jr) S:18

Meigs, Sarah C - Died 1920 Born
1835 (buried with Ezekiel Sturgis) S:8

Mellen, Elizabeth Walker - Died

Mellen (Cont.)
   1977 Nov 20 Born 1898 Sept 27
   (with George H Mellen Jr) S:17

Mellen, George H Jr - Died 1969
   July 27 Born 1889 Jan 5 (has 2
   stones) From Massachusetts,
   was Capt in US Army during
   World War II (with Elizabeth
   Walker Mellen) S:17

Melody, Mildred Noce - Died 1968
   Born 1923 "He left a great heritage" S:11

Merchant, Huldah - Died 1828 Nov
   19 in her 74th yr Widow of
   James S:1

Merrifield, May S - Died 1955 Born
   1883 S:13

Merrill, Eliza Parson - Died 1957
   Feb 17 Born 1869 May 6 (with
   Joshua Merrill) (next to Francis
   W Parsons) S:12

Merrill, Joshua - Died 1943 Dec 21
   Born 1869 June 21 (with Eliza
   Parsons Merrill) S:12

Merritt, James L - Died 1951 Jan 6
   Born 1891 June 10 From
   Massachusetts, was Pvt in 301
   Sup, Tn 76 Div during World
   War I S:18

Mershon, Eliza H - Died 1956 Sept
   4 Born 1875 June 22 S:11

Meserve, Evelyn - Died (still living
   1991?) Born 1916 Wife of
   Monroe Palmer (listed with him)
   S:12

Meserve, Harold M - Died 1960
   Born 1888 (next to Evelyn Meserve & Monroe E Palmer) S:12

Messenger, Kenneth L - Died 1969
   Born 1892 (with Marie E Messenger) S:20

Messenger, Marie E - Died 1980
   Born 1889 (with Kenneth
   Messenger) S:20

Messer, Margaret C - Died 1985
   Born 1897 (undertaker plaque
   only) S:19

Michaelis, Lester Myles - Died
   1973 Born 1898 S:16

Miller, Frank Roy - Died 1952 Born
   1893 (next to Ruth Marguerite
   Miller) S:18

Miller, G (George) J - Died (no
   dates) (with possible wife, Malinda W Miller) S:21

Miller, Gladys - Died 1979 Born
   1897 Wife of Eugene Exman
   (next to him) S:11

Miller, Helen Barrett - Died 1989
   Born 1906 (listed with Samuel
   Winters Miller) S:16

Miller, Malinda W - Died 1869
   March 1 Born 1837 April 27
   Wife of George J Miller (with a G
   J Miller) S:21

Miller, Ruth Marguerite - Died
   1953 Born 1894 (next to Frank
   Roy Miller) S:18

Miller, Samuel Winters - Died (still
   living 1991?) Born 1900 (with
   Helen Barrett Miller) S:16

Miller, Sarah A - Died 1863 Feb 10
   Age 25 years, 5 months Died in
   Cape Town, Africa Wife of Capt
   Edwin Miller S:8

Milne, Thomas - Died 1985 May 27
   Born 1894 June 18 Was in
   Massachusetts Wagoner 103
   Field Hospital during World War
   I (he has an American Legion
   star at his grave) S:13

Milou, Maria - Died 1983 Born
   1885 S:18

Milstead, Century Allen Jr - Died
   1989 Born 1932 Was a Sargeant
   in US Marine Corps during Korea
   (with Lois Higby & Dana Lee
   Milstead) S:20

Milstead, Dana Lee - Died 1987
   Born 1963 (with Lois Higby &
   Centry Allen Milstead Jr) S:20

Miner, Dorothea E - Died 1962 Aug
   8 Born 1902 Sept 21 S:19

Minor, Ella C - Buried 1909 Located in section O, lot, 10, grave 4
   S:14R

Minor, Julia F - Died 1964 Born
   1885 (with Wesley C Minor Next
   to Wesley & Ella Minor) S:14

Minor, Milton Forrest - Died 1882
   Nov 12 Age 3 years, 2 months, 6
   days (small childs stone) Son of
   Wesley & Ella Minor(also listed
   on parents stone) S:14

Minor, S Vernon - Died 1915 Born 1884 (with Wesley & Ella Minor) S:14

Minor, Wesley L - Died 1935 Born 1853 (with wife, Ella C Minor & others) S:14

Minor, Wesley, C (or F) - Died 1977 Born 1880 (with Julia F Minor next to Wesley & Ella Minor) S:14

Miranda, Sabino J - Died 1989 Aug 23 Born 1894 Dec 31 Was CST in US Navy during World War I & II S:15

Mitchell, Ada M - Died (no dates) Wife of Winthrop C Mitchell (with him & Carrie Brown Mitchell & others) S:18

Mitchell, Antonette - Died 1903 Born 1895 (with Thomas W & Sarah F Mitchell & others) S:18

Mitchell, Carrie Brown - Died (no dates) Daughter of Winthrop & Ada Mitchell (with them & Dwight Harrington Mitchell & others) S:18

Mitchell, Dwight Harrington - Died (no dates) Son of Winthrop & Ada Mitchell (with them & Marjorie Clark Mitchell & others) S:18

Mitchell, Eliza - Died 1889 Born 1808 (with Emma L Mitchell & others) S:18

Mitchell, Emma L - Died 1932 Born 1841 (with Thomas W Mitchell & others) S:18

Mitchell, Herbert B - Died 1890 Born 1888 (with Sarah F Mitchell & others) S:18

Mitchell, James Bradbury - Died (still living 1990) Born 1908 (rock marker) (with Ruth Seabury Mitchell) S:11

Mitchell, James J - Died 1940 Born 1871 (with wife, Bridget T King) S:31

Mitchell, John E - Died 1968 Born 1880 (with Rose O Mitchell) S:17

Mitchell, John James - Died 1979 Born 1892 (listed with Rosanna Ruth Mitchell) S:16

Mitchell, Joseph - Died 1929 Born 1849 (with Sarah F Mitchell & others) S:18

Mitchell, Josephine - Died 1927 Born 1871 (with Antonette & Sarah F Mitchell & others) S:18

Mitchell, Marjorie Clark - Died (no dates) Daughter of Winthrop & Ada Mitchell (with them & Sidney Clark & others) S:18

Mitchell, Oliver L - Died (no date) Born 1918 Wife of O David Sampson (with him & Roger A Sampson) S:21

Mitchell, Rosanna Ruth - Died (still living 1991?) Born 1902 (listed with John James Mitchell) S:16

Mitchell, Rose O - Died 1981 Born 1895 (with John E Mitchell) S:17

Mitchell, Ruth Seabury - Died 1972 Born 1904 (with James Bradbury Mitchell) S:11

Mitchell, Sadie - Died 1888 Born 1883 (with Sarah F Mitchell & others) S:18

Mitchell, Sarah F - Died 1912 Born 1854 (with Willie H Mitchell & others) S:18

Mitchell, Thomas W - Died 1879 Born 1829 (with William J Mitchell & others) S:18

Mitchell, Thomas W - Died 1903 Born 1880 (with Antonette & Sarah F Mitchell & others) S:18

Mitchell, Veda F - Died 1953 Born 1886 (with Josephine & Sarah F Mitchell & others) S:18

Mitchell, William H - Died 1926 Born 1878 S:21

Mitchell, William J - Died 1899 Born 1837 (with Josephine Linnell & others) S:18

Mitchell, Willie H - Died 1882 Born 1874 (with Sarah F Mitchell & others) S:18

Mitchell, Winthrop C - Died (no dates) (with wife, Ada M Mitchell & others) S:18

Mitte, Frank D - Died 1951 Born 1893 (with Louise G Mitte) S:16

Mitte, Louise G - Died 1936 Born

Mitte (Cont.)
1897 (with Frank D Mitte) S:16

Moisio, Katherine J - Died 1983 Born 1907 (with Vaino Moisio) S:20

Moisio, Vaino I - Died 1980 Born 1901 (with Katherine J Moisio) S:20

Molony, Samuel J - Died 1950 Born 1880 (with Annie O'Donnell) S:16

Moniz, Lena R - Died (still living in 1991?) (no dates) (listed with Manuel H Moniz) S:15

Moniz, Manuel H - Died 1980 Born 1897 (with Lena R Moniz) S:15

Monro, Karen A - Died 1988 Born 1901 (with Leith D Monro) S:18

Monro, Leith D - Died (still living 1991?) Born 1899 (listed with Karen A Monro) S:18

Monroe, Clifton V - Died (still living 1991?) Born 1909 (listed with Nellie, Joseph & Willie Baxter) S:21

Montaque, Ellen J - Died 1938 Born 1889 (next to Thomas F Montaque) S:16

Montaque, Thomas F - Died 1973 April 25 Born 1887 April 5 From Massachusetts, was PVT in US Army during World War I (with Ellen J Montaque) S:16

Monteiro, Antonio A - Died 1962 Born 1881 (with Marion Monteiro) S:16

Monteiro, Florence I - Died 1987 Born 1887 (100 years old) (with Joseph B Monteiro) S:18

Monteiro, John B - Died 1951 Born 1888 (with Mary R Monteiro) S:16

Monteiro, Joseph - Died 1976 Born 1892 (with Florence I Monteiro) S:18

Monteiro, Marion - Died 1959 Born 1891 (with Antonio A Monteiro) S:16

Monteiro, Mary R - Died 1980 Born 1892 (with John B Monteiro) S:16

Mooney, Alice M - Died 1927 Born

Mooney (Cont.)
1902 Wife of Charles S Dodge (with him) S:31

Moore, Ernest A - Died 1967 Jan 29 Born 1893 Nov 25 Was a Corporal in Co C, 101 Engineers in World War I (flag at stone) (next to Katharine G Moore) S:11

Moore, Ina L - Died 1963 Born 1882 (with Kate E Moore) S:14

Moore, Kate E - Died 1895 Born 1860 (with Ina L Moore) S:14

Moore, Katharine G - Died 1962 Born 1895 S:11

Moore, Mabel M Pelton - Died (still living 1991?) Born 1921 Feb 18 (listed next to William R Moore) S:20

Moore, Marvin A - Died 1966 Born 1878 S:17

Moore, William R - Died 1984 Born 1918 Was an ENC in US Navy during World War II (next to Mabel M Pelton Moore) S:20

Moores, Leon A - Died 1962 Born 1884 (he was a Mason) S:14

Moors, George A - Died 1979 Born 1910 (with William T Casey) Stone says, "Friends" S:13

Moran, Elva S - Died 1990 Born 1907 (with James Albert Moran) S:13

Moran, James Albert - Died 1963 Oct 23 Born 1900 July 24 Was a PFC in Massachusetts US Army during World War I (with Elva S Moran) S:13

Moran, Josephine - Died (still living 1991?) Born 1899 Sept 29 (with husband, Napoleon Moran) S:16

Moran, Napoleon - Died 1949 Dec 3 Born 1875 Dec 31 (with wife, Josephine Moran) S:16

Morch, Anna M - Died 1967 Born 1895 S:20

Mores, Barzilliai - Died 1928 Born 1849 (with Lilla G Mores) S:18

Mores, Forrest - Died (no dates) (with Mary Jane & Lynda Mores & Stephen McGrew) S:20

Mores, Forrest B - Died 1952 Born 1877 (with Lilla & Barzilliai

Mores (Cont.)
Mores) S:18

Mores, Lilla G - Died 1930 Born 1855 Wife of Barzilliai Mores (with him & Forrest Mores) S:18

Mores, Lynda - Died 1953 Born 1902 Wife of Stephen McGrew (with him & others) S:31

Mores, Mary Jane - Died 1926 Born 1876 Wife of Forrest Mores (with him & others) S:31

Morey, Elizabeth A - Died 1974 Born 1896 (with Lester Morey & Hattie & Daniel Nickerson) S:19

Morey, Lester F - Died 1967 Born 1899 (with Elizabeth Morey & others) S:19

Morgan, Herbert - Died 1987 Born 1905 (with Laura W Morgan) S:20

Morgan, James Anthony - Died 1906 March 8 Born 1875 or 1878 May 21 (with Thomas Henry Morgan & others) S:31

Morgan, Laura W - Died 1981 Born 1903 (with Herbert Morgan) S:20

Morgan, Leigh Ferry - Died 1970 Born 1890 S:14

Morgan, Mary Howard - Died 1905 Feb or April? 22 Born 1841 May 19 (with James Anthony Morgan, Patrick Morgan & others) S:31

Morgan, Patrick - Died 1907 Jan 26 Born 1830 March 17 (with Mary Howard Morgan & others) S:31

Morgan, Thomas Henry - Died 1891 July 28 Born 1864 Dec 15 (with Patrick Morgan & others) S:31

Morin, John E or F - Died 1927 (next to Mary M Morin) S:31

Morin, Mary M - Died 1921 (next to John E Morin) S:31

Morner, John D - Died 1972 Oct 7 Born 1893 May 14 From Wisconsin, was a Pvt in Air Service during World War I S:17

Morrill, Addie M - Died 1904 Born 1850 Stone says,"Mother" (with Estus A Morrill) S:18

Morrill, Bertha F - Died 1929 Born 1889 (with Leander Morrill) S:8

Morrill, Charles Sumner - Died 1947 Born 1880 (next to Addie M Morrill) S:18

Morrill, Estus A - Died 1937 Born 1845 Stone says,"Father" (with Addie M Morrill) S:18

Morrill, Leander C - Died (no death listed) Born 1860 (with Bertha F Morrill) S:8

Morris, Bridget - Died 1903 Born 1822 (with Charles Daniel & others) S:31

Morris, Edith M - Died 1961 Born 1876 Wife of Emery Morris (with him) S:18

Morris, Emery H - Died 1950 Born 1871 (with wife, Edith M Morris) S:18

Morris, Henry Charles - Died 1977 Born 1887 (next to wife, Ivy M Dauce) S:11

Morris, Margaret G - Died 1941 Born 1879 Wife of William J O'Neil (with him & Richard M O'Neil & others) S:16

Morris, William O - Died 1982 Born 1898 S:15

Morrison, Marion H - Died 1980 Born 1903 (next to W Chester Morrison) S:13

Morrison, W Chester - Died 1971 Born 1900 (he was a Mason) (next to Marion H Morrison) S:13

Morry, Hannah - Died 1733 Apr 8 (Hinckley Ceme records #5R say Age was 90 and the daughter of Job Bourne of Sandwich, Massachusetts) S:5

Morse, James Herbert - Died 1923 May 21 Born 1841 Oct 8 (with wife, Lucy Gibbons) S:14

Morse, James Herbert - Died 1943 June 14 Born 1875 July 8 (with wife, Jean Howe Atwater) S:14

Morse, Marjorie D - Died 1978 Born 1904 (next to James Herbert Morse) S:14

Morse, Pearl V - Died 1978 Born 1898 S:15

Morse, Warren Baker - Died 1965

Morse (Cont.)
Aug 23 Born 1895 Sept 4 From Massachusetts, was a Cpl in Co E, 104th Inf during World War I (DSCPhOlc) S:15

Morse, William Gibbons - Died 1969 Born 1877 (with Marjorie Dewey) S:14

Mortimer, Henry Coit - Died 1912 Sept 30 in Barnstable Born 1849 Dec 2 in New York S:11

Mortimer, Henry Coit Jr - Died 1943 May 6 in Barnstable Born 1876 Mar 2 in New York S:11

Mortimer, Laurence - Died 1956 May 7 in Barnstable Born 1878 Sept 26 in New York City S:11

Mortimer, Mary - Died 1964 June 15 in Barnstable Born 1881 Dec 21 in New York S:11

Mortimer, Mary Katherine - Died 1933 June 29 in Barnstable Born 1848 July 18 in Boston Wife of Henry Coit Mortimer S:11

Morton, Amanda - Died 1908 Born 1830 S:21

Morton, Caroline - Died 1928 Feb 27 Born 1837 July 17 S:8

Morton, Catherine M - Died 1972 Born 1898 (undertaker plaque only) S:15

Morton, Charles Edward - Died 1835 Dec 3 Age 6 months Son of Charles C & Bethia R Morton S:10

Morton, Charles H - Died 1897 Sept 27 Born 1842 Apr 19 S:5

Morton, Ebenezer E - Died 1904 July 15 Born 1829 Apr 10 (with Caroline Morton) S:8

Morton, Edwin Francis - Died 1840 May 21 Age 13 months Son of Charles C & Bethia R Morton S:10

Mosher, Loren K - Died 1972 Dec 20 Born 1882 Oct 4 Was Pvt in US Army during World War I S:17

Mosher, Nancy C - Died 1864 March 26 Age 26 (next to Warren A Mosher) S:13

Mosher, Warren A - Died 1859 (?) Jan 12 Age 66 (next to Nancy C Mosher Stone broken and on the ground, worn badly) S:13

Motherway, Mary - Died 1973 Born 1888 Wife of Walter Dana Rogers (with him) S:15

Mott, Dorothy E - Died (still living in 1991?) Born 1924 Feb 2 (listed with Robert G Mott) 3 S:13

Mott, Elmo C - Died 1971 Born 1890 (he was a Mason) (with Jennie C Mott) S:12

Mott, Jennie C - Died 1944 Born 1891 (with Elmo C Mott) S:12

Mott, Robert G - Died 1978 Feb 20 Born 1919 March 25 Was a Lieutenant in US Army during World War II (listed with Dorothy E Mott) S:13

Moulaison, Edward J - Died 1983 Born 1896 (with Margaret Moulaison) S:20

Moulaison, Ellen S - Died (still living 1991?) Born 1912 (listed with Hilaire Moulaison) S:20

Moulaison, Hilaire A - Died 1985 Born 1905 (with Ellen Moulaison) S:20

Moulaison, Margaret M - Died (still living 1991?) Born 1903 (listed with Edward & next to Hilaire Moulaison) S:20

Mouleton, Lucretia Berry - Died 1892 Oct 20 Born 1853 Nov 2 (stone says mother) Wife of George Greenleaf Pratt S:5

Moultrie, Anna - Died 1956 Born 1888 S:17

Mowry, Margaret A - Died 1967 Born 1884 (with George M Black) S:11

Moynihan, William P - Died 1971 Born 1900 S:16

Mullaney, Angeline G - Died 1844 Born 1879 (with Owen & Ruth Mullaney) S:18

Mullaney, Owen J - Died 1951 Born 1881 (with Angeline & Ruth Mullaney) S:18

Mullaney, Rebecca K - Died 1909

Mullaney (Cont.)
Sept 16 Age 56 years, 10 months, 9 days (stone is down from vandals) (next to Owen, Angeline & Ruth Mullaney) S:18

Mullaney, Ruth - Died (still living 1991?) Born 1910 (listed with Owen & Angeline Mullaney) S:18

Mulligan, Bertha E - Died 1944 Born 1873 S:16

Mulloy, Lawrence E - Died 1961 Born 1900 S:14

Muncherian, David Steven - Died 1985 Born 1955 Son of Stanley & Mary Muncherian (with them) S:20

Muncherian, Mary - Died (still living 1991?) Born 1921 Stone says, "Mother" (with Stanley & son, David Muncherian) S:20

Muncherian, Stanley S - Died (still living 1991?) Born 1912 Stone says, "Father" (with Mary & David Muncherian) S:20

Munro, Alexander - Died 1958 Born 1877 S:13

Munroe, Abigail - Died 1844 May 1 Born 1753 Jan 30 Relict of the late, Daniel Munroe of Boston Oldest dau of Jona Parker of Roxbury, Mass Early devoted as a christian,her life was tranquil and happy Her death peaceful & resigned (in Munroe plot) S:10

Munroe, Elizabeth - Died 1922 Born 1831 (in Munroe plot) S:10

Munroe, John - Died 1879 Feb 26 Born 1784 Oct 11 (in Munroe plot) S:10

Munroe, Nancy - Died 1880 Jan 27 Born 1791 Nov 19 (in Munroe plot) S:10

Munroe, Sarah - Died 1822 (?) May 28 Born 1822 April 26 (in Munroe plot) Daughter of John & Nancy Munroe (small stone) S:10

Munson, Florence O - Buried 1985 April 6 Age 99 Located in section 3, lot 41, grave 5 S:15R

Munz, Rose L - Died 1960 Born 1874 (next to Marian Munz

Munz (Cont.)
Warren) (stone are alike) S:20

Murdy, Anne B - Died 1971 Born 1901 (with C Gerald Murdy) S:16

Murdy, C Gerald - Died 1983 Born 1900 (has 2 stones) Was a SK2 in US Navy during World War I & II (with Anne B Murdy) S:16

Murphy, Alice B - Died 1944 May 31 Born 1866 Oct 20 (with William T Murphy & others) S:31

Murphy, Annie C - Died 1945 Born 1868 Wife of Hugh Murphy (next to him) S:31

Murphy, Caroline Doane - Died 1941 Born 1866 (with Francis William Murphy & others) S:31

Murphy, Edward T - Died 1983 Born 1903 Was a Pvt in US Army during World War II (next to Ruth E Pelton Murphy) S:20

Murphy, Elizabeth F - Died 1919 Born 1880 S:31

Murphy, Francis William - Died 1910 Born 1907 (with William Shields & others) S:31

Murphy, Frederick Edmund - Died 1927 Born 1859 (with Caroline Doane Murphy & others) S:31

Murphy, Hattie M - Died 1940 Born 1867 (next to Lester W Murphy) S:18

Murphy, Hugh - Died 1952 Born 1870 (next to wife, Annie C Murphy) S:31

Murphy, James (Jim) P - Died 1977 Born 1897 (with Marie Luise L (Blanche) Murphy) S:15

Murphy, James Jr - Died 1948 Born 1900 (with parents, & Patrick Murphy & others) S:20

Murphy, James Leo - Died 1990 Born 1916 (a rock stone) (with Lutie Lucas Murphy) S:20

Murphy, James S - Died 1941 March 24 Born 1860 April 2 (with Alice B Murphy & others) S:31

Murphy, Jan E - Died 1972 May 9 Born 1894 Sept 2 S:15

Murphy, Jeremiah A - Died 1970

Murphy (Cont.)

July 14 Born 1896 May 9 From Massachusetts, was Private in BTRY 74, Artillery CAC during World War I S:14

Murphy, Lester W - Died 1960 Born 1896 (with Hattie M Murphy) S:18

Murphy, Lutie Lucas - Died (still living 1991?) Born 1917 (listed with James Murphy) S:20

Murphy, Marie Louise L (Blanche) - Died 1981 Born 1897 (with James P Murphy) S:15

Murphy, Mary - Died 1908 April 20 Born 1838 Nov 1 (with Patrick N Murphy & others) S:31

Murphy, Mary Eagles - Died 1988 Born 1916 S:20

Murphy, Patrick - Died 1866 Aug 16 Born 1832 April 16 (with Mary Murphy & others) S:31

Murphy, Patrick N - Died 1932 Born 1867 (with wife, Sarah V Murphy & others) S:31

Murphy, Ruth E Pelton - Died 1989 March 26 Born 1917 April 20 (next to Edward Murphy) S:20

Murphy, Ruth Elizabeth (Menchin) - Died 1961 Born 1908 S:19

Murphy, Sarah V - Died 1945 Born 1869 Wife of Patrick Murphy (with him & James Jr & Sr Murphy & others) S:31

Murphy, Vincent T - Died 1960 Nov 9 Born 1898 Dec 17 Massachusetts Cpl Co B9 Engineers Training BN WWII (next to Hugh & Annie Murphy) S:31

Murphy, William Edmard - Died 1987 Born 1898 Was a Major in US Army during World War II S:16

Murphy, William T - Died 1948 Born 1863 (with James Murphy Jr & others) S:31

Murray, Archibald - Died 1916 Born 1849 (next to Margaret A Murray) S:18

Murray, Arthur David - Died 1957 March 30 Born 1883 June 1 From Massachusetts, was LCDR

Murray (Cont.)

in US Navy during World War I & II (next to Effie Taylor Murray) S:18

Murray, Catherine D - Died 1949 Born 1859 (with David L Bryant & others) S:18

Murray, Charlotte A - Died 1940 Born 1860 Wife of Joseph R Murray (with him & Ira D H Murray & others) S:18

Murray, Chester A - Died 1969 July 12 Born 1889 Dec 23 (next to Mildred H Murray & others) From Massachusetts, was Ensign in US Navy during World War I S:18

Murray, Christine - Died 1980 March 1 Born 1900 March 13 (next to Jesse Murray) S:13

Murray, Doris E - Died (still living 1991?) Born 1900 (listed with Frederick L Murray) S:15

Murray, Doris Emerson - Buried 1987 Feb 20 Age 88 S:15R

Murray, Effie Taylor - Died 1986 Dec 26 Born 1895 April 20 (next to Arthur David Murray) Stone says,"Mother of Arlene T Kenneth & Thelma E" S:18

Murray, Ella M - Died 1962 Born 1888 (with Mary M Murray & others) S:18

Murray, Francis G - Died 1972 Born 1889 (next to Margaret C Murray) S:15

Murray, Frederick L - Died 1973 Born 1896 (with Doris E Murray) S:15

Murray, Gertrude A - Died 1956 Born 1887 (with Mildred H & Ira DH Murray & others) S:18

Murray, Ira DH - Died 1952 Born 1886 (with wife, Gertrude A Murray & Charlotte A Murray & others) S:18

Murray, Jesse - Died 1984 Jan 10 Born 1892 Jan 20 He was in MM2 US Navy during World War 1 (next to Christine Murray) S:13

Murray, John D - Died 1954 July 3

Murray (Cont.)
Born 1887 May 22 (with Capt
George N Fuller & others) S:14

Murray, Joseph R - Died 1933
Born 1858 (with wife, Charlotte
A Murray) S:18

Murray, Karin A - Died 1983 Born
1895 (with Patrick Murray) S:15

Murray, Margaret A - Died 1921
Born 1854 (next to Archibald
Murray) S:18

Murray, Margaret C - Died 1972
Born 1890 (next to Francis G
Murray) S:15

Murray, Maria Ellen - Died 1943
Born 1857 (with Robert B
Murray & others) S:18

Murray, Mary M - Died 1964 Born
1893 (with Catherine D Murray
& others) S:18

Murray, Mildred H - Died 1963
Born 1889 (with Gertrude A
Murray & others) S:18

Murray, Nina L - Died 1954 July 24
Born 1878 April 11 (with Capt
George N Fuller & others) S:14

Murray, Patrick - Died 1988 Born
1894 (with Karin A Murray) S:15

Murray, Robert B - Died 1911 Born
1900 (with Ella M Murray &
others) S:18

Murray, Robert P - Died 1934 Born
1856 (with Maria Ellen Murray
& others) S:18

Murray, Rosamond M Johnstone -
Died 1961 Born 1886 (with
Minnie M Flexon) S:18

Murzic, Mary - Died 1898 Born
1892 Stone says, "Mother" (next
to John S Nunes, possible
husband) S:15

Mutsch, Marie (Eauri) - Died 1902
Born 1835 (with Freeman C
Adams & others) S:12

Mutsch, Mathilde L - Died 1969
Born 1873 (with Freeman C
Adams & others) S:12

Myers, Agnes T - Died 1987 Born
1896 (with James E Myers) S:16

Myers, Elizabeth Hopkins - Died
1912 Born 1834 (with Margarette Dwight Ward & others)

Myers (Cont.)
S:18

Myers, James E - Died 1988 Born
1901 (with Agnes T Myers) S:16

Myers, Sara - Died 1968 Born 1887
(with Mishey Burgess) S:17

Myles, J Maude - Died 1969 Born
1892 S:15

Nash, Emily S - Died 1953 Born
1875 (possibly daughter of Caleb
& Drusilla Whitford, buried with
them and other family members
with later dates as, Hatch) S:8

Nash, Harold, W - Died 1979 Born
1890 (next to wife, Harriot M
Waldron) S:11

Nathan West - Died 20th (stone
worn, not clear) Son of Nathan &
Sarah West S:12

Needham, James J - Died 1922
Born 1857 (perpetual care)
(buried with Mildred L Douglas)
S:8

Neil, Donald R - Died 1968 Born
1912 (with Douglas A Neil &
others) S:19

Neil, Douglas A - Died 1990 Born
1911 (with Raymond Neil &
others) S:19

Neil, Raymond J - Died 1942 Born
1888 (with wife, Mabel G Dimery
& others) S:19

Nelson, Albert - Died 1868 Born
1868 (with Charles & Annie
Nelson & Charlotte Rogers) S:19

Nelson, Annie Maria - Died 1873
Born 1871 (with Charles, Albert
Nelson) S:19

Nelson, Carl R - Died 1982 Born
1897 (with Greta Nelson) S:13

Nelson, Charles Franklin - Died
1874 Born 1862 (with Annie
Maria Nelson & others) S:19

Nelson, Edward B Sr - Died 1972
Born 1906 Stone says,"The
White Chief" (with Savva &
Elisabeth Kulakovs) S:17

Nelson, Greta - Died 1987 Born
1906 (with Carl R Nelson) S:13

Nelson, Josephine M - Died 1940
Born 1875 S:8

Nelson, Lilliam - Died 1978 Born

Nelson (Cont.)
1897 (next to Peter Francis
Nelson) S:15

Nelson, Peter Francis - Died 1964
Jan 4 Born 1898 Jan 7 From
Massachusetts, was PFC in
Quartermaster Corps during
World War I (next to Lillian
Nelson) S:15

Nelson, Rosanna - Died 1887 Feb
19 Age 40 Wife of William Nelson
(on same stone) S:11

Nelson, William - Died 1879 Nov 11
Age 65 (with Rosanna Nelson,
his wife) S:11

Nelson, William J - Died (no dates)
Born 1878 (with wife, Mary T
Doyle & next to William M
Nelson) S:19

Nelson, William M - Died 1952
Born 1902 (also has Barnstable
Fire Dept plaque) (next to Wil-
liam J Nelson & Mary T Doyle)
S:19

Nese, William - Died 1991 Born
1914 (a small plaque in ground,
no stone yet) S:13

Nevala, Esa - Died 1974 Born 1893
(next to Olivia P Nevala, wife)
S:18

Nevala, Olivia P - Died 1970 Born
1886 Wife of Esa Nevala (with
him) S:18

Neves, Joseph D - Died 1959 Born
1893 (with Olivia E Neves) S:16

Neves, Olivia E - Died 1970 Born
1888 (with Joseph D Neves) S:16

Newell, Elmer F (Rev) - Died 1929
Born 1864 (buried with wife,
Lucy P Hallett) S:8

Newell, Frederick William - Died
1892 Born 1892 Son of Rev
Elmer F Newell & Lucy Hallett
(buried with them) S:8

Newell, Harriet - Died 1827 March
1 Age 1 year, 6 months Daughter of Maxan(?) & Lydia Coleman
S:14

Newell, Mary E - Died 1974 Born
1879 S:15

Newton, Adeline - Died 1975 Born
1899 Wife of John E Newton

Newton (Cont.)
(with him) S:14

Newton, John E - Died 1968 Born
1897 (he was a Mason) From
Massachusetts, was a MM2
USNRF during World War I (with
wife, Adeline Newton) S:14

Nicholas, Anthony - Died (still
living 1991?) Born 1897 (with
wife, Catherine C Foster) S:15

Nichols, Ann - Died (no dates)
(between John McGinlay & Isaac
DeGrace) S:18

Nichols, Blanche E - Died 1977
Born 1895 S:17

Nicholson, Mabel A - Died 1913
Born 1885 (with James Harold
Foote & others) S:31

Nickerson, (baby) - Died 1871 Oct
7 (next to Chester W Nickerson)
S:14

Nickerson, (infant) - Died (not
listed) Child of Roland & Emily
Nickerson (with Susan and Seth
Nickerson, brother & sister) S:14

Nickerson, (infant) - Died (not
listed) Child of Roland & Emily
Nickerson (with Susan & Seth
Nickerson, brother & sister) S:14

Nickerson, (infant) - Died 1873
June 17 (with Carlton & Luella
Nickerson) S:14

Nickerson, A Ernest - Died 1952
Born 1869 (with William Henry
Bearse) S:12

Nickerson, Aaron - Died 1866 Jan
8 Born 1792 Oct 15 (next to
Martha Nickerson, her stone
leaning against his) S:14

Nickerson, Aaron - Died 1889 Feb
27 Born 1816 May 2 (with Caroline O Nickerson) (Mosswood
cemetery records say death date
was 1869?) S:14

Nickerson, Abby (Abigail) - Died
1876 Nov 13 Age 75 years, 3
months, 7 days (next to husband, Leander W Nickerson)
S:14

Nickerson, Abigail - Died 1907
Born 1817 (with Daniel Nickerson) S:14

Nickerson, Abigail C - Died 1861 July 5 Age 43 years, 1 month, 18 days (next to David P Nickerson) S:14

Nickerson, Adaline Died 1880 July 20 Age 59 years, 11 months Stone says,"Mother" Wife of Joseph Nickerson (next to Asa N Nickerson) S:14

Nickerson, Addie - Died 1882 Sept 22 Age 11 months, 3 days Daughter of Luther & Vila Nickerson(next to them) S:14

Nickerson, Addie Linnell - Died 1952 Born 1874 (with William Henry Bearse) S:12

Nickerson, Adelaide M - Died 1925 Born 1843 Wife of George Nickerson (with him) S:14

Nickerson, Albert B - Died 1878 Born 1853 (with Ann R Nickerson) S:14

Nickerson, Albert B - Died 1948 Born 1882 (with Jessie F Nickerson) S:14

Nickerson, Alexander E - Died 1910 Born 1841 (with Hepsie R Nickerson) S:14

Nickerson, Alfred P - Died 1858 June 6 Age 2 years, 1 month, 1 day Son of Franklin & Ruth B Nickerson S:4

Nickerson, Alice B - Died 1970 Born 1894 Wife of Fred T Nickerson (with him) S:19

Nickerson, Alice M - Died 1880? March 28 (Mosswood cemetery records say 1850) Dau of Isaiah & Adalaid Nickerson (next to Millisa A Nickerson) S:14

Nickerson, Amelia - Died 1890 Aug 5 Age 86 or 56? Wife of Thomas Brooks Nickerson (next to him) S:19

Nickerson, Andrew C - Buried 1919 Jan 29 Located in section O, lot 21, grave 1 S:14R

Nickerson, Ann ? Died (small stone, info all worn off, next to others, Clara & Hannah Nickerson) S:14

Nickerson, Ann M - Died (no dates)

Nickerson (Cont.)
Infant (Mosswood ceme records, bur 30 April 1889) (with Ruth & Ensign Nickerson) S:14R

Nickerson, Ann R - Died 1845 Born 1843 (with Caroline O Nickerson) S:14

Nickerson, Annie S - Died 1935 Born 1848 (with Samuel Nickerson & Frank M C Nickerson) S:18

Nickerson, Asa N - Died 1889 Dec 11 Age 43 years, 1 month, 1 day (next to Adaline Nickerson d1880) S:14

Nickerson, Augusta W - Died 1933 July 26 Born 1855 Jan 31 (with Charles & Effie Norris) S:18

Nickerson, Augustus F - Died 1852 ? June 4 Age 46 years, 7 months ? Son of Samuel & Lydia Nickerson (next to mother) S:14

Nickerson, Aurilla C - Died 1917 Born 1861 Wife of Charles S Breed (with him) S:14

Nickerson, Benjamin F - Died 1887 May 14 Age 15 years, 1 month (next to Benjamin F Nickerson d1888) S:14

Nickerson, Benjamin F Jr - Died 1888 April 26 Age 10 months, 8 days (stone small & worn) Son of Benjamin F & Camie (?) Nickerson (next to Benjamin F Nickerson d1887) S:14

Nickerson, Carlton B - Died (no date) Born 1816 April 18 (with Luella Nickerson) S:14

Nickerson, Caroline A - Died 1950 Born 1855 Wife of William Crocker (with him & Charlotte L Parker) S:14

Nickerson, Caroline D - Buried 1886 Sept 1 Located in section R, lot 35, grave 2 S:14R

Nickerson, Caroline O - Died 1903 Aug 29 Born 1817 Mar 8 (with Aaron Nickerson) S:14

Nickerson, Charles (?) - Died 18?? Sept 20 Age ? years, ? Months, 15 days (stone worn) Son of Shedrick & Lucinda Nickerson

Nickerson (Cont.)
(next to brother, Charlie S
Nickerson) S:14

Nickerson, Charles A - Died 1967
March 20 Born 1894 Sept 11
(with Nellie & Gustavas Nickerson) S:14

Nickerson, Charles F - Died 1988
Born 1902 (with wife, Maude Y
Nickerson) S:15

Nickerson, Charlie S - Died 1862
July 28 Age 11(?) years, 10
months, 20 days Son of Shedrick & Lucinda Nickerson (next
to them) S:14

Nickerson, Charlotte W - Died
1953 Born 1873 (with Collins E
& Annie Clark) S:11

Nickerson, Chester T - Died 1917
Born 1895 (with Matthew H
Nickerson & others) S:21

Nickerson, Chester W - Died 1866?
(small stone, worn) (next to
(Baby) Nickerson, d1871) S:14

Nickerson, Clara - Died (no info,
small stone, next to other small
stones, Ann ?, & Hannah Nickerson) S:14

Nickerson, Clara H - Died 1909
Oct 21 Age 86 (next to Horace
Nickerson) S:14

Nickerson, Clarentine J - Died
1831(?) Sept 4 Age 9 months
Son of Leander & Abigail Nickerson (next to mother, Abby Nickerson) S:14

Nickerson, Clarentine J - Died
1875 Born 1837 (with Julius &
Helen Linnell) S:14

Nickerson, Clarissa - Died 1869
Mar 5 Age 70 Wife of Leonard
Nickerson (next to him) S:14

Nickerson, Claude S - Died 1962
Sept 30 Born 1891 Mar 8 From
Massachusetts, was Corporal in
CoF, 301 Sup Tn 76th Division
during World war I (with wife,
Myrtle Savery) S:14

Nickerson, Crisylda(?) - Died 1843
Mar 28 Age 30 (stone worn) Wife
of Isaiah Nickerson (next to
David P Nickerson) S:14

Nickerson, Daniel - Died 1884
Born 1811 (with Minerva H
Nickerson) S:14

Nickerson, Daniel H - Died 1943
March 4 Born 1870 Jan 22 (with
wife, Hattie L Nickerson & others) S:19

Nickerson, Daniel R - Died 1898
Born 1893 (with Chester T
Nickerson & others) S:21

Nickerson, Dann E - Died 1898
Feb 1 Born 1892 Aug 17 (small
stone) (last name looks like
Nickerson, next to Harry M
Nickerson) S:21

Nickerson, David - Died 1898 Oct
22 Age 78 (with Mary A Nickerson, his wife) S:11

Nickerson, David P - Died 1886
May 4 Age 72 years, 6 months, 8
days (next to Abigail C Nickerson) S:14

Nickerson, Debor Lia(?) - Died
1826 April 23 Age 5 months, 18
days Dau of Leander & Abigail
Nickerson (next to brother,
Clarentine J Nickerson) S:14

Nickerson, Deliah B - Buried 1916
Located in section O, lot 13,
grave 9 S:14R

Nickerson, Ebenezer - Died 1829
Aug 17 Age 26 Born 1803 Nov 9
in Harwich, Mass Stone says,
"Friend & Phycisian neer can
save the mortal body from the
grave nor will the grave confine
it here when christian judgement shall appear" S:14

Nickerson, Edgar - Died 1855 Oct
25 Son of Isaiah & Adalaid
Nickerson (next to Alice A Nickerson) S:14

Nickerson, Edson W - Died 1924
Born 1858 (with Mary A Nickerson) S:14

Nickerson, Eldridge S - Buried
1925 Located in section O, lot
25, grave 1 (found in cemetery
#14, died 1925, born 1895 and
is next to Ella L Nickerson)
S:14R

Nickerson, Eliza C - Died 1857

Nickerson (Cont.)

June 23 Age 10 years, 2 months, 20 days Daughter of Oliver A & Nancy C Nickerson (next to William F Nickerson, brother) S:14

Nickerson, Eliza J - Died 1873 July 30 Age 38 years, 9 months, 25 days Wife of Leander W Nickerson Jr (next to him) S:14

Nickerson, Eliza W - Died 1914 Born 1864 (next to Harry C Nickerson) S:14

Nickerson, Elizabeth F - Died 1931 Apr 27 Born 1848 Oct 29 (buried next to Samuel Nickerson) (two small stones next to them the initials on one is, O C) S:8

Nickerson, Elizabeth M - Died (still living 1991?) Born 1894 (listed with Shirley E Nickerson) S:15

Nickerson, Ella C - Died 1849 April 25 Age 13 months Daughter of Seth & Rozilla Nickerson Died at sea on board ship, Massachusetts (listed next to parents) S:14

Nickerson, Ella Doane - Died 1899 Sept 12 Born 1894 Sept 30 (with William R Nickerson & others) S:18

Nickerson, Ella L - Died (info under ground) (a very small childs stone next to Gilbert C Nickerson) (Mosswood cemetery burial records say 11 Sept 1878) S:14

Nickerson, Ella R - Died 1857 June 30 Age 7 years, 9 months Daughter of Oliver A & Nancy C Nickerson (next to Elva W Nickerson, sister) S:14

Nickerson, Ellen C - Died 1834 Oct 21 Age 1 year, 1 month Daughter of Samuel & Lydia Nickerson (next to family) S:14

Nickerson, Elva W - Died 1857 June 26 Age 5 years, 8 months, 15 days Daughter of Oliver A & Nancy C Nickerson (next to Eliza C Nickerson, sister) S:14

Nickerson, Elvira - Died 1915 Born 1832 Wife of Charles Hallett (with him & others) S:19

Nickerson, Emeline A - Died 1896 March 8 Born 1841 July 18 (with Joseph F Nickerson) S:21

Nickerson, Emily F - Died 1905 Feb 15 Born 1828 July 1 (with husband, Roland T Nickerson) S:14

Nickerson, Ensign - Died 1848 Aug 29 Age 64 (next to wife, Rebecca Nickerson) S:14

Nickerson, Ensign - Died 1880 Nov 24 Born 1814 Sept 18 (with Ruth A Nickerson) S:14

Nickerson, Eunice M - Died 1910 Oct 25 Born 1850 May 17 (with Shubael A Nickerson) S:14

Nickerson, Eva I - Died 1943 Born 1872 (with Luther M Nickerson) S:14

Nickerson, Eva N - Died 1979 Born 1882 (with George W Nickerson) S:14

Nickerson, Everett W - Died 1848 Oct 1 Age 11 months, 4 days Son of Samuel & Lydia Nickerson (next to family) S:14

Nickerson, Fanny - Died 1866 May 23 Age 75 years, 5 months (stone worn) (next to seth Nickerson, d1892) S:14

Nickerson, Frank MC - Died 1956 Born 1877 (with Samuel & Annie Nickerson) S:18

Nickerson, Fred T - Died 1961 Born 1891 (with wife, Alice B Nickerson) S:19

Nickerson, Frederic A - Died 1856 Oct 16? Age 1(?) year (stone worn) Son of Charles Nickerson (next to Clarissa Nickerson) S:14

Nickerson, Freeman M - Died 1952 Born 1887 (with Genevieve M Nickerson) S:14

Nickerson, Genevieve M - Died 1952 Born 1886 (with Freeman M Nickerson) S:14

Nickerson, George W - Died 1948 Born 1878 (with Eva N Nickerson) S:14

Nickerson, George W (Capt) - Died 1879 Born 1840 Buried at sea (listed with wife, Adelaide M

Nickerson (Cont.)
Nickerson) S:14

Nickerson, Gilbert C - Died 1915 Born 1845 (next to Ella L Nickerson) S:14

Nickerson, Gladys R - Died (still living 1990?) Born 1896 Wife of Harold F Nickerson (large Holmes/Nickerson stone with family) S:11

Nickerson, Gustavus C - Died 1925 June 5 Born 1866 Sept 12 (with Nellie B Nickerson) S:14

Nickerson, Hannah - Died 1900? Born 1833 or 83? (stone worn and small next to other small stones, Ann? & Clara Nickerson) S:14

Nickerson, Hannah E - Died 1921 Oct 14 Born 1835 Nov 6 (stone is perpetual care) (buried with Joseph W Hinckley) S:8

Nickerson, Harold F - Died 1962 Born 1895 Member of the Barnstable Fire Dept, plaque & flag (large Holmes/Nickerson stone with family) S:11

Nickerson, Harold M - Died 1948 Born 1901 (with Daniel R Nickerson & others) S:21

Nickerson, Harriet S - Died 1942 Born 1862 Wife of Thomas Nickerson (with him & Ella Nickerson & others) S:18

Nickerson, Harry C - Died 1954 Born 1873 (next to Henry W Nickerson) S:14

Nickerson, Harry M - Died 1961 Born 1897 (with Henry T Nickerson & others) S:21

Nickerson, Hattie C - Died 1886 May 7 Age 34 years, 4 months, 12 days Wife of Capt Wendell Nickerson S:12

Nickerson, Hattie L - Died 1936 Nov 17 Born 1870 May 5 Wife of Daniel H Nickerson (with him & Lester & Elizabeth A Morey) S:19

Nickerson, Henry Francis - Died 1858 Jan 14 Age 3 years, 6 months Son of Franklin & Ruth B Nickerson S:4

Nickerson, Henry T - Died 1935 Born 1865 (with wife, Ellen McKinley & others) S:21

Nickerson, Henry W - Died 1913 Born 1851 (next to Lizzie F Nickerson) S:14

Nickerson, Hepsie R - Died 1921 Born 1844 (with Alexander E Nickerson) S:14

Nickerson, Herbert - Died 1948 Sept 26 Born 1876 July 27 From Massachusetts, was CMM in USNRF during World War I S:14

Nickerson, Horace - Died 1883 April 3 Age 62 years, 9 months, 12 days (next to Clara H Nickerson) S:14

Nickerson, Horace W - Died 1940 June 28 Born 1854 Feb 24 (with wife, Ida C Lang) S:14

Nickerson, Howard E - Died 1852 Sept 4 Age 1 year, 9 months, 8 days Son of Samuel & Lydia Nickerson (next to family) S:14

Nickerson, Ina F - Died 1951 Born 1862 (next to Victor H Nickerson) S:14

Nickerson, Irene C - Died 1972 Born 1906 (with Nathan C Nickerson) S:11

Nickerson, Isabel T - Died 1928 Oct 30 Born 1848 May 29 (next to Julius Nickerson) S:14

Nickerson, Jarvis R - Buried 1892 Located in section O, lot 13, grave 8 S:14R

Nickerson, Jennie M - Died 1934 Born 1857 (with Capt Willis T Nickerson) S:14

Nickerson, Jessie F - Died 1962 Born 1883 (with Albert B Nickerson) S:14

Nickerson, Joseph - Died 1877 Born 1852 (On 2 stones) (with Robert Nickerson & Thomas Brook Nickerson) S:19

Nickerson, Joseph F - Died 1934 Dec 29 Born 1835 Jan 21 (with Emeline A Nickerson) S:21

Nickerson, Judson V - Died 1878 Nov 6 in Sterling, Kansas Age 23 Son of Samuel & Ursalind A

Nickerson (Cont.)
Nickerson (listed next to mother)
His stone says, "His sun went
down in manhood morn" S:14

Nickerson, Julius - Died 1920 Jan
13 Born 1855 Sept 22 (next to
Isabel T Nickerson) S:14

Nickerson, Katie G - Died 1943
Born 1872 (with Thomas & Ella
Nickerson) S:18

Nickerson, Laura D - Buried 1875
Oct 4 Located in section O, lot
12, grave 4 S:14R

Nickerson, Leander W - Died 1884
Oct 10 Age 80 years, 7 months
(next to wife, Abby Nickerson)
S:14

Nickerson, Leander W - Died 1895
June 21 Age 62 years, 5 months,
2 days (next to wife, Eliza J
Nickerson) (he is listed as Jr on
wife's stone) S:14

Nickerson, Leonard (Capt) - Died
1854? Aug 9 Age 60 (next to
wife, Clarissa and listed with
Mulford Nickerson) S:14

Nickerson, Lester W - Died 1923
Born 1880 (with Roland D
Nickerson) S:14

Nickerson, Levi P - Died 1912 Born
1834 (with Thankful S Nickerson) S:14

Nickerson, Lizzie F - Died 1944
Born 1857 (next to Henry W
Nickerson) S:14

Nickerson, Lucinda J - Died 1872
July 18 Age 50 years, 3 months,
11 days Wife of Shedrick (next to
him) S:14

Nickerson, Luella - Died 1904 Feb
27 Born 1806 Dec 20 (with
Carlton B Nickerson) S:14

Nickerson, Luella C - Buried 1933
Located in section S, lot 2, grave
5 S:14R

Nickerson, Luther - Died 1893 May
3 Born 1848 Nov 20 (next to
wife, Vila Nickerson) S:14

Nickerson, Luther M - Died 1951
Born 1874 (with Eva I Nickerson) S:14

Nickerson, Lydia S - Died 1852

Nickerson (Cont.)
Sept 22 Age 41 Wife of Samuel
Nickerson (next to him) S:14

Nickerson, Martha - Died 1861
Sept 13 Born 1790 April 10
(stone leaning against Aaron
Nickerson) S:14

Nickerson, Martha A - Died 1899
March 2 Age 75 years, 6
months, 15 days Wife of Shubael
Nickerson (next to him) S:14

Nickerson, Martha B - Died 1929
Born 1827 (next to Shedrick
Nickerson) S:14

Nickerson, Mary A - Died 1868 Jan
9 Age 39 Wife of David Nickerson
(with him) S:11

Nickerson, Mary A - Died 1944
Born 1858 (with Edson W Nickerson) S:14

Nickerson, Mary Annette - Died
1933 June 4 Born 1855 June 28
Wife of Sidney E Nickerson (next
to him) S:18

Nickerson, Mary E - Died 1910
Born 1846 Wife of William J
Nickerson MD (with him) S:18

Nickerson, Mary Handren - Died
1944 Born 1864 Wife of Benjamin Small (with her) S:14

Nickerson, Matthew H - Died 1958
Born 1899 (with Harry M Nickerson & others) S:21

Nickerson, Maude Y - Died (still
living 1991?) Born 1898 (with
husband, Charles F Nickerson)
S:15

Nickerson, Mazeppa - Died 1912
June 26 Born 1837 Dec 13
(large stone) (buried with Mary
Williams Crosby-wife) S:8

Nickerson, Melinda F - Buried
1919 Located in section O, lot
13, grave 10 S:14R

Nickerson, Melissa A - Died 1885
Born 1848 (with Albert B Nickerson) S:14

Nickerson, Millisa A - Died 1818
Oct (Mosswood ceme records say
1848?) Daughter of Isaiah &
Adalaid Nickerson (next to Alice
M Nickerson) S:14

Nickerson, Minerva H - Died 1835 Born 1818 (with Daniel Nickerson) S:14

Nickerson, Minerva M - Died 1914 April 29 Born 1843 or 1848 17th (with Shubael Baxter & others) S:13

Nickerson, Mulford - Died 1838 July 23 at Brewster, Massachusetts Age 21 Son of Leonard Nickerson (with him) S:14

Nickerson, Nancy C - Died 1895 Nov 14 Age 76 Wife of Oliver A Nickerson (next to him) S:14

Nickerson, Nathan C - Died 1972 Born 1891 (with Irene C Nickerson) S:11

Nickerson, Nellie B - Died 1950 June 5 Born 1866 Dec 23 (with Gustavus & Charles Nickerson) S:14

Nickerson, Oliver A - Died 1852 April 9 Age 35 years, 8 months, 12 days Who was drowned in Cotuit Harbour & found on Squino(?) Island on 10 June (next to wife, Nancy C Nickerson) S:14

Nickerson, Orin P - Died 1935 Born 1854 (with wife, Nellie V Makepeace) S:14

Nickerson, Rebecca - Died 1866 April 16 Age 76 wife of Ensign Nickerson (next to him) S:14

Nickerson, Rebecca H - Died 1880 Born 1811 Wife of Richard Handy (with him) S:14

Nickerson, Rhoda - Died 1866 Jan 9 Wife of Samuel Nickerson (next to him) S:14

Nickerson, Robert - Died 1890 Born 1857 (with Joseph Nickerson & Thomas Brook Nickerson) S:19

Nickerson, Rodney W - Died 1847? May 31 Age 2 years, 9 months Son of Samuel & Lydia Nickerson (next to mother) S:14

Nickerson, Roland D - Died 1973 Born 1889 (with Lester W Nickerson) S:14

Nickerson, Roland T - Died 1905

Nickerson (Cont.)
Feb 17 Born 1826 Sept 19 Stone says, "Father" (with wife, Emily F Nickerson) S:14

Nickerson, Rose W - Died (no dates) Infant (with Ruth & Ensign Nickerson) S:14

Nickerson, Rosilla - Died 1886 Feb 15 Age 65 years, 6 months Stone says, "Mother" Wife of Seth Nickerson (with him) S:14

Nickerson, Ruth - Died 1883 Born 1815 Wife of Alexander Crowell (with him) S:21

Nickerson, Ruth A - Died 1865 Mar 8 Born 1819 Sept 15 (with Ensign Nickerson) S:14

Nickerson, Ruth A - Died 1940 Born 1870 (with William N Gilbert Clark, husband) S:14

Nickerson, Samuel - Died 183? Jan 19 Age 70 (stone not clear) (next to wife, Rhoda Nickerson) S:14

Nickerson, Samuel - Died 1884 Jan 15 Age 74 years, 7 months (between both wifes, Ursalind & Lydia Nickerson) S:14

Nickerson, Samuel - Died 1927 Jan 7 Born 1846 Oct 27 (buried with Elizabeth F Nickerson) S:8

Nickerson, Samuel B - Died 1895 Born 1841 (with Annie S Nickerson) S:18

Nickerson, Seth - Died 1892 Mar 2 Age 77 years, 8 months, 12 days Stone says, "Father" (next to wife, Rosilla Nickerson) S:14

Nickerson, Seth Lincoln - Died 1868 Sept 10 Age 4 months, 23 years Son of Roland & Emily Nickerson (with sister, Susan A Nickerson) S:14

Nickerson, Shedrick - Died 1883 July 18 Age 66 years, 2 months (next to wife, Lucinda J Nickerson) S:14

Nickerson, Shirley E - Died 1967 Born 1881 (listed with Elizabeth M Nickerson) S:15

Nickerson, Shubael A - Died 1916 June 11 Born 1847 April 26

Nickerson (Cont.)
(with Eunice M Nickerson) S:14

Nickerson, Shubaul - Died 1879
Dec 21 Age 65 years, 2 months,
6 days (next to wife, Martha A
Nickerson) S:14

Nickerson, Sidney E - Died 1927
Oct 6 Born 1848 March 29 (next
to wife, Ella W Howes & wife,
Mary Annette Nickerson) S:18

Nickerson, Stanley A - Died 1877
Aug 31 Born 1877 Feb 10 (with
Carlton & Luella Nickerson) S:14

Nickerson, Stanley V - Died 1861
Sept 25 Age 5 years, 5 months,
25 days Son of Seth & Rozilla
Nickerson (next to them) S:14

Nickerson, Susan Addie - Died
1865 July 25 Age 6 months, 25
days Daughter of Roland T &
Emily F Nickerson (with brother,
Seth L Nickerson) S:14

Nickerson, Susan Eda - Died 1911
Born 1885 S:14

Nickerson, Tamson B - Died 1911
May 24 Born 1867 July 24
Stone says, "At rest" (with Capt
Wendall F Nickerson) S:14

Nickerson, Thankful S - Died 1913
Born 1833 (with Levi P Nickerson) S:14

Nickerson, Thomas Brooks - Died
1896 Feb 4 Age 77 Wife of
Amelia Nickerson (next to her)
S:19

Nickerson, Thomas W - Died 1938
Born 1862 (with Ella & Harriet
Nickerson & others) S:18

Nickerson, Ursalind A - Died 1914
Born 1824 Wife of Samuel
Nickerson (next to him) S:14

Nickerson, Victor H - Died 1934
Born 1858 (next to Ina F Nickerson) S:14

Nickerson, Vila - Died 1926 Born
1850 Stone says, "The angel
came and took her away" (next
to husband, Luther Nickerson)
Was the present wife of Thomas
Jones) S:14

Nickerson, Vila R - Died 1954 Born
1886 Wife of Joseph Brigham

Nickerson (Cont.)
(with him) S:14

Nickerson, Vincent - Died 1851
Dec 1 Age 79 yrs 9 mos Born
1778 (Stone not clear) S:3+3R

Nickerson, Violet E - Died (still
living 1990) Born 1916 Wife of
Winfield M Nickerson (next to
him) S:11

Nickerson, Wallace - Died (dates
worn off, small stone next to
Eliza & Leander Nickerson) S:14

Nickerson, Wendall F (Capt) - Died
1942 Born 1852 (with Tamson B
Nickerson) S:14

Nickerson, William F - Died 1843
June 17 Age 14 months Son of
Oliver A & Nancy C Nickerson
(next to father) S:14

Nickerson, William J (MD) - Died
1918 Born 1844 (with wife, Mary
E Nickerson) S:18

Nickerson, William R - Died 1875?
(small worn stone next to Frederic A Nickerson) Son of William(?)
Nickerson S:14

Nickerson, William R - Died 1942
Born 1871 (with Ella & Katie
Nickerson & others) S:18

Nickerson, Willis C - Died (still
living 1991?) Born 1891 (listed
with, Mary & Edson Nickerson)
S:14

Nickerson, Willis T (Capt) - Died
1928 Born 1850 (with Jennie M
Nickerson) S:14

Nickerson, Winfield M - Died 1971
Born 1916 (next to wife, Violet E
Nickerson) S:11

Nickula, Ruth L - Died (still living
1991?) Born 1923 S:20

Nicol, Alex (Brigadier) - Died 1981
Born 1890 Stone says,"Salvation
Army" (with Brigadier, Ethel A
Nicol) S:18

Nicol, Ethel A (Brigadier) - Died
1971 Born 1894 Stone
says,"Salvation Army" (with
Brigadier, Alex Nicol & next to
May L Nicol) S:18

Nicol, May L - Died 1984 Born
1898 (with William A Nicol) S:18

Nicol, William A - Died 1955 Born 1881 (with May L Nicol) S:18

Niskala, Jonas - Died 1957 Born 1881 (with Mary N Niskala) S:11

Niskala, Mary N - Died (still living 1990?) Born 1883 (death date not filled in) (listed with Jonas Niskala) S:11

Nordling, Anna - Died 1971 Born 1882 (with Gustaf A Nordling) S:12

Nordling, Gustaf A - Died 1979 Born 1887 (with Anna Nordling) S:12

Norris, (infant) - Died 1866 May 11 Age 1 day (with Elizabeth Norris, wife of Charles Norris, possible parents) S:18

Norris, Abby F Mrs - Died 1843 Nov 23 Age 31? Wife of Charles Norris (near him & next to other wife, Margaret Norris) S:18

Norris, Almena - Died 1925 Born 1846 (with Capt Robert Norris & others) S:18

Norris, Charles - Died 1891 Dec 27 Age 85 years, 2 months, 24 days (next to Huldah Norris) S:18

Norris, Charles W - Died 1908 Nov 2 Born 1850 Oct 25 (with Augusta Nickerson & Effie Norris) S:18

Norris, Chester R - Died 1963 April 17 Born 1893 Dec 4 From Massachusetts, was a SFC in 488 Aero Sq during World War I S:14

Norris, Effie C - Died 1892 Feb 7 Born 1875 Dec 1 (with Augusta Nickerson & Charles Norris) S:18

Norris, Elijah H - Died 1887 Born 1837 (with Robert Norris) S:18

Norris, Elizabeth - Died 1866 May 20 Age 39 years, 6 months Wife of Charles Norris (with infant Norris d1866 & next to Husband) S:18

Norris, Elza - Died 1910 Born 1845 (with Almena Norris & others) S:18

Norris, Emma H - Died 1843 June

Norris (Cont.)
14 Age 9 months, 15 days (stone worn) Daughter of John & Hope Norris (next to James or Harris Norris) S:21

Norris, Ernest B - Died 1967 Nov 15 Born 1888 March 4 (has 2 stones) From Massachusetts, was Cpl in Co 5, 151 Depot Brig during World War I (with H Avis Norris) S:18

Norris, Florence Bliss - Died 1885 July 24 Age 37 years, 2 months (next to Theodore Norris) S:18

Norris, H Avis - Died 1959 Born 1898 (with Ernest B Norris) S:18

Norris, Hope S - Died 1884 Dec 30 Age 73 years, 3 months, 14 days (next to husband, Capt John Norris) S:21

Norris, Huldah - Died 1904 July 10 sage 74 years, 11 months, 11 days (next to Charles Norris) S:18

Norris, James B - Died 1882 Aug 6 Born 1856 May 17 (next to possible mother, Louisa Leavitt) S:21

Norris, James or Harris? - Died 1845 Sept 22 Age 10 months?, 2 days Son of John & Hope Norris (next to them) S:21

Norris, Jane M - Died 1859 Jan 15 Age 28 years, 6 months Wife of William Norris S:4

Norris, John (Capt) - Died 1887 May 15 Age 73 years, 11 months, 19 days (next to wife, Hope S Norris) S:21

Norris, John Edward - Died 1906 Feb Born 1848 May Age 57 years, 9 months, 27 days (next to Capt John & Hope Norris) S:21

Norris, Love - Died 1881 Born 1802 (with Robert Norris & others) S:18

Norris, Margaret - Died 1854 Aug 4 Age 31 years, 6 months Wife of Charles Norris (next to him) S:18

Norris, Mary - Died 1830 May 25 in her 52nd yr Wife of Peter Norris

Norris (Cont.)
S:4

Norris, Mary H - Died 1832 Oct 12 Age 1 year, 10 months Daughter of Robert & Love Norris S:4

Norris, Peter - Died 1865 Oct 4 in his 89th yr S:4

Norris, Robert - Died 1873 Born 1833 (with Capt Robert Norris & Elijah H Norris & others) S:18

Norris, Theodore - Died 1903 Jan 24 Age 59 years, 11 months (with Florence Bliss Norris) S:18

Norris, Thomas (Capt) - Died 1843 Sept 1 S:4

Norris, Willhelmina - Died 1846 Aug 8 Age 6 months, 12 days Daughter of Peter & Louisa L Norris (with mother, Louisa L Leavitt) S:21

Norris, William Sherman - Died 1858 Oct 26 Age 15 years, 3 months Son of Peter & Louisa L Norris (next to James B Norris & others) S:21

Northrop, Gladys E - Died 1977 Born 1900 (with Henry S Northrop) S:15

Northrop, Henry S - Died 1974 Born 1898 (with Gladys E Northrop) S:15

Norton, Francis Carlton - Died (still living 1991?) Born 1918 April 5 (listed with Natalie Tolman K Norton & others) S:19

Norton, Frederick Thomas - Died 1969 March 13 Born 1912 Aug 9 (2 stones) Stone says," Beloved Brother" (with William Paul Kunze & others) S:19

Norton, George F - Died 1975 Born 1909 Stone says "Beloved Husband" (between Vera Norton & Frederick Thomas Norton) S:19

Norton, George Francis - Died 1975 Sept 27 Born 1909 Dec 23 (with Francis Carlton Norton & others) S:19

Norton, Judith M - Died 1989 Born 1945 Stone says,"Beloved sister" S:19

Norton, Natalie Tolman K - Died 1962 Jan 4 Born 1905 April 22 (with Donald Wayne Kunze & others) S:19

Norton, Vera B - Died (still living 1991?) Born 1909 Stone says,"Beloved mother" (next to George F Norton) S:19

Novak, Joseph J - Died (still living 1990) Born 1912 (with Elizabeth L Bratton) A Veteran in Army, American Legion in World War II S:11

Novak, Stephen C - Died 1966 Born 1883 Interred at Tulocay Cemetery, Napa, California (on same stone with Elizabeth L Bratton) S:11

Noyes, Alberta H - Died (still living 1991?) Wife of Alfred B Noyes (listed next to him) S:19

Noyes, Alfred B - Died 1974 Aug 22 Born 1892 Sept 27 (has two stones) Was a Sargeant in US Army (with Archie Whitman & Marion Wood & next to wife, Alberta H Noyes) S:19

Nuciforo, Norberto - Died 1988 Born 1939 (undertaker plaque) S:20

Nunes, John S - Died 1987 Born 1897 Stone says,"Father" (next to possibly wife, Mary Murzic) S:15

Nunes, Julia R - Died 1981 Born 1898 (with Manuel J Nunes) S:16

Nunes, Manuel J - Died 1962 Born 1893 (with Julia R Nunes) S:16

Nurney, Thomas J - Died 1968 Born 1899 S:16

Nute, Beatrice J - Died 1916 Born 1894 (next to Christena Nute) S:13

Nute, Christena - Died 1946 Born 1872 (next to Beatrice J Nute) S:13

Nute, Edson A - Died 1936 Born 1907 S:13

Nute, Leslie F - Died 1982 Born 1904 S:13

Nute, Willis F - Died 1912 Born

Nute (Cont.)
1865 (next to Christena Nute) S:13

Nye, (daughter) - Died 1872 May 5 Age 1 year, 5 months Daughter of Marsus & Mary Nye (next to them, small stone) S:11

Nye, Abagail - Died 1838 Dec 5 in her 81st yr Widow of Stephen Nye S:5

Nye, Abigail - Died 1764 Dec 23 Age 17 Wife of Benjamin Nye S:5R

Nye, Abigail - Died 1858 Dec 5 in her 57th yr Widow of Stephen Nye S:6

Nye, Anne T - Died 1876 Dec 10 Born 1800 April 3 S:13

Nye, Annie H - Died 1924 Born 1859 S:10

Nye, Asa - Died 1859 Nov 12 Age 18 years, 10 months, 10 days S:5

Nye, Asa Mr - Died 1840 Apr 25 Age 76 years, 6 months S:5

Nye, Augustus B - Died 1926 Born 1857 (with Mabel l Nye & others) S:18

Nye, Betsey - Died (underground, stone very small) Daughter of Jabez & Polly (many stones missing in this row starting right next to this Betsey) S:11

Nye, Caroline - Died 1920 Born 1863 S:10

Nye, Chester B - Died 1935 Born 1885 (with Hiram Nye & others) S:18

Nye, Crocker - Died 1891 April 30 Age 63 years, 3 months Stone says- "Father" S:10

Nye, Eliza L - Died 1907 Born 1827 (with Peleg Nye) S:18

Nye, Elizabeth - Died 1788 Apr 13 Age 28 Born 1760 Daughter of Lemuel & Rebekah Nye S:5

Nye, Elizabeth C - Died 1860 Sept 28 Born 1867 July 9 (stones next to her are styled the same, they are, Mary Ann Nye & Marsus M Nye) S:11

Nye, Hannah - Died 1797 Aug 25

Nye (Cont.)
(buried next to Lot) Consort & wife of Lot Nye S:5

Nye, Hannah - Died 1897 Apr 28 Age 88 Born 1809 Mar 17 Wife of Stephen Nye S:5

Nye, Helen - Died 1893 May 12 Age 64 years, 7 months Daughter of Lot Nye & Abigail Otis S:9R

Nye, Hiram - Died 1913 Born 1816 (with Sarah Nye & others) S:18

Nye, J Lovell - Died 1942 Born 1888 (buried with Russell & Lena Nye, parents) S:8

Nye, Jabez - Died 1866 April 29 Age 85 years, 6 months S:11

Nye, James E - Died 1850 Sept 18 Age 1 year, 10 months, 16 days Son of James & Mary Nye (stone has perpetual care) S:11

Nye, James M - Died 1890 July 15 Born 1809 Oct 16 (family plot & stones has perpetual care) S:11

Nye, Josih - Died 1788 Oct 20 in his 20th yr Son of Lemuel & Rebekah Nye (buried next to them) S:5

Nye, Julia - Died 1866 Nov 2 Age 77 Wife of Salmon Nye (in family plot with perpetual care) S:11

Nye, Julia A - Died 1853 April 18 Born 1811 Mar 29 Wife of Capt William Loring (buried with him and others) S:11

Nye, Julia Ann - Died 1848 July 12 Age 44 Wife of Benjamin Nye & daughter of Ezra & Deborah Crowell S:11

Nye, Lemuel - Died 1814 July 1 in his 81st yr (buried next to wife, Rebekah) S:5

Nye, Lemuel - Died 1830 Feb 19 Age 50 S:5

Nye, Lena L - Died 1928 Born 1863 (buried with husband, Russell Nye) S:8

Nye, Lot - Died 1797 Aug 31 in his 67th yr (also listed in 5R records) S:5

Nye, Lydia - Died 1892 Feb 9 Born 1805 Nov 11 (stone knocked over on side) (next to Jabez Nye)

330

Nye (Cont.)
S:11

Nye, Mabel L - Died 1914 Born 1858 (with Chester B Nye & others) S:18

Nye, Mamie or Maurice - Died 1872 May 5 Age 1 year, 5 months Daughter of Marcus & Mary A Nye S:11R+26R

Nye, Marcy - Died May 3 (year not clear) Daughter of Stephen & Abigail Nye (Hinckley Ceme records #5R say death was 1784 Age 10 months, 16 days) S:5

Nye, Marion C - Died 1986 Born 1903 (next to husband, Richard C Nye) S:15

Nye, Marsus M - Died 1902 Oct 28 Born 1826 Nov 25 (next to Mary Ann Nye & Elizabeth C Nye, stones are styled the same) S:11

Nye, Mary Ann - Died 1924 May 1 Born 1846 Sept 15 (next to Elizabeth C Nye & Marsus M Nye, stones have same style) S:11

Nye, Mary C - Died 1966 Born 1869 (this grave overlooks the cemetery on the highest hill there) S:10

Nye, Mary J - Died 1886 Nov 28 Born 1813 Jan 30 Wife of James M Nye (buried next to him & others, plot has perpetual care) S:11

Nye, Mary M - Died 1919 Dec 12 Born 1814 May 2 (in family plot with perpetual care) S:11

Nye, Mary N - Died 1873 Oct 14 age 46 years, 1 month Wife of Crocker Nye (buried next to him) (stone says, "Mother") S:10

Nye, Mercy - Died 1851 June 8 age 82 years, 10 months Widow of Asa Nye S:5

Nye, Oliver - Died 1805 May 28 Son of Jonathan & Achsah Nye S:5

Nye, Paulie C - Died 1850's Oct 20 Age 68 (next to Jabez Nye) S:11

Nye, Peleg - Died 1896 Born 1817 (with Eliza L Nye) S:18

Nye, Polly C - Died 1900 Jan 5 Born 1812 Mar 8 (with Calvin Stetson) S:10

Nye, Polly G - Died 1858 Oct 28 Age 68 Wife of John Nye (this could be Jabez, she is buried next to him and so is children?) (Hinckley Ceme records #11R say death was 1853) S:11

Nye, Rachel - Died 1825 Feb 20 Age 23 Wife of Lieut Stephen Nye S:5

Nye, Rachel H - Died 1825 Oct 8 Age 8 months Daughter of Lieut Stephen & Rachel Nye S:5

Nye, Rachel H - Died 1897 April 18 Born 1831 Feb 1 (next to Temperance Nye) S:11

Nye, Rebecah - Died 1817 June 4 in her 82nd yr Widow of Lemuel Nye S:5

Nye, Rebekah - Died 1737 Feb Age 9 Daughter of Lemuel & Rebekah Nye S:5

Nye, Rebekah - Died 1787 Feb 7 Age 21 Daughter of Lemuel & Rebekah Nye S:5R

Nye, Richard C - Died 1974 Oct 10 Born 1898 April 8 (has 2 stones) Was a Pvt in US Army (next to wife, Marion C Nye) S:15

Nye, Russell - Died 1930 Born 1860 (buried with wife, Lena L Nye) S:8

Nye, Sarah - Died 1910 Born 1823 (with Hiram Nye & Chester B Nye & others) S:18

Nye, Stephen - Died 1791 Mar 25 in his 35th yr S:5

Nye, Stephen C - Died 1844 Oct 20 Age 42 Born 1802 Apr 11 S:5

Nye, Temperance - Died 1831 Aug 29 Age 51 Wife of Lemuel Nye S:5

Nye, Temperance - Died 1895 Oct 31 Born 1823 July 18 (next to Rachel H Nye) S:11

Nye, Thomas Hinckley - Died 1947 Born 1873 S:11

O'Brien, Andrew T - Died 1959 Feb 12 Born 1863 Dec 19 (with Mary C O'Brien) S:15

O'Brien, Blanche M - Died 1978 Born 1900 S:15

O'Brien, Elizabeth M - Died 1987 Born 1909 (with John J O'Brien) S:15

O'Brien, Ethel W - Died 1959 Born 1888 (Plaque sáys, "Womens relief Corp #175 WRC Dep MT") (with George H O'Brien) S:21

O'Brien, George H - Died 1943 Born 1887 (Plaque says,"Iyanough Tribe #14 Hyannis") (with Ethel W O'Brien) S:21

O'Brien, Helen - Died 1972 Born 1889 S:20

O'Brien, John J - Died 1965 Born 1900 (with Elizabeth M O'Brien) S:15

O'Brien, Mabel F - Died 1962 Born 1898 (with William G O'Brien) S:17

O'Brien, Margaret C - Died 1964 Born 1899 S:15

O'Brien, Mary C - Died 1972 Oct 30 Born 1881 July 5 (with Andrew T O'Brien) S:15

O'Brien, Mary Mollie - Died 1932 Born 1910 Niece of John & Margaret Hanlon (with them) S:16

O'Brien, William G - Died 1965 Born 1893 (with Mabel F O'Brien) S:17

O'Connell, Anne J - Died 1991 Born 1908 S:13

O'Connell, Denis - Died 1986 Born 1896 S:15

O'Donnell, Annie - Died 1964 Born 1879 (with Samuel J Molony) S:16

O'Donnell, Mary E - Died 1936 Born 1856 (with Margaret A Austin) S:16

O'Neal, Bartholomew - Died 1879 March 5 Age 36 b 1843 Buried with Margaret B O'Neal S:2

O'Neal, Margaret B - Died 1886 Aug 26 Age 48 Buried with Bartholomew O'Neal S:2

O'Neil, A Milan - Died 1982 Born 1898 (next to Emma, John, Agnes O'Neil) S:31

O'Neil, Agnes - Died 1971 Born 1885 (with Julian O'Neil & others) S:31

O'Neil, Agnes K - Died 1941 Born 1852 (with William D O'Neil & others) S:31

O'Neil, Agnes M - Died 1985 Born 1898 (next to A Milan O'Neil) S:31

O'Neil, Alice M - Died 1991 Born 1898 S:17

O'Neil (O'Neal), Bartholomew - Died 1879 March 5 in his 36th yr (next to Margaret B. & Ida O' Neil) S:31

O'Neil, Bertha H - Died 1964 Born 1888 (with Dennis O'Neil & others) S:31

O'Neil, Charles B - Died 1925 Born 1882 (with Mary A O'Neil & others) S:31

O'Neil, Dennis - Died 1917 Born 1852 (with Agnes K O'Neil & others) S:31

O'Neil, Dennis - Died 1940 Born 1940 (with Dennis O'Neil & others) S:31

O'Neil, Emma - Died 1931 Born 1861 (next to John O'Neil) S:31

O'Neil, Frank S - Died 1940 Born 1877 (with Julia M O'Neil & others) S:31

O'Neil, Ida H or N(?) - Died 1957 Born 1876 (next to Bartholomew & Margaret O'Neil) S:31

O'Neil, Ida N - Died 1957 Born 1876 (next to Bartholomew & Margaret O'Neil) S:20

O'Neil, James B - Died 1916 Born 1885 (with Charles B O'Neil & others) S:31

O'Neil, Jennie May - Died 1899 Aug 3 Born 1878 April 1 (with James B O'Neil & others) S:20

O'Neil, John - Died 1944 Born 1858 (next to Agnes M O'Neil) S:31

O'Neil, John V - Died 1954 Born 1878 (with Bertha H O'Neil & others) S:31

O'Neil, Julia M - Died 1949 Born 1887 (with John V O'Neil &

O'Neil (Cont.)
others) S:31

O'Neil, Julian - Died 1988 Born 1917 (with Rosa M O'Neil & others) S:31

O'Neil, Margaret B - Died 1886 Aug 26 Age 48 years, 6 months (next to Bartholomew & Ida O'Neil) S:31

O'Neil, Mary A - Died 1957 Born 1870 (with Owen O'Neil & others) S:31

O'Neil, Mary E - Died 1904 Jan 31 Born 1849 June 1 (with Jennie May O'Neil & others) S:31

O'Neil, Owen - Died 1916 Born 1847 (with Mary E O'Neil & others) S:31

O'Neil, Richard M - Died 1976 Born 1908 (with wife, Mildred Linnell & others) S:16

O'Neil, Rosa M - Died 1884 Born 1884 (with Agnes O'Neil & others) S:31

O'Neil, William D - Died 1882 Born 1881 (with Rosa M O'Neil & others) S:31

O'Neil, William J - Died 1957 Born 1877 (with Margaret G Morris & others) S:16

O'Neil, William J - Died 1983 Born 1905 (with wife, Margaret Quinn & others) S:16

O'Shea, Timothy S - Died 1954 Born 1885 (with wife, Margaret E Foley & others) S:16

O'Sullivan, Honora - Died 1940 Born 1844 (with Robert & Annie Cross) S:16

O'Toole, Florence V - Died 1968 June 9 Born 1899 Mar 11 S:15

O'Toole, William B - Died 1975 Jan 25 Born 1894 Feb 13 S:15

Oakes, Lucy A - Died 1894 Born 1812 (with Charles & Sarah Welch & others) S:18

Odell, James E - Died 1939 Born 1865 (with wife, Hannah M Crocker & others) S:20

Odell, James E - Died 1936 Born 1865 (with wife Mary) S:31

Odell, Mary - Died 1947 Born 1866

Odell (Cont.)
(with husband James) S:31

Odence, Marion N - Died 1975 Born 1905 (next to husband, Meyer Odence) S:15

Odence, Meyer - Died 1965 Born 1886 (next to wife, Marion N Odence) S:15

Oikelmus, Bertha J - Died 1979 April Born 1919 May S:20

Olander, Dorothy P - Died 1976 Born 1921 Wife of N Robert Olander (with him & Linnea Olander) S:20

Olander, Linnea G - Died 1981 Born 1944 (with Dorothy & N Robert Olander) S:20

Olander, N Robert - Died (still living 1991?) Born 1919 (with wife, Dorothy & Linnea Olander) S:20

Olander, O Karl - Died 1976 Born 1909 S:20

Olfson, Jean M - Died 1973 Born 1911 Wife of Robert Olfson (next to him) S:11

Olfson, Robert - Died 1990 Born 1909 (next to wife, Jean M Olfson) S:11

Oliva, Elizabeth N - Died 1972 Born 1887 (with Elmiro A Oliva) S:15

Oliva, Elmiro A - Died 1972 Born 1884 (with Elizabeth N Oliva) S:15

Oliver, Arthur J - Died 1936 Born 1903 (with Agnes M Young & others) S:31

Oliver, Eleanora - Died 1964 Born 1886 S:15

Oliver, Eliza A - Died 1924 Aug 26 Born 1858 Sept 26 (with Lindsey N Oliver) S:18

Oliver, John B - Died 1941 Born 1869 (with Mary T Oliver & others) S:31

Oliver, John L - Died 1975 March 24 Born 1897 Oct 5 Was a 2nd Lt in US Army during World War I & II S:15

Oliver, Lindsey N - Died 1945 Aug 31 Born 1959 April 20 (with

Oliver (Cont.)
Eliza A Oliver) S:18

Oliver, Mary F - Died 1919 Oct 22 Born 1830 March 31 (next to Eliza A Oliver) S:18

Oliver, Mary T - Died 1929 Born 1873 (with Arthur J Oliver & others) S:31

Omans, Clarissa G - Died 1875 Feb 20 Age 50 Born 1825 Wife of Albert Omans S:5

Omsby, John CB - Died 1858 Feb 9 25 years Born 1833 S:4

Omyrich, John S - Died 1979 Born 1900 Was a Pvt in US Army S:17

Onnell, John - Died 1781 Jan 7 in his 79th yr S:3R

Oragone, Pasquale Sr - Died 1952 Born 1887 S:16

Orechia, Alice M - Died (still living 1991?) Born 1897 (has an American Legion plaque) (with William Orcehia) S:20

Orechia, William J - Died 1967 Born 1895 (With Alice Orechia) S:20

Ormsby, Arthur T - Died 1987 Born 1899 (with Thomas L Ormsby & others) S:16

Ormsby, Catharine - Died 1894 July 16 b 1867 March 5 S:2

Ormsby, Catherine L - Died 1857 May 21 Born 1855 Jan 27 (with Mary E Ormsby & others) S:20

Ormsby, Catherine S - Died 1894 July 16 Born 1867 March 5 (with Margaret Ormsby & others) S:20

Ormsby, Edwin - Died 1917 Born 1899 Son of William & Mary Ormsby (with them & Catherine Ormsby & others) S:20

Ormsby, Eliza J - Died 1871 March 5 Born 1870 Oct 21 (with William & Mary Ormsby & others) S:20

Ormsby, Katherine - Died 1980 Born 1894 (with David H Sullivan) S:16

Ormsby, Margaret - Died 1837 or 1897 March 20 Born 1862 Dec 27 (with William U Ormsby &

Ormsby (Cont.)
others) S:20

Ormsby, Mary - Died 1902 or 1908? Born 1824 or 1826 (stone not clear) (with Catherine Ormsby & others) S:31

Ormsby, Mary E - Died 1862 Oct 21 Born 1861 Jan 23 or 29 (with Eliza J Ormsby & others) S:20

Ormsby, Mary E - Died 1932 Born 1855 Wife of William F Ormsby (with him & son, Edwin Ormsby & others) S:31

Ormsby, Thomas L - Died 1936 Born 1859 (with wife, Mary Coan) S:16

Ormsby, William F - Died 1941 Born 1857 (with wife, Mary E Ormsby & others) S:31

Ormsby, William U - Died 1902 Born 1824 (with Mary Ormsby & others) S:20

Orr, Addie - Died 1974 May 19 Born 1899 March 16 (listed with Luther Orr) S:15

Orr, Harriet M - Died 1965 Born 1906 Wife of Loomis Kinney (next to him) S:12

Orr, Luther - Died (still living 1991?) Born 1898 Dec 25 (listed with Addie Orr) S:15

Osborne, Allen G - Died 1981 Born 1893 (undertaker plaque only) S:15

Osborne, Annie S - Died 1985 Born 1899 (with Raymond C Osborne) S:17

Osborne, James Lawrence - Died 1976 Born 1910 S:11

Osborne, Raymond C - Died 1973 Born 1903 He was a Mason (with Annie S Osborne) S:17

Ossenbeck, Margaret L - Died 1968 Born 1884 S:16

Ostrander, MC - Died (no dates) (small stone) Wife of A H Ostrander S:18

Ostrowski, Lisa A - Died 1988 Born 1969 (Undertaker plaque only) S:20

Otis, (son) - Died 1745 Jan Son of James Esq & Mary Otis S:5R

Otis, (son) - Died 1779 Feb 3 (died same day) Son of Joseph Esq & Maria Otis S:5R

Otis, (widow) - Died 1737 Dec 10 Age 78 Widow of Honorable John Otis Esq (there was a note which says, Mercy Bacon) S:5R

Otis, Abagail - Died 1885 Apr 1 Age 82 years, 7 months Wife of Lot Nye Otis S:9

Otis, Abigail - Died 1757 May 16 Born 1757 May 4 Daughter of Joseph Esq & Rebecca Otis S:5R

Otis, Abigail - Died 1766 Mar 18 Age 22 Daughter of Hon James & Mary Otis S:5

Otis, Abigail - Born 1736 June 6 (stone not clear) Daughter of James & Mary Otis (Hinckley Ceme records #5R says death was 1738 July 31) S:5

Otis, Amos - Died 1771 Dec 6, perished in a snow storm at Nantucket and is buried there (listed on stone with Catherine Otis) S:10

Otis, Amos - Died 1830 April 23 Age 71 S:10

Otis, Anna - Died 1870 Sept Born 1800 Oct Wife of Capt John Otis (with him) S:19

Otis, Catherine - Died 1819 Feb 28 Born 1743 Sept 3 Widow of Amos Otis (listed on her stone) S:10

Otis, Hetty - Died 1899 May 12 in her 64th yr Dau of Lot Nye & Abagail Otis S:9

Otis, James Honorable - Died 1778 Nov 9 in his 77th yr He was listed as a Patriot S:5

Otis, Jane - Died 1772 Nov 18 in her 76th yr Wife of Solomon Otis Esq S:9R+22R

Otis, Jane - Died 1779 May 18 Wife of Solomon Otis (buried next to him) S:9

Otis, John - Died 1854 July 16 Born 18?1 Apl 22 S:5

Otis, John (Capt) - Died 1829 Jan Born 1798 Dec (with wife, Anna Otis) S:19

Otis, John Honorable - Died 1727 Sept 23 in his 70th yr S:5

Otis, Joseph - Died 1761 May 28 Born 11 Feb (no year listed) Son of Joseph Esq & Rebecca Otis S:5R

Otis, Joseph Esq - Died 1810 Sept 27 Age 85 years, 6 months Born 1725 Feb 22 at Barnstable Second son of the Late Hon James Otis S:5

Otis, Lot Nye - Died 1878 Oct 22 in his 79th yr S:9

Otis, Lucy Ann - Died 1858 Aug 12 Born 1823 April 7 Daughter of Amos & Sally Otis S:19

Otis, Maria - Died 1826 Sept 19 in Hingham, Massachusetts Buried 1827 Jan 10 Widow of Joseph Otis Esq & daughter of Rev Nathaniel Walter of Roxbury Age was 84 years Says, "member of parish for 57 years" S:5R

Otis, Maria - Died 1895 Sept 15 Born 1816 Aug 2 (with George Fisher) S:13

Otis, Martha - Died 1736 Nov 25 Age 1 months, 16 days Daughter of James & Mary Otis S:5

Otis, Mary - Died 1800 Jan 25 Daughter of Robinson T & Alice Otis S:11

Otis, Mary Jane - Died 1880 Nov 4 Age 43 years, 3 months Wife of William H Otis S:9

Otis, Mercy - Died 1737 Widow of Hon John Otis S:5

Otis, Mercy Elizabeth - Died 1844 Oct 13 Age 22 months, Consort & daughter of Rev Otis & Lucy (not sure if Otis is last name?) S:7

Otis, Nancy - Died 1808 Sept 5 in her 34th yr Wife of Amos Otis (next to him) S:10+26R

Otis, Nathan - Died 1743 May 1 Age 24 days Son of James & Mary Otis S:5

Otis, Nathaniel - Died 1729 Nov 25 in his 40th yr S:11R+26R

Otis, Otis - Died 1745 Jan Son of James & Mary Otis Esq S:5

Otis, Rebecca - Died 1766 Apl 7 in her 31st yr Wife of Joseph Otis Esq S:5

Otis, Rebecca - Died 1898 Nov 4 Age 70 years, 8 months (stone broken but repaired with cement) Wife of Job W Handy (next to him) S:19

Otis, Sally - Died 1868 April 11 Born 1778 Aug 7 Widow of ? (next to Solomon Otis) S:10

Otis, Samuel - Died 17?2 located in row 7 S:11R

Otis, Samuel B - Died 1803 located in row 7 S:11R

Otis, Samuel B - Died 1863 Nov 16 at Beaufort, South Carolina Stone erected by friends to faithful soldier in 1873 He was a member of the Company E, 10th Massachusetts Infantry He was 20 years old S:11

Otis, Sarah - Died 1742 May 6 Age 26 days Daughter of James & Mary Otis S:5

Otis, Solomon - Died 1778 Jan 2 or 9 in his 82nd yr S:9

Otis, Solomon - Died 1780 May 15 Age 47 S:10+26R

Otis, Solomon - Died 1821 June 11 Age 50 S:10

Otis, Susannah - Died 1782 May 24 Age 47 S:10

Otis, William H - Died 1893 Dec 1 Age 59 years, 8 months (died Runta Gorda?, Florida) Son of Lot Nye & Abagail Otis S:9

Pailler, Eugene G Died 1970 Born 1883 (with Grace C Pailler) S:17

Pailler, Grace C - Died 1955 Born 1888 (with Eugene G Pailler) S:17

Paine, Bethiah - Died (year not given) 8 July (date underground) Wife of James Paine (next to him) & daughter to late Honorable, John Thatcher Esq (Hinckley Ceme records #11R says death was 1734? July 8 at age 63) S:11+26R

Paine, Edwina R - Died 1960 Born 1868 (buried next to Nancy C

Paine (Cont.)
Paine) S:8

Paine, James - Died 1711 July 13 Age 20 (next to James Paine d1778?) S:11+26R

Paine, James - Died 1728 Nov 12 Born 1665 July 6 S:11R

Paine, James - Died 1741 located in row 12 S:11R

Paine, James - Died 1778 ? (stone worn) (next to James Paine d1711?) S:11

Paine, James Mr - Died 1728 located in row 12 S:11R

Paine, John - Died 1849 April 9 Age 50 S:11

Paine, John Henry - Died 1903 Born 1823 (large Paine, Titcomb & Brown stone) S:11

Paine, Nancy C - Died 1921 Born 1838 (buried next to Edwina R Paine) S:8

Paine, Rebekah - Died 1838 July 10 Age 39 Wife of John Paine (next to him) S:110

Paine, William Homer - Died 1916 Born 1835 (on large Paine, Titcomb & Brown stone) S:11

Pakstys, Mykolas - Died 1987 Born 1897 S:16

Palmer, Bathia A - Died 1974 Born 1892 Stone says,"Mother" (next to Samuel G Palmer) S:17

Palmer, George W - Died 1955 Born 1874 (with Sarah M Palmer) S:17

Palmer, Monroe E - Died 4 Sept 1970 Born 4 March 1917 Was Staff Sargeant in Massachusetts 4255 Base Unit AAF during World War II (he has military stone also) (with his wife, Evelyn Meserve,) S:12

Palmer, Samuel G - Died 1967 Born 1888 Stone says, "Father" (next to Bathia A Palmer & Mary E Toner) S:17

Palmer, Sarah M - Died 1966 Born 1894 (with George W Palmer) S:17

Palmieri, Norma - Died (still living 1991?) Born 1904 (listed with

336

Palmieri (Cont.)
Oreste Palmieri) S:18

Palmieri, Oreste - Died 1990 Born 1893 Was a PFC in US Army during World War I (listed with Norma Palmieri) S:18

Paltsios, George Died 1982 Dec 22 Born 1893 June 14 Stone says, "Father" S:15

Paltsios, George - Buried 1982 Dec 23 Age 90 Location in section 2, lot 14, grave 5 S:15R

Palumbo, Louis - Died 1952 Born 1908 S:13

Panesis, James L - Died 1970 Born 1886 (with wife, Roubiny (?) S Panesis) S:15

Panesis, Roubiny (?) S - Died 1979 Born 1893 (with husband, James L Panesis) S:15

Pano, Nicolas - Died 1971 Born 1894 S:15

Park, Grace Burtt - Died 1962 Born 1876 (next to J Edgar Park) S:14

Park, J Edgar - Died 1956 Born 1879 (next to Grace Burtt Park) S:14

Parker, ali(?) - Died 1727 Aug in his 45th yr (stone is broken) (Hinckley Cemetery records #5R say she died on the 20th and that her first name was Alice) S:5

Parker, AF Bearse - Died 1976 April 9 Born 1897 Mar 23 (with Florence J Parker) S:14

Parker, Abba H - Died 1862 Born 1861 (with Edward C Parker & others) S:18

Parker, Abigail - Died 1833 or 1853? Mar 17 in her ? yr Born 1783 June 28 Wife of Ebenezer Parker (next to him) S:12+12R

Parker, Abigail G - Died 1818 Dec 20 Age 1 year, 6 days Daughter of Joseph & Mihitable Parker S:5

Parker, Almira - Died 1830 Aug 27 Age 22 Born 1808 Aug 7 Daughter of Ebenezer & Abigail Parker S:12+12R

Parker, Amelia - Died 1892 Born 1841 (with Abba H Parker &

Parker (Cont.)
others) S:18

Parker, Andeline P - Died 1922 Born 1828 (on stone with Danford P Parker & others) S:11

Parker, Anna L - Died 1906 April 20 Born 1840 Aug 6 (with Frederick E Parker & others) S:12

Parker, Benjamin Franklin - Died 1847 Sept 5 Born 1842 July 12 Son of Benjamin & Keziah C Parker (Hinckley Cemetery records say death was in 1849) S:5

Parker, Benjamin O - Died 1831 Nov Age 18 years, 9 months Lost at sea Son of Benjamin & Ruth Parker S:6

Parker, Caroline B - Died 1805 Feb 16 Daughter of Benjamin & Keziah C Parker (Hinckley Cemetery records says death was in 1857 April 15 and birth as 1845, is it same person?) S:5

Parker, Charles F - Died 1904 Born 1854 (with Emma Matthews Parker) S:12

Parker, Charles HB - Died 1846 April 21 Age 6 years, 10 months, 4 days Son of Seth & Mary A Parker S:5R

Parker, Charles W - Died 1971 Born 1896 (with Helen M Parker) S:16

Parker, Charlotte L - Died 1971 Born 1882 Wife of Charles Parker (with William & Caroline Nickerson) S:14

Parker, Clara - Died 1908 Born 1826 (with Capt William & Ruthie Parker) S:18

Parker, Clorida A - Died 1926 Aug 20 Born 1844 Dec 14 (next to Frank C Parker) S:12

Parker, Cordelia - Died 1846 Sept 4 Age 4 years, 8 months, 16 days Daughter of Daniel Parker Sr S:5

Parker, Custavus B - Died 1846 June 14 Age 7 years Son of Benjamin & Elizabeth Parker S:5

Parker, Cynthia - Died 1842 Sept 18 Born 1841 Oct 9 Daughter of

Parker (Cont.)

? & Abigail P Smith S:11

Parker, Cynthin - Died 1853 Nov 29 in her 77th yr Wife of Seth Parker S:5

Parker, Daisy - Died (nothing filled in, still living ?) (on same stone with Danford A Parker & others) S:11

Parker, Danford P - Died 1908 Born 1834 (large Parker Family monument on dirt road with others listed) S:11

Parker, Daniel - Died (died on the 20th) (stone worn, not clear) (next to his wife, Mary Parker) S:11

Parker, Daniel - Died 1715 Sept 23 Age 20 S:11R

Parker, Daniel - Died 1847 Apl 18 in his 76th yr S:5

Parker, Daniel - Died 1886 May 10 in his 85th yr S:5

Parker, Daniel Dr - Died 1809 Feb 18 in his 75th yr S:5

Parker, Daniel Esq - Died 1728 Dec 23 Age 59 (inscription destroyed) S:11R

Parker, David - Died 1788 June 24 Age 89 S:5R

Parker, David - Died 1868 Aug 6 Age 85 S:5R

Parker, David - Died 1869 Born 1850 (stone says, "Lost at sea") (with James Parker & others) S:13

Parker, David Esq - Died 1813 Feb 28 in his 73rd yr S:5

Parker, Desire - Died 1781 July 6 Age 71 Wife of Samuel Parker S:5R

Parker, Desire - Died 1825 Dec 10 in her 76th yr Relict of Freeman Parker S:5

Parker, Ebenezer - Died 1851 July 9 Age 71 Born 1780 July 5 S:12

Parker, Edna N (or R) - Died 1885 Oct 15 Age 6 weeks (stone is down) Daughter of Edgar & Eva Parker (next to mother) S:14

Parker, Edward - Died 1852 Oct 4 Age 19 years, 9 months Son of

Parker (Cont.)

Joseph & Methitable Parker (Hinckley Ceme records say death was 1832) S:5

Parker, Edward C - Died 1904 Born 1858 (with Josiah C Parker & others) S:18

Parker, Elisha - Died 1731 Oct 27 in the 52nd yr S:11+26R

Parker, Eliza - Died 1872 Sept 2 Born 1798 March 29 (next to Mrs. Olive Ames) S:12R

Parker, Elizabeth - Died 1839 Nov 24 Born 1826 May 24 (on same stone with Danford A Parker & others) S:11

Parker, Elizabeth C - Died 1916 Born 1834 (with James Parker & others) S:13

Parker, Elizabeth M - Died 1839 Oct 11 in her 24th yr Wife of Robert Parker S:5

Parker, Elmira - Died 1882 Jan 16 Born 1790 July 20 Widow of Arthur B Crocker (buried next to him) S:6

Parker, Elva B - Died 1936 Born 1860 (with Zeno S Parker) S:14

Parker, Emeline - Died 1873 July 30 Age 64 years, 5 months Wife of Frederick Parker S:5

Parker, Emily W - Died 1849 Aug 24 Age ? years, ? months, 24 days Daughter of Jonathan & Maria Parker (stone not clear) S:12

Parker, Emma B - Died 1888 Apr 3 Born 1840 Sept 16 Wife of Seth Parker Jr S:5

Parker, Emma Matthews - Died 1898 Born 1848 Stone says,"God is all" (with Charles F Parker) S:12

Parker, Eunice - Died 1838 Jan 16 Relict of Rev Samuel Parker of Provincetown, Mass S:5

Parker, Eva L - Died 1888 Dec 5 Age 23 years, 14 days Wife of Edgar L Parker (next to daughter, Eva N Parker) S:14

Parker, Eva N - Died 1887 Sept 18 Age 4 months Daughter of Edgar

Parker (Cont.)
& Eva Parker (next to mother) S:14

Parker, Ferdinand A - Died 1875 Born 1838 (with James Parker & others) S:13

Parker, Ferdinand N - Died (no face to stone, next to James Parker) S:12

Parker, Florence J - Died 1968 May 27 Born 1893 Dec 2 (with AF Bearse Parker(?)) S:14

Parker, Frank C - Died 1876 June 10 Born 1841 Mar 22 (next to Clorida A Parker) S:12

Parker, Freddie - Died 1866 Sept 3 Age 8 years, 10 months, 18 days Son of Frederic & Emeline S:5

Parker, Frederick - Died 1882 Feb 11 Born 1815 June 11 S:5

Parker, Frederick E - Died 1922 Oct 19 Born 1844 June 19 (with Anna L Parker) S:12

Parker, Frederick Horace - Died 1856 July 19 Age 16 (lost at sea off Cape Horn) Son of Frederick & Emeline Parker S:5

Parker, Freeman - Died 1776 Sept 18 Age 27 Born 1749 Oct 15 Son of Samuel Parker S:5R

Parker, Gustavus B - Died 1846 June 14 Age 7 Son of Benjamin & Mrs Kezia C Parker S:5R

Parker, Hannah - Died 1715 Oct 13 Age 14 S:11R

Parker, Hannah - Died 1830 Mar 12 in her 86th yr S:5

Parker, Hannah D - Died 1877 Dec 30 Age 69 years, 9 months Widow of Timothy Parker (next to him) S:13

Parker, Hannah Miss - Died 1800 Jan 1 Age 65 Daughter of Samuel Parker S:5R

Parker, Harriet S - Died 1915 April 9 Born 1842 April 17 S:12

Parker, Helen M - Died 1970 Born 1891 (with Charles W Parker) S:16

Parker, Henrietta Belden - Died 1847 Sept 27 Age 5 years, 3 months Daughter of Frederic &

Parker (Cont.)
Emeline Parker S:5R

Parker, Henry Matthews - Died 1951 Born 1878 (with Charles F Parker) S:12

Parker, Horace S - Died 1956 April 13 Born 1864 Nov 28 With Lillian S Parker, Wife & Capt William Parker & others S:12

Parker, Ida May - Died 1858 Feb 19 Age 8 months, 24 days Daughter of James H Parker & Velina Lovell (next to brother, Russell Lovell Parker) S:12

Parker, Isabella F - Died 1873 Born 1834 (with Amelia Parker & others) S:18

Parker, Isaiah - Died 1829 Apr 29 in his 77th yr S:5

Parker, Isaiah - Died 1874 June 10 Age 83 years, 5 months, 16 days S:5

Parker, Jacob - Died 1811 Sept 17 in his 16th yr He died at sea Son of Jehiel & Sarah Parker S:3

Parker, James - Died (no face to stone, next to Ferdinand N Parker) S:12

Parker, James - Died 1759 Oct 4 Age 51 (Hinckley Cemetery records say death year was 1752) S:5

Parker, James - Died 1871 Born 1789 (with wife, Temperance H Parker) S:13

Parker, James H - Died 1869 May 26 Born 1824 June 10 Lost overboard near Montauk Point while in command of the schooner, Abbie Bursley (listed with wife, Velina Lovell) S:12

Parker, Jehiel - Died 1809 April 12 in his 39th yr S:3+3R

Parker, Jehiel - Died 1826 Dec 15 in his 23rd yr Died at Port Royal, Meritime (Nova Scotia, Canada) Son of Jehiel & Sarah Parker S:3

Parker, Jennie A - Died 1919 Oct 3 Born 1839 Sept 12 Wife of Capt William Parker (with him & other wife, Sophia) S:12

Parker, John S - Died 1886 Feb 4

Parker (Cont.)
Age 89 years, 6 months S:5

Parker, Jonathan (Capt) - Died 1873 May 21 Age 74 years, 7 months (next to wife, Maria Parker) S:12

Parker, Joseph - Died (nothing is filled in, still living?) (on same stone with Danford A Parker & others) S:11

Parker, Joseph - Died 1810 Aug 8 in his 80th yr S:5

Parker, Joseph - Died 1821 Sept 27 in his 16th yr Died at Norfolk, Virginia Son of Jehiel & Sarah Parker S:3

Parker, Joseph - Died 1846 Aug 8 Age 80 (mentioned on Mercy Parker, his wife's stone) S:5R

Parker, Joseph - Died 1847 Nov 21 in his 75th yr S:5

Parker, Joseph - Died 1862 Apl 1 Born 1880 Dec 9 (on same stone with Danford A Parker & others) (Hinckley Cemetery records say age was 61 years, 3 months and notation on stone says, "sleep dearest father") S:11+26R

Parker, Joseph H - Died 1855 July 28 Born 1855 May 18 Son of Joseph H & Rose D L Parker S:4

Parker, Joseph H - Died 1864 Oct 9 Age 2 years, 3 months, 14 days S:4

Parker, Joseph N - Died 1897 July 31 Born 1856 July 20 (on same stone with Danford A Parker & others) S:11

Parker, Josiah C - Died 1875 Dec 26 Age 76 years, 4 months, 29 days S:4

Parker, Josiah C - Died 1900 Born 1826 (with Isabella F Parker & others) S:18

Parker, Keziah C - Died 1846 Apl 7 in his 27th yr Wife of Benjamin Parker S:5

Parker, Lilla V - Died 1928 Oct 10 Born 1858 Feb 14 (on same stone with Danford A Parker & others) S:11

Parker, Lillian S - Died 1939 Dec

Parker (Cont.)
10 Born 1880 June 19 Wife of Horace S Parker (with him & Capt William Parker & others) S:12

Parker, Lucy - Died 1818 May 6 in her 37th yr Wife of Daniel Parker S:5

Parker, Lucy - Died 1858 Oct 14 Age 54 Born 1804 Aug 6 (on same stone with Danford A Parker & others) S:11+26R

Parker, Lucy J - Died 1902 Nov 30 Age 97 years, 3 months, 5 days Wife of Daniel Parker S:5

Parker, Maria - Died 1862 Dec 8 Age 58 years, 3 months Wife of Jonathan Parker S:12

Parker, Maria L - Died 1875 Sept 9 Age 75 years, 4 months, 20 days Wife of Josiah C Parker S:4

Parker, Maria Louisa - Died 1855 Oct 21 Age 25 years, 11 months Daughter of Jonathan & Maria Parker stone says, "Closed her early life" S:12

Parker, Marie Louisa - Died 1849 Jan 3 Age 10 years, 5 months, 22 days Daughter of Josiah C & Maria A Parker S:4

Parker, Marion - Died 1860's Mar 27 Age 2 years, 9 months, 13 days Daughter of Joseph H & Rose DL Parker (stone not very clear) S:4

Parker, Mary - Died 1737 Feb 12 Age 32 Wife of David Parker S:5

Parker, Mary - Died 1744 in her 74th yr (stone worn) (another stone next to her worn off so you cannot read it)(the day of death could be the 17th) Relict of Daniel Parker (next to her) (Hinckley Ceme records #11R say death was on Nov 17 and she was the relict of Daniel Esq) S:11+26R

Parker, Mary Ann - Died 1882 Sept 10 Born 1803 Sept 2 Wife of Seth Parker S:5

Parker, Mary Mrs - Died 1774 located in row 7 S:11R

Parker, Mary N - Died 1869 May 18 Age 82 years, 10 months, 6 days (next to Timothy Parker) S:13

Parker, Mehitable - Died 1848 Oct 9 in her 68th yr Widow of Joseph Parker S:5

Parker, Mercy - Died (date not clear) Wife of Joseph Parker & the daughter of Mary & Joseph Bursley (Hinckley Ceme records say death was 1796 Sept 16 age 20) S:5

Parker, Mercy - Died 1785 14th day (stone not clear) Wife of David Parker (Hinckley Ceme records #5R says death was in May at age 82) S:5

Parker, Mercy - Died 1812 Sept 24 in her 76th yr Wife of Dr Daniel Parker S:5

Parker, Olive - Died 1821 June 5 in her 33rd yr Wife of David Parker of Boston, Mass & daughter of Andrew Olive Garrett S:5

Parker, Patient Miss - Died 1824 S:5

Parker, Rose DL - Died 1855 Aug 30 Born 1855 May 18 Daughter of Joseph H Rose & D L Parker S:4

Parker, Russell Lovell - Died 1861 April 22 Age 2 years, 3 months, 1 days Son of James H Parker & Velina Lovell (next to sister, Ida May Parker) S:12

Parker, Ruth G - Died 1878 Mar 2 Age 53 years, 11 months Wife of George Parker S:6

Parker, Ruthie H - Died 1889 Born 1868 (with Capt William & Clara Parker) S:18

Parker, Samuel - Died 1766 March 5 Age 62 years, 1 month S:5R

Parker, Samuel - Died 17?8 April 29 (stone badly worn) Son of Benjamin Parker ? S:11

Parker, Sarah - Died 1836 July 21 in her 87th yr Relict of Isaiah Parker S:5

Parker, Sarah Miss - Died 1845 Aug 10 in her 59th yr S:5

Parker, Sarah N - Died 1830 April

Parker (Cont.)
25 Age 18 Born 1812 April 14 Daughter of Ebenezer & Abigail Parker S:12

Parker, Seth - Died 1856 Mar 15 in his 80th yr S:5

Parker, Seth - Died 1891 July 9 Born 1805 Feb 23 S:5

Parker, Silas B - Died 1895 Born 1845 (listed on large Scudder stone in their family plot) S:11

Parker, Sophia B - Died 1872 Feb 14 Born 1842 Jan 31 Wife of Capt William Parker (with him) S:12

Parker, Sophronia - Died 1835 April 17 in her 35th yr Born 1800 April 25 Wife of Ebenezer Parker (next to him) S:12+12R

Parker, Temperance - Died 1864 Feb 20 Age 81 Wife of David Parker S:5R

Parker, Temperance H - Died 1900 Born 1807 Wife of James Parker (with him & others) S:13

Parker, Theodore E - Died 1967 Born 1895 Stone says,"She walked with the lord" (next to husband, William H Parker) S:15

Parker, Timothy - Died 1871 Sept 14 Age 76 (between Hannah D & Mary N Parker) S:13

Parker, Uriel - Died 1835 Jan 8 Age 20 years, 6 months Son of Joseph & Mehitable Parker S:5

Parker, Velina - Died 1959 Born 1870 Wife of Horace Manley Crosby (with him) S:12

Parker, William B (Capt) - Died 1903 Aug 17 Born 1836 Oct 29 With wife, Sophia B Parker S:12

Parker, William E (Capt) - Died 1891 Born 1826 (with Clara & Ruthie Parker) S:18

Parker, William H - Died 1979 Born 1889 (next to wife, Theodora E Parker) S:15

Parker, Zeno S - Died 1928 Born 1853 (with Elva B Parker) S:14

Parmenter, Fred S - Died 1947 Born 1863 (with Lena G Hinckley, his wife) S:11

Parris, Elias - Died 1881 Born 1812 (with Nancy Parris) S:8

Parris, Nancy - Died 1894 Born 1822 (with Elias Parris) S:8

Parry, Rees Henry - Died 1948 Born 1856 S:8

Parsil, Anna D - Died 1987 Born 1900 (with Helen D Queenan) S:16

Parsinell, James - Died 1797 Jan 23 Age 86 (Percival could be his last name because of note in records) S:5R

Parsiuell, John - Died 1793 Jan (stone not clear) S:5

Parsley, Grace A - Died 1974 Born 1927 (next to Wayne P Parsley) S:11

Parsley, Wayne P - Died 1980 Born 1946 Was a Sgt in US Air Force in Vietnam (next to Grace A Parsley) S:11

Parsons, Francis W - Died 1924 June 1 Born 1833 Jan 5 (metal plaque on rock) S:12

Pate, Helena Stewart - Died 1850 Born 1869 (located in Pate plot) S:8

Patterson, (infant) - Died 1888? Nov 6 Born 1887 Oct 6 (near Patterson plot) Stone says, "Our Baby" (near Calvin & Marcia Patterson) S:8

Patterson, Alice - Died 1958 Born 1872 (with Phoebe Patterson) S:17

Patterson, Calvin - Died 1902 Jan 28 Born 1847 July 2 (Paterson plot) (buried with Marcia L Patterson) S:8

Patterson, Marcia L - Died 1936 Jan 20 Born 1849 June 7 (Patterson plot) (buried with Calvin Patterson) S:8

Patterson, Phoebe - Died 1988 Born 1908 (with Alice Patterson) S:17

Patterson, Ralph H - Died 1973 Born 1898 S:14

Pattison, Addie C - Died 1946 Born 1891 (next to Dexter B Pattison) S:13

Pattison, Alice B - Died 1937 Born 1859 (with Thomas Pattison) S:13

Pattison, Alice C - Died 1928 Born 1917 (with Dexter B Pattison) S:13

Pattison, Dexter B - Died 1932 Born 1889 (with Alice C Pattison) S:13

Pattison, Millicent L (Millie) - Died 1882(?) March Born 1880 Daughter of Thomas & Alice Pattison (next to them) S:13

Pattison, Thomas - Died 1916 Born 1854 (with Alice B Pattison) S:13

Paull, Hannah Mrs - Died 1872 May 27 Age 68 years, 2 days Daughter of Rev Simeon Coombs S:4

Payan, Constance K - Died 1980 Born 1895 (with Herbert E Payan) S:15

Payan, Herbert E - Died 1973 Born 1893 (with Constance K Payan) S:15

Payette, Albert - Died 1951 Born 1882 (with Emma W Payette) S:18

Payette, Emma W - Died 1970 Born 1884 (with Albert Payette) S:18

Payne, Lucy - Died 1776 May 28 in her 22nd yr Consort of William Payne & Daughter of Capt William Taylor (buried next to father) S:10+26R

Pazakis, Dyonisia R - Died 1950 Born 1860 S:8

Peacock, John D - Died 1989 Born 1898 S:15

Peak, Alice Gorham - Died 1979 Born 1901 (with Genevieve H Doe & others) S:18

Peak, Amveladams - Died 1824 June 16 in the 42nd yr S:4

Peak, Ellen Crocker - Died 1870 Born 1847 (with Alice Josephine Peak & others) S:18

Peak, Esther R - Died 1947 Born 1873 (stone says, "Peak") (with Irvin E Peak) S:12

Peak, Grace D - Died 1934 Born 1855 (with John A Sr & Jr Peak) S:18

Peak, Howard F Jr - Died 1982 Born 1891 (with Marion Blake Peak) S:18

Peak, Irvin E - Died 1958 Born 1871 (with Esther R Peak) S:12

Peak, John - Died 1886 Sept 6 Age 80 Stone says,"Father" (with Martha Peak) S:18

Peak, John A - Died 1891 Born 1890 (with Grace & John A Peak) S:18

Peak, John A - Died 1920 Born 1848 (with Grace D & John A Jr Peak) S:18

Peak, Josephine - Died 1930 Born 1851 (with William H Peak & others) S:18

Peak, Lillian - Died 1969 Born 1890 (with Nicholas Spitz) S:18

Peak, Lydia - Died 1897 March 7 Born 1839 Feb 2 Wife of William H Peak (listed with her) S:18

Peak, Lydia - Died 1947 Born 1873 (with husband, Thomas Peak & next to son, Willis Peak) S:18

Peak, Marion Blake - Died 1970 Born 1893 (with Howard F Peak Jr) S:18

Peak, Martha - Died 1896 April 11 Age 81 Stone says,"Mother" (with John Peak) S:18

Peak, Mary Gorham - Died 1967 Born 1879 (with Alice Gorham Peak & others) S:18

Peak, Mary L - Died 1918 Jan 2 Born 1839 Aug 13 (with Samuel A Peak) S:18

Peak, Miron Richard - Died 1911 Born 1841 (with Ellen Crocker Peak & others) S:18

Peak, Sally - Died 1899 Apl 28 Age 16 years, 8 months S:4

Peak, Samuel A - Died 1906 Nov 9 Born 1838 April 23 (with Mary L Peak) S:18

Peak, Thomas - Died 1957 Born 1869 (with Lydia Peak) S:18

Peak, William H - Died 1873 Nov 1 Age 39 Died at sea (listed with

Peak (Cont.) wife, Lydia Peak) S:18

Peak, William H - Died 1957 Born 1874 (with Mary Gorham Peak & others) S:18

Peak, Willis - Died (underground) Born 1891 Dec Son of Thomas & Lydia Peak (next to him) S:18

Pease, Esther I - Died (no dates) Wife of Gerald E Pease Sr (listed with him & son, Gerald E Pease Jr) S:20

Pease, Gerald E Jr - Died (still living 1991?) Born 1947 (listed with parents, Gerald Sr & Esther I Pease) S:20

Pease, Gerald E Sr - Died (still living 1991?) Born 1920 (listed with wife, Esther I & son, Gerald Jr) S:20

Peaslee, Clarence A - Died 1981 Born 1898 Was Pvt in US Army during World War I (next to Katherine M Peaslee) S:15

Peaslee, Katherine M - Died 1986 April 13 Born 1897 Nov 10 (next to Clarence A Peaslee) S:15

Pece, Cecelia V - Died 1973 Born 1896 S:15

Peck, Ida L - Died 1873 April 16 Age 32 years, 5 months, 23 days Stone says, "A kind loving wife, mother, daughter and sister" Wife of Alfonso D Peck S:18

Pedro, Gabriel - Died 1975 Born 1898 (with Geleste Pedro) S:20

Pedro, Geleste - Died 1981 Born 1902 (with Gabriel Pedro) S:20

Peeler, George W - Died 1814 Aug 26 Age 35 S:10

Peirce, (infant daughter) - Died 1847 Sept 29 Born 1847 Sept 22 Daughter of Sumner & Elizabeth D Peirce (stone knocked over) S:10

Peirce, (infant daughter) (Twin) - Died 1844 April 13 Born 1844 April 11 Daughter of Sumner & Elizabeth D Peirce (buried with twin brother) S:10

Peirce, (infant son)(Twin) - Died 1844 Sept 3 Born 1844 April 11

Peirce (Cont.)
Son of Sumner & Elizabeth D
Peirce (buried with twin sister)
S:10

Peirce, Elizabeth D - Died 1887 Oct
7 Born 1804 Jan 30 Wife of
Sumner Peirce (buried next to
him) S:10

Peirce, Mary - Died 1758 Feb 17 in
her 44th yr Wife of Joseph Peirce
S:11R+26R

Peirce, Sumner - Died 1857 Oct 11
at Callao, SA (South Africa?)
Interned here on 31 Jan 1858
Born 1802 July 18 at Portland,
Maine S:10

Peixoto, Ameila - Died 1962 Born
1872 S:16

Peixoto, Serena A - Died 1958
Born 1900 (two stones away
from Ameila Peixoto) S:16

Peli, Anastasia - Died 1988 Born
1902 (undertaker plaque only)
(next to Joyce K Anderson) S:19

Pelletier, Eva M - Died 1969 Born
1889 Wife of Ulfren J Pelletier
(with him) S:16

Pelletier, Ulfren J - Died 1953
Born 1877 (with wife, Eva M
Pelletier) S:16

Pelliconi, Marguerite - Died (still
alive 1990?)(no markings on
stone) Wife of George K Coggeshall (next to him) S:11

Pelton, Alice L - Died 1943 Born
1874 (next to Charles W Pelton)
S:18

Pelton, Charles W - Died 1949
Born 1880 (next to Alice Pelton)
S:18

Pelton, Ellen D - Died (still living
1991?) Born 1918 Aug 3 (be-
tween Irving Ivar Peltonen & Ivar
Pelton) S:20

Pelton, Ivar - Died 1973 May 3
Born 1887 Dec 9 Stone says,
"Father" (next to Karin Maria
Pelton) S:20

Pelton, Karin Maria - Died 1978
March 17 Born 1893 Dec 2
Stone says, "Mother" (next to
Ivar Pelton) S:20

Peltonen, Irving Ivar - Died 1959
June 9 Born 1916 April 29 Was
in Massachusetts BM2, USNR
during World War II (next to
Ellen D Pelton & other Pelton's)
S:20

Peltz, Saul - Died 1975 Born 1892
S:15

Pendleton, Dorothy - Died 1956
Born 1934 (with Phillip L Pendleton & others) S:20

Pendleton, Herbert F - Died 1961
Born 1910 (with Dorothy Pendleton & others) S:20

Pendleton, Phillip L - Died 1956
Aug 25 Born 1934 Dec 25 (has 2
stones) From Massachusetts,
was YNSN in USNR (also listed
with Herbert F Pendleton &
others) S:20

Pendleton, Sharon - Died 1960
(small baby lamb stone) (with
Dorothy Pendleton & others)
S:20

Penn, Eda E - Died 1975 Feb 11
Born 1899 July 29 (Jewish
section) S:15

Pennala, Aino - Died 1974 Born
1889 S:20

Penniman, Ethel C - Died 1979
Born 1884 (with Thomas Chase
& others) S:18

Pentti, Karolina - Died 1962 Born
1889 (with John & Amalia
Witikainen) S:18

Percival (son) - Died 1855 Dec 29
Son of Nathaniel & Rebecca C
Percival (with sister, d1852 Mar
1) (Hinckley Ceme records #11R
say death year was 1835) S:11

Percival, (daughter) - Died 1832
Mar 1 Daughter of Nathaniel &
Rebecca C Percival (Hinckley
Ceme records #11R say death
date was 1832) S:11+26R

Percival, ? - Died 1758 Feb 2 Age
44 (stone broken) (next to Sarah
Loring) S:11

Percival, Daniel W - Died 1875
Born 1841 To the memory of
him who died at sea S:10

Percival, Edward - Died 1873 May

Percival (Cont.)
15? Age 40 years, 1 month (with wife, Olive D Percival & others) S:19

Percival, Franklin - Died 1846 Dec 30 Age 41 years, 2 months (with Sally D Percival & others) S:19

Percival, Franklin - Died 1891 June 20 Age 56 years, 5 months (with Edward Percival & others) S:19

Percival, James - Died 1891 located in row 9 possibly lot 2 S:11R

Percival, James F - Died 1821 Dec 20 Age 5 years, 3 months Son of Thomas & Mary Percival (died same day as brother Thomas & buried with him) S:11

Percival, John (Capt) - Died 1802 Aug 10 Born 1740 Jan 6 S:5

Percival, John (Capt) - Died 1862 Sept 17 Born 1779 Apr 3 (stone says- Known as Mad Jack in command of Old Ironsides who went on 52,279 mile voyage around the world 1844-1846) S:5

Percival, John (Capt) - Died 1862 Sept 17 Born 1779 Apr 3 S:5

Percival, John W - Died 1869 Sept 30 Age 29 years, 10 months Lost at sea on the voyage from Valparaiso to New York (listed with Franklin Percival & others) S:19

Percival, John W - Died 1870 Aug 15 Age 13 months, 24 days Son of Joseph & Lucy E Percival (with them) S:19

Percival, Joseph S - Died 1870 Nov 6 Age 33 years, 2 months (with wife, Lucy E Percival & others) S:19

Percival, Lucy E - Died 1911 Jan 13 Age 69 years, 7 months Wife of Joseph Percival (with him & Franklin Percival & others) S:19

Percival, Maria - Died 1857 Sept 13 Age 64 Born 1793 Aug 9 Wife of Capt John Percival & daughter of David Smith Pinkerton of Trenton, New Jersey S:5

Percival, Maria - Died 1882 Born

Percival (Cont.)
1818 Wife of Sylvanus Jaggar (buried next to him & family) S:8

Percival, Mary - Died 1841 Jan 21 Born 1743 April 3 Stone says "Respected & beloved by all her friends & acquaintances" S:5

Percival, Mary A - Died 1888 Feb 17 Born 1820 Apr 15 S:5

Percival, Nathaniel (Capt) - Died 1882 Mar 12 Age 72 years, 6 months (next to wife, Rebecca C Percival) S:11

Percival, Olive D - Died 1882? Aug 6 Age 53 years, 8 months (with John W Percival & others) S:19

Percival, Penelope - Died 1825 March 10 in Providence Age 33 Born 1792 April 7 Wife of Isaac Percival & daughter of Benjamin & Abigail Halled S:12

Percival, Rebecca - Died 1803 located in row 10 S:11R

Percival, Rebecca - Died 1918 located in row 9 (could this be Rebecca d 1818?) S:11R

Percival, Rebecca C - Died 1818 Oct 12 Age 72 years, 7 months Daughter of Nathaniel & Rebecca Percival S:11

Percival, Rebecca C - Died 1863 Oct 30 Age 72 years, 10 months Wife of Capt Nathaniel Percival S:11

Percival, Sally D - Died 1894 May 13 Age 86 years, 7 months (with Franklin & Lucy Percival & others) S:19

Percival, Sylvanus - Died 1905 Apr 21 Born 1820 Feb 8 S:5

Percival, T - Died (no dates, but located on street level in large crypt with metal door) S:10

Percival, Thomas - Died 1821 Dec 20 Age 7 years, 11 months Son of Thomas & Mary Percival (with James F Percival) S:11

Percival, Thomas - Died 1891 located in row 6 possibly lot 2 S:11R

Pereira, Emerlinda - Died 1960 Born 1893 (with Ernest Pereira)

Pereira (Cont.)
S:16

Pereira, Ernest - Died 1953 Born 1884 (with Emerlinda Pereira) S:16

Perkins, F Newton - Died 1963 Born 1908 (with wife, Winifred M Perkins) S:20

Perkins, Florence - Died 1953 Born 1876 Stone says,"Mother" (next to F Newton Perkins & her children, James & Hazel Perkins) S:20

Perkins, Hazel - Died 1956 Born 1904 Stone says,"Sister" (next to Florence Perkins) S:20

Perkins, James - Died 1956 Born 1898 Stone says,"Brother" (next to Hazel Perkins, sister) S:20

Perkins, Jennie J - Died 1965 Born 1885 (with Jesse H Perkins) S:17

Perkins, Jesse H - Died 1964 Born 1883 (with Jennie J Perkins) S:17

Perkins, Mary - Died 1837 Jan 18 in her 50th yr Wife of Abram Perkins S:4

Perkins, Winifred M - Died (still living 1991?) Born 1911 Wife of F Newton Perkins (with him) S:20

Perna, Camillo - Died 1957 Born 1881 S:16

Perry, Benjamin Sr - Died 1955 Born 1874 (with wife, Mary F Perry) S:16

Perry, Florence Ethel - Died 1940 Born 1872 (with Walter & Minnie Perry) S:18

Perry, Henry - Died 1974 June 27 Born 1887 July 18 Was a Pvt in US Army (between Helen P & John S Cunha Sr) S:15

Perry, Irene G - Died (still living 1991?) Born 1915 (listed with Joseph & Palmeida Gracia) S:14

Perry, Izabel - Died 1938 Born 1856 (with Emilio & Roza Silva) S:31

Perry, John - Died 1870 Aug 9 Age 26 S:8

Perry, Joseph - Died 1899 Born

Perry (Cont.)
1864 (with Philomena J Perry) S:16

Perry, Joseph - Died 1960 Born 1896 (with Julia M Perry) S:16

Perry, Julia M - Died 1982 Born 1897 (with Joseph Perry) S:16

Perry, Lester Manton - Died 1956 Aug 15 Born 1894 Sept 14 From Massachusetts, was Sargeant in Quartermaster Corps during World War 1 S:14

Perry, Lewis C - Died 1952 Born 1865 (buried with Mary R Perry) S:8

Perry, Mary F - Died 1961 Born 1890 Wife of Benjamin Perry Sr (with him) S:16

Perry, Mary R - Died 1957 Born 1867 (buried with Lewis C Perry) S:8

Perry, Minnie Florence - Died 1912 Born 1885 (with Walter Ellis & Florence Ethel Perry) S:18

Perry, Philomena J - Died 1956 Born 1867 (with Joseph Perry) S:16

Perry, Ralph F (or L) - Died 1981 Born 1892 Was a PFC in US Army during World War I S:15

Perry, Walter Ellis - Died 19?? (no other date) Born 1878 (listed with Minnie Florence Perry) S:18

Perry, Walter Linwood - Died 1972 Born 1894 S:13

Person, Emm - Died 1915 Dec 9 Born 1873 Oct 5 (buried next to Frank G Phinney) S:8

Persson, A Charlotta - Died 1828 Jan 19 Born 1861 Jan 17 S:8

Persson, Augusta - Died 1960 Born 1870 (wife of Charles Doubtfire, with him) S:8

Peterson, Aurila - Died 1928 Born 1845 (with Elijah Hallett & others) S:18

Peterson, Christian - Died 1850 Aug 4? (dates under ground) Son of Peter & Christine Peterson) S:21

Petrakis, Kaliope - Died 1967 Born 1892 (with Mikall Petrakis) S:15

Petrakis, Mikall - Died 1964 Born 1890 (with Kaliope Petrakis) S:15

Petrillo, Elisa B - Died 1980 Born 1895 (with Joseph Petrillo Sr) S:16

Petrillo, Joseph Sr - Died 1987 Born 1890 (with Elisa B Petrillo) S:16

Pezet, Helen Leghorn - Died 1985 Born 1891 S:13

Pfifer, Mary Barbara - Died 1975 Nov 3 Born 1923 May 27 "A Great Lady" S:11

Pfister, Helen Goffe - Died 1936 Dec 31 Born 1857 Jan 1 (next to Mary Josephine Goffe) S:8

Phalan, John Laurence - Died 1983 Born 1907 (with Katherine D Phalan) S:13

Phalan, Katherine D - Died 1989 Born 1917 (with John Laurence Phalan) S:13

Philbrook, Harry R - Died 1967 May 5 Born 1899 July 5 (He has two stones with Veteran plaque) From Massachusetts, was Pvt in 101 Inf during World War I (with wife, Lillian C Philbrook) S:19

Philbrook, Lillian C - Died 1991 Born 1901 Wife of Harry R Phil brook (with him) S:19

Philips, Annie - Died 1929 Born 1849 S:13

Phillips, (Baby) - Died 1926 Born 1926 (next to John Phillips) S:19

Phillips, Charles W - Died 1964 Born 1899 (with Grace D Phillips) S:17

Phillips, Grace D - Died (still living 1991?) Born 1896 (with Charles W Phillips) S:17

Phillips, Harvey O - Died 1967 Dec 22 Born 1899 April 21 From Massachusetts & was a PVT in STU Army, TNG Corps during World War I S:15

Phillips, John - Died 1928 Born 1879 (next to (Baby) Phillips) S:19

Phillips, Philip - Died 1952 June 21 Born 1915 Sept 15 S:11

Phillips, William A - Died 1892 Born 1844 (Stone says, "To live in the hearts of those we love is not to die") S:8

Phiney, David - Died 17?3, ? 23rd (stone broken) S:11

Phiney, Mary - Died Nov 11 (broken stone) Wife of ? (next to David Phiney) S:11

Phiney, Seth - Died 1744 Jan 2 Age 17 months, 23 days Son of Ebenezer & Rebeckah Phiney S:11

Phinney, (Baby) - Died (no dates or markings, except Baby) (buried next to Adelia Phinney & others) S:8

Phinney, (child) - Died (no dates) (next to Temperance & Timothy Phinney) S:10

Phinney, (child) - Died (no dates) (child of Timothy & Temperance Phinney in 1700's) S:10

Phinney, (child) - Died (no dates) (child of Timothy & Temperance Phinney in 1700's) S:10

Phinney, (infant son) - Died 1825 Mar 17 Age 7 weeks, 3 days Son of Alvan & Olive Phinney S:4

Phinney, (infant son) - Died 184? Aug 17 (stone not clear) Son of L Phinney & DC Phinney (buried with Mercy Phinney and others) S:8

Phinney, (infant) - Died 1878 Nov 12 Age 5 days Daughter of Joseph & Ida Phinney (3 stones away) S:18

Phinney, ? A - Died 1844 Sept 26 Born 1822 Dec 16 (child) of Seth R & Betsey Phinney (buried next to Augusta A Phinney on back road near metal fence) S:10

Phinney, A Marion - Died 1947 Born 1894 Wife of Clarence Phinney (buried next to him) S:8

Phinney, Abbie E - Died 1931 Born 1841 (next to Charles G Phinney) S:14

Phinney, Abigail - Died 1765 Aug 28 in her 25th yr Daughter of Thomas & Reliance Phinney S:3

Phinney, Adelia - Died 1896 Oct 12 Born 1827 Apr 16 (buried with Harrison Phinney) S:8

Phinney, Albro W - Died 1862 Nov 9 in his 20th yr Died at Signe Howe Hospital near Harpers Ferry Was in Co D 125th Regiment of Penn Vols Son of William & Emily Phinney (buried next to William S Phinney) S:8

Phinney, Alonzo L (Capt) - Died 1897 May 3 Born 1835 April 11 (next to wife, Sarah B Childs) S:14

Phinney, Alvan - Died 1825 Jan 14 Age 1 years, 11 months Son of Alvan & Olive Phinney S:4

Phinney, Alvin (Capt) - Died 1831 Dec 19 in his 39th yr Son of Solomon & Anna Phinney S:4

Phinney, Alzada - Died 1910 Born 1829 (with Effie & Ebenezer Phinney) S:18

Phinney, Andrew - Died 1884 Born 1815 S:7

Phinney, Anna - Died 1840 Oct 19 Age 79 years, 2 months, 7 days Husband or father was Solomon Phinney (stone for last name was not clear, but next to Solomon Phinney) S:3

Phinney, Annie O - Died 1946 Born 1877 (new stone with perpetual care) (buried with John A Phinney, husband) S:8

Phinney, Arthur - Died 1862 Nov 22 Age 3 years, 6 months (stone is down) Son of George & Cordelia Phinney (two stones away from them) S:19

Phinney, Arthur A - Died 1946 Born 1860 Stone says, "Father" (buried next to Louvie A Phinney) S:8

Phinney, Arthur S (Capt) - Died 1871 Born 1822 (buried with Deborah E Phinney) S:8

Phinney, Asa S - Died 1864 Born 1823 (buried with Desiah Phinney) S:8

Phinney, Augusta A - Died 1848 Sept 1 Born 1826 July 31

Phinney (Cont.)
Daughter of Seth R & Betsey C Phinney (buried next to them) S:10

Phinney, Betsey - Died 1848 Sept 1 Born 1826 July 31 S:26R

Phinney, Betsey C - Died 1883 Oct 25 Age 87 years, 11 months Wife of Seth Phinney (buried next to him) S:10

Phinney, Betsey S - Died 1871 Born 1812 S:7

Phinney, Braddock Capt - Died 1839 Sept 17 in his 25th yr (with Orgn Phinney) S:3R

Phinney, Bradock - Died 1858 Mar 23 Born 1858 Feb 15 Son of L & D C Phinney (buried with Mercy Phinney) S:8

Phinney, Charles - Died 1856 Jan 21 Age 57 years, 1 month, 4 days S:8

Phinney, Charles G - Died 1938 Born 1851 (stone broken in half, metal bar holding it together) (next to Abbie E Phinney) S:14

Phinney, Charles H - Died 1811 Nov 10 Son of Edward & Desire Phinney S:10

Phinney, Chauncey Marston - Died 1907 Nov 20 Born 1882 Sept 18 (with Irving & Mary Phinney) S:14

Phinney, Clara - Died (no info, small white childs stone next to parents, Harrison C & Eliza J Phinney) S:14

Phinney, Clarence A - Died 1956 Born 1883 (buried next to wife, A Marion Phinney) S:8

Phinney, Content - Died 1796 Oct 27 in her 56th yr Wife of Joseph Phinney S:3

Phinney, Cordelia Hildreth - Died 1838 June 16 Age 5 years, 4 months S:9R

Phinney, Cynthia - Died 1976 Born 1888 (undertaker plaque only) (between Henry S Haskins & Joseph B Folger) (Mosswood cemetery records say, age 88, location block A, lot 7, grave 5)

Phinney (Cont.)
S:14

Phinney, David - Died 1793 Nov 23 Age 83 years, 5 days S:11R

Phinney, David - Died 1797 Nov 11 Age 85 Wife of David Phinney S:11R

Phinney, Deborah - Died 1777 March 10 in her 17th yr Daughter of Eli and Mary Phinney S:3R

Phinney, Deborah C - Died 1906 Born 1820 (buried with Luther Phinney) S:8

Phinney, Deborah E - Died 1899 Born 1825 (buried with Capt Arthur S Phinney) S:8

Phinney, Desiah - Died 1863 Born 1833 (buried with Lucy Phinney) S:8

Phinney, Desire - Died 1756 May 5 in her 24th yr Wife of Isaac Phinney S:3+3R

Phinney, Ebenezer - Died 1905 Born 1827 (with Alzada & Effie Phinney) S:18

Phinney, Edith C - Died 1930 Born 1851 (buried next to Horace F Phinney) S:8

Phinney, Edward - Died 1769 Mar 6 Age 3 (he was a twin) Son of Eli & Mary Phinney S:3

Phinney, Effie H - Died 1864 Born 1856 (with Alzada & Ebenezer Phinney) S:18

Phinney, Eli - Died 1777 Feb 3 in his 51st yr (next to Mary Phinney) S:3R

Phinney, Eli - Died 1799 June 30 in his 17th yr Son of Solomon & Anna Phinney S:3

Phinney, Eli - Died 1888 Born 1825 (buried with Mercy B Phinney) S:8

Phinney, Eliza C - Died 1865 July 25 Age 57 years, 6 months Wife of S B Phinney S:9R

Phinney, Eliza J - Died 1911 Born 1847 (next to Harrison C Phinney) S:14

Phinney, Elizabeth - Died 1765 Aug 22 inn her 23rd yr Daughter of Thomas & Reliance Phinney

Phinney (Cont.)
S:3

Phinney, Elizabeth W - Died 1924 Born 1846 (buried with L Etta Phinney & others) S:8

Phinney, Elmer W - Died 1953 March 28 Born 1882 Nov 16 From Massachusetts, in CBM, USNRF during World War I S:18

Phinney, Emily Phillips - Died 1891 Born 1821 (buried with Julia E Phinney & others) S:8

Phinney, Ernest G - Died 1924 Born 1869 (with Marcaret S Phinney) S:19

Phinney, Esther - Died 1840 July 30 Age 33 Wife of Grafton Phinney (next to him) S:14

Phinney, Esther F - Died 1906 Born 1837 (with Capt George N Fuller & others) S:14

Phinney, Eunice - Died 1892 Born 1823 (large stone) Stone says, "Mother" (buried with Nelson Phinney & others) S:8

Phinney, Francis E - Died 1839 Dec 29 Age 2 years, 9 months Daughter of Grafton & Esther Phinney (next to Hellen M Phinney) S:14

Phinney, Frank E - Died 1885 Born 1854 S:8

Phinney, Frank G - Died 1945 Born 1856 (large stone) (buried with Mary Lovell, his wife & others) S:8

Phinney, Freeman - Died 1826 July 19 Age 28 Stone says, "Father" (buried with wife, Harriet Phinney) (there is another Freeman, same info but in cemetery #3?) S:8

Phinney, Freeman - Died 1826 July 19 Age 29 Died at Bridgeport (Connecticut?) (there is another Freeman in ceme #8?) S:3

Phinney, George - Died 1894 Jan 11 Age 72 (next to wife, Gordelia Gorham) S:19

Phinney, George H - Died 1923 Oct 18 Born 1865 Oct 20 Son of

Phinney (Cont.)

Capt Eli Phinney (buried next to him) S:8

Phinney, George Ward - Died 1852? Nov 13 Age ? years, 9 months (stone off base) Elder son of George & Cordelia Phinney (three stones away from them) S:19

Phinney, Grace E - Died 1939 Born 1861 (buried next to Louvie A Phinney) S:8

Phinney, Grafton - Died 1862 Jan 1 Age 57 (between both wives, Esther & Sarah Phinney) S:14

Phinney, Harriet - Died 1876 Mar 8 ? (stone not clear) Age 76 Stone says, "Mother" (buried with husband, Freeman Phinney) S:8

Phinney, Harrison - Died 1884 June 19 Born 1822 Oct 6 (buried with Marry L Phinney & others) S:8

Phinney, Harrison C - Died 1913 Born 1842 (with Eliza J Phinney) S:14

Phinney, Helen M - Died 1844 Dec 19 Age 1? year, 1? day (small stone) (next to Walton F Phinney) S:14

Phinney, Hellen M - Died 1840 Jan 6 Age 9 months Daughter of Grafton & Esther Phinney (next to mother) S:14

Phinney, Henery A - Died 1826 Aug 19 Age 5 months Son of Alvan & Olive Phinney S:4

Phinney, Henry - Died (stone not marked) It says, "Our Baby" (buried next to Lydia W Phinney) S:8

Phinney, Horace F - Died 1934 Born 1850 (buried next to Mabel E Phinney) S:8

Phinney, Howard M - Died 1928 Born 1854 (with Mary A Phinney) S:14

Phinney, Irving B - Died 1931 Aug 22 Born 1842 March 3 (with Mary MacKenzie Phinney) S:14

Phinney, Isaac - Died 1862 July 21 Age 65 years, 3 months (next to

Phinney (Cont.)

wife, Sarah P Phinney) S:14

Phinney, Jabez - Died 1776 Dec 1 Age 68 S:3

Phinney, James(?) D - Died 1925 Dec 21 Born 1839 Sept 10 (with Sarah A Phinney & others) S:14

Phinney, Jane - Died 1797 July Widow of Jabez Phinney S:3+3R

Phinney, Jane - Died 1856 May 16 in her 77th yr Widow of William Phinney S:3

Phinney, John A - Died 1926 Born 1864 (buried with Annie O Phinney-new stone & perpetual care) S:8

Phinney, John Deacon - Died 1746 Nov 27 in his 82nd yr (next to his wife Sarah) S:3R

Phinney, Joseph - Died 1829 in his 85th yr S:3

Phinney, Joseph - Died 1890 Born 1828 S:8

Phinney, Joseph H - Died 1916 Born 1845 (also has a undertaker plaque) Was a Civil War Veteran, 16th Massachusetts Battery (with wife, Ida Hatch & Agnes Smith, daughter) S:18

Phinney, Joseph T - Died 1899 Born 1856 (buried with Eunice & Nelson Phinney & others) S:8

Phinney, Julia - Died 1836 May 20 Age 2 years, 9 months, 7 days S:8

Phinney, Julia A - Died 1810 March 30 (stone worn) Wife of Lewis Phinney S:14

Phinney, Julia A - Died 1894 Born 1813 (large monument with Capt Lot Phinney) S:12

Phinney, Julia Ann - Died 184? May 11 Age 31? (stone upside down laying on ground) S:12

Phinney, Julia E - Died 1926 Born 1844 (buried with William S Phinney & others) S:8

Phinney, Julia F - Died 1921 Born 1837 (buried with William W Hallett, small stones in back of them which say, Willie & Jamie) S:8

Phinney, L Etta - Died 1898 Born 1870 (buried with Elizabeth W Phinney & others) S:8

Phinney, Laura Henshaw - Died 1841 Oct 8 Age 14 months S:9R

Phinney, Letitia W - Died 1957 Born 1881 (on large Whelden family stone with William Herring Phinney & others) S:11

Phinney, Levi - Died 1821 Nov 23 Age 53 (next to wife, Naome Phinney) S:14

Phinney, Lot (Capt) - Died 1881 May (large monument) (with Julia A Phinney) S:12

Phinney, Louise G - Died 1927 Born 1856 Wife of Toilston F Phinney (with him) S:18

Phinney, Louvie A - Died 1889 Aug 29 Age 28 years, 2 months Stone says, "At Rest" (buried next to Grace E Phinney) S:8

Phinney, Lucia G - Died 1891 Jan 24 Age 77 Wife of S B Phinney S:9R

Phinney, Lucy - Died 1870 Born 1859 (buried with Desiah Phinney) S:8

Phinney, Lucy - Died 1892 June 11 Age 92 years, 1 month, 12 days Daughter of Charles & Lucy Phinney buried next to a Charles Phinney S:8

Phinney, Luella M - Died 1953 Born 1878/9? (a cross marker) (with Maurice R Phinney Sr) S:20

Phinney, Luther - Died 1902 Born 1817 (stone has large "P" on top) (buried with Deborah C Phinney) S:8

Phinney, Lydia W - Died 1948 Born 1829 (buried with Mercy B & Eli Phinney) S:8

Phinney, Mabel E - Died 1962 Born 1878 (buried next to Horace F Phinney) S:8

Phinney, Mabel S - Died 1964 Born 1886 S:18

Phinney, Marcy - Died 1820 April 12 Age 35 Wife of Richard Phinney S:3

Phinney, Margaret S - Died 1923 Born 1886 (with Ernest G Phinney) S:19

Phinney, Marry L - Died 1928 Apr 9 Born 1861 Nov 27 (buried with Mary A Lovell & others) S:8

Phinney, Marry Leslie - Died 1859 ? 21 (month not clear) Age 4 years, 9 days (stone very badly worn) (buried next to Russle Lovell Phinney) S:8

Phinney, Mary - Died 1797 Nov 11 Age 85 Wife of David Phinney (located at Lothrop's Hill) S:26R

Phinney, Mary - Died 1821 Feb 12 Age 86 Husband or father was Eli Phinney Stone says, "Relict" S:3

Phinney, Mary - Died 1890 May 24 Age 25 years, 9 months Daughter of George Phinney & Gordelia Gorham (next to them) S:19

Phinney, Mary A - Died 1930 Born 1855 (with Howard M Phinney) S:14

Phinney, Mary MacKenzie - Died 1916 Jan 25 Born 1853 Oct 8 (with Irving B Phinney) S:14

Phinney, Maurice R Jr - (a cross marker) S:31

Phinney, Maurice R Sr - Died 1949 Born 1878 (with Luella M Phinney) S:20

Phinney, Mehitable - Died 1838 Jan 28 Age 73 Paul Phinney Stone has the letters, "Relict of" S:3+3R

Phinney, Mercie M - Died 1921 Born 1856 (with Nellie M Bauch & others) S:19

Phinney, Mercy - Died 1844 Oct 4 Born 1843 Apr 21 Dau of L & D C Phinney (buried with Bradock Phinney and others) S:8

Phinney, Mercy B - Died 1902 Born 1828 (buried with Eli Phinney) S:8

Phinney, Minerva D - Died 1873 Aug 31 Age 37 years, 4 months Wife of Alonzo Phinney (next to him & other wife) S:14

Phinney, Naome Mrs - Died 1834

Phinney (Cont.)
Feb 17 Age 62 Wife of Levi
Phinney (next to him) S:14

Phinney, Nelson - Died 1885 Born
1820 (large stone) Stone says,
"Father" (buried with Eunice
Phinney & others) S:8

Phinney, Nora C - Died 1957 Born
1872 S:16

Phinney, Olive - Died 1831 June
28 in her 44th yr Wife of Timothy Phinney Jr S:9R+26R

Phinney, Olive - Died 1831 Sept 1
in her 35th yr Wife of Capt Alvan
Phinney She was the daughter of
Ebenezer & Martha Case S:4

Phinney, Olive C - Died 1908 Born
1840 S:7

Phinney, Oliver - Died 1803 April
24 Age 3 months Son of Solomon & Anna Phinney S:3

Phinney, Olivia MacKenzie - Died
1975 Jan 12 Born 1882 Sept 18
(with Irving & Mary Phinney)
S:14

Phinney, Orgn - Died 1831 Feb 11
who drowned at sea Age 18
(listed on Capt Braddock Phinney's stone) S:3R

Phinney, Paul - Died 1835 Jan 14
in his 71st yr S:3

Phinney, Polly - Died 1796 Sept 13
in her 25th yr Wife of Edward
Phinney S:10+26R

Phinney, Poly Sturges - Died 1796
Sept 14 Age 10 months Daughter
of Solomon & Anna Phinney S:3

Phinney, Prince - Died 1844 Sept
26 Born 1822 Dec 16 S:26R

Phinney, Priscilla - Died 1776 July
24 Age 14 months Daughter of
Eli & Mary Phinney S:3

Phinney, Reliance - Died 1784 Jan
27 in her 84th yr Wife of Thomas
Phinney (next to him) S:3

Phinney, Richard - Died 1765 Aug
23 b 1775 Feb 2 Son of Eli &
Mary Phinney S:3

Phinney, Richard - Died 1820 Sept
22 Age 6 months, 14 days Son of
Richard & Marcy Phinney S:3

Phinney, Richard - Died 1840 Oct

Phinney (Cont.)
11 in his 56th yr S:3

Phinney, Robert - Died 1776 Dec
18 in his 4th yr Son of Eli &
Mary Phinney S:3

Phinney, Rodger - Died 1817(?)
June 23 Age 29 (stone worn)
S:14

Phinney, Russle Lovell - Died 1875
Aug 2 Age 10 months, 9 days
Son of Harrison & Adelia Phin-
ney S:8

Phinney, Sally H - Died 1816 June
3 in her 3rd yr Daughter of
Warren & Martha Phinney S:3

Phinney, Sarah - Died 1753 May 5
in her 81st yr Wife of Deacon
John Phinney (next to him) S:3R

Phinney, Sarah - Died 1902 Nov 1
Born 1821 July 27 Wife of
Grafton Phinney (next to him)
S:14

Phinney, Sarah A - Died 1913 Oct
7 Born 1842 Feb 26 (with James
Phinney & others) S:14

Phinney, Sarah G - Died 1858 Oct
20 Age 41 Daughter of Timothy
& Olive Phinney S:9R

Phinney, Sarah P (or E) - Died
1894 March 4 Age 90 years, 4
months, 14 days Wife of Isaac
Phinney (next to him) S:14

Phinney, Seth - Died 1883 Oct 25
in her 87th yr S:26R

Phinney, Seth - Died 1744/5 Jan 2
Age 17 months, 23 days Son of
Ebenezer & Rebeckah Phinney
S:11R

Phinney, Seth R - Died 1894 June
30 Age 98 years, 20 days S:10

Phinney, Solomon - Died 1824
April 7 Age 91 years, 10 months,
19 days S:3+3R

Phinney, Sumner I - Died 1896
Dec 26 Born 1977 Aug 19 (with
Irving & Mary Phinney) S:14

Phinney, Susan Crosby - Died
1902 Born 1830 S:8

Phinney, Susanna - Died 1765 Aug
20 Born 25 Sept 1757 Daughter
of Eli & Mary Phinney S:3

Phinney, Susannah - Died 1863

Phinney (Cont.)
Born 1778 S:7

Phinney, Temperance - Died 1863 July 4 Age 67 Wife of Elijah Phinney (next to Isaac Phinney) S:14

Phinney, Thomas - Died 1784 June 10 Age 89 (next to Reliance Phinney) S:3R

Phinney, Timothy - Died 1777 Aug 7 Son of Timothy & Temperance Phinney S:10

Phinney, Timothy - Died 1780 Son of Timothy & Temperance Phinney S:10

Phinney, Timothy - Died 1883 Sept 25 Age 99 years, 3 months Born 1784 June 13 Consort of Olive C Phinney S:9R

Phinney, Toilston F - Died 1927 Born 1852 (with wife, Louise G Phinney) S:18

Phinney, Victor W - Died 1852 Dec 22 Age 17 Son of Lot & Julia Phinney (next to them) S:12

Phinney, Walter Bourne - Died 1895 May 20 Born 1868 Jan 15 Died at Saltpond, West Coast of Africa (next to George Ward Phinney) S:19

Phinney, Walton F - Died 1821 Born 1846 (next to Francis E Phinney) S:14

Phinney, Warren - Died 1815 May 14 Noted on Sally H Phinney's stone that Warren, her father was, "drowned at sea" Wife was Martha S:3

Phinney, William - Died 1777 Feb 23 Age 10 Son of Eli and Mary & brother of Edward Phinney S:2R

Phinney, William - Died 1852 April 26 in his 73rd yr S:3

Phinney, William - Died 1892 Born 1811 (buried with Emily Phillips Phinney & others) S:8

Phinney, William Herring - Died 1931 July 9 Born 1870 Aug 22 (large Whelden family stone in middle of ceme with others) S:11

Phinney, William S - Died 1929 Born 1854 (buried with Julia E

Phinney (Cont.)
Phinney) S:8

Pickard, Edward C - Died 1958 Born 1887 (with Isaac & Hattie Hopkins) S:18

Pickering, Daniel P - Died 1896 Born 1822 (with Julia A Pickering & others) S:21

Pickering, Julia A - Died 1850 Born 1849 Daughter of Daniel & Julia A Pickering (with them & Julia M Pickering) S:21

Pickering, Julia A - Died 1922 Born 1828 (with Julia A Pickering, daughter & others) S:21

Pickering, Julia M - Died 1856 Born 1854 (there is a stone behind this one) Daughter of Daniel & Julia A Pickering (with them) S:21

Plearce, Samuel - Died 1818 Feb 16 in his 72nd yr S:7

Pierce, David H - Died 1962 July 6 Born 1901 March 14 (with Evelina E Pierce) S:16

Pierce, David H Jr - Died 1932 Born 1923 S:31

Pierce, Emma - Died 1880 Nov 3 Age 40 years, 10 months Wife of Myron E Pierce & Daughter of Allen & Sophia Bearse (between parents) S:21

Pierce, Esther H - Buried 1983 March 6 Age 85 Located in section A, lot 28, grave 4 S:14R

Pierce, Ethel E - Died 1968 Born 1900 (with James W Pierce) S:17

Pierce, Evelina E - Died 1978 May 18 Born 1897 Nov 10 (with David H Pierce) S:16

Pierce, Florence B - Died 1972 Born 1886 Wife of Heman Pierce (with him & Florence & Francis Pierce) S:18

Pierce, Francis C - Died 1913 Born 1906 (with Heman, Grace & Florence Pierce) S:18

Pierce, Garry C - Died 1960 Born 1890 (with wife, Esther B Hammond) S:14

Pierce, Grace M - Died 1912 Born 1878 Wife of Heman F Pierce

353

Pierce (Cont.)
(with him & Florence & Francis Pierce) S:18

Pierce, Heman F - Died 1960 Born 1881 (with wifes, Grace, Florence Pierce also with Francis C Pierce) S:18

Pierce, James W - Died 1979 Born 1893 (with Ethel E Pierce) S:17

Pierce, John W - Died 1953 Feb 6 Born 1898 Jan 4 S:17

Pierce, Louise BV - Died (still living 1991?) Born 1904 (listed with Neal A Pierce) S:17

Pierce, Maude Ethel - Died 1953 July 8 Born 1895 Dec 21 Wife of Shirley Savery Evans (with him) S:12

Pierce, Meredith - Died 1943 Jan 3 Born 1927 May 14 S:12

Pierce, Neal A - Died 1987 Born 1900 (listed with Louise BV Pierce) S:17

Pierce, Nora - Died 1973 Born 1879 Wife of Lorenzo Gifford (with him) S:14

Pigeon, Emma K - Died 1972 Born 1883 (with Richard Pigeon) S:14

Pigeon, Richard - Died 1970 Born 1882 (with Emma K Pigeon) S:14

Piggott, Albina S - Died 1944 Born 1860 (with Bertha E Piggott) S:13

Piggott, Bertha E - Died 1961 Born 1880 (with Albina S Piggott) S:13

Pigott, Roy - Died 1980 Born 1912 Military stone that says, "BMLC US Coast Guard - Korea" S:12

Pihl, Louise G - Died 1966 Born 1898 (with Roland T Pihl) S:17

Pihl, Roland T - Died 1976 Born 1898 (with Louise G Pihl) S:17

Pillion, Gladys M - Died (still living 1991?) Born 1904 (listed with William F Pillion) S:16

Pillion, William F - Died 1989 Born 1895 (listed with Gladys M Pillion) S:16

Pina, Antone - Died 1974 Born 1888 (listed with Mary E Pina) S:13

Pina, C C - Died 1931 Born 1867

Pina (Cont.)
(stone not clear & in the bushes located in back of cemetery) S:20

Pina, Caesar - Died 1981 Born 1897 S:16

Pina, Charles M - Died 1936 Born 1878 (with Mary SR Pina) S:16

Pina, Clara B - Died 1970 Born 1893 (a large church glass candle light with many flowers still around the grave) S:15

Pina, Ethel - Died 1987 Born 1896 (with daughter, June Costa) S:16

Pina, John B - Died 1953 Born 1897 S:16

Pina, Joseph L - Died 1923 Nov 9 Born 1878 Nov 1 Stone says, "Erected by his friend, John J Rosary" S:31

Pina, Mary E - Died (still living 1991?) Born 1906 (listed with Antone Pina) S:13

Pina, Mary SR - Died 1964 Born 1887 (with Charles M Pina) S:16

Pina, Peter G - Died 1944 Born 1896 S:16

Pinkham, Catherine J - Died 1915? Born 1833 Wife of James Blagden (next to him) S:21

Pinkham, Dorothy H - Died 1974 June 17 Born 1919 Aug 2 Stone says, "Mother" (located between Harry L & Robert L Jones) S:19

Pinson, Laurence W - Died 1964 Born 1947 Stone says, "My son, Boy Scouts of America Life scout unit 60 Plaque says, 13 Aug 1947 to 24 July 1964 (next to Margaret E Pinson) S:20

Pinson, Margaret E - Died (no dates) Stones says, "Mother" (Rishe Levine Anderson on reverse side of her stone) (next to Laurence W Pinson) S:20

Pipeling, Althea J - Died 1970 Born 1897 S:17

Pitcher(?), Hannah G - Died 1914 Born 1822 Stone says, Wedded 60 years, 30 March 1907 (large rock with plaque) (with Samuel Pitcher MD) S:18

Pitcher(?), Samuel (MD) - Died

Pitcher (Cont.)

1907 Born 1821 (large rock with plaque) (with wife, Hannah G Pitcher) Stone says, "Wedded 60 years, 30 March 1907" S:18

Pitcher, Chloe - Died 1855 Born 1794 (with Nathan A Pitcher & others) S:18

Pitcher, Nathan A - Died 1863 Born 1840 (with Samuel Pitcher & others) S:18

Pitcher, Samuel - Died 1866 Born 1789 (with Chloe Pitcher & others) S:18

Pitts, Cora E - Died 1941 Born 1873 (stone is under perpetual care) (listed on Crowell stone with Julia Crowell & others) S:8

Planz, G G - Died 1931 Born 1867 S:31

Pocius, August - Died 1943 Born 1885 (next to Hedwig Pocius) S:17

Pocius, Hedwig - Died 1964 Born 1898 (next to August Pocius) S:17

Pocknett, Benjamin F - Died 1921 Born 1875 (with Caroline E Pocknett) S:18

Pocknett, Caroline E - Died 1941 Born 1869 (with Benjamin F Pocknett) S:18

Poirier, Stephen J - Died 1978 April 9, 29 days (with William J & Maria Robie) S:20

Polette, Edna H - Died 1982 Born 1898 S:18

Pollard, Agnes - Died 1892 March 24 Age 80 (with Elizabeth McDonald) S:14

Pollock, Dalwyn K - Died 1985 Born 1905 (located in Henderson plot) Was Cpl in US Army during World War II S:18

Pollock, Gertrude F - Died 1975 Born 1897 (Henderson plot) (with Mattie May Henderson & Walter B Pollock Sr & others) S:18

Pollock, Walter B Sr - Died 1966 Oct17 Born 1894 Sept 19 (has 2 stones) (Henderson plot) From

Pollock (Cont.)

Massachusetts, was E3 in USNRF during World War I (with Mattie May Henderson & others) S:18

Polto, Helia G - Died 1937 Born 1896 (a large family stone with others) S:11

Polto, John A - Died 1941 Born 1870 (a large family stone with others) S:11

Polto, Mamie S - Died 1977 Born 1902 Wife of Kenneth D Greene (with him) S:11

Polto, Seraphena - Died 1924 Born 1869 (a large family stone with others) S:11

Pompey, Rhodella M - Died 1954 Born 1881 Stone says, "Grand-mom" (next to Onida P Ridley) S:18

Pooler, Alice May - Died 1933 Born 1912 S:18

Pope, John James Otis - Died 1935 Born 1868 (buried with Guest family) S:8

Pope, Lucie A - Died 1938 Born 1863 Wife of George Guest (buried with him) S:8

Porgie, Rose M - Died 1991 Born 1900 (undertaker plaque only) S:15

Porier, Naomi L - Died 1869 Dec 17 Born 1834 Nov 7 Wife of Sylva-nus Porier (next to son, Willie S Porier) S:14

Porier, Willie S - Died 1877 April 22 Age 15 years, 11 months (stone is down) Son of Sylvanus Porier (next to possible mother, Naomi L Porier) S:14

Porter, Sophonia - Died 1815 July 25 ? Wife of Josiah Scudder (next to him) S:12

Post, Clarence W - Died 1969 Born 1886 (he was a Mason) (with Cleone C Rich Post & others) S:18

Post, Cleone C - Died (still living 1991?) Born 1821 (with Cleone C Rich Post & others) S:18

Post, Cleone C Rich - Died 1976

Post (Cont.)
Born 1889 (with Ethel M Hallett
& others) S:18

Potter, EM - Died (no dates) (with
Hattie Potter, Sarah A Phinney &
others) S:14

Potter, Hattie L - Died 1948 Dec 21
Born 1875 July 9 (with E M
Potter, Sarah A Phinney &
others) S:14

Powell, Arthur A - Died 1941 Born
1863 S:8

Power, Emma - Died 1960 Aug 16
Born 1865 April 5 S:16

Power, Grace C - Died (no dates
listed) (located between Jeanette
Hassett & Robert Gill) S:16

Powers, Charles F - Died 1951
Born 1874 (with Elizabeth B
Powers) S:13

Powers, Elizabeth B - Died 1962
Born 1883 (with Charles F
Powers) S:13

Powers, George - Died 1985 Born
1915 (listed with Lou Powers)
S:20

Powers, Lou - Died (still living
1991?) Born 1920 (listed with
George Powers) S:20

Powers, W - Died (no dates) (next to
John Reposa) S:31

Powers, William E - Died 1985
Born 1904 (with wife, Ruth L
Cornish & others) S:19

Prada, Beth A - Died 1963 Aug 21
Stone says, "Baby" S:20

Prada, Edward A Sr - Died 1974
Aug 12 Born 1906 May 1 (has 2
stones) Was a CCOMM in US
Coast Guard (with Elizabeth
Prada) S:20

Prada, Elizabeth E - Died 1986
Born 1908 (with Edward Prada)
S:20

Prantes, Spiros A - Died 1981 June
Age 85 Born 1895 Stone says,
"Peace" (some of the above info
from the Mosswood cemetery
records) S:15

Pratt, (son) - Died 1817 May Son of
Rev Enoch Pratt (is listed with
Joseph Field Pratt) S:5R

Pratt, Charlie K - Died 1853 Sept 5
Born 1844 Feb 8 Son of Rev
Enoch & Lucy Pratt S:5

Pratt, Enoch Rev - Died 1860 Feb
20 Born 1781 July 31 at Mid-
dleborough, Mass Ordained
pastor of Congregational Church
of West Barnstable 1807 Resigned in 1835 S:5

Pratt, Ernest - Died 1890 May 6
Born 1809 Jan 8 Son of George
& Lucretia Moulton S:5

Pratt, Eva Ardelle - Died 1968 Oct
3 Born 1896 Feb 13 (large stone
says Pratt) S:8

Pratt, Frances G - Died 1833 Feb 7
Age 15 months Son of Rev
Enoch & Mercy S Pratt S:5

Pratt, Francis Alexander - Died
1835 March 1 Age 7 weeks S:5R

Pratt, George Greenleaf - Died
1890 May 3 Born 1842 May 6
(stone says father) S:5

Pratt, Ida Hyde - Died 1840 July 2
Age 20 months, 6 days Daughter
of Rev Enoch & Lucy Pratt (stone
says, A Lovely Flower) S:5

Pratt, John Edward - Died 1935
Feb 5 Born 1850 Nov 11 (with
Sarah Louisa Pratt) S:8

Pratt, Joseph Field - Died 1816
June 29 Age 13 weeks Probable
parents are Mary & Rev Enoch
Pratt Buried next to Mary Pratt
which says her father was
Joseph Field S:5

Pratt, Josephine S - Died 1830
July 3 Daughter of Rev Enoch &
Mercy Pratt S:5

Pratt, Lucretia Berry Moulton -
Died 1892 Oct 20 Born 1853
Nov 20 Wife of George Greenleaf
Pratt S:5R

Pratt, Lucy Jenkins - Died 1896
May 28 Age 96 Born 1800 Jan
10 Wife of Rev Enoch Pratt S:5

Pratt, Mary - Died 1826 July 18
Born 1782 Oct 28 in Boston,
Mass Married on 1809 Apl 27
Wife of Rev Enoch Pratt Daugh-
ter of Dea Joseph Field of Bos-
ton, Mass S:5

Pratt, Mercy S - Died 1839 Mar 13 Stone also says, Who infant daughter Rebeca Age 16 days, erected to the memory Husband was Rev E Pratt S:5

Pratt, Rebeca - Stone says, Age 16 days, erected to the memory Written on her mothers stone, Mercy S Pratt d: 1839 Father was Rev E Pratt S:5

Pratt, Sarah Louisa - Died 1903 Jan 15 Born 1853 Sept 1 (buried with Eva Ardelle Pratt) S:8

Pratt, Viola - Died 1982 Born 1910 Wife of Nelson L LeGrand (with him) S:17

Prayer, Julius - Died 1970 Born 1895 S:17

Preble, Josephine M - Died 1937 Born 1873 Wife of William Preble (buried next to him) S:8

Preble, William P - Died 1951 Born 1863 S:8

Prentice, Mary - Died 1780 July 8 in her 26th yr "A sincere mistiaul affectionate companion, an agreeable friend" Wife of William Prentice and daughter of Col. David Gorham S:26R

Prentice, Mira - Died 1863 Nov 1 Age 69 Widow of James F Prentice & daughter of Ezra & Deborah Crowell S:11

Prentice, William Henry - Died (still living 1991?) Born 1896 (others listed too, but later dates) S:14

Prentiss, Lillian P - Died 1988 Born 1909 (with Elmer Jackson) S:20

Price, Elizabeth - Died 1967 Born 1888 (next to William Price) S:15

Price, Ruth L - Buried 1983 Jan 21 Age 93 Located in section C, lot 2, grave 5 S:14R

Price, William - Died 1969 Born 1892 (next to Elizabeth Price) S:15

Princi, Margaret Bergin - Died 1990 March 19 Born 1949 Sept 18 S:20

Prior, Gladys Gifford - Died 1969

Prior (Cont.) Born 1892 (next to Reginald Austin Prior) S:14

Prior, Reginald Austin - Died 1965 Born 1892 (next to Gladys Gifford Prior) S:14

Pritchard, Mildred Hart - Died 1924 Born 1891 (has 2 stones) (with Marion Hart Cronin) S:18

Pvy, John William - Died 1954 Born 1903 S:20

Pye, Elmer - Died 1989 Nov 25 Born 1909 April 20 (also has a US Service plaque) Was a TEC 3 in US Army during World War II (next to Henry Pye) S:20

Pye, Henry - Died 1964 March 1 Born 1907 May 31 (also has plaque of Veterans of Foreign Wars) Was a Pvt, PW Camp 1460 SCU during World War II (next to Elmer Pye) S:20

Pyy, Chris - Died 1981 Born 1962 (there are music notes all over his stone) S:19

Pyyny, Jane T - Died 1984 Born 1919 S:20

Pyyny, Wendla F - Died 1957 Born 1875 S:20

Queenan, Helen D - Died 1987 Born 1902 (with Anna D Parsil) S:16

Quigley, Rachel M - Died 1958 Born 1865 S:11

Quinn, Margaret - Died 1989 Born 1910 Wife of William J O'Neil (with him & others) S:16

Quinn, Ruth Nye - Died 1981 Feb Age 81 Born 1899 (with Thomas J Quinn) (some of the above info is from the Mosswood cemetery records) S:15

Quinn, Thomas J - Died 1972 Born 1893 (with Ruth N Quinn) S:15

Quinn, Thomas J Jr - Died (still living in 1991?) Born 1905 Jan 11 (listed with Hellen V Foster, wife) S:15

Rabbitt, Emma E - Died 1953 Born 1881 S:16

Ragine, Dism? - Died March? Born May 28 (stone not clear, it was

Ragine (Cont.)
also hand written on cement)
S:20

Ramoska, Joseph - Buried 1982
Oct 7 Age 89 Located in section
8, lot 120, grave 8 S:15R

Ramsay, Anne F - Died 1981 Born
1889 (Mosswood Ceme records
#15 say burial was 1981 March
27 at age 91) S:15

Ramsay, Sherburn - Died 1913
Born 1846 (with Luther & Eva
Nickerson) S:14

Rand, Lottie Edson - Died 1920
July 28 Born 1875 Nov 12 Wife
of Walter C Clark (next to Richard Henry Rand & Jane E
Edson) S:19

Rand, Richard Henry - Died 1909
June 9 Born 1875 June 12 (next
to wife, Lottie Edson Rand) S:19

Randall, (no first name) - Died
1929 Born 1926 (Randall is
placed on stone as if it were a
last name, but possibly same as
Randall N Brown) S:31

Rankin, Dorothy - Died 1988 Born
1907 S:12

Ransden, Alberto M - Died 1971
Born 1899 He was a Mason
(next to wife, Mildred P Ransden)
S:14

Ransden, Mildred P - Died 1968
Born 1900 Wife of Alberto M
Ransden (next to him) S:14

Ranson, Maude B - Died 1979
Born 1893 Stone says,"Much
loved" S:14

Ranta, Emil - Died 1961 Born 1892
S:20

Ranta, Tarmo E - Died 1955 May 9
Born 1923 Jan 1 From Massa-
chusetts, was a Pvt in Bty H, 83
CA (AA) during World War II
S:20

Ravi, Helena Margherita Chesia -
Died 1974 Feb 21 Born 1884
Aug 27 at San Giorgio a Cremo-
na,Italy Daughter of Salvatore
Vincenzo Ravi & Mary William-
son Booth (with Harry Louis
Bailey) S:14

Rawson, Dorothy - Died 1683 Dec
28 Age 2 years, 4 months (metal
brace holding stone together,
very clear inscription) Daughter
of William & Ann Rawson S:11

Raymond, Bessie W - Died 1913
Born 1876 (with Ben & Elizabeth
Baxter) S:18

Raymond, Byron D - Died 1976
July 22 Born 1898 Aug 4 Stone
says, "Father" (next to Eva &
Frances Raymond) S:17

Raymond, Eva M - Died 1976 Aug
4 Born 1900 Sept 26 Stone says,
"Mother" (between Frances &
Byron Raymond) S:17

Raymond, Frances M - Died 1990
Dec 22 Born 1895 March 28
Stone says, "Mother" (next to
Eva M Raymond) S:17

Ready, John H - Died 1939 Born
1856 (with Mary A Ready) S:18

Ready, Mary A - Died 1928 Born
1856 (with John H Ready) S:18

Reavis, Germon A - Died 1966
Born 1882 S:17

Reavis, Mary E - Died 1958 June
25 Born 1884 Dec 20 S:18

Rebello, Antonio B - Died 1946
Born 1872/3 (with wife, Maria
Clara & son, Antonio B Rebello
Jr) S:31

Rebello, Antonio B Jr - Died 1922
Born 1897 (with parents, Anto-
nio Sr & Maria Clara Rebello)
S:31

Rebello, Maria Clara - Died 1954
Born 1878 Wife of Antonio
Rebello (with him & son, Antonio
Jr) S:31

Reddick, Eliza M - Died 1959 Born
1875 (with Robert Reddick) S:18

Reddick, Robert H - Died 1956
Born 1881 (with Eliza M Reddick) S:18

Reed, Lillian L - Died 1968 Born
1875 S:17

Reed, Sherman W - Died 1972
Born 1890 S:15

Reedmon, Anna - Died (still living
1991?) Born 1899 Wife of John
M Kasper (listed with him) S:17

358

Regan, Patrick - Died 1898 Oct 12 in Barnstable, Massachusetts Born in Ireland S:20

Reguera, Galan - Died 1965 May 11 Born 1896 Nov 26 From Massachusetts, was Corporal in 575 Tech Sch Sq AAF during World War I & II S:14

Reichert?, Emma A - Died 1953 Born 1868 (Stone down from vandals) (with Ezra D Marchant) S:18

Reid, Ivy Janet Capener - Died 1986 Born 1899 S:17

Reid, John - Died 1973 Born 1888 (next to Margaret J Reid) S:14

Reid, Margaret J - Died 1966 Born 1885 (next to John Reid) S:14

Reimann, George P - Died 1971 Born 1902 (with I Margaret Reimann) S:20

Reimann, I Margaret - Died 1979 Born 1904 (with George Reimann) S:20

Reis, Antone P - Died 1952 Born 1891 From the Cape Verde Islands (stone down from vandals) (between Lillian M MacElhinney & William A Treen) S:18

Reis, Manuel P - Died 1968 Born 1893 (with Mildred J Reis) S:16

Reis, Mildred J - Died 1984 Born 1910 (with Manuel P Reis) S:16

Rennie, Elsie E - Died 1925 Born 1866 Wife of Thomas D Rennie (with him) S:14

Rennie, Helen M - Died 1979 Born 1885 (next to W Christie Rennie) S:14

Rennie, Thomas D - Died 1936 Born 1864 (rock marker) (with wife, Elsie E Rennie) S:14

Rennie, W Christie - Died 1956 Born 1887 (next to Helen M Rennie) S:14

Replogle, Anna C - Died 1979 Born 1889 (undertaker plaque only) S:15

Reposa, ? (Diane?) - Old worn stone located in back of Joaquina J Reposa's stone) S:31

Reposa, Albert D - Died 1943 Feb 4

Reposa (Cont.)
Born 1916 March 17 From Massachusetts, was Sergeant in US Army Air Forces during World War II (next to Manuel & Mary J Reposa) S:31

Reposa, John Died 1924 Born 1886 (a small white stone) S:31

Reposa, Manuel D - Died 1926 Born 1892 (with Mary Julia Reposa) S:31

Reposa, Mary Julia - Died 1971 Born 1894 (with Manuel D Reposa) S:31

Revan, Constantine A - Died 1977 Born 1899 S:15

Reynolds, Elizabeth F - Died 1948 Born 1866 Wife of Horton Reynolds (with him) S:14

Reynolds, Horton L - Died 1940 Born 1863 (with wife, Elizabeth F Reynolds) S:14

Rhodehouse, Mamie - Died 1863 Aug 15 (year/month not clear 3 days?) Has Civil War star 1861-65 Dau of Nelson & Rebecca Rhodehouse (next to them) S:14

Rhodehouse, Mary - Died 1863 Born 1863 (with Nelson Rhodehouse & Rebecca Burgess) S:14

Rhodehouse, Melinda Ann - Died 1950 Born 1859 (with Nelson Rhodehouse & Rebecca Burgess) S:14

Rhodehouse, Nelson - Died 1906 (or 1908?) Born 1830 (with Rebecca Burgess) S:14

Rhodehouse, Nelson Jr - Died 1859 Born 1856 (with Nelson Rhodehouse & Rebecca Burgess) S:14

Rhodehouse, Rebecca B - Buried 1889 Located in section 7, lot 4, grave 10 S:14R

Rhodehouse, Rebecca Burgess - Buried 1899 S:15R

Ricci, Louis D - Died 1961 June 24 Born 1877 Dec 17 S:16

Rice, Louis E - Died 1936 Born 1852 S:19

Rice, Patrick J - Died 1971 May 26 Born 1900 Jan 1 From

Rice (Cont.)
Massachusetts, was Pvt in CoE,
31st Med Reg during World War
II S:15

Rich, Augusta L - Died 1893 June
30 Born 1835 May 15 (next to
Seth Rich) S:12

Rich, Benjamin F - Died 1821 Born
1852 He was a Mason (with
Eunice B Rich & others) S:18

Rich, Carrie M - Died 1936 Born
1872 Wife of Frank H Williams
(with him) S:12

Rich, Eunice B - Died 1941 Born
1861 (with Clarence W Post &
others) S:18

Rich, Florence - Died 1961 Born
1870 (with husband, Adrian
Chadwick) S:12

Rich, Seth - Died 1897 May 9 Born
1826 May 29 (next to Augusta L
Rich) S:12

Rich, Walter Irwing - Died 1899
Sept 14 Born 1867 Aug 24 S:12

Richard, Alfred A - Died 1951 Born
1881 S:16

Richards, Jennie Sophia - Buried
1984 July 6 Age 84 Located in
section L, lot 4, grave 2 S:14R

Richards, Linda A - Died 1946
Born 1886 (with Stephen S Richards) S:14

Richards, Stephen S - Died 1948
Born 1883 (with Linda A Richards) S:14

Richardson, Abigail - Died 1834
Feb 15 Age 25 Wife of Josiah
Richardson & daughter of
Ebenezer & Betsey Scudder
(buried with William Richard-
son-infant, in same grave) S:7

Richardson, Alexina - Died 1861
May 27 Born 1828 Jan 30
(buried with Elizabeth Matthews
& others) S:8

Richardson, Annie Dutcher - Died
1965 Born 1875 S:15

Richardson, Emma S - Died 1892
Sept 15 Born 1867 Jan 17
Daughter of John O A & Sarah
Richardson S:8

Richardson, Ephraim - Died 1873

Richardson (Cont.)
Dec 31 Born 1808 Mar 31
(buried next to Ephraim Richardson & buried with Jane
Richardson) S:8

Richardson, Ephraim(?) - Died
1815 June 28 (stone not clear)
(buried next to Ephraim Richardson) S:8

Richardson, Hannah - Died 1861
Jun7 Age 82 years, 3 months,
12 days Wife of John Richarson
S:3

Richardson, Jane - Died 1911 Feb
18 Born 1813 Jan 17 (buried
with Ephraim Richardson) S:8

Richardson, John - Died 1842 Dec
31 in his 78th yr S:3

Richardson, John OA - Died 1870
Feb 16 Age 58 years, 1 month
Was in Company F, 48th Regi-
ment, Massachusetts Wife was
Sarah S (buried next to him) S:8

Richardson, Sarah S - Died 1886
Sept 8 Born 1844 Jan 15 Wife of
John O A Richardson (buried
next to him) S:8

Richardson, William - Died 1835
Age 19 Died at Marine Hospital
on Staten Island, New Jersey
(NY?) Son of John Richardson
S:3+3R

Richardson, William - Died 1834
Feb 12 Age 3 days (buried with
mother, Abigail) Son of Josiah &
Abigail Richardson) S:7

Richer, Alice D - Died 1968 Born
1898 (with Leo T Richer) S:15

Richer, Leo T - Died 1964 Born
1900 (with Alice D Richer) S:15

Richmond, Mildred E - Died 1982
Born 1897 Wife of Walter
Richmond (with him) S:18

Richmond, Walter E - Died 1945
Born 1884 (with wife, Mildred E
Richmond) S:18

Richter, Jeannette - Died 1924 Nov
19 S:21

Rider, John S (Capt) - Died 1849
Sept 22 at Staten Island ? Age
42 S:11

Ridley, Evelyn S - Died 1889 Born

Ridley (Cont.)
1889 (with Catherine S Lewis & others) S:18

Ridley, John - Died 1966 Born 1888 From Massachusetts, was Pvt in Hq TRP 92 Div during World War I S:17

Ridley, Marietta L - Died 1930 Born 1859 (with Evelyn S Ridley & others) S:18

Ridley, Onida P - Died 1968 Born 1899 Stone says,"Mother" (next to Rhodella M Pompey) S:18

Riedell, Carl F - Died 1988 Born 1902 (with Charles Parker)`S:12

Riedell, Ethel Parker - Died (still living 1991?) Born 1906 (with Charles Parker) S:12

Ring, Hattie A - Died 1892 May 18 Age 22 years, 9 months Wife of William D Ring (between Adelia & Isaiah B Linnell) S:21

Riordan, William G - Died 1989 Born 1919 Was a Lt JG in US Navy during World War II S:20

Ritchie, Alfred C - Died 1957 Born 1907 (with Loton Cannon & others) S:18

Rivers, Henry L - Died 1965 Sept 11 Born 1884 July 15 (next to Ida J Rivers) S:16

Rivers, Ida J - Died 1981 Aug 20 Born 1887 Jan 10 (next to Henry L Rivers) S:16

Robbins, Abbott L - Died 1926 Born 1852 (with Fannie A Robbins) S:12

Robbins, Abigail - Died 1848 Aug 22 Born 1845 Oct 24 Daughter of Joseph & Persis Robbins Within Linnell plott S:12

Robbins, Albert H - Died 1930 Aug 27 Born 1887 Feb 28 From Massachusetts, Pvt in CoK, 165 th Inf during World War I (near James Robbins & others) S:18

Robbins, Albert S - Died 1978 Born 1895 Was a Private in US Army during World War I (next Gladys E Robbins) S:14

Robbins, Alice - Died 1974 Born 1876 (with James Robbins &

Robbins (Cont.)
others) S:18

Robbins, Alton E - Died 1962 Born 1884 (with wife, Emma E Robbins & David Welch) S:18

Robbins, Bertha R - Died 1973 Born 1882 Stone says,"Mother" S:14

Robbins, Della - Buried 1890 Jan 16 Located in section O, lot 13, grave 4 S:14R

Robbins, E F (Capt) - Died 1917 Born 1842 (with wife, Charlotte B Boyek) S:14

Robbins, Edith M - Died 1947 Born 1856 Wife of Charles Crosby (with him) S:12

Robbins, Edward II - Died 1914 Born 1884 (with Lillian F Robbins & others) S:18

Robbins, Elia (?) - Died 1890 Jan 16? Age 20 years, 6 months, 15 days (stone worn bad) (next to Washington E Robbins) S:14

Robbins, Elisha - Died 1928 Born 1880 (with William H Robbins) S:14

Robbins, Eliza Freeman - Died 1918 July 19 Born 1865 Nov 7 (with George F Robbins & next to Nelson F Robbins) S:21

Robbins, Emily - Died 1876 Born 1832 (with Lemuel Marchant & others) S:21

Robbins, Emma E - Died 1986 Born 1889 Wife of Alton E Robbins (with him & David A Welch) S:18

Robbins, Fannie A - Died 1941 Born 1860 (with Abbott L Robbins) S:12

Robbins, Genieve - Died 1862 Aug 17 Born 1861 Sept Daughter of Joseph & Persis Robbins (located in Linnell plot) S:12

Robbins, George F - Died 1929 Born 1885 (with Eliza Freeman Robbins) S:21

Robbins, Gladys E - Died 1986 March 17 Born 1898 Feb 12 (next to Albert S Robbins) S:14

Robbins, Honora - Died 1901 Born

Robbins (Cont.)
1863 S:21

Robbins, Horace L - Died 1974 Born 1902 (with Sylvia Mae Robbins) S:16

Robbins, James H - Died 1914 Born 1850 (with Mary E Robbins & others) S:18

Robbins, Joseph - Died 1841 April 21 Born 1839 April 24 Located in Linnell plot S:12

Robbins, Joseph - Died 1888 Mar 2 Born 1807 July 8 S:12

Robbins, Kenneth Michael - Died 1960 June Born 1959 Dec Stone says, "We know your gods little angel now" S:13

Robbins, Lillian F - Died 1965 Born 1889 (with Alice Robbins & others) S:18

Robbins, Marcy - Died (date underground) Daughter of John Robbins (located between Henry Bacon & James Lothrope) S:10

Robbins, Marshall F Jr - Died 1969 Born 1891 (with Marshall F Robbins & Caroline Coleman) S:14

Robbins, Marshall F Sr - Died 1942 Born 1866 (with Capt EF Robbins & Charlotte Boyek & wife, Caroline W Coleman) S:14

Robbins, Mary E - Died 1902 Born 1855 (with William A Robbins & others) S:18

Robbins, Nellie W - Died 1860 May 14 Born 1860 Mar 29 Daughter of Joseph & Persis Robbins (located in Linnell plot) S:12

Robbins, Nelson F - Died 1930 Born 1860 (next to Eliza Freeman Robbins) S:21

Robbins, Persis - Died 1855 Feb 2 Born 1850 Nov Daughter of Joseph & Persis Robbins (located in Linnell plot) S:12

Robbins, Persis H - Died 1905 Mar 8 Born 1817 April 6 Wife of Joseph Robbins Stone says, "To meet the loves gone before" S:12

Robbins, Rebecca J - Died 1910 (or 1916) Born 1851 (stone

Robbins (Cont.)
crumbling, in bad condition) (with Washington E Robbins) (next to Sylvester Jones) S:14

Robbins, Richard Freeman - Died 1910 Born 1879 (with Mabel Evans) S:12

Robbins, Samuel - Died 1726 Nov 8 Age 7 months, 2 days Son of Nathan? & Rebeccan Robbins S:5R

Robbins, Sophornia - Died 1855 Feb 14 Born 1854 Mar Daughter of Joseph & Persis Robbins (located in Linnell plot) S:12

Robbins, Sylvia Mae - Died 1948 Born 1889 (with Horace L Robbins) S:16

Robbins, Timothy - Died 1864 Born 1827 (with Emily Robbins & others) S:21

Robbins, Washington E - Died 1906 Born 185? (stone crumbling, bad condition) (with Rebecca J Robbins) (next to Sylvester Jones) S:14

Robbins, William A - Died 1913 Born 1880 (with Edward H Robbins & others) S:18

Robbins, William LG - Died 1886 Born 1852 (Crowell stone) (with Eugene Crowell & others) S:14

Robbins, Williams Henry - Died 1954 Born 1881 (with wife, Alice T Smalley) (some of above info from Mosswood cemetery records) S:14

Robello, Antone B - Died 1966 May 6 Born 1892 Jan 23 S:14

Robello, Maria H - Died 1926 Born 1866 Wife of John Rogers (with him) S:14

Roberick, Alfred C - Died 1972 Born 1911 (next to Rita G Roderick) S:20

Roberts, James C - Died 1975 Dec 8 Born 1900 Dec 25 Was a Pvt in US Army during World War II S:17

Roberts, Laura - Died 1951 June 22 Born 1875 Aug 3 Wife of Edwin Thomas (with him) S:11

Roberts, Martha - Died 1940 Born 1860 Wife of Robert Dight (with him) S:14

Robichaud, Genevieve - Died 1963 Born 1883 Wife of Joseph Robichaud (with him) S:16

Robichaud, Joseph - Died 1957 Born 1881 (with wife, Genevieve Robichaud) S:16

Robie, Maria L - Died (still living 1991?) Born 1921 (with William Robie & Stephen Poirier) S:20

Robie, William J - Died 1982 Born 1917 Was in US Army during World War II (with Maria Robie & Stephen J Poirier) S:20

Robin, Emil W Died 1935 Born 1891 (with Selma Rodin) S:18

Robinson, Abbie - Died 1933 Born 1863 (with husband, Francis R Robinson) S:18

Robinson, Abigail - Died 1853 Feb 1 in her 63rd yr Wife of Thomas Robinson S:5

Robinson, Adeline - Died (no dates) Wife of Simeon N Robinson (listed with him) S:21

Robinson, Almond - Died 1869 May 18 Born 1858 Sept 26 (with Edmund Robinson & others) S:21

Robinson, Asa - Died 1940 Born 1860 (with Emmeline P Robinson & others) S:21

Robinson, Caroline - Died 1911 Born 1836 (with Jonathan Hallett & next to Asa W Robinson) S:21

Robinson, Edmund - Died 1915 Jan 22 Born 1839 Oct 20 (with Mary F Robinson & others) S:21

Robinson, Eliot Harlow - Died 1942 Born 1884 (with wife, Helen W Bradlee) S:14

Robinson, Eliza F - Died 1863 Sept 29 Born 1860 Nov 18 (with Almond Robinson & others) S:21

Robinson, Ella F - Died 1861 Nov 11 Born 1858 Sept 26 (with Eliza F Robinson & others) S:21

Robinson, Emmeline P - Died 1929 Born 1855 (with Harry W Robinson & others) S:21

Robinson, Etta D - Died 1951 Born 1885 Wife of George F Robinson (with him & others) S:18

Robinson, Francis R - Died 1928 Born 1855 (with wife, Abbie Robinson) S:18

Robinson, George F - Died 1958 Born 1880 (with wife, Etta D Robinson & others) S:18

Robinson, Hannah Mrs - Died 1854 Jan 29 Age 77 Widow of James Robinson S:12

Robinson, Harry S - Died 1960 Oct 23 Born 1888 July 19 at Georgia Was a 1st Lieutenant in Dental Corps during World War I S:14

Robinson, Harry W - Died (no date) Born 1886 (with Joseph H Hallett & others) S:21

Robinson, Henry W - Died 1960 Born 1885 (with Francis & Abbie Robinson) S:18

Robinson, John W - Died 1884 Nov 17 Age 30 years, 2 months, 23 days Son of William & Sally Robinson (next to them) S:21

Robinson, Marguerite F - Died 1935 Born 1907 S:20

Robinson, Mary A - Died 1973 Born 1888 S:16

Robinson, Mary F - Died 1923 March 18 Born 1839 April 4 (with Willie A Robinson & others) S:21

Robinson, Olive C - Buried 1981 Nov 27 Age 90 Located in section 3, lot 23-13 1/2, grave 2 S:15R

Robinson, Sally W - Died 1893 March 26 Age 69 years, 5 months, 11 days (next to John W Robinson) S:21

Robinson, Simeon N - Died 1904 Dec 3 Age 62 years, 9 months (with wife, Adeline Robinson) S:21

Robinson, Thomas W - Died 1866 Feb 7 in his 86th yr S:5

Robinson, Walter - Died 1961 Born 1877 (with wife, Annie Ledger) S:19

Robinson, William - Died (stone down & not clear of name) Son

Robinson (Cont.)
of William & Sally Robinson
(next to them) S:21

Robinson, William - Died 1892
April 17 Age 71 years, 4 months,
9 days (next to Sally W Robinson) S:21

Robinson, Willie A - Died 1894
June 6 Born 1873 May 29 (with
Almond Robinson & others) S:21

Rocha, Joseph B - Died 1949 Born
1893 (with wife, Mary Rocha)
S:16

Rocha, Mary - Died 1968 Born
1889 Wife of Joseph B Rocha
(with him) S:16

Roche, Frederick L - Died 1957
Born 1889 (with Katherine
Roche) S:16

Roche, Katherine - Died 1965 Born
1887 (with Frederick L Roche)
S:16

Roderick, Alfred C - Died 1972
Born 1911 (next to Rita G Roderick) S:31

Roderick, Joseph C - Died 1969
Born 1883 (with wife, Mary C
Roderick) S:17

Roderick, Louisa - Died 1980 Born
1890 (with Manuel Roderick)
S:15

Roderick, Manuel - Died 1980
Born 1876 (with Louisa Roderick) S:15

Roderick, Mary - Died 1974 Born
1882 Wife of Conrad Fernandes
(with him) S:16

Roderick, Mary C - Died 1974
Born 1893 Wife of Joseph C
Roderick (with him) S:17

Roderick, Rita G - Died 1953 Born
1915 (next to Alfred C Roderick)
S:31

Rodin, Mildred M - Died 1939 Born
1897 (with Walter O Rodin) S:31

Rodin, Selma - Died 1935 Born
1869 Stone says, "Mother" (next
to Emil W Robin) S:18

Rodin, Walter O - Died 1931 Born
1894 (with Mildred M Rodin)
S:31

Rodrick, Francis J - Died 1955

Rodrick (Cont.)
Born 1885 (with Mary Rodrick)
S:16

Rodrick, Mary - Died 1985 Born
1893 (with Francis J Rodrick)
S:16

Rodrigues, Antonio - Died 1986
Born 1894 S:15

Roe, Ella Frances - Died 1894 Born
1851 S:5

Rogeberg, Karen M - Died 1987
Born 1896 Wife of Fred Williams
(next to him) S:12

Rogers, (baby boy, stillborn) - Died
1850 May 8 Located in section
R, lot 13, grave 3 S:14R

Rogers, (child) - Died 1835 Dec 3
Born 1835 Nov 21 Daughter of
David & Deborah Rogers (next to
other infants) S:14

Rogers, (child) - Died 1837 May 29
Born 1837 May 20 Daughter of
David & Deborah Rogers (next to
other infants) S:14

Rogers, (child) - Died 1838 Sept 26
Born 1838 Sept 19 Daughter of
David & Deborah Rogers (next to
other infants) S:14

Rogers, (child) - Died 1842 April 7
Born 1842 April 4 Daughter of
David & Deborah Rogers (next to
others infants) S:14

Rogers, (daughter) - Died 1845 May
5 Born 1845 April 28 Dau of
David & Deborah Rogers (next to
other infants) S:14

Rogers, (infant dau) - Died 1850
May 7 Dau of David & Deborah
Rogers (next to mother) S:14

Rogers, (infant son) - Died 1848
Oct 13 Age 6 weeks Son of H W
& Eliza Ann Rogers (with mother) S:14

Rogers, (infant) - Died (death date
possibly same as birth) Born
1848 April 20 Son of David &
Deborah Rogers (with another
infant) S:14

Rogers, (infant) - Died (no death
date, possibly same as birth)
Born 1846 May 17 Daughter of
David & Deborah Rogers (with

Rogers (Cont.)
another infant) S:14

Rogers, (infant) - Died 1832 Sept 2 Age 19 days Son of Russell & Ann Rogers S:6

Rogers, (son) - Died 1843 July 31 Born 1843 July 17 Son of David & Deborah Rogers (next to others infants) S:14

Rogers, Albert P - Died 1980 Born 1921 Was an ETM2 in US Navy during World War II S:20

Rogers, Alfred - Died 1975 Born 1897 (with Mary C Rogers) S:15

Rogers, Alma - Died (not listed) Daughter of Frederick & Patience Rogers (with brother, Charlie Rogers) S:14

Rogers, Ann Russell - Died 1851 June 1 Age 17 years, 4 months Daughter of Russell & Ann Rogers S:6

Rogers, Anna J - Died 1852 Mar 5 Age 42 years, 6 months Wife of Russell Rogers & daughter of John & Ann Bassett S:6

Rogers, Annie - Died 1938 Born 1865 S:16

Rogers, Catherine C - Died 1941 Born 1864 Wife of Hugh A Rogers (with him) S:16

Rogers, Charles - Died 1933 Born 1844 S:31

Rogers, Charles Bassett - Died 1845 Dec 6 Age 13 months, 2 days Son of Russell & Ann Rogers S:6

Rogers, Charlie - Died (not listed) Son of Frederick & Patience Rogers (with sister, Alma Rogers) S:14

Rogers, Charlotte - Died 1951 Born 1881 (with Charles, Annie & Albert Nelson) S:19

Rogers, Christine - Died 1959 Born 1886 (next to Eliza & Ernest Rogers) S:14

Rogers, Clement C - Died 1973 Born 1893 (with Elsie C Rogers) S:18

Rogers, David - Died 1845 Sept 19 Age 63 (next to Martha Rogers)

Rogers (Cont.)
S:14

Rogers, David W - Died 1830 July 20 Age 38 years, 2 months (next to Frederick Rogers d1880) S:14

Rogers, Deborah M - Died 1880 Aug 17 Age 68 years, 2 months, 25 days Wife of David (next to many infant babies) S:14

Rogers, Eliza - Died 1961 Born 1892 (with Ernest Rogers) S:14

Rogers, Eliza A - Died 1923 Born 1871 (next to James & Hannah Rogers) S:12

Rogers, Eliza Ann - Died 1848 Sept 7 Age 18 Wife of HW Rogers (with infant son) S:14

Rogers, Elsie C - Died 1978 Born 1894 (with Clement Rogers) S:18

Rogers, Emogene Clifford - Died 1849 July 28 Age 3 months, 5 days Daughter of Russell & Ann Rogers S:6

Rogers, Ernest - Died 1961 Born 1891 (with Eliza Rogers) S:14

Rogers, Freddie - Died 1874 April 8 Age 20 years, 7 months Son of Frederick & Patience Rogers (next to mother) S:14

Rogers, Frederick - Died 1880 Feb 4 Age 61 years, 4 months Stone says, "Our Dear Father" (next to wife, Patience A Rogers) S:14

Rogers, Hannah K - Died 1917 Born 1853 (with James N Rogers) S:12

Rogers, Hugh A - Died 1939 Born 1856 (with wife, Catherine C Rogers) S:16

Rogers, Jack - Died 1943 Born 1873 (with wife, Maria Rogers) S:16

Rogers, James N - Died 1927 Born 1857 (with Hannah K Rogers) S:12

Rogers, John - Died 1922 Born 1868 (with wife, Maria H Robello) S:14

Rogers, John F - Died 1885? Born 1882 S:19

Rogers, John J - Died 1960 Born 1891 (with Lillian L Crooks) S:17

Rogers, Jordan - Died 1954 Born 1893 (with wife, Theresa Rogers) S:14

Rogers, Maria - Died 1950 Born 1875 Wife of Jack Rogers (with him) S:16

Rogers, Martha - Died 1844 Oct 13 Age 61 (next to David Rogers) S:14

Rogers, Mary B - Died 1980 Born 1892 (with Joseph J Keane) S:16

Rogers, Mary C - Died (still living 1991?) (listed with Alfred Rogers) S:15

Rogers, Patience Alma - Died 1896 Feb 5 Age 82 years, 4 months Stone says,"Our Dear Mother" Wife of Frederick Rogers (next to him) S:14

Rogers, Russell - Died 1891 Nov 8 Born 1808 Oct 19 (buried next to wife, Anna J Rogers) S:6

Rogers, Samuel - Died 1920 Jan 7 Born 1898 Aug 11 From Massachusetts, was in 4th Coast Artillery during World War I (next to John Rogers & Maria H Robello) S:14

Rogers, Terence A - Died 1985 Born 1900 Was an E3 in US Navy during World War I S:15

Rogers, Theresa - Died 1942 Born 1894 Wife of Jordan Rogers (with him) (a large glass church candle has been placed at grave, red glass) S:14

Rogers, Walter Dana - Died 1967 Born 1888 From Massachusetts, was Major in US Army during World War I (with Mary Motherway, wife) S:15

Rooney, Dora - Died 1932 Born 1878 (with James Dahill & others) S:31

Rooney, Genevieve - Died 1960 Born 1876 (with John F Rooney) S:16

Rooney, John F - Died 1951 Born 1869 (with Genevieve Rooney) S:16

Roper, Harold M Sr - Died 1977 Born 1897 Was an E2 in US

Roper (Cont.)
Navy during World War I S:15

Ropes, Charlotte Sherburne - Died 1972 April 6 Born 1909 March 31 (with Edward Jackson Lowell Ropes) S:14

Ropes, Edward Jackson Lowell - Died 1988 Dec 8 Born 1909 Jan 22 (with Charlotte Sherburne Ropes) S:14

Rosa, Frances G - Died 1948 Born 1868 (with Joseph, John & Lucy Rosa) S:20

Rosa, John - Died 1967 Born 1900 (with Lucy, Joseph & Frances Rosa) S:20

Rosa, Joseph G - Died 1928 Born 1864 (with Frances G & John & Lucy Rosa) S:20

Rosa, Lucy E - Died 1961 Born 1903 (with John, Joseph & Frances Rosa) S:20

Rosario, Sebastian - Died 1951 Born 1874 (with Josepha F Rosary & others) S:16

Rosary, Joaquin J - Died 1977 Born 1896 (with Sebastian Rosario & others) S:16

Rosary, John J - Died 1950 Born 1877 (with Josepha F Rosary his wife & others) S:16

Rosary, Joseph - Died 1958 Nov 21 Born 1882 Sept 12 S:16

Rosary, Josepha F - Died 1947 Born 1877 Wife of John J Rosary (with him & others) S:16

Rosary, Mary M - Died (still living 1991?) Born 1899 (with Joaquin J Rosary & others) S:16

Rosary, Profirio - Died 1964 Born 1895 Stone says,"Godfather" S:14

Rose, Elnora P - Died 1963 Born 1886 (with Louis Rose) S:18

Rose, Louis L - Died 1954 Born 1885 (next to Elnora P Rose) S:18

Rosenbaum, August A - Died 1984 Born 1898 (with Nancy K Rosenbaum) S:17

Rosenbaum, Nancy K - Died 1986 Born 1899 (with August A Rosenbaum) S:17

Rosengren, Amanda W - Died 1944 Born 1866 S:8

Ross, Charles W - Died 1958 Born 1878 (has 2 stones) (with to Margaret A Ross) S:17

Ross, John W - Died 1970 May 23 Born 1891 Feb 10 From Massachusetts, was PFC in US Army during World War II S:18

Ross, Margaret A - Died 1974 Born 1882 (with Charles W Ross) S:17

Rotch, Arthur Grinnell - Died 1962 Born 1880 (with Margaret M Fernald) S:11

Rowe, Leslie N - Died 1985 Born 1892 (undertaker plaque only) S:15

Rowell, Fred M - Died 1975 April 18 Born 1900 Mar 8 Was a LCDR in US Navy during World War I & II S:15

Rowsell, Madeline Rive - Died 1988 Born 1900 (next to Philip Rowsell) S:15

Rowsell, Philip - Died 1982 Born 1897 (next to Madeline Rive Rowsell) S:15

Roycroft, Ann M - Died 1975 Born 1908 (with George Wirtanen) S:20

Roza, (no name) - Died 1953 March 27 (listed with Donald Roza, has no name listed on stone) S:31

Roza, Donald A - Died 1935 Jan 21 Born 1931 Nov 15 (listed with someone who died 1953 March 27, no name listed) S:31

Roza, John Clarence - Died 1918 Born 1917 (a small white stone) S:31

Roza, Joseph P - Died 1918 Born 1862 (next to Mary P Roza) S:31

Roza, Mary P - Died 1927 Born 1865 (next to Joseph Roza) S:31

Rubin, Elizabeth - Buried 1982 May 2 Age 82 Located in section 9, lot 19-13 1/2, grave 6 S:15R

Rubin, Samuel E - Died 1978 Born 1896 (Jewish section) Was a RM3 in US Navy during World War I S:15

Ruedy, Viola Heaman - Died 1986

Ruedy (Cont.)
Oct 20 Born 1899 June 13 (next to Charles F Heaman) S:15

Ruhan, Kathryn L (Lt Col) - Died 1963 Born 1887 Was an Army Nurse Corps S:16

Rumrill, Lucretia Handy - Died 1986 Born 1891 S:14

Rupp, Joseph W - Died 1960 Born 1890 (with Marion Pease Rupp) S:16

Rupp, Marion Pease - Died 1960 Born 1881 (with Joseph W Rupp) S:16

Ruppert, Mary Jordan - Died 1972 Born 1899 S:15

Rusengren, Kusta V - Died 1975 Sept 3 Born 1898 July 22 Was a Pvt in US Army during World War II S:20

Ruska, John S - Died 1959 Born 1889 S:20

Russel, (daughter) - Died 1787 June (stone not clear) Daughter of John & Mary Russel S:11

Russel, Ame - Died 1729/30 Feb 5 in her 23rd yr Stone says, "Beneath this marble stone doth lye two subjects of deaths tyranny, the mother who in close tomb sleeps with the issue of her womb (with Leonard Russel, infant) (Hinckley Ceme records #11R says death was 1729/30) S:11+26R

Russel, Bethiah - Died 1763 Mar 31st (stone worn) in her 65th yr Widow of Samuel Russel (next to him) (Hinckley Ceme records says death was 1763 March 31) S:11+26R

Russel, John Dr - Died 1765 Dec 24 in his 36th yr S:5

Russel, Leonard - Died 1722 Feb 2, died 17 days after birth Infant son of Anna Russel (buried with her) S:11

Russel, Lothrop - Died 1745 July 16 Age 21 Bachelor of Arts at Harvard College, Boston, Mass S:11

Russel, Mehetable Mrs - Died 1746

Russel (Cont.)
Mar 17 Age 45 Consort to Dr John Russel (a stone buried in tree trunk next to her, cannot read) S:11

Russel, Samuel - Died 1753 ? 4th Age 36 or 56 years, 5 months, 4 days (worn) (stone next to him cannot be read) S:11

Russel, William - Died 2nd (rest is worn off) Son of John & Mary Russel (next to a sister d1787) S:11

Russell, (still born baby) - Died 1700 Child of Rev Jonathan & Mercy Russell S:5

Russell, (still born baby) - Died 1724 Nov 10 Child of Rev Jonathan & Mercy Russell (also listed in #5R records) S:5

Russell, (stillborn) - Died 1737 Feb 28 Son of Rev Jonathan & Mercy Russell S:5R

Russell, Dinah Mrs - Died 1773 March 3 in her 74th yr Consort of Deacon Moody Russell S:11R +26R

Russell, Elizabeth - Died 1790 Dec 3 Born 1727 Aug 4 Listed as a Widow S:5

Russell, Hannah C - Died 1911 Born 1865 Stone says,"Wife" Wife of James C Russell (next to him) S:19

Russell, Hazel A - Died 1975 Born 1899 (Ames stone) (with Samuel & Mother Ames & others) S:12

Russell, Helen - Buried 1981 June 23 Age 82 Located in section N, lot 12, grave 2 S:14R

Russell, Hittey - Died 1787 June 2 Age 9 years, 3 months Daughter of John & Mary Russell S:11R

Russell, James C - Died 1898 Born 1860 Stone says,"Husband" (next to wife, Hannah C Russell) S:19

Russell, John - Died 1748 Aug 1 in his 25th yr S:11R+26R

Russell, John - Died 1760's Mar 17 Age 1 year, 10 months, 26 days Son of Jonathan & Elizabeth

Russell (Cont.)
Russell (Hinckley Ceme records say death year was 1761) S:5

Russell, John Dr - Died 1765 Dec 24 Age 36 S:5R

Russell, Jonathan - Died 1729/30 Mar 18 Son of Jonathan & Mercy Russell S:5

Russell, Jonathan - Died 1759 Sept 16 Age 8 years, 4 months Son of Jonathan & Elizabeth Russell S:5

Russell, Jonathan Rev - Died 1710/11 Feb 21 Age 56 "Minister of Church of Barnstable who breathed out his soul Feb 21 1710/11" (from latin translation) S:11R

Russell, Jonathan Rev - Died 1759 Sept 10 First ordained pastor in Barnstable 1712 Oct 29 He followed his father S:5

Russell, Lothrop - Died 1745 July 16 in his 21st yr Bachelor of Arts of Harvard College S:11R +26R

Russell, Martha - Died 1756 Aug 30 Daughter of Rev Jonathan & Mercy Russell (Hinckley Ceme records say death year was 1736) S:5

Russell, Mehetable Mrs - Died 1746 March 17 in her 45th yr Consort of Dr John Russell of Barnstable S:11R+26R

Russell, Mercy - Died 1729/30 Mar 23 Age 2 years, 3 months, 3 days Dau of Jonathan & Mercy Russell S:5

Russell, Mercy - Died 1750 May 23 in her 58th yr Wife of Rev Jonathan Russell S:5

Russell, Mercy - Died 1766 Mar 22 Age 7 months Daughter of Jonathan & Elizabeth Russell S:5

Russell, Mercy - Died Possibly-1739 Mar 9 Born 1700 Daughter of Jonathan & Mercy Russell (Hinckley Ceme records #5R says death was 1734 Jan 7 and birth was 1732 March 9) S:5

Russell, Oakes - Died 1797 July 30

Russell (Cont.)
in the 34th yr S:5

Russell, Otis - Died 1797 July 30
Age 34 S:5R

Russell, Raymond H - Died 1977
Born 1899 Was in Cem US Navy
during World War II S:15

Russell, Samuel - Died 1755 Sept 4
Age 56 years, 4 months, 4 days
S:11R

Russell, Warren King - Died 1962
Aug 12 Born 1897 Dec 17 From
Massachusetts, was 2nd Lieu-
tenant in FA, Res during World
War I S:14

Russell, William - Died 1772 Oct 2
Age 7 months Son of John &
Mary Russell S:11R

Russo, Felix - Died 1961 Born
1872 (buried with Freida A
Russo, wife) S:8

Russo, Freida A - Died 1933 Born
1869 Wife of Felix (buried next
to him) S:8

Russo, Henry - Died (still living
1991?) Born 1895 (listed with
Josephine Bell) S:16

Ruuska, Heleena - Died 1934 May
2 Born 1858 Jan 28 S:11

Ruuska, Kalle - Died 1935 June 27
Born 1857 Mar 25 (listed with
Heleena Ruuska) S:11

Ruuska, Lulia - Died 1905 Feb 10
Born 1901 Feb 5 (stone broken
at base) Daughter of Charles &
Helten? Ruuska S:11

Ryan, W - Died (no other markings
on stone) S:20

Ryder, Albert E - Died 1936 Born
1859 (next to Lucy & Annie
Ryder) S:14

Ryder, Annie W - Died 1946 Born
1860 (next to Lucy H Ryder)
S:14

Ryder, Ausil I - Died 1986 Born
1905 Chief of Barnstable Fire
Dept flag & plaque (with Natralie
M Ryder) S:11

Ryder, Bertram F - Died 1960 Born
1884 (with wife, Florence Haskins) S:14

Ryder, Caroline E - Died 1925

Ryder (Cont.)
Born 1866 (with Horace C Ryder
& others) S:19

Ryder, Caroline S Mrs - Died 1849
Sept 22 Age 42 years, 9 months
at Staten Island, New York
(husband died on way there to
get her remains) Wife of Capt
John S Ryder (next to him)
(Hinckley Ceme records #11R
says death was 1849) S:11+26R

Ryder, Charles C - Died 1937 Born
1864 (Star marker says, "Barnstable Fire Chief" (not sure if it is
for Charles or Warren Ryder)
(with Lucretia G Hallett & others) S:19

Ryder, Emily - Died 1907 March 1
Age 73 (with Louise Ryder) S:14

Ryder, Eunice H - Died 1888 Sept
15 Born 1808 Jan 12 Wife of
Isaiah Ryder S:5

Ryder, Horace C - Died 1955 Born
1857 (with Warren Ryder &
others) S:19

Ryder, Horace J - Died 1956 Born
1882 S:18

Ryder, John S (Capt) - Died 1850
June 18 Was from Provincetown,
Mass He died of Small Pox
incountered while talune(?) the
remains of his wife in Staten
Island, N Y (she is next to him)
(Hinckley Ceme record #11R
says death year was 1850) S:11
+26R

Ryder, Joshua H - Died 1879 Nov 9
Age 55 (with Emily Ryder) S:14

Ryder, Louise - Died 1877 Feb 8
Age 7 (with Emily & Joshua
Ryder) S:14

Ryder, Lucy H - Died 1954 Born
1892 (next to Annie W Ryder)
S:14

Ryder, Malcolm E - Died 1983
Born 1896 Was MM2 in US Navy
during World War I S:14

Ryder, Marjorie B - Died 1981 Sept
15 Born 1906 May 4 Widow of
Charles F Clagg (on same stone)
S:11

Ryder, Mary N - Died 1987 Born

Ryder (Cont.)
1893 Wife of Harry P Azadian
(with him & others) S:19

Ryder, Myron D - Died 1962 May
31 Born 1897 Nov 29 From
Massachusetts, was wagoner in
9th Co, 151 Depot Brigade
during World War I (next to
Wallace Ryder & Laura Clayton)
S:14

Ryder, Natralie M - Died 1973 Born
1913 (with Ausil I Ryder) S:11

Ryder, Paul T - Died Oct 25 - Nov 2
1966 S:11

Ryder, Viola E - Died 1982 Born
1888 S:18

Ryder, Wallace - Died 1954 Born
1862 (with wife, Laura B Clayton) S:14

Ryder, Wallace Jr - Died 1969 Aug
17 Born 1890 Sept 13 (also on
main family stone) (with wife,
Marjorie Bowen) From Massachusetts, was PFC Col, 59th
Infantry during World War I S:14

Ryder, Warren G - Died 1986 Born
1905 (with wife, Marjorie I Dolliver & others) S:19

Ryder, Warren H - Died 1910 Born
1828 (with wife, Susan A
Gorham & others) S:19

Saari, Ida - Died 1961 May 24 Born
1891 Sept 13 (stone is a rock)
(with Onni Saari) S:20

Saari, Onni - Died 1976 Dec 18
Born 1890 Dec 30 (stone is a
rock) (with Ida Saari) S:20

Sacca, Clara Belle - Died 1973
Born 1909 S:13

Saint, William - Died 1951 Born
1864 (a rock marker) (with
Carrie Saint & others) S:18

Sala, Estelle H - Died 1973 Born
1896 (listed with Martin M Sala)
S:16

Sala, Martin M - Died (still living
1991?) Born 1900 (listed with
Estelle H Sala) S:16

Salminen, Hilda F - Died (still
living 1991?) Born 1900 (listed
with Ivar Salminen) S:17

Salminen, Ivar - Died 1965 Born

Salminen (Cont.)
1900 (listed with Hilda F Salminen) S:17

Salo, Albert V - Died 1974 Aug 17
Born 1914 March 25 Was a
Sargeant in Army Air Forces
(next to Henry Salo) S:20

Salo, Anna O - Died 1967 Born
1896 (with Henry Salo) S:20

Salo, Ava G - Died 1973 Born 1917
(a large marble seat with name
on it) (next to Albert V Salo &
others) S:20

Salo, Henry - Died 1975 Born 1886
(with Anna O Salo) S:20

Samos, Martha A - Died 1956 Born
1883 (with Ann L Washburn)
S:18

Sampson, (baby) - Died 1950 S:21

Sampson, Abigail - Died 1866 Jan
7 Age 70 years, 6 months (next
to Oliver Sampson) S:21

Sampson, Augusta C - Buried 1896
Located in section O, lot 11,
grave 4 S:14R

Sampson, Benjamin T - Died 1854
Aug 5 Age 25 years, 4 months, 2
days (next to wife, Joanna L
Sampson) S:14

Sampson, Charles E - Buried 1873
Located in section O, lot 11,
grave 5 S:14R

Sampson, Charles W - Buried 1848
Located in section O, lot 11,
grave 2 S:14R

Sampson, Freeman H - Died 1850
June 5 at Sacramento City,
California Age 25 years 2
months (with Nancy Sampson)
S:14

Sampson, Hannah B - Buried 1871
Sept 25 Located in section R, lot
10, grave 6 S:14R

Sampson, Hannah H - Died 1839
June 19 Age 19 Wife of Josiah
Sampson (near him) S:14

Sampson, James T - Died 1856
Jan 18 Age 38 years, 10 months
(with wife, Mary H Sampson)
S:14

Sampson, Joanna L (or B) - Died
1859 Nov 29 Age 33 Widow of

Sampson (Cont.)

Benjamin T Sampson (next to him) Daughter of James & Elizabeth Childs S:14

Sampson, Josiah - Died 1861 Aug 3 Age 39 (There is a broken & crumbled stone next to him that cannot be read) (by Hannah(?) Sampson, wife) (age could also be 70?) S:14

Sampson, Josiah (Esq) - Died 1829 July 14 in his 76th yr (buried next to wife, Sarah) S:7

Sampson, Lucy T (or F) - Died 1851 Mar 11 Age 21 (next to Nancy Sampson) S:14

Sampson, Mary - Died 1795 Mar 16 in her 36th yr Consort of Josiah Sampson S:7

Sampson, Mary C - Died 1845 Nov 18 Age 30 (next to William Sampson) S:14

Sampson, Mary H - Died 1852 Dec 12 Age 27 years, 9 months, 10 days Wife of James T Sampson (next to him) S:14

Sampson, Nancy - Died 1818 Oct 5 Age 29 years, 1 month, 22 days (with Freeman h Sampson) S:14

Sampson, Nancy - Buried 1848 Oct 8 Age 29 Located in section R, lot 10, grave 2 S:14R

Sampson, Nancy C - Buried 1845 Nov 21 Age 30 Located in section B, lot 10, grave 4 S:14R

Sampson, O David - Died (no date) Born 1908 (with Olive L Mitchell, wife) S:21

Sampson, Oliver - Died 1844 Dec 21 Age 47 years, 4 months (next to Abigail Sampson) S:21

Sampson, Orie D W Jr - Died 1952 Born 1928 Was a Corporal in US Army during Korea S:21

Sampson, Roger A - Died 1962 Born 1945 Son of O David Sampson & Olive Mitchell (with them) S:21

Sampson, Sarah - Died 1844 Feb 12 Age 88 years, 7 months, 10 days Relict of Josiah Sampson Esq (buried next to him) S:7

Sampson, Southworth - Died (dates & info not clear) (buried next to Mrs Jedidah Samson) (Hinckley Ceme records #9R says death was 1802 Feb 9 in his 66th yr and first name was Samson) S:9+26R

Sampson, William - Died 1834 Sept 27 Age 48 (next to Mary C Sampson) S:14

Sampson, William - Buried 1854 Located in section O, lot 11, grave 3 S:14R

Samson, (child) - Died (not clear) (possibly parents are William & Abigail Samson) S:10

Samson, (child) - Died (stone not clear) (possible parents are William & Abigail Samson, another unnamed child stone next to this one) S:10

Samson, Abigail - Died 1817 Sept 16 in her 57th yr Wife of William Samson S:10+26R

Samson, Jedidah (Mrs) - Died (dates & info not clear) (next to Southworth Sampson, husband) (Hinckley Ceme records says death was 1801 Jan 7 in his 67th yr) S:9+26R

Samson, Jemima - Died 1773 Nov 15 in her 5th yr Daughter to Southworth and Jedidah Samson (located at Cobb Hill East Cemetery)(Goodspeed or Meeting House Hill East) S:26R

Samson, John - Died (dates not clear, badly worn) Son of william & Abigail Samson S:10

Samson, Josiah - Died (dates not clear) Son of Southworth & Jedidah Samson (buried next to them) (Hinckley Ceme records #9R says death was 1772 Jan 9 in his 6th yr) S:9+26R

Samson, William - Died (no date) Son of William & Abigail Samson S:10

Samson, William - Died 1822 May 3 in his 63rd yr S:10+26R

Sanborn, Dorothy B - Died 1975 Born 1888 S:15

Sanit, Carrie - Died (no dates) (a rock marker) (with William Saint & others) S:18

Sargent, Edith Hoovan - Died 1990 Born 1900 (next to husband, J Bradford Sargent Jr) S:15

Sargent, J Bradford Jr - Died 1989 Born 1896 Was Ensign in US Navy during World War I (next to wife, Edith Hoovan Sargent) S:15

Saulnier, Dorothy A - Died 1973 Born 1902 (listed with J Gustave Saulnier) S:15

Saulnier, J Gustave - Died (still living 1991?) Born 1896 (listed with Dorothy A Saulnier) S:15

Saunders, Robert T - Died 1896 Sept 15 Born 1870 Feb 14 S:11

Savage, Adelaide - Died 20 March 1827 Age 20 yrs 6 mos Consort of W H Savage S:26R

Savage, Hope - Died 1792 Oct 20 Age 4 mos 5 days Daughter to Samuel and Hope Savage S:26R

Savage, Hope - Died 1830 Dec 22 Age 75 Wife of Dr Samuel Savage and daughter of Col Elisha Doan of Wellfleet S:26R

Savage, Howard E - Died 1949 Born 1879 S:14

Savage, John - Died 1788 July 26 Age 11 weeks 5 days Son of Dr Samuel and Hope Savage S:26R

Savage, John - Died 1811 Oct 5 Etatis 22 Student of law Son of Samuel and Hope Savage "Insatiate archer could not one suffice. Thy shafts flew thrice and thrice my peace was slain" S:26R

Savage, Joseph - Died 1791 Aug 19 Age 5 mos 18 days Son of Samuel and Hope Savage S:26R

Savage, Samuel Dr - Died 1831 June 28 in his 83rd yr "An eminent physician, a patriotic citizen, beloved and respected in all the relations of social and domestic life" (This following is an inscription on his stone in honor of his wife, Hope Doane who died 22 Dec 1830) "In her piety,

Savage (Cont.) sincerity, charity, politeness and affability were so happy united with elegance of person and polish of mind as rendered her respected and esteemed by all who knew her. From a grateful sense of her affectionate tenderness and excellent deportment as a wife. This stone is erected by him who knew her worth and laments her loss" S:26R

Savage, Samuel Hay - Died 1901 Oct 21 at Boston Born 1827 Mar 8 at Barnstable,Mass (in Bowles plot near church, stone has large crest at top) S:10

Savage, Susan - Died 1825 May 10 in her 35th yr Born 1790 Aug Wife of Charles Savage, American Consul to Guatemala and daughter to Gen A Wood of Wiscasset, Maine S:26R

Savage, Tyler - Died 1796 Feb 13 Age 1 yr 3 mos 9 days Son of Samuel and Hope Savage S:26R

Savery, Alonzo G (or C) - Died 1926 Born 1865 (with wife, Myra C Edson) S:14

Savery, Burleigh H - Died 1965 Born 1878 (with Viola M Savery) S:14

Savery, Edson Raymond - Died 1951 Born 1889 (with Alonzo Savery & Myra Edson & wife, Ellen Savery) S:14

Savery, Ellen Frances - Died 1973 Born 1888 Wife of Edson Raymond Savery (with him) S:14

Savery, Ellen M - Died 1956 Born 1886 (with Leon Goodspeed Savery) S:14

Savery, George H - Died 1949 Born 1873 (with Louise A Savery) S:14

Savery, Ida May - Died 1906 Born 1858 Wife of Edgar Robert Evans (with him) S:12

Savery, Leon Goodspeed - Died 1954 March 11 Born 1887 Aug 3 From Massachusetts, was a PFC in Co E in 101 Supply TN during World War I ((with Ellen M

Savery (Cont.)

Savery) S:14

Savery, Lizzie F - Died 1917 Born 1881 S:14

Savery, Louise A - Died 1976 Born 1889 (with George H Savery) S:14

Savery, Lovelin - Buried 1916 Located in section 7, lot 1, grave 1 S:14R

Savery, Mary B - Died 1853 Aug 21 Age 18 With of Samadrus Savery (next to him) (stone repaired which was cracked in half at one time before) S:14

Savery, Myrtle - Died 1971 Born 1900 Wife of Claude Nickerson (with him) S:14

Savery, Samadrus - Died 1888 Dec 11 Age 56 years, 4 months (next to wife, Mary B Savery) S:14

Savery, Viola M - Died 1968 Born 1877 (with Burleigh H Savery) S:14

Savory, Catherine - Died 1848 April 20 Age 55 years, 6 months, 26 days (there is a very small marker next to her with the face worn off) Wife of George Savory (next to him) S:14

Savory, George - Died 1888 Aug 16 Born 1798 April 8 (next to wife, Catherine Savory) S:14

Sawyer, Bernice - Died 1980 Born 1895 S:18

Sawyer, Eleanor Conway - Died 1985 Born 1902 (with Mildred Sawyer) S:13

Sawyer, Lucy AE - Died 1961 Born 1891 Wife of Wilton Crosby (with him) S:12

Sawyer, Mildred - Died 1956 Born 1896 (with Eleanor Conway Sawyer) S:13

Schaefer, Sarah Budd - Died 1971 Born 1886 S:15

Schall, Leroy A - Died 1985 Born 1892 (doctor sign over name) was 1st Lt.in US Army during World War I (flag at stone)(with wife, Mabel f Schall) S:11

Schall, Mabel F - Died 1963 Born

Schall (Cont.)

1895 Wife of Leroy A Schall (with him) S:11

Schlegel, William - Died 1986 Born 1899 Was PTR3 in US Navy during World War I S:15

Schoeck, Alice E - Died (still living?) Born 1906 (listed with Gustav J Schoeck) S:18

Schoeck, Gustav J - Died 1987 Born 1899 (listed with Alice E Schoeck) S:18

Schofield, Dorothy L - Died (still living 1991?) Born 1926 (with John R Schofield) S:20

Schofield, John R - Died 1990 Born 1924 (has 2 stones) Was a RDM2 in US Navy during World War II (with Dorothy L Schofield) S:20

Schwab, Jane E - Died 1962 Born 1872 (with Frances A Glancy) S:16

Scocco (Slocco), Joseph L - Died 1975 Born 1897 S:16

Scott, Howard W Sr - Died 1968 March 15 Born 1900 July 28 From Massachusetts, was S1 in USNRF during World War I S:15

Scudder, (baby boy) - Died 1964 (birth left blank) S:13

Scudder, (infant) - Died (dates broken off stone) Daughter of Erastus & Olive Scudder (near them & with Ebenezer Scudder) S:12

Scudder, (infant) - Died 1844 July 27 Age 5 days Daughter of Josiah & Sophronia Scudder S:12+12R

Scudder, (infant) - Died 1845 or 1815 Nov 2 Age 17 days Son of Josiah & Sophronia Scudder S:12+12R

Scudder, (infant) - Died 1855 Oct 12 Born 1855 Sept 24 Son of Josiah & Augusta Scudder (next to them) S:12

Scudder, ? Lovell - Died 1816 Aug 24 (small stone & worn) (next to James N Lovell, d1865) S:12

Scudder, ? - Died 1841 Aug (stone

Scudder (Cont.)
not clear, but next to Henry Scudder, d1838 and possible child of Philander & Jane Scudder) S:12

Scudder, Abby C - Died 1934 Sept 26 Born 1842 (listed in family plot) S:11

Scudder, Abigail - Died 1803 Apr 8 in her 41st yr Consort of Capt Ebenezer Scudder Jr(buried next to him) S:7

Scudder, Abigail - Died 1881 Feb 1 Age 69 years, 6 months Wife of Nelson Scudder S:11R

Scudder, Abigail R - Died 1836 June 3 Age 6 months Daughter of Philander & Jane Scudder S:12

Scudder, Albert - Died 1861 June 11 Age 58 years, 8 months, 25 days (buried next to Asenath L Scudder) S:8

Scudder, Albert - Died 1907 Nov 28 Born 1846 Nov 21 (with Fannie L Wiley & others on Wiley/Scudder stone) S:12

Scudder, Alexander - Died 1862 March 12 Born 1793 March 12 (next to wife, Mary Bourne) S:14

Scudder, Alice Cordelia - Died 1840 Feb 7 Age 3 years, 5 months (top of stone broken off by vandals) (with Eugenia J Scudder & others) S:18

Scudder, Anna - Died 1822 July 24 in her 84th yr Widow of Samuel Scudder S:3

Scudder, Ansel H - Died 1825 July 26 Age 1 year, 28 days Son of Josiah & Sophronia Scudder S:12

Scudder, Apphia D - Died 1906 Nov 26 Born 1828 May 22 S:7

Scudder, Arthur - Died 1820? Mar 8 (stone badly worn) (next to Eliza Hall 9 S:8

Scudder, Asa - Died 1910 Nov 13 Born 1838 April 17 S:11

Scudder, Asa (Capt) - Died 1822 May 25 in his 51st yr (next to wife, Sally Scudder, d1868)

Scudder (Cont.)
S:11+26R

Scudder, Asenath L - Died 1895 Mar 19 Age 89 years, 1 month, 6 days Stone says, "She had done what she could" (buried next to Albert Scudder) S:8

Scudder, Augusta - Died 1894? April Born 1880? August (stone overgrown, not clear) Only daughter of Charles & Dora Scudder S:12

Scudder, Augusta H - Died 1909 Feb 17 Born 1819 Sept 8 (with Josiah Scudder) S:12

Scudder, Benjamin F - Died 1876 Apr 7 in his 73rd yr S:7

Scudder, Bertha B - Died 1931 Born 1858 Wife of J Porter Scudder (with him) S:12

Scudder, Bessie Curtis - Died 1954 Born 1879 S:18

Scudder, Bethia - Died 1916 Feb 13 Born 1831 July 16 S:11

Scudder, Bethiah - Died 1884 Jan 12 Born 1813 May 26 Wife of Daniel Scudder (in same plot with him) S:11

Scudder, Betsey - Died 1848 Sept 14 Born 1776 Oct 17 Widow of Ebenezer Scudder S:7

Scudder, Cephas - Died 1811 Nov 30 Age 6 mos 14 days Son of Isaac & Lydia Scudder S:12R

Scudder, Charles Noble - Died 1886 March 7 Born 1858 Jan 8 Son of Joseph & Augusta Scudder S:12

Scudder, Content D - Died 1835 Jan 5 Age 26 Wife of Isaac Scudder S:12

Scudder, Cora Atla - Died 1880 Sept 2 Age 37 Wife of Franklin Young S:12

Scudder, Cordelia - Died 1871 May 21 Age 65 years, 11 months (top of stone broken off by vandals) Wife of Frederick Scudder (with him & Alice Cordelia Scudder & others) S:18

Scudder, Daniel - Died 1773 Oct 2 in his 48th yr S:3+3R

Scudder, Daniel - Died 1881 May 22 Born 1813 Oct 27 (large family plot with stone pillars around it) S:11

Scudder, Daniel - Died 1898 Oct 2 Born 1842 Aug 7 (in family plot with others) S:11

Scudder, David - Died 1837 Aug 6 Age 37 (with Lucinda Scudder & others) S:18

Scudder, David Esq - Died 1819 Jan 17 in his 56th yr S:4

Scudder, Desire - Died 1850 May 27 Age 83 years, 4 months, 16 days Relict of David Scudder Esq S:4

Scudder, Ebenazer - Died Apr 6 Age 41 (Hinckley Ceme records #9R says death year was 1737) S:9+26R

Scudder, Ebenezer - Died 1814 Nov 7 Age 20 Born 1794 Son of Ebenezer & Abigail Scudder S:7

Scudder, Ebenezer - Died 1818 June 8 Age 84 years, 3 days S:3

Scudder, Ebenezer - Died 1829 Born 1815 S:2

Scudder, Ebenezer - Died 1839 Sept 22 Age 6 months, 15 days (stone is down) son of Erastus & Olive M Scudder (near them and with infant Scudder) S:12

Scudder, Ebenezer (Capt) - Died 1847 Aug 28 Age 86 years, 15 days S:7

Scudder, Ebenezer H - Died 1836 Mar 3 Age 3 years, 6 months Son of Isaac & Content Scudder S:12

Scudder, Edward - Died 1866 Dec 11 Born 1804 Aug 27 (stone broken at base) S:11

Scudder, Edward - Died 1878 Oct 16 Age 36 years, 8 months Son of Edward & Rebecca Scudder S:11

Scudder, Edwin - Died 1923 Born 1845 Stone says "Phinney" (buried with Grace Howes) S:8

Scudder, Elazer - Died 1881 Nov 9 Born 1805 Oct 6 (on stone with Hattie & Eliza T Scudder) S:4

Scudder, Eleazer - Died 1811 Dec 7 Age 75 S:4

Scudder, Eleazer Jr - Died 1805 Sept 12 Age 38 S:4

Scudder, Elisha G - Died 1822 Oct 11 Age 31 S:9

Scudder, Eliza - Died 1869 Aug 3 Born 1793 Feb 7 Wife of Elisha Scudder & daughter of Ebenezer Bacon S:9

Scudder, Eliza - Died 1873 Nov 5 Age 55 Wife of Alfred Scudder S:12

Scudder, Eliza - Died 1933 Born 1861 (with James G Small, Sophia Hinckley & James C Small) S:13

Scudder, Eliza A - Died 1883 Age 48 Born 1835 (Hinkley does not list birth off stone)(listed on large stone in family plot) S:11+26R

Scudder, Eliza T - Died 1900 March 13 Born 1808 Sept 25 (on stone with Elazer & Hattie Scudder) S:4

Scudder, Elizabeth - Died 1746 April 7 in her 19th yr S:9R+26R

Scudder, Elizabeth H - Died 1829 Mar 1 Born 1807 Dec 30 Wife of Freeman L Scudder (with him in large Scudder plot) S:12

Scudder, Ella - Died 1843 May 3 Age 6 months, 3 days Daughter of Alfred & Eliza Scudder S:12

Scudder, Ellen Wiley - Died 1941 Mar 22 Born 1853 Sept 8 Wife of Albert Scudder (with him & others on Wiley/Scudder stone) S:12

Scudder, Emma Adeline - Died 1932 Jan 21 Born 1838 May 12 Daughter of Alexander & Mary Scudder (two stones away) S:14

Scudder, Erastus - Died 1884 Dec 30 Age 71 years, 5 months, 13 days S:12

Scudder, Ervin - Died 1923 Born 1845 (buried with Eunice & Nelson Phinney & others) S:8

Scudder, Ethel Murray - Died 1965 Born 1891 (next to Frederic Freeman Scudder) S:12

Scudder, Eugenia J - Died 1906 Sept 13 Age 73 (top of stone broken off by vandals) (with Cordelia Scudder & others) S:18

Scudder, Eunice M - Died 1934 Born 1846 (with Gustavus Scudder) S:14

Scudder, Frederic Bryant - Died 1983 Born 1921 (next to Ethel Murray Scudder) S:12

Scudder, Frederic Freeman - Died 1949 Born 1891 (next to Walter Scott Scudder) S:12

Scudder, Frederick - Died 1878 Feb 4 Age 73 years, 2 months (top of stone broken off by vandals) (with wife, Cordelia Scudder & others) S:18

Scudder, Freeman L - Died 1832 Dec 3 Born 1805 Mar 16 (in large Scudder plot with wife Elizabeth H Scudder and others) S:12

Scudder, Freeman L - Died 1901 Dec 28 Born 1833 Mar 19 (metal maker next to Harriet Davis Scudder) S:12

Scudder, George - Died 1851 Nov 4 Born 1792 Dec 2 S:7

Scudder, Granville - Died 1837 Sept 2 Age 10 months, 26 days Son of Harvey & Perimlin (Premella) (with her) S:12

Scudder, Gustavus - Died 1920 Born 1844 (with Eunice M Scudder) S:14

Scudder, Hannah - Died 1797 Jan 27 in her 33rd yr Wife of Asa Scudder and daughter of James Huckins S:3R

Scudder, Hannah - Died 1802 Sept 20 Age 4 mos 6 days (listed with mother, Lydia Scudder, d 1802) (located at Lothrop's Hill) S:26R

Scudder, Hannah Mrs - Died 1844 Sept 17 Age 64 Wife of Deacon, Josiah Scudder (with him & others in large Scudder plot) S:12

Scudder, Hannah P - Died 1829 Born 1787 S:2

Scudder, Hannah R - Died 1903

Scudder (Cont.) Sept 11 Born 1839 Sept 22 (buried next to Windall Scudder) S:8

Scudder, Harriet Davis - Died 1917 Born 1833 (next to Freeman L Scudder) S:12

Scudder, Harriet Ellen - Died 1989 Born 1918 S:12

Scudder, Hattie - Died 1862 Jan 15 Age 15 years, 15 days Born 1847 Jan 1 Daughter of Eleaser & Eliza Scudder (on stone with Elazer Scudder) S:4

Scudder, Henrietta - Died 1875 Feb 16 Age 80 Died in her home of her birth 7th daughter of Benjamin Hallett (next to him) S:12

Scudder, Henry - Died 1814 Nov 13 Age 24 (died in Halifax, Nova Scotia, Canada) Son of Ebenezer & Abigail Scudder S:7

Scudder, Henry - Died 1838 Feb 16 Age 4 months, 11 days Son of Philander & Jane Scudder S:12

Scudder, Henry A - Died 1892 Jan 29 Born 1819 Nov 25 (large coffin crypt in cement boarder Scudder plot) Graduated from Yale 1842 Entered the Bar 1844 Was a Judge 1869 S:12

Scudder, Isaac - Died 1797 Oct 27 Age 11 months Son of Ebenezer & Abigail Scudder S:7

Scudder, Isaac (Capt) - Died 1847 Sept 22 Age 49 S:12

Scudder, Isabel - Died 1828 Aug 16 Age 14 months, 13 days Daughter of Josiah & Sophronia Scudder S:12

Scudder, Isabella T - Died 1846 Dec 12 Age 18 Daughter of Alexander & Mary B Scudder (next to sisters, Lucinda & Mary C Scudder) S:14

Scudder, Isaiah - Died 1852 June 1 Age 84 (next to wife, Lydia & son, Isaiah Jr Scudder) S:13

Scudder, Isaiah - Died 1866 Mar 25 Lost at Sea Born 1850 Sept 14 (this inscrption is listed on

Scudder (Cont.)

back of mother, Asenath L Scudder's stone) Son of Albert & Asenath L Scudder S:8

Scudder, Isaiah Jr Mr - Died Age 40 (dates not listed) (next to Lydia Scudder) (Stone down & broken) S:13

Scudder, J Porter - Died 1933 Born 1852 (with wife, Bertha B Scudder) S:12

Scudder, James - Died 1778 Aug 30 in his 15th yr Son of Ebenezer and Rose Scudder (next to brother Thomas) S:3R

Scudder, James - Died 1829 Born 1809 S:2

Scudder, James D - Died 1840 Born 1779 S:2

Scudder, James H - Died 1835 Jan 5 Age 3 months, 10 days Died of smallpox Son of Harvey & Perivella Scudder S:12

Scudder, Jane Mrs - Died 1858 April 2 or 21 Born 1806 April 21 Wife of Philander Scudder (next to him) S:12

Scudder, John W - Died 1872? Apr 9 in his 72nd yr (buried next to wife, Eliza Hall) S:8

Scudder, Joseph - Died 1864 May 3 at home Born 1839 Feb 11 Enlisted 7 Aug 1862 in Company E, 40th Regiment of the Massachusetts Volunteers Disabled by sickness & honorably discharged on 27 April 1864 S:12+12R

Scudder, Joseph Franklin - Died 1931 Born 1930 S:12

Scudder, Joseph W - Died 1888 Apr 19 Age 85 years, 28 days S:7

Scudder, Josiah - Died 1877 Dec 29 Born 1802 Feb 12 (with Augusta H Scudder) S:12

Scudder, Josiah (Deacon) - Died 1851 Mar 26 Age 75 (with wife, Hannah Scudder & others in large Scudder plot) S:12

Scudder, Josiah Porter - Died 1851 April 15 Age 11 Son of Josiah &

Scudder (Cont.)

Sophonia Scudder (next to mother) Drowned, capsized Bark San?eehy tornado going to New York (stone says "Erected" in memory of) S:12 +12R

Scudder, Lot - Died 1839 Mar 31 Age 68 Wife was Sophia Scudder S:3

Scudder, Louisa - Died 1833 Sept 15 Age 6 months, 12 days Daughter of Philander & Jane Scudder S:12

Scudder, Lucinda - Died 1850 April 7 Age 18 Daughter of Alexander & Mary B Scudder (next to sister, Mary C Scudder) S:14

Scudder, Lucinda - Died 1877 Jan 4 Age 79 Wife of Prentiss Scudder (with him & David Scudder & others) S:18

Scudder, Lydia - Died 1778 June 18 in her 79th yr Widow of Ebenezer Scudder S:3

Scudder, Lydia - Died 1797 Jan 27 Age 21 hours Daughter of Asa & Hannah Scudder S:3

Scudder, Lydia - Died 1802 Sept 20 Age 18 years, 8 months, 16 days Consort to Asa Scudder (Hinckley Ceme records #11R says death was 1802 Sept 20 at age 18 years, 8 months, 16 days) S:11+26R

Scudder, Lydia - Died 1854 Aug 13 Age 79 Widow of Isiah Scudder (next to Mr Isaiah Scudder Jr) (stone is down & broken) S:13

Scudder, Lydia - Died 1923 Mar 5 Born 1834 July 7 (stone is down) S:11

Scudder, Lydia A - Died 1858 July 11 Age 28 (in Davis plot) Wife of Prentiss W Scudder & daughter of Joseph & Phebe Davis S:10

Scudder, Marcia F - Died 1887 Aug 12 in her 76th yr Wife of Benjamin Scudder (buried next to him) S:7

Scudder, Marietta H - Died 1881 May 9 Age 48 years, 11 months (next to Freeman L Scudder)

Scudder (Cont.)
S:12

Scudder, Mary - Died (listed on large Smith stone with Charles H Smith) S:10

Scudder, Mary - Died 1878 Born 1804 (with Capt Zenas Marston) S:18

Scudder, Mary C - Died 1858 July Age 23(?) (stone worn) Daughter of Alexander & Mary B Scudder (next to Lucinda Scudder, sister) S:14

Scudder, Mary Crosby - Died 1949 Born 1864 S:12

Scudder, Mary E - Died 1877 Born 1838 Buried with Charles Smith, husband (a very large stone approx 5 feet high & 3 feet square) S:8

Scudder, Mary Miss - Died 1837 Sept 4 in her 65th yr S:4

Scudder, Mary Mrs - Died 1813 Jan 13 in her 76th yr Relict of Eleazer Scudder S:4

Scudder, Maude C - Died 1955 Jan 23 Born 1875 Dec 22 Daughter of Daniel & Abby Scudder (in family plot) S:11

Scudder, Mildred Fisher - Died 1935 Born 1900 (with Eleanor Lumbert & Edson Fisher) S:14

Scudder, Nannie B - Died 1893 Born 1822 (in large boarder Scudder plot) (possibly wife of Henry A Scudder) S:12

Scudder, Nelson - Died 1887 March 19 Age 75 yrs 11 mos Born 1811 (in family plot with others)(Hinkley did not list birth off stone) S:11+26R

Scudder, Olive M - Died 1876 Oct 29 Age 61 years, 8 months Wife of Erastus Scudder (next to him) S:12

Scudder, Otis - Died 1844 Aug 13 Age 4 months Son of Philander & Jane Scudder S:12

Scudder, Permella Y - Died 1842 Aug 7 Age 51 years, 5 months, 2 days Wife of Harvey Scudder (with infant, Russell Scudder)

Scudder (Cont.)
S:12

Scudder, Persis - Died 1840 April 8 Age 5 years Daughter of Josiah & Sophronia Scudder S:12

Scudder, Persis C - Died 1889 Oct 6 Age 49 Wife of Warren Cammett (next to him) S:13

Scudder, Philander (Capt) - Died 1889 or 1839 April 17 Born 1800 Dec 20 S:12

Scudder, Polly - Died 1860 Mar 19 in her 86th yr Relict of Eleazer Scudder S:4

Scudder, Prentiss - Died 1828 Nov 17 Age 34 (with Prentiss W Scudder & others) S:18

Scudder, Prentiss W - Died 1906 Aug 9 Age 78 (with David Scudder & others) S:18

Scudder, Rachel - Died 1776 June 16 in her 23rd yr Wife of Samual Scudder S:3+3R

Scudder, Rebecca - Died 1878 April 8 Born 1808 Jan 24 Wife of Edward Scudder (stone leaning against his) S:11

Scudder, Rose - Died 1784 May 2 Age 9 days Daughter of Ebenezer and Rose Scudder S:3R

Scudder, Rose - Died 1812 April 17 Age 72 years, 1 month, 12 days Wife of Ebenezer Scudder S:3

Scudder, Rose Delap - Died 1784 May 2 Age 9 days Daughter of Ebenzer & Rose Delap (other stones say that Ebenzer & Rose's last name is Scudder?) S:3

Scudder, Rufus - Died 1771 June 10 Son of Samual & Rachel Scudder S:3

Scudder, Russell - Died 1842 Aug 22 Age 24 days (infant) (with Permella Y Scudder) S:12

Scudder, Russell - Died 1842 Born 1817 S:2

Scudder, Sally - Died 1813 located in enclosed area S:11R

Scudder, Sally - Died 1841 Nov 14 Age 26 Born 1815 Sept 19 Daughter of Asa & Sally Scudder

Scudder (Cont.)
S:11

Scudder, Sally - Died 1868 Mar 22 Age 80 Widow of Capt Asa Scudder S:11

Scudder, Samuel - Died 1808 Mar 22 in his 79th yr S:3

Scudder, Samuel Jr - Died 1824 Feb 26 in his 55th yr S:3

Scudder, Sarah A - Died 1922 Born 1838 Wife of Silas (listed with him on large stone in family plot) S:11

Scudder, Sophia - Died 1855 Mar 16 in her 84th yr Widow of Lot Scudder S:3

Scudder, Sophronia - Died 18?6 July 25 Age ?3 yrs (not clear) Wife of Josiah Scudder (stone says) Erected in memory of S:12R

Scudder, Sophronia Augusta - Died 1855 Feb 8 Born 1818 April 21 Daughter of Josiah and Augusta ? S:12+12R

Scudder, Stuart Franklin - Died 1946 Born 1895 (with Mary Crosby Scudder) S:12

Scudder, Susan D - Died 1900 Mar 16 Age 87 Wife of Isaac Scudder S:12

Scudder, Thomas - Died 1778 Oct 3 Age 13 Son of Ebenzer & Rose Scudder S:3

Scudder, Walter Crosby - Died 1986 Born 1911 (next to Joseph Franklin Scudder) S:12

Scudder, Walter Scott - Died 1942 Born 1860 (next to Mary Crosby Scudder) S:12

Scudder, William - Died (stone not clear) Son of David & desire Scudder Esq S:4

Scudder, William - Died 1928 Born 1845 (stone says,"Husband) (with Mary A Bacon) S:12

Scudder, Windall - Died 1839 Sept 28 Age 4 years, 2 months, 9 days Son of Albert & Asenath C Scudder S:8

Scudder, Zenas L - Died 1864 Sept 12 Age 27 Born 1836 Sept 30

Scudder (Cont.)
(next to Erastus Scudder) S:12

Scudder, Zeno (honorable) - Died 1857 June 26 Born 1807 Aug 18 Was a sailor,studied medicine & law Entered Bar 1836 1848 was President to Mass Senate 32,33rd sessions An Accident ended his career (large Scudder stone, cement boarder) S:12

Scuder, James - Died 1778 Aug 30 in his 15th yr Son of Ebenzer & Rose Scuder S:3

Seabury, Augusta A - Died 1894 Born 1833 (listed with Reuben G Seabury) S:11

Seabury, Bertha (Berttie) R - Died 1879 Mar 15 Age 33 years, 8 months Wife of David M Seabury (next to him) S:11+26R

Seabury, David E - Died 1951 Born 1876 (with Carrie Lothrop) S:11

Seabury, David M - Died 1921 Born 1843 (next to wife, Bertha R Seabury) S:11

Seabury, George G - Died 1951 Born 1866 (with Mallie G Hinckley, wife & others) S:11

Seabury, Reuben G - Died 1908 Born 1830 (with Augusta A Seabury) S:11

Seaman, Frederick - Died 1975 Born 1900 (he was a Mason) (with Gladys F Seaman) S:15

Seaman, Gladys F - Died (still living 1991?) Born 1909 (with Frederick Seaman) S:15

Sears, Alice Blaisdell - Died 1974 Feb 23 Born 1890 Dec 23 (next to husband, Philip Fowle Sears) S:15

Sears, Auren - Died 1842 Sept 18 Age 10 months,11 days Son of Capt Snow Y & Sylvana Sears S:11

Sears, Benjamin F - Buried 1921 Nov 15 Located in section O, lot 19, grave 6 S:14R

Sears, Carl L - Died 1926 Born 1925 (with Annie R Hardy & others) S:18

Sears, Catherine J - Died 1958

Sears (Cont.)
Born 1863 S:11

Sears, Cynthia H - Died 1924 Born 1844 (with Henry V Sears) (bottom of stone **says**, "To live in hearts we leave behind is not to die) (with Stephen Lewis also) S:8

Sears, Edith B - Died 1979 Born 1883 Wife of Luther H Sears Sr (with him & son Luther Jr & others) S:18

Sears, Elsie E - Died 1988 June 30 Born 1897 Dec 31 S:18

Sears, Henry V - Died 1920 Born 1846 (with Cynthia H Sears) S:8

Sears, Isaiah G - Died 1926 Born 1853 (with Sarah P Sears & others) S:18

Sears, Lillian Parker - Died 1910 Born 1882 (with Isaiah G Sears & others) S:18

Sears, Luther H - Died 1955 Born 1874 (with wife, Edith Sears & Luther Sears Jr & others) S:18

Sears, Luther H Jr - Died 1963 Born 1911 (with parents, Luther Sr & Edith Sears & others) S:18

Sears, Mary A - Died 1955 Born 1873 Wife of Ellis G Cornish (with him & William Powers & Ruth L Cornish) S:19

Sears, Nellie C - Died 1892 Born 1862 (with William A Hallett & others) S:18

Sears, Nellie M - Died 1963 Born 1883 (between Baby Girl Cusick & William Cusick) S:19

Sears, Orin - Died 1874 March 26 Age 27 years, 6 months Drowned in the Potomac River Son of Snow K Sears (next to him) S:18

Sears, Parker - Died 1937 Born 1900 (with Isaiah G Sears & others) S:18

Sears, Philip Fowle - Died 1973 April 7 Born 1888 Nov 26 From Massachusetts, was S1 in USNRF during World War I (next to wife, Alice Blaisdell Sears) S:15

Sears, Sarah E - Died 1977 Born 1886 S:15

Sears, Sarah P - Died 1920 Born 1853 (with William C Sears & others) S:18

Sears, Snow K - Died 1855 Sept 25 Age 49 at Havana (he was a Mason)(stone worn) (next to son Orin Sears & next to Sylvia Sears) S:18

Sears, Stella Lucinda - Buried 1912 Jan 8 Located in section O, lot 19, grave 7 S:14R

Sears, Sylvia - Died 1907 Jan 24 Born 1818 Oct 15 (next to Snow K Sears) S:18

Sears, William C - Died 1933 Born 1882 (with Lillian Parker Sears & others) S:18

Sears?, ? - Died 1742 (stone worn & broken) Daughter of ? & Martha Sears ? (next to Hannah Crocker) S:11

Seavey, (Phinney), Elvira Alvah - Died 1904 Born 1859 (buried next to Susan Crosby Phinney) S:8

Seavey, Eleanor S - Died 1890 May 19 Age 36 Wife of Alonzo H Seavey & daughter of Owen & Eleanor Bacon S:18

Selff, James Frank - Died 1974 Born 1892 (with wife, Mae Margaret Selff) S:18

Selff, Mae Margaret - Died 1953 Born 1886 Wife of James Frank Selff (with him) S:18

Selinger, Ethel Ormsby - Died 1943 Born 1891 (with Thomas L Ormsby & others) S:16

Semple, Grace - Died 1973 Born 1882 Wife of Louis Burlington (with him) S:12

Senteio, Frank - Died 1949 Born 1878 (with Palmira Hutchins & Gregory Senteio) S:16

Senteio, Gregory - Died 1963 Born 1892 From Massachusetts, was a Pvt in Co D, 367th Inf during World War I (with Frank Senteio & Palmira Hutchins) S:16

Seppanen, Sennia - Died 1955

Seppanen (Cont.)
March 5 Born 1900 May 8 Wife
of Waino Seppanen (with him)
S:18

Seppanen, Waino - Died 1949 Dec
19 Born 1891 Jan 19 (with wife,
Sennia Seppanen) S:18

Sessions, Elliott H - Died 1969 Nov
22 Born 1894 Mar 28 From
Massachusetts & Corporal in 224
Aero Sq during World War I S:13

Sethares, Costas Constantine -
Died 1987 Born 1895 (with Mary
C Sethares) S:15

Sethares, Mary C - Died 1965 Born
1911 (with Costas Constantine
Sethares) S:15

Sethares, Nicholas H - Died 1974
Feb 18 Born 1891 Dec 19 From
Massachusetts, was Pvt in US
Army during World War I S:15

Shalvey, Bernadette - Died (still
living 1991?) Born 1893 (listed
with Loretta C Shalvey) S:15

Shalvey, Loretta C - Died 1972
Born 1892 (with Bernadette
Shalvey) S:15

Sharp, John F - Died 1824 Nov 10
(stone still standing but broken)
Twin son of William & Elizabeth
P Sharp (next to Sadie Sharp)
S:18

Sharp, Sadie - Died 1878 (Stone
vandalized) Daughter of William
& Elizabeth Sharp (next to John
F Sharp) S:18

Sharpe, Ernest R - Died 1932 Born
1862 S:18

Shattuck, Frances E - Died 1973
Born 1893 (with James P Shattuck) S:15

Shattuck, James P - Died 1983
Born 1894 (with Frances E
Shattuck) S:15

Shaw, Alice P - Died 1980 Born
1901 (next to husband, William
B Shaw) S:15

Shaw, Elisabeth - Died 1772 June
6 in her 39th yr Wife & Consort
of Rev Oakes Shaw S:5

Shaw, Josephine A - Died 1894 Apr
9 Born 1853 Nov 21 S:8

Shaw, Lucy Mrs - Died 1853 Oct 9
Age 82 Relict of Rev Philander
Shaw of Eastham, Massachu-
setts S:14

Shaw, Maude J - Died 1937 Born
1872 Wife of Jehiel Crosby
(buried next to him) S:8

Shaw, Oakes Rev - Died 1802 Feb
11 Born 1736 at Bridewater,
Mass He was a graduate of Harvard in 1758 Ordain 1760
(buried next to Miss Rhoda
Shaw Lovell) (Hinckley Ceme
records #5R says death year was
1807) S:5

Shaw, Rebecca - Died 1802 July 16
Age 71 Widow S:12+12R

Shaw, Sarah Miss - Died 1792 July
16 in her 23rd yr S:5

Shaw, William B - Died 1987 Born
1893 (was a Mason) (next to
wife, Alice P Shaw) S:15

Shea, Gertrude C - Died 1966 Born
1898 (next to John F Shea) S:15

Shea, John F - Died 1979 Born
1898 (next to Gertrude C Shea)
S:15

Shea, Lillian U - Died 1973 Born
1899 (with Ralph J Shea) S:15

Shea, Lynne A - Died 1990 Born
1947 S:13

Shea, Ralph J - Died 1990 Born
1900 (with Lillian U Shea) S:15

Shearer, Mabel Williams - Died
1984 Dec 29 Born 1893 Mar 5
S:15

Shedd, Margurite Danforth - Died
1970 Born 1897 (with Robert
Lemuel Shedd) S:14

Shedd, Robert Lemuel - Died 1975
Born 1902 (with Margurrite
Danforth Shedd) S:14

Sheehan, George D - Died 1979
Oct 12 Born 1898 Aug 2 Was a
Pvt in US Army during World
War II S:15

Shelton, Flora Lumbert - Died
1944 Born 1873 (with Oliver &
Deborah Lumbert) S:14

Shepherd, Darrell R - Died (still
living 1991?) Born 1907 (listed
with Sarah Shepherd) S:19

Shepherd, Jeannett E - Died 1983 Born 1900 (with Charles Eldridge) S:18

Shepherd, Sarah W - Died 1969 Born 1902 (with Darrell R Shepherd) S:19

Sherman, Charles E - Died 1929 April 24 Born 1851 Sept 27 (with Emma E Sherman) S:18

Sherman, Charles H - Died 1910 Born 1822 (with Harriet B Sherman) S:18

Sherman, Eliza (Lida) - Died 1969 March 1 Born 1883 Oct 21 (next to Lula Sherman Lumbert) S:18

Sherman, Emma E - Died 1921 Nov 3 Born 1857 March 5 (with Charles E Sherman) S:18

. **Sherman**, Gladys M - Died 1968 Sept 21 Born 1898 April 7 (has 2 stones) (with Walter Henry Sherman) S:17

Sherman, Harriet B - Died 1908 Born 1827 (with Charles H Sherman) S:18

Sherman, Harriet W - Died 1888 Dec 6 Age 71 years, 3 months S:18

Sherman, Henry L - Died 1950 Born 1868 (with Irma W Sherman) S:18

Sherman, Irma W - Died 1926 Born 1874 (with Henry L Sherman) S:18

Sherman, Joseph E - Died 1897 Born 1822 (with Susan L Sherman & others) S:18

Sherman, Laura A - Died 1921 Born 1855 (with Joseph E Sherman & others) S:18

Sherman, Margaret Azoy - Died 1974 Nov 19 Born 1890 Oct 1 (listed on back of stone of Harriot Freeman & Charles Austin Groves) S:8

Sherman, Robert A - Died 1986 Born 1897 S:18

Sherman, Ruby L - Died 1943 Born 1882 S:17

Sherman, Susan L - Died 1907 Born 1822 (with Wallace C Sherman & others) S:18

Sherman, Wallace C - Died 1946 Born 1858 (with Laura A Sherman & others) S:18

Sherman, Walter Henry - Died 1965 Jan 26 Born 1894 June 23 (has 2 stones) From Massachusetts, was COX in USNRF during World War I (with Gladys M Sherman) S:17

Sherwood, Frederick M - Died 1984 Born 1903 (he was a Mason) (with wife, Harriette R Sherwood & Carol Fay) S:20

Sherwood, Harriette R - Died (no dates) (also listed as Mason) Wife of Frederick M Sherwood (listed with him & Carol Fay) S:20

Shields, Agnes - Died 1933 Born 1868 (with James Shields) S:31

Shields, Ellen Hyland - Died 1913 Born 1829 (with Frederick Edmund Murphy & others) S:31

Shields, James - Died 1951 Born 1869 (with Agnes Shields) S:31

Shields, William - Died 1907 Born 1832 (with Ellen Hyland Shields & others) S:31

Shortley, May Weeks - Died 1968 Born 1881 (on family stone with Hiram Weeks) S:12

Showell, Charles Batchelor - Died 1974 May 16 Born 1892 April 10 (next to wife, Zelia Thompson Showell) S:14

Showell, Zelia Thompson - Died 1964 March 1 Born 1892 Jan 5 Wife of Charles Batchelor Showell (next to him) S:14

Shuley, Mary T - Died 1974 Born 1887 (with Michael F Shuley) S:16

Shuley, Michael F - Died 1949 Born 1876 (with Mary T Shuley) S:16

Shuman, Charles - Died 1974 April 16 Born 1900 Oct 27 (Jewish section) Husband of Rose S:15

Shuttleworth, Walter - Died 1929 Born 1879 (with Walter Shuttleworth Jr & others) S:31

Shuttleworth, Walter Jr - Died 1955 Feb 25 Born 1916 Feb 9

Shuttleworth (Cont.)
From Massachusetts, was in
Company F, 801 SIG, SUC
Regiment during World War II
(with Bridget Shuttleworth Walls
& others) S:31

Sibley, Addie R - Died 1905 Born
1869 Stone says, "Cervus
Alces"(?) (with Dora & Frank
Sturgis) S:14

Siddall, Clarence O - Died 1972
July 12 Born 1896 April 29
From Massachusetts and a CE
in USNRF during World War 1
(next to Cora G Siddall) S:13

Siddall, Cora G - Died 1990 Jan 18
Born 1905 Oct 19 (next to
Clarence O Siddall) S:13

Silhavy, John Frank - Died 1984
Born 1897 Age 81 (next to
Marion Otis Silhavy) (buried at
block 8, lot 65 F 1/2, grave 3)
(some of the above info is from
Mosswood cemetery records)
S:15

Silhavy, Marion Otis - Died 1978
Born 1901 (next to John F
Silhavy) S:15

Silva, Alice M - Died 1982 Born
1901 Wife of Daniel J Silva (with
him & others) S:14

Silva, Daniel J - Died 1974 April 4
Born 1896 Oct 5 From Massa-
chusetts, was a Major in US
Army Air Force during World
War I & II (with George W Brew-
ster) S:14

Silva, Emilio R - Died 1946 Born
1865 (with Roza Silva & Izabel
Perry) S:31

Silva, Mary - Died (under ground)
Born 1894 July 21 (next to Mary
Silva) S:20

Silva, Mary - Died 1909 June 16
Born 1861 Feb 28 Stone says
"Wife" (next to Mary Silva) S:31

Silva, Roza A - Died 1936 Born
1862 (with Emilio Silva & Izabel
Perry) S:31

Silver, George W - Died 1897 Dec 2
Born 1864 May 3 (next to
Joseph C Silver) S:21

Silver, Joseph C - Died 1928 Born
1850 (with Rebecca C Silver)
S:21

Silver, Rebecca C - Died 1939 Born
1858 (with Joseph C Silver) S:21

Silvia, Frederick - Died 1969 Born
1883 (undertaker plaque only)
S:17

Simmons, Alice - Died 1923 Born
1850 (with Nellie May Bond &
others) S:18

Simmons, Caroline - Died 1826
July 10 Age 6 months, 20 days
Daughter of Lemuel B & Tem-
perance Simmons (next to them)
S:21

Simmons, Charles - Died 1827 Jan
19 Age 1 year, 11 days Son of
Jehiel & Rachel Simmons S:4

Simmons, Daniel B - Died 1840
Jan 7 Age 20 months, 5 days
Son of Capt Lemuel B & Tem-
perance Simmons (next to them)
S:21

Simmons, Eliza A - Died 1889
Born 1816 Wife of LB Simmons
(with him & others) S:21

Simmons, Ella Jessup - Died 1952
Born 1866 (with Elizabeth Chase
& others) S:18

Simmons, George Crary - Died
1875 Oct 3 Born 1874 March 21
Son of Levi & Hersilia Simmons
(next to them) S:18

Simmons, Hannah - Died 1863
July 27 Age 96 years, 1 month,
13 days Widow of Sylvanus
Simmons (next to him) S:21

Simmons, Haratio - Died 1958
Born 1872 (with Ella Jessup
Simmons & others) S:18

Simmons, Hersilia B - Died 1882
Aug 15 Age 41 Wife of Levi L
Simmons (next to him) S:18

Simmons, Horatio - Died 1855 May
17 Age 19 years, 4 months, 20
days Born 1835 Dec 27 (with LB
Simmons) S:21

Simmons, Jehiel - Died 1878 Dec 8
Age 83 yrs 11 mos S:4

Simmons, L B - Died 1892 Born
1802 (with wifes, Temperance

Simmons (Cont.)
Simmons & Eliza A Simmons) S:21

Simmons, L(Lemuel) B (Capt) - Died 1892 April 22 Born 1802 April 19 (with Eliza, LB & Temperance Simmons) S:21

Simmons, Levi L - Died 1886 Aug 23 Age 53 (with Mary L Simmons, wife) (stone down & broken in half due to vandals) (next to Hersilia B Simmons, other wife) S:18

Simmons, Louisa H - Died 1881 April 21 Born 1841 Aug 8 (stone down due to vandals) (with Sylvanus Simmons) (between Charles C Crocker & family & Mertiel L Simmons) S:18

Simmons, Lurane Lovell - Died 1822 May 21 Age 8 months, 4 days Daughter of Jehiel & Rachel Simmons S:4

Simmons, Mary L - Died 1863 Aug 5 Age 29 years, 2 months, 13 days Wife of LL Simmons (Levi) (next to him) (stones are broken in half by vandals, next to Hersilia B Simmons) S:18

Simmons, Mertiel L - Died 1888 May 25 Born 1870 Feb 9 (next to Sylvanus & Louisa Simmons whos stone is down) S:18

Simmons, Rachel - Died 1865 Apl 8 Age 60 years, 11 months Wife of Jehiel Simmons S:4

Simmons, Sylvanus - Died 1856 March 22 Age 86 (next to wife, Hannah Simmons) S:21

Simmons, Sylvanus - Died 1899 Jan 17 Born 1841 July 7 (stone down due to vandals) (with Louisa H Simmons) S:18

Simmons, Temperance - Died 1841 Born 1803 Wife of LB Simmons (with him & others) S:21

Simpson, Cora C - Died 1986 Born 1890 (with Thomas & Catherine Baker) S:14

Simpson, E F - Died 1976 Born 1896 (with Henry B Baker) S:14

Sims, Earl K - Died 1962 Born

Sims (Cont.)
1886 (next to Mary W Sims) S:13

Sims, Mary W - Died 1981 Born 1884 (next to Earl K Sims) S:13

Sippola, Johanna - Died 1981 Born 1891 Wife of Axel Ahonen (with him) S:20

Sisk, Cora - Died 1984 Born 1918 S:11

Sjoblom, Hilma T - Died 1974 Born 1898 (with John Sjoblom) S:15

Sjoblom, John - Died 1973 Born 1897 (with Hilma T Sjoblom) S:15

Skelly, Elizabeth P (Bannon) - Buried 1981 Aug 11 Age 85 Located in section 3, lot 66, grave 4 S:15R

Slack, Lucy J - Died 1929 Born 1853 (in with John & Lucy Linnell & family) S:14

Slade, Elizabeth - Died 183? (stone worn) Wife of William S:14

Slade, Elizabeth - Died 1870 Aug 3 Age 39 Wife of Willard Slade (next to him) S:14

Slade, Willard E - Died 1900 Jan 26 Born 1825 Jan 24 (next to wife, Elizabeth Slade) S:14

Slavin, Amy Childs - Died 1988 Feb 3 Born 1896 Nov 2 (next to Richard F Slavin) S:31

Slavin, Margaret - Died 1895 Sept 15 Age 72 Born at Phtown, County Kilkenny, Ireland (with Mary Slavin & others) S:31

Slavin, Mary A - Died 1932 Born 1855 (with Matthias Slavin & others) S:31

Slavin, Mary E - Died 1936 Born 1863 (with Thomas P Slavin) S:20

Slavin, Matthias - Died 1913 March 17 Born 1891 March 25 (with Gertrude M Eldridge & others) S:31

Slavin, Matthias P - Died 1916 Dec 6 Born 1858 March 1 (with wife, Mary A McKinley & others) S:31

Slavin, Richard F - Died 1970 Feb Born 1893 Nov 26 (military stone) From Massachusetts, was

Slavin (Cont.)
a Corporal in Company L, 325th Infantry during World War I (next to Amy Childs Slavin) S:31

Slavin, Thomas - Died 1874 June 18 Age 55 Born at Nenagh, County Tipperary, Ireland (with Margaret Slavin & others) S:31

Slavin, Thomas P - Died 1944 Born 1862 (with Mary E Slavin) S:20

Small, Abner L - Died 1895 Jan 20 Age 82 years, 6 months, 19 days (next to wife, Betsey A Small) S:14

Small, Alfred T - Died 1937 Born 1867 (with wife, Carrie M Bacon) S:18

Small, Allcotts - Died 1851 Dec 6 Age 13 Stone says, "Little Allcotts grave" Son of Gyrenus & Thankful Small S:12

Small, Benjamin (Capt) - Died 1876 Aug 23 Age 87 years, 2 months, 28 days (between both wifes, Polly & Eliza Small) S:14

Small, Benjamin Merrill - Died 1938 Born 1863 (with Mary Handren Nickerson, wife) S:14

Small, Betsey A - Died 1853 Jan 5 Age 36 years, 6 months, 10 days Wife of Abner L Small (next to him) S:14

Small, Edward F - Died (still living 1991?) Born 1900 S:15

Small, Eliza - Died 1871 Nov 1 Age 75 Wife of Benjamin Small (next to him) S:14

Small, Elizabeth W - Died 1987 Born 1911 (has military stone also) (with Henry E Small) S:12

Small, Everett - Died 1932 Born 1872 (with wife, Anna J Lynde) S:12

Small, Gyrenus - Died 1898 Nov 5 Born 1819 Jan 5 S:12

Small, Harriet - Died 1821 Dec 30 Daughter of Benjamin & Polly (next to sister, Mary Small) S:14

Small, Henry E - Died 1977 Born 1915 (has military stone) Was a PFC in US Army during World War II in Company F, 101

Small (Cont.)
Infantry, 26 Division (with Everett Small & Anna J Lynde) S:12

Small, Imogene Sturgis - Died 1979 Born 1881 (stone is perpetual care) (buried with Elias Parris, also the Parris's are listed on same stone with the Sturgis family) S:8

Small, J Webster - Died 1961 July 24 Born 1910 April 16 S:12

Small, James Cyrenus - Died 1865 Born 1865 (with Eliza Scudder & Sophia Hinckley & James G Small) S:13

Small, James Godfrey - Died 1913 Born 1837 (with Sophia Hinckley) Military stone too, which says, "US Navy 1861-1865" S:13

Small, Lester A - Died 1902 Feb 11 Born 1851 Sept 22 My husband (next to Melissa L Small) S:14

Small, Maria - Died 1826 Aug 29 Daughter of Benjamin & Polly Small (next to them) S:14

Small, Marilyn - Died 1988 Born 1934 Wife of Donald I Anderson (next to Robert P Small and Madelyn A Coffin) S:12

Small, Mary - Died 1826 Aug 25 Age 10 years Daughter of Benjamin & Polly Small (next to sister, Maria Small) S:14

Small, Mary H - Died 1897 June 25 Born 1826 April 29 (with Henry A Waitt) S:12

Small, Mary R - Died 1892 Jan 11 Age 69 years, 2 months The daughter of a king Wife of Capt Abner L Small (next to him) S:14

Small, May - Died 18?? May 6 (a very small stone, like for a child) (between Grace Williams & James Parker) S:13

Small, Melissa L - Died 1857 Sept 21 Age 19 years, 8 months Daughter of Abner & Betsey Small (next to them) S:14

Small, Polly - Died 1855 June 16 Age 65 Wife of Capt Benjamin Small (next to him) S:14

Small, Robert P - Died 1978 Born 1901 (with Madelyn A Coffin) S:12

Small, Sarah - Died 1849 Born 1816 (with Warren Small) S:12

Small, Sarah W - Died 1924 Born 1839 (with Warren Small) S:12

Small, Warren - Died 1908 Born 1815 (with Sarah Small) S:12

Small, Warren D - Died 1850 Born 1849 (with Warren Small) S:12

Smalley, Alice T - Died 1971 Born 1878 Wife of William Robbins (with him) S:14

Smart, Albert J Jr - Died 1975 July 9 Born 1890 March 26 (next to Annah Potter Smart) Was 2nd Lt in US Army during World War I S:15

Smart, Annah Potter - Died 1981 Feb 7 Born 1892 Oct 6 (next to Albert J Smart Jr) S:15

Smith, (daughter) - Died 1866 Oct 30 Daughter of Edmund Smith (listed with him & others on family stone) S:11

Smith, (infant) - Died 1840 S:11R

Smith, ? Parker - Died 1842 Sept 18 Born 1841 Oct 9 Child of Henry & Abigail P Smith S:11

Smith, ? - Died (small broken stone) (next to Charles Smith, son of James & Susanna Smith) S:11

Smith, Abagail N - Died 1812 Dec 2 Age 7 years, 10 months (buried with Stephen N Lothrop) Daughter of Mathias & Chloe Smith S:5

Smith, Abbie C - Died 1916 July 15 Born 1842 July 4 (with William C Welden & others & next to Willie Smith & others) S:18

Smith, Agnes P - Died 1975 Born 1887 Daughter of Joseph Phinney & Ida Hatch (with them) S:18

Smith, Alan H - Died 1944 Aug 23 Born 1925 Oct 19 From Massachusetts, was a Private in 38th Armd, Infantry Bn, 7 Amd Div during World War II S:18

Smith, Albert H - Died 1883 March

Smith (Cont.)
3 Born 1866 Nov 17 (with Willie Smith & next to John H Smith & others) S:18

Smith, Albert N - Died 1970 June 11 Born 1892 Aug 29 From Massachusetts, was a Private in US Army during World War I (next to Annie A Smith) S:14

Smith, Alice May - Died 1926 Born 1866 (with Beatrice Smith & others) S:18

Smith, Amasa - Died 1829 Jan 6 Age 51 years 8 months S:10

Smith, Amy F - Died 1929 Born 1870 (with Phebe G Smith) S:18

Smith, Andronicus C - Died 1832 Sept 19 Age 3 weeks, 4 days Child of Mary Smith (Hinckley Cem records #11R says day of death was the 9th of Sept at age 3 weeks, 4 days) S:11+26R

Smith, Anna E - Died 1898 Dec 7 Born 1845 Oct 23 Wife of Reuben Smith (next to him) S:11

Smith, Anne - Died 1722 July 2 Age 53 Wife of Joseph Smith S:5R

Smith, Annie A - Died 1972 Jan 24 Born 1891 Sept 27 (next to Albert N Smith) S:14

Smith, Annie C - Died 1878 Aug 2 in her 35th yr Wife of Cyrus B Smith S:9

Smith, Augusta P - Died 1903 Dec 17 Age 55 years, 7 days S:19

Smith, Beatrice - Died 1895 Born 1895 (with John Bayard Smith & others) S:18

Smith, Bertha H - Died 1933 Born 1883 (with Chauncey H Smith & others) S:18

Smith, Bethier Mrs - Died 1811 July 6 Age 31 or 38? Wife of James Smith (next to James Smith, d1832) S:11

Smith, Betty/Betsey - Died 1833 Dec 20 in her 58th yr Widow of Solomon Smith (next to him) S:11+22R

Smith, Carl Hallett - Died 1900 Oct 12 Born 1900 Sept 25 (with

Smith (Cont.)

James & Satilla Smith) S:18

Smith, Caroline H - Died 1880 Sept 5 Age 61 years, 8 months Wife of Daniel Smith (next to him) S:11

Smith, Caroline J - Died 1907 Born 1845 Wife of Isaac Smith (with him & Eliza F Smith & others) S:18

Smith, Celestia F - Died 1917 April 4 Born 1842 March 1 Wife of George A Smith (next to him) S:19

Smith, Charles - Died 1800 July 15 Age 1 years, Son of James & Sylvana Smith (stone in very bad condition) S:11

Smith, Charles - Died 1811 Feb 2 Age 6 months Son of James & Bethier Smith S:11R

Smith, Charles - Died 1820 July 15 Age 11 years 8 months 8 days (stone broken in half) Son of James & Susanna Smith S:11

Smith, Charles - Died 1984 Born 1895 Was a Cpl in US Army during World War I (next to possible wife, Josephine C Smith) S:15

Smith, Charles E - Died 1954 Born 1878 (with Charlotte S Smith, wife & others) S:18

Smith, Charles F - Died 1956 Born 1878 (with Georgia Johnson & Christine Drisko) S:18

Smith, Charles H - Died 1870 ? Born 1828 ? (stone badly worn) (a very large stone approx 5 feet high & 3 feet square, buried with Mary E Scudder) (there is also a listing at #10 cemetery?) S:8

Smith, Charles H - Died 1870 Born 1828 (large square stone, 2' X 2' X 4' with others) (there is also another listing at #8 cemetery?) S:10

Smith, Charles Howard - Died 1880/90 ? Born 1827 ? (buried with Charles Smith & Mary Scudder) S:8

Smith, Charlotte - Died 1850 Oct 2 Age 68 Widow of David Smith

Smith (Cont.)

(stone leaning against his) S:11

Smith, Charlotte S - Died 1965 Born 1878 Wife of Charles E Smith (with him & Eliza F Smith & others) S:18

Smith, Chauncey H - Died 1949 Born 1886 (with Herbert A Smith & others) S:18

Smith, Clifford E (Cappy) - Died 1985 Nov 25 Born 1922 Aug 20 S:20

Smith, Cynthietta - Died 1842 Sept 18 Born 9 Oct 1841 Daughter of Henry & Abigail Smith located in row 5 possibly lot 2 S:11R+26R

Smith, Cyrus B - Died (Year?) May 13 Age 73 years, 4 months, 26 days S:9

Smith, Daniel - Died 1844 Mar 18 Age 15 Infant(?) son of Daniel Smith (next to him) S:11

Smith, Daniel - Died 1859 Aug 10 Age 41 years, 2 months S:11

Smith, Daniel - Died 1894 located in row 6 S:11R

Smith, Daniel Baker - Died 1851 July 16 Age 3 years, 1 day Son of Elish & Abby Smith S:4

Smith, Daniel Freeman - Died 1859 Nov 7 in Boston Age 18 years, 23 days Only son of Freeman & Sarah C Smith (next to them) S:11+26R

Smith, Dannie - Died (small stone with no markings, but listed with Fannie Smith) S:11

Smith, David - Died 1824 Mar 13 Age 46 S:11

Smith, David (Capt) - Died 1838 Aug 27 Age 31 S:11

Smith, Deborah I - Died 1900 Aug 28 Born 1827 May 1 (with John Smith) S:18

Smith, Deborah P - Died 1840 Mar 25 Age 4 years 5 months 6 days Born 1835 Sept 17 Daughter of James & Mehitable Smith S:11

Smith, Desire Mrs - Died 1824 Feb 1 in her 86th yr Relict of ? S:11 +26R

Smith, Eben - Died 1842 Mar 19

Smith (Cont.)
Born 1841 Feb 22 Son of
Edmund Smith (listed on family
stone with others) S:11

Smith, Ebenezer - Died 1876 July
22 Born 1809 Jan 28 (stone
says Age 67 yrs 6 mos) (Hinkley
did not record birth from
stone)(large family stone with
others) S:11+26R

Smith, Edmund - Died 1835 July 7
Age 11 years, 5 months Son of
Reuben & Mary Smith (next to
father) S:11

Smith, Edmund - Died 1873 Oct
17 Age 37 Born 1836 Aug 5 son
of Ebenezer & Lydia Smith
(Hinkley did not record birth off
stone)(listed on family stone with
others) (Hinckley Ceme records
#11R says death was 1873)
S:11+26R

Smith, Elijah - Died 1800's (stone
not clear) (next to Daniel Smith)
S:11

Smith, Elijah - Died 1802 Oct 21
Age 65 yrs 7 mos 21 days
(between Julia & Mrs Mary
Smith) S:11

Smith, Elijah - Died 1865 April 17
Age 69 years, 7 months (Hinckley Ceme records #11R says
death was 1865) S:11+26R

Smith, Elisha - Died 1863 Dec 18
Age 42 years, 10 months (he was
a Civil War Veteran, 1861-65,
flag at grave) S:11

Smith, Eliza - Died 1874 Born
1811 (with Levi L Smith & other
& next to Levi Smith & others)
S:18

Smith, Eliza F - Died 1943 Born
1881 (with Charles E Smith &
others) S:18

Smith, Ellen P - Died 1965 Born
1880 (with Percy E Smith) S:15

Smith, Elsie C - Died 1934 Born
1891 (next to Harold F Smith)
S:18

Smith, Elvin - Died 1805 June 28
Age 13 years, 10 days Son of
Mathias & Chloe Smith

Smith (Cont.)
(Hinckley Ceme records #5R
shows a Ervin at age 3) S:5

Smith, Emily B - Died 1924 Born
1832 (with Levi L Smith & others) S:18

Smith, Ernest R - Died 1985 Born
1916 (with Mary E Donaghy &
James Ensor) S:13

Smith, Estella A - Died 19- (no
other date listed) Born 1861 Wife
of Charles A West (with him &
daughter, Eva Estella West) S:18

Smith, Fannie - Died (no markings
on stone, but listed with Dannie
Smith) S:11

Smith, Flavill A - Died 1908 Born
1828 (with Kimball R Smith &
others) S:11

Smith, Flora K - Died 1931 Born
1852 (with Kimball R Smith &
others) S:11

Smith, Frances Maria - Died 1853
Sept 13 Born 1852 Dec 6
Daughter of Elisha & Abby
Smith S:4

Smith, Frank - Died 1931 (?) Born
1868 (large Smith stone with
Charles H Smith) S:10

Smith, Freeman - Died 1891 June
13 Age 75 years, 3 months, 18
days (next to wife, Sarah C
Smith, d1879) S:11

Smith, Gail D - Died (still living
1991?) Born 1943 Nov 22 Wife of
James A Goff (listed with him)
S:12

Smith, George A - Died 1922 Nov
23 Born 1840 July 6 (next to
wife, Celestia F Smith) S:19

Smith, George A - Died 1970 Born
1896 (with Mary McCormick
Smith, wife) S:16

Smith, George H - Died 1901 April
11 Born 1839 Sept 17 (with
Abbie C Smith & others) S:18

Smith, Hannah - Died 1868 Oct 31
Age 84 Widow of Amasa Smith
(next to him) S:10

Smith, Harold F - Died 1929 Born
1889 (next to Elsi C Smith) S:18

Smith, Harold L - Died 1911 Born

Smith (Cont.)
1867 (with Mary Rhodehouse) S:14

Smith, Harold L - Buried 1901 Located in section 7, lot 4, grave 7 S:14R

Smith, Harriet D - Died 1858 Oct 7 Age 18 years, 8 months S:5

Smith, Harvey J - Died 1977 Born 1899 S:15

Smith, Helen M - Died 1872 Aug 9 Age 25 Daughter of Elisha & Abby Smith S:11R

Smith, Henry - Died 1847 Oct 28 in his 30th yr Son of Levi & Love Smith S:6

Smith, Herbert A - Died 1943 Born 1857 (with Isabel K Smith & others) S:18

Smith, Isaac - Died 1886 Born 1834 (with wife, Rebecca Smith & others) S:18

Smith, Isabel K - Died 1947 Born 1860 (with Bertha H Smith & others) S:18

Smith, Isabella - Died 1909 Born 1834 (on same stone with Thomas Smith) S:11

Smith, Isaiah H - Died (none) Born 1865 Feb 7 Was in the Spanish American War, Veteran of Cuba (has a cross marker) S:19

Smith, James - Died 1832 Sept 19 Age 56 (next to Bethier & Susan Smith, both wifes) S:11

Smith, James - Died 1883 May 7 Born 1800 Nov 13 (next to wife, Mehitable Smith) S:11

Smith, James Newell - Died 1938 Nov 24 Born 1858 May 12 (with Satilla & Carl Smith) S:18

Smith, James P - Died 1911 Born 1846 (large Smith family stone) S:11

Smith, John - Died 1900 Aug 27 Born 1822 Jan 10 (with Deborah I Smith) S:18

Smith, John - Died 1963 Born 1881 (with Maria & Mary E Smith) S:20

Smith, John Bayard - Died 1975 July 3 Born 1899 May 14 (has 2

Smith (Cont.)
stones) Was a Pvt in US Army during World War I (with Prince Bearse Smith & others) S:18

Smith, John H - Died 1907 Born 1830 (with Emily B Smith & others) S:18

Smith, Josephine C - Died 1977 Oct 4 Born 1899 May 30 Stone says,"Wife" (next to possible husband, Charles Smith) S:15

Smith, Josiah C - Died 1882 June 13 Age 64 years, 2 months 1817 Apr S:5

Smith, Julia - Died 1809 April 18 Age 1 year 6 months, 8 days Daughter of Reuben & Mary Smith S:11

Smith, Julia M - Died 1978 Born 1897 (undertaker plaque only) S:17

Smith, Kimball - Died 1865 located in row 9 possibly lot f S:11R

Smith, Kimball R - Died 1851 Born 1850 (with Medora Smith & others) S:11

Smith, Kimball R - Died 1863 Born 1804 (with Flavill A Smith & others) (Hinckley Ceme records says age was 59 years, 3 months) S:11

Smith, Kimball R - Died 1938 Born 1858 (with Flora K Smith & others) S:11

Smith, Levi - Died 1863 Sept 3 Age 90 years, 1 month S:6

Smith, Levi - Died 1864 Born 1864 (with Orville B Smith & others) S:18

Smith, Levi L - Died 1875 Born 1804 (with Eliza Smith & others) S:18

Smith, Lillian - Died 1921 Born 1862 (with Levi Smith d1864 & others) S:18

Smith, Lizzie A - Died 1929 Jan 8 Age 83 years, 4 months, 22 days Wife of Thomas J Smith (listed with him & son, Thomas W Smith & others) S:19

Smith, Love - Died 1864 Oct 23 Age 84 years, 1 month Widow of

Smith (Cont.)
Levi Smith S:6

Smith, Lucy C - Died 1891 Mar 28 Age 68 years, 7 months S:5

Smith, Lydia - Died 1820 April 11 in her 79th yr Widow of Capt Samuel Smith (buried next to him) S:10+26R

Smith, Lydia - Died 1899 April 8 Born 1815 July 26 Wife of Ebenezer Smith (listed on large family stone with others) S:11

Smith, Lydia F - Died 1887 Aug 15 Age 87 years, 3 months, 3 days S:9

Smith, Mabel C - Died 1965 Born 1884 Stone says,"Aunties" (with Margaret G Smith) S:16

Smith, Margaret G - Died 1964 Born 1889 Stone says,"Aunties" (with Mabel C Smith) S:16

Smith, Margaret V - Died 1964 Born 1887 S:17

Smith, Maria - Died 1977 Born 1885 (with John & Mary E Smith) S:20

Smith, Marietta W - Died 1884 Nov 22 Age 40 years, 3 months Wife of George A Smith S:5

Smith, Martha - Died 1846 Oct 14 in her 69th yr Wife of Samuel Crosby (next to him)

Smith, Mary - Died 1727 ? 19th (stone badly worn) Wife of Jabez (she is possibly a Smith?) S:11

Smith, Mary - Died 1827 March 16 Age 88 Widow of Elijah Smith S:11

Smith, Mary - Died 1838 Aug 18 Age 51 Widow of Reuben Smith (next to him) S:11

Smith, Mary E - Died (still living in 1991?) Born 1925 (with John & Maria Smith) S:20

Smith, Mary K - Died 1837 located in row 9 possibly lot 2 S:11R

Smith, Mary McCormick - Died 1990 Born 1890 Wife of George A Smith (with him) S:16

Smith, Mary Mrs - Died 1827 Mar 16 in her 88th yr Widow of Elijah Smith S:11+26R

Smith, Mary R - Died 1835 Feb Age 16 months Daughter of ? & Mary Smith (father's name underground) S:11

Smith, Mary W - Died 1881 Born 18?? (buried with Charles Smith & Mary Scudder) S:8

Smith, Matthias - Died 1838 Mar 19 Age 69 S:5

Smith, Medora - Died 1878 Oct 10 Born 1854 Feb 20 (with William W Smith & others) (Hinckley Ceme records #11R says death was on Oct 10 and birth was on Feb 20) S:11+26R

Smith, Mehitable - Died 1890 Mar 24 Born 1806 Aug 30 Wife of James Smith (stone styled same as husbands & Reuben R Smith & Anna E Smith) S:11

Smith, Nathan - Died 1818 Dec 17 in his 81st yr S:5

Smith, Nellie - Died (no markings, but next to Elisha Smith, stone is knocked down) S:11

Smith, Newton - Died 1975 Jan 24 Born 1895 Sept 15 Was in US Army during World War I S:15

Smith, Orlando - Died 1813 located in row 5 S:11R

Smith, Orlando - Died 1878 Dec 5 Age 28 (stone badly worn) S:11+26R

Smith, Orlando - Died 1873 (?) Dec 5 Age 72 ? (Hinckley Ceme records says death was 1878 at age 28) S:11

Smith, Orville B - Died 1870 Born 1861 (with Washington J Smith & others) S:18

Smith, Pauline - Died 1878 Born 1801 Wife of Rhotire Smith (with him & Isaac Smith & others) S:18

Smith, Percy E - Died 1966 Born 1876 (with Ellen P Smith) S:15

Smith, Phebe G - Died 1964 Born 1865 (with Amy F Smith) S:18

Smith, Prince Bearse - Died 1945 Born 1859 (with Alice May Smith & others) S:18

Smith, Rebecca - Died 1871 Born

Smith (Cont.)

1831 Wife of Isaac Smith (with him & Caroline J Smith & others) S:18

Smith, Reuben - Died 1829 Nov 18 in his 47th yr (next to wife, Mary Smith) (Hinckley Ceme records says age was 47) S:11+26R

Smith, Reuben R - Died 1906 Feb 15 Born 1839 Aug 19 (next to James & Mehitable Smith) S:11

Smith, Reuben R (Capt) - Died 1834 March 15 at sea From Schooner, Columbia on passage from Alexandria to New York age 31 years S:11

Smith, Rhash - Died 1880 (?) Born 1879 (stone not clear) (on large Smith stone with Charles H Smith) S:10

Smith, Rhotire - Died 1895 Born 1808 (with Pauline Smith & others) S:18

Smith, Richard L - Died 1834 Dec 4 in his 31st yr S:5

Smith, Robert W - Died 1914 Sept 24 Born 1838 Nov 2 (next to Tryphena Smith) S:19

Smith, Rosella - Died 1900 Aug 2 Born 1846 Jan 11 Daughter of Ebenezer & Lydia Smith (listed on family stone with others) S:11

Smith, Sallie Gorham - Died 1934 Born 1855 (on Smith stone with James P Smith & others) S:11

Smith, Sally E - Died 1860 Feb 7 Age 50 years, 7 months, 11 days Wife of Isaac Smith S:4

Smith, Samuel (Capt) - Died 1817 Sept 4 in his 74th yr (buried next to wife, Thankful Smith) S:10+26R

Smith, Sarah C - Died 1879 May 25 in Boston, Age 58 years, 1 month, 7 days Wife of Freeman Smith (next to him) S:11

Smith, Sarah Mrs - Died 1827 July 12 in her 56th yr Wife of Benjamin Smith (on same stone with Richard Smith) S:5

Smith, Satilla Hallett - Died 1937 Aug 7 Born 1868 April 5 (with

Smith (Cont.)

Carl & James Smith) S:18

Smith, Solomon - Died 1813 Dec 12 in his 16th yr Son of Solomon & Betsey Smith S:11+26R

Smith, Solomon - Died 1814 April 2 in his 45th yr (Erected in memory of) S:11+26R

Smith, Solomon - Died 1815 Dec 12 Age 10 or 16 ? Son of Solomon & Betty Smith S:11

Smith, Solomon (Capt) - Died 1839 April 17 Age 27 years, 9 months Born 1811 July 12 in Barnstable, Mass Lost in the schooner, "Sachein" while going as passenger from Provincetown Mass to Boston Stone says "adieu my wife and child so young" S:11

Smith, Solomon J (Capt) - Died 1866 March 28 Age 27 years, 3 months Stone says,"Husband" S:19

Smith, Stephen I - Died 1970 Born 1892 (has 2 stones) From Pennslyvania, was a Pvt in US Army during World War I S:16

Smith, Susan - Died 1822 Jan 28 Age 88 years, 8 months Widow of James Smith (Hinckley Ceme records says death was 1872) S:11

Smith, Susan - Died 1872 Jan 28 Age 88 years,8 months Widow of James Smith S:11

Smith, Susan - Died 1880 May 7 Born 1802 Oct 26 Stone says, "At Rest" Wife of Thomas Smith (with him) S:11

Smith, Tabitha - Died 1850 Oct 2 Age 68 Widow of David Smith S:11R

Smith, Thabatha - Died 1860 located in row 9 S:11R

Smith, Thankful - Died 1799 Sept in her 35th yr Wife of Capt Samuel Smith S:10+26R

Smith, Thomas - Died 1860 Sept 10 Born 1800 June 14 (with Susan Smith) S:11

Smith, Thomas Eldridge - Died 1836 April 23 Age 6 months, 11

Smith (Cont.)
days Son of Capt Thomas & Susan Smith S:11

Smith, Thomas J - Died 1873 Oct Age 35 years, 5 months Stone says "In Consequence of the wreck of SShy at Guatemala on Tonala Baron, a passage from Panama to Acapulco" (listed with wife, Lizzie A Smith & others) S:19

Smith, Thomas Jefferson - Died 1836 April 23 Age 6 months, 11 days Son of Capt Thomas & Susan Smith S:11

Smith, Thomas M - Died 1866 June 20 Age 67 years, 10 months, 13 days S:9R

Smith, Thomas W - Died 1875 Sept 12 Age 8 years, 3 months Son of Thomas & Lizzie Smith (with them & Capt Allen Howes & Temperance Howes) S:19

Smith, Tryphena L - Died 1894 July 6 Born 1840 Sept 23 (next to Robert W Smith) S:19

Smith, Wallace J - Died 1858 May 7 Age 2 years, 3 months, 10 days Son of George Smith & Rebecca E Easterbrook (next to mother) S:19

Smith, Washington J - Died 1875 Born 1855 (with Lillian Smith & others) S:18

Smith, William F - Died 1988 Born 1927 (undertaker plaque only) (located between Russell Gibson & Alberta Noyes) S:19

Smith, William W - Died 1893 Born 1856 (with Medora Smith & others) S:11

Smith, Willie - Died 1865 May 22 Born 1864 April 29 (with Albert H Smith) S:18

Snelling, Pinckney W (MD) - Died 1965 Oct 30 Born 1897 March 15 (with Sarah J Snelling) S:13

Snelling, Sarah J - Died 1975 May 15 Born 1899 Aug 12 (with Pinckney W Snelling MD) S:13

Snow, (infant) - Died (dates under ground) Son of Nathaniel D &

Snow (Cont.)
Rieann Snow (next to infant Snow d1831?) S:21

Snow, (infant) - Died 1831? Son of Nathaniel D & Rieann Snow (next to Jane D Snow) S:21

Snow, Adaline - Died 1839 Aug 3 Age 23 years, 6 months Wife of Jonathan Snow S:4

Snow, Alice E - Died 1962 Born 1887 (with Leslie B Snow) S:18

Snow, Almira - Died 1870 May 5 Age 72, 10 months, 5 days S:4

Snow, Alvan - Died 1861 Sept 22 Age 64 years, 2 months, 10 days S:4

Snow, Annie Crocker - Died 1932 Born 1858 Wife of George Snow (with him and others on same stone) S:26R

Snow, Aren - Died 1842 Sept 18 Age 11 days Son of Capt Snow & Mrs Sylvanus Sears S:11

Snow, Daniel B - Died 1914 Born 1837 (with Mary J Snow) S:8

Snow, Doane (Capt) - Died 1842 Feb 25 Age 55 (next to wife, Jane Snow) S:21

Snow, Esther - Died 1851 Jan 17 Age 18 years, 2 months, 20 days Daughter of Alvan & Almira Snow S:4

Snow, Frank - Died 1856 Born 1855 (with Samuel Snow & others) S:18

Snow, Frank - Died 1893 Born 1858 (with Frank Snow d1856 & others) S:18

Snow, George - Died 1927 Born 1854 (with Annie Crocker, his wife and others) S:26R

Snow, George Henry - Died 1952 Born 1877 Son of George & Annie Snow & husband to Jennie (on same stone) S:26R

Snow, Grace L - Died 1960 Born 1875 S:21

Snow, Helen K - Died 1971 Born 1894 Wife of Herbert Snow (next to him) S:14

Snow, Herbert L - Died 1973 Born 1895 (next to wife, Helen K

Snow (Cont.)
Snow) S:14

Snow, Jane D - Died 1841 March
18 Daughter of Nathaniel D &
Rieann Snow (next to them) S:21

Snow, Jane Mrs - Died 1838 May
15 Age 51 Wife of Done (Doane)
Snow (next to him) S:21

Snow, Jennie - Died 1965 Born
1882 Wife of George Henry Snow
(on same stone) S:26R

Snow, Jonathan (Capt) - Died 1845
Feb 16 Age 67 years, 9 months
S:4

Snow, Leslie B - Died 1965 Born
1884 (next to Alice E Snow) S:18

Snow, Mary J - Died 1907 Born
1840 (with Daniel B Snow) S:8

Snow, Maryanna - Died 1843 July
13 Age 31 (stone worn) Widow of
Capt Nathaniel Snow (next to
him) S:21

Snow, Nathaniel (Capt) - Died
(dates broken off stone, also
stone broken in half) Age 31
years, 3 months (next to wife,
Maryanna Snow) S:21

Snow, Phebe H - Died 1933 Born
1861 (with Mary & Daniel Snow)
S:8

Snow, Ruth - Died 1939 Born 1887
Daughter to George & Annie
Snow (on same stone) S:26R

Snow, Samuel - Died 1837 July 29
in his 69th yr S:4

Snow, Samuel - Died 1910 Born
1828 (with Sarah J Snow &
others) S:18

Snow, Sarah J - Died 1910 Born
1834 (with Frank Snow & others) S:18

Snow, Sylvanus A (Capt) - Died
1861 July 20 Age 31, 9 months,
13 days Died at Harrison Landing, Virginia S:4

Snowdon, Irene Mabel - Died 1986
Born 1898 (with husband,
Russell M Snowdon) (buried 10
Feb 1986 Age 88, section 3, lot
47-4th1/4, grave #2) (some of
above from Mosswood cemetery
records) S:15

Snowdon, Russell M - Died 1966
Born 1890 (with wife, Irene M
Snowdon) S:15

Snyder, Anthony J - Died 1971
Born 1893 (listed with Lucy R
Snyder) S:17

Snyder, Bryon - Died 1966 Born
1895 Son of Ernest & Lida
Snyder (with them) S:12

Snyder, Ernest - Died 1936 Born
1872 (with Lida E Snyder) S:12

Snyder, George H - Died 1941 Born
1867 (with Nellie Lawson) S:11

Snyder, Lida E - Died 1957 Born
1874 Wife of Ernest Snyder (with
him) S:12

Snyder, Lucy R - Died (still living
1991?) Born 1903 (listed with
Anthony J Snyder) S:17

Soares, Alice M - Died 1991 Born
1911 (undertaker plaque only)
S:20

Soares, Isabel M - Died 1973 Born
1889 (with Manuel C Soares) S:16

Soares, Jaoquin F - Died 1947
Born 1885 S:16

Soares, Manuel C - Died 1949 Born
1889 (with Isabel M Soares) S:16

Soininen, Irja H - Died 1970 Born
1929 S:20

Somerville, A Neil - Died 1957
Born 1887 S:13

Somes, Helen A - Died 1881 Sept
23 Age 41 years, 5 months Wife
of Rev A H Somes S:5

Soule, Richard W - Died 1951 Born
1901 (with George Bradford &
others) S:18

Soule, William W - Died 1968 Nov 1
Born 1899 June 19 From
Massachusetts, was CMM in US
Navy during World War II S:17

Sousa, Manuel - Died 1945 Born
1870 (with Mary M Sousa) S:16

Sousa, Mary M - Died 1944 Born
1872 (with Manuel Sousa) S:16

Southward, Florence M - Died
1849 May 26 Wife of John P
Southward S:8

Southward, John P - Died 1926
Born 1843 (buried next to wife,
Florence M Southward) (his

Southward (Cont.)
stone says, A Mason) S:8

Southworth, Jemima - Died 1773
Nov 15 Age 5 Daughter of
Samson & Jedidah Southworth
S:9R

Souza, Antone R - Died 1919 Born
1883 (with Virginia R Souza)
S:31

Souza, Frank - Died 1929 Born
1871 Stone says,"Father" (with
Mary R Souza) S:31

Souza, Georgina - Died (still living
1991?) Born 1892 (listed with
John R Souza) S:14

Souza, Isabel F - Died 1967 Born
1905 (with Manuel Souza) S:16

Souza, John Bettengourt - Died
1967 Born 1892 (with wife, Anna
Josephine Grundell) S:12

Souza, John M - Died 1930 July
Born 1890 April (with wife,
Isabel Souza Marshall) S:14

Souza, John R - Died 1974 Born
1892 (with Georgina Souza) S:14

Souza, Manuel - Died 1985 Born
1897 (with Isabel F Souza) S:16

Souza, Mary A - Died (still living
1991?) Born 1925 - (listed with
Georgina & John R Souza) S:14

Souza, Mary A - Died 1988 Born
1897 (next to Roland R Souza)
S:14

Souza, Mary L - Died 1939 Born
1874 Wife of Nickolas Souza
(with him) S:31

Souza, Mary M - Died 1986 Sept 23
Born 1896 June 30 S:15

Souza, Mary R - Died 1964 Born
1874 Stone says, "Mother" (with
Frank Souza) S:31

Souza, Nickolas - Died 1919 Born
1868 (with wife, Mary L Souza)
S:31

Souza, Olivia V - Died (worn stone
located in corner of cemetery,
but near Frank & Mary Souza)
S:31

Souza, Robert Franklin - Died 1941
Born 1923 (called Bobby) (with
Anna J Grundell & John B
Souza) (he has another stone

Souza (Cont.)
that says, Bobby) S:12

Souza, Roland R - Died 1965 Born
1895 (next to Mary A Souza)
S:14

Souza, Rose Dorothy - Died 1969
March 14 Born 1900 Aug 10
S:15

Souza, Virginia R - Died 1980 Born
1886 (with Antone R Souza) S:31

Souza, William - Died 1952 Born
1893 S:16

Sowle, Lucy J - Died 1954 Born
1869 Daughter of George Smith
& Rebecca Easterbrook (with
mother & next to brother, Wallace J Smith) S:19

Sparrow, Sarah - Died 1735 Feb 11
in her 94th yr Wife of Jonathan
Sparrow of Eastham & her 1st,
her first husband was James
Cobb She was the daughter of
George Lewis the emigrant
S:9R+26R

Spear, Sarah - Died 1851 Aug 7
Age 9 years, 3 months Daughter
of Seth & Sophia Hallett (next to
them) S:21

Spencer, Data W - Died 1851 Nov 7
Age 26 years, 5 months, 25 days
Wife of Capt James Spencer S:4

Spencer, Lyndon - Died 1981 Born
1898 Was VADM in US Coast
Guard during World War II S:20

Sperry, Louise Black - Died 1985
Born 1929 (next to William
Sperry) S:20

Sperry, William C - Died 1990 Born
1916 (next to Louise Sperry)
S:20

Spilsted, Caroline S Mrs - Died
1849 Oct 5 Age 27 Wife of
Thomas Spilsted & daughter of
Lot & Rebecca Hinckley (Hinckley Ceme records #11R says
death was 1849) S:11+26R

Spinney, (?) Lizzie P - Died 1889
Oct 24 Age 30 years, 5 months
Wife of Stillman C Spinney (?)
S:12

Spinney, Byron C - Died 1958
Born 1878 (stone is leaning)

Spinney (Cont.)
(with Frank & Ora Spinney) S:21

Spinney, Frank H - Died 1940 Born 1852 (with wife, Ora E Spinney & Byron Spinney) S:21

Spinney, Ora E - Died 1924 Born 1861 Wife of Frank H Spinney (with him & Byron C Spinney) S:21

Spitz, Nicholas - Died 1944 Born 1888 (with Lillia Peak) S:18

Spooner, Edward P - Died 1912 Born 1853 (with Ellen F Sponner) He was a Mason S:12

Spooner, Ellen F - Died 1934 Born 1851 S:12

Spooner, Gordon Medbury - Died 1978 Feb 27 Born 1907 May 4 (on same stone with Isabel Sparrow Spooner & others) S:11

Spooner, Isabel Sparrow - Died 1975 Mar 6 Born 1899 Oct 27 (with Gordon Medbury Spooner & others) S:11

Sprague, Ellen M - Died 1901 Jan 13 Age 80 years, 4 months Widow of Rev Davis Cobb S:4

Sprague, Evelyn M - Died 1966 Born 1900 (next to Fon L Sprague) S:18

Sprague, Fon L - Died 1976 Born 1891 (next to Evelyn Sprague) S:18

St Coeur, ? - Died (no other markings, but located just five feet from the stone of Doris St Coeur) S:11

St Coeur, Doris - Died 1985 Born 1899 (located just five feet from another St Coeur with no markings) S:11

St Coeur, Peter B - Died 1983 Mar 28 Born 1926 Aug 18 He was a PHM3 in US Navy during World War II (near Doris & Wilfred O St Coeur) S:11

St Coeur, Suzanne - Died (still living in 1990?) Born 1921 (listed on same stone with Charles H Howes) S:11

St Coeur, Wilfred O - Died 1975 Mar 30 Born 1896 Jan 19 He

St Coeur (Cont.)
was in Sea 2, US Navy during World War II (a veteran plaque is also there) (next to Doris St Coeur) S:11

St Peter, Caroline M - Died 1976 Born 1883 (with Joseph St Peter) S:16

St Peter, Joseph - Died 1966 Born 1884 (with Caroline M St Peter) S:16

Stackpole, Burton O - Died (still living in 1991?) Born 1891 (listed with Lillian M Stackpole) S:15

Stackpole, Lillian M - Died 1972 Born 1892 (listed with Burton O Stackpole) S:15

Staffen, John - Died 1943 June 14 Born 1884 Aug 29 (with wife, Ludwika Staffen) S:16

Staffen, Ludwika - Died 1964 Feb 24 Born 1884 May 27 Wife of John Staffen (with him) S:16

Stansifer, C Marion - Died (still living 1991?) Born 1914 (with Charles M Stansifer & others) S:19

Stansifer, Charles M - Died 1980 Born 1912 (with CMarion Stansifer & Bertha & Isaiah Ellis) S:19

Stapleton, Etta L - Died 1935 Nov 5 Born 1881 July 10 (with James H Lothrop & others) S:18

Starbuck, Eliza C - Died 1870 Sept 16 Age 18 years, 8 months, 8 days Daughter of Abraham & Betsey Hinckley S:9

Starbuck, Martha Crocker - Died 1903 Born 1813 (on same stone with Capt William Crocker & Ellen Crocker) (probably married into Starbuck family after Crocker died) S:5

Starch, (Mother) - Died 1925 Born 1866 (buried next to husband, (Father) Starck/Starch & Albert B Starch, b1909 d 1934) S:8

Starck, (Father) - Died 1926 Born 1868 (buried next to (Mother) Starck/Starch) S:8

Starr, Corinna (Crowell) - Died 1939 Born 1849 (with Forest Eugene Starr) S:21

Starr, Dorothy Maitland - Died 1987 Born 1902 Wife of Leopold E Starr (next to him) S:19

Starr, Forest Eugene - Died 1939 Born 1855 (with Corinna (Crowell) Starr) S:21

Starr, Leopold E - Died 1990 Born 1896 Stone says,"Husband" (next to wife, Dorothy Starr) S:19

Starratt, Arthur W - Died 1940 Born 1876 (with Amma Matthews Goss & others) S:18

Starratt, Lizzie F - Died 1943 Born 1878 (with Arthur W Starratt) S:18

Stasinakis, Apostolos - Died 1984 Born 1894 (with Dora Stasinakis) S:15

Stasinakis, Dora - Died 1990 Born 1902 (with Apostolos Stasinakis) S:15

Stauber, Anna - Died 1970 Born 1874 S:15

Stearns, Emily E - Died 1926 Born 1838 Wife of Capt Edwin Fuller (with daughter, Emma E Fuller) S:14

Steele, Alice Howitt - Died 1933 Born 1853 (in Allen Plot with Caroline H Allen & others) S:12

Steele, Elaine Ball - Died 1986 Sept 11 Born 1921 Dec 17 S:13

Stemson, Nabby - Died 1800 May 24 Age 23 Relict of Capt Jeremiah Stemson S:11

Stennes, Carrie M - Died 1990 Born 1898 (with Peder M Stennes) S:15

Stennes, Peder M - Died 1973 Born 1897 (with Carrie M Stennes) S:15

Stetson, Galvin - Died 1860 May 3 Born 1799 Sept 27 (with Polly C Nye) S:10

Stetson, Hitty S - Died 1855 Sept 24 Age 59 Daughter of Thomas & Mary Stetson S:10

Stetson, Mary - Died 1832 Aug 16 in her 65th yr Wife of Thomas

Stetson (Cont.)
Stetson (next to him) S:10+26R

Stetson, Polley - Died 1779 Feb 10 Age 37 years, 9 months Daughter of Thomas & Susannah Stetson S:9R

Stetson, Susannah - Died 1785 Feb 8 Age 43 Wife of Thomas Stetson S:9R

Stetson, Thankful - Died 1853 April 11 Age 19 Widow of Timothy Stetson (stone missing next to her but was Thomas Stetson which was found laying in next row broken on the ground) S:10

Stetson, Thomas - Died 1785 Oct 23 Age 52 years, 6 months S:9R

Stetson, Thomas - Died 1842 Nov 19 Age 84 S:10

Stetson, Thomas - Died 1844 Feb 22 Age 1 year 8 months 23 days Son of Calvin & Polly C Stetson (buried next to them) S:10

Stetson, Thomas - Died 1856 July 28 Age 48 (his stone should be next to Thankful Stetson but is broken off laying in next row) S:10

Stetson, William - Died 1769 March 5 Age 4 months Son of Thomas & Susannah Stetson S:9R

Stevens, Abbie T - Died 1909 Born 1831 (next to Augustine W Stevens) S:14

Stevens, Anna L - Died 1958 Born 1875 Wife of William Kinney MD (in Kinney plot with him & others) S:12

Stevens, Asa - Died 1859 Oct 30 Age 60 years, 10 months, 26 days (stone is knocked down & broken) S:8

Stevens, Asa W - Died 1907 June 7 Born 1834 June 8 (buried next to wife, Dorcas m Stevens) S:8

Stevens, Augustine W - Died 1859 Feb 9 at Galveston, Texas Age 33 (next to Abbie T Stevens) S:14

Stevens, Bennie - Died 1865 May 15 Born 1864 Apr 6 (buried next to Edgar Stevens) S:8

Stevens, Burton R - Died 1986 Born 1907 Was a Private in US Army during World War II (there is also a Veteran star there) S:13

Stevens, Carroll E - Died 1917 Born 1896 (with Mildred Stevens & others) S:18

Stevens, Charles B - Died 1927 Born 1858 (on same stone with wife Isabel B & other family members) S:8

Stevens, David A - Died 1973 Oct 12 Born 1893 Nov 28 From Massachusetts, was Colonel in US Army during World War I & II S:15

Stevens, Dorcas M - Died 1891 Aug 10 Born 1837 Jan 5 (stone is knocked down) Wife of Asa W Stevens (buried next to him) S:8

Stevens, Edgar - Died 1900 Nov 2 Born 1877 Jan 25 (buried next to Sylvia Stevens & others) S:8

Stevens, Edward E - Died 1931 Born 1862 (with Emily C Stevens & others) S:18

Stevens, Elizabeth M - Died 1955 Born 1870 Wife of Henry A Stevens (on same stone with him & family) S:8

Stevens, Emily C - Died 1951 Born 1861 (with Carroll E Stevens & others) S:18

Stevens, Grace W - Died 1943 Born 1863 (buried next to Mary M Stevens) S:8

Stevens, Henry A - Died 1945 Born 1867 (on same stone with family) S:8

Stevens, Henry C - Died (Stone not clear) Age 25 years, 8 months, 11 days Born 1864 Mar 6 Stone says, Father S:8

Stevens, Irene A - Died 1989 Born 1909 (with Burton R Stevens) S:13

Stevens, Isabel B - Died 1946 Born 1869 Wife of Charles B Stevens (he & family on same stone) S:8

Stevens, Mary M - Died 1910 Oct 28 Age 83 years, 8 months, 10 days Wife of Henry Stevens

Stevens (Cont.) (buried next to her) Stone says, Mother S:8

Stevens, Mildred - Died 1967 Born 1894 (with Edward Stevens & others) S:18

Stevens, Richard A - Died 1984 Born 1904 (next to Burton & Iren Stevens) S:13

Stevens, Sylvia L - Died 1866 Jan 26 Age 29 years, 5 months, 25 days (buried next to Edgar Stevens) S:8

Stevenson, Thomas - Died 1727 Oct 13 Age 25 Son of Robert Stevenson S:9

Steward, Phinehas (Capt) - Died 1825 Mar 17 in his 33rd yr Was drowned at sea S:4

Stewart, Catherine M - Died 1988 Born 1927 (next to Roy & Marjorie Stewart) S:19

Stewart, Charles Elton - Died 1953 Born 1904 (buried with Janet Humes Stewart) S:8

Stewart, Eleanor G - Died 1979 Born 1906 (with Nellie G Watson) Stone says, "Bambi" S:13

Stewart, Janet Humes - Died 1950 Born 1877 (on same stone with Charles Elton Stewart) S:8

Stewart, Marjorie Ross - Died 1977 Born 1901 Wife of Roy Bryson Stewart (with him & next to Catherine M Stewart) S:19

Stewart, Mary H - Died 1833 June 14 in her 30th yr Daughter of Silvanus & Mary Steward S:4

Stewart, Roy Bryson (DMD) - Died (still living 1991?) Born 1896 (listed with wife, Marjorie Ross Stewart) S:19

Stewart, Samuel T (Major) - Died 1855 Born 1879 (buried with wife, Edith Koebel) S:8

Stewart, Sylvanus Jr - Died 1811 June 26 in his 10th yr Son of Sylvanus & Polly Stewart S:4

Stickney, Alice E - Died 1919 Born 1862 Wife of Albert Bacon (with him) S:18

Stiff, Abbie F - Died 1950 Jan 7

Stiff (Cont.)
Born 1879 Feb 6 (with Albert E
Stiff) S:18

Stiff, Albert E - Died 1907 Nov 20
Born 1900 Jan 14 (with Abbie F
Stiff) S:18

Stiff, Edwin C - Died 1908 Age 75
years, 3 months, 14 days Born
1833 S:5

Stiff, Eunice Macy - Died 1879 May
19 Age 43 years, 2 months, 8
days Wife of Edwin C Stiff S:5R

Stiff, Flora Josephine - Died 1868
Mar 25 Age 6 years, 11 months,
20 days Daughter of Edwin &
Eunice Stiff S:5

Stimson, Ellen - Died 1898 Born
1827 (on same stone with Henry
W Stimson & others) S:11

Stimson, Francis - Died 1900 Born
1829 (on same stone with Henry
W Stimson & others) S:11

Stimson, Frederick D - Died 1899
Born 1826 (on same stone with
Henry W Stimson & others) S:11

Stimson, Henry - Died 1850 Born
1820 (on same stone with Henry
W Stimson & others) S:11

Stimson, Henry W - Died 1870
Born 1797 (large pillar on dirt
road Others listed) S:11

Stimson, Jeremiah - Died 1821 Age
2 yrs 1 mon Born 1819 (on stone
with Henry Stimson & others)
S:11+26R

Stimson, Jeremiah W - Died 1834
Born 1831 (on same stone with
Henry W Stimson & others) S:11

Stimson, Mabby - Died 1800 located in row 1 S:11R

Stimson (Stimcon ?), Mary A - Died
1870 Oct 6 73 yrs 3 mos Born
1797 Wife of Henry W Stimson
(next to him & others) S:11+26R

Stimson, Nabby Mrs - Died 1800
May 24 Age 23 (obit) Relict of
Capt Jeremiah Stimson &
daughter of Ebenezer Hinckley
S:11R

Stockman, William Watson - Died
1918 Born 1842 S:12

Stokes, Mary Jane - Died 1984

Stokes (Cont.)
Born 1898 S:18

Stone, D Earle - Died 1961 Born
1887 (with wife, Eleanor M
Stone) S:14

Stone, Eleanor M - Died 1985 Born
1897 Wife of D Earle Stone (with
him) S:14

Stone, George W - Died 1969 Born
1888 (next to Grace F Stone)
S:15

Stone, Grace F - Died 1981 Born
1888 (next to George Stone) S:15

Storer, Ammi Park - Died 1900
Sept 1 Born 1891 May 24 (with
Iva & Ferdinand Storer) S:18

Storer, Ferdinand I - Died 1903
Sept 27 Born 1841 Oct 22 (he
was a Mason) (with Iva & Ammi
Storer) S:18

Storer, Iva M - Died (no date) Born
1855 May 1 (with Ammi &
Ferdinand Storer) S:18

Story, Dorothy C - Died 1969 Born
1889 Wife of Edward Covell (with
him) S:16

Stout, Victor - Died 1969 June 18
Born 1908 Aug 18 From Massachusetts, was Lt Col in US Army
during World War II S:20

Stowers, Mary L - Died 1872 Oct 5
Age 29 years, 1 month, 8 days
Wife of Charles A Stowers S:5R

Stratecaros, Sotireos - Died 1938
Born 1867 S:8

Stratton, Carrie C - Died 1962
Born 1847 (with Elmer W
Lapham & others) S:14

Strawbridge, Abby Hallen - Died
1930 Born 1851 (in Allen plot
with Nathan Hastings Allen &
others) S:12

Stromberg, Edna G - Died 1967
Born 1895 S:15

Strother, Homer D - Died 1967 Nov
19 Born 1879 April 24 From
Massachusetts, was Cpl in 10th
Artillery Corps Band during the
Spanish American War S:17

Stuart, Charles A - Died 1966 Jan
13 Born 1913 Feb 13 From New
York, AERM1, USNR during

Stuart (Cont.)
World War II S:20

Stuart, Mary - Died 1908 Born 1850 (on corner lot of cemetery) Daughter of John & Sarah Wilson S:10

Studley, Florence A - Died 1951 April 24 Stone says,"Mother" (with Isaiah S Studley) S:18

Studley, Isaiah S - Died 1972 Born 1877 Stone says,"Father" (with Florence A Studley) S:18

Sturges, Adelaide F - Died 1925 Born 1843 Wife of Isaac C Sturges (next to him) S:14

Sturges, Amie H - Died 1959 Born 1863 (with Harrie J Gifford) S:14

Sturges, Charlotte F - Died 1987 April 2 Born 1899 Oct 12 (with George W Sturges near pond in back of cemetery) S:18

Sturges, Eliza B - Buried 1902 Jan 31 Located in section S, lot 4, grave 1 S:14R

Sturges, Ella F - Died 1926 Feb 15 Born 1853 Oct 25 (located near pond in back of cemetery) S:18

Sturges, George W - Died 1966 Nov 21 Born 1889 Nov 30 (located near pond in back of cemetery with Charlotte F Sturges) From Massachusetts, was a Cpl in 204th Co, MPC during World War I (has 2 stones) S:18

Sturges, Hannah - Died 1843 Aug 5 Age 54 Wife of Moses Sturges (next to him) S:3R

Sturges, Hannah L - Died 1900 Dec 30 Born 1829 May 9 Stone says,"Mother" (next to Laban T Sturges) S:14

Sturges, Hannah L - Buried 1900 Dec 30 Located in section S, lot 1, grave 1 S:14R

Sturges, Henry L - Died 1945 Born 1867 (next to Laban & Hannah Sturges) S:14

Sturges, Isaac C - Died 1890 June 8 Born 1838 Feb 16 Stone says, "Father" (next to wife, Adelaide F Sturges) S:14

Sturges, Laban T - Died 1905 Jan

Sturges (Cont.)
5 Born 1826 Mar 11 Stone says,"Father" (with Hannah L Sturges) S:14

Sturges, Lydia - Died 1825 April 9 Age 87 Wife of Samuel Sturgis (next to him) S:10

Sturges, Lydia P - Died 1886 Born 1832 (with William H Sturges) S:14

Sturges, Mary F - Buried 1908 Jan 24 Located in section S, lot 2, grave 2 S:14R

Sturges, Moses - Died 1841 Oct 9 Age 69 (next to wife Hannah) S:3R

Sturges, Prizilla ? - Died 1802 Aug 8 Wife of Capt Ezekiah Sturges S:12

Sturges, RC - Died 1899 August Born 182? Jan (with wife, Susan A Sturges) S:14

Sturges, Samuel (Capt) - Died 1762 Aug 19 Age 26 S:10

Sturges, Susan A - Died 1886 April 14 Born 1832 Jan 6 Age 51 years, 3 months, 8 days Wife of RC Sturges (with him) S:14

Sturges, Willa Miriam - Buried 1890 July Located in section S, lot 2, grave 4 S:14R

Sturges, William A - Buried 1894 Located in section S, lot 2, grave 1 S:14R

Sturges, William A (Capt) - Died 1894 March at Rio de Janeiro, Brazil Born 1854 Aug (listed with Mary H Fuller, wife) S:14

Sturges, William H - Died 1926 Born 1828 (with Lydia P Sturges) S:14

Sturges, Winnie Williey - Buried 1887 July Located in section S, lot 2, grave 3 S:14R

Sturgess, Hannah - Died 1843 Aug 5 Age 54 Wife of Moses Sturgess S:3

Sturgess, Lucy P - Died 1860 Feb 6 Age 51 years, 7 months S:3+3R

Sturgess, Moses - Died 1841 Oct 9 in his 60th yr S:3

Sturgis, ? - Died (stone badly worn)

Sturgis (Cont.)

Child of Samuel Sturgis (next to John Sturgis) S:11

Sturgis, ? - Died (stone worn badly, next to Lucas Sturgis d 1708) S:11

Sturgis, ? - Died 1751 Age 19 (stone worn bad and covered with moss) (between Thomas Sturgis d 1763 & Russel Sturgis) S:11

Sturgis, ? - Died 1756 May 14 Age 21 (stone badly worn) Wife of Samuel Sturgis (next to son, John Sturgis) S:11

Sturgis, Abigail - Died (underground) Daughter of John & Abigail Sturgis Esq S:11

Sturgis, Abigail - Died 1737 Oct 21 Age 3 weeks Daughter of John & Abigail Sturgis Esq S:11

Sturgis, Abigail - Died 1740 Sept 23 Age 19 days Daughter of John & Abigail Sturgis Esq (they tried naming their child 3 times, Abigail) S:11

Sturgis, Abigail - Died 1751 Dec 4 Age 19 years, 4 months, 12 days Daughter of Thomas & Martha Sturgis S:11R

Sturgis, Abigail - Died 1751? May Age 19 Daughter of Thomas & Mary Sturgis ? (stone covered heavily with moss) S:11

Sturgis, Abigail - Died 1752 Dec 10 in her 42nd yr Consort of John Sturgis Esq (next to him) S:11+26R

Sturgis, Abigail - Died 1753 May 28 Age 6 months Daughter of John Esq & Abigail Sturgis S:11R

Sturgis, Abigail Mrs - Died 1794 Oct 16 S:26R

Sturgis, Abigail Mrs - Died 1723 Oct 4 in her 63rd yr S:11R+26R

Sturgis, Abner - Died (no dates, but located in row 15) S:11R

Sturgis, Ada R - Died 1895 Born 1887 Daughter of William & Adelaide Sturgis (on same stone) S:10

Sturgis, Adeline C - Died 1908 April 4 Age 76 years, 11 months Wife of Charles Sturgis (next to him) S:19

Sturgis, Agnes F - Died 1890 Feb 21 Age 20 years, 8 months, 1 day Wife of Edward E Sturgis S:13

Sturgis, Allen R - Died 1909 Born 1847 (buried with Moses Sturgis & others) S:8

Sturgis, Annis M - Died 1958 Born 1875 (with Rebecca Davis Sturgis) S:8

Sturgis, Annis Parris - Died 1944 Born 1852 (Parris may be her maiden name) (with Rebecca Davis Sturgis) S:8

Sturgis, Caroline - Died 1821 Aug 12 Age 8 months 20 days Daughter of David & Hannah Sturgis S:10

Sturgis, Charles - Died 1899 Jan 17 Age 82 years, 11 months (next to wife, Adeline Sturgis) S:19

Sturgis, Corae(?) - Died 1870(?) Age 11 months Born (not clear) Says, parents are Dennis & Mary W Sturgis S:8

Sturgis, Daniel H - Died 1914 May 8 Born 1832 June 2 (has two markers) (with wife, Eliza L Bowman) S:14

Sturgis, David - Died 1862 Dec 14 Age 72 S:10

Sturgis, Dennis C (Capt) - Died 1920 Dec 27 Born 1824 June 4 (with wife, Mary W Bearse) S:8

Sturgis, Dora K - Died 1946 June 13 Born 1859 Aug 10 Wife of Frank L Sturgis (with him) S:14

Sturgis, Eben - Died 1831 Dec 5 Age 2 yrs Son of Nathaniel Sturgis S:26R

Sturgis, Eben - Died 1837 Dec 25 Age 4 months, 10 days Son of David & Eliza Sturgis S:10

Sturgis, Ebenezer - Died 1740 Jan 12 Age 1 year, 11 months, 8 days Son of John & Abigail Sturgis Esq S:11

Sturgis, Ebenezer - Died 1824 June 1 in his 70th yr S:26R

Sturgis, Edward - Died 1748 Jan 5 in his 64th yr (next to a child names Edward Sturgis Gorham) S:11+26R

Sturgis, Edward - Died 1856 Dec 26 Age 37 Lost at sea (stone is down) (with Nathaniel Sturgis) S:19

Sturgis, Edward E - Died 1902 Born 1864 Son of Daniel Sturgis & Eliza Bowman (with them) S:14

Sturgis, Edward S - Died 1923 Born 1884 Son of William & Adelaide Sturgis (on same stone) S:10

Sturgis, Edwin E - Died 1928 Born 1841 (buried with Sarah Sturgis & others) S:8

Sturgis, Elery - Died 1863 Born 1860 Son of Daniel Sturgis & Eliza Bowman (with them) S:14

Sturgis, Eliza Mrs - Died 1845 Jan 5 Age 40 Wife of David Sturgis (next to him) S:10

Sturgis, Elizabeth - Died 1713 located in row 15 S:11R

Sturgis, Elizabeth - Died 1715 May 13 Age 22 years, 5 months S:11R

Sturgis, Elizabeth - Died 1721 Aug 22 Age 2 months, 10 days Daughter of Thomas & Martha Sturgis S:11R

Sturgis, Elizabeth Mrs - Died 1748 Feb 19 in her 65th yr S:11R+ 26R

Sturgis, Ellen G - Died 1914 May 16 Born 1836 Aug 25 Wife of Russell Sturgis (with him) S:18

Sturgis, Elva Weston - Died 1862 Oct 9 Age 5 years, 2 months, 8 days Daughter of Russell & Ellen Sturgis (with them) S:18

Sturgis, Ezekiel - Died 1810 Mar 2 Age 33 S:3

Sturgis, Ezekiel - Died 1870 Born 1818 (buried with Sarah C Meigs) S:8

Sturgis, Francis - Died (date

Sturgis (Cont.)
underground) (small stone) Daughter of Thomas & Elizabeth Sturgis S:10

Sturgis, Frank L - Died 1940 July 14 Born 1861? Dec 28 (with wife, Dora K Sturgis) S:14

Sturgis, Grace Cammett - Died 1937 Born 1865 (with Franklin Cammett) S:14

Sturgis, Hannah E - Died 1819 Dec 11 Age 79 S:10

Sturgis, Hannah Eliza - Died 1836 Aug 20 Age 5 weeks Daughter of David & Eliza Sturgis S:10

Sturgis, Hannah Mrs - Died 1829 Feb 16 Age 39 Wife of David Sturgis S:10

Sturgis, Harriet B - Died July 26 18?? Born 1866 Aug 31 (stone badly worn) (buried next to husband, Benjamin F Davis) S:8

Sturgis, Horace W - Died 1944 Born 1851 (with M Annis Parris Sturgis) S:8

Sturgis, Howard Smith - Died 1969 Born 1886 (with wife, Frances Easterbrook & Lt Col Russell Sturgis) S:19

Sturgis, Jackson - Died 1829 April 29 at Loghouse Landing, North Carolina Born 1789 Dec 1 son of Thomas & Elizabeth Sturgis (listed on their large stone coffin) S:10

Sturgis, John - Died 1773 Sept 6 Age 41 years, 9 months S:11R

Sturgis, John - Died 1752 Mar 25 Bachelor of Arts at Harvard College, Boston, Mass (possible son of John & Abigail Sturgis Esq) (buried near them) (Hinckley Ceme records #11R says death day was the 25th at age 21) S:11+26R

Sturgis, John - Died 1758 Aug 22 Age 10 months, 8 days Son of Samuel & Abigail Sturgis S:11R

Sturgis, John - Died 1759 April 12 Age 13 months, 6 days Son of John & Mehetable Sturgis Esq S:11

401

Sturgis, John - Died 1841 Sept 18 in his 62nd yr S:4

Sturgis, John ? - Died (stone worn) Son of Samuel Sturgis (next to another child Sturgis) S:11

Sturgis, John Esq - Died 1754 ? (stone worn) (next to wife, Abigail Sturgis d1752) S:11

Sturgis, John Esq - Died 1759 Aug 10 in his 55th yr S:11R+26R

Sturgis, L Adelaide - Died 1942 Born 1852 or 1854? (listed with husband, William R Sturgis & Children on same stone) S:10

Sturgis, Lois B - Died 1925 Born 1866 Wife of Edward Landers (with him) S:14

Sturgis, Lucas - Died 1708 June 30 Age 48 (stone worn) S:11

Sturgis, Lucas (?) - Died (stone worn blank, next to Lucas Sturgis, d1708) (also another stone next to this one, small & worn off) S:11

Sturgis, Lucy - Died 1855 July 13 Age 67 Born 1788 June 7 (stone down & broken) Wife of Nathaniel Sturgis (four stones away from him) S:19

Sturgis, Lucy C - Died 1949 March 28 Born 1862 Dec 14 Daughter of Charles & Adeline Sturgis (next to them) S:19

Sturgis, Lydia - Died 1825 April 9 in her 87th yr Widow of Samuel Sturgis S:26R

Sturgis, Martha - Died 1742 March 9 Age 24 years, 4 months Daughter of Thomas & Martha Sturgis S:11R

Sturgis, Martha - Died 1774 June 17 in her 78th yr Daughter of Jonathan Russel & Relict to Thomas Sturgis (between two Thomas Sturgis, one d1785, other d1763) S:11+26R

Sturgis, Mary - Died 1721 April 15 in her 15th yr Daughter of Samuel & Mary Sturgis (buried next to mother) S:9+26R

Sturgis, Mary - Died 1755 June 23 or 25 in her 86th yr S:9+26R

Sturgis, Mary - Died 1850 May 9 Born 1847 July 26 (small stone says, little Mary, next to main Sturgis family stone) S:8

Sturgis, Mattie A - Died 1982 Born 1909 Wife of John Davies (with him & Jacquelyn Long & others) S:19

Sturgis, Mehitable - Died 1739 located in row 8 S:11R

Sturgis, Moses - Died 1889 Born 1819 (buried with Sarah Sturgis & others) S:8

Sturgis, Moses Jr - Died 1921 Born 1848 (buried with Moses Sturgis & others) S:8

Sturgis, Nathaniel - Died 1710 Jan 20 Age 12 Son of Samuel & Mary Sturgis S:11R

Sturgis, Nathaniel - Died 1780 June 14 in his 68th yr S:26R

Sturgis, Nathaniel - Died 1858 May 29 Born 1786 Aug 5 (stone is down) (with Edward Sturgis) S:19

Sturgis, Olive - Died 1756 located in row 7 S:11R

Sturgis, Olive - Died 1756 May 14 in her 21st yr Wife of Samuel Sturgis S:11R+26R

Sturgis, Owen - Died 1863 Oct 24 Born 1861 Feb 15 (stones is in back of Sturgis family stone) S:8

Sturgis, Perry C - Died 1895 (a very small stone - a baby) S:14

Sturgis, Rebecca Davis - Died 1912 Born 1887 (with Annis M Sturgis) S:8

Sturgis, Russel - Died (small stone and badly worn) Son of William & Sarah Sturgis S:11

Sturgis, Russel - Died 14th ? (stone very small & badly worn) Son of William & ? Sturgis (Hinckley Ceme records #11R says death was 1773 March at age 14 months and mother's name was Sarah) S:11

Sturgis, Russell - Died 1873 Oct 23 Age 48 years, 6 months (with wife, Ellen G & daughter Elva Weston Sturgis) S:18

Sturgis, Russell B (Lt Col) - Died 1953 Born 1908 (with Howard Smith Sturgis & Frances Easterbrook) S:19

Sturgis, Ruth D - Died 1900 March 25 Age 95 Wife of William W Sturgis (next to him) S:19

Sturgis, Sally - Died 1843 Apl 22 Age 66 Wife of Samuel Sturgis S:4

Sturgis, Samuel - Died 1762 March 8 in his 33rd yr S:11R +26R

Sturgis, Samuel - Died 1769 Jan 26 in his 86th yr (Hinckley Ceme records #9R says death was 1762) S:9+26R

Sturgis, Samuel - Died 1932 Born 1858 (Crocker stone with Eleanor Crocker) S:11

Sturgis, Samuel Capt - Died 1762 Aug 19 in his 26th yr S:26R

Sturgis, Sarah - Died 1910 Born 1821 (buried with Moses Sturgis & others) S:8

Sturgis, Sarah Mrs - Died 1772 Dec 10 Age 44 years, 2 months, 24 days Wife of Capt Thomas Sturgis (next to him) (Hinckley Ceme records #11R says death was 1772) S:11+26R

Sturgis, Sarah Mrs - Died 1779 Dec 10 Wife of Capt Thomas Sturgis S:11

Sturgis, Thankful - Died 1773 Aug 9 Age 16 yrs 6 mos S:11R+26R

Sturgis, Thankful - Died 1824 May 2 in her 68th yr Wife of Ebenezer Sturgis S:26R

Sturgis, Thomas - Died 1708 June 30 Age 48 years, 6 months S:11R

Sturgis, Thomas - Died 1763 Dec 18 in his 78th yr S:11

Sturgis, Thomas - Died 1785 Oct 16 in his 64th yr (buried next to wife, Mrs Sarah Sturgis) S:11+26R

Sturgis, Thomas - Died 1792 Sept 6 Age 10 months Son of Thomas & Elizabeth Sturgis (buried next to sister, Francis Sturgis) S:10

Sturgis, Thomas - Died 1821 Sept

Sturgis (Cont.)
16 Born 1754 April 5 (a large stone coffin with Elizabeth Jackson & children) S:10

Sturgis, Thomas - Died 1835 Jan 20 at Canton, China Born 1795 June 24 Son of Thomas & Elizabeth Sturgis (listed on their large stone coffin) S:10

Sturgis, Willa Mariam - Buried 1890 July Located in section S, lot 2, grave 4 S:14R

Sturgis, William A - Buried 1894 Located in section S, lot 2, grave 1 S:14R

Sturgis, William R - Died 1906 Born 1852 (stone located street level at back entrance) (with L Adelaide Sturgis) S:10

Sturgis, William W - Died 1891 Jan 21 Age 91 (next to wife, Ruth D Sturgis) S:19

Sturgis, Winnie Williey - Buried 1887 July Located in section S, lot 2, grave 3 S:14R

Sturtevant, Rev Josiah - Died 1825 Jan 23 in his 46th yr S:3+3R

Suhonen, Anna - Died 1964 Born 1895 Wife of Matti E Suhonen (with him) S:17

Suhonen, Matti E - Died 1976 Born 1890 (has 2 stones) Was PFC in US Army during World War I (with wife, Anna Suhonen) S:17

Sulkala, Erick - Died 1953 Born 1882 (this is a large family stone with others) S:11

Sulkala, Fanny M - Died 1942 Born 1893 (on large family stone with others) S:11

Sulkala, Kalervo A - Died 1958 Born 1919 (on large family stone with others) S:11

Sullivan, Aina M - Died 1985 Born 1911 Wife of Francis Sullivan (listed with him & daughter, Joan Sullivan) S:20

Sullivan, Alice G - Died 1987 Born 1895 (with John A Sullivan) S:16

Sullivan, Bradford E - Died (still living 1991?) Born 1931 Son of Winthrop & Margaret Sullivan

Sullivan (Cont.)
(listed next to them) S:19

Sullivan, David H - Died 1981 Born
1900 (has 2 stones) Was SP1 in
US Navy during World War II
(with Katherine Ormsby) S:16

Sullivan, Dorothy - Died 1938 Born
1904 (with Antone P George &
others) S:31

Sullivan, Francis J - Died (still
living 1991?) Born 1903 (with
wife, Aina & daughter, Joan
Sullivan) S:20

Sullivan, Joan Marie - Died 1968
Born 1933 Daughter of Francis
& Aina Sullivan (with them) S:20

Sullivan, John A - Died 1980 Born
1894 Was a CYN in US Navy
during World War I (with Alice G
Sullivan) S:16

Sullivan, John Joseph - Died 1985
Feb 20 Born 1924 March 29
Was a SP1 in US Navy during
World War II S:20

Sullivan, Leon F - Died 1983 Born
1894 Was a Capt in US Army
during World War I S:15

Sullivan, Margaret S - Died 1974
Born 1902 Wife of Winthrop
Sullivan (next to him & son,
Bradford E Sullivan) S:19

Sullivan, Mary E - Died 1987 Born
1903 (with Winifred G Sullivan)
S:16

Sullivan, Mary Rita - Died 1982
Born 1888 Stone says,"Mother"
S:15

Sullivan, William F - Died 1965
Feb 6 Born 1891 May 15 From
Massachusetts, was a Sgt in
CoE, 401 Telegraph Bn during
World War I (with wife, Helen E
Butler) S:16

Sullivan, Winifred G - Died 1980
Born 1899 (with Mary E Sullivan) S:16

Sullivan, Winthrop E - Died 1957
Jan 7 Born 1897 Feb 16 From
Massachusetts, was a 2nd Lt Ph,
in Infantry during World War I
(next to wife, Margaret S Sullivan) S:19

Sumner, Margaret Claude - Died
1974 Aug 21 Born 1892 April 25
S:14

Sundelin, Ida M - Died 1961 Born
1880 Wife of Rev Veijo V Sundelin (next to him) S:20

Sundelin, Orvo E - Died 1988 Born
1905 S:20

Sundelin, Veijo V (Rev) - Died 1962
Born 1877 (next to Ida M Sundelin, wife) S:20

Sunderman, Beth - Died 1958 Oct
22 (listed with Eleanor Hathaway & Rebecca & Herbert
Sunderman) S:20

Sunderman, Herbert J - Died (no
dates) (listed with Eleanor
Hathaway & Beth & Rebecca
Sunderman) S:20

Sunderman, Rebecca - Died 1961
Nov 13 (with Eleanor Hathaway
& Beth & Herbert Sunderman)
S:20

Sundman, Carl V - Died 1963 Nov
1 Born 1893 July 27 From
Massachusetts, was a Pvt in Bty
D, 336 Field Arty during World
War I S:20

Sundman, Hilda L - Died 1968
Born 1882 S:20

Sundquist, Axel M - Died 1969
Born 1893 (with Stina AF
Sundquist) S:15

Sundquist, Stina AF - Died 1975
Born 1902 (with Axel M Sundquist) S:15

Sunquist, Gunnar N - Buried 1983
April 7 Age 92 Located in section
4, lot 98-4th1/4, grave 1 S:15R

Supple, Joseph I - Died 1990 Born
1898 (has 2 stones) Was a Pvt in
US Army during World War I
S:15

Suthergreen, Effie S - Died 1902
Born 1855 (with Wesley S
Suthergreen) S:12

Suthergreen, J Edward - Died
1930 Born 1906 Stone says,
"Brother" (new flat metal marker)
(next to Mildred Suthergreen)
S:12

Suthergreen, Mildred - Died 1905

404

Suthergreen (Cont.)
Born 1902 Stone says, "Sister"
(new flat metal marker) (next to
J Edward Suthergreen) S:12

Suthergreen, Wesley S - Died 1881
Born 1844 (with Effie S Suthergreen) S:12

Sutherland, Hugh M - Died 1975
June 2 Born 1889 Feb 6 (with
wife, Leola A Sutherland) S:17

Swain, Martha F - Died 1848 Oct
30 in her 25th yr Wife of Charles
C Swain S:7

Swan, Henry L - Died 1905 Born
1843 (with Horace L Swan) S:14

Swan, Horace L - Died 1903 Born
1841 (with Henry L Swan) S:14

Swan, Susan L - Died 1894 Born
1817 (with Valentine, Henry &
Horace Swan & others) S:14

Swan, Valentine J - Died 1865
Born 1812 (with Susan L Swan
& others) S:14

Sweet, Bertha A - Died 1970 Born
1897 (with Walter H Sweet) S:15

Sweet, Walter H - Died 1974 Born
1897 (with Bertha A Sweet) S:15

Sweetser, Albert N - Died 1884 Nov
30 Born 1851 Aug 15 S:8

Sweetser, Albert R - Died 1940
Sept 12 Born 1861 July 5
(buried next to Carrie Sweetser)
S:8

Sweetser, Carrie K - Died 1952
Sept 9 Born 1862 Sept 11 (a
veteran star is place at grave)
(buried next to Albert R Sweetser) S:8

Sweetser, Daniel (Capt) - Died
1857 Jan in his 39th yr Lost at
sea (listed on same stone with
Sophia Sweetser) S:8

Sweetser, Sophia - Died 1871 Feb
2 in her 53rd yr S:8

Swenson, Allan C - Died 1966 Born
1904 (with Ruth E Swenson)
S:11

Swenson, Ruth E - Died 1966 Born
1901 (with Allan C Swenson)
S:11

Swift, (nameless) - Died 1797 Oct 3
Infant S:26R

Swift, (nameless) - Died 1799
March 2 Infant S:26R

Swift, Agusta F - Died 1856 Apr 6
Born 1825 Sept 13 S:2

Swift, Benjamin H - Died 1922
Born 1845 Was in Company I,
33rd Regiment Massachusetts
Volunteers (with Clara & Harrison Swift) S:18

Swift, Clara F - Died 1892 Born
1856 (with Benjamin & Harrison
Swift) S:18

Swift, Edgar F - Died (no date listing for death) Born 1852 (listed
with wife, Isabell F Swift) S:13

Swift, Harrison Bl - Died 1895
Born 1880 (with Benjamin &
Clara Swift) S:18

Swift, Isabell F - Died 1940 Born
1854 Wife of Edgar F Swift
(listed with him) S:13

Swift, Jonathan - Died 1810 Jan
23 Age 10 weeks 4 days Son of
Ebenezer and Lucy Swift S:26R

Swift, Joseph F - Died 1960 Born
1887 (with Margarite Swift) S:16

Swift, Lottie E - Died 1888 May 18
Age 31 years, 7 months Wife of
Henry N Swift S:19

Swift, Lucy - Died 1811 July 15 in
her 34th yr Wife of Ebenezer
Swift S:26R

Swift, Lydia - Died 18?0 March 28
4 mos 21 days Daughter of
Ebenezer and Lucy Swift S:26R

Swift, Margarite - Died 1969 Born
1885 (with Joseph F Swift) S:16

Swinerton, Ellen A - Died 1936
Born 1839 (small stone gone
next to her, looks like it could
have been a child) Wife of
Sumner P Gorham (with him)
S:19

Swinerton, Hannah Otis - Died
1860 April 3 Born 1777 May 20
Widow of Solomon Swinerton
S:10

Swinerton, Sarah - Died 1880
Born 1815 Daughter of Solomon
& Hannah Swinerton & (possible
wife of Otis Nye - stone worn)
S:10

Swinerton, Solomon Otis - Died 1800 July 24 Age 1 year, 10 months Son of Solomon & Hannah Swinerton S:10

Swinerton, Timothy - Died 1881 Aug 5 Born 1798 June 29 Stone says,"Our father" S:10

Sylvester, Manuel L - Died 1934 Born 1876 S:16

Sylvester, Mary P - Died 1912 Born 1826 S:4

Sylvia, Anthony - Died (stone worn and not clear) S:31

Sylvia, Anthony - (between David H Pierce & Charles Rogers, stone is worn) S:31

Sylvia, Anthony Oliver - Died 1957 Feb 5 Born 1894 Nov 15 From Massachusetts, was a Pvt in 128 Casual Co, during World War I S:16

Syrjala, Anni - Died 1956 Born 1877 (next to John Syrjala) S:18

Syrjala, John - Died 1936 Born 1877 (next to Anni Syrjala) S:18

Tait, Anna - Died 1903 Born 1842 S:8

Tallant, Andrew - Died (no dates listed) (a broken stone next to him) Son of Nathaniel & Lydia Tallant (next to father) S:11

Tallant, Eben W - Died (stone not clear) Son of Nathaniel & Lydia Tallant S:11

Tallant, Frances - Died 1834 Sept 22 Age 5 Daughter of Nathaniel & Lydia Tallant (stone broken and laying about) (with James M Tallant) S:11+26R

Tallant, James M - Died 1828 July 2 Age 1 at Hallowell Son of Nathaniel & Lydia Tallant (with Frances Tallant) S:11+26R

Tallant (Tallaut ?), Lydia - Died 1890 Born 1806 Wife of Nathaniel Tallant (next to him) S:11+26R

Tallant, Nathaniel - Died 1871 April 20 Age 76 (top of his stone has draftman & tools overhead) S:11+26R

Tallman, (Baby) - Died 1917 (in

Tallman (Cont.)
Tallman plot) (next to M Elaine Andrews & Myrtle I Tallman) S:12

Tallman, Alina Alice - Died 1863 Sept 6 Age 4 months, 3 days Daughter of Stephen & Mary Tallman (next ? Tallman, d185?) S:14

Tallman, Ariel H - Died 1958 Born 1879 (next to Catherine V tallman) S:12

Tallman, Aurilla J - Died 1905 Born 1837 (with Charles S Tallman) S:13

Tallman, Beatrice B - Died 1971 Born 1892 (with Julius W Howland & others in Tallman plot) S:12

Tallman, Catherine V - Died 1970 Born 1891 (next to Ariel H Tallman) S:12

Tallman, Charles S - Died 1889 Born 1825 (with Aurilla J Tallman) S:13

Tallman, Charlotte B - Died 1972 Born 1905 (with Leonard S Tallman) S:13

Tallman, Edward - Died 1855 Jan 7 Age 2 years, 10 months, 2 days Son of Stephen & Mary Tallman (with sister, Mary Ella Tallman) S:14

Tallman, Ella B - Died 1900 Born 1892 (in Tallman plot with others) S:12

Tallman, Ellen C - Died 1943 Born 1851 (with Joseph W Tallman & others in Tallman plot) S:12

Tallman, Harry L - Died 1951 Born 1875 (he was a Mason) (in Tallman with Philip D Andrews & others) S:12

Tallman, Joseph W - Died 1935 Born 1848 (in Tallman plot with Ellen C Tallman & others) S:12

Tallman, Joseph W Jr - Died (still living 1991?) Born 1889 (listed in Tallman plot with others, he would be 102 years if still living?) S:12

Tallman, Leonard S - Died 1982

Tallman (Cont.)
Born 1901 Has military stone too that says,"WT1 in US Navy during World War I (with Charlotte B Tallman) S:13

Tallman, Mary B - Died 1904 Born 1823 (with Mary B Tallman) S:14

Tallman, Mary Ella - Died 1853 July 21 Age 4 months, 1 day Daughter of Stephen & Mary Tallman (with ? Tallman, son of Stephen & Mary) S:14

Tallman, Myrtle I - Died 1959 Born 1876 (in Tallman plot with Harry L Tallman & others) S:12

Tallman, Stephen B - Died 1905 Born 1828 (with Mary B Tallman) S:14

Tannatt, Mary Hedge - Died 1878 Sept 14 Born 1797 Dec 1 (next to Isaac G Hedge) S:19

Tant, Anna C (or R) - Died 1984 Born 1898 Age 86 (buried 17 May 1984, block 8,lot 74-1st 1/2, grave #1) (some of the above info from the Mosswood cemetery records) S:15

Tayler, Jasper - Died 1773 Sept 11 Age 2 years, 2 months, 4 days Son of Mr Jasper & Mary Tayler S:11R

Tayler, Josiah - Died 1770 June 28 in his 98th yr (next to Seth? Tatler) S:9

Tayler, Mary Mrs - Died 1846 April 18 Age 96 years, 4 months Born 1749 Dec 17 Widow of Mr Jasper Tayler S:11R

Tayler, Seth(?) - Died 1775 Feb 3 in his 29th yr (stone not clear for name) (next to Josiah Tayler) S:9

Taylor, (infant child) - Died (stone not clear) Child of Lewis & Mary Taylor S:4

Taylor, Abigail - Died 1760 June 10 Age 11 years, 9 months, 27 days Daughter of William & Desire Taylor S:9R

Taylor, Abigail B - Died 1917 Aug 28 Born 1837 Feb 13 Wife of Freeman Taylor (two stones

Taylor (Cont.)
away from him) S:19

Taylor, Achsah Miss - Died 1848 May 30 Age 83 S:10

Taylor, Ansel E - Died 1938 Born 1869 (between Amily & E Raymond Taylor) S:18

Taylor, Azubah Y - Died 1846 Oct 13 Age 22 years, 9 months Wife of Reuben Taylor S:21

Taylor, Barbara Clarke - Died 1979 Born 1912 (with Wilfred Taylor) S:20

Taylor, Benjamin E - Died 1971 Born 1898 (with Helen C Taylor) S:18

Taylor, Carlton T - Died 1979 Born 1895 Was a cook in US Army during World War I (with wife, Irma A Coleman) S:14

Taylor, Charles H - Died 1901 Feb 14 Born 1832 Oct 22 (with Sarah A Taylor & others) S:18

Taylor, Christina - Died 1897 Nov 4 Born 1820 Oct 5 (with Dustin Taylor) S:21

Taylor, Desire - Died 1800 April Born 1722 April Consort to Capt William Taylor (buried two stones away from him) S:10

Taylor, Dorah H - Died 1866 Nov 25 Born 1863 Oct 15 (with Charles H Taylor & others) S:18

Taylor, Doris E Knight - Died 1984 Born 1898 (next to Carlton Taylor & Irma A Coleman) S:14

Taylor, Dustin - Died 1895 June 25 Born 1819 July 12 (with Christina Taylor) S:21

Taylor, E Raymond - Died 1986 Born 1899 (next to Ansel E Taylor) S:18

Taylor, Ebenezer - Died 1760 March 13 in his 23rd yr Bachelor of Arts of Harvard College S:9R

Taylor, Ebenezer - Died 1785 May 18 in his 74th yr S:10+26R

Taylor, Ebenezer - Died 1832 Nov 6 Age 72 (buried next to Miss Hannah Taylor & Miss Achsah Taylor) S:10

Taylor, Edwin - Died 1912 Born 1838 (with Phebe S Taylor & others) S:21

Taylor, Eliza A - Died 1890 Feb 3 Age 58 years, 1 month, 29 days Wife of Eben E Taylor S:6

Taylor, Elizabeth P - Died 1868 April 27 Age 93 Born 1775 April 26 (next to Mary Taylor, d1846) S:11

Taylor, Ella B - Died 1961 Born 1881 Wife of Willis Taylor (with her) S:18

Taylor, Elmer B - Died 1949 Born 1893 Son of George W Taylor & Cordelia C Davis & Maude McCray & others on large Taylor stone) S:12

Taylor, Emily B - Died 1922 Born 1875 (next to Ansel E Taylor) S:18

Taylor, Francis - Died 1953 Born 1895 (also has Barnstable Fire Dept plaque) (next to Helen D Taylor) S:19

Taylor, Frank - Died 1892 Oct 18 Age 53? years, 2 months (also has a Civil War Veteran star marker, 1861-65) S:19

Taylor, Fredrick - Died 1907 Born 1867 (with Sarah Taylor, wife & Cecile M Bylund) S:21

Taylor, Freeman - Died 1908 Oct 27 Born 1828 Nov 4 (next to wife, Sarah Taylor) S:19

Taylor, George L - Died 1859 April 16 Born 1857 May 17 (with Dorah H Taylor & others) S:18

Taylor, George W - Died 1908 Born 1861 (on large Taylor stone with Cordelia C Davis & others) S:12

Taylor, Hannah Miss - Died 1832 Nov 13 Age 62 S:10

Taylor, Helen C - Died 1957 Born 1900 (with Benjamin E Taylor) S:18

Taylor, Helen D - Died 1976 Born 1892 (next to Francis Taylor) S:19

Taylor, Herbert F - Died 1873 Dec 20 Age 21 years, 9 months Son of Freeman & Sarah Taylor (next to them) S:19

Taylor, Howard G - Died 1913 Born 1859 (with Phebe E Taylor) S:21

Taylor, Isaac L - Died 185? Nov Son of Lewis & Mary A Taylor S:4

Taylor, Jacob - Died 1777 Dec 27 in his 73rd yr (buried with Leverett Taylor) S:1

Taylor, Jasone - Died 1896 Sept 21 Born 1844 Mar 27 Son of Lewis & Mary Taylor S:4

Taylor, Jasper - Died 1773 Sept 11 Age 2 years, 2 months, 4 days Son of Jasper & Mary Taylor S:11

Taylor, John - Died 1874 Feb 1 Age 23 years, 1 month Son of William & Desire Taylor (next to William A & William Taylor) S:19

Taylor, John B - Died 1874 Sept 11 Age 20 years, 9 months (with Simeon Taylor) S:18

Taylor, Josiah - Died 1770 June 28 in his 28th yr S:9R+26R

Taylor, Joyce - Died 1926 Born 1858 (with Susie E Taylor & others) S:18

Taylor, Leverett - Died 1776 May 6 Age 38 Wife of Jacob Taylor Buried with him S:1

Taylor, Lewis - Died 1863 Sept 24 in his 42nd yr S:4

Taylor, Marth F - Died 1912 Dec 3 Born 1832 Oct 7 S:6

Taylor, Mary - Died 1792 Feb 13 in her 81st yr S:1

Taylor, Mary - Died 1846 April 18 Age 96 years, 4 months Born 1749 Dec 17 Widow of Jasper Taylor (next to son, Jasper) S:11

Taylor, Mary A - Died 1899 Dec 19 Born 1824 June 20 Stone says "Gone Home" S:4

Taylor, Mary L - Died (stone not clear) Daughter of Lewis & Mary Taylor S:4

Taylor, Mary Mrs - Died 1791 March ? Age 77 Widow of Ebenezer Taylor S:10

Taylor, Phebe E - Died (no date) Born 1861 (with Howard G

Taylor (Cont.)
Taylor) S:21

Taylor, Phebe S - Died 1915 Born 1835 (with Eliza E Baker & others) S:21

Taylor, Rowland - Died 1752 Nov 30 in his 32nd yr S:1

Taylor, Ruth M - Died 1955 Born 1898 (next to Emily Taylor) S:18

Taylor, Sarah - Died 1862? Feb 17 Age 35 Wife of Capt Freeman Taylor (next to him) S:19

Taylor, Sarah - Died 1929 Born 1874 Wife of Frederick Taylor (with him & Cecile M Bylund) S:21

Taylor, Sarah A - Died 1902 Sept 12 Born 1830 July 30 (with George L Taylor & others S:18

Taylor, Sarah Elizabeth - Died 1884 Nov 9 Born 1844 Jan 7 Wife of James L Taylor S:11

Taylor, Sarah Mrs - Died 1778 Dec 21 in her 29th yr S:10+26R

Taylor, Seth - Died 1775 Feb 3 in his 29th yr S:9R+26R

Taylor, Simeon - Died 1885 Dec 18 Born 1822 Nov 2 S:6

Taylor, Simeon - Died 1902 May 17 Age 80 years, 4 months (with Unity Taylor & others) S:18

Taylor, Susan - Died 1907 Born 1825 Wife of John Henry Paine (with him on large Paine, Titcomb & Brown stone) S:11

Taylor, Susie E - Died 1935 Born 1863 (with Aurila Peterson & others) S:18

Taylor, Unity - Died 1892 May 21 Age 73 years, 9 months (with Martha J Baker & others) S:18

Taylor, Wilfred - Died (still living 1991?) Born 1908 (with Barbara Clarke Taylor) S:20

Taylor, William - Died 1757 June 29 Age 5 years, 9 months, 15 days Son of William & Desire Taylor S:9R

Taylor, William - Died 1802 Sept 14 in his 91st yr S:10+26R

Taylor, William - Died 1874 June 5 Age 73 years, 11 months (next to

Taylor (Cont.)
William A & John Taylor) S:19

Taylor, William A - Died 1862 July 2 Age 15 years, 10 months, 5 days (stone is down) Son of William & Desire Taylor (between William & John Taylor) S:19

Taylor, Willis C - Died 1942 Born 1879 (with Ella B Taylor, wife) S:18

Teasee, Manuel M - Died 1968 July 30 Born 1895 May 3 From Massachusetts, was Pvt in CoK, 63rd Pioneer Infantry during World War I S:17

Tedesco, Anthony J - Died 1989 Born 1891 S:19

Tedesco, S Joyce - Died 1972 Born 1896 (with A J Tedesco) S:19

Teixeira, Julius M - Died 1953 Born 1893 (with Ruby M Teixeira) S:18

Teixeira, Ruby M - Died 1988 Born 1908 (with Julius M Teixeira) S:18

Tejidor, Roberto - Died 1909 July 14 Born in Mexico (stone is down) S:31

Tenney, Harry W - Died 1983 Born 1899 (with Lida B Tenney) S:15

Tenney, Helen L - Buried 1980 Nov 25 Age 87 Located in section O, lot 22, grave 4 S:14R

Tenney, Lida B - Died (still living 1991?) Born 1912 (with Harry W Tenney) S:15

Tenney, William R - Died 1980 Born 1894 (with wife, Helen Adams) S:14

Terpos, Christ - Died 1988 Born 1893 (listed with Olga Terpos) S:15

Terpos, Elias C - Died 1975 Born 1900 (with Helen Terpos) S:15

Terpos, Helen - Died 1968 Born 1911 (with Elias C Terpos) S:15

Terpos, Olga - Died (still living 1991?) Born 1911 (with Christ Terpos) S:15

Terry, Adeline Z - Died (still living 1990) Born 1903 (with Carl A Terry) S:11

Terry, Carl A - Died 1977 Born 1893 (with Adeline Z Terry) S:11

Terry, Edith F - Died 1986 July 6 Born 1892 Aug 2 (next to John Leary Terry) S:16

Terry, George E - Died 1908 Born 1853 (with wife, Susan A Terry & next to Elizabeth Terry Leckie) S:19

Terry, John Leary - Died 1962 May 13 Born 1892 Nov 28 From Massachusetts, was a Sgt in Med Depot during World War I (next to Edith F Terry) S:16

Terry, Mary A - Died 1915 Born 1874 S:31

Terry, Susan A - Died 1915 Born 1850 Wife of George E Terry (with him & next to Elizabeth Terry Leckie) S:19

Tesee, (TESEE) - Died No dates Stone says "We loved you because you were you" Located at side of cemetery near railroad tracks This stone could be for one just in front of it, Teresa Marie McMakin - see her listing S:19

Tetrault, Amedee - Died 1974 Born 1894 Was PM, 3C in US Navy during World War I (next to Nell Dilger) S:15

Teuyaw, Byron H - Died 1943 Born 1878 (with Joseph Burlingame & Inez Garder) S:14

Thacer, Lewis - Died 1825 Feb 24 Age 5 months, 21 days Son of Lewis & Sally Thacer S:4

Thacer, Sally H - Died 1873 Nov 14 in her 86th yr S:4

Thacher, Angie C - Died 1939 March 4 Born 1860 Nov 14 (with George L Thacher) S:18

Thacher, Anthony - Died 1742 Aug 29 Age 18 years, 3 months, 12 days Son of Elisha & Phebe Thacher S:9R

Thacher, Betsey - Died 1889 July 28 Age 63 years, 6 months S:8

Thacher, Clara S - Died 1887 May 28 Age 25 years, 9 months Wife of Charles Thacher S:19

Thacher, Content - Died 1773

Thacher (Cont.)
March 20 in her 60th yr Wife of John Thacher S:26R

Thacher, Cotie - Died (date not clear) March 31 (stone worn) (small childs stone) Child of George & Fannie Thacher (next to them & stepmother Lizzie Thacher) S:18

Thacher, Edward C Jr - Died 1982 Born 1915 Was in US Army S:31

Thacher, Eleanor R - Died 1913 Born 1839 (next to Florence & Franklin Thacher & others) S:18

Thacher, Fannie E - Died 1911 Born 1847 Wife of George L Thacker (next to him) S:18

Thacher, Florence H - Died 1944 Born 1879 (with Frank G & next to Eleanor R Thacher & others) S:18

Thacher, Frank G - Died 1953 Born 1876 (next to Winslow & Frank Thacher & others & with Florence H Thacher) S:18

Thacher, Franklin - Died 1921 Born 1842 (next to Eleanor R Thacher & others) S:18

Thacher, George L - Died 1901 Born 1834 (stone over from vandals) (between wifes, Fannie & Lizzie Thacher) S:18

Thacher, George L - Died 1919 Aug 12 Born 1860 Oct 1 (with Angie C Thacher) S:18

Thacher, John Honorable Esq - Died 1764 March 26 in his 90th yr "After a long life of influence & faithfullness in several military & civil officers" S:9R+26R

Thacher, Lewis Esq - Died 1825 Sept 11 in his 45th yr S:4

Thacher, Lizzie C - Died 1869 Sept 5 Age 23 years, 11 months, 25 days (stone over from vandals) Wife of George Thacher (next to him 9) S:18

Thacher, Martha - Died 1806 Aug 4 in her 23rd yr Daughter of Jethro & Hannah Thacher of Lee, Massachusetts S:10+26R

Thacher, Oliver - Died 1866 July 8

Thacher (Cont.)
Age 34 years, 1 month S:21

Thacher, Phebe - Died 1742 Sept 24 Age 15 years, 6 months, 14 days Daughter of Elisha & Phebe Thacher S:9R

Thacher, Rebeckah Miss - Died 1870 Sept 14 in her 67th yr S:26R

Thacher, Remember - Died 1795 April 26 Age 37 Wife of John Thacher S:26R

Thacher, Samuel - Died 1761 May 26 Age 2 years, 24 days Son of John & Content Thacher S:9R

Thacher, Samuel Sturgis - Died 1741 Feb 14 Age 3 months, 4 days Son of Elisha & Phebe Thacher S:9R

Thacher, Sarah - Died 1834 Feb 15 Age 73 Widow of John Thacher S:26R

Thacher, Winslow K - Died 1963 Nov 15 Born 1878 March 19 From Massachusetts, was a Cpl in Motor Trans Corps during World War I (next to Frank G Thacher & others) S:18

Thatcher, Anthony - Died 1806 Jan 8 Age 63 (buried next to wife, Elizabeth Thatcher) S:10

Thatcher, Elisha - Died 1785 March 12 in her 84th yr (date underground) (located next to Phebe Thatcher and Elisha Thatcher) S:10+26R

Thatcher, Elisha - Died 1774 Dec 6 in his 76th yr S:10

Thatcher, Elizabeth - Died 1818 Aug 6 Age 78 Widow of Anthony Thatcher (next to him) S:10

Thatcher, John V - Died 1968 Born 1882 S:15

Thatcher, Lot (Capt) - Died 1763 Feb 14 Age 30 Died at Charleston, North Carolina S:9

Thatcher, Martha - Died 1802 Jan 7 in her 67th yr Wife of Capt Lot Thatcher (his stone next to her) S:9+26R

Thatcher, Mary Mrs - Died 1814 April 28 Age 62 Wife of John

Thatcher (Cont.)
Thatcher Esq S:10

Thatcher, Mercy Mrs - Died 1853 Feb 24 Age 73 Widow of Capt Pegleg Thatcher (next to him) S:10

Thatcher, Peleg (Capt) - Died 1817 Aug 12 in his 66th yr S:10+26R

Thatcher, Phebe - Died (date underground) Widow of Elisha Thatcher (between Elisha & Elisha Thatcher) S:10

Thayer, (child?) - Died 1834? June 1 (stone badly worn) Child of Joseph & Catherine Thayer (next to them) S:19

Thayer, (child?) - Died 1841? March 8 (stone badly worn) (possible child of Joseph & Catherine Thayer Next to them) S:19

Thayer, Alva - Died 1907 Born 1826 (with Sophia Thayer & others) S:18

Thayer, Anna J - Buried 1981 Nov 7 Age 83 Located in section 8, lot 97-1st1/2, grave 3 S:15R

Thayer, Catherine - Died 1883 Feb 19 Wife of Joseph Thayer (next to him & 2 children who's stones are badly worn) S:19

Thayer, Gladys Brooks - Died 1976 May 1 Born 1882 Feb 1 S:15

Thayer, Henrietta - Died 1893 Feb 16 Age 76 years, 5 months, 24 days (stone off base & down) (listed with husband, Horatio N Thayer) S:21

Thayer, Henry E - Died 1850 July 22 Son of Horatio & Henrietta Thayer (next to their stone) S:21

Thayer, Horatio N - Died 1860 May 12 Age 53 Lost at sea (listed with wife, Henrietta Thayer) S:21

Thayer, Joseph - Died 1875 July 5 Age 75 years, 3 months (stone worn) (next to wife, Catherine Thayer) S:19

Thayer, Laura - Died 1876 Oct 19 Age 41 years, 8 months, 6 days Wife of Wendell P Baxter S:21

Thayer, Lawrence A - Died 1956

Thayer (Cont.)
Born 1905 (large anchor in-graved in stone) Belonged to Massachusetts, BM2 USNR in World War II PH 1941-45 Veter-an plaque & service stone (next to Mary C C Thayer) S:12

Thayer, Mary C C - Died 1984 Born 1892 (next to Lawrence A Thayer) S:12

Thayer, Ophella? - Died (dates under ground) Daughter of Horatio N & Henrietta Thayer (next to brother, Henry E Thay-er) S:21

Thayer, Sophia - Died 1915 Born 1826 (with Alva Thayer & Henry & Ellen Hallett) S:18

Thomas, Almeda K - Died 1963 Born 1883 S:17

Thomas, Delina C - Died 1984 Born 1899 (with Ronald Thomas) S:20

Thomas, Edwin - Died 1966 Mar 18 Born 1875 Nov 26 (with Laura Roberts, his wife) S:11

Thomas, Florence B - Died 1986 Feb 14 Born 1930 July 30 Wife of Richard C Thomas (with him) S:11

Thomas, J Harold - Died 1959 Born 1901 Member of the Barn-stable Fire Dept (flag at grave) S:11

Thomas, James Stacey - Died 1969 Jan 2 Born 1921 Nov 21 From Massachusetts, was a Sargeant in Med Dept during World War II S:20

Thomas, John Harold - Died 1959 April 5 Born 1901 Mar 31 Son of Edwin & Laura Thomas (with them) S:11

Thomas, Joseph - Died (still living 1991?) Born 1910 (with Lembi Thomas) S:20

Thomas, L Vernelle - Died 1984 Born 1901 (next to Mabel E Thomas) S:11

Thomas, Lembi E - Died 1984 Born 1910 (with Joseph Thomas) S:20

Thomas, Mabel E - Died 1959 Born

Thomas (Cont.)
1883 (next to L Vernelle Thomas) S:11

Thomas, Nathan - Died 1884 April 2 Age 69 years,10 months (with Warren Thomas, his brother) S:13

Thomas, Patience - Died 1809 May 8 Age 32 Wife of Lemuel Thomas S:12

Thomas, Richard C - Died (still living 1990) Born 1924 Dec 11 (with Florence B Thomas, wife) S:11

Thomas, Robert Newell - Died 1972 June 16 Born 1896 Sept 27 From Massachusetts, was EM2 in US Navy during World War I S:18

Thomas, Roby Scott - Died 1983 Mar 28 Born 1960 Aug 21 "Our Carpenter" (next to Richard C & Florence B Thomas) S:11

Thomas, Ronald C - Died 1966 Born 1899 (with Delina Thomas) S:20

Thomas, Samuel C - Died 1905 Feb 1 Born 1874 Apr 5 (buried next to Frederick Bearse) S:8

Thomas, Sarah - Died 1884 June 28 at So Boston Age 32 years, 11 months Wife of George Thomas S:18

Thomas, Warren - Died 1874 Nov 23 Age 67 (with Nathan Thomas, his brother) S:13

Thompson, Betsey - Died 1834 Nov 25 Age 22 years, 5? months, 7 days Wife of James Thompson S:21

Thompson, Edna Williams - Died 1984 June 23 Born 1889 April 24 (listed with Howard Dow Thompson) S:15

Thompson, Edward R - Died 1973 Born 1964 (next to John W Thompson) S:13

Thompson, Eleanor Handy - Died 1981 Born 1900 S:14

Thompson, Frances T - Died 1889 Nov 2 Age 38 years, 2 months, 19 days (located under a tree,

Thompson (Cont.)
stone is worn) Wife of William
Thompson S:14

Thompson, Howard Dow - Died
1973 March 9 Born 1892 Oct 19
Died in Mandeville, Jamaica,
West Indies (listed with Edna
Williams Thompson) S:15

Thompson, John - Died 1830 Nov
23 Age 42, formerly of Boston,
Mass S:10

Thompson, John W - Died 1989
Born 1951 (next to Edward R
Thompson) S:13

Thornton, Grace Jane - Died 1905
April 10 Born 1832 Aug 10 Wife
of John Buckley (with him &
Timothy Buckley & others) S:31

Thurber, Mary A - Died 1923 Born
1834 S:19

Tibbetts, Elizabeth C - Died 1951
Born 1871 (with George W
Tibbetts) S:12

Tibbetts, George W - Died 1946
Born 1875 (with Elizabeth C
Tibbetts) S:12

Tiebout, Todd G - Died 1971 Born
1898 S:15

Till, Agnes Elizabeth - Died (no
dates) Daughter of Alexander &
Agnes Till (next to them) S:12

Till, Agnes G - Died (no markings)
Wife of Alexander Till (next to
him) S:12

Till, Alexander - Died 1909 Jan 8
in Osterville, Massachusetts
Born 1857 Oct 6 in England
(next to wife, Agnes G Till) S:12

Tillinghast, Joseph - Died 1886
Feb 15 Born 1809 Sept 13 Stone
says, "At rest" S:19

Tilson, Lydia - Died 1800 Nov 18
Born 1798 Nov 3 Daughter of Mr
Tilson & Jemima Wood S:5R

Tinney, May R - Died (still living
1991?) Born 1902 (with Walter
Tinney) S:20

Tinney, Walter R - Died 1978 Born
1896 (with May R Tinney) S:20

Titcomb, Edward - Died 1914 Born
1844 (on large Paine, Titcomb &
Brown stone) S:11

Tivenan, Marguerite M - Died 1989
Born 1895 S:16

Tobey, Francis - Died 1835 Dec
Born 1829 Jan 30 Son of Jonathan B & Polly Tobey S:10

Tobey, Freeman C - Died 1863 Nov
26 Age 55 years, 6 months S:4

Tobey, Jonathan B - Died 1829
Dec 15 Born 1794 May 30 S:10

Tobey, Lydia B - Died 1818 June 4
Age 11 months 4 days Infant
daughter of Jonathan B & Polly
Tobey S:10

Tobey, Lydia B - Died 1825 Sept 26
Age 6 years 2 months Daughter
of Jonathan B & Polly Tobey
(next to father) S:10

Tobey, William - Died 1821 Sept 12
Son of Jonathan B Tobey S:10

Todd, Catherine H - Died 1973
Born 1900 (with Randolph H
Todd) S:15

Todd, Randolph H - Died 1981
Born 1898 Was FN in US Navy
during World War I (has 2
stones) (with Catherine H Todd)
S:15

Toffey, Hannah Catherine - Died
1986 Dec 24 Born 1986 Sept 29
S:19

Tolby, Frederick M - Died 1962
Born 1882 S:20

Tolchinsky, Odyssea Olvan - Died
1983 Born 1891 S:14

Tomlinson, Bertram - Died 1981
April 21 Born 1895 March 22
Was a PFC in US Army during
World War I (next to Nona Myers
Tomlinson) S:19

Tomlinson, Bertram L Jr - Died
1985 Sept 26 Born 1923 June 6
Was a Sargeant in US Army Air
Corps during World War II (next
to Bertram & Nona Tomlinson)
S:19

Tomlinson, George W - Died 1956
Feb 11 Born 1879 Oct 20 in
Connecticut Was a Wagoneer in
Co A, 6 regiment Infantry during
the Spanish American War (next
to Georgia Tomlinson) S:14

Tomlinson, Georgia - Died 1966

Tomlinson (Cont.)
Born 1869 (next to George W Tomlinson) S:14

Tomlinson, Nona Myers - Died 1983 Feb 9 Born 1896 July 18 (with Bertram L Tomlinson Jr) S:19

Tompkins, Cora Thacher Drew - Died 1981 Born 1894 S:17

Tompkins, Ethel M - Died 1971 Born 1889 (with Stanley A Tompkins) S:18

Tompkins, Miles Richard - Died 1986 Aug 11 (small lamb stone) S:20

Tompkins, Stanley A - Died 1933 Born 1881 (with Ethel M Tompkins) S:18

Toner, Mary E - Died 1985 Born 1899 Stone says,"Aunt" (next to Samuel & Bathia Palmer) S:17

Toney, Florence - Died 1961 Born 1888/9 (has 2 stones) (next to George W Toney) S:17

Toney, George W - Died 1952 Born 1878 (next to Florence Toney) S:17

Tongberg, Carl O - Died 1962 Born 1906 (next to Emma & Otto Tongberg) S:13

Tongberg, Emma - Died 1971 Born 1878 (with Otto Tongberg) S:13

Tongberg, Otto - Died 1939 Born 1872 (with Emma Tongberg) S:13

Tonks, Arthur W - Died 1949 Born 1872 (next to Ruth Fenn Tonks) S:11

Tonks, Gerald F - Died 1986 Born 1901 (stone has circle that says,"Green Gross For safety") S:11

Tonks, Ruth Fenn - Died 1976 Born 1896 (next to Gerald F Tonks) S:11

Toppin, Elizabeth A - Died 1974 Born 1893 (with Francis V Toppin) S:15

Toppin, Francis V - Died 1967 Born 1894 (with Elizabeth A Toppin) S:15

Torrey, Edwin G - Died 1895 Born

Torrey (Cont.)
1852 (buried next to wife, Elnora B Torrey) S:8

Torrey, Elnora B - Died 1917 Born 1853 Wife of Edwin (stone says "Mother, At Rest") S:8

Toscano, Anna R - Died (still living 1991?) Born 1899 Nov 18 Wife of Nazzareno Toscano (with him) S:16

Toscano, Nazzareno A - Died 1981 Sept 10 Born 1899 March 31 (with wife, Anna R Toscano) S:16

Towse, Barbara Scudder - Died 1975 Born 1923 (next to Harriet Ellen Scudder) S:12

Tracy, Ollia M - Died 1962 Born 1898 (Charles Cloutier is listed as her husband) S:15

Travers, Doris B - Died (still living 1990) Born 1911 Wife of Frank Travers (next to him) S:11

Travers, Frank - Died 1967 Born 1906 Member of Barnstable Fire Dept (next to Doris B Travers) S:11

Trayser, Donald G - Died 1955 Born 1902 (rock marker) (with Annabel Jerauld) S:11

Treco, Dorothy Stimson (Elizabeth) - Died 1986 Born 1898 Age 87 (buried 4 March 1986, section 11, lot 65-4th1/4, grave #3) (some of the above info is from the Mosswood cemetery records) S:15

Treen, William A - Died 1926 Born 1862 S:18

Trefry, Laurence D - Died 1976 Jan 5 Born 1896 July 14 Was a Captain in Army Air Force during World War I & II S:18

Trefry, Millicent Bassett - Died 1962 Born 1897 (with Bertram Johnson & Mildred Bassett) S:18

Trimble, Gladys M - Buried 1982 Nov 2 Age 82 Located in section 4, lot 47-2nd 1/2, grave 2 S:15R

Tripp, Harold J - Died 1974 Born 1892 (with Kathryn Tripp) S:15

Tripp, Katherine E - Died (no dates) Wife of Warren A Tripp (listed

Tripp (Cont.)
with him & William A Maher &
others) S:31

Tripp, Kathryn - Died 1980 Born
1896 (with Harold J Tripp) S:15

Tripp, Warren A - Died (no dates)
(listed with wife, Katherine E
Tripp & others) S:31

Trott, John Alden - Died (no dates)
(with Sallie Sturgis Trott & John
Clapp Trott) S:11

Trott, John Clapp - Died (no dates)
(with Sallie Sturgis Trott & John
Alden Trott) S:11

Trott, Sallie Sturgis - Died 1913
(large Trott stone with John
Clapp & John Alden Trott) S:11

Trowbridge, Cornelius Miller Jr -
Died 1972 Jan 8 at Evanston,
Illinios (has 2 stones) Born 1901
Sept 8 (with Catherine F Crane)
S:20

Trumbull, Elisabeth Weaver - Died
1985 Aug 5 Born 1911 Sept 10
(next to Ralph W Trumbull) S:11

Trumbull, Ralph William - Died
1973 Dec 25 Born 1901 Dec 15
S:11

Tsiknas, George E - Died 1945
Born 1862 (buried with Mary V
Tsiknas) S:8

Tsiknas, Mary V - Died 1949 Born
1881 Wife of George Tsiknas S:8

Tuck, Caroline - Died 1889 Jan 28
Born 1815 Feb 1 (next to Dr
Henry Tuck) S:9

Tuck, Elizabeth J - Died 1884 Jan
18 Born 1810 June 11 Daughter
of Henry & Caroline Tuck
(buried next to them) S:9

Tuck, Henry MD - Died 1845 June
21 Born 1808 Feb 16 S:9

Tucker, Lazarus Dr - Died 1812
March 24 Age 36 S:5R

Tuohy, Catherine V - Died 1918
Oct 12 Born in County Mayo,
Ireland Wife of George F Aylmer
(with him & Henry J Aylmer &
others) S:31

Tuominen, Charles I - Died 1964
Born 1887 (next to Hilma J
Tuominen, wife) S:18

Tuominen, Hilma J - Died 1954
Born 1887 Wife of Charles I
Tuominen (with him) S:18

Tupper, Abigail - Died 1802 March
31 in her 70th yr Widow of
Mordecai Tupper S:26R

Tupper, Allen - Died 1827 Feb 23
in his 27th yr S:10+26R

Tupper, Lothrop - Died 1827 April
5 in his 71st yr S:10+26R

Tupper, Mercy - Died 1825 June
23 in her 64th yr Wife of Lothrop
Tupper (buried next to him)
S:10+26R

Tupper, Mordecai - Died 1790 July
21 in his 72nd yr S:26R

Tupper, Ruth - Died 1825 Aug 27
Age 27 Daughter of Lothrop &
Mercy Tupper S:10

Tupper, Ruth - Died 1829 July 27
Age 31 Wife of William Tupper
S:12

Turner, Albert H - Died 1875 Born
1854 (with Charles W Turner &
others) S:14

Turner, Albert H - Died 1950 Born
1887 (with Francis J Turner &
others) S:14

Turner, Charles W - Died 1936
Born 1859 (with Cora S Turner
& others) S:14

Turner, Cora S - Died 1933 Born
1863 (with Albert H Turner &
others) S:14

Turner, Deborah l - Died 1892 Jan
5 Born 1882 Apr 4 Wife of
Washburn Turner S:5

Turner, Elihu F - Died 1871 Born
1824 (with Julia A Turner) S:14

Turner, Francis J - Died 1962 Born
1894 (with Albert H Turner &
others) S:14

Turner, James Varnum - Died
1898 Nov 5 Born 1864 June 9
(has 2 stones) (with Augusta P
Turner) Daughter of Benjamin &
Caroline Crocker (with them &
others) S:18

Turner, Julia A - Died 1884 Born
1830 (with Willis H Turner &
others) S:14

Turner, Mary - Died 1891 Dec 29

Turner (Cont.)
Born 1804 May 18 S:5

Turner, Wellington Jesse - Died
1982 July 20 Born 1900 June
17 Age 82 (buried 23 July 1982,
section 8, lot 95-2nd1/2, grave
#1) (some of the above info is
from the Mosswood cemetery
records) S:15

Turner, Willis H - Died 1851 Born
1851 (with Albert H Turner &
others) S:14

Turpin, James Clifford - Died 1966
Born 1886 (stone has Wright
Brothers plane ingraved on it
1908-12, he was a pioneer
aviator with the Wright Brothers)
(in Turpin plot) S:11

Turtle, Harry Francis - Died 1935
Born 1864 (next to Martha
Potter Turtle) S:8

Turtle, Martha Potter - Died 1945
Born 1857 S:8

Twombley, Helen H - Died 1976
Born 1909 (next to Winfield H
Twombley) S:11

Twombley, Winfield H - Died 1966
Born 1880 (next to Daisy J
Twombley & Helen H Twombley)
S:11

Twombly, John S - Died 1922 Born
1848 (with Lillie C Twombly) S:12

Twombly, Lillie C - Died 1930 Born
1856 (with John S Twombly)
S:12

Underwood, Elizabeth J - Died
1980 Born 1928 Wife of Wilton
Crosby Jr (next to his listing)
S:12

Uniacke, Gerald V - Died 1972 July
29 Born 1896 Aug 1 From
Massachusetts, was a Pvt in US
Army during World War I S:15

Vallis, John Weldon - Died 1971
Born 1890 (with Beatrice Haskell) S:11

Van Amrince, Loretta S - Died
1968 Born 1894 (with Roy F Van
Amrince) S:16

Van Amrince, Roy F - Died 1965
Born 1890 (with Loretta S Van
Amrince) S:16

Van Bibber, Arthur E - Died 1929
March 4 Born 1920 Oct 3 Son of
Arthur E Van Bibber & Isabel H
Hinckley (with mother & John-
nie Hinckley & others) S:18

Van Buren, Esther H - Died 1986
Born 1906 Wife of Kenneth Van
Buren (with him) S:19

Van Buren, James A - Died 1964
Sept 28 Born 1893 June 29 Was
a Corporal in Btry B, 334 Field
Arty during World War I S:19

Van Buren, Kenneth - Died 1970
Born 1897 (with wife, Esther H
Van Buren) S:19

Van Duzer, Arlene A - Died 1978
Born 1910 (with Clyde Van
Duzer) S:19

Van Duzer, Clyde E - Died 1989
Born 1910 (with Arlene A Van
Duzer) S:19

Van Knox, James - Died 1927 Born
1871 S:12

Van Leeuwen, Alida - Died 1972
Born 1883 Wife of Peter Van
Leeuwen (with him) S:13

Van Leeuwen, Peter - Died 1954
Born 1882 (with Alida Van
Leeuwen) S:13

Van Sickle, John - Died 1989 Born
1904 S:11

Van Sickle, Lucy B - Died 1988
Born 1914 (next to John Van
Sickle) S:11

Vanduzer, Floyd C - Died 1987
Born 1899 Was PFC in US Army
during World War I (next to
Helen E Vanduzer) S:11

Vanduzer, Helen E - Died 1979
Born 1902 Stone says, "Mother"
(next to Helen C Vanduzer
Holmes) S:11

Vaughn, Elizabeth - Died 1891 Mar
8 Born 1855 Mar 14 Daughter of
George & Olivia Buckinster
Bacon S:9

Verner, Bertha Whateley - Died
1989 Oct 10 Born 1900 Oct 9
S:15

Vezin, Cornelia Ransom - Died
1976 Dec 28 Born 1891 Nov 30
(with Russell K Vezin) S:14

Vezin, Russell King - Died 1946 July 7 Born 1876 April 30 (with Corenlia Ranson Vezin) S:14

Viehmann, John C L - Died 1987 Born 1895 (with Meta A Viehmann) S:15

Viehmann, Meta A - Died (still living 1991?) Born 1899 (listed with John C L Viehmann) S:15

Vieira, John M - Died 1974 Born 1891 (undertaker plaque) S:16

Vieira, Manuel A - Died 1963 Dec 20 Born 1897 April 8 S:15

Volkheimer, Dorothea M - Died (still living 1991?) Born 1899 (listed with Hugo C Geissele) S:16

Von Colln, Gustaf William - Died 1977 Born 1896 (has 2 stones) Was a LCDR in US Navy during World War II (also has plaque that says, 1941-45) (with Irma H Von Colln) S:19

Von Colln, Irma H - Died (still living 1991?) Born 1909 (listed with Gustaf Von Colln) S:19

Vose, Norma B - Died 1986 Born 1901 Wife of Benjamin Lewis (buried with him) S:8

Waats, Florence G - Died 1977 Born 1904 Wife of Sargent P Watts Sr (with him & son, Sargent P Watts Jr) S:19

Wagoner, Althea B - Died 1977 Born 1893 (with Frederick Wagoner) S:18

Wagoner, Frederick G - Died 1932 Born 1894 (with Althea B Wagoner) S:18

Wagoner, George W - Died 1938 Born 1869 (with Isabella Wyer, his wife) S:21

Waitt, Anna Schoeps - Died 1923 Oct 20 Born 1867 April 1 "She followed him" S:11

Waitt, Arthur M - Died 1920 Nov 10 Born 1858 Oct 24 Stone says, "He Was Beloved" S:11

Waitt, Ellen Hinckley - Died 1911 Aug 11 Born 1831 Dec 17 (on large Waitt stone) S:11

Waitt, Henry A - Died 1856 Aug 3

Waitt (Cont.)
Born 1814 May 22 (with Mary H Small) S:12

Waitt, Hubert Mitchell - Died 1900 May 7 Born 1824 Aug 6 (on large Waitt stone) S:11

Waitt, Isabel Cushman - Died 1908 Sept 21 Born 1898 Jan 27 (large Waitt stone) S:11

Waitt, Penelope - Died 1907 Jan 17 Born 1827 Mar 5 Wife of Samuel Wiley (with him & others on Wiley/Scudder stone) S:12

Walcott, Henry R - Died 1954 Born 1896 (next to Lilla Nickerson Walcott) S:14

Walcott, Lilla Nickerson - Died 1904 Born 1869 (next to Henry R Walcott) S:14

Waldron, Harriot M - Died 1979 Born 1890 Wife of Harold W Nash (next to him) S:11

Waldrop, Warren A - Died 1988 Born 1922 Was in the US Army during World War II S:13

Walker, Albert H - Died 1918 Born 1888 (with Hannah M Walker) S:21

Walker, Alton A - Died 1957 Born 1875 (next to Joseph Walker) S:17

Walker, Angie - Died 1979 Born 1895 Wife of John F Clowery (with him) S:11

Walker, Betsey N - Died 1912 Jan 24 Born 1837 Nov 14 (with Joseph Walker & others) S:18

Walker, Hannah M - Died (no date) Born 1842 (with Albert H Walker) S:21

Walker, Irving W - Died 1915 Oct 7 Born 1892 April 9 (with Charles Wyman & Joseph Walker & Betsey Walker) S:18

Walker, Joseph - Died 1897 March 15 Born 1833 July 13 (with Betsey N Walker & others) S:18

Walker, Joseph - Died 1956 Born 1866 (next to Alton A Walker) S:17

Wallace, Earl T - Died 1989 Jan 3 Born 1923 Dec 1 (also has West

Wallace (Cont.)
Barnstable Fire Dept plaque)
Was a Sargeant in US Army Air
Corps during World War II (listed
with Joan Wallace) S:20

Wallace, Edwin - Died 1868 Apr 12
Age 9 years, 6 months Son of
Edwin C & Eunice C Wallace
(this parents last name are really
Stiff?) S:5

Wallace, Frances (Haelen) - Died
1983 Born 1889 (with Wilfred
Wallace) S:11

Wallace, Joan M - Died (still living
1991?) Born 1925 Dec 30 (listed
with Earl Wallace) S:20

Wallace, Sarah E - Died 1852 Sept
17 Age 14 years, 6 months
(stone is off its foundation)
Daughter of Jacob T & Mehitable
S Wallace S:11

Wallace, Wilfred - Died 1954 Born
1891 (plaque on rock says,
"Semper Fidelis") (with Frances
Wallace (Haelen)) S:11

Wallen, Janice A - Died 1985 Oct
11 Born 1929 July 3 (with
Richard K Wallen, they died the
same day) S:12

Wallen, Richard K - Died 1985 Oct
11 Born 1924 Jan 13 (with
Janice A Wallen) S:12

Waller, John H - Died 1968 Born
1883 (with Susanna K Waller)
S:20

Waller, Susanna K - Died 1969
Born 1889 (with John Waller)
S:20

Walley, Ann S - Died 1895 Aug 2
Age 60 (stone off base) (next to
William & Charles Walley) S:21

Walley, Charles H - Died 1920
June 17 Age 82 (next to Ann &
William Walley) S:21

Walley, Julius A - Died 1950 Born
1865 (with wife, Bertha C Gray)
S:18

Walley, William - Died 1862 Oct 2
Age 32 (stone down) (next to
Anne & Charles Walley) S:21

Walls, Beatrice L - Died 1962 Born
1923 (with Francis E Walls) S:19

Walls, Bridget Shuttleworth - Died
1960 Born 1884 (with Sally
Shuttleworth Coombs & others)
S:31

Walls, Francis F - Died 1974 Born
1908 (with Beatrice L Walls)
S:19

Walsh, Clyda Rae - Died 1981 Aug
12 Born 1901 Feb 1 Wife of
Michael Walsh (with him & next
to Joseph Thomas Walsh) S:20

Walsh, Edwin A - Died 1967 Oct 6
Born 1895 Aug 17 From Massachusetts, was MM1 in USNRF
during World War I S:15

Walsh, Elizabeth M - Died 1961
Born 1897 Wife of Joseph Walsh
(with him) S:16

Walsh, Joseph F - Died 1967 Born
1899 (with wife, Elizabeth M
Walsh) S:16

Walsh, Joseph Thomas - Died 1982
Born 1924 (has 2 stones) Was
GMMCA in US Navy during
World War II, Korea & Vietnam
(next to Mattie Walsh) S:20

Walsh, Mattie M - Died 1991 Born
1918 (next to Joseph Walsh)
S:20

Walsh, Michael Joseph - Died 1976
Feb 12 Born 1900 July 27 (has 2
stones) Was a PFC in US Marine
Corps during World War I (with
wife, Clyda Rae Walsh) S:20

Walter, Katherine M - Died 1983
Born 1900 S:18

Walton, Bessie M - Died 1944 June
18 Born 1888 May 23 (next to
Edward S Greene) S:18

Ward, John HR - Died 1973 Born
1900 (with Josephine M Ward)
S:15

Ward, Josephine M - Died (still
living 1991?) Born 1903 (listed
with John HR Ward) S:15

Ward, Margarette Dwight - Died
1907 Born 1841 (with Elizabeth
Hopkins Myers & others) S:18

Ward, William - Died 1959 May 8
Born 1895 Jan 20 Was in South
Carolina as Private in US Army
during World War I (next to

Ward (Cont.)
other military stones like, David
Davis Grew) S:18

Wardwell, Silas J - Died 1938 Born
1875 S:8

Warner, David A - Died 1865 Jan
21 Son of Albert & Henrietta
Warner (next to mother) S:14

Warner, Henrietta - Died 1865 Feb
19 Age 25 years, 1 month Wife of
Albert Warner (next to child,
David & Rufus Warner) S:14

Warner, Irene A - Died 1983 Born
1891 (with Irving S Warner) S:17

Warner, Irving S - Died 1962 Born
1889 (with Irene A Warner) S:17

Warner, Rufus B - Died 1860 Sept
18 (small stone) Son of Albert &
Henrietta Warner (next to David
A Warner) S:14

Warren, Gladys M - Died 1981
Born 1893 (with Hartley O
Warren) S:14

Warren, Hartley O - Died 1964 Jan
3 Born 1893 Jan 20 From
Massachusetts, was a Private in
Air Service during World War I
(next to Gladys M Warren) S:14

Warren, Helen C - Died 1986 Born
1890 (next to Hartley & Gladys
Warren) S:14

Warren, Marian Munz - Died 1987
Born 1902 (next to Rose L Munz)
(stones are alike) S:20

Warren, Mary Lincoln - Died 1966
Born 1873 Wife of Rev Alfred
Hussey (with him) S:11

Wartiainen, Hilma K - Died 1971
Born 1893 Wife of Peter Wartiainen (with him) S:20

Wartiainen, Peter V - Died 1964
Born 1887 (with wife, Hilma K
Wartiainen) S:20

Washburn, Ann L - Died 1947 Born
1930 (with Martha A Samos)
S:18

Washburn, Charles P - Died 1839
Feb 6 Age 1 years, 9 months Son
of John P & Patience Washburn
S:6

Washburn, John P - Died 1841 Feb
12 Age 9 months, 23 days Son of

Washburn (Cont.)
John P & Patience Washburn
S:6

Washburn, John P - Died 1886
April 14 Age 75 S:9

Washburn, Patience W - Died 1875
Sept 14 Age 68 years, 7 months,
10 days Wife of John Washburn
S:9

Washington, George T - Died 1958
Born 1853 (with wife, Josephine
D Washington) S:18

Washington, Hanson - Died (still
living 1991?) Born 1892 (with
wife, Jessie Bell & Sallie L
Crudup) S:18

Washington, Josephine D - Died
1941 Born 1859 Wife of George
T Washington (with him) S:18

Waterman, Ellen Gray - Died 1883
Jan 19 Age 51 years, 5 months,
6 days Wife of Charles Waterman S:5

Waterman, Helen - Died 1963 Born
1883 (next to Henry Waterman)
S:18

Waterman, Henry - Died 1932
Born 1872 (next to Helen
Waterman) S:18

Watson, Nellie G - Died 1957 Born
1874 (with Eleanor G Stewart)
Stone says, "Nana" S:13

Watt, Alice B - Died 1975 Born
1924 (in Watt plot) S:13

Watt, Robert A - Died 1979 Born
1921 Was a LCDR in US Army
during World War II & Korea (in
Watt plot) S:13

Watt, Robert Stephen - Died 1980
Born 1946 Son of Robert A &
Alice B Watt (next to them) (in
Watt plot) S:13

Watts, Julia A - Died 1899 Born
1809 (has 2 stones) Wife of
William D Watts (with him &
Henry Goodspeed & others) S:18

Watts, Sargent P Jr - Died (still
living 1991?) Born 1946 (with
Sargent P Sr & Florence G
Watts) S:19

Watts, Sargent P Sr - Died 1986
Born 1911 (with wife, Florence G

Watts (Cont.)
Watts & Sargent P Watts Jr)
S:19

Watts, William D - Died 1891 Born
1812 (has 2 stones) (also with
Julia A Watts & Charles & Sarah
Goodspeed & others) S:18

Weatherhead, Bertha L - Died
1974 Born 1882 S:17

Weaver, George F - Died 1880 Aprl
2 Born 1833 Aug 7 (on same
stone with wife, Marg B Weaver)
S:8

Weaver, Julia H - Died 1918 Born
1855 Wife of Robert Fuller (with
him) S:14

Weaver, Mary G - Died 1909 Oct 1
Born 1869 May 29 (buried with
George & Mary Weaver) S:8

Weaver, Mary B - Died 1927 Sept
11 Born 1832 Nov 10 Wife of
George Weaver (buried with her)
S:8

Webb, Abbie - Died 1896 Born
1839 (with Anna W Bodfish)
S:14

Webb, James W - Died 1918 Born
1834 (with Anna W Bodfish)
S:14

Webb, Sarah - Died 1875 July 1
Age 75 Wife of William Webb
S:14

Webber, Erastus - Died 1917 Born
1840 (with Sarah Webber &
others) S:18

Webber, Sarah A - Died 1917 Born
1837 (with Albert Chase & others)
S:18

Weber, Arthur F - Died 1985 Born
1893 Was a Veteran in 5th Division during World War I (also
has veteran star) S:13

Weber, Martha J - Died 1987 Born
1901 S:20

Week, Edward R - Died 1846 Sept
13 Age 3 years, 8 months Son of
Robinson & Sylvia L Week S:7

Weeks, Alice - Died 1870 Nov 24
Born 1861 Oct 5 Daughter of
Robinson & Sylvia L Weeks S:7

Weeks, Alice E - Died 1889 Feb 17
Age 33 years, 11 months Wife of

Weeks (Cont.)
George H Weeks S:5

Weeks, Alven - Died 1841 Oct 18
Age 10 years, 6 months Son of
John & Hannah Weeks (Hinckley
Ceme records #5R says death
was 1844) S:5

Weeks, Barzillia - Died 1805 Nov 7
Age 73 S:5R

Weeks, Benjamin C (Capt) - Died
1859 June 10 Age 46 years, 8
months S:5

Weeks, Celestia B - Died 1870 Born
1830 (with Hiram H Weeks on
family stone) S:12

Weeks, Celia - Died 1856 Feb 18
Age 81 years, 6 months Widow
of Zenas Weeks S:5

Weeks, Content A - Died 1893
March 28 Age 76 years, 11
months Wife of Capt Seth Weeks
S:5R

Weeks, Edward H - Died 1867 Jan
12 Son of Robinson & Sylvia L
Weeks S:7

Weeks, Eleazer - Died 1881 Sept 9
Born 1795 July 25 S:5

Weeks, George W - Died 1902 Born
1835 (with father, Zenas Weeks
Jr) S:13

Weeks, Henry H - Died 1848 May
18 Age 2 years, 7 months Son of
Robinson & Sylvia l Weeks S:7

Weeks, Hiram H - Died 1889 Born
1822 (on Weeks stone with
Celestia B Weeks) S:12

Weeks, John - Died (stone not
clear, located between Alven &
Tryposa Weeks) S:5

Weeks, John - Died 1865 Nov 12
Age 69 S:5R

Weeks, Lucy - Died 1864 Aug 18
Born 1808 June 13 Wife of
Eleazer Weeks S:5

Weeks, Lydia - Died 1804 Oct 17
Age 20 S:5R

Weeks, Mary Λ - Died 1908 Born
1842 (on family stone with
Hiram Weeks) S:12

Weeks, Mary Elma - Died (date not
clear) 19 years, 4 months, 22
days Daughter of Robinson &

Weeks (Cont.)
Sylvia L Weeks S:7
Weeks, Orville D - Died 1955 Born
1859 (on family stone with
Hiram Weeks) S:12
Weeks, Robinson - Died 1904 Born
1816 (entire family buried next
to each other) (wife was Sylvia L
Weeks) S:7
Weeks, Sarah S - Died 1886 Apr 13
Age 76 years, 5 months Widow
of Benjamin Weeks S:5
Weeks, Seth (Capt) - Died 1887
Sept 12 Age 84 years, 6 months
S:5R
Weeks, Sylvia L - Died 1904 Born
1822 (died same year as hus-
band, Robinson, family next to
each other) S:7
Weeks, Tryposa A - Died 1883 Mar
18 Age 6 months Daughter of
John & Louisa W Weeks S:5
Weeks, William Marston - Died
1928 Born 1859 Son of Robin-
son & Sylvia L Weeks S:7
Weeks, Zenas - Died 1840 Oct 15
in his 65th yr S:5
Weeks, Zenas Jr - Died 1876 Born
1804 (with son, George W
Weeks) S:13
Weitlich, Helen M - Died 1972
Born 1892 (with William W
Weitlich) S:15
Weitlich, William W - Died 1969
Born 1891 (with Helen M Weit-
lich) S:15
Welch, Angenora - Died 1867 Born
1837 (with Charles & Esther
Welch) S:18
Welch, Charles W - Died 1894 Born
1824 (with Melvina Welch) S:18
Welch, David A - Died 1952 Born
1860 (with Alton E Robbins)
S:18
Welch, Esther A - Died 1896 Born
1827 (with Charles Welch &
Jacob Hawes & others) S:18
Welch, Julia J - Buried 1984 Dec
24 Age 84 Located in section 8,
lot 109,4th 1/4, grave 1 S:15R
Welch, Melvina - Died (no
dates)(with Charles & Angenora

Welch (Cont.)
Welch & others) S:18
Welch, Sarah - Died (no dates)
(with Charles Welch & Lucy A
Oakes & others) S:18
Welden, Emily - Died 1871 Sept 20
Born 1818 Feb 8 (with George H
Smith & others) S:18
Welden, William C - Died 1885
July 10 Born 1818 Dec 3 (with
Emily Welden & others) S:18
Wellman, Anne B - Died 1972 Born
1883 (with Margaret & F Well-
man) S:20
Wellman, F - Died 1975 Born 1882
(with Anne & Margaret Wellman)
S:20
Wellman, Margaret B - Died (still
living 1991?) Born 1909 (with
Anne & F Wellman) S:20
Welsh, Mary E - Died 1967 Born
1894 Wife of Horace Crosby
(with him) S:12
Wennergren, Frank O - Died 1966
Born 1868 (next to Hulda A
Wennergren) S:20
Wennergren, Hulda A - Died 1963
Born 1875 (next to Frank O
Wennwergren) S:20
Wes, Augustar - Died 1946 Born
1864 Wife of Charles M Jones
(next to him) S:12
Wesselhoeft (Wesselhoelf), Frances
G - Died 1973 Born 1887 (with
Conrad Wesselhoeft) S:11
Wesselhoeft, Conrad - Died 1962
Born 1884 World War I plaque,
1917-18 with flag (with Frances
G Wesselhoelf/Wesselhoeft) S:11
Wesson, Bernice S - Died 1972
Born 1888 S:15
West, Benjamin G (Deacon) - Died
1924 Nov 22 Born 1829 Dec 13
(with Eliza H West stone says,
"Asleep in Jesus") S:13
West, Bennie - Died 1869 Oct 2 Age
4 years, 4 months Son of
Benjamin & Eliza West (two
stones away from them) S:13
West, Bertha - Died 1962 Born
1895 Daughter of Nathan &
Sara West (with them) S:12

West, Charles A - Died 1860 or 1866 Dec 10 (stone worn bad) Son of Nathan & Sarah West S:12

West, Charles A - Died 19 (no other date listed) Born 1862 (listed with wife, Estella A Smith & Eva Estella West, their daughter) S:18

West, Charles Albert - Died 1857 Jan 10 Age 12 years, 3 months Son of James & Temperance West (next to sister, Susan E West) S:13

West, Charlotte A - Died 1864 Aug 27 Age 35 years, 26 days Wife of Benjamin G West (next to him) S:13

West, Christine - Died 1972 Born 1890 Daughter of Nathan & Sara West (with them) S:12

West, Eliza H - Died 1922 June 20 Born 1834 Apeil 14 (with Dea Benjamin G West) S:13

West, Elizabeth Davis - Died 1977 Aug 2 Born 1900 June 28 (next to Howard E West) S:15

West, Esther P - Died 1880 Nov 8 Age 81 years, 8 months Wife of Capt Frances West (next to him) S:12

West, Eva Estella - Died 1928 Born 1887 (with parents, Charles A West & Estella A Smith) S:18

West, Frances (Capt) - Died 1872 Mar 11 Age 76 years, 11 months S:12

West, Frances H - Died 1855 Nov 14 Age 31 years, 10 months He died at Carthagelia SA & removed here 1 July 1869 (next to wife, Josephine S West & Capt Frances & Esther P West) S:12

West, Hannah - Died 1866 July 17 Age 74 years, 7 days Wife of Stephen West (next to him) (stone broken in half, then cemmented back together) S:13

West, Henry J - Died 1976 Born 1894 (with Mary AE West) S:14

West, Howard E - Died 1977 Born 1897 Was Pilot in 402, Lt US

West (Cont.)
Navy (next to Elizabeth Davis West) S:15

West, James - Died 1903 Born 1822 (next to wife, Temperance West) S:13

West, Josephine S - Died 1881 Nov 16 Age 46 years, 7 days Wife of Frances H West (next to him) S:12

West, Mary AE - Died 1966 Born 1893 (with Henry J West) S:14

West, Maryanna - Died 1857 Sept 19 Age 2 years, 9 months Daughter of James & Tryphosa P West (next to mother) Stone says, "Born to suffer and to die" S:13

West, Mehitable S - Died 1874 Born 1825 Stone says, "Mother" (with Robert C West) S:13

West, Nathan E - Died 1928 Born 1864 (with Sara A West) S:12

West, Nathan E (Capt) - Died 1913 Born 1822 (with Sarah P West) S:12

West, Robert C - Died 1862 Born 1827 Stone says,"Father" (with Mehitable S West) S:13

West, Sara A - Died 1927 Born 1869 Wife of Nathan E West (with him) S:12

West, Sarah P - Died 1909 Born 1826 Stone says, "At rest" (with Capt Nathan E West) S:12

West, Stephen - Died 1863 June 9 Age 78 years, 9 months, 9 days (next to Hannah West) S:13

West, Susan Ellen - Died 1848 Aug 20 Age 13 months Daughter of James & Temperance West (next to father) S:13

West, Temperance - Died 1818 Sept 27 Age 28 Wife of James West (next to him) (stone down & broken) S:13

West, Theodore V - Died 1951 Born 1852 (buried with to wife, Ella D Hamlin) S:8

West, Tryphosa P - Died 1909 Born 1819 Wife of James West (next to Maryanna West, daughter)

West (Cont.)
S:13

Westgate, Bryan R - Died 1983 Feb 5 Born 1955 June 28 Stone says, "Beloved husband" S:20

Wetherbee, Edith L - Died 1986 Born 1917 Wife of Frederick D Wetherbee (with her & others) (has Military stone too Says, "Edith Nordling Wetherbee") S:12

Wetherbee, Frederick D - Died 1974 Sept 14 Born 1908 April 16 (there is a military stone too, "OM1 US Navy") (with Frederick E Parker & wife, Edith L Wetherbee & others S:12

Wetherbee, Hattie M - Died 1936 Born 1870 (with Frederick E Parker & others) S:12

Wetherbee, J Duncan - Died 1935 Born 1871 (with Frederick E Parker & others) S:12

Wetherbee, Marion Estella - Died 1914 Apr 16 Born 1853 Aug 29 (buried next to Chloe J Hamblin) S:8

Wheeler, Agnes M - Died 1964 Born 1891 S:17

Wheeler, Bradley Hall - Died 1989 July 2 Born 1063 Aug 4 (a golf club,glove & ball were left at grave) Stone says, "Life flies by so fast You hardly get a chance to realize it So get a hold of what you can, and make the best of it" S:11

Wheeler, Harold W - Died 1986 Born 1901 Was a Pvt in US Army during World War II (has 2 stones) (with wife, Nellie F Wheeler & daughter, Barbara Jenkins) S:20

Wheeler, Herbert W - Died 1987 Born 1920 (has 2 stones) Was a Sgt in US Army (with Jean A Wheeler) S:20

Wheeler, Jean A - Died (still living 1991?) Born 1923 (listed with Herbert W Wheeler) S:20

Wheeler, Nellie F - Died 1985 Born 1901 Wife of Harold Wheeler

Wheeler (Cont.)
(with him & daughter, Barbara Jenkins) S:20

Whelden, Abigail T - Died 1910 Oct 9 Born 1836 Dec 14 (buried with Elizabeth Matthews & others) S:8

Whelden, Anna M - Died 1864 Sept 21 Age 28 years, 1 month, 3 days (a tall white monument near church) S:10

Whelden, Asenath - Died 1835 Mar 15 in her 65th yr Wife of Eben Whelden (buried next to him) S:5

Whelden, Bela - Died 1849 Oct 11 in the 58th yr S:5

Whelden, Berinthia D - Died 1858 Feb 26 in her 56th yr Wife of Chipman Whelden S:5

Whelden, Calvin - Died 1839 Apr 22 in his 2nd yr Son of Eben & Eliza Whelden S:5

Whelden, Chester H - Died 1955 Born 1874 (with Flora B Whelden & others) S:18

Whelden, Chipman - Died 1878 Oct 30 Age 73 years, 8 months S:5

Whelden, Clarissa - Died 1872 Oct 27 in her 78th yr Widow of Bela Whelden (stone not clear) S:5

Whelden, Clarissa Mrs - Died 1849 Oct 11 Age 58 Widow of Bela Whelden S:5R

Whelden, Eben - Died 1887 Nov 11 Age 78 years, 7 months S:5

Whelden, Ebenezer - Died 1844 Dec 23 in his 85th yr (buried next to wife Asenath) S:5

Whelden, Eliza A - Died 1845 Nov 20 in her 39th yr Wife of Eben Whelden S:5

Whelden, Eliza D - Died 1872 Feb 2 Age 67 Born 1805 Jan 10 S:5

Whelden, Emily E - Died 1928 Born 1851 (with Chester H Whelden & others) S:18

Whelden, Frederick - Died 1839 Apr 19 Age 4 Son of Eben & Eliza Whelden S:5

Whelden, Frederick - Died 1912 Sept 11 Born 1844 Dec 2 (a

Whelden (Cont.)
large family stone in middle of
cemetery, with Isadore Smith
Whelden & others) S:11

Whelden, George H - Died 1871
Nov 14 Age 51 years 4 months
12 days Stone says,"Fruitful to
the end" (a tall white monument
near church) S:10

Whelden, Hannah - Died 1816 Mar
24 Wife of Peter Whelden (buried
next to him) S:5

Whelden, Herbert Walter - Died
1856 Sept 13 Age 9 months 20
days Son of George H & Mary C
Whelden S:10

Whelden, Isaac - Died 1893 Dec 1
Age 94 years, 6 months Born
1799 May 26 S:5

Whelden, Isaac H - Died 1863 Nov
20 (Hinckley Ceme records #5R
says death was at age 26) S:5

Whelden, James F - Died 1876
Born 1847 (with Emily E Whelden & others) S:18

Whelden, Joseph W - Died 1866
July 8 Age 44 years, 6 months,
24 days Died at sea on board the
ship USS Macedonian (listed
next to wife, Lorena S Whelden)
S:21

Whelden, Lorena S - Died 1868
April 23 Age ? (stone worn) Wife
of Joseph W Whelden (next to
him) S:21

Whelden, Mary C - Died 1858 June
16 Age 26 years, 9 months (A
tall white monument near
church) S:10

Whelden, Peter - Died 1846 Apr 26
in his 75th yr S:5

Whelden, Samuel P - Died 1890
Apr 10 Age 41 Born 1849 (Hinckley Ceme records #5R says death
was 1880) S:5

Whelden, Serena - Died 1882 Born
1822 (with James F Wheldon &
others) S:18

Whelden, Susan Miss - Died 1853
Oct 22 in her 60th yr S:5

Whelden, Walter H - Died 1856
Sept 13 Age 9 months 20 days (a

Whelden (Cont.)
tall white monument located
near church) S:10

Whelden, William G (or C) - Died
1891 Oct 23 Age 47 S:5

Whelden, Zelia L - Died 1902 Born
1814 Widow of Chipman Whel-
den S:5

Wheldon, Anna M - Died 1864 Sept
21 Age 28 years,1 month,3 days
(next to Walter H Wheldon) S:10

Wheldon, Arunah - Died 1898 Born
1820 (with Serena Whelden &
others) S:18

Wheldon, George H - Died 1871
Nov 14 Age 51 years 4 months
12 days Stone says, "Faithful to
the end" (next to Mary C Wheldon) S:10

Wheldon, Mary C - Died 1858 June
16 Age 26 years, 9 months S:10

Wheldon, Samuel - Died 1876 Feb
1 Age 53 years, 8 months, 11
days S:6

Wheldon, Walter - Died 1839 Sept
11 Age 23 S:6

Whihtman, Emma - Died 1853
Sept Daughter of John & Emma
Whihtman (?) S:10

Whitcomb, Franklin L - Died 1949
July 26 Born 1862 Mar 5 (A
large crypt with others there who
died a recent date) S:8

White, ?eso Cyrus C - Died 1843
Age 21 days (stone not clear)
Son of Evander & Eliza White
(with mother) S:21

White, Abby I Mrs - Died 1836 Sept
5 Age 34 (there is a stone missing next to her) Wife of Evander
C White (near him) S:21

White, Azubah F - Died 1928 Born
1873 (buried with Horace M
Bearse) S:8

White, Betsey B - Died 1894 Jan
16 Age 74 years, 28 days Stone
says, "Only gone home" (next to
Zenas M White) S:21

White, Donald P - Died 1981 Born
1932 Was a Sargeant in US
Army in Korea (has Korea plaque
too) S:19

White, Donald Seymour - Died 1990 Born 1896 Was 2nd Lt in US Army during World War I S:15

White, Edna S - Died 1963 Born 1913 (there is an old stone cross near her with no markings) S:31

White, Eliza Ann Mrs - Died 1843 Dec 31 Age 31 Wife of Evander C White (next to him & with ?eso Cyrus C White, her son) S:21

White, Euphena M - Died (no date) Born 1847 (listed with Nelson C White) S:21

White, Evander C - Died 1885 Dec 8 Age 76 years, 3 months, 27 days (next to wife, Eliza Ann White) S:21

White, George - Died 1887 Apr 1 Age 59 years, 10 months S:5

White, Joan Marie - Died 1968 Aug 15 Born 1933 Feb 12 From Massachusetts, FFC? US Army S:20

White, John D - Died 1935 Born 1852 (with wife, Minnie C White) S:18

White, Lucy C - Died 1873 Apr 17 Age 38 years, 4 months Wife of George White S:5

White, Mary Lizzie - Died 1878 Jan 18 Age 15 years, 3 months, 16 days Daughter of Lucy White S:5

White, Minnie C - Died 1927 Born 1871 Wife of John D White (with him) S:18

White, Nelson C - Died 1913 Born 1839 (with Euphena White) S:21

White, Rebecca N - Died 1923 Born 1853 (with Richard B, Copeland) S:18

White, Walter H - Died 1960 Born 1888 (with wife, Zora Coffin) S:12

White, Zenas M - Died 1834? Jan 10 Age 18 months Son of Evander & Abby White (next to possible sister, Betsey B White) S:21

Whitehead, Anna M Fouquett - Died 1953 Jan 6 Born 1894 Sept 20 Stone says, "Mom" S:16

Whitehead, Della - Died 1944 Born 1880 (with Silas V Whitehead) S:12

Whitehead, Frances Tripp - Died 1976 Born 1897 S:11

Whitehead, Silas V - Died 1952 Born 1874 (with Della Whitehead) S:12

Whiteley, A Hope - Died (still living in 1991) Born 1921 Wife of Leonard Cloud (listed with him) S:13

Whiteley, Ada - Died 1966 Born 1888 Wife of Henry A Whiteley Sr (with him & Julia O McGlothlin) S:13

Whiteley, Elmer S - Died 1979 Born 1905 (with Florence M Whiteley) S:12

Whiteley, Florence M - Died (still living in 1991?) Born 1905 Wife of Elmer S Whiteley (listed with him) S:12

Whiteley, Helen M - Died 1980 Born 1893 (next to William T Whiteley) S:12

Whiteley, Henry A Sr - Died 1955 Born 1890 (with Ada Whiteley) S:13

Whiteley, William T - Died 1958 Dec 29 Born 1893 Jan 3 Also, a veteran plaque which says, "Private in Massachusetts Company F, 307 Engineers during World War 1" (next to Helen M Whiteley) S:12

Whitford, Caleb E - Died 1904 Born 1842 (very large family stone) Was in Battery E, RI Light Artillery (buried with possibly, wife, Drusilla Whitford) S:8

Whitford, Drusilla D - Died 1949 Born 1950 (buried with Caleb Whitford) S:8

Whitford, Elbert S - Died 1935 Born 1868 (buried with Grace w Whitford & others) (back of this stone says "Phinney") (Grace was his wife) S:8

Whitford, Grace W - Died 1928 Born 1872 Wife of Elbert S Whitford, buried with him &

Whitford (Cont.)
others Stone says, "Phinney" S:8

Whiting, ? - Died 1974 July 11 (stone not clear) Daughter of William & Laura Whiting (next to Walter R Whiting Jr) S:19

Whiting, Henry J - Died 1977 Born 1910 S:20

Whiting, Phillips C - Died 1988 Born 1898 (undertaker plaque only) S:15

Whiting, Walter R Jr - Died 1969 Feb 17 Born 1893 Aug 20 (also has Veteran plaque) Was a Sargeant in US Army during World War I, from Massachusetts (next to ? Whiting) S:19

Whitman, Archie R - Died 1967 Born 1897 (with Marion Wood, wife) S:19

Whitman, Bertha - Died 1879 Feb 23 Born 1878 Dec 10 S:5

Whitman, Bertha - Died 1879 Feb 23 Born 1878 Dec 10 S:5

Whitman, Bertha Florence - Died 1870 Jan 25 Age 2 years, 11 months, 10 days Daughter of Josiah B & Lydia A Whitman S:5

Whitman, Clarence Herbert - Died 1883 Feb 5 Age 8 years, 6 months, 27 days Son of Josiah B & Lydia A Whitman S:5

Whitman, Cyrus F - Died 1864 Oct 7 Age 16 years, 6 months, 26 days Son of Jonas & Lydia Whitman S:5

Whitman, George Herbert - Died 1848 Aug 21 Age 3 years, 8 months, 14 days Son of Isaac & Eliza Whitman S:6

Whitman, George W - Died 1864 Jan 20 Age 23 years, 9 months, 14 days (at Gold Hill, Nevada) Son of Jonas & Lydia Whitman S:5

Whitman, Henry - Died 1877 Nov 6 Born 1877 Nov 4 Son of H & E Whitman S:5

Whitman, Isaac - Died 1865 Feb 27 Age 61 years, 3 months, 20 days S:6

Whitman, Isaac Henry - Died 1849

Whitman (Cont.)
Oct 26 Age 19 years, 21 days (died in Liverpool, England) Son of Isaac & Eliza Whitman (stone next to fathers) S:6

Whitman, John Esq - Died 1816 Sept 6 in his 34th yr S:5

Whitman, Jonas - Died 1805 Age 18 years, 11 months, 2 days Born 1787 Apr 8 Son of Dr Jonas Whitman S:5

Whitman, Jonas Dr - Died 1824 July 21 in his 75th yr S:5

Whitman, Mercy G - Died 188? Sept 10 (stone not clear) Age 63 S:5

Whitman, Rachel - Died 1851 Aug 30 Born 1802 Feb 8 Widow of Samuel Whitman S:5

Whitman, Samuel - Died 1842 Mar 14 Born 1779 April 1 (buried next to wife, Rachel) S:5

Whitney, Ernest W - Died 1960 Born 1904 Chief of Barnstable Fire Department (flag at stone) S:11

Whitney, Gladys C - Died 1969 Born 1887 (with William B Whitney) S:18

Whitney, William B - Died 1955 Born 1888 (with Gladys C Whitney) S:18

Whitted, Julian H - Died 1976 Born 1897 Was a Corporal in US Army during World War I S:18

Whittemore, Augustus W - Died 1925 Born 1857 (with Hattie L Whittemore) S:21

Whittemore, Betsey - Died 1897 Born 1822 (with Joseph Whittemore) S:19

Whittemore, Ellen - Died 1934 Born 1850 S:31

Whittemore, Hattie L - Died 1941 Born 1858 (with Augustus W Whittemore) S:21

Whittemore, Hiram - Died 1903 Nov 3 Born 1860 Oct 1 (with wife, Nellie F Whittemore & others) S:19

Whittemore, Joseph - Died 1894 Born 1819 (with Betsey

Whittemore (Cont.)
Whittemore) S:19

Whittemore, Lorena T - Died 1983
June 15 Born 1900 Feb 5 S:15

Whittemore, Louisa - Died 1891
Born 1852 (with Maria Whittemore & next to Joseph Whittemore) S:19

Whittemore, Maria - Died 1857
Born 1854 (with Louisa Whittemore) S:19

Whittemore, Nellie F - Died 1933
Dec 10 Born 1861 Sept 29 Wife
of Hiram Whittemore (With him
& Ida & Leo Butterfield) S:19

Wholey, John T Sr - Died 1984
Born 1906? Husband of Helen C
Wholey S:16

Wiinaikainen, Wilhemina - Died
1957 Born 1882 (with Otto
Wiinikainen in family plot) S:11

Wiinikainen, Arvi A - Died 1972
April 2 Born 1909 Mar 22 (in
family plot) S:11

Wiinikainen, L Mary - Died (still
living 1991?) Born 1907 (with
Victor Wiinikainen) S:20

Wiinikainen, Olavi V - Died 1987
Born 1920 (another large family
stone with name on it) He was a
TEC 5, US Army during World
war II Flag at grave S:11

Wiinikainen, Otto - Died 1943
Born 1874 (with Wilhemina
Wiinikainen in family plot) S:11

Wiinikainen, Otto E - Died 1956
Jan 18 Born 1916 Jan 16 He
was a Cpl in 78th Airdrome,
Squad AAF, Mass during World
War II (flag at grave, in family
plot) S:11

Wiinikainen, Victor A - Died 1965
Born 1909 (with L Mary Wiinikainen) S:20

Wilbar, Chester H - Died 1942 Born
1869 (with Nellie E Wilbar &
others) S:18

Wilbar, Leonard Goodrich - Died
1919 Born 1901 (with Chester H
Wilbar & others) S:18

Wilbar, Nellie E - Died 1937 Born
1865 (with Leonard Goodrich

Wilbar (Cont.)
Wilbar & others) S:18

Wilcox, Delores E - Died 1990 Born
1927 Stone says,"She gave so
much & asked so little" S:20

Wilcox, Josephine - Died 1917 May
23 Age 77 years, 11 months, 7
days S:21

Wilcox, M Eleanor - Died 1989
Born 1914 (a large rose quartz
stone with a Wilcox plaque put
on it) S:20

Wilder, Thomas - Died 1846 June
24 Age 59 S:1

Wiley, David - Died 1840 July 1
Age 3 months Son of Samuel
Wiley (with David F & Esther P
Wiley) S:12

Wiley, David F - Died 1836 April 18
Age 1 month Son of Samuel
Wiley (with Esther P & David
Wiley) S:12

Wiley, Esther P - Died 1836 Mar 17
Age 4 Daughter of Samuel Wiley
(with David F Wiley) S:12

Wiley, Fannie L - Died 1855 Mar
10 Born 1851 Oct 15 Daughter
of Samuel Wiley & Penelope
Waitt (with them and others on
Wiley/Scudder stone) S:12

Wiley, Lucy H - Died 1879 June 19
Born 1799 Oct 30 Wife of
Samuel A Wiley (next to him)
S:12

Wiley, Samuel A - Died 1885 Sept
23 Born 1798 Jan 23 (with wife,
Lucy H Wiley) S:12

Wiley, Samuel S - Died 1856 May
22 Born 1827 Aug 13 (On
Scudder/Wiley stone) (with
Penelope Waitt & others) S:12

Wilkins, Rose A - Died 1854 Sept 1
Age 22 years, 1 month, 4 days
Wife of Capt Charles Wilkins S:6

Willbur (or Willbair), Abby Ann -
Died 1841 Jan 12 Age 15
months, 20 days (last name not
clear) Daughter of George & Eliza
Willbur or Willbair (next to Esek
& George A Willbur or Willbair)
S:21

Willbur (or Willbair), Esek H - Died

Willbur (Cont.)
1837 Oct 7 Age 2 years, 2 months, 15 days Died at North Providence Son of George & Eliza Willbur or Willbair (next to sister, Abby Ann Willbur or Willbair) S:21

Willbur (or Willbair), George A - Died 1845 Aug 30 Age 30 months (stone not clear, worn) Son of George & Eliza Willbur or Willbair (with Esek? H Willbur or Willbair) S:21

William, Evelyn C - Died (still living) Born 1912 Mar 19 Wife of James Goff (with him) S:12

Williams, Abbie L - Died 1941 Born 1865 (with George Williams) S:12

Williams, Albert D - Died 1937 Born 1886 (with John W Williams & others) S:13

Williams, Alonzo S - Died 1889 Born 1886 (with John W Williams & others) S:13

Williams, Anna L - Died 1971 Born 1888 (with John W Williams & others) S:13

Williams, Bessie S - Died 1956 Born 1868 (with John W Williams & others) S:13

Williams, Cornelia - Died 1903 Born 1838 Widow of Nathaniel Bacon (with him) S:18

Williams, Edith B - Died 1984 Born 1893 S:12

Williams, Edward C - Died 1966 Born 1876 (listed with Placide Davis & Margaret M Williams) S:17

Williams, Edward O - Died 1936 Born 1865 (with wife, Joetta F Williams & others) S:19

Williams, Elizabeth E - Died 1943 Born 1864 S:18

Williams, Ethel M - Died 1948 Born 1876 Stone says,"Mother" (with John P Williams) S:18

Williams, Florence M - Died 1978 Aug 19 Born 1896 Nov 3 (with husband, Lester W Williams) S:15

Williams, Frank H - Died 1940 Born 1860 (with Carrie M Rich) S:12

Williams, Fred L - Died 1942 Born 1883 (next to wife, Karen M Rogeberg) S:12

Williams, Frederick A - Died 1911 Born 1866 (with Susan A Williams) S:14

Williams, George - Died 1944 Born 1863 (with Abbie L Williams) S:12

Williams, George Jr - Died 1894 Born 1894 (with George Williams) S:12

Williams, Grace - Died 1953 Born 1874 S:13

Williams, Hannah L - Died 1898 Dec 10 Born 1830 March 20 (between John H & Isabel H Williams) S:13

Williams, Helen Steans - Died 1983 Born 1892 S:13

Williams, Isabel H - Died 1888 Dec 29 Age 38 years, 2 months, 21 days (next to Hannah L Williams) S:13

Williams, Jiell - Died 1825 Aug 25 Age 22 1/2 months Daughter of Zenas D & Mary Bassell (next to this stone is Mary Howland, widow of same parents above? Error? Is this person a Howland or Williams?) S:4

Williams, John H - Died 1905 June 30 Born 1816 July 2 (next to Hannah L Williams) S:13

Williams, John P - Died 1932 Born 1875 Stone says,"Father" (with Ethel M Williams) S:18

Williams, John W - Died 1935 Born 1852 (with Bessie S Williams) S:13

Williams, Lester W - Died 1973 Dec 3 Born 1893 Oct 25 (with wife, Florence M Williams) S:15

Williams, Margaret M - Died 1961 Born 1874 (with Edward C Williams & Placide Davis) S:17

Williams, Millie P - Died 1970 Born 1879 (with Richard Soule & others) S:18

Williams, Olieve - Died 1957 Born 1899 (undertaker plaque only) S:17

Williams, Ralph R - Died 1974 Born 1899 (with Edith B Williams) S:12

Williams, Susan A - Died 1958 Born 1871 (with Frederick Williams) S:14

Williams, Victor - Died 1890 Born 1890 (with George Williams) S:12

Williams, Williams, Joetta F - Died 1963 Born 1870 Wife of Edward O Williams (with him & Clifford H Howe & others) S:19

Williamson (Harper), Florence May - Died 1962 Born 1881 S:12

Williamson, Anton - Died 1961 Born 1880 (with Selma C Williamson) S:14

Williamson, Selma C - Died 1970 Born 1879 (next to Anton Williamson) S:14

Willis, Abbie - Died 1937 Jan 18 Born 1858 Nov 14 Daughter of Uberto C & Mary Crosby S:8

Willison, Rachel - Died 1874 Nov 10 Age 33 years, 6 months Wife of John Willison S:9

Willman, Filemon - Died 10 P 1977 Kudli Marrask (death date) Born, 15 P 1892 Ref Synt Kesak (this must be in their foreign language) (next to Maria Willman) S:11

Willman, Maria - Died Death, 9 P 1927 Kudli MuHTiK Born, 20 P 1890 Ref Synt Tammik (this entry must be in their foreign language) (next to Filemon Willman) S:11

Willppey, Hannah M - Died 18?? April 21 (stone not clear) (next to Hurly J Willppey) S:12

Willppey, Hurly J - Died 1884? (stone not clear) (possibly was in service corps) (next to Hannah M Willppey) S:12

Wills, John - Died 1891 Born 1807 Unitarian minister of this church for 5 years S:9

Wilson, Clarisa - Died 1922 Jan 22 Born 1836 Jan 31 (with William Wilson & others) S:18

Wilson, Cleveland I (Rev) - Died 1962 (listed with Estelle M Wilson (Howard)) S:13

Wilson, Estelle M (Howard) - Died (still living 1991?) (listed with Rev Cleveland I Wilson) S:13

Wilson, Gertrude A (Major) - Died 1975 May 10 Born 1895 July 30 Was in Nurse Corps, in US Army during World War II (with Capt Marion E Foley) S:16

Wilson, John - Died 1868 Born 1814 (next to John R Wilson) S:10

Wilson, John R - Died 1921 Born 1846 S:10

Wilson, Sarah (Bourne) - Died 1901 Born 1823 S:10

Wilson, William H - Died 1897 Nov 30 Born 1828 Oct 7 (with Clarisa Wilson & others) S:18

Winchell, Alfred L - Died 1976 Born 1902 S:19

Winchell, Elvin D - Died 1934 Born 1876 (with wife, Jessie Libby) S:19

Winchell, George - Died 1976 Born 1938 (next to Vicki L Winchell) S:19

Winchell, Vicki L - Died 1971 Aug 13 Born 1971 June 16 (next to George Winchell) S:19

Wing, Albert Baker - Died (no date) Born 1881 (with wife, Lena Lewis & son, Albert Baker) S:18

Wing, Charles H - Died 1917 Born 1850 (with wife, Isabel M Wing) S:18

Wing, Isabel M - Died 1945 Born 1859 wife of Charles H Wing (with him) S:18

Wing, Mary E - Died 1953 Born 1898 (with Eunice Mildred Crocker) S:14

Wing, Roselle A - Died 1984 Born 1896 (others listed with later dates) (with Russell M Wing) S:14

Wing, Russell M - Died (still living

Wing (Cont.)
1991?) Born 1898 (with Roselle A Wing) S:14

Wing, Thomas B - Died 1825 Sept 8 Age 21 (written in pencil in records) S:26R

Winkelmann, Herbert A Dr - Died 1985 June 6 Born 1893 May 3 (on same stone with Danford A Parker & others) S:11

Winkelmann, Marion (Parker) - Died 1965 Dec 14 Born 1890 Dec 14 (on same stone with Danford A Parker & others) S:11

Winship, Edward C - Died 1807 Sept 27 Age 7 months Son of Damuel & Polly Winship S:10

Winship, Mary Mrs - Died 1809 Aug 31 in her 26th yr Wife of Samuel Winship S:10

Winslow, Nathan F - Died 1862 Born 1839 Was in Company #11, 35th Regiment of the Massachusetts Volunteers S:2

Wintringham, John S - Died 1987 Born 1910 (next to Kathryn F Wintringham) S:11

Wintringham, Kathryn F - Died 1964 Born 1910 (next to John S Wintringham) S:11

Wirtanen, George E - Died 1980 Born 1911 (with Ann M Roycroft) S:20

Wirtanen, Richard - Died 1958 Born 1886 (with William Wirtanen) S:20

Wirtanen, William - Died 1977 Born 1881 (with Richard Wirtanen) S:20

Wirth, Clarence E - Died 1961 Born 1873 (with Sarah L Wirth) S:8

Wirth, Sarah L - Died 1946 Born 1880 S:8

Wiseman, George P - Died 1970 Nov 2 Born 1899 March 30 From Massachusetts, was E2 in US Navy during World War I S:16

Withington, Elida A - Died 1878 April 26 Age 19 (stone not clear) Daughter of James & Ablfe? Withington (next to Abigail B

Withington (Cont.)
Taylor) S:19

Witikainen, Amalia - Died 1951 Born 1886 Wife of John Witikainen (with him & Karolina Pentti) S:18

Witikainen, John - Died 1947 Born 1882 He was a Mason (with wife, Amalia Witikainen) S:18

Wittenmeyer, Bessie H - Died 1962 Born 1903 (with Harold F Wittenmeyer) S:21

Wittenmeyer, Harold F - Died 1963 Born 1904 (with Bessie H Wittenmeyer) S:21

Witton, Charles J - Died 1966 Aug 18 Born 1893 March 3 From Massachusetts, was Pvt in CoA, Millitary Police during World War I (next to Dora Witton) S:17

Witton, Dora - Died 1986 Born 1896 (next to Charles J Witton) S:17

Wolf, Harvey F - Died 1951 Born 1890 (with son, Richard E Wolf & Harvey F Wolf) S:18

Wolf, Harvey F - Died 1967 Born 1892 (with Harvey F & Richard E Wolf) S:18

Wolf, Richard E - Died 1940 Born 1919 (Coat of Arms on stone) Son Harvey & Dora Wolf (with father & Harvey F Wolf) S:18

Wolsieffer, Martha J - Died 1976 Born 1887 S:15

Wood, Abby - Died 1889 May 8 Age 75 years, 3 months Wife of Browning K Wood (with him & others) S:18

Wood, Ada W - Died 1880 Born 1855 S:2

Wood, Browning K (Capt) - Died 1885 May 18 Age 72 years, 11 months (next to wife, Abby Wood & others) S:18

Wood, Coloss - Died 1879 Oct 12 Age 79 years, 4 months, 18 days S:2

Wood, Edward E - Died 1928 Born 1855 (with Capt Browning K Wood & others) S:18

Wood, Luther S - Died 1882 Jan 5

Wood (Cont.)
Born 1847 Aug 17 S:2

Wood, Marion - Died 1987 Born 1896 Wife of Archie Whitman (with him & Alfred B Noyes) S:19

Wood, Martha - Died 1765 (rest of stone not clear) (next to Infant, Bacon, daughter of John & Eliza Bacon) S:9

Wood, Martha A - Died 1904 Born 1832 S:7

Wood, Mary W - Died 1933 Born 1862 (next to Edward E Wood & others) S:18

Wood, Temperance - Died 1842 Jan 19 in her 77th yr Widow of Ansell Wood S:4

Wood, Waterman W - Died 1896 Born 1834 S:7

Woodbury, Colin P - Died 1928 Born 1890 (with Mae E Woodbury) S:18

Woodbury, George O - Died 1925 March 21 S:18

Woodbury, Hammon - Died 1914 Born 1838 (buried next to Charles Lee Howe) S:8

Woodbury, Lillian - Died 1955 Born 1890 S:30R

Woodbury, Mae E - Died 1941 Born 1889 (with Colin P Woodbury) S:18

Woodbury, Marston - Died 1953 Born 1883 S:30R

Woodland, Carolyn J - Died (still living 1991?) Born 1912 (with Louis Woodland) S:20

Woodland, Louis A - Died (still living 1991?) Born 1909 (listed with Carolyn J Woodland) S:20

Woodruff, Ann I Creelman - Died 1980 Born 1904 S:19

Woodruff, Victor D - Died 1981 Feb 5 Born 1898 Aug 8 Was in US Navy during World War I S:15

Woods, Emeline - Died 1873 Aug 25 Age 69 years, 1 month, 16 days S:2

Woodward, Gertrude S - Died 1964 Born 1891 (with husband, James A Woodward) S:15

Woodward, James A - Died 1973

Woodward (Cont.)
Born 1889 (with wife, Gertude S Woodward) S:15

Woodworth, Henry - Died 1864 Born 1847 (on large Paine, Titcomb & Brown stone) S:11

Woodworth, Marcia - Died 1935 Born 1860 (on large Paine, Titcomb & Brown stone) S:11

Worrell, Elisha Bacon - Died 1943 June 6 Born 1858 Sept 6 (buried with Helen F W Hill, husband) S:8

Worrell, Hannah R - Died 1894 Nov 26 Born 1816 Aug 24 (stone says "Precious in the sight of the lord is the death of his saints") S:8

Worrell, James - Died 1887 May 21 Born 1813 Jan 1 (stone says- I am the resurrection and the life) S:8

Worrell, Josiah - Died 1860 Jan 3 Age 6 years, 5 months, 15 days (stone says- ? of the kingdom of god) Son of James & Hannah Worrell (buried next to them) S:8

Woungberg, Mollie Davis - Died 1939 Born 1881 (buried with Henry Davis, very large stone) S:8

Wright, Alice May - Died 1915 Born 1876 (with Wesley L Wright) S:14

Wright, Benjamin - Died 1843 Sept 2 Age 68 (buried with daughter, Chloe Wright - On same stone) S:5

Wright, Benjamin (Capt) - Died 1817 Feb Age 43 Lost at sea (listed with Benjamin C Wright) S:13

Wright, Benjamin C - Died 1854 June 14 Age 20 (with William W & Capt Benjamin Wright) S:13

Wright, Blanche - Died 1942 Born 1878 (buried with Claribel & Herbert Wright) S:8

Wright, Chloe - Died 1833 Apr 16 Age 10 Daughter of Benjamin Wright (buried with him) S:5

Wright, Claribel - Died 1922 Born

Wright (Cont.)
1846 (buried with Herbert G
Wright & Blanche Wright) S:8

Wright, Delacy Jr - Died 1984 Born
1896 Was a Private in US Army
during World War 1 S:18

Wright, Donald D - Died (no date)
Born 1897 (listed with Gladys M
Wright) S:18

Wright, Eliza A - Died 1875 April 3
Age 23 years, 5 months, 6 days
Wife of Robert L Wright S:18

Wright, Eunice C - Died 1889 Nov
20 Age 80 years,6 months,16
daus Wife of Capt Benjamin
Wright (listed with him) S:13

Wright, Gladys M - Died 1988 Born
1897 (with Donald D Wright)
S:18

Wright, Herbert G - Died 1938
Born 1846 (buried with Claribel
Wright) S:8

Wright, Isaiah - Died 1863 Born
1822 (Hinckley Cem records #5R
says "He was shot and instantly
killed near his own home on the
evening of Jan 10 at age of 41
years, 7 months") S:5

Wright, Mary E - Died 1835 Nov 28
Age 28 years, 4 months, Wife of
Asa Wright S:4

Wright, Mary H - Died 1834 July 5
Age 13 years, 6 months Daughter of Asa & Mary E Wright S:4

Wright, Preston A - Died 1928 Born
1863 (with Teresa Daniel Wright)
S:31

Wright, Sarah G - Died 1885 May
18 Age 64 years, 9 months Wife
of Capt Zenas W Wright S:5R

Wright, Teresa Daniel - Died 1973
Born 1884 (with Preston A
Wright) S:31

Wright, Wesley L - Died 1950 Born
1869 (with Alice May Wright)
S:14

Wright, Wilhelmina C - Died 1957
Born 1870 S:17

Wright, William - Died 1836 Jan 1
Age 4 years, 5 months, 15 days
Son of Asa & Mary H Wright S:4

Wright, William W - Died 1884 Aug

Wright (Cont.)
3 Age 17 Killed falling from ship,
Crissa in the Indian Ocean
(listed with Ben C & Capt Ben
Wright) S:13

Wyer, Adalaide C - Died 1919 Born
1867 (with William F Wyer &
others) S:21

Wyer, Adelena - Died 1880 April 24
Age 2 years, 2 months Born
1878 (has two stones) Daughter
of William & Adalaide Wyer (with
them) S:21

Wyer, Isabella - Died (no dates)
Wife of George Wagoner (listed
with him) S:21

Wyer, Phebe S - Died 1873 Feb 14
Age 71 years, 9 months S:18

Wyer, William F - Died 1907 Born
1860 (with Adelena Wyer &
others) S:21

Wyer, William Jay (Capt) - Died
1913 Born 1822 (with Adalaide
C Wyer & others) S:21

Wyman, Charles G - Died 1910
June 9 Born 1847 July 14 (with
Irving W Walker & others) S:18

Wyman, Mary E - Died 1966 Born
1889 S:15

Xinogaly, (Baby) - Died 1929 Feb 6
(with Philip & Lillian Xinogaly)
S:19

Xinogaly, Lillian B - Died 1987
Born 1906 (with Philip & (Baby)
Xinogaly) S:19

Xinogaly, Philip C - Died 1976
Born 1906 (with Lillian & (Baby)
Xinogaly) S:19

Yakola, August J - Died 1966 Born
1885 (with Lena Yakola) S:20

Yakola, Frank - Died 1985 Born
1915 (with Frank August Yakola)
S:20

Yakola, Frank August -. Died 1956
Feb 4 Born 1937 May 5 From
Massachusetts, was A3C in
3665 BSC Militia TNG, GP AF
(with Frank Yakola) S:20

Yakola, Lena - Died 1968 Born
1882 (with August Yakola) S:20

Yankus, Dominick - Died 1960
Born 1881 S:16

Yankus, Margaret - Died 1958 Born 1878 Wife of Peter Yankus (with him) S:16

Yankus, Peter - Died 1947 Born 1875 (with wife, Margaret Yankus) S:16

York, Emily E - Died 1906 Born 1859 (with John York & others in York plot on street) S:13

York, Florence B - Died 1927 Born 1866 Wife of Herbert York (with him & others in York plot on street) S:13

York, Herbert W - Died 1932 Born 1864 (with John York & others in York plot on street) S:13

York, Hilton W - Died 1904 Born 1893 (with John York & others in York plot on street) S:12

York, Jane D - Died 1965 Born 1891 Wife of Herbert W York (with him & others on street) S:13

York, John - Died 1876 Born 1816 (large York plot on street with others) S:13

York, John W - Died 1861 Born 1857 (with John York & others on street in York plot) S:13

York, Julia E - Died 1909 Born 1823 Wife of John York (with him & others on street in York plot) S:13

Youdell, Margaret I - Died 1879 Sept 15 Age 59 years, 4 months Stone says, "Rest, sister" S:5R

Young, (infant) - Died 1822 April 11 Daughter of A & SOE ? (between Betsey & Deborah Young) S:10

Young, (male) - Died (stone very small & broken at ground level) Son of Joseph Young S:10

Young, za?(Louisza?) - Died (stone is very small and front worn off) Daughter? of Bangs & Hannah Young S:10

Young, Abbie E - Died 1893 Born 1866 (next to George Young) S:19

Young, Agnes M - Died 1983 Born 1894 (with John B, Mary T &

Young (Cont.)
Arthur J Oliver) S:31

Young, Albertina - Died 1972 Born 1907 Wife of Irving F Coleman (with him) S:13

Young, Alexander - Died 1935 Born 1888 S:16

Young, Alice AH - Died 1904 Jan 23 Born 1850 July 9 S:12

Young, Anjenette - Died 1874 July 30 Born 1838 Feb 26 Stone says, "Beloved wife of Franklin Young, A true wife and a fond mother" S:12+12R

Young, Asa - Died 1872 Mar 23 Born 1788 Oct 13 S:10

Young, Bangs - Died 1804 Sept 13 Age 48 S:26R

Young, Bethiah - Died 1799 Oct 27 in her 37th yr (stone down & covered in grass) Wife of Moses Young (The entire Young plot area is in bad condition with many broken & missing stones) S:10

Young, Betsey - Died 1830 Aug 12 Age 37 Daughter of Bangs & Hannah Young S:10

Young, Collin ? - Died (front of stone worn off) Son of Bangs & Hannah Young S:10

Young, Deborah - Died 1807 Nov 16 (next to infant Young d1822) S:10

Young, Edward S - Died 1953 Oct 26 Born 1884 Nov 16 (with wife, Ina B Young) S:19

Young, Frances L - Died 1928 Born 1883 Child of John & Annie M Young (listed on family stone) S:11

Young, Francis H - Died 1922 Born 1889 Child of John & Annie Young (listed on family stone) S:11

Young, Franklin - Died (Only says, 2 weeks) Son of Franklin Young & Cora Atla Scudder (next to mother) S:12

Young, George - Died 1893 Born 1865 (next to Abbie E Young) S:19

Young, Hannah - Died 1839 Aug 31 Age ?4 (daughter or wife of Bangs Young?) (stone not clear) S:10

Young, Harold F - Died 1972 Born 1889 (with Ruth P Young) S:15

Young, Henry C - Died 1930 Born 1899 (with Nellie & John Young) S:31

Young, Henry Koebel - Died 1952 Born 1894 (buried with Edith Koebel & Samuel Stewart) S:8

Young, Ina B - Died 1973 April 8 Born 1886 April 20 Wife of Edward Young (with him) S:19

Young, John - Died 1918 Born 1843 (large family stone with American flag) S:11

Young, John F - Died 1927 Born 1875 (with Nellie & Henry Young) S:31

Young, LeRoy - Died 1975 Born 1902 He was a Mason (with Nellie Young) S:20

Young, Louiza Miss - Died (underground) Daughter of Bangs & Hannah Young S:10

Young, Mary - Died 1883 Oct 15 Born 1799 Feb 10 S:7

Young, Mary - Died 1892 Born 1835 S:7

Young, Nellie E - Died 1981 Born 1904 (with LeRoy Young) S:20

Young, Nellie T - Died 1918 Born 1878 (with John & Henry Young) S:31

Young, Olive Mrs - Died (stone broken, only top remains) 3rd daughter of Bangs & Hannah Young S:10

Young, Ruth P - Died 1965 Born 1897 (with Harold F Young) S:15

Young, Susan Otis - Died 1846 Dec 11 Born 1788 April 25 Daughter of John & Rebecca Easterbrook & wife of Asa Young (buried next to him) S:10

Zandiotes, Harry - Died 1963 Born 1895 S:15

Zappey, Arthur Franklin - Died (no information) (with Maude Ella Zappey) S:11

Zappey, Maude Ella - Died (no information) (with Arthur Franklin Zappey) S:11

Zborowski, Edna R - Died 1987 Born 1897 (with Severyn A Zborowski) S:18

Zborowski, Severyn A - Died 1978 Born 1896 (with Edna R Zborowski) S:18

Zompas, Charles A - Died 1970 April 26 Born 1894 Sept 24 From Massachusetts, was Pvt in US Army during World War I S:15

Zwicker, Borden A - Died 1969 Born 1910 (he was a Mason) S:13

Zybon, Dorothy A - Died 1962 Born 1907 (next to Ernest E Zybon) S:13

Zybon, Ernest E - Died 11 Feb 1991 Born 1908 Also has military stone which says, "Massachusetts Private in 17th Infantry, TNG Regiment during World War II" S:13